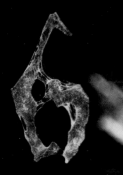

RESIDENT EVIL

TABLE OF CONTENTS

The content of this strategy guide is based on the research of BradyGames.

PART I: BRIEFING

This chapter provides a complete introduction to the characters, world, and rules of *Resident Evil 6* by Capcom. In this guide you'll learn how to control the game, play online with others, and obtain expert tips and tricks to help you master the game. The goal of this chapter, as well as this entire guide, is to prepare any player of any skill level for the challenges offered by *Resident Evil 6*.

INTRODUCTION

Resident Evil 6 is the ninth "main" installment of the series of games that debuted on the Sony PlayStation in 1996. The franchise also includes more than eleven spin-off games, five blockbuster live-action films, and two feature CG animated films. The table below lists the main games in order of release date, in contrast to the period in which the story of each is set:

RESIDENT EVIL GAMES ORDERED BY RELEASE DATE VS. PLOT TIME PERIOD

GAME	PLOT TIME PERIOD
Resident Evil	1998
Resident Evil 2	1998, two months later
Resident Evil 3: Nemesis	1998, same time as RE2
Resident Evil Code: Veronica X	1998, three months after RE2 and RE3
Resident Evil Zero	1998, just before RE1
Resident Evil 4	2004
Resident Evil 5	2009
Resident Evil: Revelations	2005
Resident Evil 6	2013

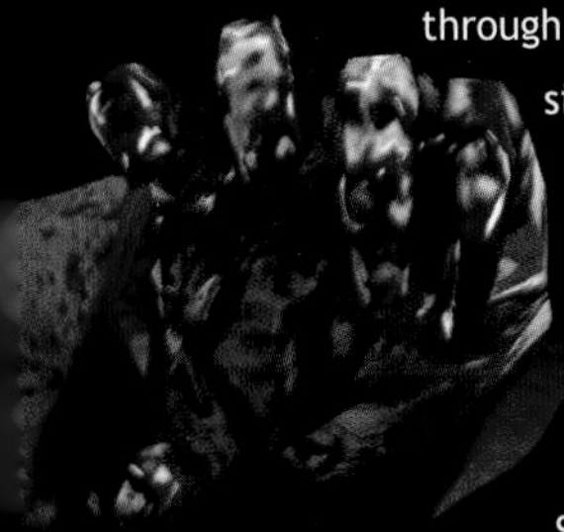

The story of *Resident Evil 6* picks up in the year 2013, four years after the events of *Resident Evil 5*. Told non-sequentially through three separate campaigns, each with a different player-character team, the plot follows the attempts of the sinister new organization “Neo-Umbrella” as it attempts to take over the world via bioterrorist attacks. These shadowy enemies of humankind have perfected a new C-Virus with which to infect the population, turning citizens into dangerous mutants that will mindlessly carry out Neo-Umbrella’s will.

To quell rising incidents of bioterrorism, U.S. President Adam Benford plans to reveal the official truth behind the “Raccoon City Incident” of 1998 and the subsequent cover-up. Standing witness for the president is Leon S. Kennedy, a survivor of Raccoon City, Field Operations Support (FOS) agent, and the President’s personal friend. Unfortunately, Neo-Umbrella learns of Benford’s plans and responds by releasing the old “tried and tested” T-Virus on the population, transforming them into flesh-eating zombies. Through their separate campaigns, series heroes Leon S. Kennedy, Chris Redfield, and Sherry Birkin team up with new characters Helena Harper, Piers Nivans, and Jake Muller. They must infiltrate Neo-Umbrella’s secret lair and undo these evil machinations before the villains take over the world and kill all who oppose them.

OBJECTIVE OF THE GAME

The objective of *Resident Evil 6* is to complete three full-length campaigns through combat prowess and survival skills. Doing so unlocks a secret fourth campaign in which the mysterious double-agent Ada Wong is the main character. Completing Ada’s Campaign unlocks an additional, secret ending. Campaigns can be played solo offline or co-op online with friends and random players. Certain stages called “crossover events” during campaigns allow for four players to team up and work together (or not) for a short period of time. Furthermore, completing any campaign unlocks “Agent Hunt mode,” wherein players can invade the games of others and kill them, allowing for player vs. player assassinations. Players can improve their characters’ skills by replaying the game as well as “The Mercenaries,” a timed mode played solo or multiplayer online wherein the goal is to work together (again, or not) to survive the longest against wave after wave of monsters. By unlocking and clearing all campaigns and upgrading all skills to maximum levels, the player “masters” *Resident Evil 6* and stands a better chance of dominating online matches of all kinds.

PROFILES

The protagonists of *Resident Evil 6* are mostly, but not always, heroes who put everything on the line for the greater good of humankind. Each of the characters is described in this section.

LEON S. KENNEDY

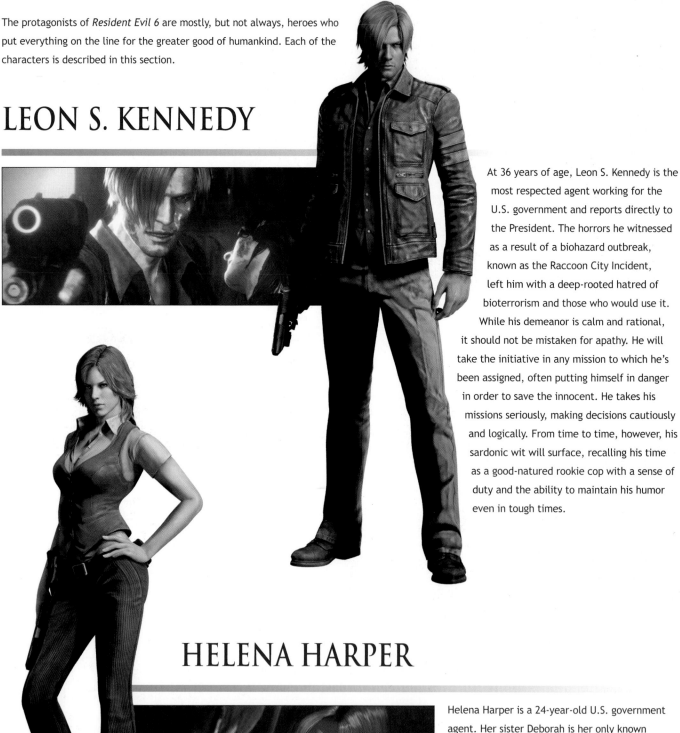

At 36 years of age, Leon S. Kennedy is the most respected agent working for the U.S. government and reports directly to the President. The horrors he witnessed as a result of a biohazard outbreak, known as the Raccoon City Incident, left him with a deep-rooted hatred of bioterrorism and those who would use it. While his demeanor is calm and rational, it should not be mistaken for apathy. He will take the initiative in any mission to which he's been assigned, often putting himself in danger in order to save the innocent. He takes his missions seriously, making decisions cautiously and logically. From time to time, however, his sardonic wit will surface, recalling his time as a good-natured rookie cop with a sense of duty and the ability to maintain his humor even in tough times.

HELENA HARPER

Helena Harper is a 24-year-old U.S. government agent. Her sister Deborah is her only known living relative. During the Tall Oaks terrorist attack, the U.S. Secret Service dispatched her to protect President Benford. She is a strong woman with strong moral convictions and is sympathetic to the plight of others, although she does let her emotions get the better of her from time to time.

CHRIS REDFIELD

Chris Redfield is a 39-year-old BSAA (Bioterrorism Security Assessment Alliance) operative working for its North American branch. He was the leader of Alpha Team until he suffered post-traumatic amnesia and wound up a belligerent drunk in the underbelly of Eastern Europe.

Around this time, a biohazard outbreak in China shocks the world. Piers Nivans, his teammate on Alpha, finds Chris and convinces him to resume his leadership role in the BSAA. Despite his memory loss, Chris retains the fortitude and leadership skills that make him one of the BSAA's top agents.

PIERS NIVANS

Piers Nivans is a 26-year-old BSAA operative working for its North American branch. Chris Redfield is his commanding officer.

His hand-eye coordination and concentration skills are without equal, making him the BSAA's top-ranking sniper. He reacts quickly to the changing conditions on a battlefield and, as a result, he will usually find a way to complete his mission despite adverse conditions. A serious and determined man in battle, he still has time to offer a kind word for his fellow soldiers. It is these qualities that prompt his C.O. to comment that the future of the BSAA rests on the shoulders of men like him. Piers prefers not to think of his team as subordinates but as members of a big family. He believes that the strength of the BSAA hinges on the bonds of all its agents. He holds Captain Redfield in the highest regard, and Captain Redfield trusts him implicitly.

JAKE MULLER

Jake Muller is a 20-year-old professional mercenary under the employ of rebel forces in Edonia. Despite his youth, his combat experience is extensive and his survival skills are formidable. His cynicism creates an unapproachable aura, and even his fellow mercenaries consider him to be moody and distant. The only thing he trusts in this world is cold, hard cash, and he has no time for the concerns of others. He is the consummate mercenary, selling his services to the highest bidder without any concern for the ideologies of the groups that employ him.

SHERRY BIRKIN

Sherry Birkin is a 26-year-old U.S. agent working under the direct command of a U.S. Presidential aide. She is one of only a handful of people to survive the Raccoon City Incident in 1998. During the incident, Sherry was infected by the G-Virus. While she survived exposure to the virus itself, the U.S. government took her into custody to monitor how the virus would affect her physiology. Thus began her time as a human guinea pig, poked and prodded by curious scientists and government officials.

In 2009, she was inexplicably offered a position as a special agent in the employ of the United States. She quickly assented in order to escape her life of forced imprisonment, even though in practice she was still under the watchful eye of the government.

She lacks the experience of more seasoned agents, but she can still hold her own against Jake Muller and is capable of providing the emotional support he has lacked for most of his life. Despite the tragedy she has witnessed, she still believes deeply in the good of people.

ADA WONG

Not much is known about the international spy Ada Wong, including her age or whom she works for. Even her true name, as well as her aims, remains a mystery. What is known is that no matter how difficult her missions may be, she has the brains and the physical ability to pull them off without a hitch. While there is stoicism in her demeanor, it is her poise and sangfroid that she is known for. She appears to be working toward a specific goal and, once she accomplishes it, she is the type that would have no qualms about betraying her handlers.

In 1998, she went to Raccoon City with the intent of secreting out a sample of the G-Virus. It was there that she first met Leon S. Kennedy, a rookie cop at the time. Following the events of Raccoon City, she has been known to offer aid to Leon on his missions but mostly as a ploy to enlist his help.

Currently, Ada has snuck aboard a submarine after being contacted by Derek Simmons, a man she hasn't heard from since the Raccoon City Incident. While on the submarine, she discovers a mission that was never fielded to her and a terrible secret that will spur her to act. What forms those actions will take is anybody's guess.

CONT

The following are the default co

PLAYSTATION 3 DEFAULT MENU CONTROLS

CONTROL	FUNCTION
Left Stick/ Directional Pad	Move cursor/toggle option
START	Open main menu
✕	Select highlighted choice
○	Cancel/Go back/exit screen
R1	Next page/Next scene
L1	Previous page/Previous scene

PLAYSTATION 3 DEFAULT NAVIGATION CONTROLS

CONTROL	FUNCTION
Left Stick	Move character
Left Stick + ✕	Dash
Right Stick	Rotate camera view/Aim
START	Pause game
SELECT	Game menu/Skip cinema
Directional Pad Left/Right	Switch weapon
Directional Pad Up/Down	Switch item
✕	Reset camera, Action (context determinate)
○	Partner Action
○ + L1	Praise partner
○ + R1	Thank partner
○ + ↑	Move ahead/Attack indicated enemy when aiming
○ + →	Wait at current position
○ + ←	Follow or return to player character
□	Reload/Pick up item
△	Item menu
L1	Directional beacon, view objective
R1	Take Health Tablet
R2	Melee attack/Counter attack/Stomp
L2	Ready weapon/Aim
L2 + R2	Fire weapon

XBOX 360 DEFAULT MENU CONTROLS

CONTROL	FUNCTION
Left Stick/ Directional Pad	Move cursor/toggle option
START	Open main menu
A	Select highlighted choice
B	Cancel/Go back/exit screen
R	Next page/Next scene
L	Previous page/Previous scene

XBOX 360 DEFAULT NAVIGATION CONTROLS

CONTROL	FUNCTION
L	Move character
L + A	Dash
R	Rotate camera view/Aim
START	Pause game
BACK	Game menu/Skip cinema
Directional Pad Left/Right	Switch weapon
Directional Pad Up/Down	Switch item
A	Reset camera, Action (context determinate)
B	Partner Action
B + LB	Praise partner
B + RB	Thank partner
B + D-pad (up)	Move ahead/Attack indicated enemy when aiming
B + D-pad (right)	Wait at current position
B + D-pad (left)	Follow or return to player character
X	Reload/Pick up item
Y	Item menu
L	Directional beacon, view objective
R	Take Health Tablet
RT	Melee attack/Counter attack/Stomp
LT	Ready weapon/Aim
LT + RT	Fire weapon

ONSCREEN DISPLAY

The images below show the kinds of markers, gauges, and readouts displayed onscreen while playing the game and controlling your character. Note that playing as different characters changes the appearance, layout, and navigation of the onscreen display.

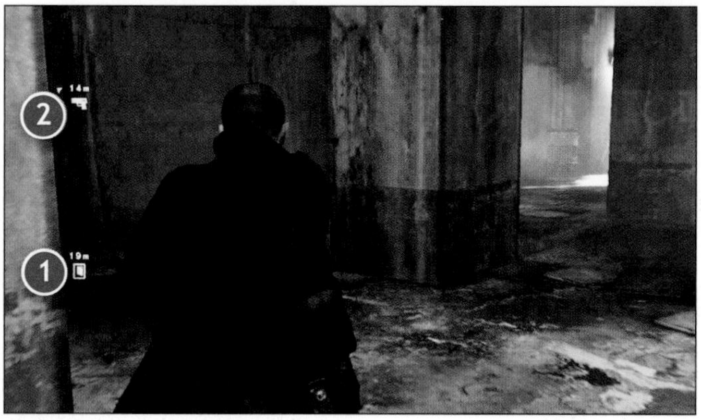

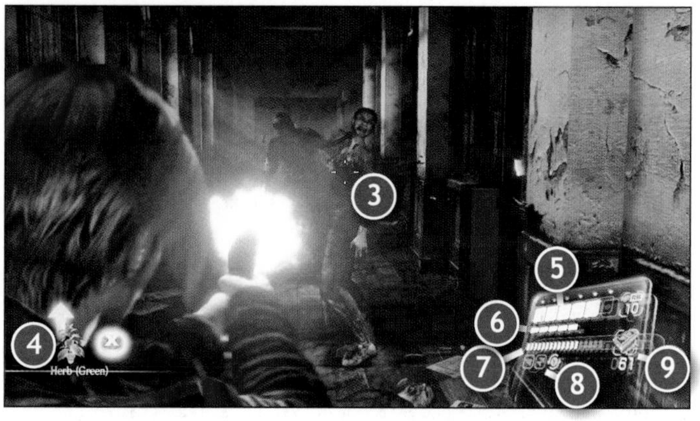

1. **Objective Marker:** Indicates position of nearest objective, usually a door, with distance numbered in meters.

2. **Weapon Marker:** Indicates position of a new weapon, with distance to object numbered in meters.

3. **Crosshair:** Appears when a firearm is aimed, indicating bullet trajectory. For greater accuracy, move the crosshair over an enemy body part before firing.

4. **Item Pickup:** Indicates an item is within reach. Press button displayed to pick up. Icon with a cross-out mark indicates no room remaining in inventory.

5. **Life Gauge:** Displays amount of life remaining. Damage sustained is indicated by red segment portions. If no further damage is sustained, red segment soon heals. When empty, character enters dying mode. Refill by taking Health Tablets on hand.

6. **Combat Gauge:** Displays stamina remaining for use in melee attacks. When empty, character cannot use melee and holds side in exhaustion. Refills automatically over time but refills faster when standing still.

7. **Magazine Gauge:** Displays number of bullets remaining in chamber of current weapon as well as the total magazine size. Press Reload to refill magazine when additional ammo is on hand.

8. **Weapon Modes:** Multiple icons displayed in this area indicate that the currently equipped weapon features multiple modes of fire. While aiming the weapon, press Ⓨ or △ to switch modes of fire.

9. **Additional Ammo:** Displays amount of additional ammo used in currently equipped weapon beyond what is currently loaded in the clip. Pressing Reload reduces this number; picking up more ammo increases it.

STARTING A CAMPAIGN

After booting up *Resident Evil 6* and logging into online profiles as needed, press the Start button to skip the cinema and arrive at the title screen. Press Start again to proceed to the main menu.

From the main menu, select Play Game and press the Action button to proceed to the Play Game screen. The other options on this screen allow you to navigate other menus:

Options: Change controller functions, camera behavior, game settings such as subtitles, HUD position, and laser sight color, display settings for brightness, and audio settings.

Credits: View the game's credits roll, which is also displayed following completion of each campaign.

Records: View personal records regarding amount of game played, weapons used, enemies defeated, medals earned by completing chapters, and records achieved in extra modes.

Special Features: View special content unlocked, such as action figures collections (unlocked by shooting Serpent Emblems hidden throughout stages) or review previously seen cinemas from the various campaigns, arranged in chronological order to provide a better picture of the overall narrative.

Marketplace: Look for new downloadable content for *Resident Evil 6* or download additional content already purchased.

THE PLAY GAME SCREEN

Selecting Play Game from the main menu takes you to the Play Game screen. Select Campaign to start a new game or select one of the other options available. More content for the Dog Tags and Extra Content screens becomes available as you progress in campaigns:

Dog Tags: View and customize Dog Tag elements unlocked by completing chapters within campaigns, which help you identify yourself uniquely in online matches.

Extra Content: Play Agent Hunt or The Mercenaries. Agent Hunt is unlocked by clearing any one campaign when you are connected online.

THE CAMPAIGN SCREEN

At first, the only option on this menu is to start a new game. You must complete the short Prelude, and then you will unlock the Leon, Chris, and Jake campaigns.

After completing the Prelude and returning to this screen, more options are available:

Continue: Select Continue to pick up from your last save point (the game saves your progress automatically at key locales).

Chapter Select: Restart from a new or previously completed chapter in any campaign.

Join Game: Join another player's game, via online connection.

Skill Settings: Purchase and equip Skills in three skill sets. At first, only one three skill set is available. Clear any campaign to make eight skill sets available and to equip any skill set on the fly during a campaign from the game menu.

CAMPAIGN SELECTION

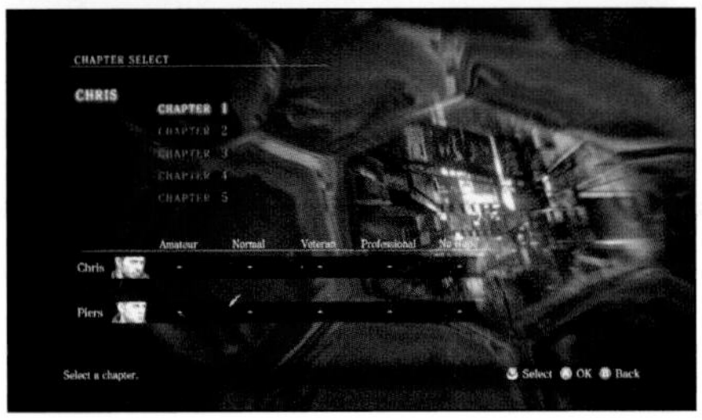

After completing the short and action-packed Prelude, you return to the Campaign Select screen. Select Leon, Chris, or Jake to begin any campaign. You can also replay the Prelude.

Selecting any campaign to begin takes you to the Chapter Select screen. Only Chapter 1 of a campaign is available to start. Complete chapters in sequential order to unlock more chapters in this screen. At the bottom, your best time and ranking medals are displayed for each difficulty mode you attempt.

IMPROVE YOUR TIME AND INVENTORY THROUGH REPLAY

Replaying chapters that you previously completed allows you to improve your completion times and chapter ranking. When you restart a chapter, you still possess all the ammo, items, and weapons you had on hand from completing subsequent chapters. As a result, you can replay chapters with better weaponry, more items, and more ammo!

DIFFICULTY AND CO-OP SELECTION

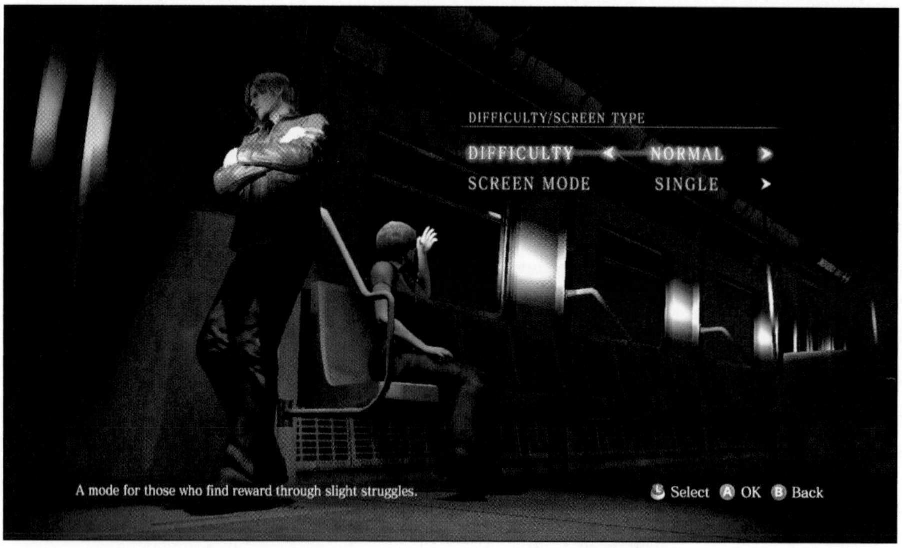

After choosing a campaign and chapter to play, the Difficulty/Screen Type screen appears. Use the Left Stick or directional pad of your controller to toggle through each of the settings, and then press the Action button to proceed.

DIFFICULTY

Four difficulty modes are available from the start: Amateur, Normal, Veteran, and Professional. Completing a campaign in Professional difficulty unlocks the No Hope difficulty for that campaign. Selecting harder modes changes the behavior, stamina, and health of enemies across the board in the following ways:

- Increased enemy walk/run speed.
- Decreased time before downed enemy rises.
- Increased frequency of enemy attacks.
- Increased number of hits during a multiple-hit attack.
- Decreased chance of dazing an enemy with shots.
- Decreased time of dazed effect inflicted by gunshots.
- Decreased time of dazed effect inflicted by Flash Grenades.
- Increased number of accurate shots fired by armed enemies.
- Decrease in interval between stationary gunshots.
- Increased chance of J'avo mutation.
- Increased speed of grapple attacks.
- Increased number of hits delivered during a grapple.
- Decrease in time a Rasklapanje stays immobilized after defeat of all body parts.

SCREEN MODE

Screen mode determines whether you play alone, control one character, or play with a friend in co-op mode via split screen and a second controller connected to player 2.

CHARACTER SELECT

The Leon, Chris, and Jake campaigns each feature two playable characters. In single-screen offline mode, the character you do *not* choose becomes a partner controlled by AI. The partner follows the player character except in times of forced separation. Partner Action commands can be issued to change the partner's behavior or command the partner to move or attack, depending on whether the current locale and situation allows.

PLAY AS BOTH CHARACTERS

As you navigate through a campaign, you notice areas that the main character (Leon, Chris, or Jake) is unable to explore and that only the usual partner character (Helena, Piers, or Sherry) has access to. For this reason, it is wise to replay each scenario as the partner character. Some hidden collectibles are accessible only by the partner, and they won't collect them if you're not in control!

SYSTEM SETTINGS

The final screen of options shown when selecting a campaign determines how you play: offline or online; with or without a partner; which countries you are available to play with; whether you want to complete all the objectives or not; whether your partner reacts to your attacks if struck; whether you want skills that allow infinite ammo to be used or not; and whether other players can enter your game as monsters in Agent Hunt mode. When you are finished determining the criteria of your match, select the Start Game option at the bottom. If playing offline, you begin immediately; if playing online, you then proceed to the lobby and can select a game or join the next match randomly.

NAVIGATION

This section discusses the basics of exploring and searching your environment.

MOVEMENT AND TURNING

Use the Left Stick and Right Stick simultaneously to move and turn your character at the same time. While tilting the Left Stick moves the character in any direction, angle the camera in the direction the character is moving in order to see better. Keep your thumbs on both controls while your fingers hover over the shoulder buttons. Be ready to raise your weapon and fire it at a moment's notice.

CAMERA RESET

Press the Action button while standing still to reset the camera position to waist level behind your character. The camera reset position can be changed in the Options menu.

DASHING

Hold the Action button while moving to dash across long stretches at faster speed. The camera falls to a lower angle behind the character but can still be angled mid-dash using the Right Stick. Dashing is effective for traversing long, empty areas quickly or for evading constant gunfire such as from machine guns.

While dashing, the character also performs certain actions automatically, such as jumping across gaps, climbing ladders, dropping from ledges, hopping through windows, and sliding across countertops.

ACTION BUTTON FUNCTIONS

As was mentioned previously, the function of the Action button changes depending on the circumstances, such as the environmental object the character is facing. You encounter the following types of environmental objects to interact with on a regular basis plus additional control panels and levers with special functions:

CLIMBING LADDERS AND LEDGES

Press Action when standing at the base of a solid ladder or a waist-level ledge to climb up. If you find you cannot climb a ladder, examine it more closely to determine if it is broken higher up or perhaps raised out of reach. In the case of raised ladders, find a way to reach the top end of the ladder and press Action to make it drop down. Then you can use it.

DROPPING FROM LEDGES

When standing at an open ledge with clear ground below, press Action to drop to the lower level. Your character will drop over ladders as well. You'll be surprised by some of the heights your character can drop from. If you move to an open ledge and the Action button icon does not display, then it is not safe to drop from the ledge at that spot. Find another area from which to drop safely.

HOPPING THROUGH WINDOWS

Approach any window, barricade, or waist-level wall opening and press Action to hop over. Your character can jump safely over the low wall if the area on the other side is clear of furniture and obstacles, even if it means smashing through a glass pane. If the Action button is not displayed, the wall or barrier may be slightly too high to jump over.

SLIDING ACROSS SURFACES

Approach any counter or waist-high table and press Action to slide across the surface. Doing so where papers or objects are stacked can have a dramatic effect. Sliding over a counter is a great way to approach an enemy quickly during an attack.

OPENING DOORS, SUITCASES, AND CHESTS

Most other environmental interactions are also handled with the Action button: opening doors, suitcases, item chests, and windows; pulling levers; pushing buttons; and so forth. When you open a door, press Action once to open it quietly or press Action twice quickly to kick it open loudly. Doing so can sometimes knock down an opponent standing on the other side of the door.

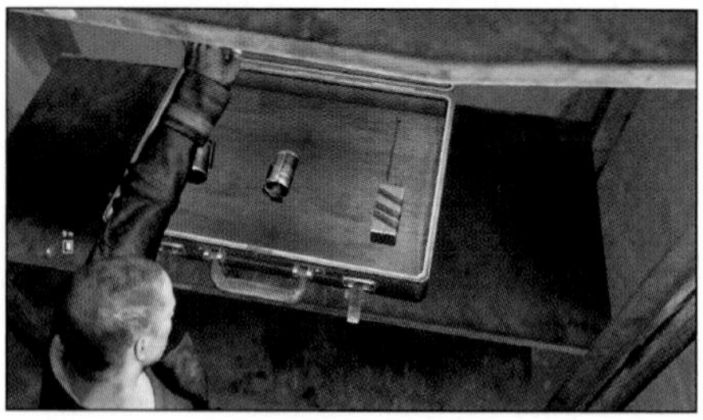

Note that some doors, levers, and buttons can be used only via Partner Action, with both your character and your partner performing the action at the same time.

SMASHING ITEM CRATES

Throughout stages, you find breakable crates, barrels, vases, and boxes of various colors and sizes. Approach any of these and press the Fire button to smash the container. This does not reduce the Combat Gauge as long as the action is used to smash an object, whereas kicking at air does reduce your gauge. These breakable objects contain valuable items such as ammo, herbs, and Skill Points that you can use to purchase and upgrade skills between chapters.

PICKING UP ITEMS

When you find an item—either by locating it on a table, shelf, or in a dead person's hand or by smashing an item crate—move toward the item until the item's icon appears in the lower-left corner of the screen. Press the Reload/Pick Up button to collect the item and to add it to your inventory. If the item icon is crossed out, then no room is available in your inventory. Press the Item Menu button and combine or discard items to make room, and then try again to pick up the new supply.

SKIPPING CINEMAS

If you have already seen a cinema play, either through death or chapter replay, press the Select or Back button to skip the scene and resume control of the game. Scenes previously viewed can be viewed again in the Special Features menu.

THE IN-GAME MENU

Press Select or Back (depending on your console) to open the game menu. You won't use the game menu often, but it's still handy. Unlike pausing the game (accomplished by pressing Start), time does not stop while you view this menu. Therefore, open the game menu only in a safe and enemy-free location.

Like the onscreen display, the game menus change form depending on the character played. Some characters' game menus are displayed as square tablet devices while others' are rotating wheels. But the functionality of the icons displayed remains the same:

Resume Game (curved-back arrow): Return to controlling the character. It is also accomplished by pressing Select/Back or the Cancel button.

Restart from Checkpoint (thumbtack): Restart the game from the last checkpoint with the weapons, items, and health available at the time. Look for "Checkpoint" to appear onscreen while you move through areas to help identify the location of the previous checkpoint.

Display Another Player's Records (graph): Display the Records screen (same as seen on the main menu) for another player currently playing in your campaign, including partner and Agent Hunt players.

Change Game Settings (tools): Change the same settings available in the Options of the main menu. With some exceptions, they are not changeable mid-game.

Equip Skills (crosshair): Switch to another of eight skill sets you've already built prior to starting a chapter. The skills in each set are displayed to the left. This is not available until at least one campaign is cleared.

End Game Session (power sign): Leave the campaign and return to the Play Game screen. In online mode, the player leaves the match.

Using Items

This section discusses how to use items in the field and also how to manage your item and weapon menus.

Green Herbs and Red Herbs

After finding more than one Green Herb, or a Green Herb and Red Herb, press the Item Menu button to open your item slots. The game does not stop or pause while the Item Menu is open, so do not attempt this in a hostile environment unless the situation is critical and unavoidable.

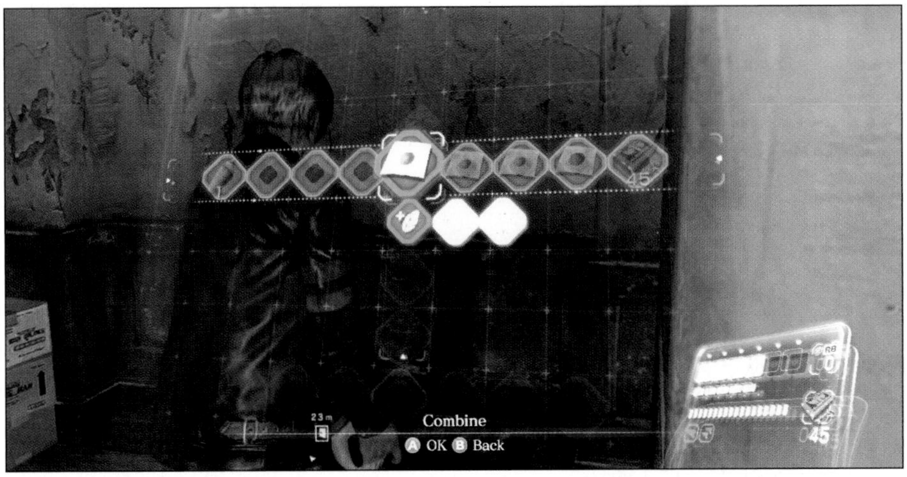

To combine herbs, use the directional pad to select a Green Herb powder and press Action. Up to three options are displayed, depending on other items in your inventory. If you possess more than one herb, the Combine command is available. Press Action to select this, then select another herb on hand to mix with. The Store command moves the herb or mixture to the case in the form of Health Tablets to be used during combat. The discard command removes the item from inventory, and it cannot be reclaimed.

Your character can carry up to 16 Health Tablets in the case. However, the only way to carry this amount is to refill the case with a six-powder mixture when carrying ten Health Tablets already. Use the following table to help you mix herbs for the best results:

Green Herb and Red Herb Combinations

Herbs Combined	Result	# Health Tablets
Green	1 Powder	+1 Health Tablet
Green + Green	3 Powders	+3 Health Tablets
3 Powders + Green	6 Powders	+6 Health Tablets
Green + Red	6 Powders	+6 Health Tablets

Health Tablets

After creating Health Tablets from Green and Red Herbs and moving them to the tablet case, press the Health Tablet button (R1 or RB) to consume tablets and restore health. Each tablet you consume restores one block of health. Therefore only six Health Tablets can be consumed at a time. Press the button six times rapidly to recover full health quickly.

If your Health Tablet case is empty, press R1 or RB and Reload to refill the case, which automatically converts Green and Red Herbs on hand to tablets. This method picks the best combination available, in the following order of preference:

1. Green + Red
2. 3 Powders + Green
3. Green + Green
4. Single Green

Switching Weapons and Items

Press right or left on the directional pad to switch weapons you carry. If you switch to an empty weapon with additional ammo available, your character automatically reloads. Be aware of this and make sure your character is a safe distance from enemies before equipping an empty weapon that can be reloaded.

Press up or down on the directional pad to switch to holding an item in possession, such as a First-Aid Spray, Remote Bomb, or any type of grenade. Each type of item is used differently, so familiarize yourself with those differences.

Rearranging Weapons

Whether you miss a weapon lying in the field or even find them in the order available in a campaign, weapons may not be ordered to your liking. To rearrange weapons, press the Item Menu button to open your item slots, and then press R1 or RB to switch to your weapons. While viewing the weapons this way, press the Reload button to select a weapon you want to move. The change slot icon appears below this weapon. Now scroll left or right to the place you want the weapon to go and press Action. The two selected weapons switch slots.

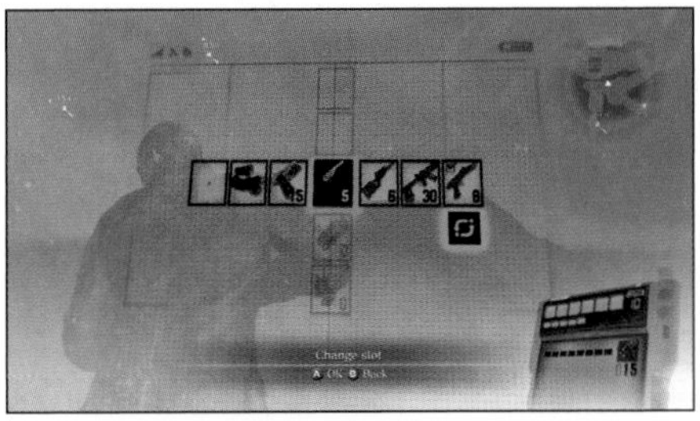

For example, Jake finds the Shotgun extremely late in his campaign—last, in fact. If you're more comfortable with this weapon being closer to your Nine-Oh-Nine handgun in the selection order, then move the cursor to select the Shotgun and press Reload. While the Shotgun is marked with the switch slots icon, move to, say, the Elephant Killer and press Action. This moves the Shotgun to your second slot and your Elephant Killer to last place. This may be preferable for dealing with a mixture of weak and strong enemies simultaneously, such as J'avo and Strelats in the same location. But if, later on, you are dealing with close-range and long-range enemies simultaneously, move the Sniper Rifle next to the Nine-Oh-Nine via the same method. Rearrange your weapons often depending on the combat situation. Avoid cycling through several weapons before arriving at the right one.

FIRST-AID SPRAY

First-Aid Spray provides full healing instantaneously, both to you and to all allies within touching range. Equip a First-Aid Spray on hand by pressing D-pad Up or D-pad Down, then press Fire to use it to restore your health and physical Combat Gauge. Use it while you are near your partner to restore their health too.

GRENADES

You can find a variety of thrown explosive devices in the field. To equip a grenade, press D-pad Up or D-pad Down until the desired type appears in hand. To throw a grenade, hold the Ready/Aim button, and then press Fire to toss it. Before throwing a grenade, use the Right Stick to adjust your arc of trajectory, which is visible onscreen as a series of red dots, until the final dot is near the enemy's feet.

Different grenades affect enemies in various ways upon detonation, and some enemies are particularly vulnerable to them:

GRENADE EFFECTS BY TYPE

TYPE	NOTES
Hand Grenade	Detonates on impact, damaging all surrounding foes and allies.
Flash Grenade	Blinds all enemies for several seconds, rendering them vulnerable to throws, stealth hits, and melee attacks; highly effective against enemies that hatch from chrysalid cocoons.
Incendiary Grenade	Creates flames in a wide radius around the target, setting all enemies and allies within range on fire and causing them to suffer flame damage for several seconds afterward; highly effective against zombies and Rasklapanje.

REMOTE BOMBS

Remote Bombs are explosive C4 devices that can be planted by hand and then triggered via remote control. While equipped with a Remote Bomb in your hand, press Ready/Aim to plant the Remote Bomb where you are standing.

Move a safe distance away and press Ready/Aim and Fire at the same time to detonate the device, inflicting intense damage to all targets, and allies, within a short range of the bomb.

After planting a Remote Bomb, many actions can be performed prior to detonation, such as picking up other items, overturning tables, sliding across table surfaces, climbing ladders, etc. You can also switch to a different weapon or grenade, use it, and then re-equip the detonator. Therefore, don't feel that planting a Remote Bomb limits your combat abilities in any way.

PARTNER ACTIONS

The three main campaigns require that two-person teams work together and cooperate to survive. Many doors, levers, buttons, and hatches display the Partner Action button icon when approached, indicating that the object can only be interacted with or used by two people who work in unison. Whenever you encounter a door that displays the Partner Action icon, pressing the Partner Action button automatically calls your partner over to help. While they approach you may be vulnerable to enemy attack, so only use this in clear or safe areas.

PARTNER COMMANDS

Throughout stages, your partner follows you and attacks enemies automatically. However, there may be times that you do not want them to follow you, or to attack enemies, for fear of giving your position away. Partner Commands allow you to give instructions to your partner, whether they are controlled by computer AI or another player.

If your AI partner responds in the negative to a partner command, then the situation may not permit such action at the time. Reassess and determine whether another partner command will work better.

Holding down the Partner Action button allows you to locate your partner in the environment. Even if your partner is in another room and cannot reach you, his/her location is marked with a special cursor.

MOVE IN

Hold the Partner Action button and press D-pad Up to direct your partner to move ahead of you, attack an enemy in front of you, or attack one you've targeted while aiming with your laser sight. This order is basically a command to be aggressive and fight to the last bullet, but it fails if no enemies are present. Issue this order when entering major combat situations and boss fights. Your partner works their hardest to reduce the damage you sustain as well as the number of bullets you use.

CALL

Hold Partner Action and press D-pad Down to call your partner to your position. This command also changes the partner's attack behavior, instructing them to disengage if they are fighting an enemy.

WAIT

Hold Partner Action and press D-pad Left to direct your partner to stay in a certain location when not in battle. The partner will wait in the spot you left them while you explore ahead. This command may be cancelled if you move too far out of the partner's range or if you enter a situation where your partner is necessary.

FOLLOW ME

Hold Partner Action and press D-pad Right to direct your partner to follow after you. Your partner moves to your flank and resumes the default behavior of following you from area to area, attacking enemies at random. This command is also effective for moving your partner out of your way.

THANKS AND PRAISE

Hold Partner Action and press R1/RB or L1/LB to congratulate or flatter your partner for recent actions. Doing so sometimes bolsters the partner's willingness to attack with more powerful weaponry when the next Move In command is issued.

COMBAT

The following section of this chapter discusses all topics relating to combat actions, including controls used and button timing required to defeat enemies efficiently and stylishly.

PHYSICAL COMBAT

Due to the lack of ammunition, mixing firearm use with melee attacks and self-defense tactics is critical to survival. Press the Fire button to perform a melee attack against nearby enemies. Physical attacks are more effective when the enemy is stunned or lying prone.

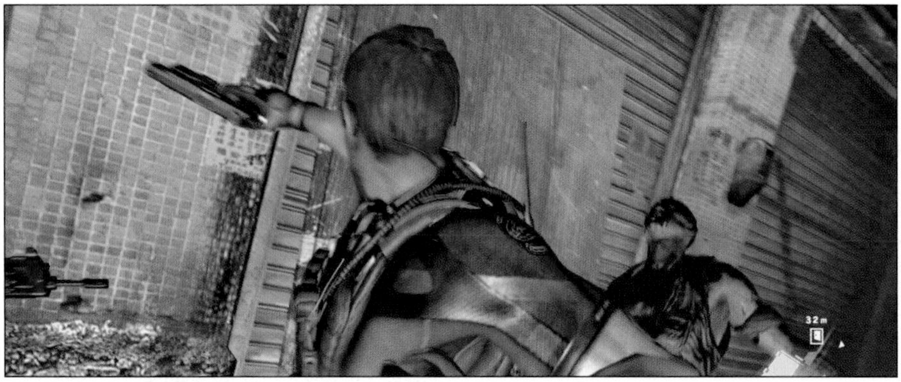

To daze an enemy, use a firearm and shoot them in either arm. You see the effectiveness of your shot when a change occurs in the enemy's posture. When the enemy bends over or cringes in pain, lower your weapon and rapidly approach them. If the Fire button icon appears onscreen, the enemy is dazed and ready to be hit with a melee attack. Press the Fire button to knock the enemy to the ground with a devastating blow.

If the first melee attack is not enough to kill the enemy, stand near the enemy's head. If doing so causes the Fire button to appear again, then press it another time to stomp on the enemy's head, smashing their skull. Stomp on an enemy from the side or their feet may cause you to stomp on their torso instead, which is highly damaging but may not kill them.

All physical attacks deplete the Combat Gauge. The Combat Gauge refills gradually over time as long as no further physical exertion occurs. The gauge refills even more quickly if the character stands completely still and performs no action.

If the Combat Gauge drops to empty through repeated use of melee, then the character may begin to hold their side in pain and pant. The Combat Gauge turns pink and fills slowly. The panting condition will not abate until the pink bar fills completely and goes away. This condition reduces movement speed and prevents dashing. Additional recovery time is required to allow the pink gauge to refill and go away and also to allow the Combat Gauge to refill. Therefore, you must use physical melee attacks sparingly and wisely to avoid this crippling condition. Jake Muller possesses additional Hand-to-Hand combat moves that do not use stamina or deplete the Combat Gauge.

STEALTH HITS

By approaching an unaware enemy from behind, you can execute a stealth hit. Sneak within a few feet of an enemy's back and the Fire button icon appears. Press Fire to execute a Stealth Hit attack that kills the enemy instantly. Be aware that using a Stealth Hit is not completely silent in itself, and the noise may alert surrounding enemies to your presence.

THROWS

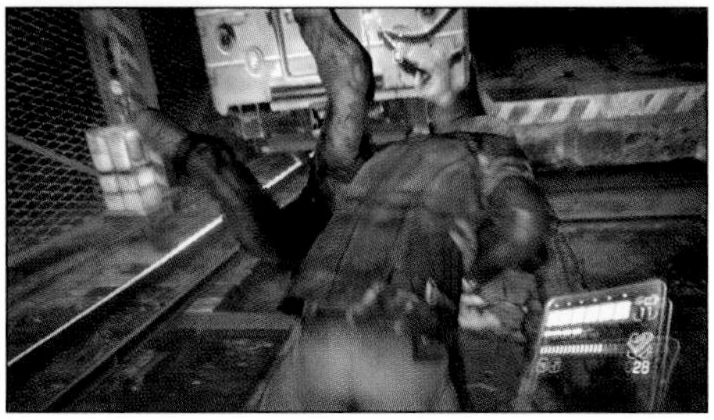

After you shoot an enemy in the face or throw a Flash Grenade so that it detonates in front of an enemy, they may begin staggering in pain and holding their eyes. While the enemy is in this condition, lower your weapon and approach them quickly. When the Fire button icon appears, press Fire to execute a Throw maneuver. Your character seizes the enemy by the head and performs a special suplex-style throw or head slam attack that kills the enemy instantly.

COUNTERS

Certain enemy attacks can be countered by pressing the Fire button with just the right timing during the attack. Approach enemies that are raising their weapons or rearing back to strike. The Fire button appears briefly during such enemy attacks. Press Fire while the icon is still onscreen to execute a counter. Your character performs a special move to throw off the attack with enough power to kill most regularly encountered foes.

PARTNER COMBOS

By performing melee attacks on an enemy that your partner is also attacking, you may trigger instances of partner combos. When this occurs, as indicated by a chime sound, press the button shown onscreen (either Fire or Partner Action, usually). Perform a devastating team-up attack against an enemy and take them out instantly!

AIMING AND FIRING

To aim a firearm, Stun Rod, or Combat Knife, press and hold the Ready/Aim button to raise your weapon. The character changes posture and prepares to attack. When using a melee weapon such as the Stun Rod or knife, you must be extremely close to your enemy and aiming is not much of a factor. With most firearms, an aiming crosshair appears onscreen. You can change this crosshair to a laser sight in the Options menu. While aiming, adjust your targeting using the Right Stick. When the laser aligns with your target, press and release the Fire button to attack.

A variety of other actions can be performed while aiming or readying a weapon.

DUCKING

While aiming a weapon, press the Action button to duck quickly and then stand back up. This move is extremely effective for dodging most enemy attacks that are launched at your character's torso or head. Some enemies such as Strelats, however, fire projectile shots at your legs and ducking these attacks provides no benefit.

TAKING COVER

While aiming a weapon and standing near a waist-high object or barrier, press Action to crouch behind the barrier in a cover position. This crouch makes it more difficult for enemies to target and shoot you. Crouching behind cover may provide no defense against explosive devices or grenades, however, so relocate quickly if needed.

CORNER COVER

When approaching any corner, press and hold the Ready/Aim button to press your shoulder against the wall near the corner. While pressed against the wall, use the Left Stick to turn left or right, move to the edge of the corner, and peek around the edge. You can also step out and aim at an enemy around the corner, reducing your exposure to return gunfire while you shoot or throw a grenade. This is a valuable method for surveying what's around the next corner while maintaining your advantage, a good alternative to running in blind, bumping into enemies, and losing the advantage.

OVERTURNING TABLES

You can overturn certain heavy tables to provide adequate cover against enemy fire. When approaching a table, see if the Ready/Aim button icon appears with a cover icon. When this occurs, press Ready/Aim to overturn the table and take cover behind it. Overturning a table works better than hiding behind it, since enemies can shoot between the table legs to hit you.

LEAP AND ROLL MANEUVERS, AIMING FROM THE GROUND

When aiming a weapon, press the Action button while moving the Left Stick to perform a variety of evasive maneuvers against enemies. When moving forward or to either side while aiming, press Action to roll in that direction. The character rolls onto his or her back and then aims from the ground. Or press Action while aiming and moving backward to jump and land on your back without the roll. Aiming from the ground is an effective tactic against most types of bipedal and crawling enemies. While on your back, tilt the Left Stick to one side or the other and press Action again to roll in that direction. Then strike another aiming-from-the-ground pose.

WEAPON MODES

While you equip a weapon, see whether small, square icons appear below your Magazine Gauge. If so, then the weapon has multiple modes of fire. Press Ⓨ or △, depending on your console, to switch weapon modes while aiming.

Leon's Wing Shooter and the Bear Commander are two weapons with multiple firing modes. Switching modes with the Wing Shooter allows you to equip two guns at once and fight two-fisted. Switching modes with the Bear Commander, on the other hand, allows you to switch from firing bullets to firing 40mm Explosive or Acid Rounds.

RELOADING

Press the Reload button to refill your weapon's clip if it is less than full and if you have additional ammo on hand. Attempting to fire an empty weapon causes your character to reload automatically, and this can sometimes leave them exposed, outside of cover, while they jam a new clip in the gun. Reloading manually in clear areas or while behind cover is much wiser because it allows you to pop up and fire at your next enemy with a full clip every time. Reload often, reload safely.

QUICK RECOVERY

When an enemy's attack knocks you down, press the Action button repeatedly to get back up on your feet quickly. In some cases, you may roll right off the ground without missing a beat. Doing so puts you back in the action and prevents your enemies from injuring you further with follow-up attacks. Quick Recovery does not work if a powerful shot or explosion sends you spinning through the air and out of control.

IMMOBILIZATION

Certain enemy attacks may hold you or immobilize you on the spot. Sometimes an enemy grabs you in a powerful bear hug or in their giant hand. You must rotate the Left Stick rapidly to break free. Other enemies spew a sticky webbing or liquid that paralyzes you on the spot for several seconds without reprieve. However, during this time you are free to aim and shoot, provided your hands are free. Afterward, equip your knife and aim downward at your own legs to cut yourself free.

QUICK SHOT

One of the most effective ways to knock an enemy off balance is with the Quick Shot attack. Press and release Ready/Aim and Fire simultaneously to perform a Quick Shot when an enemy is within medium range and you have stamina remaining in your Combat Gauge. Your character fires a quick shot into the enemy's abdomen, causing them to change stance. Quickly approach the enemy and knock them down with a melee attack, and then follow with additional stomps or bullets.

Quick Shots are a highly effective way to conserve ammo and make the most of each bullet, especially when you're low. Sometimes performing two Quick Shots on an enemy in succession can knock them to the ground or even kill them. However, performing a Quick Shot consumes stamina, which reduces the Combat Gauge.

QUICK TIMING EVENTS

During certain combat situations, special commands may appear onscreen with a timer gauge. You must press the button or buttons displayed before the timer hand reaches the end of the gauge or face the consequences. Some instances require pressing a button rapidly for a long period in order to reach safety.

At other times—such as when you hang from a ledge, drive a flats boat through debris, or you're held in a large enemy's grip—you must rotate the Left Stick rapidly clockwise or counterclockwise to break free and avoid disaster.

Although many of these instances are highlighted in the campaign walkthroughs contained in **Part II: Campaign Analysis** in this guide, there may be other instances we can't predict in which you step too close to a ledge or fail to act in time. Always be prepared to lift your left hand off the side of the controller and start jamming your finger on buttons repeatedly to survive!

REVOLVING ACTION COMMAND PROMPTS

Occasionally during the heat of action, a revolving action command prompt will appear onscreen, usually corresponding to the operation of something mechanical. When this occurs, a ring appears around a button icon in the center of the screen with an endlessly rotating timer hand, which moves through green-blue areas repeatedly. As the timer hand moves through the colored area, press the button shown to clear that area. Wait until the timer hand rotates around again, and be ready to hit the next colored area. Hitting the button too soon or too fast can spell failure, and you must try over again from the beginning.

ENEMY MUTATIONS

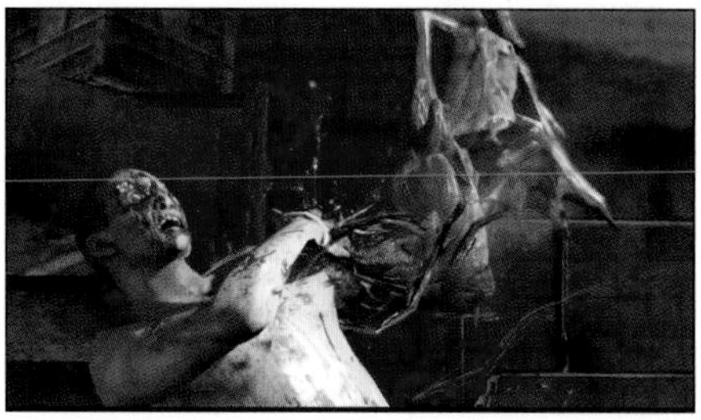

The J'avo infected by the C-Virus can be either easy to deal with or hard, especially when they mutate. Some J'avo are programmed to change and grow new body parts when you shoot them in the arms, torso, head, or legs. During a mutation, the J'avo becomes invulnerable to attack, so avoid wasting bullets. After the mutation occurs, new body parts grown by the J'avo are resistant to damage and gunfire, with the exception of the head. A head mutation usually leaves the head even weaker than before, so target the head. J'avo with mutated arms, however, can use their new appendages to shield themselves from attacks. Shoot targets around the shielding limb, such as the feet or head, to take them out. Explosions also work well against mutated J'avo.

CHRYSALID TRANSFORMATIONS

While mutations occur on the spot, some J'avo encase themselves in chrysalid cocoons. After a short period of time, the creature inside the chrysalid transforms into a new monster and breaks out of its shell to attack. Shooting a chrysalid during the transformation speeds the process and also weakens the resulting creature.

CHRYSALID HATCHLINGS HATE THE LIGHT

Creatures that emerge from chrysalids, such as Mesets, Strelats, and more, all share one thing in common: light sensitivity. Since they've just clawed their way out of an extremely dark cocoon, bright light is their weakness. Throw Flash Grenades at creatures that have emerged from chrysalids to daze them for long periods of time or even kill them.

DYING STATUS

A player character whose health is reduced to zero falls into Dying status. During this time, the screen turns completely red, the character falls to the ground, and movement is restricted. The character can aim and fire the weapon they have in hand but cannot change weapons or heal themselves. Any further damage sustained by the character results in death and the end of game.

When a character is dying, a gauge appears at the bottom of the screen. If the character survives until this gauge fills completely, then he or she will stand up and be able to move again but remain in Danger status. If a partner character can get to the player character and administer aid, then the character can get up immediately. But they will still be in Danger status unless related skills apply.

In online mode, revive a dying player character by approaching them and pressing the Partner Action or Take Health Tablets buttons.

DANGER STATUS

A character revived from Dying status by a partner may still be without health, even when they're on their feet. This is known as Danger status. The screen remains somewhat blurry and tinged red, and the character holds their side while walking. Dashing and melee attacks are prohibited, and aiming is extremely shaky. Any hit you sustain while in this condition will put you right back in Dying status again. Administer aid to yourself at the first opportunity to get out of Danger status and regain all of your movement and combat abilities.

CHAPTER COMPLETION

At the completion of a chapter, the player is evaluated based on several criteria and then awarded an overall rank. Clear time, enemies killed, firing accuracy, and number of player deaths all factor into the overall rank. While the highest ranking for each criteria is A, the highest overall ranking is S, followed by A, B, C, or D. Achieving S Ranking in many chapters can unlock new bonus content.

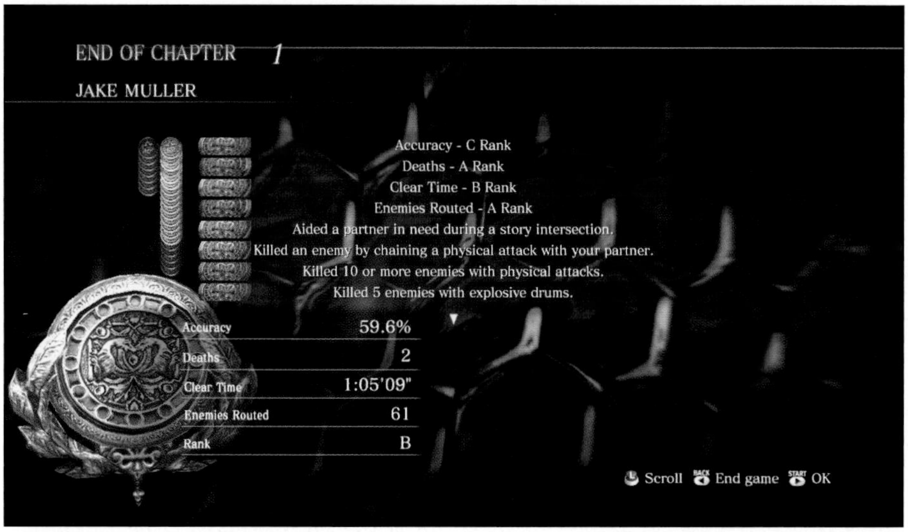

Additionally, each completed chapter unlocks new Dog Tags, and each campaign cleared unlocks new modes and maps for The Mercenaries. Clearing all three campaigns unlocks the fourth Ada campaign. Clearing all four campaigns unlocks a secret ending and several infinite ammunition skills, although with heavy Skill Point price tags.

SKILL SETTINGS

After viewing the Chapter Ranking screen, press the Start button to continue to the Skill Setting screen. Here you can purchase new skills using Skill Points accumulated during the previous chapter or upgrade already purchased skills with multiple experience levels. You can also equip different skills before heading out on your next mission.

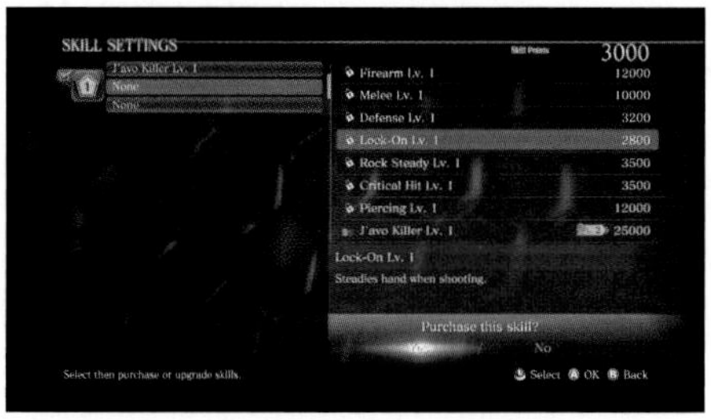

At first, only one three-skill set is available for your first entire game. This prohibits you from changing skills during a chapter. However, after clearing any single campaign, you can equip up to eight three-skill sets. Mix and match skills in all three sets to change how you fight and the amount of items enemies drop, improve how your partner heals you from dying, and more. With eight skill sets at your command, you can switch skill sets at any time during a chapter in the game menu.

The Skill Settings screen does not appear upon completion of a campaign.

NEW GAME+

When you clear a campaign, the Continue option on the Play Game menu is replaced by New Game+. Normally, you can replay any previously cleared chapter with all of the weapons and items you've acquired and even more powerful weaponry found in later chapters. However, in New Game+ you can start a campaign from scratch without the weapons you've acquired. This will not affect other character's weapons and items in other campaigns. This provides a way to experience the joy of playing a campaign from scratch, unlocking all chapters, and finding everything all over again.

If you do not choose the New Game+ option, and instead replay a chapter or start a different campaign, then the top option returns to "Continue" until you clear Chapter 5 from another campaign.

UNLOCKING EXTRA CONTENT

Complete any campaign at any difficulty to unlock Agent Hunt mode. By completing each campaign, you also unlock a new map in The Mercenaries. These extra play modes are available in the Extra Content screen of the Play Game menu.

ACHIEVEMENTS/ TROPHIES

By clearing chapters or fulfilling certain bonus criteria, you may unlock Xbox 360 Achievements or PlayStation 3 Trophies. Complete lists of these awards are contained in **Part V: Appendices**, along with a bevy of other information regarding enemies, weapons, items, and more.

Part II: Campaign

Introduction

This portion of the book covers the four campaigns of *Resident Evil 6* in thorough detail, with helpful screenshots and maps marking the locations of weapons, items, and supplies throughout every stage.

Regarding Strategies Provided

Tactics are provided for the enemies you face at any given moment, including unique "boss" monsters that are extremely difficult to defeat. All strategies, enemy appearances, and item placement notes are based on playing the game in Normal difficulty mode, in a single-player offline game. Changes that may occur when playing online in cooperation with other players or against player monsters in Agent Hunt mode are not accounted for. In other words, if the text refers you to conduct a task with your partner, then it is assumed that you are playing with an AI partner who will follow commands and assist you in key undertakings. Since the game is multi-platform and controls can be reconfigured, button controls are identified in most cases by their proper name rather than the controller icon.

Standard Campaign Progression

As explained in **Part I: Briefing**, players must first complete the short tutorial Prelude campaign, which consists of less than half of a stage. Completing the Prelude unlocks three campaigns simultaneously: Leon's, Chris', and Jake's. Because you can play the campaigns in any order, and because certain events happen in more than one campaign, some tips and boss strategies are conveniently repeated in several places within this guide.

Completing all three campaigns unlocks the secret fourth campaign for Ada. Each campaign is divided into five chapters. After each chapter, the player is ranked according to their playing speed and combat abilities. The criteria that determine your individual and overall rankings are listed at the end of each chapter description in this guide.

Completing all four campaigns unlocks a hidden ending that plays after the normal ending. Additional extras are unlocked for each chapter of each campaign completed, such as Dog Tags for online identification, Agent Hunt mode, and extra maps in The Mercenaries.

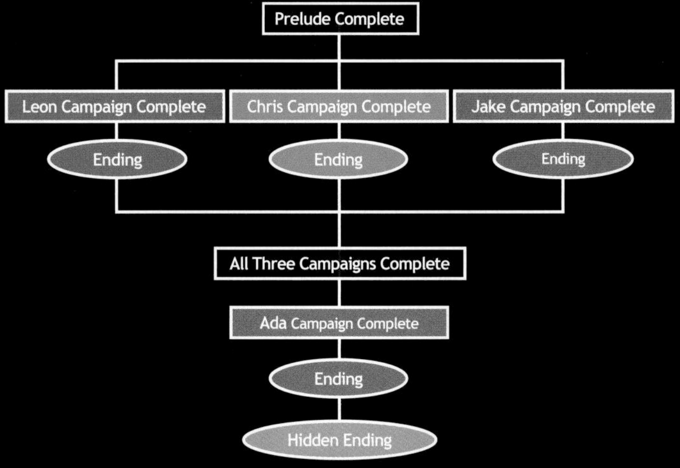

A NOTE ON STORY

The events of *Resident Evil 6* are revealed out of chronology, and the story is divided among the three campaigns so that all four must be played to completely understand the full story. For this reason, the story can become a bit confusing when you're just starting out in your first campaign. However, if you prefer to start at the beginning and get a better initial sense of the story, then it is advised that you start with Jake. Chris' Campaign starts six months later but soon backtracks to the same time that Jake's Campaign starts. Leon's Campaign starts six months later than the other two. The hidden Ada Campaign actually begins earlier than any of the other campaigns but, as noted, cannot be played until the other three campaigns are cleared.

CAMPAIGN DIFFERENCES

Each campaign features some unique enemies and settings that distinguish them from the others. Leon's Campaign starts off slower and somewhat more gothic and creepy in atmosphere and may be more accessible for newcomers. However, Leon's situation soon becomes tricky to survive since ammunition is scarce. Chris' Campaign is probably the most combat-oriented of the initial three and requires greater ammunition conservation tactics and melee abilities. Players who have purchased and upgraded a lot of skills prior to playing Chris' Campaign will find the undertaking easier. Jake's Campaign is in many ways the most straightforward except for a short portion of Chapter 3 where the player must escape from captivity using stealth tactics. Ada's Campaign is the most difficult to complete without dying often and also features a greater number of stealth-oriented situations.

SERPENT EMBLEM NOTES

Throughout the walkthroughs in this section of the guide, you'll see notes regarding the locations of, and tips for shooting, hidden Serpent Emblems. Each emblem you shoot unlocks a file in the Collections screen of the Special Features menu. By shooting all the Serpent Emblems in a campaign, you unlock complete biographies on all characters, enemies, and situations, providing a better understanding of the game and the story. By completing rows and columns of files on the collection screen, you obtain action figures of all the characters. Use the notes provided throughout the walkthrough to help you locate and shoot all of the Serpent Emblems.

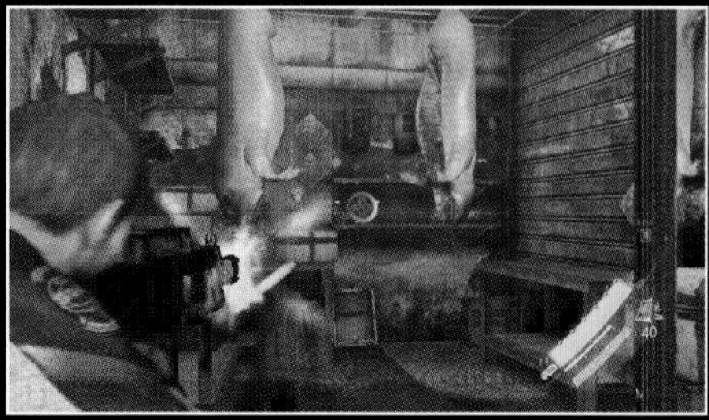

PARTNER CHARACTER NOTES

There are two playable characters for every scenario: the main character for which the campaign is named and the secondary "partner" character who is also playable. The main character is always right-handed, and the partner character is always left-handed. If the left-handed aiming bothers you, press down on the Right Stick to switch hands. Whenever a door or mechanism must be operated by both characters simultaneously, the main character must examine the left side of the machine or door while the partner must move to the right.

During Partner Actions, the main character always boosts the partner character to higher ledges. For this reason, it is both interesting and beneficial to play a campaign as both characters, since the partner sometimes gets to explore areas that the main character does not. Some hidden items and a couple of Serpent Emblems can only be found or shot by the partner character. An AI-controlled partner character always has the same inventory and weaponry as the main character. However, when replaying chapters as the partner character, you need to collect weapons all over again.

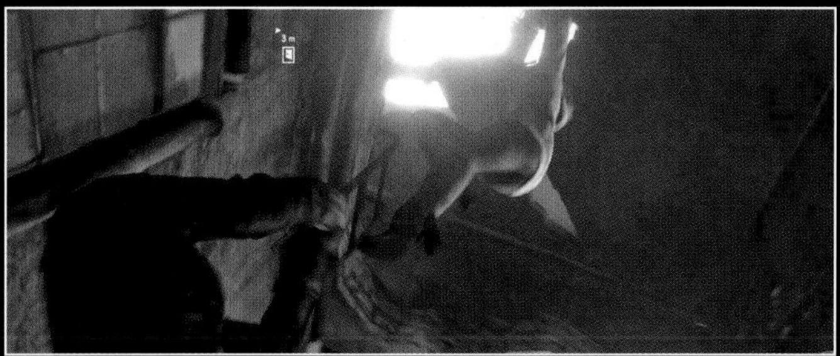

PRELUDE

CITY MAP

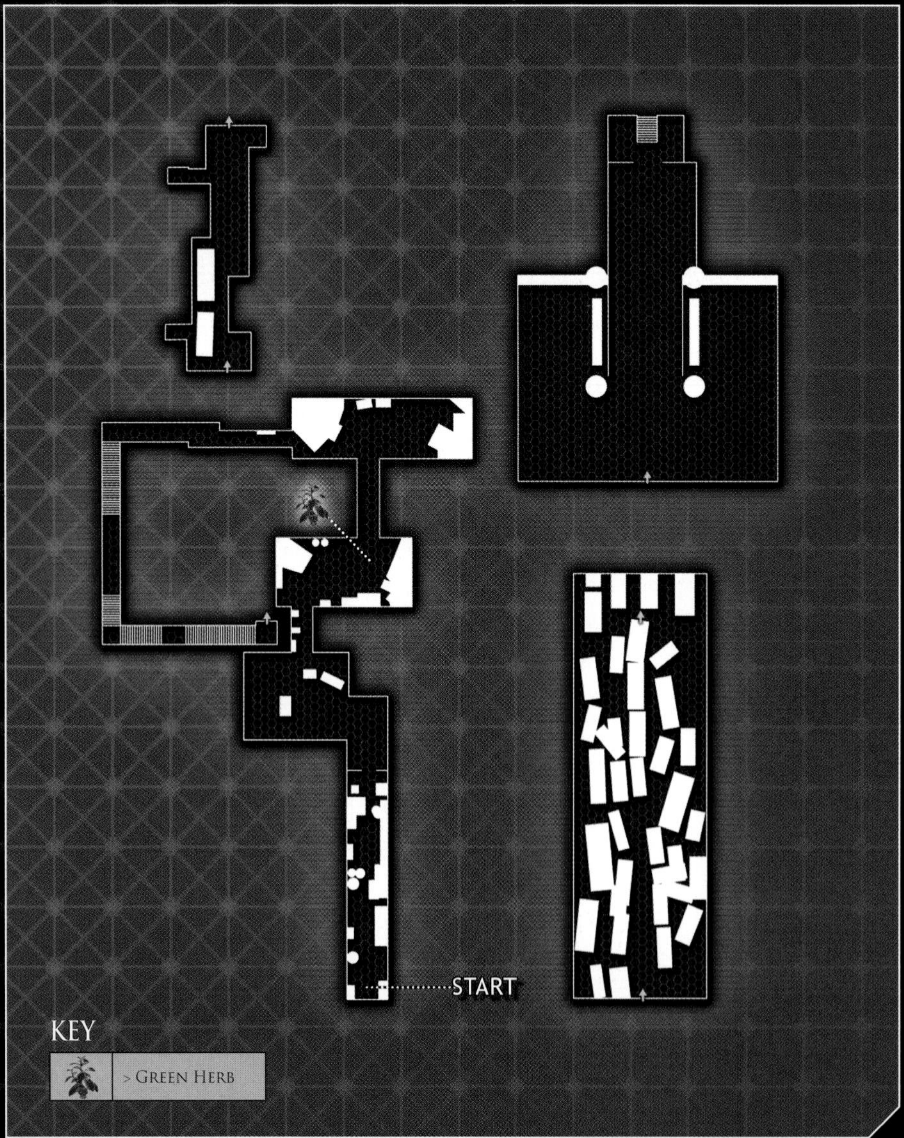

IN WITH A BANG

The streets of an unknown city run rampant with chaos, with the infected undead attempting to kill innocent civilians. The BSAA, unable to distinguish human from monster, open fire on everyone. Carnage ensues. Leon S. Kennedy and Helena Harper are caught in a blast and knocked unconscious. You are playing as Leon.

Leon regains his feet and moves to Helena. Tap the Action button repeatedly to drag her out of the street, and move the Right Stick to look around the area while doing so.

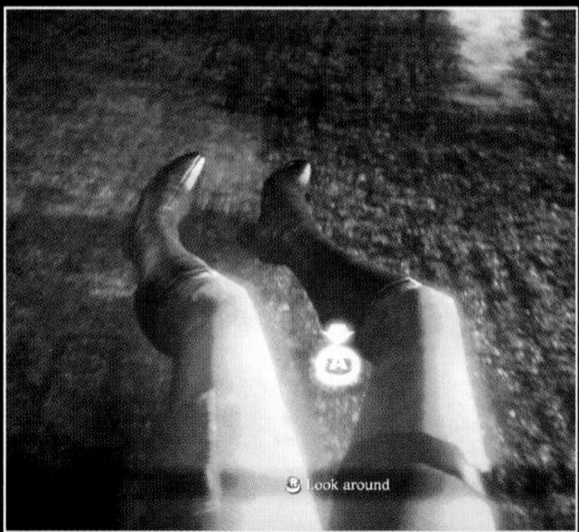

RESCUE YOUR PARTNER

When the helicopter flies off, Leon faces a debris-strewn alley. Tilt the Left Stick in any direction to navigate through the narrow wreckage. After a fall, press the Partner Action button to take Helena's hand and pull her back up.

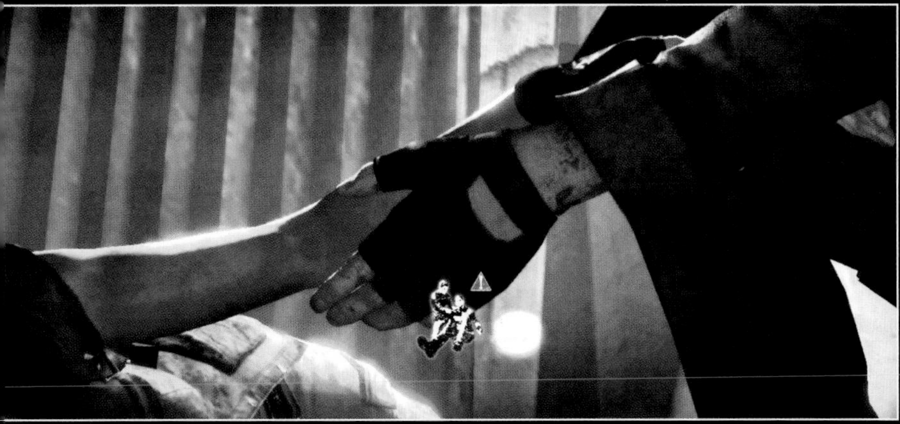

PRY THE DOOR WITH REVOLVING COMMAND PROMPTS

Continue moving down the alley until you reach a door. Press the Action button to open it—you find it is locked. Leon spots an iron bar, so press Action to pick it up. When Leon inserts the iron bar behind the door bar, a revolving command prompt appears onscreen. The timer hand circles the gauge repeatedly, moving through a small area of color. When the timer hand touches the colored area, press Reload to pry the door open. Do this repeatedly until you are successful.

EXAMINE THE CRIME SCENE

Tilt the Left Stick in any direction to move through the trashed room. Upon reaching the body near the windows, press Action to examine it. Afterward, continue moving into the next room

FIND A HEALTH ITEM

Leon leaves Helena by the door. Move to the driver's side of the parked truck and press Action to look through the windows. Leon spots a **Green Herb** inside. Press Action to smash the window, and then Reload/Pick Up to claim the herb.

MIX UP A REMEDY

Move back to Helena while Ingrid Hunnigan radios Leon. Press the Item Menu button to open your item slots. Select one of the powder mixtures in your possession and press Action, then select the other herb on hand and press Action again to combine them. Select the three-powder mixture that is formed and press Action twice to send it to your Health Tablet Case. Then, press the Health Tablet button (R1 on PlayStation 3, RB on Xbox 360) to administer aid.

GRASP OF THE DEAD

A disheveled soldier interrupts Leon. This soldier is infected with the same virus that has turned everyone else into zombies. You have a split second in which to raise your weapon and fire, but it's a waste of bullets. Unfazed, the zombie grabs you momentarily. Rapidly rotate the Left Stick counterclockwise to break free of the initial grasp. Unfortunately, Leon falls to the floor with the zombie, which grabs him again. Rotate the Left Stick again. This time, a second gauge appears—as the timer hand moves through the colored area, press the Fire button to kill the zombie with a finishing move.

LET THE BEACON POINT THE WAY

Return to Helena and press the Health Tablet button again to administer aid. With your partner back on her feet, start moving toward the objective marker (a small white door icon) that indicates the direction of the exit. Hold the Directional Beacon button (L1 on PlayStation 3, LB on Xbox 360) to bring up a digital pointer that will set you on the right path.

Press Action to open the door and descend the stairs. Approaching the door at the bottom prompts the Partner Action button icon to display. This always indicates that you cannot move on without your partner. Press Partner Action to summon your partner to help you open the door.

TAKE THE SITUATION IN HAND

Leon and Helena emerge into the chaos of the city near the site of an airplane crash. Press Action to hop over the stair rail and drop to the street below. Upon hitting the ground, immediately shoot the zombie on your left. The best tactic for dealing with enemies that get too close is the Quick Shot. Press and release the Aim and Fire buttons simultaneously to pump a quick round into the zombie, which causes it to stagger. Then move up to the monster and press the Fire button to kick it to the ground. Afterward, press Fire again to stomp on its head while it's down. Then, pick up the ammunition that it may drop.

EQUIP A BETTER WEAPON!

The crowded street situation quickly becomes challenging. Press right on the directional pad to switch to one of Leon's stronger weapons, which are now available. Each weapon has only one full clip, although you may pick up additional ammo dropped by zombies. The Shotgun is an excellent choice for close-quarters crowd control. Equip it and start blasting your way into the crowd.

Be wary of crawling zombies that may leap up from the ground—either crush in their heads or blast them on the ground from a safe distance. Aim for headshots as much as possible to conserve your ammo and reduce the need to switch to other weapons.

RUN!

Keep fighting your way up the street between the parked cars until reaching such a distance that the airplane lodged in the building behind you breaks free and crashes to the ground. As the resulting fireball begins to spread through the city blocks, tilt the Left Stick downward and hold the Action button to dash away from the spreading flames and flying cars.

A BSAA helicopter hovers into a low position directly ahead. Tilt the Left Stick upward and continue holding Action to dash over car hoods and rooftops to reach the chopper. Leon barely manages to grab the landing skid, and a zombie clutches onto his leg. Rotate the Left Stick to shake the ghoul free.

FLY CRAZY

Now inside the helicopter, Leon must take control when the pilot falls ill. Press the Reload button repeatedly to fill the gauge before the timer needle swings to the left side. Failure results in instant death and the end of the game.

The pilot resurrects as an undead and attacks Helena. Leon aims his gun into the cabin, and a revolving command prompt appears. Press the Fire button to shoot the zombie as the timer needle moves through the small, colored part of the dial. If you miss the first time, you have a few more tries. However, the zombie eventually eats Helena if you fail to shoot it in time, and that too means game over.

With the onboard situation resolved, rotate the Left Stick rapidly to regain control of the chopper. Unfortunately, it's no use: the aircraft crashes into a building and the partners spill out onto a glass floor. Press the Action button before the timer runs out. Get off the glass floor before the helicopter collapses on top of you.

WHERE ARE WE NOW?

Catch your breath and then head for the exit door. Press Partner Action to open the door together. Leon and Helena find that they have arrived at a rather strange, yet altogether relevant area. Press Action one last time to hop over the rail and drop to the floor below. Proceed toward the central monolith to complete the Prelude.

LEON

NORMAL DIFFICULTY

The walkthrough provided for Leon's Campaign has been simplified to cover only Normal difficulty mode, in single player, offline. Most of the strategies described herein pertain to playing as Leon and not as Helena. The occasions in which the partners must work separately are covered but only from Leon's perspective. Therefore, we recommend playing as Leon during your first attempt at this campaign in order to follow this walkthrough more closely.

The walkthrough does not account for changes due to gaming online with other players.

LEON CHAPTER 1

JUNE 29, 2013

Tall Oaks, U.S.A.

Facing off against a U.S. President-turned-zombie, Leon S. Kennedy of the FOS (Field Operations Support) has no choice but to shoot his longtime friend, President Adam Benford. Witness to his act of self-defense is Helena Harper, vetted Secret Service agent and President Benford's assigned protector. Leon and Helena must now escape the campus where Benford was set to speak and get out of town safely. Then it's time to track down the people responsible for President Benford's transformation and bring them to justice.

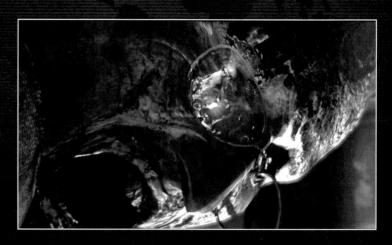

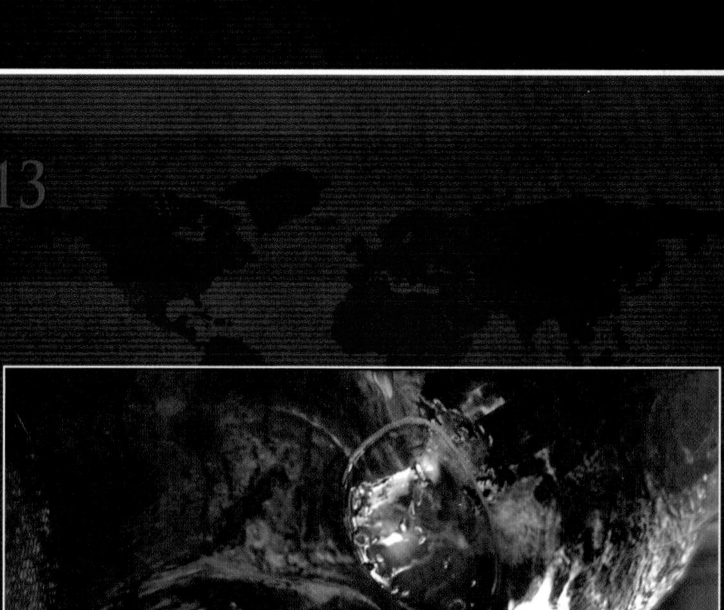

CAMPUS—VISITORS ROOM

VISITORS ROOM MAP

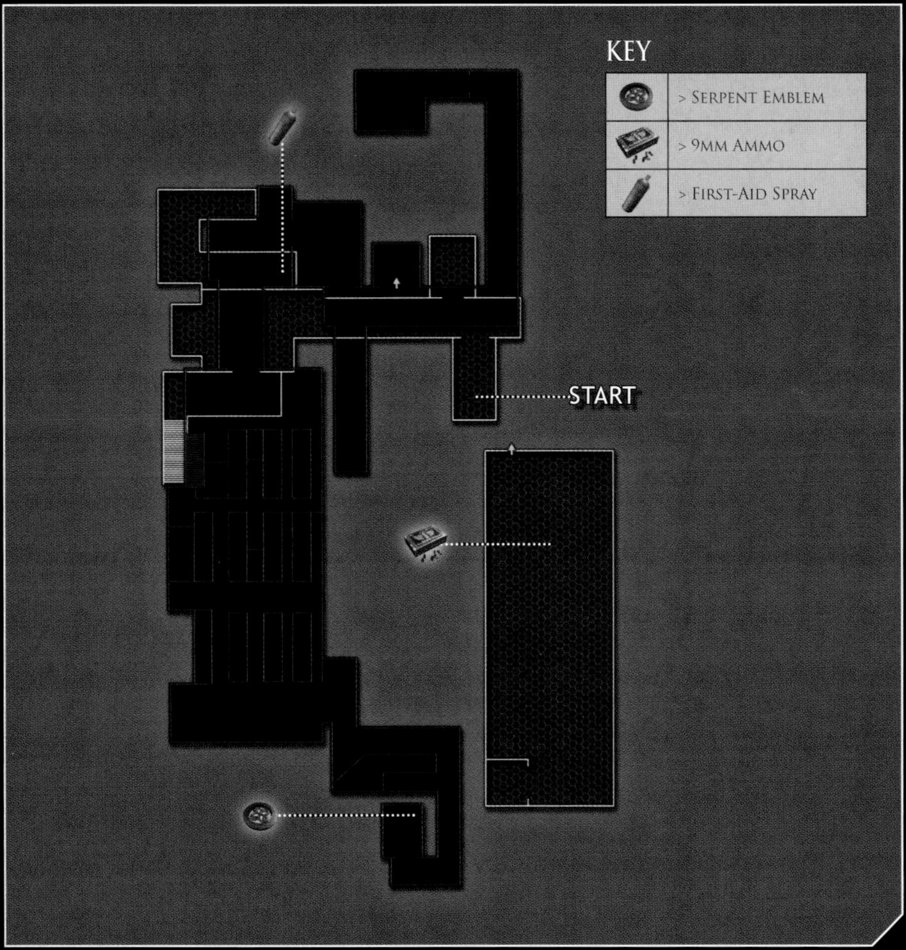

THE OBJECTIVE MARKER

The little, white objective marker changes shape to show you whether your objective is a door or a point in space that you must cross in order to proceed. Your distance from the objective is also displayed in meters. The objective marker is one method of determining where you need to go next, but you don't always want to go to the objective marker first. Sometimes exploring side areas proves more beneficial in terms of acquiring new items and weapons.

GET MOVING

Tilt the Left Stick to move and exit the room. You may opt to enter the room across the hall. Approaching the desk causes the person slumped in the chair to fall over.

Continue down the corridor and examine the elevator on the right to determine that power is out. You need to get the elevator power back on throughout this level in order to get off this floor. Follow the corridor all the way down to the reception area then head toward the small, white objective marker, which is on the door on your left.

PARTNER UP TO OPEN DOORS

Approach the door. The Partner Action button icon appears, indicating that both you and your partner must open the door at the same time to continue. Press Partner Action to touch the door and call out to your partner. In Single mode offline, your AI-controlled partner should immediately run to you. In online mode, this is determined by the other player. If you find yourself waiting on someone else, press Partner Action again to call out their character name. Repeat until they stop what they are doing and join you.

NAVIGATE THE BANQUET HALL

Head right, trot down the steps, follow the balcony to the end, and go down the stairs on your left. You spot another survivor running away at the other end of the banquet hall. The aisles between the nearest tables are cluttered by chairs and impassable, so move down the hall to the back rows. When you reach the middle of the banquet hall, more cluttered chairs force you to go back to the right to find a clear aisle to pass. Go left at the end and through the open doorway on the far side.

DON'T BE AFRAID...

Turn right and enter the kitchen. Judging by the loud noises, you're on the right path to find either the survivor or more zombies. Head left through the kitchen and right through the open exit door. Follow the connecting corridor around the corner to the right and open the door at the end with a Partner Action.

At this point you encounter Robert, a scared university employee who is looking for his daughter, Liz. With Helena's help, you must make time to reunite Robert with his missing daughter before making your escape.

SERPENT EMBLEM: CLOSET IN ROBERT'S ROOM

Following Robert's departure from the room, face the exit door. Turn to your left and move to the open closet doorway. Even from outside the closet, you easily spot a giant blue crest on the highest shelf. This is a **Serpent Emblem.** Shoot this and other emblems hidden throughout each chapter. The emblems unlock additional content for Leon's Campaign in the Collections screen of the Special Features menu. You can collect four Serpent Emblems in every chapter.

FOLLOW ROBERT

Head back through the kitchen to the banquet hall, which is now veiled in darkness. Proceed into the hall. Leon and Helena automatically turn on flashlights, providing limited visibility. Flashes of lightning from the storm brewing outside also help you make your way back through the clear aisles.

Robert waits on the other end of the banquet hall, where he is nearly crushed by a falling chandelier. Move to the double doors behind him and press the Action button to open them. Robert proceeds to the door on the right. However, if you go up the stairs across from the door and follow the balcony to the end, you find a can of **First-Aid Spray** next to a dead body.

KNOW HOW TO USE YOUR FIRST-AID SPRAY

To use a First-Aid Spray, press up or down on the directional pad of your controller until the First-Aid Spray is selected. With the item in hand, press the Fire button to heal yourself. In online play, First-Aid Spray used in close proximity to your partner will heal both of you. However, since finding First-Aid Spray is rare, conserve these items for major battles and boss fights, and use herbs in the form of Health Tablets to recover instead.

FIND LIZ

Return down the stairs and join Robert near the opposite doors. He opens the portal for you and will open other doors in the next several areas. Follow Robert into the small museum. After a coughing fit, he moves across the room and opens the exit door for you. Follow him through the passages until you find another elevator without power. Robert claims to have the keys that turn on the power and will use them as soon as you find Liz.

Continue to follow Robert down the corridor to the door at the end. When he backs away, move to the door and open it with a Partner Action. You find his daughter Liz, who is infected and in bad shape. Robert carries Liz back down the corridor to the elevator.

When Robert encounters some fallen boards blocking the path, move ahead of him and push the boards aside by pressing the Partner Action button. Afterward, move ahead of Robert into the open elevator car.

TIME TO CLOCK IN

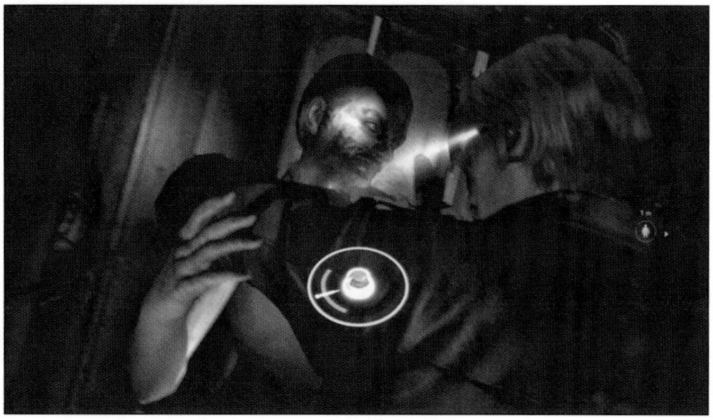

Following a brief blackout, Liz turns into a zombie and attacks you. A semi-circle gauge appears onscreen, and a timer hand begins moving from left to right. Situations like this are known as QTEs (Quick Timing Events), and you encounter several varieties of these sudden crisis situations throughout the game. Rotate the Left Stick rapidly in a counterclockwise motion to break free of the zombie's grip before the timer hand moves all the way to the right. Failure to fill the gauge before the timer hand reaches the end means that Liz might pull you to the ground and chew through your throat; this spells an instant game over. However, your partner can also intervene in such situations, cutting off the Quick Timing Event.

When she is done grappling with you, Liz tackles Helena. Hold the Ready/Aim button (L2 on PlayStation 3, LT on Xbox 360) to raise your weapon. Tilt the Right Stick downward to aim at Liz, and press Fire (R2 on PlayStation 3, RT on Xbox 360) to shoot her. This intervention allows Helena to reverse the situation and shoot the zombie Liz in the head.

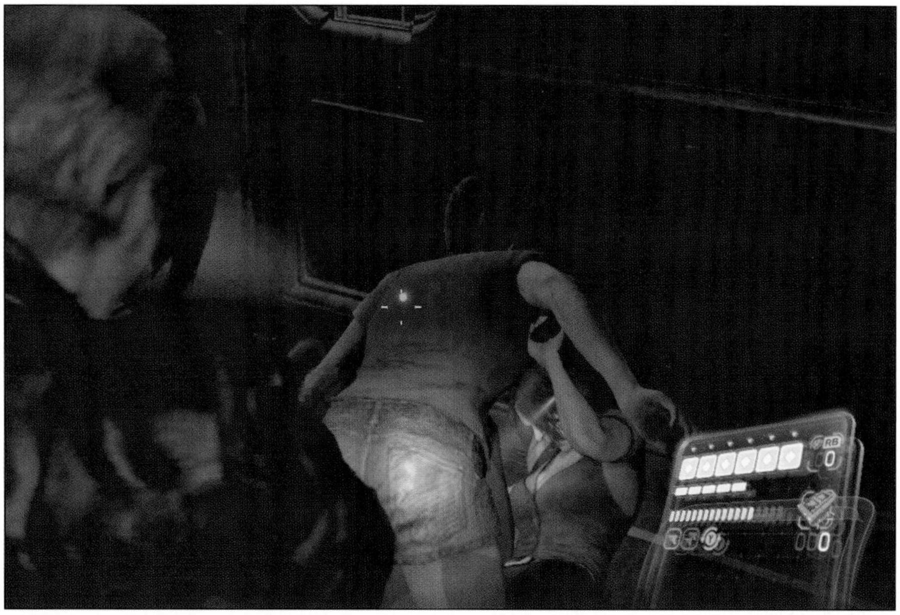

IT'S DIFFERENT, PLAYING AS THE PARTNER

As you may have noticed while starting up this campaign, you have the option of playing all of Leon's chapters as Helena. In situations like this, you see events from her perspective and may have to react to them differently. Because Helena is left-handed (like all the partners in the other campaigns) an additional challenge is added to the game. While this walkthrough doesn't cover these differences in detail, playing through as Leon should provide you the experience necessary to re-play as Helena, to improvise whenever needed, and to complete her unique actions and objectives.

HARSH GREETING

A few seconds after Liz is killed, the elevator doors open and a throng of zombies barges in. They don't react immediately, so raise your weapon and open fire. Shoot the closest zombie in the head to daze it, and then release the Aim button to lower your weapon. While the dazed zombie staggers, the Fire button icon appears onscreen along with a melee attack image. When you are close to a dazed zombie, press Fire whenever this image appears to perform a melee attack—you'll knock it to the ground. Any other zombies caught in the radius of Leon's roundhouse kick are also knocked to the ground, regardless of dazed status beforehand. The zombies encountered in the elevator are weak enough that this attack combo will kill them. However, in future situations when you've knocked a zombie on the floor, you must move next to its head and press Fire to smash its skull and kill it instantly.

PICK UP DROPPED ITEMS QUICKLY!

The items sometimes dropped by defeated enemies are temporary: you must pick them up within a short amount of time—roughly two minutes—or they vanish!

CIRCUMNAVIGATE THE GARAGE

A dying man collapses on the running car parked in the center of the garage, triggering its alarm. All of the remaining zombies in the garage immediately start walking toward the noise. While they congregate in the center, move into the shadows to the far left and run behind the row of parked cars. At the end of the aisle, go diagonally to the right toward the objective marker. Open the red exit door with a Partner Action.

DON'T RISK YOUR HEALTH FOR EXTRA GOODIES

Although a box of **9mm Ammo** is lying on the central car's hood near the driver's door, the risk of attack outweighs the benefit. This is an important lesson to be learned and a rule you should follow for the rest of Leon's Campaign.

CAMPUS

CAMPUS MAP

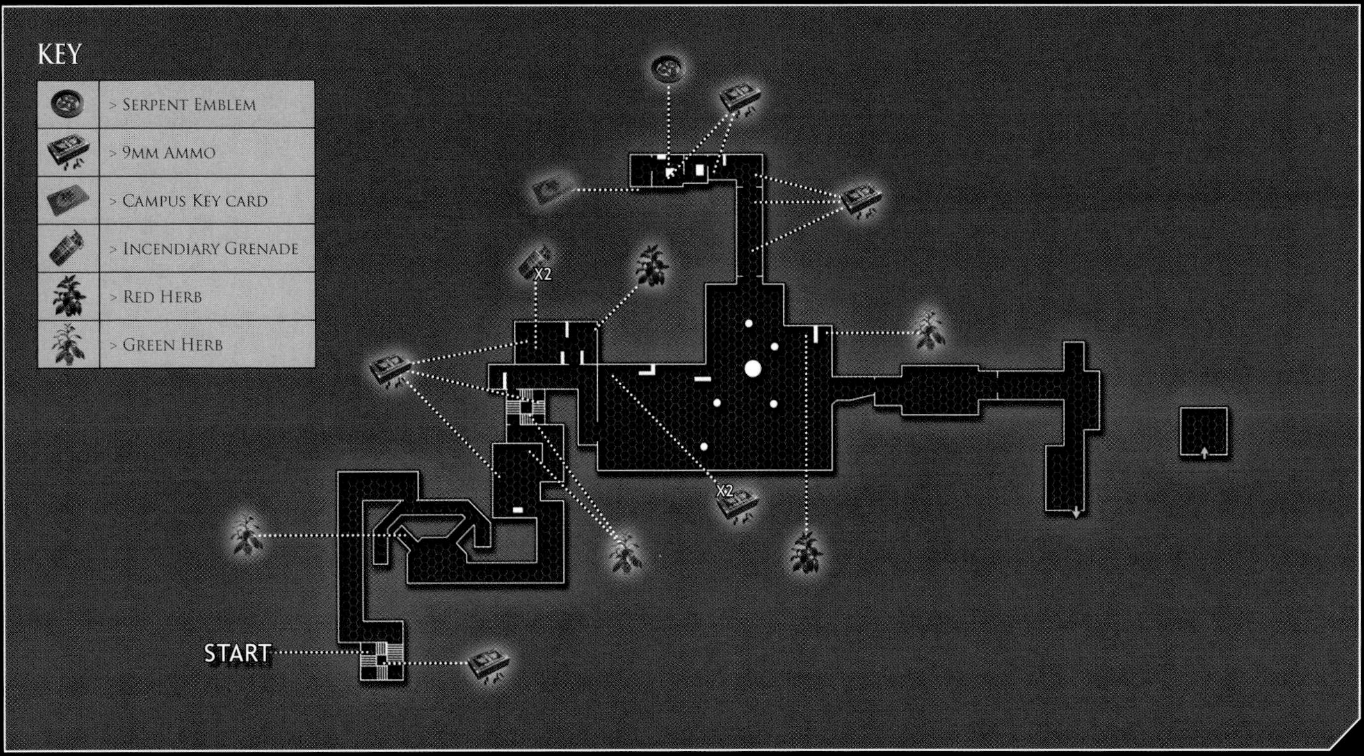

CHECK AROUND BEFORE PROCEEDING

Before going up the stairs you face, tilt the Right Stick to angle the camera to Leon's left. You spot a pack of **9mm Ammo** lying on the floor nearby. Pick it up and then ascend the stairs. The next long corridor is empty. Cross long, empty distances such as this quickly by holding the Action button to dash. Turn right at the end and open the double doors.

YOU'RE ABOUT TO GET A LECTURE...

Move to the left across the top of the lecture hall. When you reach the clear aisle down on the far side, you accidentally kick a can down the stairs, awakening a former student. Shoot this zombie as it attempts to work its way upstairs. Aim for its head to conserve bullets. The sound of your gun draws in another zombie from the left, which you should deal with the same way.

Descend the stairs to the lecture floor. Another zombie rises from behind the desk. Move to the opposite side of the desk and shoot the zombie in the head as it tries to come around. You can also press Action to climb on top of the desk to gain an advantage and shoot it from above.

When the zombies are dead, turn around and move to the top of the blocked aisle to find a **Green Herb**. Even though you can now add this to your Health Tablet case and use it to cure yourself if needed, hold out a little longer and wait to find a Red Herb to combine it with. After all, why add only one pill to the case when you can add three or six? Exit the lecture hall through the side double-doors.

TIME FOR SCHOOLING

Proceed up the next hallway until you reach a makeshift barricade that blocks the passage. Open the double doors on your left. A zombie typically leaps out and attacks you. Rotate the Left Stick quickly to throw it off before it inflicts too much damage. Hopefully Helena knocks the zombie off you. If so, immediately move to its head and press Fire to stomp the un-life out of it.

As you proceed into the classroom, a zombie woman resurrects on your left. Shoot this monster in the head a few times to kill it, and then face the back side of the desk. As indicated by the icon onscreen, you can press Action to slide over the desktop. Such actions are a good way to escape from enemies and to put a small barrier between you and potential threats, which gives you time to reload your weapon and attack.

Move toward the back of the classroom and search the second-to-last aisle on the left for **9mm Ammo**. A male zombie across the room rises. Conserve bullets by moving over to it and performing a Quick Shot (press and release Aim and Fire simultaneously). This causes the zombie to stagger, during which time you can lower your weapon, approach it quickly, and knock it to the floor with a melee hit. Stand near its head and press melee again to crush its skull. Remember this series of attacks and use it frequently to take down single zombies quickly.

COMBINE YOUR HERBS

Search behind the last row on the other side of the aisle to find another **Green Herb**. Press △ on PlayStation 3 or Ⓨ on Xbox 360 to open your Items Menu. Scroll left or right through your items until a Green Herb is selected and then press the Action button. Options appear below the herb, and the first is to combine this Green Herb with another. Press Action again and the cursor automatically moves to the other Green Herb. Press Action again to combine the two, creating a set of three green powders. Now press Action twice more to send the mixture to your Health Tablet case, resulting in three tablets. Press the Health Tablet button (R1 on PlayStation 3, RB on Xbox 360) to administer aid to yourself. Each Health Tablet consumed restores one block of your Health Gauge. If you are down more than one block, press the Health Tablet button multiple times quickly to fully heal.

STEALTH HITS SAVE TIME AND BULLETS

Open the back door of the classroom, proceed down the hall to the soda machines, and head left to the exit. Descend the stairs and stop at the bottom. Turn right and you see a zombie with its back to you. When an enemy is unaware of your presence like this, run up behind them and press Fire to perform a Stealth Hit. Stealth Hits help you take out zombies instantly, no ammo required. However, be aware that another zombie is on the floor behind the first. It rises and leaps for you. Avoid zombie leaps by holding Ready/Aim, moving backward, and pressing Action. Though the controller combo sounds complex, you can do it rather quickly to avoid attacks. Then, while lying flat on your back, continue holding Aim to keep your weapon ready and shoot the zombie. Aim for the head for quicker results. Pick up the **9mm Ammo** and **Green Herb** in the corner along with any items the monsters dropped and then proceed through the double doors.

BE CONSCIOUS OF YOUR SURROUNDINGS

Head down the corridor. An open doorway is on your left, leading to another classroom. However, around the corner on your right is a group of zombies that spots you entering the classroom and follows you there. Run behind the closest zombie in this group and perform a Stealth Hit. Get on your feet and shoot the other zombies in their heads while moving backward. If one lunges, press Action while aiming and walking backward to dodge the attack. Keep firing.

TRY DUAL-FISTED MODE

While aiming Leon's Wing Shooter, press △ on PlayStation 3 or Ⓨ on Xbox 360 to switch weapon modes. Firing two guns at once kills enemies faster, which is effective against zombie hordes. However, bear in mind this mode uses ammo faster, fires less accurately, and reloading two guns takes slightly longer.

SECOND-PERIOD CLASS

Now it's safe to turn around and enter the classroom. A **Red Herb** is in the far corner on your right. Open your Item Menu and combine this with the Green Herb you found recently to create six Health Tablets. Add them to your case. A zombie lies in the aisle and lunges as you move past it. Perform a Quick Shot to counter this move. Stomp on its head while it's down. Another zombie rises from behind the desk, and you should have enough stamina left in the Combat Gauge to take it down with a Quick Shot and melee combo. Afterward, however, your Combat Gauge needs time to recharge. While it does this naturally, the process is faster if you stand still for a few seconds. If the tactics described don't work for your situation, you can stun and damage the zombies by shooting the fire extinguisher lying on the desktop nearby. Pick up the **9mm Ammo** and **Incendiary Grenades x2** on the desk. Conserve the latter items for use against crowds in desperate situations. Exit the classroom, move to the double doors at the end of the corridor, and open them with a Partner Action.

MARAUD AND PLUNDER THE COMMONS

Leon and Helena enter an outdoor courtyard. Single zombies stand in scattered locations all over the grounds. If you ignore them or run past them, you face the risk of drawing them all to one location, where they might create a horde and cause you grief. However, you can slide across certain tables in the area to put a barrier between you and these monsters, and then shoot across. Therefore, approach and take down single zombies you encounter here with Quick Shots and melee follow-ups. Note that zombies carrying weapons are great targets for this combo, since you can grab the weapon out of the zombie's hand and use it against the thing with nasty results.

From the doorway, head to the far left toward the soda machines, where you find two packs of **9mm Ammo**. Deal with a zombie woman behind the tables here, then work your way back to the center. Move to the opposite wall of the area and follow it toward the objective marker. Perform a Stealth Hit on a zombie with its back to you, and then use the Quick Shot and melee combo on another one coming down the red carpet.

THE EXIT IS NO-GO

Proceed to the marked gate and press Action to examine it. You determine that the gate is locked and that a key is required. Ingrid Hunnigan, Leon's backup via radio, suggests looking for the key in the other wing. Turn away from the doors and head to the far right. Kill more single zombies in your path before they gather together. You find a **Green Herb** and a **Red Herb** on two separate tables in the corner. Combine and store them at the next opportunity. Continue to the double wooden doors on the wall and press Partner Action to enter the building.

DON'T TRIP OVER THE BODIES

Proceed somewhat slowly up the corridor. Partially tilt the Left Stick to reduce speed. Running over one of the corpses in this area causes you to trip and hinders movement speed. Pick up a box of **9mm Ammo** lying next to the closest body and another behind the mini-fridge on the right and farther ahead.

FULL-SCALE BREACH

Press Partner Action to open the door at the far end. An alarm is triggered, causing dozens of zombies to crash through the windows and climb into the corridor. Additional waves of foes enter the corridor as long as the alarm is going off, so you have to hold out. Shoot zombies until they fill the corridor. Press the D-pad up or down to equip an Incendiary Grenade and then toss it. Adjust your arc of trajectory prior to the throw, and make sure the grenade lands well away from you and Helena. If you run out of Incendiary Grenades, look for fire extinguishers on either side of the passage. Shoot them to blow down groups of zombies. Approach the downed group, crush a few heads, and then quickly retreat as enemy survivors struggle to rise. Save your stamina and perform Quick Shot/melee attack combos only against enemies armed with baseball bats, bottles, and axes. You can snatch these weapons away and use them for instant kills.

During the short spans between hordes, cross to the far end of the corridor and tap the Pickup button rapidly to collect all the items dropped by the zombies you killed. If Helena doesn't follow, hold the Partner Action button and press down on the D-pad to prompt her to come to you. This prevents you from having to rush in and save her from a zombie attack. If your partner is seized by a zombie, and you have the opportunity, move in close and press Partner Action to free Helena.

CLEAR THE DOOR

When Ingrid Hunnigan finally hacks the security system, you can break through the door. However, the zombies won't be shut out so easily. Aim your handgun at the heads of the two zombies poking out from behind the door and fire at them until they explode.

Note that you can pick up a pack of **9mm Ammo** while doing this. You can still pick up this ammo from the nearby bench if you miss it during the event.

SEARCH DESK DRAWERS

Go behind the counter in the student office. To find more **9mm Ammo**, press Action to open the drawer in the desk located to the left of the back door.

Continue through the small library into the back office. Move to the left side of the nearest desk and open the drawer to find **9mm Ammo**.

SERPENT EMBLEM: STUDENT OFFICE

Move around the desk cluster to the desk near the dead woman. Open the drawer to find another **Serpent Emblem** to collect.

ONE WELL-GUARDED KEYCARD

Open the back door of the back office with a Partner Action. The **Campus Keycard** rests on the shelves to the far left. Taking it causes the zombie on the floor to leap out and attack. When you hear the growl, you have a second to react by pulling a Quick Shot. Otherwise, as is most likely, the zombie drags you to the floor.

Rotate the Left Stick rapidly to break free of its hold. You see a second gauge with the Fire button displayed. Wait until the timer hand moves into the colored section. Then press Fire to strike back with tremendous force. If this doesn't kill the zombie, then shoot it or kick its head in.

BLAST YOUR WAY OUT

Revitalize yourself with a Health Tablet and return to the first office. The bodies throughout the office will rise, depending on whether you (or Helena) pass by them.

Fight your way back out to the corridor. There you face the last wave of zombies from your previous encounter. Run down to the exit to draw the attention of all the zombies, then run back to the office doorway to draw them all in. If you have Incendiary Grenades on hand, use them to torch the group, or you may shoot any remaining fire extinguishers. Otherwise, take them all down and aim for headshots.

UNLOCK THE EXIT

Head back to the locked gate and take out single zombies roaming the grounds. Don't waste bullets killing every single undead. Just focus on the ones standing between you and the objective marker. Approach the gate and press Partner Action to open it.

YOU'LL NEVER PASS SECURITY

You must move through the metal detector to proceed through the room. Your weapons set off the alarm. Proceed directly across the room and through the other metal detector. Take out the lone zombie in your way with a Quick Shot/ melee attack combo. Open the exit door with a Partner Action.

MAKE A BREAK FOR IT!

The short stretch behind the campus exit may look safe, but it will soon be flooded with enemies. Avoid fighting with zombies, and instead begin making your way out. Approach the barriers at the far end and press Action to hop over them. Move to the far wall of the next alley and run down a few feet to avoid a crowd. Dash to the other side of the alley and go left. Continue on to the end without shooting or touching anyone. If your AI partner stops to fight, hold Partner Action and press down on the D-pad. This tells Helena to disengage and to follow you. Move to the driver's door of the police car parked at the bottom of the hill.

LOOK FOR THE KEYS!

Inside the police car, move the Right Stick to search the car for the keys. Look to the far right and press Action to make Helena check the glove box. The keys are not in there, so look forward and then upward to check the sun visor. Press the Reload button to start the car and then press Fire to drive off. Press Aim to back up then Fire to drive forward again.

You don't get very far in the car, but you're safe for now. Move to the open manhole and press Partner Action to drop inside.

UNDERGROUND

UNDERGROUND MAP

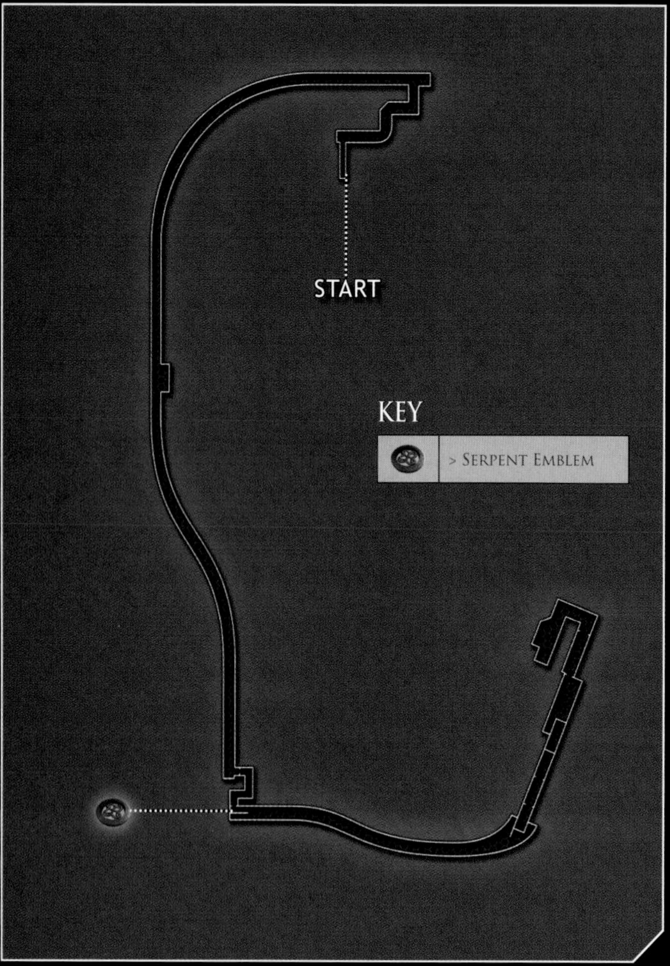

SMASH ITEM CRATES FOR RANDOM ITEMS

Move downstairs into the sewer and head right. Follow the corridor until you spot some brightly colored boxes of various sizes in the corner. Smash these boxes to obtain extra items. The items contained in item boxes are randomly determined each time you break them.

CONTROL HOW YOU OPEN DOORS

Open the door across from the item boxes. Press Action once to open it quietly as you did back at campus or press Action twice to burst through quickly. The second approach offers the advantage of allowing you to enter a room quickly and possibly stunning an enemy that stands on the other side. However, the extra noise may also attract nearby enemies.

MAKE SOME TRACKS

Drop down onto the tracks. To the right, power lines lie in water pools, so don't approach them. Instead, go the other way up the tunnel. You encounter a few zombies as you proceed. Shoot the ones that are aware of you and sneak up on the others to perform Stealth Hits.

STICK TO THE WALLS

Occasionally a train roars through this tunnel. When you see a growing light and your partner shouts, move to the nearest wall and press Reload and Action to press up against the wall. Failure to do so means instant game over. Trains have the benefit of clearing the area of zombies and allow you to pick up any dropped spoils.

COUNTER THE HOUNDS

Continue up the tunnel. As you approach a bonfire on the left, prepare to be attacked by a group of Zombie Dogs. Possibly the best way to deal with these fast little monsters is to allow them to charge at you. Press Fire at the last second, just as soon as the icon displays onscreen. This is known as a "counter," a tactic that can be used against most other enemies that perform melee attacks.

Dash through the last segment of the tunnel. You pass a zombie that is killing a civilian, but there's no way to intervene in time. You may also have to avoid another train in this area, so stay close to the wall. At the end of the line, you encounter zombies moving through water filled with electrical lines. You are unable to go that way, so ignore the zombies and climb up the ledge to the left.

Kick open the door via Partner Action and descend the dark stairs. Be ready for a few close encounters at the first corner and kick apart nearby item crates to restock supplies. Open the door at the bottom to find that you've reached another dangerous train track.

SERPENT EMBLEM: B TRACK

After opening the door at the bottom of the stairwell, drop off the platform and turn right. You spot a **Serpent Emblem** tucked below the corner of the parked train. Shoot it to collect it.

DASH THROUGH THE HORDE

Follow the tracks through the darkness for a long distance until you see light reflected on the wall ahead. A horde of zombies approaches. Rather than waste your bullets on them, run past them and stay close to the left-hand wall. *Run*—do not dash! Soon a train roars through the tunnel. If you're dashing, then you won't be able to flatten against the wall. When you avoid the train successfully, all you have to do afterward is pick up the items the dead zombies drop.

BREAK INTO THE TRAIN

After the horde is destroyed, continue up the rest of the tunnel to the end and cross to the right side. Approach the raised loading platform and climb onto it. A zombie climbs out of the floor vent behind you, so turn around and dispatch it. Then, examine the train compartment door, which you find is locked. Drop off the platform, move to the back of the train, and press Partner Action to lift Helena onto the top. Helena can then drop through the open escape hatch up top and unlock the door from the inside. Climb back onto the loading platform and rejoin her.

CLAUSTROPHOBIA SETS IN

The train is full of corpses, the nearest of which reanimates and attacks. After killing it, proceed down the aisle to the door and open it with a Partner Action. You rouse fewer zombies by moving at slow speeds through the compartments. However, in the third car all the bodies resurrect as you move through the middle of the car, no matter how slowly you move. Take them all down, proceed to the back door, and move toward the light at the far end of the last car. Stop near the open door on your left and, using headshots, kill the zombie outside.

SLIDE INTO CRATES

Drop into the tunnel, move quickly around the back end of the train, and perform a Stealth Hit on a zombie. Proceed up the tunnel and climb onto the next platform. Dash toward the far end of the platform and press Aim while sprinting, which enables you to slide into some item crates on the left side. Sliding into two or more crates to break them open is more efficient than cracking them open one at a time. Remember this important tactic during battles.

EXIT COMPLICATIONS

Press the red button on the wall next to the shutter. A woman calls out from the train behind you. Move over to the doors and open them via Partner Action. The woman runs over, opens the shutter doors, and immediately becomes food for a zombie horde. Toss an Incendiary Grenade if you have one on hand or plant a Remote Bomb and run away. Press up or down on the D-pad to select a Remote Bomb if one is available. While the bomb is in hand, move to the spot where you want to plant it and press Ready/Aim to set the bomb on the ground. The remote detonator automatically appears. Move a safe distance away, and press Aim and Fire to set off the explosive. One Remote Bomb planted in the center of the shutter door opening should take out most of the horde. Dispatch the rest with your handgun from behind the nearby boxes.

The zombies on the platform behind you reanimate and approach. Leave them behind and run up the subway stairs. Move behind the zombie standing near the turnstiles and take him down with a Stealth Hit. Move to the far right and hop over the low gate to continue. Approach the bars and press Partner Action to exit the subway.

TOWN MAP

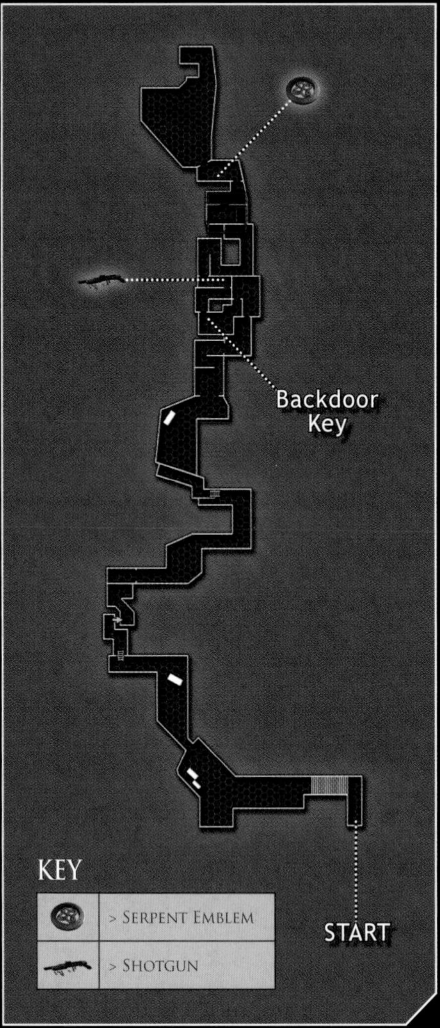

IT'S CHAOS OUT THERE

Ascend the stairs out of the subway. A zombie firefighter attacks from your right but misses. Perform a Quick Shot followed by melee attacks to take his axe and bury it in his skull.

Move up the street and give a wide berth to zombies and dead bodies you might trip over. Smash wooden barrels to either side to collect items but otherwise keep moving up the street.

Approach the cluster of cars blocking the road and press Partner Action to rescue the man pinned under an automotive bumper.

AVOID STOPPING...FOR ANYTHING

Having cleared the road, proceed up the street and resume the practice of ignoring zombies, which are otherwise distracted. Only take out those that target you and actually block your forward movement. Some of the zombies in this area are cops wearing protective body armor and firing machine guns at random. You have three choices for dealing with such zombies: leave their area as fast as possible, throw an Incendiary Grenade, or shoot them repeatedly in the face.

OVER THE MOSH PIT

Approach the burning wreckage blocking the street and continue down the alley to the left. Climb the ladder mounted to the fence, then follow the series of gantries above the zombie horde. Jump across the gap and continue on behind the idle zombie standing on the raised gantry. Move in close enough to finish this zombie with a Stealth Hit.

GET MOVING AGAIN

Drop back down to street level at the end of the gantries. Turn right and open the nearby door with a Partner Action. Even though carnage happens up ahead and the street is suddenly full of burning zombies, they will soon die. Dash through the area to avoid an armored cop zombie that is firing at random. Run diagonally to the left across the street and into the next alleyway

BREAK UP THE FEAST

Near the parked car, ignore the zombie feeding on the corpse. Instead, move up behind the unwary one on the left and perform a Stealth Hit. When the other one rises, kill it with a Quick Shot/melee attack combo.

Follow the bending alley inward and take down another approaching zombie. Smash the wooden barrels behind the ladder, and then climb onto the raised platform. Dispatch another zombie up here with a Stealth Hit. Press Partner Action to shove the heavy dumpster out of your way.

HEAD INDOORS

Climb onto the balcony to your right then move across the top of the parked bus. Drop down on the clear right side. Proceed up the street until an accident occurs and blocks your path. Turn down the alley to the right and open the double doors of the "modern RED" bar with a Partner Action.

ONE QUICK DRINK, THEN TIME TO GO

Move up to the bar and head left around the counter. Smash the item barrel in the corner and go through the door behind the bar. Cross the small outdoor yard quickly and press Action to open the back gate. The body nearby will animate and attack Helena, so help her put this zombie down. Move around the building corner and go in the back door.

FAMILY TIME

Navigate through the house and into the living room. A dead family is gathered around the TV, which shows important news happening elsewhere. Open the door on the far side of the living room and follow the corridor to the back exit. Examine the exit door to determine that it is locked. Go back into the family room and you'll spot the **Backdoor Key** in a dead woman's pocket. When you pull it out, the husband rises to stop you. Put him back down with a Quick Shot/melee combo and then return to the back door. The corpse here falls over and then attacks. You can avoid this by backing away in time. Use the key on the back door and press Action again to open it.

CAN I BORROW YOUR BOOMSTICK?

Take the **Shotgun** from the corpse in the alley. Now, smash the wooden barrels at the other end, one of which usually drops some **12-Gauge Shells**. Press Partner Action to kick open the door.

SILENCE THE SHRIEKER

With Helena in tow, you discover a dangerous new species—the Shrieker. In addition to the usual zombie-style grabbing attacks, this creature can inflate its lungs and emit a high-pitched scream that inflicts damage and renders you vulnerable to other attacks. The creature's weak spot is its chest, especially when the lungs are puffed out. The Shotgun is the most effective weapon against the Shrieker. However, shooting its puffed lungs allows it to emit a death rattle before dying. This last screaming attack affects a cone-shaped area in front of the creature, which means you can avoid the direct effects of the sound blast by running to the creature's side or rear. Shriekers drop **Skill Points (1,000)** when defeated.

As soon as you see the creature in this situation, turn right and jump through the glass window. The hallway is a much safer place to fight, or frankly to make your escape, since several zombies climb over the nearby fence if you remain outdoors.

THE LURKER ABOVE

While you proceed down the back corridor, zombies hop in through the windows on your right. Use an Incendiary Grenade or Remote Bomb to take them out, including the one hanging from the ceiling. Shoot this zombie before trying to pass under him or he will be able to grab you.

SEPARATION ANXIETY

The brick hallway leads to a small courtyard. Examine the gate on the opposite side of the yard to find that it is locked. Turn right and go up the stairs in the corner. Move to the opening in the rail and press Partner Action to toss Helena across the gap.

While Helena slowly pushes a dumpster out of her way and drops down to unlock the gate, you must contend with the zombies that invade the courtyard and begin moving up the stairs. Although you can now drop down from the gap in the railing, avoid doing so. Instead, stand at the top of the narrow stairs and make the zombies funnel their way up to you. Take out the first few with Quick Shot/melee attack combos, then back up or drop onto your back and gun down the rest with headshots. When she gets the far gate open, Helena joins you in killing off the last few at the bottom of the stairs. Enter another bar and smash the item barrel on the left. Then, go around the counter and out the front door.

SERPENT EMBLEM: AFTER HOURS BAR INTERIOR

While approaching the double doors at the exit of the bar, stop and turn to your left to spot a **Serpent Emblem.** It rests on the left end of the stool-seating section, against the wall.

THESE PEOPLE REALLY NEED HELP

Across the street from the bar entrance, a mismatched group of survivors is cornered by a zombie mob. Move in and take down the nearest zombie with a Stealth Hit. Afterward, take down zombies with headshots without moving too close to the survivors in the corner, regardless of their interpersonal dramas. The usual Quick Shot/melee attack combo tactics won't work well here due to the numbers. So move around while looking for Stealth Hit opportunities and avoid remaining stationary for too long.

After you clear out the first horde, a Shrieker appears with the second wave. Hit this creature with any remaining Incendiary Grenades or blast it in the face and puffy chest with the Shotgun. Otherwise, it will circle the area and repeatedly blast all of you with its noise.

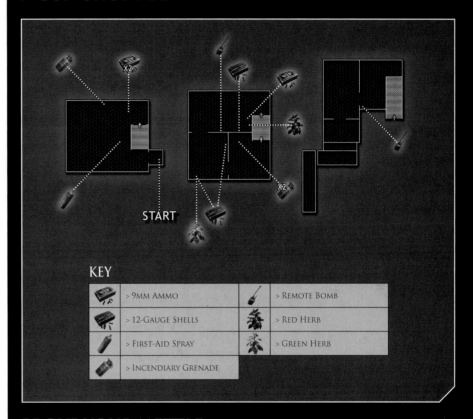

AN AMBULANCE... ATTACKS!

When the camera suddenly angles down the burning street, dash to the left to get away from the gas station. Press Action while moving sideways and try to perform a dodge roll if it's needed. An ambulance crashes into the pumps, and you can be killed or heavily injured if it runs over you. Human cops with body armor and guns spill out of the back of the ambulance and begin firing. However, the benefit of the crash is that one of the pumps begins spewing gas all over the place. Shoot the gas to destroy the station and eliminate the horde before it takes out the survivors. What a way to save people!

After the explosion, one of the cops will lead you down the alley. Pick up any dropped items you can, and follow him before burning zombies fill the area again. Approach the gate and press Partner Action to proceed.

GUN SHOP

GUN SHOP MAP

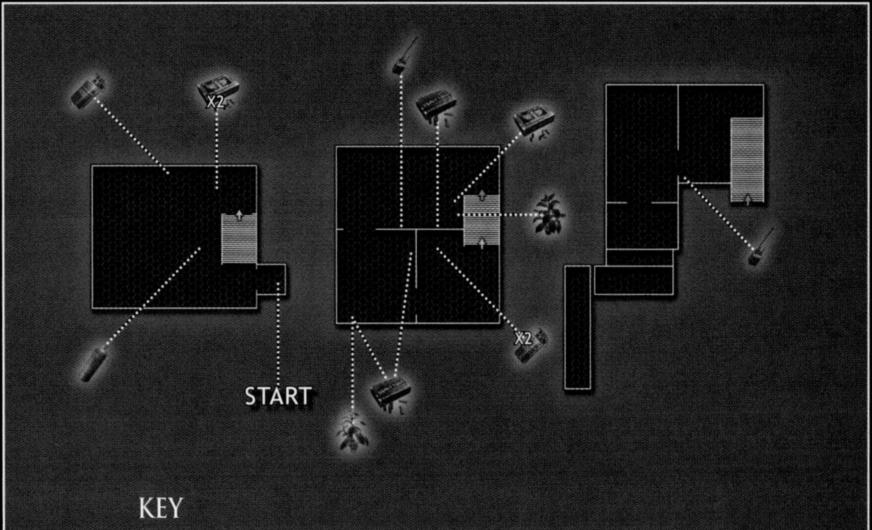

KEY

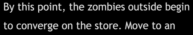

	> 9MM AMMO		> REMOTE BOMB
	> 12-GAUGE SHELLS		> RED HERB
	> FIRST-AID SPRAY		> GREEN HERB
	> INCENDIARY GRENADE		

PROVE YOUR METTLE

Enter the back door of the gun shop. The owner is upstairs, locked in his apartment, and won't let you in unless you kill all the zombies outside. Quickly search the shop for supplies, including the **Shotgun** (if you missed it earlier) on the shelves to the left, and a **First-Aid Spray** behind the counter on the right. Hop over the counter and move to the far corner of the gun case to find two boxes of **9mm Ammo**, then divert to the left to find an **Incendiary Grenade** on a small table.

By this point, the zombies outside begin to converge on the store. Move to an open window and shoot the zombies outside before they can get in. Shoot or kick zombies that climb through windows to knock them back out.

When dealing with zombies that get inside the store, check first to make sure they're not wearing body armor before you try a Quick Shot on them. Frankly, you must take down most of the enemies with gunfire to avoid depleting your Combat Gauge. Look for zombies holding weapons, or individuals that have weapons embedded in their chests—reserve your Quick Shot/melee attack combos for these specific foes.

MEET THE BLOODSHOT ZOMBIE

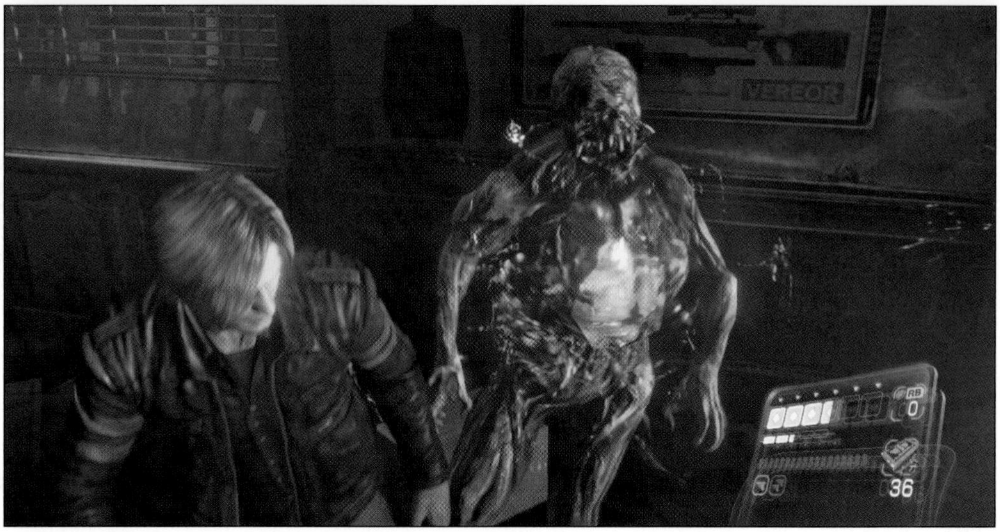

One of the survivors goes outside and starts a fight with a zombie. Unfortunately, the battle turns on the poor guy when the zombie transforms into a new species called Bloodshot. These are strong and resilient monsters that require extra shots to kill them. Shoot a Bloodshot in the legs until it kneels, revealing the weak spot in its chest. Then you can finish the monster with a Shotgun blast to the weak spot. Incendiary Grenades work really well against Bloodshots, especially when they appear among zombie hordes. Bloodshots drop **Skill Points (500)** when defeated.

As the final wave of zombies floods the store, move behind the counter and make the enemies funnel into your Shotgun blasts. If their numbers become overwhelming, turn and hop over the counter to escape.

RESTOCK QUICKLY DURING THE CHATTER

When the owner finally trips the security system and shutters drop over the windows, head upstairs. While the owner talks, approach the table on his left to pick up a **Red Herb** and **9mm Ammo**. Check the couch nearby to find a **Remote Bomb**. When the store owner moves, open the drawer in the workbench where he was standing to obtain **12-Gauge Shells**.

Soon zombies begin spilling out of the building behind yours. Fire through the windows and throw an Incendiary Grenade into the crowd gathering below the far window, especially when a Bloodshot appears.

BREAK DOWN THE WHOPPER

The owner opens the door to the next room. Move to the workbench opposite the door and pick up the **Green Herb**. Open the drawer in this workbench and take **12-Gauge Shells**. Additional **12-Gauge Shells** are in a drawer in the other workbench, which is in the opposite corner of the room.

A giant, zombie monster called a Whopper bursts into the room. This monster's weak spot is its tiny legs, so shoot it low until it falls. Also consider planting a Remote Bomb in one corner of the room, wait until the Whopper approaches, then dash to the other side of the room before detonating it. Whoppers drop **Skill Points (2,500)** when they are defeated.

THE FINAL STAND

Follow the owner into the stairwell. Turn left and enter the small closet under the stairs to find **Incendiary Grenades x2**. Now, run upstairs. Grab another **Remote Bomb** to the left of the exit, and go outside.

Zombies, Bloodshots, and Whoppers start climbing over the low fence on one side of the patio. Run to that location, plant a Remote Bomb, run away, and detonate it. Be sure to focus on shooting the Whopper in the legs to bring it down quickly.

GET ON THE BUS!

Continue shooting enemies and shoving them off you until the bus arrives and the shop owner opens the back gate. At this point, leave the remaining enemies and move through the gate. Drop over the ledge, move left on the fire escape and drop over the side. Run up the alley toward the other survivors.

A Whopper picks up the front of the bus to prevent its escape. Toss an Incendiary Grenade onto the bus hood, and rapidly shoot the Whopper in the face with your handgun and Shotgun until it lets go.

CHAPTER RANKING

After each chapter, you are awarded a rank for prowess in four criteria regardless of difficulty selected: hit accuracy percentage, player deaths suffered, total clear time, and number of enemies defeated. For each letter-grade rank obtained, a specific number of points are awarded as determined by the "Points Awarded Per Rank" table. These points are then added together to determine an overall rank for the chapter as determined by the "Total Ranking Points Table." S is a perfect score, requiring A ranking for all four criteria.

LEON CHAPTER 1: RANKING CRITERIA

RANK	ACCURACY(%)	DEATHS	CLEAR TIME(MIN)	ENEMIES ROUTED
A	70	2	85	80
B	60	5	110	60
C	50	7	130	40
D	*1	*1	*1	*1

*1 Any Below Rank C

POINTS AWARDED PER RANK (ABOVE)				
Rank	A	B	C	D
Points	25	20	15	10

TOTAL RANKING POINTS TABLE

RANK	S	A	B	C	D	E
Total	100	90	75	55	45	*2

*2 Any Below Rank D

UNLOCK AND UPGRADE NEW SKILLS

After viewing the ranking screen, you may either exit to the Play Game menu or press Start to proceed to the Skill Settings screen. Purchase Skills from the menu on the right hand side and equip them in your skill set, displayed on the left. Up to three Skills can be equipped at a time.

Good initial investments of your Skill Points include Firearm Lv. 1, Defense Lv. 1, or Zombie Hunter Lv. 1. You unlock the Zombie Hunter skill by killing 30 or more zombies, which should be no problem during Leon Chapter 1. If you're switching now to Chris' or Jake's Campaign, purchase J'avo Killer Lv. 1, which is unlocked by defeating 30 or more J'avo enemies.

By completing Leon's Campaign (or any other campaign), you will unlock the ability to create up to eight Skill Sets and switch them in the Game Menu (accessed by pressing Back/Start). So go ahead and purchase extra Skills now, even if they don't fit in the three slots currently available.

THE BUS

ONE SHORT TRIP

Leon and Helena are knocked unconscious when their bus crashes on a country road. They revive to find the vehicle under siege and zombies are everywhere. Both heroes roll onto their backs. Tilt the Left Stick downward to crawl slowly away from the approaching monsters while shooting them in the face. After creating a bit of breathing room, reload and pick up two boxes of **9mm Ammo** on the floor below you. The bus teeters on the edge of a cliff, and the yawing motion throws off your aim at least once. Immediately resume shooting zombies in their heads until the situation ends.

FOREST CEMETERY

CEMETERY MAP

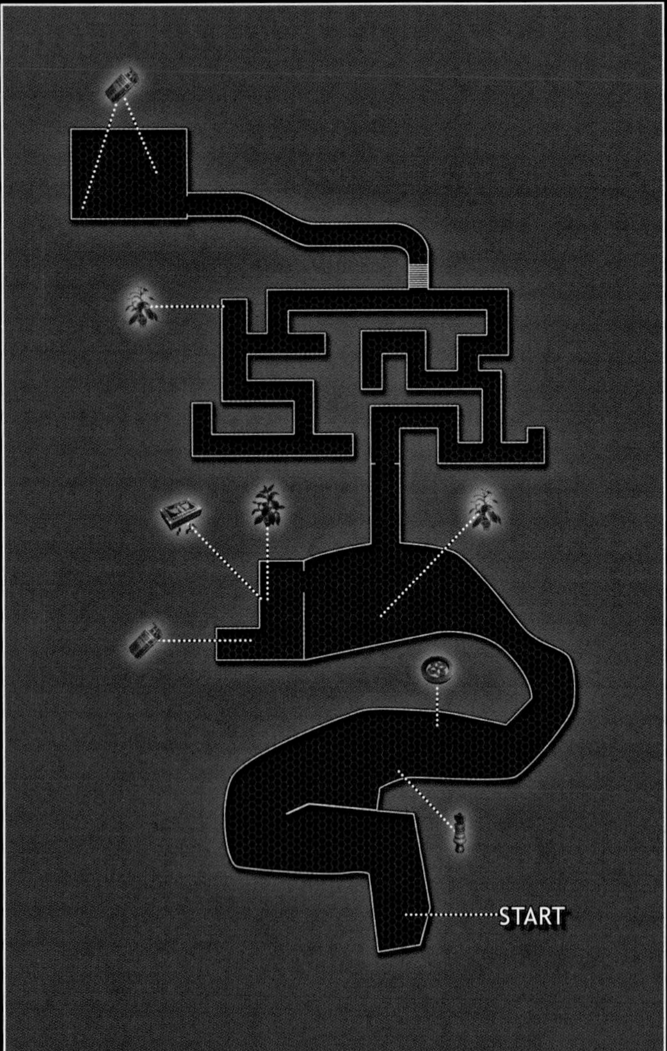

KEY

	> Serpent Emblem		> Skill Points 5000
	> 9mm Ammo		> Red Herb
	> Incendiary Grenade		> Green Herb

THIS IS A BAD IDEA...

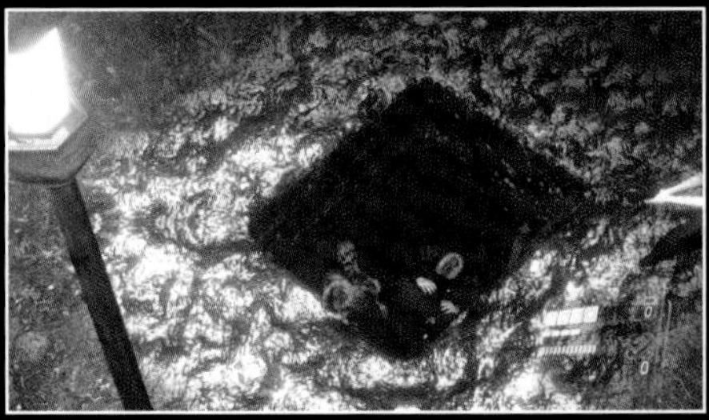

You must navigate through a cemetery to reach the cathedral, the place where Helena says there are answers. During a zombie infestation, the cemetery is the last place you want to be—for obvious reasons. Stick to the path as much as possible in order to navigate through it quickly. The resurrected corpses attack you incessantly throughout the cemetery, so move as quickly as possible. Do not leave the path to attack moving corpses or to search for items. However, do refer to the map in this section to find the locations of **Skill Points (5,000)** and a **Green Herb**, both stashed inside sarcophagi that you must force open. Also, avoid the open pits in the ground. You might slip on the mud and fall into the pit, where you will be trapped with a zombie lurking just under the water's surface.

WARNING! BEWARE OF THE LIGHTNING FLASHES!

Occasionally lightning will flashes across the sky, bright enough to blind you momentarily. During these instances when you are briefly stunned, cemetery zombies have the opportunity to ambush you with a grab. Rotate the Left Stick rapidly to escape these holds quickly and reduce the damage you sustain. If you see your partner in trouble, run over and press Partner Action to come to the rescue.

SERPENT EMBLEM: CEMETERY OBELISK

The cemetery path leads to an uphill slope with a wooden fence on the left and a stone wall on the right. Stop at the bottom of this slope, turn left, and move into the cemetery. Look for a small cluster of headstones and an obelisk next to a tree. Go to the back side of the obelisk to find a **Serpent Emblem** mounted in one of the circles. Break it to collect it.

SOLITARY CABIN IN THE WOODS LOOKS LEGIT

Continue following the stone path to the cathedral. Wipe out zombies that get in your way or that run up behind you. Eventually, you approach a small bridge that leads to the cathedral grounds. It has a gate that is locked. Turn left from the bridge toward the light of a cabin and make a break for it.

Enter the cabin and search the far-left area to find an **Incendiary Grenade**. Move to the bathroom door on the back wall and press Partner Action to open it. A frightened dog jumps out of the bathroom and runs away. Grab the **9mm Ammo** off the sink and exit the cabin.

FIND THAT DOG, FIND THAT KEY!

You see the dog that fled the cabin has a key to the bridge gate in its mouth. Run all the way back down the stone path. Blast or dodge more zombies in your way and head toward the dog.

Zombie Dogs also appear in the cemetery now, and the best way to deal with them is still a last-minute counter. The animal's location is marked with a red diamond, which also indicates your distance away from it.

Now transformed into the undead, the dog waits at the end of one of the side paths in the company of several other zombies and Zombie Dogs. Toss an Incendiary Grenade into their group to kill them. The Zombie Dogs tend to dodge this, however. Combat them using Quick Shots and counters. The Zombie Dog with the key in its mouth is harder to take down than the others, so blast him with your Shotgun repeatedly. When the beast finally dies, move to its location and pick up the **Cemetery Key**.

ENTER THE CATHEDRAL GROUNDS

Follow the path all the way back to the bridge, press Action to use the Cemetery Key to unlock the gate, then press Partner Action to open it. A lightning flash allows a zombie to knock you over a small ledge, separating you from Helena. You must navigate the rows of standing crypts to rejoin your partner. A few items and a large number of zombies wait among the crypts. You can take down many of the enemies with Stealth Hits simply by moving swiftly. However, be aware that some of the zombies are wearing armor that deflects bullets. Avoid using any Incendiary Grenades while dealing with monsters among the crypts and instead focus on stocking up on the items that they drop.

Use your directional beacon frequently to find your way through the maze-like crypt area. Press L1 on PlayStation 3 or LB on Xbox 360 to display your directional beacon and follow it to the cemetery exit.

When you arrive at the exit, pick up the **Green Herb** in the corner to the left and examine the gold door. It's locked, so backtrack a little bit to the middle aisle and go up. Follow this path to the left and continue up the stairs. The exit to the cathedral is on your right, but you should go straight in order to rescue your partner from more zombies and a Shrieker. Return to the stairs and go up. Follow the long road to the cathedral gate and ignore any enemies that follow you out of the crypts.

REFUSED ENTRY

Search the courtyard in front of the cathedral doors to find two **Incendiary Grenades**. One is on the bench near the tree to your right, and the other is on the bench in the back corner. Avoid breaking the item crates at the moment. They provide better items if you break them during a battle. Approach the cathedral doors and press Partner Action to knock on them. The inhabitants refuse you entry when a zombie horde climbs over the gate behind you.

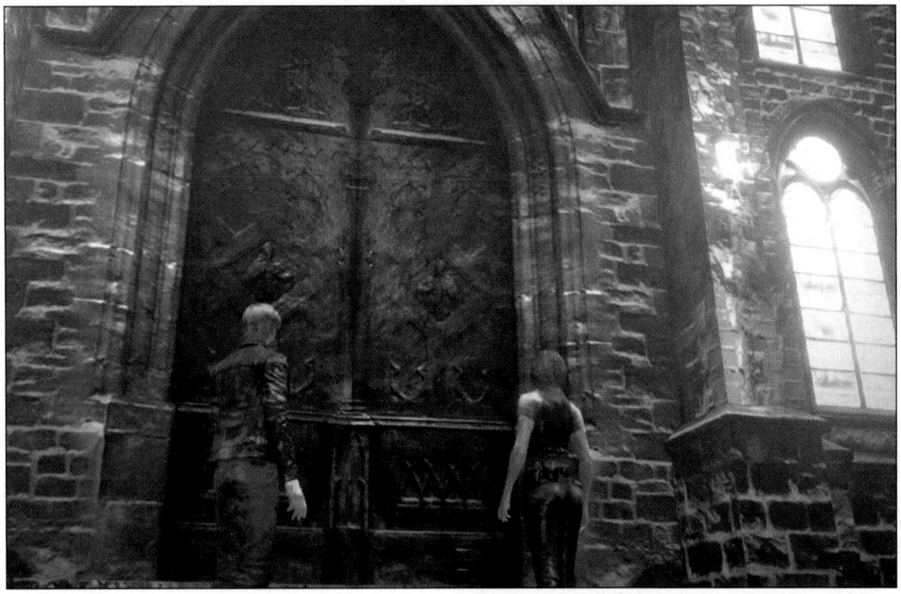

For each wave of enemies, equip an Incendiary Grenade and throw it at the base of the fence that the masses of undead climb over. With the right timing, this takes out most of the zombies, and you need only mop up the remainders. If you are short on Incendiary Grenades, then break the item crates in this area in the hopes of obtaining more. Use Quick Shot/melee attack combos against zombies holding weapons in order to use those items against their owners. You can also plant Remote Bombs next to zombie clusters, move away, and then detonate them. Shriekers also climb over the fence, and you must shoot these quickly before they scream. This inflicts damage and summons more zombies. The later waves in this courtyard also include Bloodshots—you should use Incendiary Grenades and your Shotgun against these difficult foes.

The enemies just keep coming. Eventually, the people inside the cathedral allow you to come indoors. Pick up any item drops within a reasonable distance of the doors, head back, and enter the cathedral via Partner Action.

NOT A HAPPY PLACE

Search the entire cathedral ground floor for items. Again, avoid smashing item barrels until you're in the heat of battle at a later time: you obtain better items from them (but fewer Skill Points). Among the central pews you find goodies such as a **First-Aid Spray** and a **Green Herb.**

When you are done scavenging, join your partner on the dais. Examine the strange altar. Then turn right and examine the pedestal in the corner, where you find and collect the **Madonna of Happiness**.

CONNECT TO THE SECOND LEVEL

Move to the broken ladder on the right and press Partner Action to hoist Helena up to the second-level balcony. She runs to the far end of the cathedral and knocks down an emergency ladder. Run over and climb this ladder to join her on the second floor.

Cathedral Map

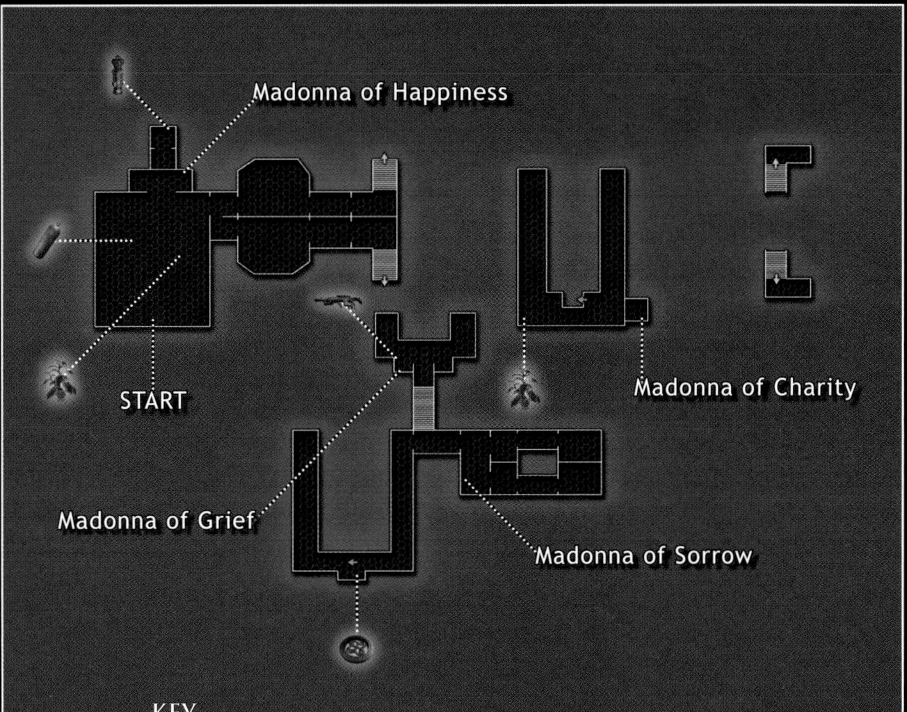

KEY

	> Serpent Emblem		> Skill Points 4000
	> Semi-Auto Sniper Rifle		> Green Herb
	> First-Aid Spray		

Turn left and run down to the end. Here you'll find another pedestal, but placing the statue here does nothing. Examine the plaque on the wall to learn a clue about the cathedral.

Turn around and head back toward the emergency ladder. Open the last door on the left and enter a small room. Break into the small chest in the back corner of this room to find and collect the **Madonna of Charity**.

Place the Madonnas

Circle around the second-floor balcony to the far side, where you locate a **Green Herb** next to an item crate in the corner. Continue toward the front of the cathedral to the pedestal, and press Partner Action to set one of the statues there. Then, wait while your partner circles back around the second floor and places the other Madonna statue on the other pedestal. A door opens on the lower level.

Trials of the Ancient Family

Drop back down to the first floor and head through the open door in the corner, which is to the right of the dais. This small room features two doors and two levers. One of the levers is marked for you. Move to the marked lever and press Partner Action to pull the levers simultaneously.

A gate comes down, dividing the room. Turn to your left to spot a statue emerging from the wall. This device tracks your location with a laser-sighted crossbow and will fire. Dash over to the statue and quickly press the Action button to deactivate it before it shoots you. After you inform your partner of what you have found, she does the same thing. The two doors open, so proceed to the next room.

Still separated from your partner by a dividing wall, you are now surrounded by a dozen or more statue panels with a statue behind each. Pull the levers on the far wall in unison, and then turn around and look for the statues that emerge—up to three at a time. You must dash around the room and quickly deactivate them. Dodge flame arrows and press statue buttons until the exit doors slide open.

POINT THE WAY WITH MIRRORS

Smash the item barrels in the next area. A dead man on your partner's side holds a gun with a laser sight, which points at a circle mirror on your side. However, the laser just misses the mirror. Equip a gun if needed, and aim your laser sight at the mirror to activate it and to open the exit door.

Continue upstairs. At the top, Helena encounters a zombie on her side. Shoot between the stone posts to help her kill it. Now move over to the archway in the corner, which overlooks the statue below. The statue holds another circular mirror. Aim your laser sight at the mirror to activate it and to open the nearby exit.

In the next room, look high on the wall on Helena's side to spot another circle mirror mounted in an alcove. Aim your laser sight at the mirror on her side to continue.

A zombie crawls on the ground in the next chamber. Move to it and stomp on its head before it lunges and finish it off. Afterward, look at the ceiling overhead to see a giant mirror that reflects the next room. Aim your laser sight at the mirror in the alcove off to the far side. The reflected laser opens the doors. Proceed into the next chamber to reunite with Helena and examine the central pedestal to find the **Madonna of Sorrow**.

THE MAN WITH THE GUN YOU NEED

One door opens leading out of the room. Go through it and continue on upstairs. At the top, go left to find a dead man holding a **Semi-Auto Sniper Rifle**. Behind the bars, another Madonna statue waits for you to collect it. First take the weapon and then smash the two wooden barrels in the opposite corner to collect **7.62mm Ammo x2.** (These barrels always yield this ammo.) Examine the plaque on the wall across from the barrels to learn an important clue. Now, proceed out onto the parapets.

SHOOT THE BELLS

As indicated by the plaque inside, five bells hang from the towers around the parapets: three large bells inside the towers and two tiny bells that spin on weathervanes on top of the towers. Go outside through the doorway near the dead man who had the Sniper Rifle. Shoot a large bell directly ahead and another off to the far right. You have to zoom in on the very top of the central tower to shoot the spinning bell. Next, you can either shoot the tiny bell or the weathervane it is on. Aim for the weathervane's chicken for the easier shot. When you are done there, go back through the interior to the parapets on the other side. Here you shoot a large bell to the left and another weathervane bell on the small tower beside it.

TAKE YOUR MADONNA AND GO

The bars blocking access to the statue rise when all five bells have been shot. Return to the pedestal and claim the **Madonna of Grief**.

When you take the statue, the door opens at the bottom of the stairs. Head back down and through the doorway on your right to the third-floor balcony overlooking the cathedral. Move to the back end of the balcony. You find two pedestals on which to place the two blue Madonna statues.

SERPENT EMBLEM: CATHEDRAL WINDOW

Before placing the two Madonna statues on the two third-floor pedestals simultaneously, look high up on the opposite wall. A **Serpent Emblem** leans inside one of the round, stained-glass windows above the cathedral entrance. At this close range, you don't even need to use a Sniper Rifle.

GRIEF AND SORROW

Before placing the two Madonna statues on the two blue pedestals, move to the far side of the third-floor balcony and smash two item barrels for goods. Then, place the pedestals simultaneously with a Partner Action. Doing so opens the secret stairway behind the dais downstairs and also unleashes something quite vile that attacks the survivors within the cathedral!

LEPOTITSA (CATHEDRAL)

This bizarre monster runs around the room and unleashes clouds of blue gas that turn the survivors within the cathedral into zombies that also attack. Therefore, the faster you bring this monster down, the fewer zombies you face. Any zombies that are killed drop extra Sniper Rifle ammo, which is greatly needed. You must stay approximately twenty feet from the boss at all times or the gas may kill you instantly.

Primarily use the Sniper Rifle to attack the boss. Switch from your Sniper Rifle to your Shotgun to blast zombies quickly, then switch back to the Sniper Rifle and resume shooting the Lepotitsa from a safe distance. Target the creature's legs to reduce its mobility. If it kneels, it's possible to dash in close for a special melee attack. However, maintaining a safe distance from the gas makes this a difficult maneuver. If the distance is too far, rush in just a bit closer and toss an Incendiary Grenade at it.

After spreading gas on the first floor, the monster climbs upstairs and circles the second-floor balcony, doing the same. Stay on the ground floor and shoot it with the Sniper Rifle whenever it stops. The monster's weak point is its tiny head, which is extremely hard to hit with the Sniper Rifle, so aim for the upper torso to make the best use of your 7.62mm rounds.

Following its tour of the second floor, the Lepotitsa drops back to the ground floor and changes tactics, attempting to approach within close range for grapple attacks. It also pursues the remaining civilians this way, turning them each into zombies. Blast it in the face with the Shotgun as it approaches while backing slowly away. If it lunges, press Action while aiming and backing up to drop on the ground and shoot from below. However, don't stay on the floor shooting. Tilt the Left Stick to roll to either side and release the Aim button to get back up. From medium range, toss Incendiary Grenades at it. Your partner will shout when the monster resumes emitting gas clouds, at which point you should dash to the other end of the cathedral and switch back to your Sniper Rifle. Continue chasing it around the cathedral and shoot it until it dies.

UNDERGROUND ACCESS

The Lepotitsa dies in the center of the cathedral floor and drops the **Underground Keycard**. Grab the item and descend the secret staircase under the altar. Examine the lighted panel on the right side of the hatch to use the keycard. In the small room beyond, smash the item barrels on the left and open the chest in the back right corner to obtain **Skill Points (4,000)**. Open the back doors with a Partner Action.

UNDERGROUND LAB

UNDERGROUND MAP

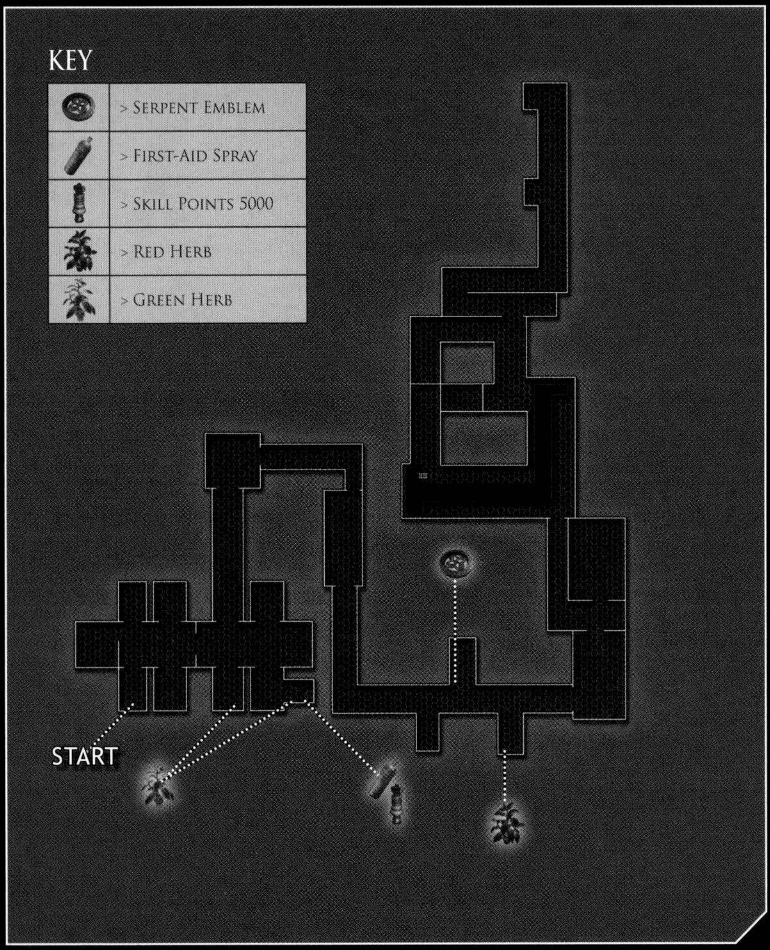

Using the panel on the upper level, you must input the room numbers as you deduce them from the partials provided. Tilt the Left Stick to move Leon's hand over the buttons and press Reload to input the desired number. Each number can be used only once in each three-letter passcode. There are two gates that you *should* open and two that you *should not* open.

OPEN:

201: Contains two item file boxes to smash. However, if you open it after 102, it contains a zombie holding a liquid nitrogen gas bottle. Shoot the bottle to freeze the zombie instantly then use a melee attack to smash it.

210: Opens the gate to the next area.

DO NOT OPEN:

012: Releases zombies. Do not open and certainly do not open first!

102: Contains a Shrieker. Do not open! The Shrieker's cries call other zombies into the area. However, if you are desperate for Skill Points, then open this chamber first and kill the Shrieker before proceeding.

TRIALS OF THE SCIENTISTS

Proceed into the next room and head left. Smash the blue file boxes on the raised platform to obtain an item and then examine the panel. You can also examine the doors arranged around the room and peek inside each one. Some rooms hold enemies. Each of the rooms bears an overhead sign with a partial number. Some of the numbers have been scratched off, leaving you to guess what they are.

MORE BAD NUMBERS

The second portion of the chamber features another number input panel and more rooms labeled with partial passcodes. This time you *should* open rooms 012, 201, and 021 for the reasons listed below:

OPEN:

012: Opens the door to the immediate left of the input panel. Contains two zombies, one holding a liquid nitrogen gas bottle that you can shoot to flash-freeze both. Also contains the door to room 201.

201: Opens the room inside room 012. Contains a **Green Herb**, two item file boxes, and a chest containing **Skill Points (5,000)** and a **First-Aid Spray**.

021: Opens the exit gate in the corner.

DO NOT OPEN:

102: Contains a Shrieker and a **Green Herb**. Do not open unless you are desperate for the herb. The Shrieker's cries will call other zombies into the area.

120: Contains a lone zombie that tends to transform into a Bloodshot. Do not open!

HELENA IN DESPERATION

Proceed down the passageway behind the gate you opened with passcode 021. Use a Partner Action to open the door at the end. Continue right and open the next door. Move slowly down the corridor because the dead corpse in the middle will reanimate and attack. Kill it quickly.

With the zombie eliminated, Helena runs ahead and starts looking for someone. Smash the item file box in the corner and go after her.

HELENA IS MAD, HELENA ISN'T LISTENING

Repeatedly issue Partner Commands to Helena at this point, while she is fervently exploring ahead, and sometimes you'll solicit a funny response.

NEVER INTERRUPT A ZOMBIE'S CONCENTRATION

Follow Helena into the next corridor section. She begins searching wildly everywhere. While she is doing so, head down the corridor. Shoot the zombie that stands up straight ahead, then go into the bathroom on the left. Smash the item file boxes in the corner to reveal a zombie sitting on the toilet. It begins to grab for you, so use your Shotgun to blast it.

SERPENT EMBLEM: LABORATORY MALE EMPLOYEE BATHROOM

In the same bathroom where the zombie sits on the toilet, examine the sink to drain the water in it. A **Serpent Emblem** is revealed.

WARNING! DON'T WASH YOUR HANDS IN THE WOMEN'S RESTROOM!

The women's bathroom farther up the corridor and on the right features an interesting trap. When you examine the sink to drain the water in it, a Shrieker appears behind you. Don't set off this trap. Instead, just take the **Red Herb** in the stall to the right and get out!

TERRIFYING PATIENTS

Helena waits for you at the end of the corridor. Move past her and open the door. A zombie woman crawls out of the vent on the wall opposite the entrance. Moving farther into the room prompts the zombie on the table to the right to reanimate and leap. Smash the file box to the right. The male zombie on the last examination table also reanimates as you move past it.

Exit through the back door of the examination room. Use a Partner Action to open the door across the hallway marked "biohazard." After a revealing scene, move to the familiar passcode input panel on the wall to the right. Punch the numbers 2, 0, and 1 to open the door at the far end of the hallway outside the room.

UNBEARABLE WORK CONDITIONS

Enter the second specimen lab and proceed through the doorway on the left in the second room. Move to the back of this room and go through the doorway on the right into a third room. This third room is a large chamber with a crackling power generator, and many of the floor sections have been removed. These floor sections are displayed on the electronic wall map to the left. Pull the lever on the right side of the wall map to raise the shutter gate that is back in the first room.

Backtrack to the first room and dispatch a few new zombies along the way. By the time you reach the first room, you face an invading horde. Retreat to the back of the second room and let them file toward you for easy takedown with a Remote Bomb or Incendiary Grenade.

LOWER THE FIRST BRIDGING SEGMENT

Move to the back of the first room and crush a file box as you go. Pull the lever on the back wall next to the electronic map. Doing so lowers the gate in the area, separating you from Helena. It also lowers a bridge segment missing from the third room.

TAKE THE UNDERPASS

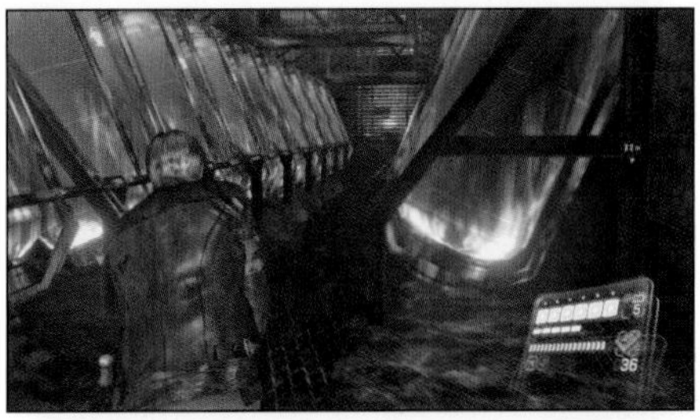

Confront or ignore a couple zombies in your room then drop through the hole in the floor to the level below. Navigate to the other end of the specimen tube aisles, where you encounter another crawling zombie. You can also shoot a Zombie Dog trapped in a cage over your head if you are bothered by the racket it makes. Climb the ladder in the corner to the right.

LOWER THE SECOND SEGMENT

Rejoin Helena and head down the stairs into the third room. You must deal with the acid-spitting zombies that are there. Fight your way through the crowd, cross the new bridge segment, and pull the lever next to the electronic map in the corner. This lowers a bridge segment on the far side of the room.

DISPATCH HELENA TO LOWER THE LAST SEGMENT

Head back across the bridge to the first corner and deal with new zombies dropping down from your left. Stand near the first lever you pulled and gun down zombies standing on top of the new bridge segment.

Move to the doorway of the new bridge segment and press Partner Action to boost Helena up. On her own, she drops down on the other side and heads for the final bridge lever. Cover her by equipping your Sniper Rifle. Take out the enemies who attack her, including a Bloodshot. Watch for new zombies sneaking up behind you while you cover Helena.

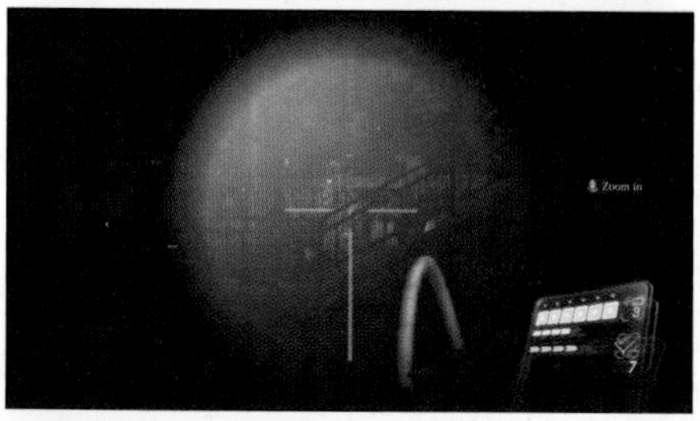

REUNITE AT THE TWIN LEVERS

Once Helena finally reaches the lever and pulls it, lowering the final bridge section, you must confront a horde of zombies on your own. Toss an Incendiary Grenade into them or use a Remote Bomb, then pick off the rest with your Wing Shooter. Remember to praise Helena for her work using Partner Commands. Join her at the exit door and press Partner Action to pull the two levers simultaneously.

FIGHT TO THE EXIT

Follow the corridor into a large warehouse. Move to the right and take out some zombies at the corner. Continue toward the objective marker. More zombies rise and others drop into the room. A Shrieker approaches from the far end, and you should snipe it before it gets too close. However, don't waste too much ammo here because the zombies will continue dropping from the hole above the exit. Approach the hatch in the wall and press Partner Action to escape from the lab.

ALTAR ENTRANCE MAP

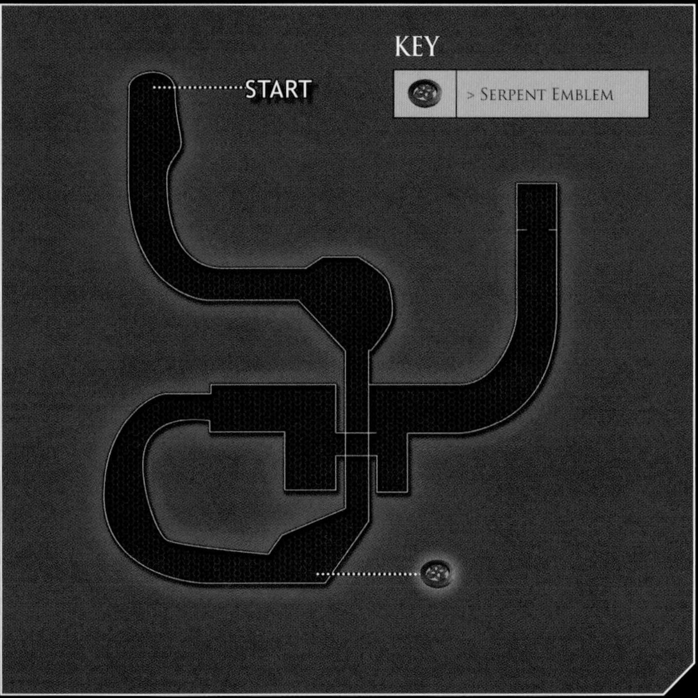

PRIMITIVE ALTAR

PRIMITIVE ALTAR MAP

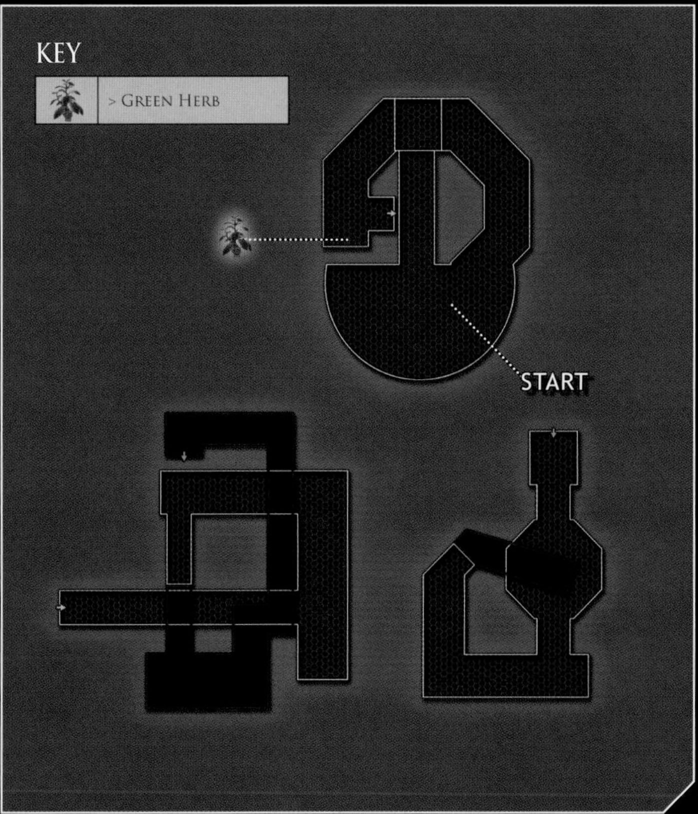

SERPENT EMBLEM: SUBMERGED AQUEDUCT

After crawling under the second archway and heading up the slope out of the water, you see a tall clay pot behind the barrier on the left. A **Serpent Emblem** rests against the cave wall behind this clay pot.

CURVY YET LINEAR PATH

Continue along the path and cross a bridge above the aqueduct that you just crawled through. Head left and be ready to gun down a zombie skeleton coming up the tunnel to the right. Proceed down this tunnel to a set of bars and break through them using a Partner Action. Helena finds her sister Deborah and leaps over to rescue her.

CLEAR THE WAY

As Leon states, Helena will carry Deborah while he is responsible for killing all of the enemies. Head down the curved path, drop over the low ledge, and grab the **Green Herb** on the table next to the clay item pot. Turn left and continue down the bridge. Run up behind the idle zombie for a Stealth Hit. Use a Quick Shot to kill the next zombie on your right, which brandishes a machete that you can use against it. Kill another acid-spitting zombie coming from the other direction and smash a clay item pot nearby.

Follow the route to the next corner. A zombie crawls out of the hole on your right. Shoot it before it sets foot on the ground. When you move onto the next bridge, a roof cave-in allows a couple zombies to run up to you. Perform Quick Shot on one of them and use a melee attack to kick them both off the bridge. Smash more item pots at the next corner and in the following room.

Perform a Stealth Hit on the zombie near the railing, then drop off the ledge to the right and smash a clay pot. Proceed down the next passage, drop over a series of small ledges, and take down a zombie at the end. Go left and smash another item pot.

MANUAL LABOR

Ingrid Hunnigan finally gets back in contact with Leon, but only briefly. Smash the pots in the area, then move to the metal dumpster and push it out of your path. When you stop, move around the circle to the right, smash a clay pot, and then head inward. Smash another clay pot in the niche to your left and watch for an acid-spitting zombie that suddenly attacks from behind. Quickly push another dumpster out of the way and perform a Stealth Hit on the zombie that spits acid at Helena and Deborah. From there, just follow Helena to the center of the area.

RACE TO THE SISTERS

Leon is separated from Helena. Zombies drop from the sky while you navigate the path downward along the curved ramp, and they will leave items for you. Drop from the low ledge at the end and smash two clay item pots at the corner. Move to the nearby ledge and press Partner Action to jump onto a rope and swing to the other side.

Smash the nearby item pot and descend another ramp. Leap the gap and drop from the next two ledges. Examine the dumpster blocking the next ledge. Helena pulls a lever to take it out of your way. Press Partner Action to swing across another rope...until Deborah unexpectedly knocks you to the floor.

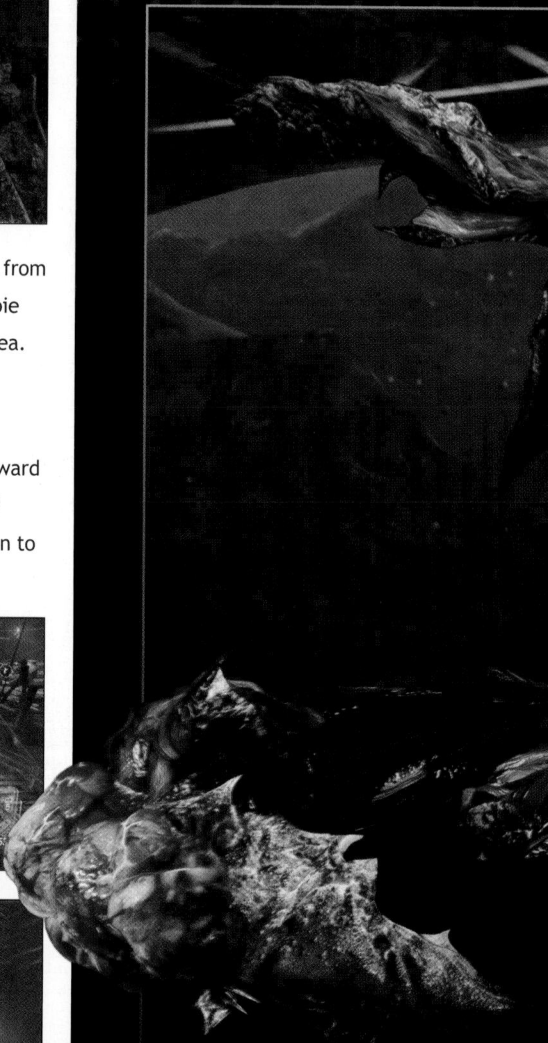

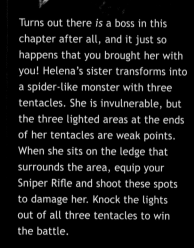

Turns out there *is* a boss in this chapter after all, and it just so happens that you brought her with you! Helena's sister transforms into a spider-like monster with three tentacles. She is invulnerable, but the three lighted areas at the ends of her tentacles are weak points. When she sits on the ledge that surrounds the area, equip your Sniper Rifle and shoot these spots to damage her. Knock the lights out of all three tentacles to win the battle.

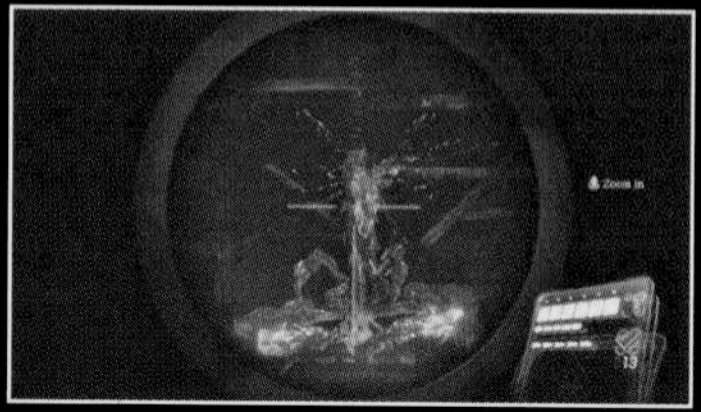

DEBORAH

Keep your focus on Deborah and not on eliminating zombies. Snipe her off the surrounding wall again at the first opportunity. When Deborah lands on the floor and extends her tentacles, switch to your Shotgun and shoot their glowing ends. Back away from her while doing so to avoid her extended whipping attacks. Shoot one tentacle until the light at the end goes out then target the others.

Deborah quickly adopts a strategy of leaping onto the ground next to you and performing a sweep kick to knock you down. If she extends her tentacles while you're down, she impales you with one and holds you there. Rotate the Left Stick to escape before suffering more damage or instant death. Change tactics to dash away from her whenever she leaps to the ground, then turn to face her and fire.

One way to use her targeting strategy to your advantage is to move next to one of the large TNT barrels when she is on the higher level. When she leaps you should move away from the TNT barrel, then turn and fire at the barrel as she extends her tentacles. The resulting explosion should take out one or more of her other tentacles.

Deborah falls to the ground floor in pain, but she soon leaps back up again. From this point forward, zombies appear on your level and attack. Eliminate them swiftly with Quick Shots from your Sniper Rifle or Shotgun and restock with the items that they drop.

ALTAR CORRIDOR

ALTAR CORRIDOR MAP

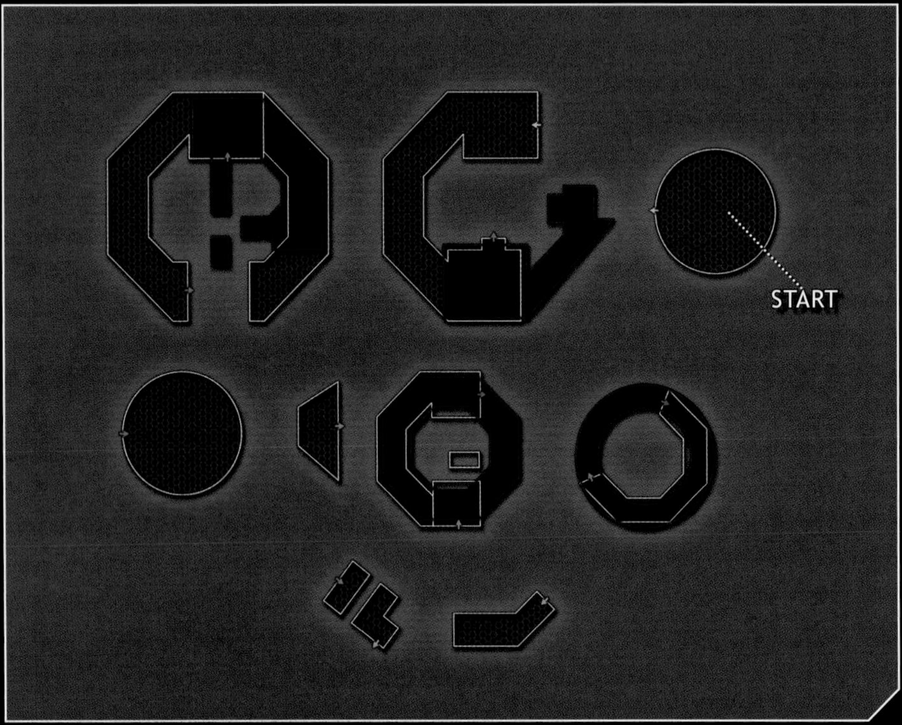

GET TO HELENA QUICKLY

Deborah takes out the floor, which drops everyone into another cavern. Quickly smash the surrounding clay item pots to restock and descend the curved ramp. Take out the zombies that get in your way. Shoot those with gas lanterns to set groups on fire. At several points, small quakes occur. Avoid dashing forward during quakes or you could suffer damage from falling debris and zombies.

MOVE THE MINE CART ONTO THE RAILS

Drop from the end, head left, and drop down again. Move to the corner where there's a break in the railing, smash the two item pots, and leap the gap. Head to the right and kill an armored zombie by shooting the lamp it holds. This zombie stands in front of a crank.

Turn the crank in order to move the mine cart that Helena fell into from the center over to the side. Then run around the corner, smash the two item pots, and jump into the mine cart with her.

DUCK!

The mine cart begins moving along a track. Press Reload and Action to duck below low overhangs, which sometimes appear twice in a row.

Deborah climbs aboard the mine cart. Use your Shotgun to shoot the glowing ends of her tentacles and to knock her off. When she starts to spin around to swing her tentacles for a strike, press Action while aiming at her to duck under her attacks.

BLAST WITH DYNAMITE

Some rocks block the track ahead. Shoot the TNT barrel stuck in the rocks to blow them off the track. Otherwise you suffer an instant game over. Duck under more low overhangs and blast more TNT barrels off the tracks before your cart runs into them. This causes you to suffer minor damage. Shoot another TNT barrel ahead to take out a group of zombies and to avoid damage.

Deborah climbs back on, so blast her tentacles and duck under her sweeping attacks until the mine cart crashes.

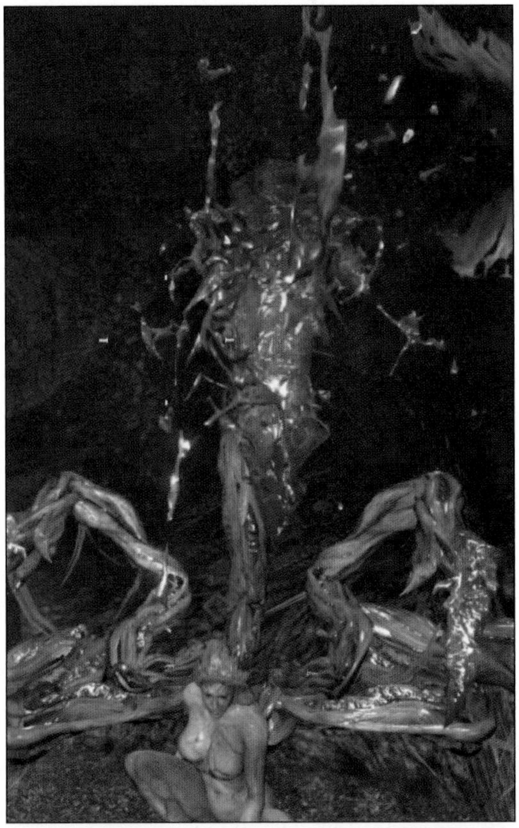

YOU GOTTA DO EVERYTHING, AND FAST!

Deborah prepares to kill Helena on another platform. Move to the end of the ledge you're on, collect the **9mm Ammo**, press Partner Action, and then equip your Sniper Rifle. Aim at Deborah's final tentacle and shoot the glowing end of it before she kills Helena.

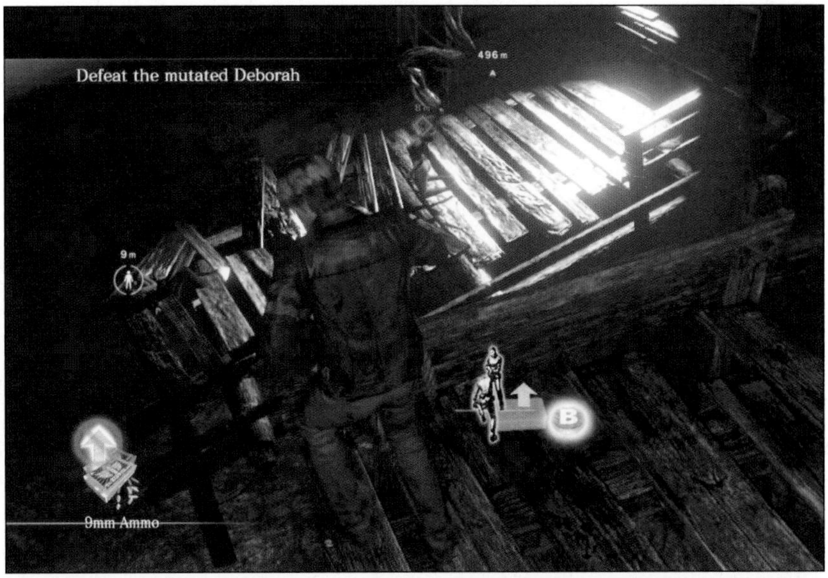

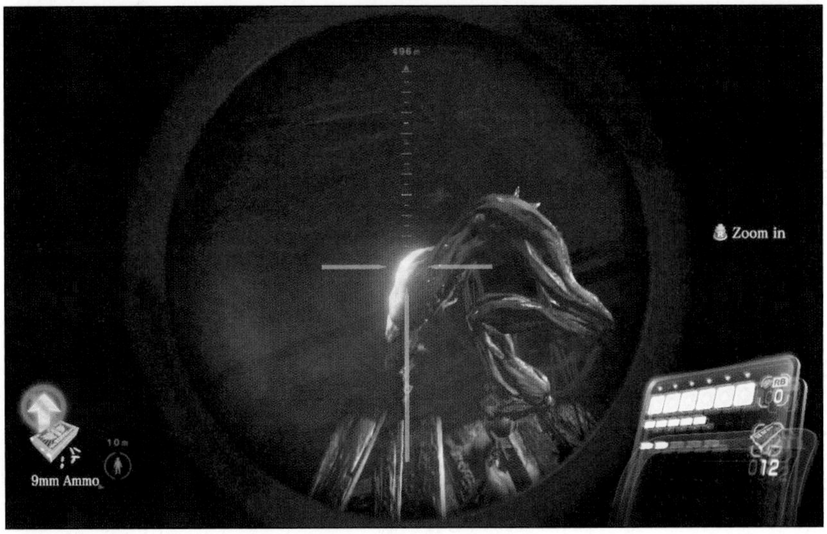

LEON CHAPTER 2: RANKING CRITERIA

RANK	ACCURACY(%)	DEATHS	CLEAR TIME(MIN)	ENEMIES ROUTED
A	70	2	80	80
B	60	5	100	60
C	50	7	120	40
D	*1	*1	*1	*1

*1 Any Below Rank C

POINTS AWARDED PER RANK (ABOVE)				
Rank	A	B	C	D
Points	25	20	15	10

TOTAL RANKING POINTS TABLE

RANK	S	A	B	C	D	E
Total	100	90	75	55	45	*2

*2 Any Below Rank D

ALTAR CORRIDOR

ALTAR CORRIDOR MAP

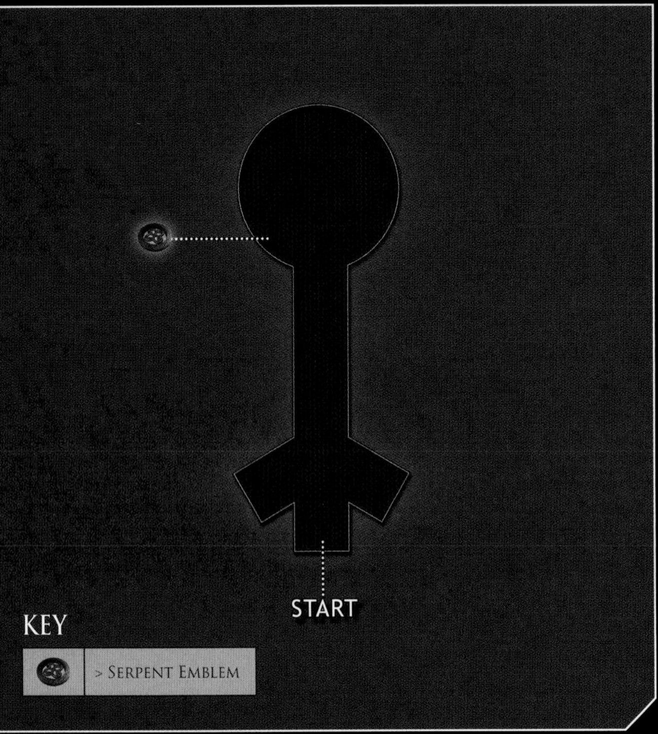

EXIT THE SCENE OF THE CRIME

Turn away from the platform ledge and head down the sloping tunnel into a wide circular room.

SERPENT EMBLEM: ALTAR CORRIDOR EXIT

Stop inside the wide circular room and use the Right Stick to rotate the camera up and to your left. A **Serpent Emblem** rests on a ledge high above.

REKINDLE THE PARTNERSHIP

Take the levers on either side of the metal doors and pull them simultaneously with a Partner Action. You enter the catacombs with Helena.

CATACOMBS

CATACOMBS MAP

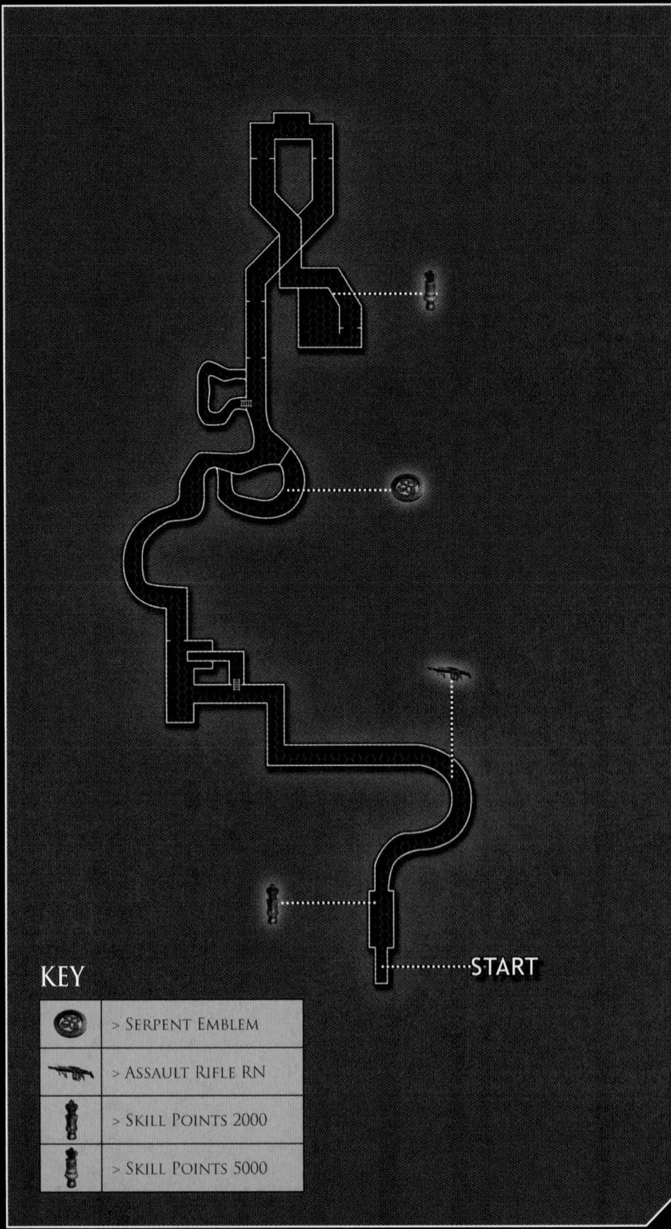

PLUNDER THE TOMBS

Proceed up the passageway and break item pots on the right and left. Open the two sarcophagi on either side at the base of the stairs by pressing Action. Tap Reload repeatedly to force the top off. The one on the left contains **Skill Points (2,000)**, and the other contains a snake that will jump out and bite you. Shoot the snake for revenge and also to add it to your enemies killed record.

Go up the steps and follow the curving ledge. Open another sarcophagus on your left to obtain the **Assault Rifle RN**. This weapon is fitted with a bayonet that makes for some nice melee takedowns.

DASH AND SLIDE UNDER SPINNING BLADES

After descending some stairs, a trap springs in the corridor ahead. Go under the spinning blades by dashing toward them and pressing Ready/ Aim to slide at the last second. Although you would normally crawl the rest of the way out, zombies start coming down the corridor. Stay under the spinning blades and allow the zombies to walk into their own deaths. When the area is clear, crawl forward and push Action to crawl faster.

WALL OF FIRE

Go around a few corners and you find that the next passage is full of flames. Run up behind the zombie near the flames and perform a Stealth Hit. Facing the flames, press Action to talk to Helena a moment. Continue to the broken ladder on the wall to your right.

Press Partner Action to send Helena on a mission to douse the flames. While she puts out the fire, watch the corridor behind you. A zombie holding a lit stick of dynamite soon approaches. Perform a Quick Shot and melee attack combo to stick the dynamite into the zombie's mouth. Run away before the stick explodes.

Helena quickly extinguishes the flames that block the corridor by killing a zombie that was turning a crank to the right. Examine the large door with a Serpent Emblem. At this point, you can use a ring that Leon received recently to unlock the door. Press Action to examine the door again to unlock it. However, the mechanism inside the ancient device turns slowly. Meanwhile, you must deal with a horde of zombies headed your way. Move to the crank and turn it to burn up a crew of zombies coming over the bridge. When zombies fall out of the ceiling all over your area, move toward the bridge and kill them all. One or more of the zombies carries dynamite, so use a Quick Shot/melee attack combo to make the first one blow up all the others. Another wave comes over the middle bridge, so turn the crank again to set them aflame. The giant door finally unlocks. Move to it and open it with a Partner Action.

BRZAK SIGHTING

Proceed into the cave. A large, nasty-looking sea creature moves through the water, but it's no threat for now. Move around the room to the left. Follow the side tunnel into the next chamber.

STEP OUT OF THE COLD WATERS

You stumble upon more sarcophagi, none of which can be opened. Move onto dry land to the left. Follow this short path to a couple item pots and a sarcophagus that you can open.

SERPENT EMBLEM: WET CAVE IN THE CATACOMBS

Open the sarcophagus that sits on dry land in the wet area to find a **Serpent Emblem**.

OPEN THE RED GEM GATE

Drop back into the water and proceed. A large gate with a red gem is down, but there appears to be no way to open it. You must split up again—move to the wall on your left and press Partner Action to send Helena to another area.

While Helena is off trying to open the gate, check the water behind you for ripples. This is a zombie swimming up to attack. Be ready to counter when it moves to strike or it will pull you underwater. If it grabs you, you can break free by the usual methods.

Soon Helena drops down on the other side of the gate and turns the crank to open it. But something unfortunate happens, and she is dragged off to another section of the cave. Although you are separated, you must still work together to help each other move through the catacombs. Begin by dashing to the top of the nearby steps, equip your Sniper Rifle, and take out the zombies that spring from the waters around her and pursue her. She soon turns a blue crank that opens the gate next to you, releasing a zombie. Take it down with a Quick Shot fired from your Sniper Rifle. Then, turn the crank with the red light to open the gate on Helena's side.

WORK SEPARATELY TO GET THROUGH THE SAME CAVE

Proceed down the path on your side. Dash forward and slide under some spinning blades, and then crawl the rest of the way beneath them. An impassable wall of spikes that repeatedly protrude from the floor blocks the passage beyond. Use your Sniper Rifle to scope the area to your left. You spot a zombie endlessly turning the crank that moves the spikes. Shoot this zombie to stop the spikes and also the zombie beyond the red gate on Helena's side.

FIND THE OLD CRANK

Examine the nearby crank panel to determine that the crank itself is missing. Some zombies appear behind you. Kill them and backtrack to the spinning blades to see some acid-spitting zombies crawling their way under. Toss an Incendiary Grenade to take them all out. One of them drops the **Old Crank**. Dash toward the blades, slide to go under again, and retrieve it.

The zombie on the right comes alive and attacks as you come back with the Old Crank. Be ready to fall on your back and fire. You must also deal with some Bloodshots that guard the crank device. Hit them with an Incendiary Grenade or plant a Remote Bomb near them. When the area is finally clear, return to the panel and use the Old Crank to raise the gate on Helena's side. In response, she comes over to your side and turns the crank to lower your gate. Shoot an approaching armored zombie in the head to prevent it from attacking Helena while she works.

TOUR HELENA'S PATH

Optionally you may backtrack to the side Helena traveled to get here. Along the route, you find sarcophagi to open, including one with a snake and another containing **Skill Points (5,000)**.

SO, YOU THOUGHT YOU WERE LEAVING?

When you are finished exploring Helena's area, return to the massive double doors and move to the lever on the left side. Press Partner Action to pull the levers in unison, which drops you into a cave!

CAVERN

CAVERN MAP

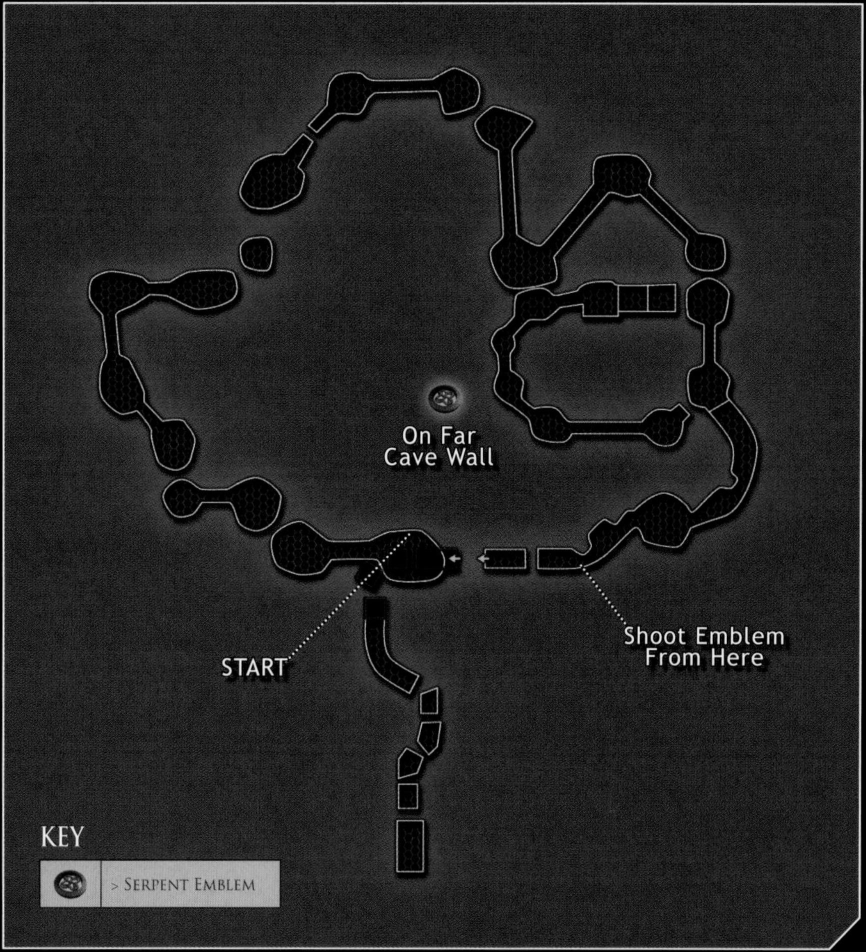

HOW FAR BACK DOES THIS CAVE GO?

With your partner, you land in a cavern that houses the remains of a temple even more ancient than the previous catacombs. Although the view is magnificent, you have no time to look around. Zombies attack you incessantly throughout this cave, so you must continue moving. Kill the two coming up the path and start down the slope.

Drop from the ledge to the lower level and continue downward. The path is linear and no items are available, so just keep moving forward.

DROP THE BRIDGE

Soon you arrive at an area with a crank. Shoot the zombie holding a gas lantern to burn him up. Then grab the crank and begin rotating it as fast as possible to lower a bridge to the next area.

Cross the bridge and kill more lantern-swinging zombies and Bloodshots. Toss an Incendiary Grenade to end this encounter quickly. After jumping across a couple of platforms, you cross a bridge that collapses. Rotate the Left Stick to climb back up and then jump the newly-formed gap.

Kill a Shrieker and any zombies it summons, then start across an unsteady rope bridge. A Whopper on the other side moves onto the bridge and attacks, and you'll have no luck trying to beat it at this point. Retreat off the bridge and shoot the Whopper in the legs as it advances.

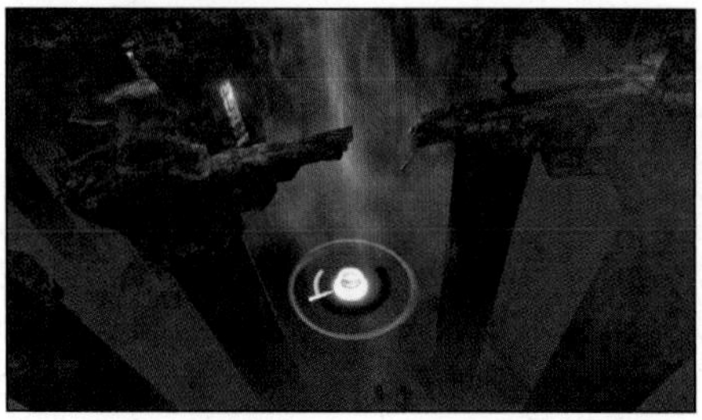

After the Whopper is dealt with, cross the cleared rope bridge. Smash some item pots in this area and be prepared for any zombies strapped with dynamite that drop into the area. Continue across the next rope bridge and body-slam an unwary zombie with a Stealth Hit. Dash across the next rope bridge to avoid a pursuing Whopper, then turn and shoot it in the legs as it tries to cross.

TOSS AND COVER HELENA

When you reach a platform with metal posts and plates, you must perform a Partner Action to hurl Helena across the gap. Her platform collapses, and she nearly slides down into a horde of crawling zombies. Equip your Sniper Rifle and help her by picking off the scavengers crawling after her. Continue tracking her with your scope and shoot a Whopper in the legs so that she can get past it. Clear your platform of attackers that hold dynamite. Then snipe a Shrieker, Bloodshots, and other zombies attacking Helena on the other side of the cave. When she begins turning a crank to lower a bridge, check your platform for more enemies. Cross the bridge when it's down to rejoin Helena.

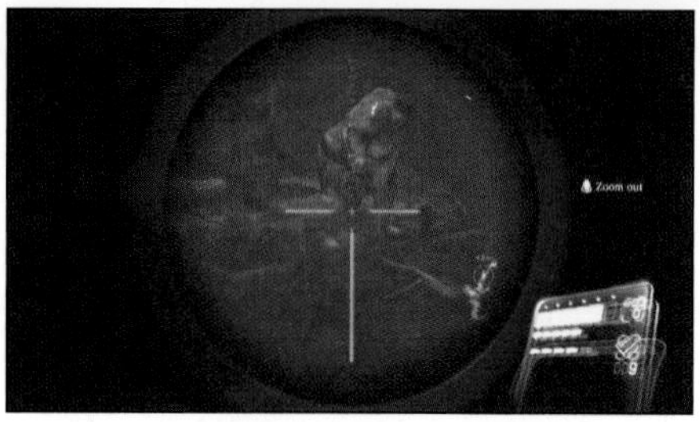

ROLL THAT BOULDER

Approach the large boulder at the back of the platform and press Partner Action to roll it out of the way. Drop over the ledge and cross a series of extremely narrow bridges. Stop and turn back afterward to make sure your partner gets across okay. Go back to help her up if she has trouble.

SERPENT EMBLEM: CAVERNS

After crossing the extremely narrow bridges on which you're likely to fall over the side, stop near a small clay item pot resting on a small block. A **Serpent Emblem** is visible on the far cave wall. Shoot it with the Sniper Rifle.

BRING ON THE COLLAPSE

Jump over a gap and then move to the crank on the left. Press Partner Action to start turning the cranks in unison. Unfortunately, zombies attack during your first attempt. Press Action to stop working and confront the enemies. When you are done, go back to turning the crank.

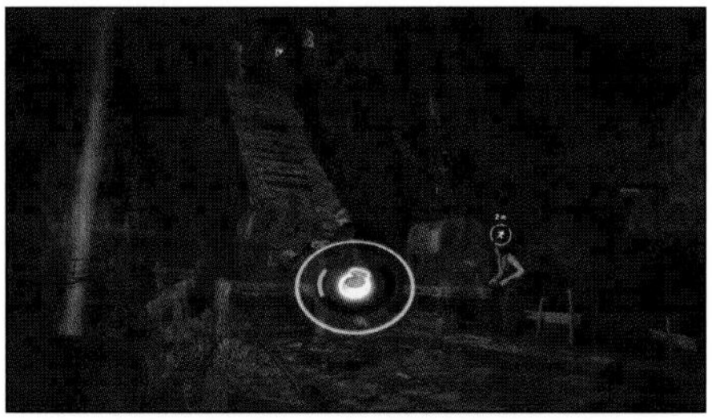

When you've lowered the bridge all the way, the platform you're standing on collapses! Dash across the remaining platforms and ignore any enemies you encounter along the way. You automatically leap over gaps and hop low obstacles while dashing. If a zombie tackles you, rotate the Left Stick quickly to shove it off or you risk going down with it. Be sure to help Helena if a zombie grabs her.

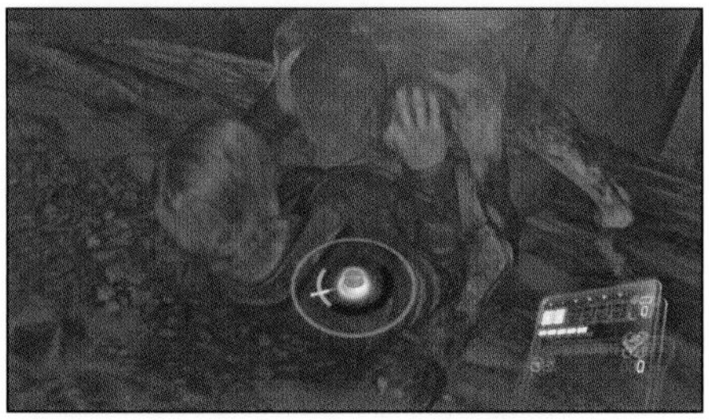

When you land on a platform blocked by a large boulder, press Partner Action to push it out of the way. Then leap across the final gap. Leon and Helena are swept away by flood waters.

UNDERGROUND WATER CHANNEL

WATER CHANNEL MAP

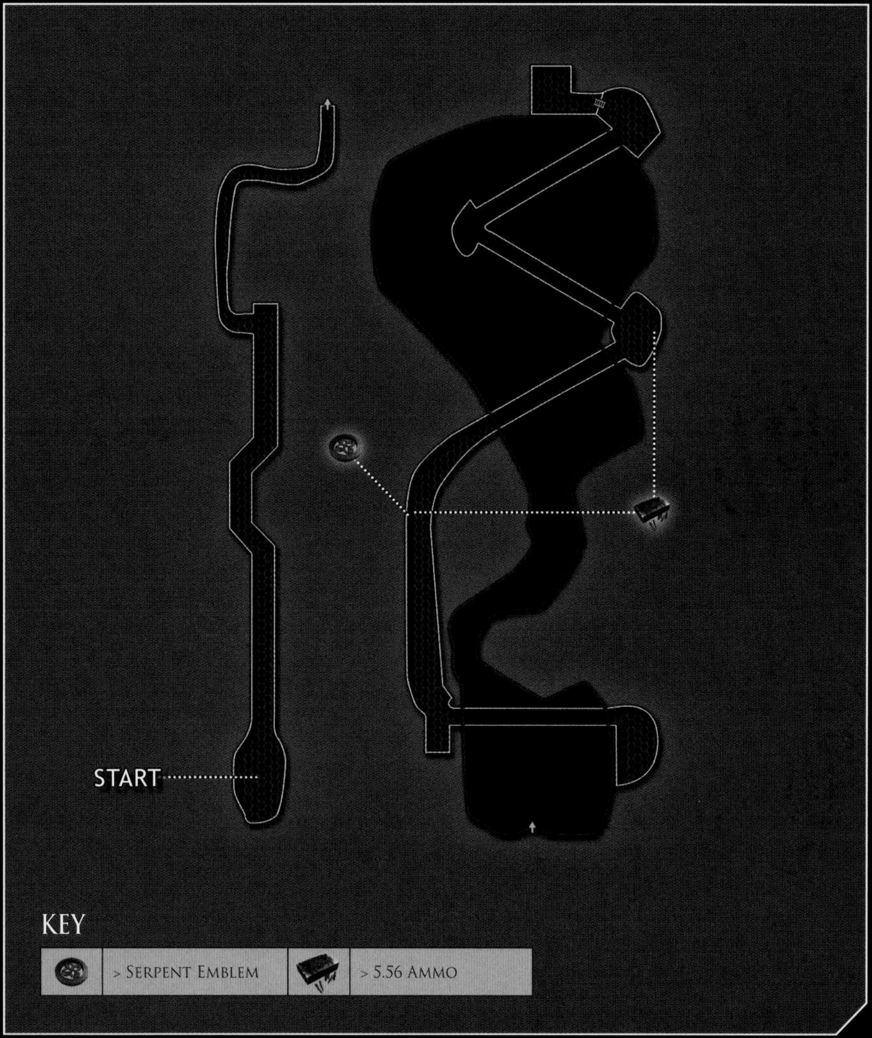

AVOID DROWNING

After a long slide, you land in an underwater tunnel. Move the Left Stick to swim forward and change your direction up or down with the Right Stick. When facing a straight area with little or no obstacles, press Action to swim faster.

GRAB SOME AIR

Your remaining oxygen is displayed as a gauge on the right side. If it empties, you begin losing health until death. Swim forward and upward toward the light in the ceiling. When prompted, press Action to surface in a tiny space. After you catch your breath, press Action to submerge and continue swimming. You must reach the next air pocket before you run out of oxygen.

After surfacing at the next air pocket, continue swimming. The giant fish monster called Brzak that you saw previously in the catacombs reappears and causes a cave-in. Swim through the new hole in the left wall.

GRIP OF THE DEAD

While swimming through the new tunnel, you start to pass floating zombie bodies. Avoid the bodies if possible or they seize you by the neck, draining your remaining air faster. Rotate the Left Stick to break free and help your partner if she is caught in a zombie's grip. The next air pocket in which you surface is rather gruesome due to all the corpses.

The distance to the next air pocket is quite far—so far, in fact, that your oxygen will drain almost completely. However, you eventually reach an iron grate. Press Partner Action to pull off the cover together and surface.

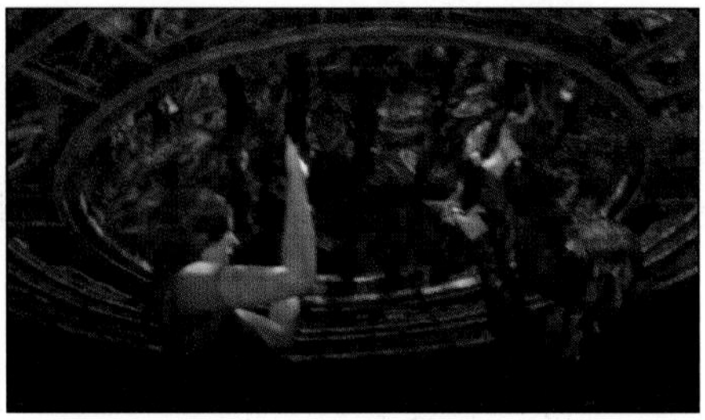

BRZAK ATTACKS!

The Brzak grabs you both and drags you away. Helena struggles to keep the big fish from biting down and then grabs a passing spear and harpoons it in the eye. You must press the buttons displayed onscreen during this Quick Timing Event to grab the fish tighter and move to its head. You eventually trade places with Helena and wind up prying the monster's jaws open. Rotate the Left Stick and then press Fire to grab the spear and stab out its other eye.

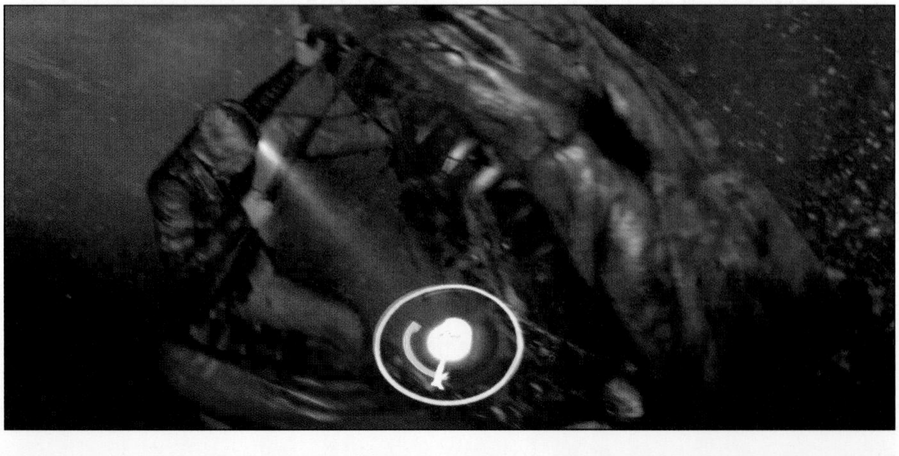

SWIM TO DRY LAND

The Brzak spits you into a cave—Helena on dry land and you in the water. Check your directional beacon and start swimming through a small cave. Swim across the surface as before by tilting the Left Stick. Hold the Action button to swim aggressively. You are stopped by some bars in your path and must wait for Helena to remove them. After the bars rise, continue swimming for the far shore.

The Brzak surfaces behind you. Tap the Action button rapidly to swim away from the fish and its bizarre tongue while Helena fires at the tongue from the shore. Eventually her shots drive the Brzak back underwater. Continue swimming to shore. When the monster surfaces again, resume tapping the Action button rapidly.

Nearing land, you have to struggle with a zombie that emerges from the water. Helena should help out by shooting it and then shooting the Brzak again when it surfaces one last time. Swim to land and climb out.

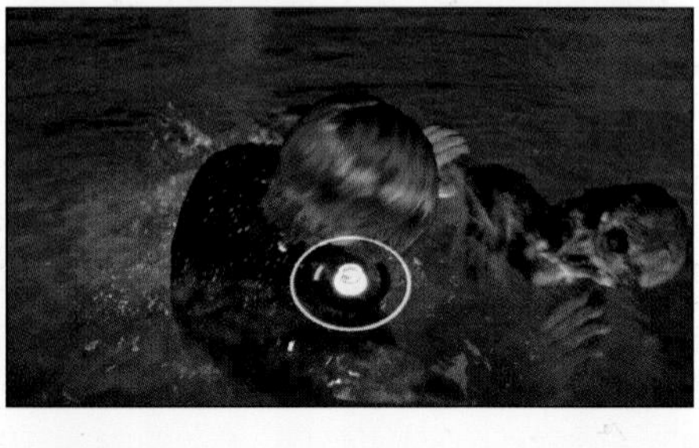

Smash some item pots nearby and move to the broken gate at the back of the area. Before moving on, consider whether you'd like to explore the upper portions of the cave for additional items.

SERPENT EMBLEM: THE BRZAK'S CAVE

Climb the ladder mounted to the side wall in the area where you finally climb out of the water. This leads to the upper paths of the caves. Cross the bridges and pick up items along the way. One of the bridges leads into a stone block tunnel. While you pass through this tunnel, look down and to your right to spot a **Serpent Emblem** at the bottom of a broken barrel.

THE BRZAK'S FINAL ASSAULT

While pushing aside the old broken gate via Partner Action, you are attacked and pulled underwater by the Brzak again. This time you slide down a tunnel and enter aiming mode automatically. Pick up **9mm Ammo** available during this event and shoot the Brzak repeatedly in its glowing tongue. Reload each time the creature slows down and backs off a bit. Shoot it again when it charges.

When Leon says to get ready, prepare to press Reload and Action to dodge the Brzak's charging bite attack. After seeing several TNT barrels bounce past uselessly, you spot one that finally might be helpful. When the game enters slow motion, aim upward and shoot the TNT barrel to blow up the Brzak.

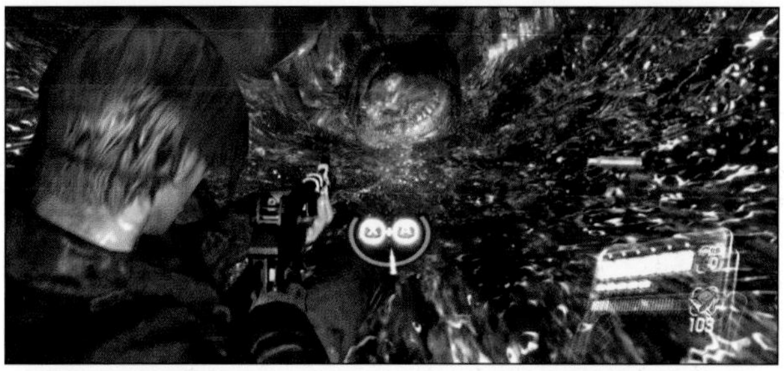

DEREK ENTERS THE STAGE

Finally clear of Twin Oaks and the ancient catacombs that run beneath the town, Leon and Helena watch in horror as the area is sanitized. This really is Raccoon City all over again. But just when they think things couldn't get any worse, Leon receives a phone call that he didn't want to hear...

LEON CHAPTER 3: RANKING CRITERIA

RANK	ACCURACY(%)	DEATHS	CLEAR TIME(MIN)	ENEMIES ROUTED
A	70	2	55	70
B	60	5	80	60
C	50	9	100	40
D	*1	*1	*1	*1

*1 Any Below Rank C

POINTS AWARDED PER RANK (ABOVE)				
Rank	A	B	C	D
Points	25	20	15	10

TOTAL RANKING POINTS TABLE

RANK	S	A	B	C	D	E
Total	100	90	75	55	45	*2

*2 Any Below Rank D

INSIDE THE AIRPLANE

AIRPLANE MAP

LEPOTITSA (COCKPIT)

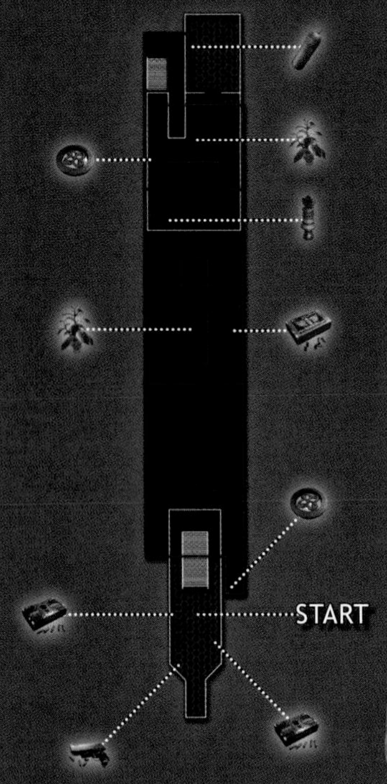

KEY

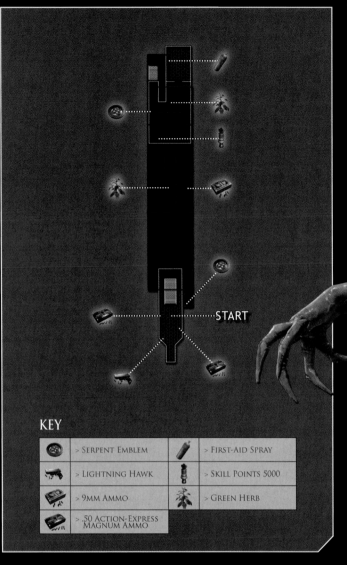

	> Serpent Emblem		> First-Aid Spray
	> Lightning Hawk		> Skill Points 5000
	> 9mm Ammo		> Green Herb
	> .50 Action-Express Magnum Ammo		

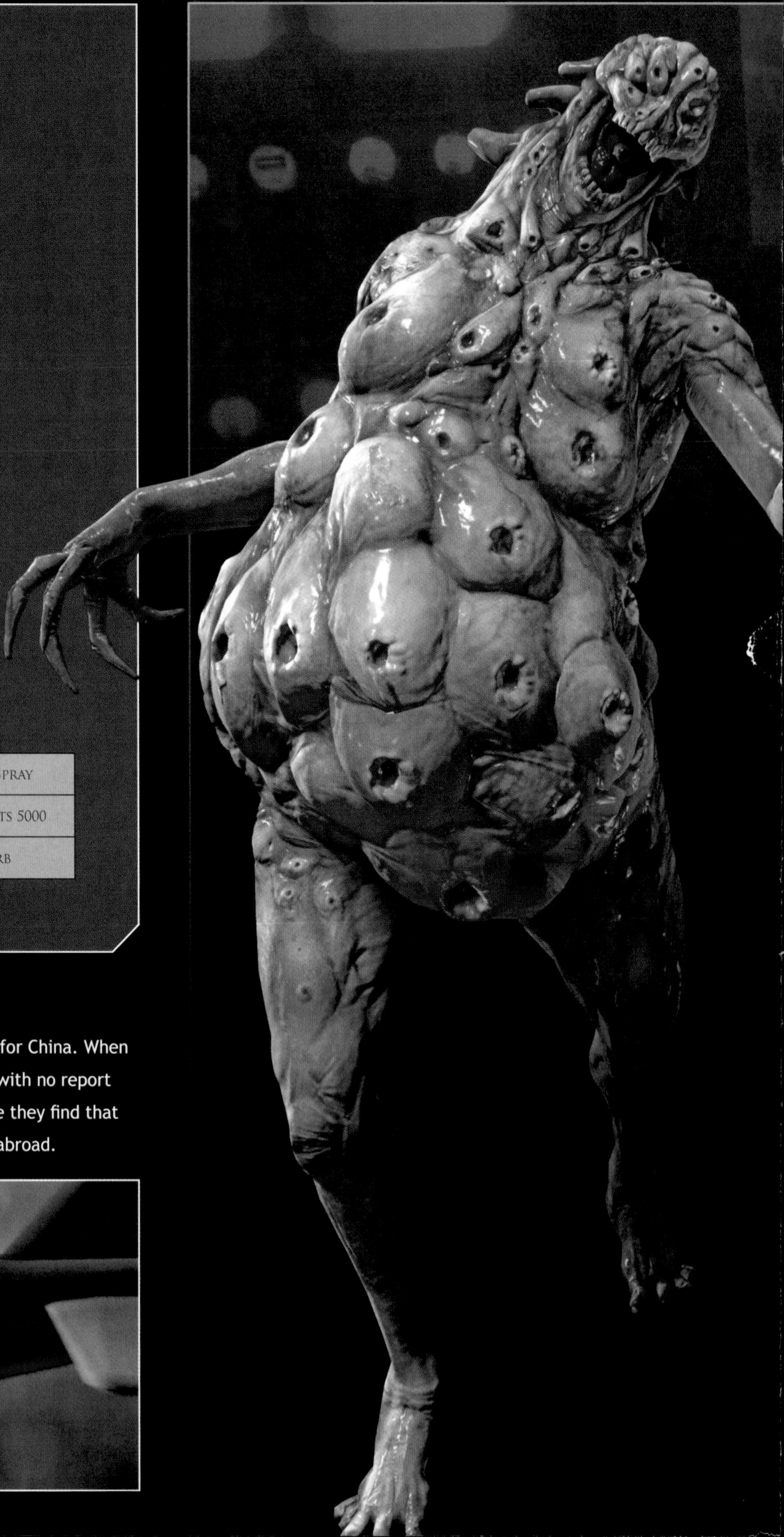

DOOMED FLIGHT

Leon and Helena board an international flight headed for China. When the plane experiences some rather strong turbulence with no report from the cockpit, the two decide to investigate. There they find that the horror unleashed in Twin Oaks has followed them abroad.

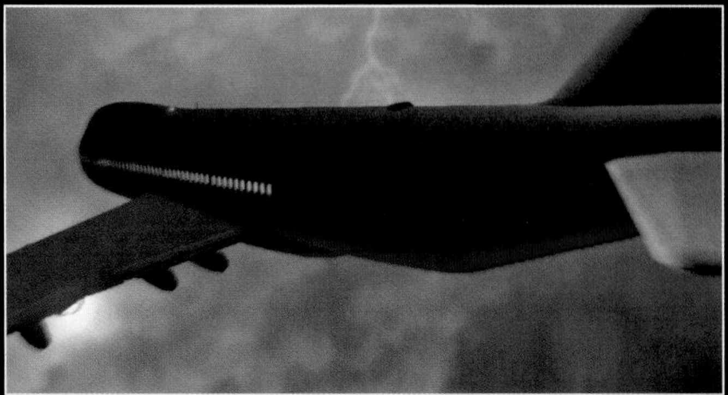

Due to the confined space, this Lepotitsa does not employ its zombie-making gas attack. Instead, it merely gives chase and performs grapple attacks. If you're weak at the time, it tackles you to the floor and kills you.

Coming straight out of a cutscene, the first strategy to employ is becoming familiar with the cockpit layout. Do not back away from the Lepotitsa or it will corner you, since the stairs are now covered and closed off by a floor shutter. Instead, turn left or right and use the small passage behind the stairs to escape from the monster. After running a few feet away, turn and toss an Incendiary Grenade or plant a Remote Bomb and detonate it from a distance.

The best weapon to use against the Lepotitsa in this confined space is on the ground near the co-pilot's seat, next to a dead agent. Pick up the **Lightning Hawk** magnum pistol. Leon equips it immediately, so defend yourself with Quick Shots or aim for the creature's head. Two or three shots fired should be enough to drive the creature into the ceiling, ending the battle for now.

FLIGHT TEAM DOWN!

Search the communications consoles to the left and right sides of the cockpit to find two boxes of **.50 Action-Express Magnum Ammo** for your new Lightning Hawk. Reload and move to the right side of the pilot's area. Press Action to examine the plane diagram on the side wall monitor and to see what's wrong. The tail section is flashing, and you must go to the back of the plane to determine the problem.

SERPENT EMBLEM: CREW LOUNGE

Descend the stairs from the cockpit and go right. Turn to face the front of the plane, where you see that the crew luggage compartment is open. A **Serpent Emblem** is visible on the right side.

NAVIGATE THE CABIN

Make your way through the first-class cabin and cross between the seat rows. An agent comforts a sick passenger in the next area. Search the table behind them to find **9mm Ammo**.

Move to the other side of the plane and enter the first open door on the right. A **Green Herb** sits in an empty chair.

Navigate through the seat rows of the main cabin. Follow the next corridor to the left and then divert into the next empty room to find another **Green Herb**. Take a moment to mix the herbs that you have on hand and recover full health. Now, enter the back stairwell of the plane and descend to the cargo level.

SERPENT EMBLEM: HAZARDOUS MATERIALS HOLD

When you enter the area where they store the big gas cylinders, examine the glass case on the right to find a **Serpent Emblem**. Smash the glass and shoot it.

CHECK THE CARGO BAY

Open the metal chest in the hazardous materials hold to find **Skill Points (5,000)**. Then, head around the corner to the left and open the compartment hatch door. Press Action, rotate the Left Stick, then press Partner Action.

Search the loading bay for a **First-Aid Spray** on the left-hand wall. Continue to the back right corner and press Partner Action to turn the red valve.

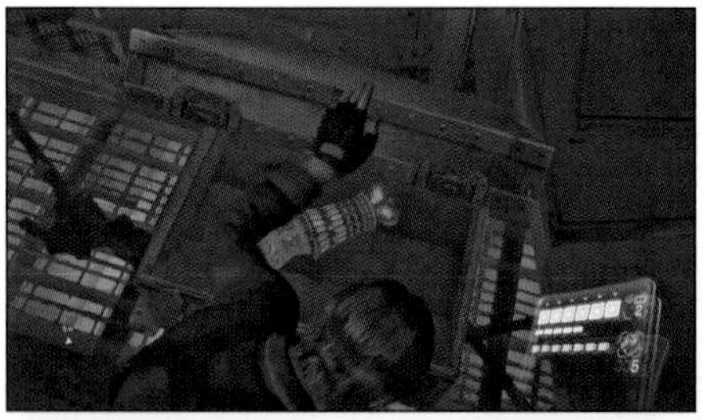

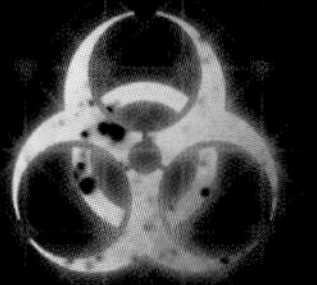

LEPOTITSA (LOADING BAY)

The monster breaks into the loading bay and attacks, this time dispensing its horrible gas, which you encountered previously at the cathedral. Fortunately, the gas isn't so thick that you die immediately. However, your health drains continually as long as the Lepotitsa remains onboard. You must eject it quickly.

Attacking the creature isn't the best strategy for beating it. Defeat the Lepotitsa by breaking into the control box near the bulkhead ramp, which is on the opposite side of the plane. Pull the lever to open the bulkhead door. To prevent the monster from chasing you while you do this, issue the "Move In" Partner Command to Helena so that she attacks the creature more aggressively. If this doesn't work, shoot the air tanks along the wall to the left side of the control box. If you do so with the proper timing, short-lived jets of air will temporarily block the Lepotitsa from approaching. If this fails, press Action to cancel breaking into the control box and run behind Helena. Then run back to the control box when the monster targets her instead of you.

Press Action to examine the control box then tap the Reload button rapidly to fill the Quick Timing Event gauge and pry the cover off. Move to the lever and press Action to open the doors. The Lepotitsa is blown out while Leon and Helena cling to the bulkhead ramp for dear life. Slowly press and release the Aim button to move your left hand. Then move your right hand the same way with the Fire button. Pressing and releasing the buttons too quickly or not in time causes you to fall back on the ramp and will essentially require you to start this Quick Timing Event over.

The central cargo container slides out of the plane. Press Reload and Action to roll out of the approaching object's path or you will plunge to your death. Afterward, continue climbing up the ramp hand over hand.

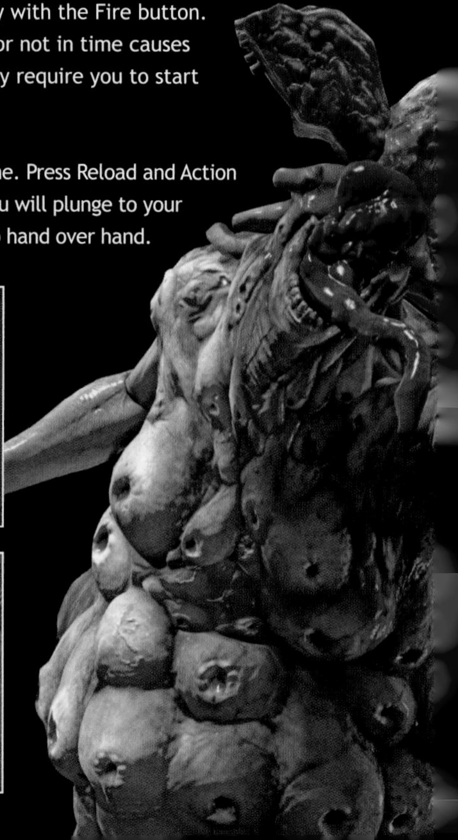

IT'S TOO LATE

Safely back onboard, you must now return to the cockpit and take control of the plane to keep it from crashing. However, the Lepotitsa's gas has turned everyone but you (and your partner) into zombies. Ascend the stairs back into the passenger cabin. There you spot the first victim of the gas around the corner. Blast the zombie with a Quick Shot to prevent it from grabbing you.

More zombies come in from around the corner. Perform a Quick Shot on the closest one and use a melee attack to kick them down. More zombies wait in the passenger aisles. Battle your way to the right side of the plane and continue to the cockpit. Dash past the zombies knocked over by turbulence, which fall and struggle to rise.

OH YEAH, IT GETS WORSE

When you reach the first-class cabin, press Partner Action to slip past the panel blocking the doorway. Cross the row into the other aisle. Extreme turbulence turns the plane on its side, flinging you into the wall.

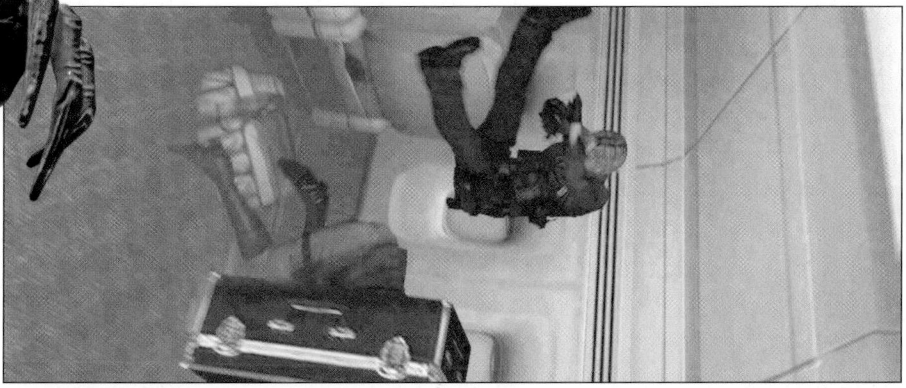

RETAKE THE COCKPIT

Recover and dash upstairs into the cockpit. The pilots have arisen, so take them out with quick Shotgun blasts. Touching the top stair triggers turbulence that throws you back down to the bottom. Dash back upstairs, finish off the zombies, and collect any items they drop.

TAKE OVER CONTROL

Approach the monitor and examine it to see what's happening with the plane now. The open bulkhead door depressurized the plane, throwing it off balance. Following Ingrid Hunnigan's report, move to the pilot's seat on the left and press Action to climb behind the controls. Meanwhile, Helena must clear the cockpit of endless zombies.

As you did previously in the police car, use the Right Stick to look around the cockpit controls. Examine the buttons overhead, and a Quick Timing Event command prompt appears. To proceed, press Reload just as the timer hand moves through the two colored sections of the gauge.

Now look down and to your right at the throttle lever. Press Action to grab it. Rapidly tap the Reload button to pull the throttle back.

The autopilot alert goes off, warning you to pull up. Look forward toward the steering controls and rapidly tap the Reload button to pull back.

AIRPLANE CRASH SITE

CRASH SITE MAP

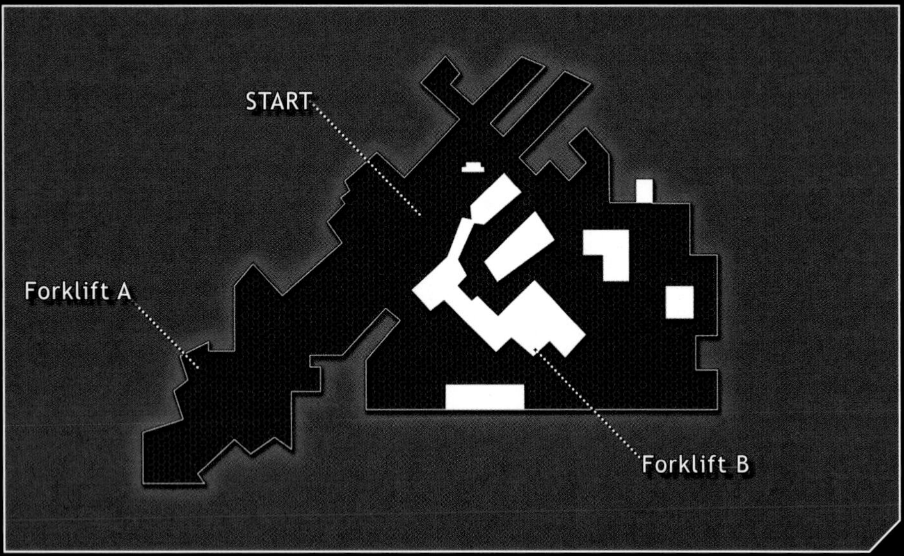

UNEXPECTED RENDEZVOUS

With no choice but to crash the plane into a major population center of China, Leon and Helena manage to survive the accident. Exiting the plane, they encounter Jake Muller and Sherry Birkin, whom Leon hasn't seen since the Raccoon City Incident 15 years ago. But there's no time to remember the old days because Sherry and her friend are being tailed by a menacing stalker. Leon and Helena must help the younger team fight off the Ustanak.

USTANAK (SHIPYARD)

The Ustanak has equipped itself for this battle with a giant cage on its back. If it catches hold of Jake, it will put him in the cage. There's no way to rescue Jake from this cage, but he usually breaks himself out. Any other character the Ustanak grabs merely suffers damage for several seconds and can break free by rotating the Left Stick. Free a partner caught in Ustanak's hold by moving beside the creature and pressing the Partner Action button when the icon is displayed onscreen. This action unlocks the "Lifesaver" Achievement/Trophy. The only other attack the Ustanak employs in the beginning is a charging shoulder butt, which knocks you down and inflicts significant damage. You roll around in pain afterward, which allows the Ustanak to scoop you up.

One of the keys to avoiding the Ustanak's grab is to stay off the ground as much as possible. At the start of the battle, turn to your left and climb the ladder mounted on the cargo container. From here you can shoot the monster repeatedly in the head, preferably with the Lightning Hawk or by tossing Incendiary Grenades. If the creature climbs onto the platform you're on then merely hop down and shoot it from below. Climb back up when the Ustanak drops down and continue playing this game of levels as much as possible.

A bin full of propane tanks is on top of the cargo container. Move behind the bin and press Action to push the container over the side, which spills the tanks on the ground. When the Ustanak is near the tanks, shoot one of them with your Wing Shooter to create a huge explosion. The blast inflicts severe damage to the monster.

You can climb the larger cargo container a few yards away from the first. Press the red button on the forklift next to the container. This lowers the forklift arms and the pallet resting on them. Hop onto the pallet, then climb on top of the container. Up here you find several item crates to smash and two more bins of propane tanks to push over the side. Hop down, stand near the tanks, and shoot the Ustanak to bait him toward your location. Then dash a few yards away and shoot the tanks before the creature runs off.

After the Ustanak suffers significant damage, the dramatic music ends and the monster runs away. Let it go and avoid wasting any bullets on it at this time. Move to the back wall of the area and press the Partner Action button to climb over.

The Ustanak returns, separating Leon and Sherry from Jake and Helena. While Helena and Jake continue fighting with the monster, Leon and Sherry must find a way to get back into combat. When playing as Leon, smash the item crates found around the enclosed area and restock. Then move to the back of the wrecked bus. Press the Partner Action button and tap Reload repeatedly to open the engine hatch. Press Partner Action again to examine the engine. You remain at the engine to fix it while Sherry runs up to the driver's seat. A revolving Quick Timing Event command prompt appears onscreen. To fix the engine, press Reload as the timer hand moves through five colored parts of the gauge. Press the button a little early for greater success. Sherry starts the engine and crashes the bus through the barrier. Dash back into the main battle area and resume fighting the Ustanak.

When the bus crashes through the barrier, a new section opens to the right. You now have access to another forklift with arms that can be lowered to reach four more bins of propane tanks. Climb up, knock the bins over, and shoot the tanks to use them against the Ustanak. After suffering additional damage, the Ustanak will retrieve its claw arm and switch it out. Thereafter, he returns and attempts to capture Jake or grab the others. Continue blowing up propane tanks around the Ustanak and shoot it in the head until you've won the battle.

HEAD FOR THE MARKET

Following the Ustanak's demise, turn away from the fallen tower and head into an alley. Smash the item crates along the way to the exit and continue onward through the use of a Partner Action.

MARKET

MARKET DISTRICT MAP

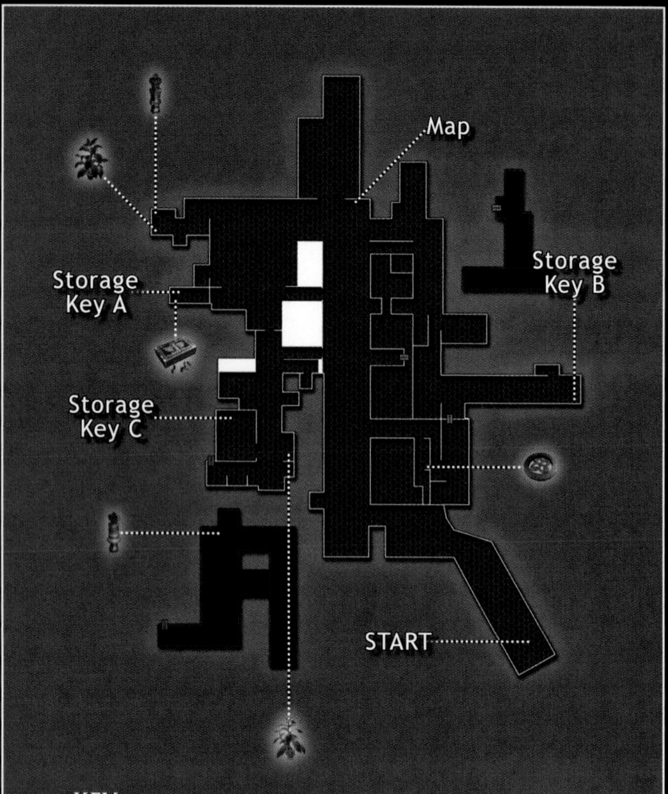

KEY

	> Serpent Emblem		> Skill Points 5000
	> 9mm Ammo		> Red Herb
	> Skill Points 2000		> Green Herb

SERPENT EMBLEM: BUILDING BEHIND THE MARKET

Ingrid Hunnigan informs Leon that he and Helena have to cut through an abandoned market area to find Simmons at the rendezvous point that he set with Sherry. Move to the first corner on the left side of the street. Equip the Sniper Rifle and look diagonally to your left. In the distance, you can barely see the top of a neon sign. Scope this area to spot a **Serpent Emblem** that can barely be seen, atop barbed wire, to the left of the neon sign. Shoot it with the Sniper Rifle.

NO ORDINARY MUGGING

Go diagonally from the entrance to the left and proceed down the center street. Ahead, some kind of monster attacks a man. Proceed up the street to the spot where he was attacked then go down the side street to the right to find and examine his dead body.

SERPENT EMBLEM: ABANDONED MARKET SHOP ON SIDE STREET

Find the dead body of the man who was attacked. Continue down the side alley a few steps, then turn right and enter a small shop. A **Serpent Emblem** rests on a messy countertop. Don't miss smashing the item crate in the short passage behind the emblem location.

FIND THE MARKET MAP

Return to the central street and make your way to the objective marker straight ahead. You determine that the exit door is locked and requires three separate keys. Using the map posted next to the door, you identify the locations of the three keys within the market. While searching for the keys, return to this map and reference the side street paths as often as needed. Memorize the most direct route to each key and do not wander about.

Unfortunately, something rather nasty crawls out of the discarded meat pile near the door. This persistent monster can be shot and blasted in half but cannot be killed. It will divide and multiply, and its parts will follow you throughout the market, complicating your efforts to find the three door keys.

RASKLAPANJE: THE ENDLESS MENACE

The tottering, gelatinous humanoid creature that falls from the discarded meat pile is called a Rasklapanje. These annoying creatures follow you everywhere and repeatedly perform grab attacks. To break free of them, you must rotate the Left Stick rapidly. However, shooting them only makes things worse since the creature's torso separates from the legs, creating two enemies that pursue you. Furthermore, both of the creature's hands might be blasted off, which creates additional creatures that crawl up and leap onto your face.

The best way to deal with the Rasklapanje is to steer clear of it. Lead it away from areas where you need to search, perform actions, or complete Partner Actions, and then dash away from it. Perform all required actions quickly before it catches up. If a Rasklapanje gets too close to you, use melee attacks to knock it back. Note, however, that even punches and kicks can cause Rasklapanje to fall apart, so use these attacks sparingly.

In Single mode, your AI partner won't be as tolerant of these creatures and opens fire at will. Monitor the situation and don't hesitate to suppress the Rasklapanje body parts created by your partner. Incendiary Grenades work well but may not suppress all body parts or may even divide the creature further. Remote Bombs detonated with proper timing can suppress all Rasklapanje body parts at once.

For easy suppression, stand on severed hands and use a melee attack to pick them up and throw them. Certain containers throughout the market can be used to dispose of severed hands in nasty ways. These include microwave ovens, fire-burning stoves, and boiling soup cauldrons. To use these devices, stand near them and allow a severed Rasklapanje hand to approach. If a full torso approaches, blast off its two hands. If you're standing within about five feet of these cooking tools, press the melee attack button to pick up the hand and quickly shut it inside.

Notice the use of the term "suppress" instead of "defeat" or "kill." The Rasklapanje's body parts revive after a few minutes and either rejoin themselves or grow into two new full-size Rasklapanje. Each body part you suppress drops items, no matter how many times it revives and is suppressed. Rasklapanje torsos sometimes drop **Skill Points (3,000)** provided that all other body parts have been suppressed previously. Therefore, when facing multiple body parts, try to leave the torso last for disposal. After successful suppression of all the parts of the Rasklapanje, leave the area as quickly as possible before they reanimate.

HEAD FOR STORAGE KEY A

Use the map above to find important items while avoiding the Rasklapanje menace and searching for the three keys. From the area map, turn left and head to the far corner. Enter the fresh seafood shop and search the back room to find a **Red Herb** and a chest containing **Skill Points (2,000)**.

Exit the seafood shop, turn right, and continue down the side street. To the right, you spot a door that is blocked by a fallen and sparking power line. This is a great location to fry Rasklapanje parts if you can bait and knock them onto the sparking wires. However, you must deactivate the power if you want to get through the door beyond. The power lever is behind the counter to the left, on the back wall. Pull the lever to deactivate the power. Then approach the door and open it via Partner Action. **Storage Key A** lies on the ground next to a dead body.

Another Rasklapanje crawls out of the vent in the nearby shop. Pick up **9mm Ammo** from the dumpster on your left and exit the small side alley quickly.

NOW FOR KEY B

Go back toward the seafood shop at the corner and divert to the right down a narrow alley. Unbar and open the door at the end, which creates another avenue of escape from pursuing Rasklapanje body parts.

Return to the map next to the exit door for direction to the next key. Turn right and head toward the butcher shop in the corner. At the corner, turn right again and go down the street to the very end. Unbar and open the gate at the end, then backtrack slightly and go down the side street to the right. At the end of this street you find **Storage Key B** near another dead body.

TAKE TO THE ROOFTOPS

Turn around and head back but notice the other dead body next to the ladder on your left. Climb up the ladder, turn right, and move to the edge of the roof. Press Partner Action to fling Helena onto the rooftop on the opposite side of the central street. Hop down from the ledge and fight off the Rasklapanje body parts. Helena navigates around the far side and opens the door on the other side of the street. If you are overwhelmed, use a Remote Bomb to suppress all the body parts at once.

RETRIEVE KEY C FROM THE BATHROOM

Enter the doorway Helena opened, proceed forward and then left, and follow the objective door marker down to the end. Search the shop across from the marked door to find a **Green Herb**. Then, open the marked door with a Partner Action. Bomb the Rasklapanje body parts squeezing their way out of the shower drains. Pick up **Storage Key C** to the right.

ONE QUICK STOP

Although it's time to leave, take this worthwhile detour on the way back—outside the bathroom, turn to your right and go around the corner to find a ladder. Climb up and cross the rooftops. At the second corner, you find a chest containing **Skill Points (5,000)**. From the chest, turn right and move to the ledge, then drop down twice to return to the central street.

BUTCHER SHOP BLOODBATH

Head back to the triple-locked door. Press Action three times to use each key while stopping to defend against the Rasklapanje as needed. Open the doors with a Partner Action.

When you move past the meat grinder in the butcher shop, a full-size Rasklapanje seizes you. Rotate the Left Stick to fill the gauge twice. Then press Fire while the creature is off-balance to knock it into the meat grinder. Good riddance! Proceed to the exit and press Partner Action to continue.

MEDICAL RESEARCH CENTER

RESEARCH CENTER MAP

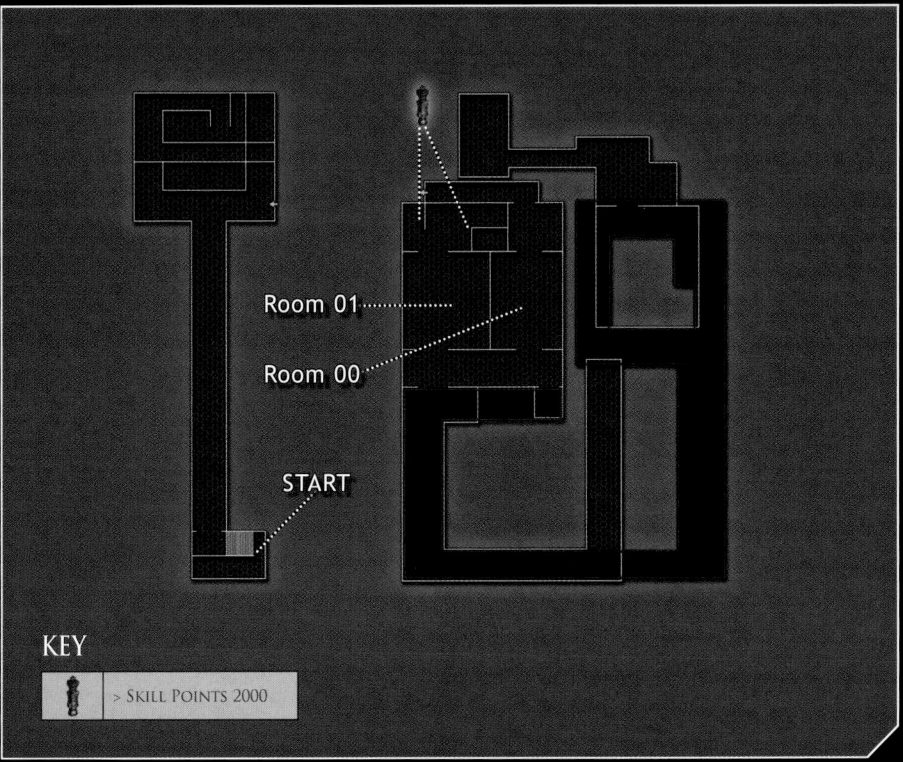

SOMETHING UNEXPECTED

Searching for Simmons at the rendezvous point, Leon and Helena encounter Ada Wong instead. Only something about her is...different. Check the door directly ahead to find that Ada locked it. Go down the stairs to the left. Enter the doorway on the right and open the door.

THE HARD DASH

You enter a long room full of test specimens. Seeing the elevator at the far end, you tell Helena to run. Dash for the far end. As you cross the halfway point, Ada activates a trap where a laser beam grid moves across the floor. Move to the right, aim and press Action to roll forward and lie flat on your back. If done correctly, you'll pass below a low gap in the array. Failure to act in time or missing the gap in the beams inflicts injury to you.

Continue dashing to the end of the room. Move to the right side of the sealed doorway and smash the glass circuit breaker with several melee attacks. Then help Helena break hers. If the BSAA troops in another room similar to yours break out of confinement first, they board the elevator before you do and get to claim some fabulous prizes. You get stuck taking the stairs, and going to Room 00. However, if you make it onto the elevator before the BSAA soldiers, the elevator will take you to Room 01. Outside Room 01 you'll find several extra item crates to smash, as well as two chests, each containing **Skill Points (2,000)**.

TAKE THE STAIRS

With no other choice after failing to make the elevator, move left around the corner and go through the door. Ascend the stairs in the next room and open the door at the top. Smash the five item crates on the left and open the door marked No. 00 with a Partner Action.

DODGE MOVING FLOOR MINES

Smash the item crates around the room and examine the exit door to find that it is locked. A moment later, moving floor mines flood the room. On contact, these mines turn red and then explode. Blast them with your Shotgun or perform a dodge roll while Aiming—simply tilt the Left Stick any direction and press Action. The second method conserves more ammo, but you risk rolling into a wall or another mine and suffering damage anyway. You can also "bump" into them while running on a curved route and continue, leaving the mine to explode harmlessly behind you.

At this point, Ada leaves. The room machinery then malfunctions, and floor mines begin moving around wildly. Dodge the remaining floor mines until they all explode and the exit door opens.

▶▶ROOM 01 MUST BE HOTWIRED

A similar scenario involving the floor mines occurs in Room 01, except it is Helena's job to hotwire the control panel at the back of the room while Leon dodges the floor mines. Set off the floor mines before they explode next to Helena, or she takes longer to accomplish her task.

PURSUE ADA

Go to the floor vent in the far-right corner of the plundered room. (The men in the other room arrived first, after all.) Press Action to kick out the vent cover. Crawl through the opening.

Ada's location is marked below. Dash along the long gantry and try to keep up with her. Allowing her to get too far ahead results in game over. Turn at the far corner and dash after her again. Turn left again, dash to the end, and drop from the edge.

HEAD TO SHERRY'S RENDEZVOUS

After a long scene in which Ada escapes, turn right and dash into the open doorway at the far end. On the desk to the left, you find a **First-Aid Spray**. Exit the room, circle the balcony level to the far side, and descend the stairs. Smash all the item crates around the large room to restock. An open doorway leads to the outside but is blocked by barrels. Examine this doorway to determine that this is where the other guys exited but you cannot.

Go through the marked door into the next room. Turn left and follow the yellow line down the street and around the corner. Dash for the door at the far end and open it with a Partner Action.

TRAIN

TRAIN MAP

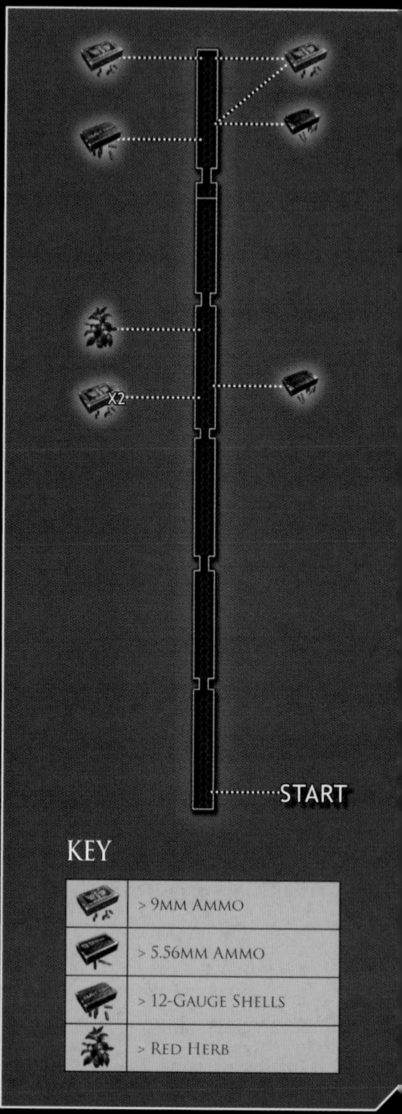

SELF-VILIFIED

Leon and Helena leap onboard a speeding train in pursuit of former White House aide Derek Simmons. Dash across the flat car and go through the first passenger car. Shove open the door and continue through another empty car. The third car is full of useful items, including **9mm Ammo**, **5.56mm Ammo**, and a **Red Herb**.

Proceed to the next car and down the aisle. The roof hatch is open and you cannot proceed beyond it. Press Partner Action to climb onto the train roof together.

SIMMONS (TRAIN)

Equip the Lightning Hawk and shoot Simmons two or three times. If you back up while firing, you encounter **9mm Ammo**.

Leon and Helena rush past Simmons and drop back inside the train and he follows. Back away from him while firing. Avoid his lunges by pressing Action to leap onto your back. Fire once or twice more then get up. Various ammo lies on the seats around you, so tap the Pickup button repeatedly to nab what you can during your fighting retreat.

Wounded, Simmons roars and climbs back on top of the train. Run back to the open roof hatch and press Partner Action twice to climb back up. As an alternative, you can run to the damaged rear of the train, pick up ammo along the way, and then climb up to the roof.

Helena suggests attacking from both sides, which is a good strategy. Dash past Simmons and fire from both sides. When you run out of magnum ammo, switch to your Sniper Rifle. Regardless of your distance from Simmons, it's your next-most powerful firearm. Remote Bombs and Incendiary Grenades are both powerful as well.

Climb in and out of the train car as needed to keep shooting Simmons in his mutated form. When he reverts to human form, perform a Quick Shot with your Sniper Rifle to make him kneel in pain. Then approach Simmons and press Fire to knock him to the floor for a beat-down. Tap the Action button rapidly to punch him repeatedly and then administer a devastating final blow. If you fail to fill the onscreen Quick Timing Event gauge before the timer hand moves to the right, Simmons can reverse your hold and damage you.

After suffering a certain degree of damage, Simmons hurls himself and Leon onto another train. After mutating into a new form, he charges you. Dash along the length of the train. Avoid crate stacks and leap automatically over low barriers.

When you reach the end, you leap back onto the first train, rejoining Helena. Press the Action button rapidly to climb onto the train and avoid an attack from Simmons' new tail.

Simmons now runs alongside the train, occasionally forming a mutated Gatling gun to fire at you. Pick up ammo in the area and shoot Simmons with any weapon more powerful than your handgun. When the mutant Gatling gun begins to glow, relocate to another spot and continue firing.

Simmons ends his chase by leaping back into the train car. Press Reload and Action to avoid his claw swipe and climb on top of the train to escape.

After you watch in horror as Simmons derails an entire passenger train on another track, equip the Assault Rifle RN. Fire on him as he heads on a collision course with your train. You must trip him up so that he does not derail your train.

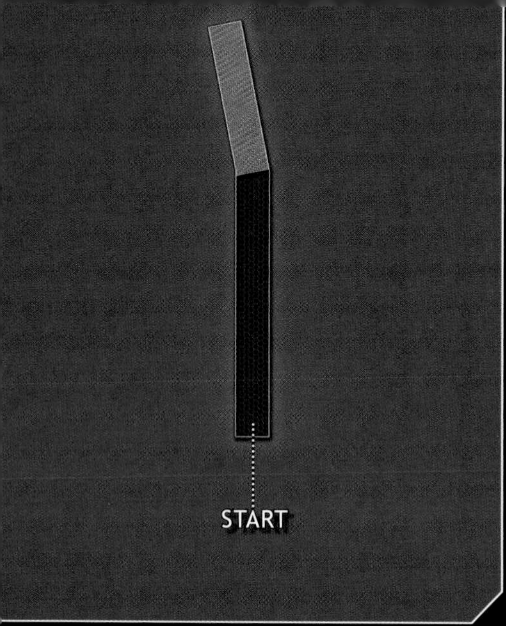

Climbing out of the water onto a dry ledge, Leon and Helena remain out of breath. Walk down the path and up the stairs to complete this chapter.

LEON CHAPTER 4: RANKING CRITERIA

RANK	ACCURACY(%)	DEATHS	CLEAR TIME(MIN)	ENEMIES ROUTED
A	70	2	75	7
B	60	5	90	5
C	50	9	110	3
D	*1	*1	*1	*1

*1 Any Below Rank C

POINTS AWARDED PER RANK (ABOVE)				
Rank	A	B	C	D
Points	25	20	15	10

TOTAL RANKING POINTS TABLE

RANK	S	A	B	C	D	E
Total	100	90	75	55	45	*2

*2 Any Below Rank D

PORT AREA

PORT AREA (FULL) MAP

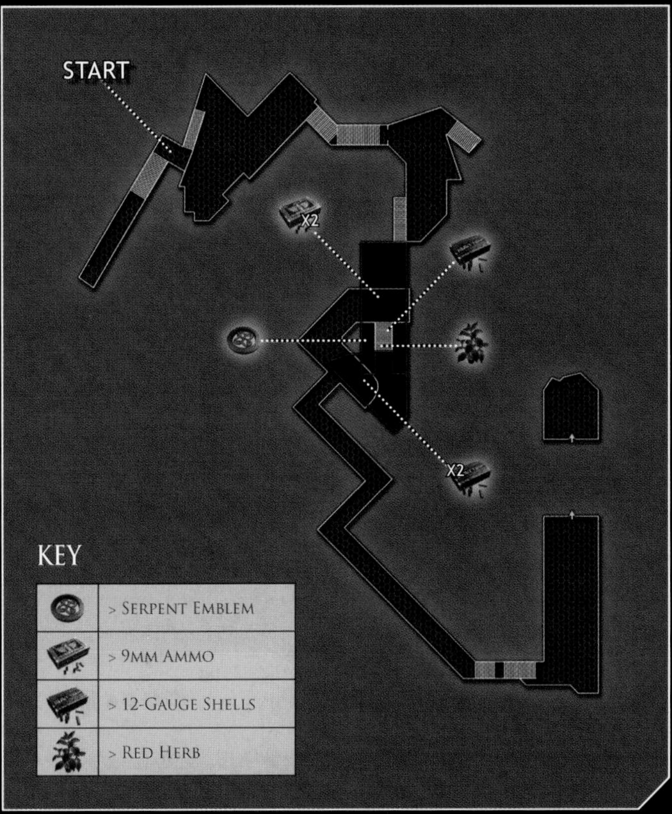

THE FOG IS COMING FOR YOU

Switch through your weapons and reload them all as you follow the BSAA soldier downstairs. Follow him up the rise while stopping to shoot a few zombies emerging from a blue fog. Reload and head up the stairs on the side of the street behind the soldier. Approach the gate at the top of the stairs and press Partner Action to open it.

Follow the soldier uphill to the right. Enter the open front door of the clothing store on the right side of the street.

LOOT THE CLOTHES SHOP

The store is about to be invaded by the fog and the zombies it creates, so move quickly. Smash the item crate and pick up two boxes of **9mm Ammo** on the low table and the **12-Gauge Rounds** near the black and white handbag. A **Red Herb** and another item crate are near the register. Pick up these items and go upstairs before the fog floods the store's first level otherwise you die instantly.

SERPENT EMBLEM:
CLOTHING STORE

A **Serpent Emblem** rests on the top shelf against the back wall of the store. Shooting this is more important than grabbing any items, so make this your priority.

ESCAPE THE STORE

Smash the item crates around the second floor while the soldier kicks the doors open. Then proceed into the corridor. Helena tends to stay and fight the zombie horde coming up the stairs. Turn around and gun them all down so she can move on.

Follow the corridor until you reach two item crates then smash them. A door bursts open and suddenly the corridor is full of zombies. Fire on them and blast the corridor clear. Ignore the enemies behind you, move to the doors, and open them with a Partner Action. Run downstairs to the military vehicle.

THE SAD SIDE OF BIOTERRORISM

After a long drive through the fog, the soldier stops in a clear area. Turn and snipe a couple zombies coming out of the fog behind you. This raises your kill count for ranking. Don't stay there long, however. Move to the overturned truck and press Partner Action to climb over it.

HIGH-RISE AREA

HIGH-RISE AREA MAP

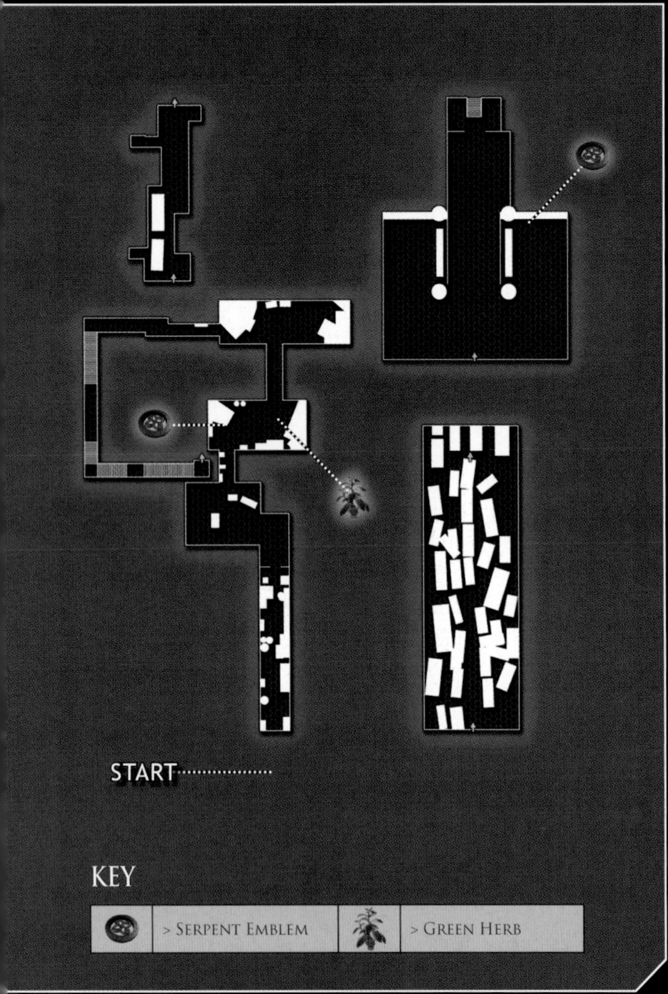

Head left around the corner. Examine the body below the window if you prefer, then turn right and crawl into the next room. Two BSAA zombies in this area wear body armor. Shoot them each in the head with your Shotgun. Smash the item crates found in the room. Then, search the open back door of the military vehicle parked nearby to find a **Green Herb**.

SERPENT EMBLEM: BSAA GARAGE

Look inside the open back of the truck, parked to the left of the entrance, to find a **Serpent Emblem**.

YOU KNOW WHERE THIS IS HEADED

Proceed down the corridor past the military vehicle. Open the last door, continue to the next corner quickly, and open fire on a horde of zombies running up the stairs from below. Toss an Incendiary Grenade to clear the stairs more quickly. Continue to the next door and open it with a Partner Action.

STREET FIGHTING II

Press Action to hop over the rail into the street. Perform a Quick Shot/melee attack combo against the zombie standing to your right, then equip your Shotgun and fight your way through the narrow space between parked cars. Wait until a zombie knocks down the rolling fence blocking your path, then take him out and continue.

FAMILIAR SIGHTS

This situation from the Prelude may seem familiar, but things are a little different here in Leon's Campaign than they were before. For one thing, both Leon and Helena are on their feet. Hit the closest zombie with a Quick Shot to knock it back, then turn right and dash into the alley. Crawl under the low horizontal post and smash an item crate on the left. Ascend the ramp and drop down. Smash another item crate and proceed to the door. Press Action to open it.

ROLLING FIREBALL

The crashed jet behind you falls from the building onto the street and explodes. Run away from the spreading fireball and hold Action to dash. A BSAA chopper hovers ahead. Continue running toward it. During liftoff, a zombie clings to your leg. Rotate the Left Stick to shake it off.

CRASH THAT CHOPPER PROPERLY!

During the helicopter flight, you are forced to take the controls. Tap the Reload button rapidly to avoid crashing. The pilot turns into a zombie and attacks Helena. Leon aims backward to shoot the pilot. Press the Fire button when the rotating timer hand moves through the colored part of the revolving command prompt. When shooting the pilot once doesn't succeed, shoot him again! Helena ejects him from the plane.

Rotate the Left Stick rapidly to avoid crashing. After side-swiping a train, the helicopter smashes into the Quad Tower's lobby—which is exactly where you wanted to go! The structure overhanging Leon and Helena's crash site threatens to fall on them. Press Reload and Action to get out of the way in time.

SERPENT EMBLEM: QUAD TOWER LOBBY

After escaping the helicopter crash, move forward and continue over to the right-hand railing. Check the shelves behind the reception desk to find a **Serpent Emblem.**

HALLOWED HALL OF NEO-UMBRELLA

Smash the available item crates and open the doors via Partner Action. Proceed down the steps. Move to the railing and press Action to hop over.

QUAD TOWER ENTRANCE

TOWER LOBBY MAP

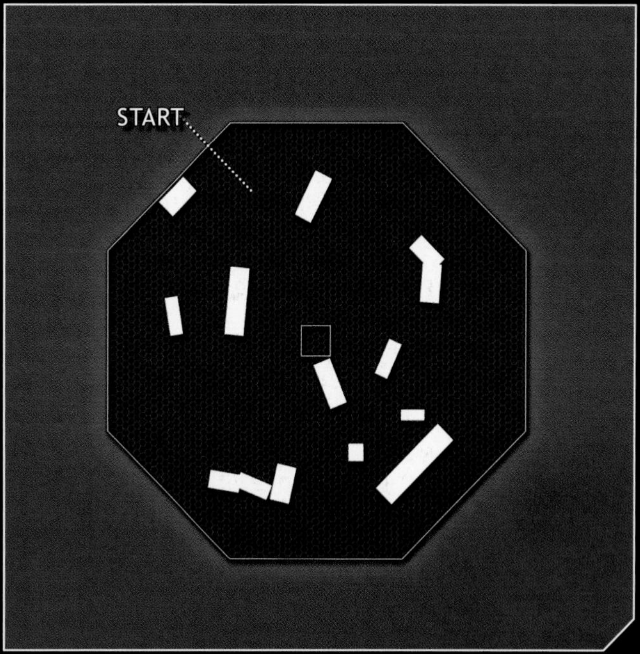

"BACK FOR MORE?"

Moving into the strange room with the infamous sigil patterned on the floor, you are confronted by a ghost of the recent past—Derek Simmons, alive but not necessarily well. The advance C-Virus now infecting his human body allows him to transform into terrifying shapes—as you're about to see!

SIMMONS (T-REX FORM)

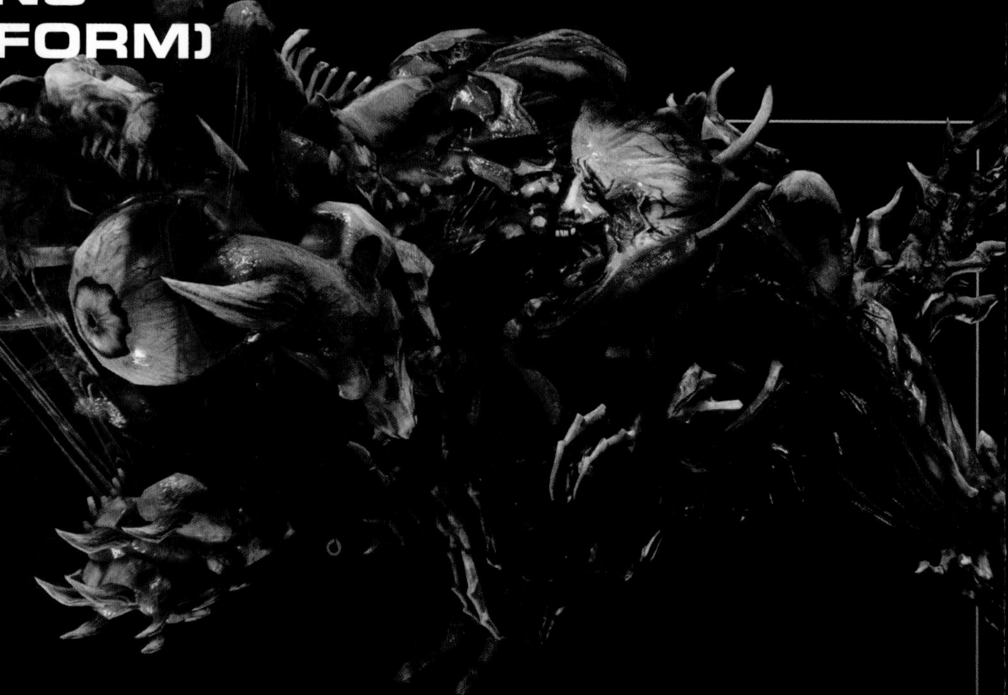

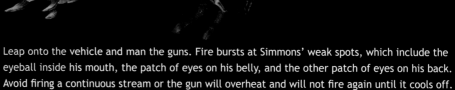

Simmons turns into a bizarre monster that vaguely resembles a Tyrannosaurus Rex. Various items are scattered around the area, which you can use to fight Simmons. Use these items and reserve your most powerful weaponry for the battles to come. Move beside one of the red exploding barrels scattered throughout the room. Bait Simmons to your position by shooting at his head with your handgun. Do this once or twice to get his attention. As the T-Rex Simmons charges your way, move away from the barrel and perform a dodge roll or slide as necessary to avoid damage. Then quickly shoot the barrel. If you need ammo, move around the outskirts of the area and smash item crates to restock.

Severe damage causes Simmons to collapse into his human form. When he finishes screaming, perform a Quick Shot/melee attack combo to knock him to his knees and push him to the ground. Start tapping the Action button rapidly before you even see the Quick Timing Event Gauge appear onscreen and pummel his face. Be sure to beat the timer hand each time to maximize the damage you inflict. After leaping off Simmons, move away quickly while reloading your weapon. He transforms back into the monstrous mutation immediately.

Repeat the strategies above and continue baiting Simmons near barrels and then shooting them. Eventually, the BSAA soldier from earlier bursts onto the scene in a vehicle specially rigged with twin machine-gun turrets on the back.

Leap onto the vehicle and man the guns. Fire bursts at Simmons' weak spots, which include the eyeball inside his mouth, the patch of eyes on his belly, and the other patch of eyes on his back. Avoid firing a continuous stream or the gun will overheat and will not fire again until it cools off.

The mutated monster Simmons throws a car, blocking the vehicle in a corner. While you're stuck, fire at his eyeballs to keep him at bay. The military vehicle breaks free of the wreckage and takes another lap around the area, allowing you to continue firing on the monster. However, the ride soon comes to an end when Simmons overturns it. Note that there is another vehicle parked in the area with a machine-gun turret. Unfortunately the T-Rex Simmons smashes the vehicle as soon as he sees you on it. Resume your previous strategy of baiting him toward barrels then shooting the barrels to wound him. If there are no more barrels, then throw Incendiary Grenades under him to damage the eyes on his belly, or place Remote Bombs in his path and detonate them when he walks over them.

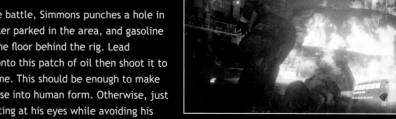

Late in the battle, Simmons punches a hole in an oil tanker parked in the area, and gasoline pools on the floor behind the rig. Lead Simmons onto this patch of oil then shoot it to set it aflame. This should be enough to make him collapse into human form. Otherwise, just keep shooting at his eyes while avoiding his attacks until the battle ends. Another tactic you may try is to simply run and hide from Simmons and allow the chopper that is firing from above to finish him off.

QUAD TOWER

TOWER EXTERIOR MAP

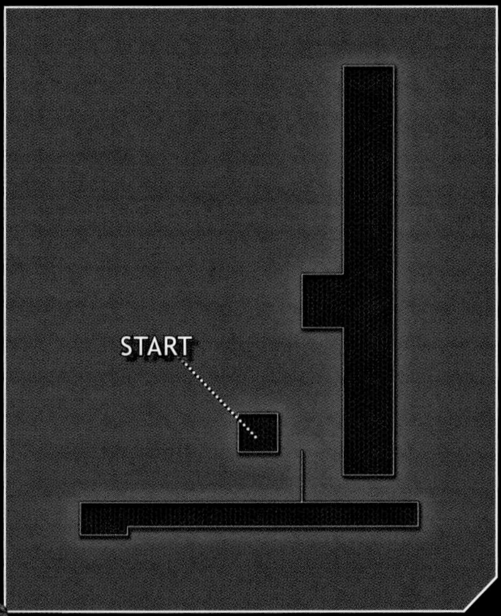

CLASH OF THE RACCOON CITY TITANS

While you attempt to reach the rooftop by elevator, chaotic circumstances force you to abandon the ride. Hanging from the elevator cables, you must climb to the top. Along the way, you notice Ada Wong and Simmons squaring off in a colossal battle.

SIMMONS (CHIMERA FORM)

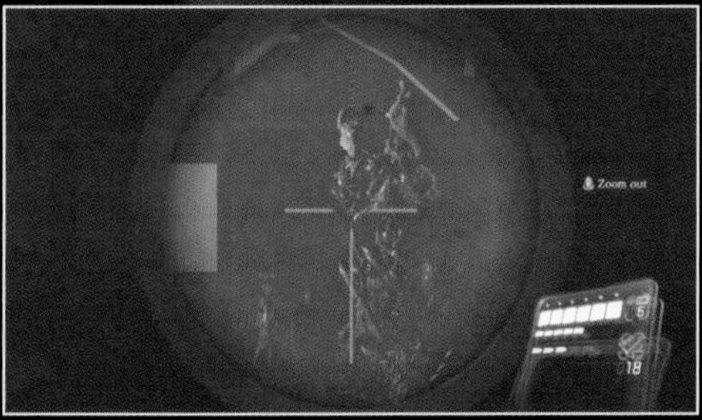

Leon and Helena begin this sequence on the sidelines, hanging from the elevator cable on the building opposite the battle taking place. Press both of the lower shoulder buttons on the controller and release one at a time as shown onscreen. Always hold one button down and alternate them to climb hand over hand up the rope. Don't climb too fast, don't release both buttons at once, and do not stop or you fall back to the bottom. Allow your fingers to move up and down on the buttons in a steady and regular rhythm. Focus on what you're doing rather than the awesome fight happening in the background.

When you reach the top of the rope, you land on the bridge segment opposite the rest of the bridge where Ada and Simmons fight. Equip your Sniper Rifle and assist Ada by shooting Simmons in his elongated head and neck, which are his weak spots. When he reverts to human form, shoot him to make him stagger so that Ada can give him a beat-down. While she does so, shoot the zombies closing in on her.

The bridge segment collapses, forcing you back onto the elevator cable. Continue climbing up by alternately releasing one shoulder button while holding the other. In hound form, Simmons leaps onto the building below you and begins climbing up. If he catches up to you, press Reload and Action to dodge his claw swipe or he throws you off the building to your death. Unless he closes the distance, ignore him and focus on climbing the rope.

When you finally reach safety, jump onto the bridge to assist Ada. Press Partner Action to pick her up and protect her from Simmons. When the camera angles toward the monster, aim your Sniper Rifle at him, zoom in, and shoot him repeatedly. If you run out of 7.62mm ammo, switch to the Assault Rifle RN and hit him with short bursts until he transforms. Leon picks up Ada and shields her against Simmons' Gatling gun attack.

Ada finally awakens and now you can fight Simmons together. As Helena suggested in the last fight, dash and slide past Simmons so that you and Ada can fire from opposite sides. Blast his extended neck with your Shotgun, Assault Rifle RN, or even your handgun but save your magnum rounds for later. Duck under Simmons' horizontal swipes and side roll away from his vertical attacks and rushing charges. Simmons rears back and extends his neck in the opposite direction prior to each style of swing.

When Simmons reverts to human form, approach him and perform a Quick Shot/melee attack combo to force him to the ground. Start tapping Action before the next gauge even appears onscreen to give him a full beat-down. Then move away quickly while he transforms back into a monster. Note that some of his transformations happen very quickly and provide you no time to take him down. Retreat if you find that this is the case.

If zombies crowd you and limit your actions, take them down with Quick Shots. Pick up items they drop, reload your weapons, and keep shooting Simmons' head and neck until Ada ends the battle in dramatic fashion.

QUAD TOWER ROOF

TOWER ROOFTOP MAP

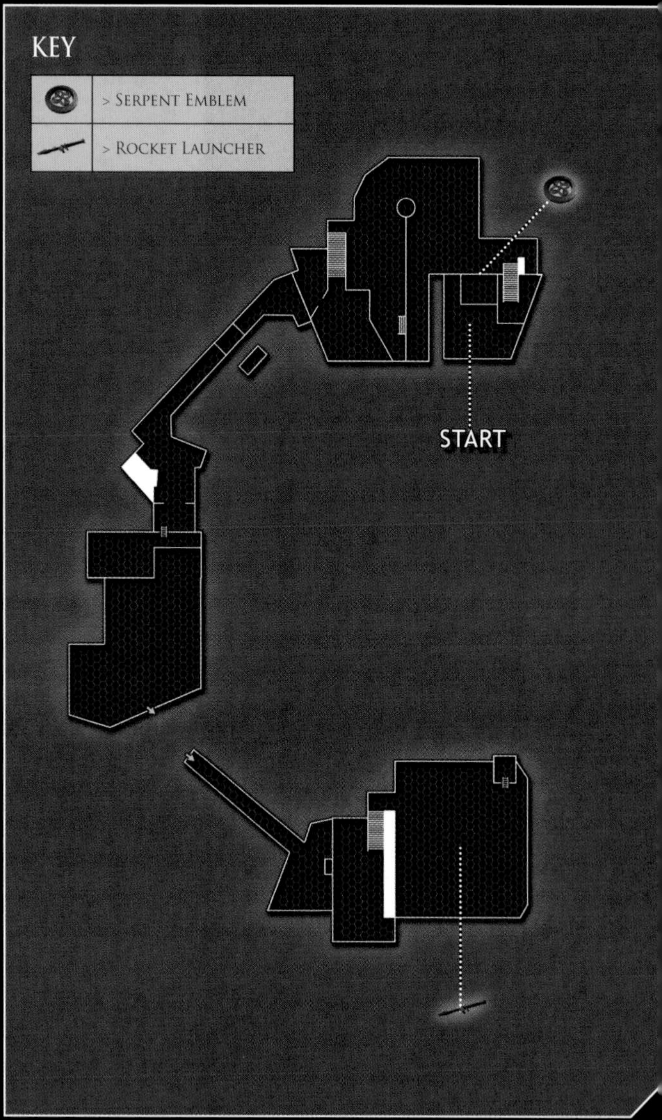

THE FINAL BATTLE

You finally reach the rooftop, where Ada parked her helicopter for you to use and left a "present." Unfortunately, you are not alone on the roof—the persistent Simmons is yet again back for more.

SIMMONS (FLY FORM)

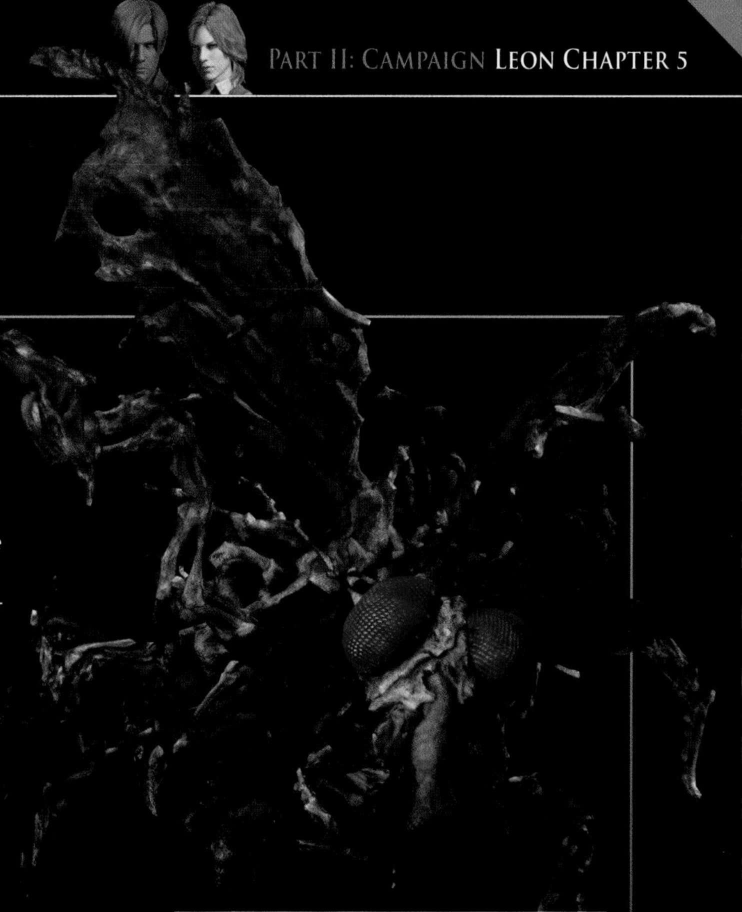

The rooftop is also full of zombies, which Simmons uses to heal himself. Blast zombies with Quick Shots but focus the majority of your shots on Simmons. Watch out for the tentacle he extends and swings horizontally and vertically as before. Dodge these attacks by rolling to the side or leaping backward as appropriate. The tentacle swings much faster this time and with less warning. You can back away to the opposite corner of the area and step outside of Simmons' range entirely. Since he is immobile, toss Incendiary Grenades under him to watch him fry. Use your handgun and Shotgun to shoot him first and save your more powerful weapons for later.

Continue shooting Simmons until he crumples in pain and is mobbed by zombies. You can then move inside the nearby stairwell. Take a moment to reload all your weapons. Go around the stairs to the right and smash the item boxes in the corner.

SERPENT EMBLEM: QUAD TOWER ROOF

The final Serpent Emblem in Leon's Campaign lies under the first set of stairs here. Look below the stairs to spot a **Serpent Emblem** on the wall outside the bars, and shoot it.

Ascend the stairs and head right. Take the next right and dash across the long platform to smash item crates at the end. Backtrack a bit and go down the side stairs. Then, head to the far right and descend the long stairs.

Smash the item crates in the far-left corner, then move to the door opposite and initiate Partner Action to open it. Inside, turn right and smash more crates. Then, climb onto the raised platform and move over to the crane. Climb onto it with a Partner Action.

One of Simmons' nasty "spitball" attacks knocks you into a construction lift. Simmons' massive new fly form is now visible, and he crawls on the previous building. Shoot him in his red, glowing eyes to keep him at bay. Helena moves the crane to the other side of the building. Relocate within the lift to avoid more of these "spitball" attacks.

Simmons takes flight and lands on the building beside you. Switch to your Shotgun and blast him in the eyes to keep him writhing in pain and to prevent him from attacking.

Leap off the crane as it collapses but climb back onto the building amid a horde of zombies. Knock back the closest one with a Quick Shot. Switch to your Wing Shooter and kill all the zombies in the area, including more that climb the fence. Smash the item crates in the corner and pick up enemy item drops to restock.

When the area is clear, move to the gate and open it via Partner Action. Smash the item crates on your left and climb the ladder on your right. Go right to the corner and smash more item crates, then approach the low railing and hop over.

Simmons feeds on zombies and makes himself so large that he can only sit on the edge of the building and attack. Note that one of the zombies in this area is impaled by a lightning rod and that item crates surround the area.

Keep the zombie population in the area low by blasting them quickly in the head with your Shotgun. This prevents Simmons from regenerating any lost legs. Continue killing zombies until the only one that Simmons can pick up is the one impaled on the lightning rod. Equip your Lightning Hawk and shoot one of Simmons' legs until it breaks off. Aim for the glowing joint on his underbody. When he consumes the zombie impaled on the lightning rod, lightning strikes him. Now you know what to do!

Clear the zombies off the roof again using your Shotgun, handgun, and melee attacks. Don't tire yourself out, however, since mobility is important. When the camera angles upward to show Simmons swinging his massive leg, press Reload and Action to avoid the attack. If you have an Incendiary Grenade on hand, press Fire to counter by running up the leg and slamming the grenade into the leg joint. If you manage to blast the leg off this way, quickly kill all the zombies so that the only one Simmons can eat is the one impaled on the lightning rod. As a mutated "fly," Simmons also performs a variation of the leg attack in which he stabs zombies on the roof. Press Reload and Action whenever you see this move displayed onscreen—you quickly flip away from this attack and avoid damage.

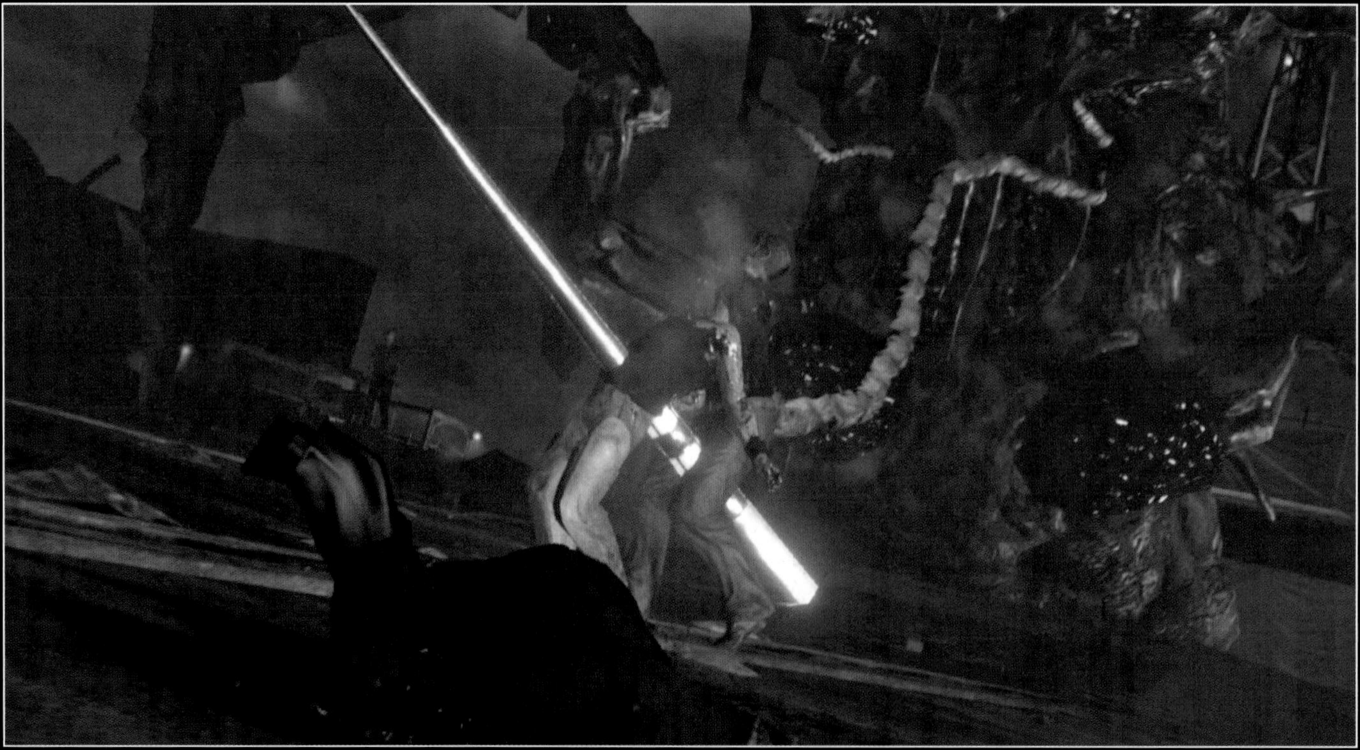

When the zombies are mostly defeated, equip your Lightning Hawk and begin blasting Simmons' leg joints as fast as possible. If your magnum runs empty too soon, switch to your Sniper Rifle and take out the rest of the legs as fast as possible. As a result, Simmons can do nothing but flop onto the rooftop like a legless maggot.

Now is the crucial moment—pick up the lightning rod, carry it over to Simmons' head, and press Fire to impale his eye with it. When he regrows his legs and stands back up this time, lightning strikes the rod. The battle appears to be over.

Now you must reach the helicopter. Ascend the broken ledge, drop from the end, climb onto the air-conditioning unit, and hop over the low rail. Run upstairs to the heliport and approach the driver's side of the chopper. The "present" Ada left you is a **Rocket Launcher**! Press Partner Action to examine the chopper and wait for Helena to join you.

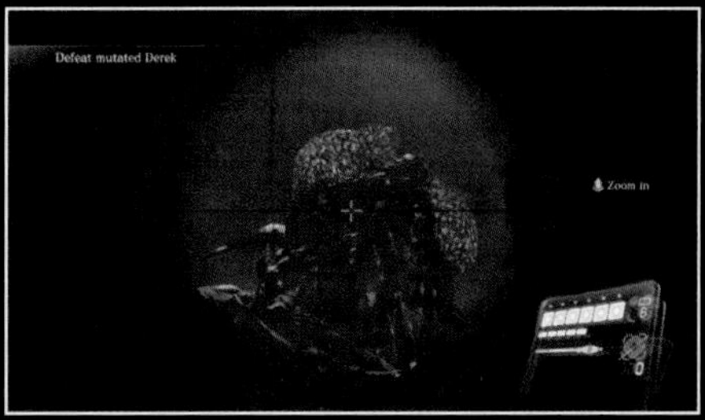

Simmons rears his ugly fly head one more time. Before he strikes, aim the Rocket Launcher at his head and fire. Perfect aim is not required.

ENDING

After viewing the ending of Leon's Campaign, you unlock a new Dog Tag just as you've done in previous chapters. If this is the first campaign you've completed, you also unlock all eight Skill Sets. You are able to choose sets and switch Skills on the fly while replaying this or other campaigns. Also, Agent Hunt is unlocked in the Extra Content menu. If you have completed all three campaigns at this time, Ada's Campaign is added to the Campaign Select menu. Complete Ada's Campaign to unlock a secret ending, which plays after the credits, and infinite ammo Skills. Equip the Infinite Rocket Launcher Ammo Skill while replaying Leon's Chapter 5. The Rocket Launcher is then permanently added to your inventory with infinite ammo!

LEON CHAPTER 5: RANKING CRITERIA

RANK	ACCURACY(%)	DEATHS	CLEAR TIME(MIN)	ENEMIES ROUTED
A	70	2	65	60
B	60	3	80	50
C	50	5	120	20
D	*1	*1	*1	*1

*1 Any Below Rank C

POINTS AWARDED PER RANK (ABOVE)				
Rank	A	B	C	D
Points	25	20	15	10

TOTAL RANKING POINTS TABLE

RANK	S	A	B	C	D	E
Total	100	90	75	55	45	*2

*2 Any Below Rank D

CHRIS

NORMAL DIFFICULTY

The walkthrough provided for Chris' Campaign has been simplified to pertain only to Normal difficulty mode, in single player, offline. Most of the strategies described herein pertain to using Chris' unique abilities. However, certain areas that are only accessible when playing as Piers are described with special notes. The walkthrough does not account for changes due to gaming online with other players. Therefore it is recommended that you play as Chris during your first attempt at this campaign in order to follow this walkthrough more closely.

CHRIS CHAPTER 1

JUNE 29, 2013

Eastern Europe

Chris Redfield is not the man he used to be. Sequestering himself in an Eastern European bar, he is getting drunk and turning belligerent on the waitstaff. An encounter with former subordinate Piers Nivans makes him realize that he has blocked the past from his memory. But even if he can't remember, he's been recalled to active duty anyway.

MAIN STREET

MAIN STREET MAP

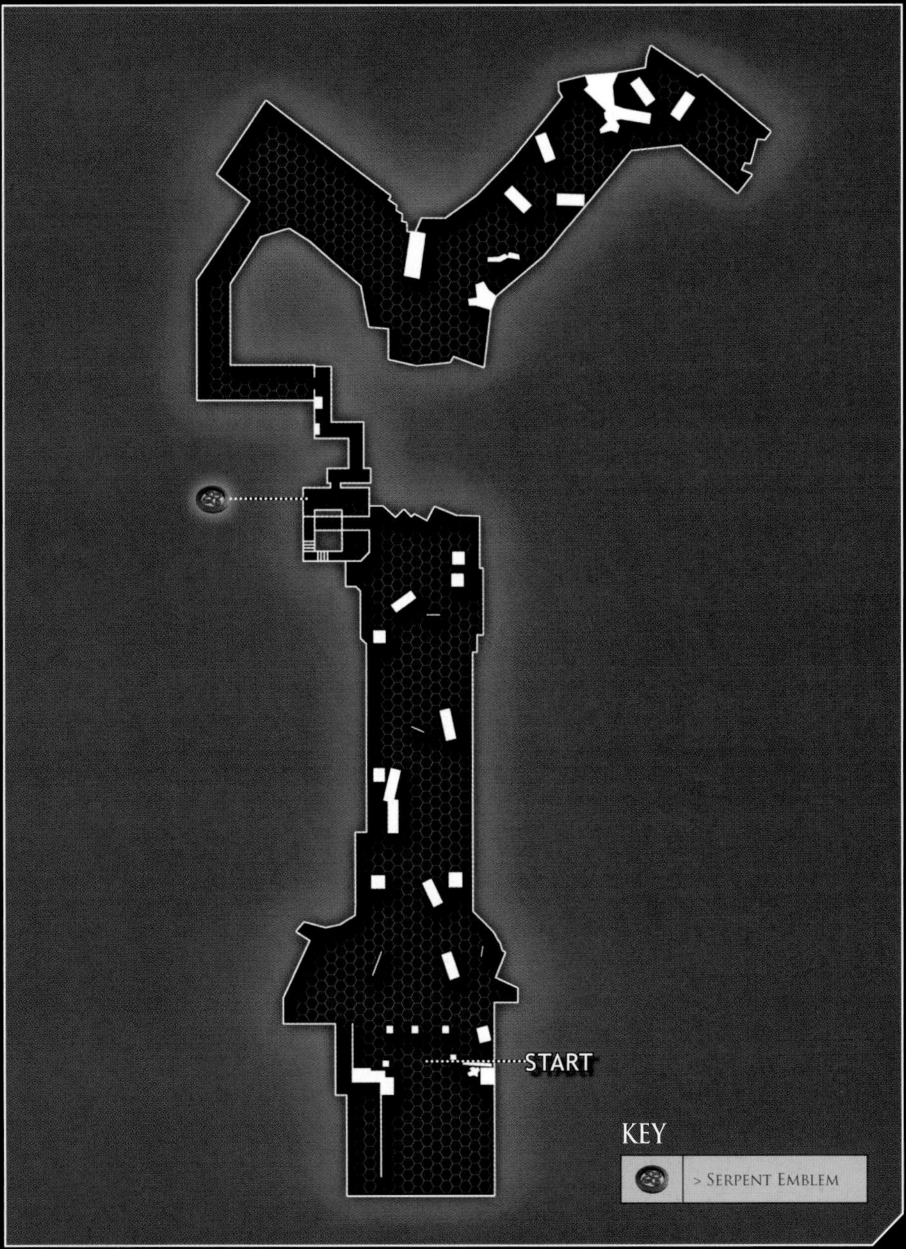

BACK ON DUTY

Waiyip, China, is under bioterrorist attack by Neo-Umbrella. When the helicopter settles in a hovering position, press Partner Action to rappel down to the rooftop.

SMASH CRATES FOR ITEMS

Follow the other BSAA soldiers to the roof edge and press Action to jump down. Turn to your left to spot an item crate. Approach it and press Fire to smash it and reveal an item. The things contained in item crates are randomly determined each time you play, but it is important to make use of any and all items you find.

TIME TO PARTNER UP

Go to the ramp and descend to the ground floor. Drop off the suspended ledge at the end of the ramp. Move over to the corner to smash two tall item crates. Then, join Piers at the double doors. Press the Partner Action button to summon Piers to help you open the doors.

PIERS CAN GET CRANKY

Sometimes Piers becomes impatient if he has to wait for you to explore. Calm him down by holding the Partner Action button and pressing left on the directional pad to issue the Wait command. After that, he'll be silent a while before mouthing off again.

TOO MUCH PRESS

Push your way through the news crew and proceed down the street past fleeing civilians and dead bodies. When you approach the barricade at the end, the cars explode. Divert left to the double doors and press Partner Action to breach the interior.

USE THE DIRECTIONAL BEACON

In the heat of combat, you sometimes lose your bearings. Press and hold L1 or LB to make the directional beacon appear in the environment. It points the way to your next destination. Use the Directional Beacon to guide your way whenever you feel lost or don't know where to go next.

PREPARE FOR INJURY

Head down the hall past your solders and continue up the stairs on your left. Arriving on the top level, head left and smash two item crates. These typically yield Green and Red Herbs.

Press the Item Menu button to open your item slots. Combine herbs by selecting one and pressing Action while the leaf icon is highlighted. Then, select another herb to mix it with—the game automatically selects a Red Herb if one is available, since it's the best choice. Combine two herbs to make three- or six-powdered mixtures. Select the result and press Action twice to send it to your Health Tablet supply. Then, whenever your health is low, press R1 or RB to swallow a tablet and recover.

FIND CHRIS' FIRST SERPENT EMBLEM

Follow the corridor around the corner, beyond windows that shatter with machine-gun fire. Entering the little butcher's kitchen, look to your left to spot something rather peculiar...

SERPENT EMBLEM: BUTCHER BLOCK

On the upper level of the first tenement building, a **Serpent Emblem** rests on the back shelves of a small butchery. Shoot this and other emblems hidden throughout each chapter. They unlock additional content in the Collections screen of the Special Features menu regarding Chris' Campaign. Four Serpent Emblems appear in every chapter.

REGENERATING ENEMIES?

Leave the butcher's block and smash the item crate on the table to the left. Open the door. Press Action once to open a door quietly or press it twice quickly to kick it open. Head right toward the balcony ledge and go through another door. More gunfire and an explosion shatter the windows as you pass.

Continue following the passage until you reach a hole in the wall on the left. A J'avo soldier executes a civilian and runs off. Drop down to street level and pursue him. Open the door at the end of the alley with a Partner Action. Chris shoots the monster in the head only to watch as the brains, skull, and face reform. Gun down the monster by shooting it in the head again.

CARNAGE EXTREME

Proceed down the street to the right beyond the burning truck. Head left and toward the parked cop cars. Further down, a J'avo with a rocket launcher fires, obliterating a BSAA helicopter. Proceed down to the end of the street. While the camera is angled upward, slide across the hoods of any cars that get in your way. The helicopter crashes to the street, blowing up the police blockade.

Move around the wreckage and go right. Spot your team outside some double doors and smash three item crates across the street before joining them. Open the doors with a Partner Action.

BACK STREET

BACK STREET MAP

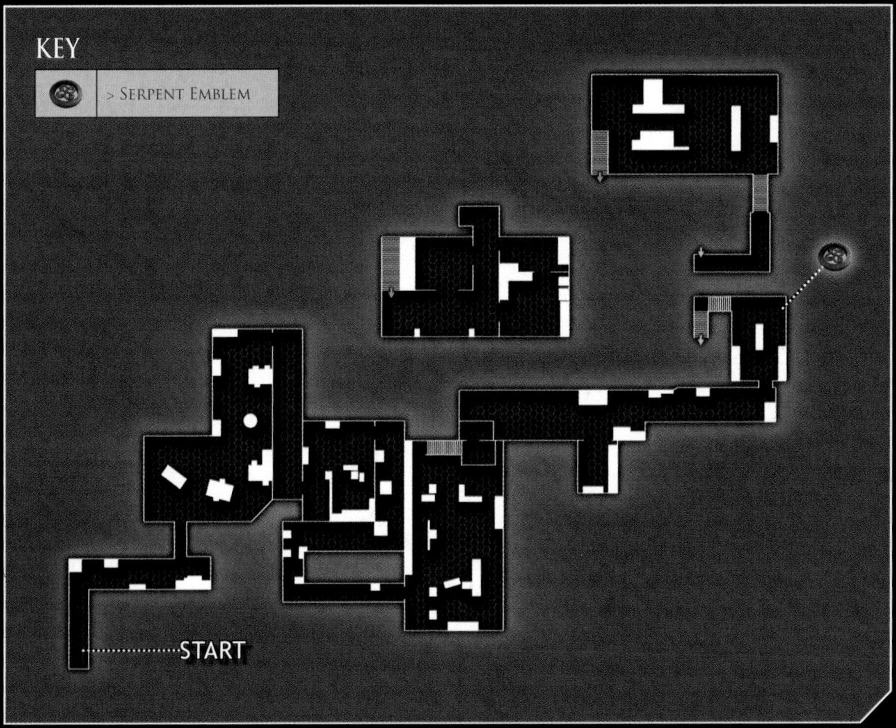

BREACH, BANG, AND CLEAR

Follow your soldiers down the alley and to the right. Follow them into a smaller alley on the left and open the door at the end with a Partner Action. From outside the doorway, shoot the J'avo that you can see inside or throw a grenade into the room and kill them all at once. Then, breach the room and use Quick Shot plus melee attacks to finish off the remainders. This will save bullets for future encounters.

LISTEN FOR THE ALL CLEAR AND SAVE TIME

The handy thing about fighting with a group of professional soldiers is that they will shout "all clear" when the enemies are eliminated. Use these verbal cues to help you move on more quickly and score a better completion time!

ENJOY THE HUNT

Jump behind the counter and move down the aisle until another J'avo bursts through the back door. Take him down with a Quick Shot and a melee attack. Let your Combat gauge recharge, then exit through the door.

Turn right, head down the alley, and open the next double doors with a Partner Action. Inside, approach the low wall opposite the door and hop over. Smash two item crates in this area, then join your team by the next door. One man kicks it open and is immediately grabbed and attacked. Gun down the J'avo when the soldier is clear. Fortunately, your fellow soldier gets back up and rejoins the fight.

THE J'AVO GET COCKY

Proceed down the alley and take cover behind the boxes stacked in the center. Another J'avo waits in ambush behind some low crates further down. Wing him in the leg or arm to bring him out of hiding and then take him down. Proceed down the rest of the alley cautiously because two more J'avo wait in ambush on your right. After dispatching them, continue past their dead bodies to the next corner. Move to the boxes stacked on your left, hold Ready/Aim to press up against them, press Action to crouch, and then move to the corner of the low box. A J'avo comes around the corner from the right, so stand up and give him a Quick Shot to knock him down. Finish with a melee attack. In the same way, take out another enemy hiding behind the crates stacked on your left.

MUTATIONS MAKE ENEMIES STRONGER

Follow your men to the next door and smash the item crates to either side before proceeding with a Partner Action. Piers shoots a J'avo in the arm then watches in horror as the arm mutates into something foul. When J'avo mutate, they are invulnerable during the process. Afterward, the mutated appendage remains resistant to bullets, so shoot them elsewhere, such as the head or legs. J'avo can mutate more than once, so be wary. Using Quick Shots, kill this J'avo and the rest in the room, including the one at the top of the stairs.

RETURN FIRE FROM COVER

Head up the steps and open the door at the top. Drop from the ledge to street level and crush the item crate on the right. Open the gate with a Partner Action. Move forward to the first box on the left and take cover behind it. While standing behind the box, aim with your weapon and then press Action to take cover. While in cover, move the Left Stick to rise up and fire short bursts. Be sure to reload between bursts. A shutter door opens on the right and J'avo with machetes rush in. Gun them all down. Advance from cover point to cover point, shooting J'avo further away whenever they pop their heads out. Switch from your Assault Rifle to your Nine-Oh-Nine as needed if ammo runs out. Smash the crates inside the shuttered area on the right to restock.

Continue to the end of the alley, smash an item crate in the right corner, and join your men at the door. Open it and smash the crate on the left and in the far right corner of the room.

SERPENT EMBLEM: BUILDING ENTRANCE

A **Serpent Emblem** is hidden behind the item crate in the corner that is formed by the two large bookshelves. Smash the crate to reveal it and shoot the emblem.

BUSTING DOORS DOWN

Ascend the stairs and open the door at the end of the hallway. Proceed upstairs above the flaming area, open the door, and breach the next building. Fire on the J'avo that scramble out of the room on your left.

Proceed through the sitting area to the corner and go upstairs. Be careful as you head down the corridor because a J'avo bursts through the door on the left. Enter the room he came out of, smash an item crate, and open the door on the right. Another J'avo smashes through the door across the hall. Take him down, then enter that room and find another item crate in the kitchen. Return to the hallway, move to the double doors at the end, and open them with a Partner Action.

ROOFTOPS

ROOFTOPS MAP

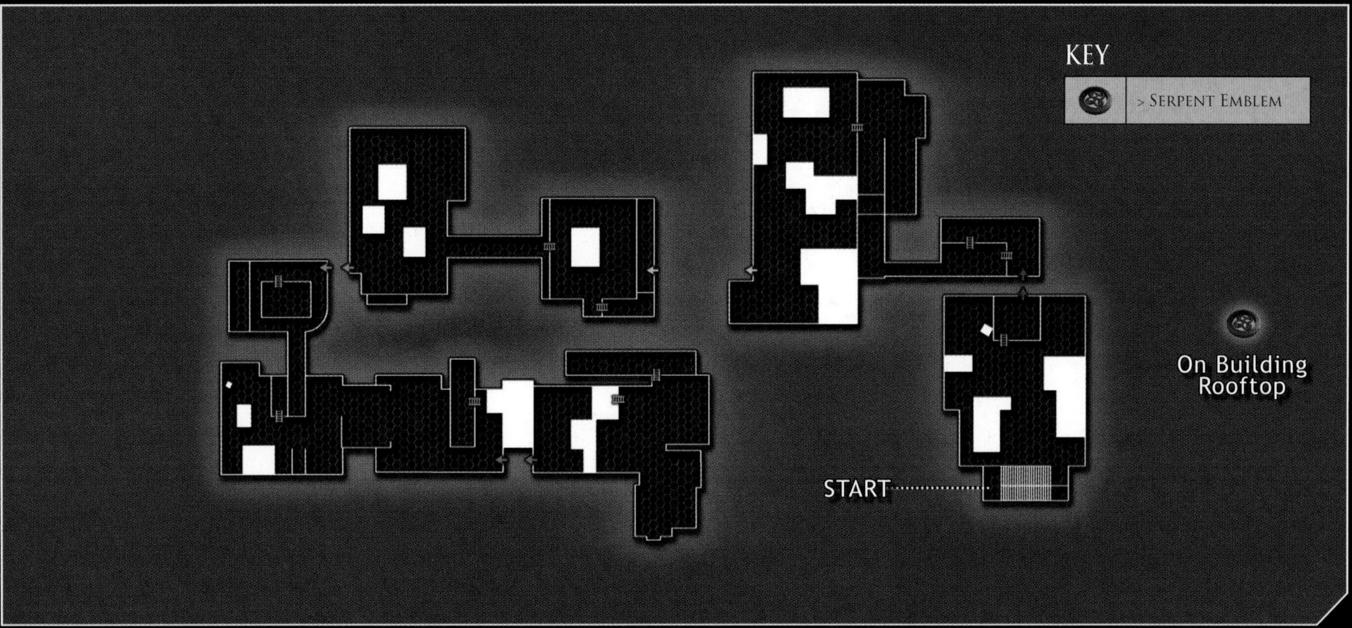

DANGERS IN THE NIGHT

Chris and his team occupy a staircase leading up to the roof. Smash the two item crates to your far left. A J'avo guard stands with his back to you on the first stair landing. Run up behind him for a Stealth Hit. Chris pushes him right over the edge! However, you have no such luck surprising the second enemy that is one flight up. But you can hit him with a Quick Shot, use a melee attack, and push him over the rail.

NOGA-LET: J'AVO THAT TAKE FLIGHT

Continue upstairs to the rooftop. HQ points out a tenement building straight ahead as being the "Ace of Spades," your target destination. A group of J'avo issue in from the far left. Climb onto the raised platform to your left and gun them down as they come. Shoot them in the legs to easily trip them up.

Some of them may mutate into flying creatures called Noga-Let. Until you find some Flash Grenades, fight these mutations by shooting at the still-human looking torso hanging below them.

After clearing the area of hostiles, climb the ladder on the far side. Move to the back ledge and jump across the gap. Take out any stragglers that dash out from behind the corner on your left. Now, climb either ladder on the little building.

SERPENT EMBLEM: CONSTRUCTION BUILDING ROOFTOP

From the vantage point of the highest roof in the first area (which is connected to the next building by a small, wooden bridge), equip the Sniper Rifle or Assault Rifle and turn away from the wooden bridge. A **Serpent Emblem** is mounted on a post rising from the top of a building under construction far away. Piers has an easier time hitting the emblem with his Sniper Rifle. However, it's still possible for Chris to shoot it with his Assault Rifle with a deep breath and a little skill...

TAKE THE HIGH GROUND

Cross the makeshift wooden bridge and drop onto the next rooftop. Make your way across the ledge to the ladder and climb it. Smash three item crates in the corners, then climb the long ladder up the side of the building. Higher up, J'avo guards spot Chris immediately. Gun them both down quickly and move to the wall beneath them. Climb onto the rise and shoot more J'avo around the corner to the left. Take out any Noga-Let with bursts of Assault Rifle fire.

ZIP LINE INTERRUPTED

Mount the orange raised platforms in the corner, and move under the slanted, horizontal pole. Press Partner Action to slide across to the next building. A J'avo fires a rocket launcher mid-slide, knocking Chris and Piers to the lower levels and separating them.

Chris catches hold of another horizontal pole. Tap the Reload button rapidly to climb hand over hand along the pole and over to the building. J'avo take positions on your flank, and it's up to Piers to gun them down. Keep moving along the pole to the next building as fast as possible.

PROCEED WITH COVER FIRE

Drop onto the scaffold and climb the very high ladder. Smash the two item crates in the niche to your left. Return fire on the J'avo on the rooftop below if you spot them before they run off.

Drop down when clear, move to the next small building, and climb the ladder mounted to it. From atop this building, shoot the J'avo in the area below you. They might mutate into Noga-Let, so stay on the roof and shoot them down.

Drop off the side of the roof and smash two item crates in the corner. Now, climb onto the rise and hop over the horizontal pole. Move onto the orange platform and jump the gap. Take out two ambushers that may mutate here. Move right and climb another ladder. Drop down on the other side, move to the right around the dividing wall, and smash two crates in the corner.

Now, cross the bridge to the next building. Shoot the ambushers on your level as well as above, and watch out for flying foes that team up. If they do so, move to the corner of the building where Piers can see you and your pursuers. He will shoot them down. Smash the item crates on this building and then climb the ladder.

Smash another item crate up high, then follow the long salvage bridge. Drop down twice at the end and you are finally reunited with Piers. At this point, you have the option to search the surrounding rooftops and to backtrack a short distance along the route he traveled to locate several item crates worth smashing for supplies.

ANOTHER BRIEF SEPARATION

When you are ready to proceed, join Piers at the metal door with the red light and open it with a Partner Action. Head right and around the corner at the end. Climb up, move onto the raised ledge, drop off, proceed to the orange platform at the edge, and jump off. Chris falls again, but only because an RPG was fired this time. Take cover behind the nearest low rise and return fire on the J'avo gathered on the next rooftop. As they cross the bridge, toss a grenade to take them all out at once. When everything is clear, smash some item crates on the back corner of this roof and cross the wooden bridge.

DON'T SHOOT THE BARRELS!

Climb the ladder on the second roof to reach a building still under construction. Move out to the end of the platform and drop down. Make your way to the orange metal door and open it with a Partner Action.

Avoid shooting any red barrels on this rooftop because they'll explode. You also need to use them against incoming enemies. Move to the corner, cross to the next roof section, and descend the stairs. **Three Flash Grenades** sit on a wide crate directly ahead and slightly to the right. Pick these up since they'll soon come in handy. Also smash the three item crates against the back wall.

OKAY, SHOOT THE BARRELS!

A bright floodlight suddenly turns on, and J'avo scatter across the area. Shoot the barrels to blow up squads of J'avo simultaneously. Stay on the move, look for lone targets of opportunity, approach them, and hit them with Quick Shots followed by melee attacks. If more than one J'avo mutates and starts to fly, equip a Flash Grenade to stun them all at once, then pull their wings off.

The BSAA sends in reinforcements! Help them mop up the last enemies, then move to the green double doors in the corner of the roof and open them with a Partner Action.

TENEMENT

TENEMENT MAP

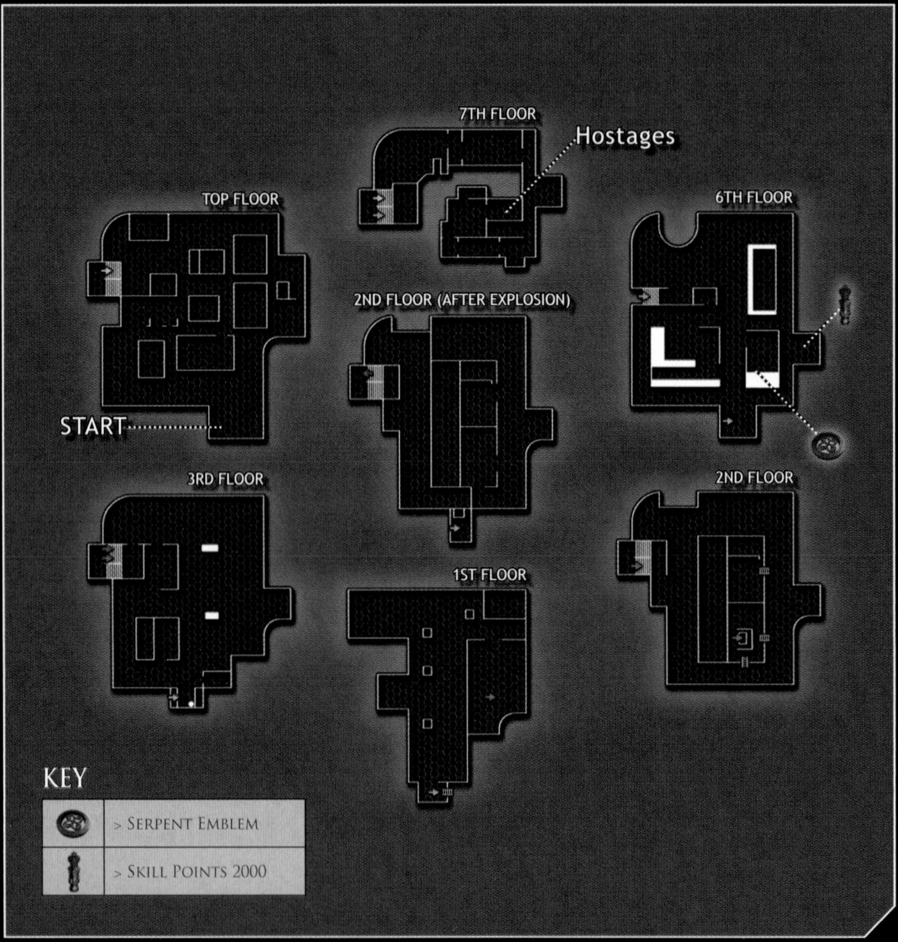

ATTACK OF THE SPIDER-MEN

Chris and his team are informed of a hostage situation within the tenement house. Join Piers at the door, kick it open, and take cover in the next area. Return fire on J'avo that flood the area, and occasionally watch your back by doing an about-face (Left Stick down + Action). Watch for J'avo that may mutate into Noga-Trchanje, which are creepy but easily killed merely by closing in and stomping on them, even when they're not down.

DOWN TO LEVEL 7

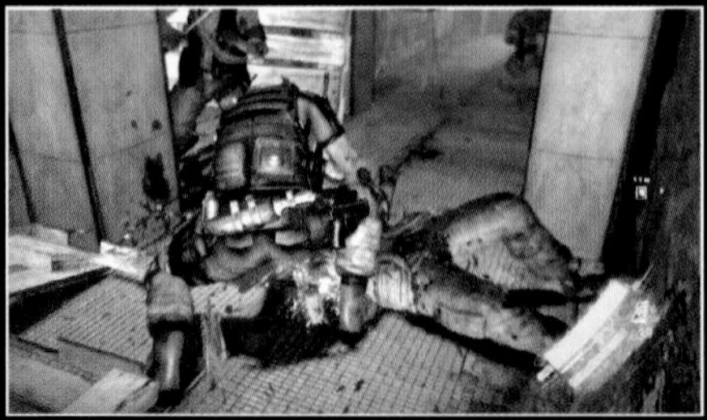

Continue fighting until all clear is reported, then use your Directional Beacon to catch up with the others at the stair door. Smash the nearby item crates and enter the stairs. Follow your men downstairs to Level 7, and kick open the door. Smash the item crate opposite, and then navigate the retail level. Engage hostiles in the corridors with your men and search side nooks for more breakable item crates.

ONE CREEPY AMBUSH

Upon reaching the next closed door on Level 7, head to the right to smash three item crates. Now, return to the door and open it for your team. Inside and to the right you encounter a ghastly sight—the ceiling is covered with Noga-Trchanje! Toss a Flash Grenade to knock them all down, then step on as many heads as possible before they recover.

HOSTAGES IN FLIGHT

Reload and move through the next few rooms behind your troops. HQ radios that the hostages are in the next room. Before opening the door that all your men are trained upon, divert to the left into the next room and smash all the item crates. Rejoin your men and press Partner Action to open the door.

Two Noga-Trchanje mutations escape the room, carrying two hostages. If you're quick enough, you can smash the second hostage-carrying monster as it leaves the room. Otherwise you must chase it around the level with the hostage it carries. Don't shoot it or you might kill the hostage. Instead, hit it with melee attacks and it should die easily.

HQ spots the other hostage-toting monster up on Level 8. While returning to the stairwell, you encounter several Noga-Trchanje sent to block your path. Take them out with melee or shoot their fleshy human parts to kill them quickly. Look out for Noga-Trchanje waiting on the ceiling for you as you reach the stairs!

Return to Level 8 and chase the Noga-Trchanje with the hostage around the level, using the blue arrow marker to guide you to its location. More of these spider-like mutants emerge from under raised shutters and vents to attack. Use melee attacks and Quick Shots aimed downward to take them out. The second hostage-carrier provides quite a chase, but you'll eventually notice a predictable pattern of movement. Use this to catch it at a corner or intersection and stomp on it.

NOW FOR LEVEL 6

With both hostages rescued, return to the stairs. This time, go all the way down to Level 6. Smash item crates on either side of the gaping hole in the floor nearby. Then, follow Piers down the center aisle.

SERPENT EMBLEM: TENEMENT LEVEL 6 BUTCHERY

As you pass down the center aisle on Level 6, you'll notice a butcher shop on the left. Stop and look behind the counter to spot another **Serpent Emblem** to shoot.

STOPPED MID-DESCENT

Behind the butcher shop, just off the center aisle, you find an item chest containing **Skill Points (2,000)**. When approaching the exit door, look to the far right to spot an item crate. Continue on to the white elevator doors and press Action to open them.

Board the elevator and press Partner Action to descend. After another communique from HQ, the elevator stops before reaching the bottom. From your fixed view of the car, move to the left corner in the foreground and press Action to find the escape hatch overhead. Press Partner Action to boost Piers up. Then press the button again so he'll pull you out of the elevator.

A J'avo above fires a rocket launcher, obliterating the elevator. Chris and Piers are safe, however. Shoot that J'avo on Piers' side. Smash the item crates on your side of the shaft, then move to the doors and press Partner Action to open them.

FULL OFFENSIVE

J'avo set up an ambush as you open the elevator shaft doors. Equip a Hand Grenade and toss it into the center of them to obliterate most of them at once. Then, jump through the doorway and take cover to the left. Throw another grenade at the second wave of J'avo that enters from the back. Check your left as well for any sneaky foes that try to move up on your flank.

Clear the level and search thoroughly. Many item crates are on this level to help you restock. When finished collecting, use your Directional Beacon to help you find the exit door.

THE FINAL HOSTAGE

Descend the stairs to Level 2 and open the door. Turn right and observe the large opening in the center of the floor. First, move around the outside of the area and smash any item crates you find. Then move into the center, drop onto the grate, and shoot the J'avo holding the woman hostage on the level below. Quickly press Partner Action to drop down. Shoot the other J'avo on the bottom level before they can kill the woman.

DESPERATE SHOT

A final J'avo drops from the ceiling and puts his machete to the hostage's throat. The game enters slow motion, and you must shoot the J'avo in the head at the first clear opportunity. Aim for either side of the woman's head and fire when the J'avo puts his face in your crosshair. If you wait too long, he slashes her throat. Collect any remaining items then open the back door of the room. Approach the BSAA soldier entering from the loading dock.

CLEAR BEFORE BOMBARDMENT

Although the hostages are safe, Chris and Piers are trapped in the building by an explosion. You must now get clear of the building. Turn around, head up the center aisle, and drop into the elevator shaft. Climb the ladder on the far side. Open the door at the top with a Partner Action.

The first missiles strike the building. Turn left and follow the railing around to the right. Dash to the far end and turn left. Now, enter the stairwell and go back up to Level 3.

The floor begins to collapse. Turn right, run to the tables near the edge of the floor chasm, and slide across them. Don't worry about fighting the J'avo on the other side because another missile soon takes them out. Pick up any items they drop and run to the opening on the far side of the room.

The floor gives way. Rotate the Left Stick counterclockwise rapidly to climb back up, then help your partner if needed. Move to the ledge and press Partner Action to jump off.

CHAPTER RANKING

As in the other campaigns, the player is awarded a rank for prowess in four criteria regardless of difficulty selected: hit accuracy percentage, player deaths suffered, total clear time, and number of enemies defeated. For each letter grade rank obtained, a specific number of points are awarded as determined by the "Points Awarded Per Rank" table. These points are then added together to determine an overall rank for the chapter as determined by the "Total Ranking Points Table," with S being a perfect score that requires A ranking for all four criteria.

CHRIS CHAPTER 1: RANKING CRITERIA

RANK	ACCURACY(%)	DEATHS	CLEAR TIME(MIN)	ENEMIES ROUTED
A	70	2	80	70
B	60	3	90	50
C	50	5	100	40
D	*1	*1	*1	*1

*1 Any Below Rank C

POINTS AWARDED PER RANK (ABOVE)				
Rank	A	B	C	D
Points	25	20	15	10

TOTAL RANKING POINTS TABLE

RANK	S	A	B	C	D	E
Total	100	90	75	55	45	*2

*2 Any Below Rank D

City in Eastern Europe

December 24, 2012

Edonia Map

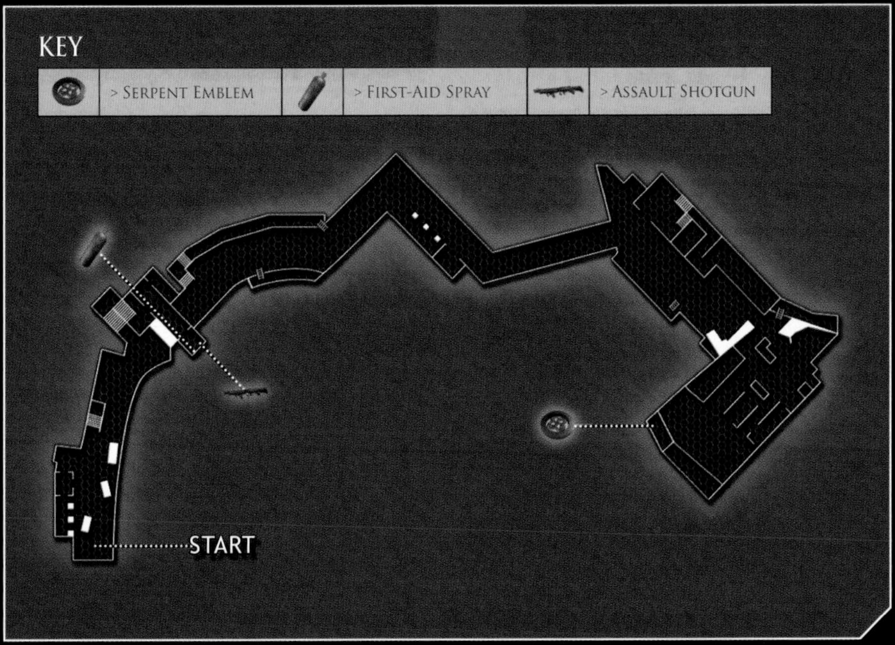

Flashback

Chris Redfield is remembering the events of six months prior to the outbreak in Waiyip, China, when he led an international BSAA team on a doomed mission to suppress a bioterrorist assault in Eastern Europe. Following intel that the enemy is using new mutating enemies called "J'avo," Redfield prepares his team to invade the occupied territory and wipe out the infestation. Now is not the time to compromise or take prisoners—kill them all!

Into the Blitz

When the BSAA convoy stops, Chris jumps out on the left side of the tank. Take cover at the right corner of the troop transport parked there and fire on J'avo farther down the street.

Clear the enemies you can from the center of the street, then move to the left side of the troop transport and continue to the covered sidewalk. Ahead is an item crate, but you must break it open quickly. Hold Action while moving to dash toward it, then press Ready/Aim within a few feet of the crate to slide into it. As a result, you'll face the doorway ahead and be ready when two J'avo attack from inside. Take them down by performing Quick Shots followed with melee attacks and head stomps. Smash another item crate in the interior, then take cover at the doorway straight ahead. Fire on any J'avo that may be taking cover behind the truck parked outside. When only one enemy is visible outside, dash forward and slide to throw it off balance, then finish with melee attacks.

Heavier Mutations

Mutating J'avo can be knocked to the ground, but otherwise you can't hurt them. Enemies that mutate their arms and limbs into wide exoskeleton shields are still easy to defeat if you approach them from behind.

Deal with the Snipers

A machine-gun turret high up and farther down the street fires on all positions. Snipers along the bridge pick off anyone dumb enough to stick their head out. Move from the building interior to the back of the parked truck, then dash up the nearby stairs and take cover along the top wall with the rest of your men. Position yourself on the wall far enough to the right to take out a sniper located in the open second-story picture window on your left.

The trucks below begin moving up. This is your cue to hop the wall and fall in behind them. The armored assault transport takes out the machine-gun emplacement on the far right. Move in behind it, then up along its right side, and take cover at the front corner. From here, open fire on the snipers along the bridge above and the building to your left.

TAKE THE BRIDGE

When the area is clear, break cover and dash up the stairs on the far left. Equip your handgun for this assault and perform Quick Shots to take down enemies. Save your Combat Gauge, however, by shooting enemies in the head while they're down. Several enemies are still within the building, and performing too many melee attacks will exhaust Chris.

Go upstairs into the interior and take cover against the inside wall. Fire on J'avo hiding in the doorway and below the windowsill of the next room. When the next room seems clear, breach it and smash three item crates to restock. Proceed up the stairs and over the bridge to the locked bell tower. As you can clearly see, a new weapon is stored inside the tower room. Press Partner Action to call Piers to help you break in. Your breach is interrupted when a gigantic B.O.W. begins smashing its way through the street.

OGROMAN (EDONIAN STREET)

Open fire on the giant monster as it approaches the bridge. Its face and the exposed umbilical muscle on its back are the weak points. Soon the monster smashes its fists onto the bridge, forcing Chris and Piers to leap off.

Continue shooting the monster in the face as it climbs over the bridge. Once it is on your side, turn around and dash for the far end of the street. In Single offline mode, ignore the ladder on the right since it connects to a wooden platform with no supplies. Instead, go up the ladder around the half-corner to the left and climb inside the building. Break the item crates in this area to resupply as you move around. While this is the better position to attack from in Single player offline mode, do note that in co-op mode a better strategy is to position one player on the wooden platform and the other inside the building to shoot the monster from both sides—in the face from the front and in the exposed umbilical from behind.

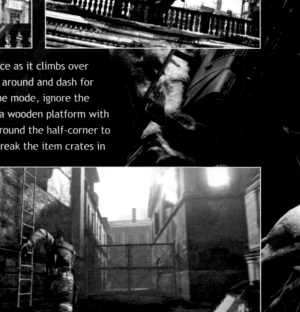

J'avo come up the stairs from the far end. Most of these are easily killed using Quick Shots and follow-up melee attacks. Many drop additional useful items. However, save the majority of your bullets for the Ogroman outside. The monster stomps down the street until it's parallel to your position and then turns to face you. Soon it raises a fist and delivers a power punch capable of knocking out walls and taking out a large portion of your health. Therefore, relocate whenever the Ogroman stops and faces your position.

Continue shooting the Ogroman in its two weak points, the face and umbilical. Stop whenever the creature reacts in pain and staggers. As you keep shooting the monster, these moments when it falls off-balance get worse until the creature topples to one side, either crashing into the building or leaning on the wooden platform opposite. If the creature leans against the wooden platform, then fight off J'avo in your vicinity until the Ogroman is back on its feet and resume shooting it. But while the creature leans against the building, move to its elbow and press fire to run onto its shoulders. Chris seizes a spine protrusion and tries to pull it out. Tap the Action button rapidly to fill the timer gauge onscreen before the timer needle swings to the right side. Good controller technique for this requires lifting your left hand off the controller and tapping the Action button rapidly with your left forefinger, taking care to lift your pointer only the minimum amount off the button between every tap. If successful, Chris rips the protrusion out of the monster and stabs it in the neck. This causes the monster to run off and ends the battle. If you fail to rip out the spine and stab the monster with it, the Ogroman will grab you and squeeze. Rotate the Left Stick rapidly to break free. You drop to the ground level and should climb back into the building as quickly as possible.

WEREN'T YOU ABOUT TO DO SOMETHING? OH YEAH...

Smash any item crates remaining inside the building's second story where you fired on the Ogroman. Then, head back down the street toward the starting position of the stage. Go up the stairs, which are now on your right. Remember that you were about to break into the tower and collect a new weapon before the Ogroman showed up. Approach the tower door and open it with Partner Action. Inside you find the **Assault Shotgun**, a **First-Aid Spray**, and another item crate to smash.

CROSS-STREET COMBAT

Drop over the side of the smashed bridge and dash up the street to catch up with your men. Fall in behind the APC as it proceeds down the narrow street, and then divert to the right into a sidewalk that goes into a small room. Take down several J'avo with Quick Shots and then follow-up shots to the head when they're down. Snipers open fire from the windows across the street, so get inside quickly and clear out the small room. Take cover at the doorway leading back to the street, and return fire on the snipers in the opposite windows. Catch up to the APC when the street is cleared.

FLANK AND AMBUSH

The APC parks at the bottom of a wide street full of J'avo. Move to the left side of the APC, then go through the doorway into the ruins to the side. Dash upstairs and take out an idle sniper on the upper level. Jump the gap, look down and to your right, and take out any J'avo that penetrated your lines. Turn left and drop into the next segment. Proceed through the next doorway and head uphill. From the doorway and windows of the last segment, you can flank and ambush J'avo in the streets while remaining protected from sniper fire.

When the area is clear, dash across the street and climb the ladder on the opposite building. Use close-quarters tactics to take out a couple snipers perched up in this area, then smash the item crates.

TAKE THE FENCE LINE

As you head up the clear street, a truck full of J'avo reinforcements arrives. Ready a Hand Grenade and toss it next to the truck to kill most of the reinforcements as they hop out. Clean up the few remainders with Quick Shots and melee attacks. Afterward, go left down the street a bit. Fin, the rookie bombardier, moves in and sets charges to blow the lock. Approach the ledge and press Action to drop into the rail yard.

SURVIVE THE KILL BOX

Fin moves ahead to set charges on a train car that is blocking the exit. Meanwhile, you must defend yourself against J'avo hordes entering the area from the far right. If you are playing as Piers, turn left and climb the ladder to reach a high sniper's perch with a couple of item crates to break. From here, use your Anti-Materiel Rifle to take out J'avo snipers on the highest level on the opposite side of the area and advancing ground soldiers. If you are playing Chris, move from cover to cover on the ground and return fire on J'avo. Don't be too hasty to advance—reinforcements fill in quickly. Instead, gun down J'avo that attempt to breach your line. Throwing grenades inside the open train cars works well, especially if multiple J'avo take positions inside them. Otherwise, continue shooting targets that pop their heads out from cover until Fin sets the charges and takes cover. Fall back to the marker position and the train car will blow up, ending the battle.

SERPENT EMBLEM: RAIL YARD

When Fin sets the charges and shouts to take cover, dash forward into the J'avo's territory within the rail yard and head to the far-right corner. A **Serpent Emblem** is visible through the windows of the small building in the back. Shoot it quickly, then turn around and dash back to Fin's position so he can destroy the train car. You should only stop to fight J'avo that take position between you and the Serpent Emblem. Hopefully you won't suffer too much damage if this occurs.

THE BRIDGE

BRIDGE MAP

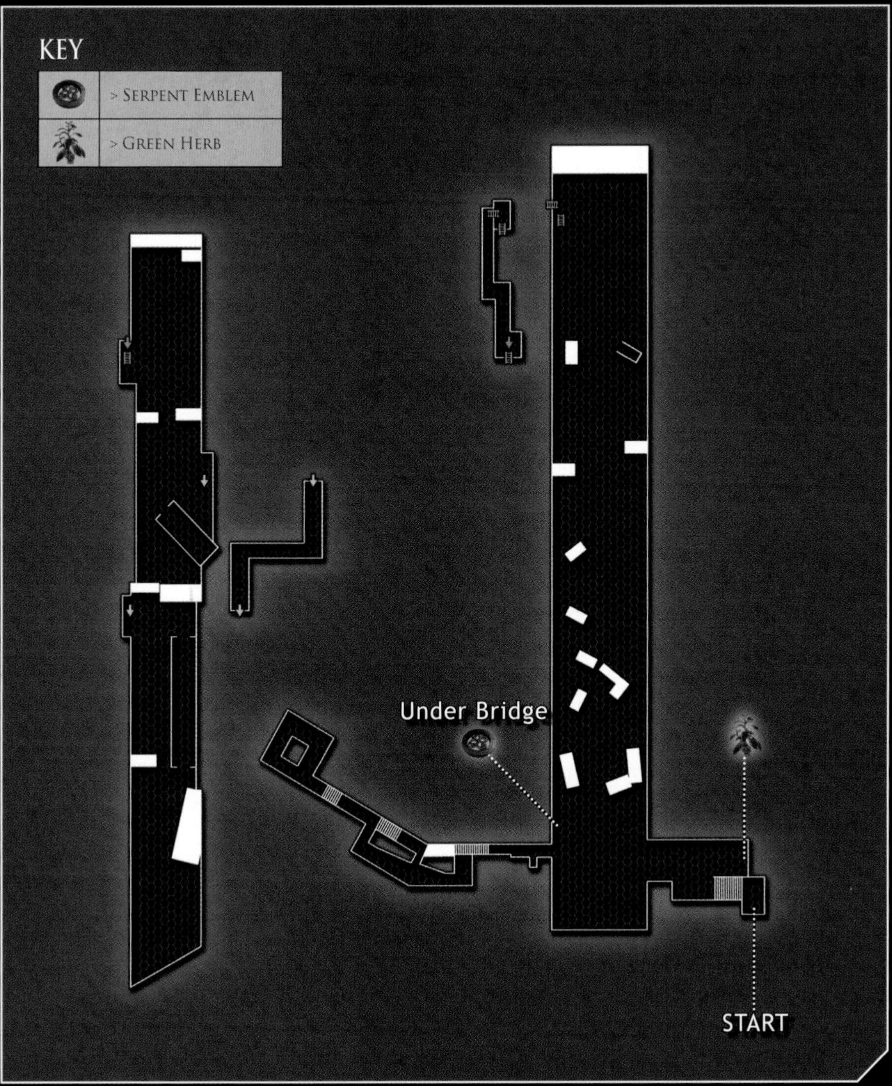

SURVIVE THE DETONATION

As Chris, begin moving up the bridge. J'avo detonate charges set, blowing up the area where you're standing. Tilt the Left Stick forward and press Action to crawl forward, using your stamina to go faster. As you approach a burning car, tilt the Left Stick to the left to roll that direction. Get out of the car's way before it explodes and slides down the collapsing bridge segment. Continue climbing to the top, using all your stamina, until Fin takes your hand.

SIT-REP

Move forward and down the stairs to the left. HQ reports a man is down on the bridge and requires extraction. However, enemies have him pinned down and they are closing in. Restock your supplies by smashing the item crates at the bottom of the stairs, and turn right to find a Green Herb sitting on some barrels.

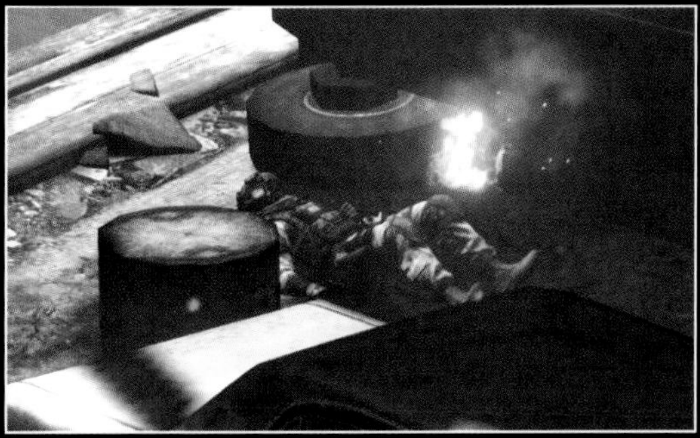

DISPATCH PIERS

Heading toward the bridge, divert left to smash another small item crate. Then, cross the street to the far side. A recon scout waits there to take Piers on a sniping expedition. Press Partner Action in this area to fling Piers across the gap. If you are playing as Piers, see the note after this section that details the sniper mission.

TAKE THE BRIDGE

The injured man is safe behind an overturned truck. While Fin looks to his injuries, move to the right corner of the truck and return fire on a couple gunners manning a turret farther up. When those enemies are dealt with, quickly dash to their position and hop the sandbags to take the point, otherwise reinforcements will continue manning the gun.

BAIT THE TANK OUT

Take cover at the left edge of the cargo container behind the turret and open fire on any mutating J'avo around the corner. Dash across the bridge to the sandbags in front of the other gun turret. Take shelter here

against shelling from the tank at the far end. Chris spots a fuel truck parked near the tank and orders Piers to take the shot. Piers cannot, however, unless the tank moves forward. Stay at the sandbags in front of this turret, stand up, and fire just two or three handgun shots at the J'avo farther down the bridge. Immediately drop back down. Repeat this until the tank moves forward and Piers shoots the fuel truck, blowing it up.

TIE UP LOOSE ENDS, THEN CLIMB

Kill any J'avo remaining on the bridge and work your way up while moving from cover to cover. A sniper may still be positioned on the ledge above the tunnel entrance at the far end, which you can take down with Assault Rifle fire. You can also aim at him and then order Piers to attack him by issuing the Move In command.

When the area is clear, move up the left side of the bridge and climb the ladder near the wreckage that blocks the end. Climb another ladder and follow the gantry to a couple item crates that you should smash. Climb a third ladder to reach the train rail level up top, which is mostly empty for the moment. Proceed up the tracks, break the item crate on the left, and kick down the emergency ladder. Then, take out a J'avo hiding in ambush inside the open derailed train car off to the side. Piers should catch up to you by this point.

SNIPER MISSION

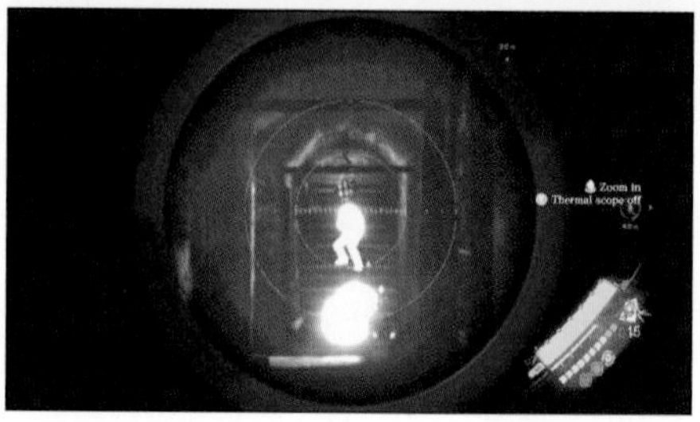

Get comfortable using the Anti-Materiel Rifle through the first part of this mission. Using it efficiently is required through Piers' part of this segment. Upon approaching the bridge, move to the far side and initiate a Partner Action. After Chris throws you across the gap, follow the recon scout into the tunnel. Before moving ahead, survey areas with your Anti-Materiel Rifle and switch modes to use the thermal scope. Before proceeding, take out enemies from a distance in long dark corridors.

Ascend the long flight of stairs at the end of the passage to reach the crow's nest. Smash the nearby item crates to restock on bullets, and then approach the open section of the window. Survey the bridge with your Anti-Materiel Rifle scope. Thermal imaging is still effective outdoors and helps you pick targets out of the environment more easily. Snipe the J'avo on the bridge, starting with the ones closest to Chris' position and working your way to the back.

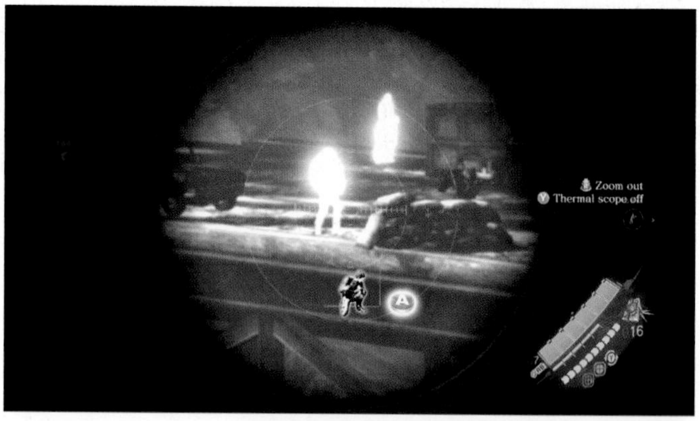

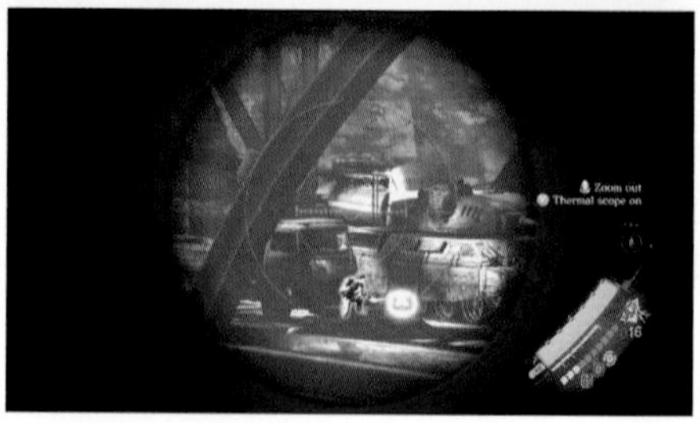

When no more targets remain, Chris radios that he needs help and Piers offers to take out the truck at the back, provided Chris can make the tank move. Keep your scope trained on the tank and switch off thermal. When the tank moves forward, shoot the red oil tanker to blow up the army tank.

The scout opens the back door of the room for you. Exit the crow's nest and proceed up the stairs toward the bridge. While walking along this path, you can stop and shoot a **Serpent Emblem** under the bridge. A squad of J'avo wait at the top of the stairs but should be easy to take out with one well-placed Hand Grenade. Smash the item crates here, and then proceed onto the upper rail level of the bridge.

Sneak up behind a J'avo near the train car for a Stealth Hit. Then, move into the doorway at the back of the parked train car and shoot two more J'avo inside. Cross through the train car, drop back down onto the rails, and then go left to a ladder and climb down.

First, sneak up behind a J'avo guard directly ahead and perform a Stealth Hit to take him down. Smash the nearby item crate and start crossing the gantries toward Chris' position. Continue to the right and stand below the raised emergency ladder until Chris arrives and lowers it. Then you can join in the fun as it continues.

SERPENT EMBLEM: BRIDGE UNDERSIDE

This Serpent Emblem can be shot only when playing as Piers. After shooting the oil tanker to blow up the enemy tank, exit the crow's nest and follow the concrete path. Before moving up the stairs, stop and look at the beams below the bridge. Just to the left of the first support column, a **Serpent Emblem** rests against a girder. Shoot it with the Anti-Materiel Rifle to add it to your collection.

TIP THE DUMPSTER

Turn around and lead Piers to the dumpster blocking the clear portion of the bridge, located to the right of some hedgehog steel-beam barricades. Dumping the dumpster triggers a full-scale assault on the upper level by J'avo, including a cannon railcar. You must hold the enemy advance until Fin can get the wounded man topside.

HOLD THE BRIDGE

Run back down the bridge and take cover at the positions closest to the derailed train car. J'avo paratroopers land on the bridge, making matters worse. Take down the paratroopers as they land and before they get on their feet. Advance and kill the soldiers inside the cargo container that has been blown on top of the ladder. Climb inside this container and shoot from the far end to take out more reinforcements.

When Fin finally delivers the wounded man, Chris orders him to blow the bridge. Continue fighting J'avo that approach at close range, then return to cover and fire on both advancing troops and the ones equipped with rocket launchers standing on the cannon train car. After Fin sets the charges and your camera automatically swings around to look at the rear of the bridge, disengage fighting and dash back to Fin's location, which is marked with a blue arrow. Move around the right side of the barriers you cleared the dumpster away from. Take cover behind the sandbags to the left. Fire on pursuing J'avo until the cannon railcar moves within blasting range. Then into the river it goes!

IN FRONT OF CITY HALL

IN FRONT OF CITY HALL MAP

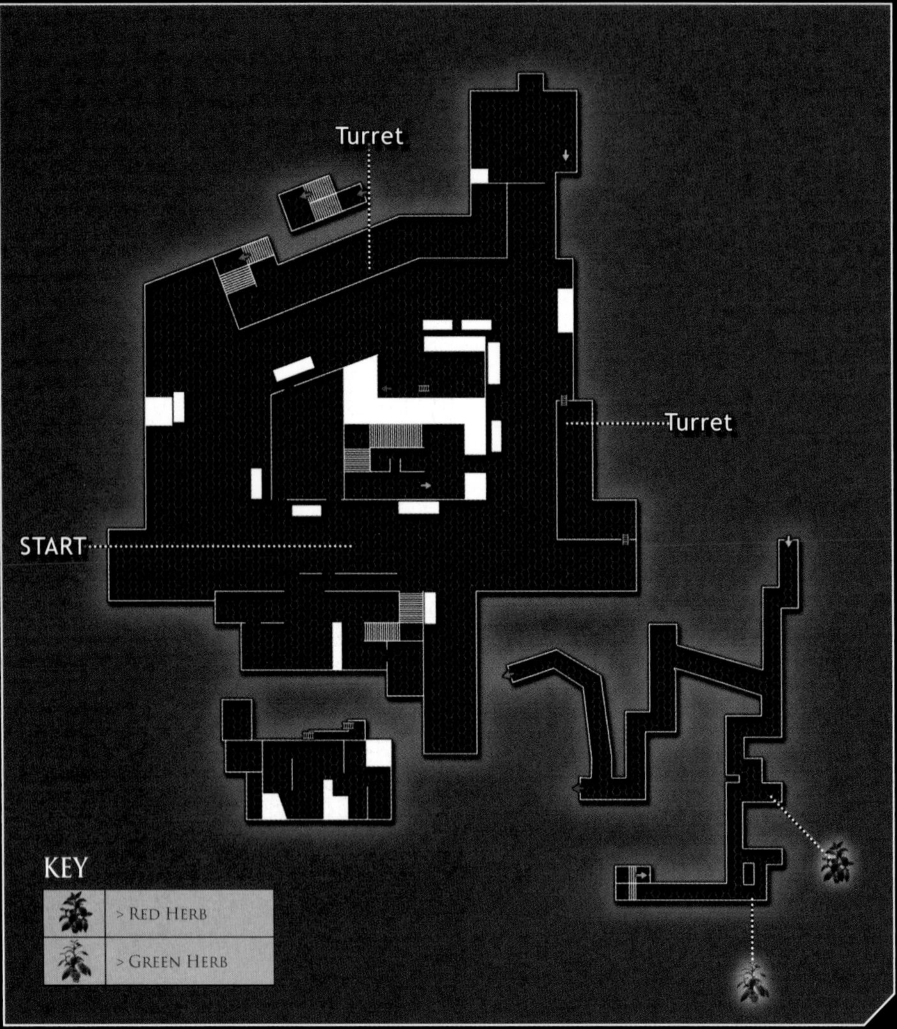

OGROMAN (X2)

J'avo forces have taken control of several anti-aircraft guns around the area, making it impossible for the BSAA to bomb the giant B.O.W. into submission. While running from the creature and fighting it, you must attack the three anti-aircraft gun positions one at a time. When Fin moves into position to plant charges on the gun, you must defend the position until the charges go off. From Chris' starting position, turn completely around and run away from the monster. Immediately divert to the right through an archway. Ascend the stairs and shoot the sniper and the anti-aircraft cannon operator at the far end. Turn left and fight your way through the kitchen, killing any J'avo in your path. However, do not remain in the kitchen since enemies endlessly drop from the ceiling until the nearby cannon is destroyed. Instead, proceed back outdoors and fire on the Ogroman, shooting its face and exposed umbilical. Ignore the J'avo except if they attack you or Fin while he is placing charges.

Aim for the Ogroman's soft tissue umbilical, which the helicopter accidentally pulled out of its back. This is its weakest spot. The face is also a weak point but not to the same degree. By shooting the umbilical or face, you may cause the monster to stagger and lean against the building. When this happens, quickly approach the creature's elbow resting on the edge. Press the Fire button to leap onto the Ogroman's shoulder and begin twisting a large bone protrusion out of its back. To succeed, tap the Action button rapidly to fill the onscreen gauge before the timer reaches the left side. As indicated before, failure to rip the bone out in time allows the Ogroman to seize Chris and crush him. To escape, rotate the Left Stick rapidly.

CHRIS FINALLY MEETS SHERRY

Taking the area near the city hall of Edonia, Chris and Piers encounter Sherry Birkin, survivor of the Raccoon City Incident and daughter of the notorious William Birkin. She is now all grown up and an agent of the FOS (Field Operations Support). With her is a petulant and yet familiar young man who appears to be affiliated with the bioterrorists. The reunion is cut short when another massive Ogroman is dropped on the scene!

The second anti-aircraft cannon is located atop an old church tower in the center of the area. At this point, you have two choices. Join Fin at the church door, which triggers his planting of charges to blow it open. Or you can dash past the church to the top end of the street, where you'll find a ladder connected to a balcony from which J'avo fire. Climb the ladder, kill the J'avo, and take control of the gun turret at the far end by holding the Aim button. Rotate the turret using the Left Stick and hold the Fire button to shoot. Hit the Ogroman's face or exposed umbilical enough times to make it lean against the building, allowing for another Quick Time Event attack. However, be warned that if the Ogroman reaches the turret, he will rear back and smash the gun turret with his fist, and you don't want to be standing there when he does. Abandon the turret if the Ogroman moves too far up the street to the left, and head over to the corner and resume shooting it in the face. Make the Ogroman stagger and lean on the building, and stab it with its own spines. In this manner, you can defeat the Ogroman and force it to drop **Skill Points (4,000)**. Collect this item from the street, and then join Fin at the church doors.

After Fin blows the church door, breach the interior and fight the J'avo descending the stairs from above. Smash crates on the ground floor, then ascend the stairs and climb the ladder to reach the roof.

Shoot the two J'avo manning the anti-aircraft cannon, and then protect the team while they set up charges on the gun. To do this effectively, you must fight enemies from two sides: endless J'avo drop from a high ledge at the back of the rooftop before the cannon is destroyed, and occasionally the Ogroman (if still alive) climbs up the side of the building and begins swatting at the soldiers. Fin will stop planting the charges in order to drive away the Ogroman. Therefore, prioritize shooting the Ogroman in its weak spot to make it climb down from the building. As a result, the bombardier can resume setting charges as quickly as possible. Take down J'avo swiftly with Quick Shots and melee follow-ups to prevent them from interfering as well.

Whether or not the first Ogroman is dead, a second one appears after the church anti-aircraft cannon is destroyed. The second Ogroman's back umbilical is not pulled out and exposed like the first one's. Do not shoot at the second Ogroman until the first is dead.

When the tower cannon is destroyed, drop down through the ceiling hole and descend the stairs. Follow the soldiers underground by dropping through the ground-floor hatch into a subterranean tunnel. Fin plants charges on the door and then you may proceed. Don't miss the **Green Herb** sitting inside the exposed drain pipe at the first corner. Smash the box across from it to clear the windowsill, and open fire on a J'avo standing in the next area. Continuing to follow your soldiers, find more item crates and items, such as a **Red Herb** near some barrels in a side niche, and collect items dropped by defeated enemies.

Eventually you reach a ladder mounted in concrete. Climb it, head right, and press Action twice to unbar and open the door. Then quickly turn around and drop back into the tunnel. Turn left and follow a short dirt tunnel to another ladder.

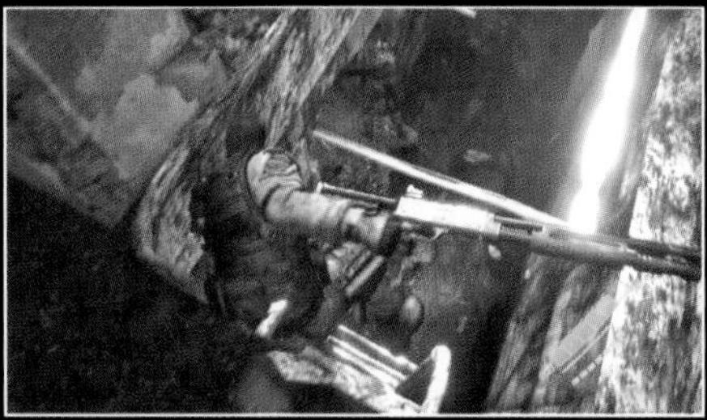

Climb the ladder and blast any J'avo at the top of the nearby stairs. Ascend the stairs and cross the exposed upper level. J'avo snipers fire from the church tower rooftop, but luckily a gun turret is nearby that you can use to kill them and fire on the Ogroman. If only one Ogroman remains, watch for it to go off to the far right while you're manning the turret. It will pick up a truck and hurl it at you. Dodge this and then man the turret again. Just remember that if the Ogroman stops in front of the gun turret, he will smash it, and you don't want to be near the turret when that happens.

Since the second Ogroman's umbilical is not exposed, shoot its head until it covers its face in pain and leans against the building. Then run onto its shoulders and rapidly rotate the Left Stick to pull out its umbilical. The timer hand moves fast, and you'll find it hard to beat, so try this little trick with the controller: release the controller with your left hand, pinch the Left Stick with all the fingers of your left hand, and then rotate it as rapidly as possible. You'll get more rotations per second this way and yank the umbilical out easily. Upon dropping to the street, dash away from the Ogroman. You did open the door across the street, right? Dash across the street and go back through the tunnel to the balcony you were on before mounting the Ogroman.

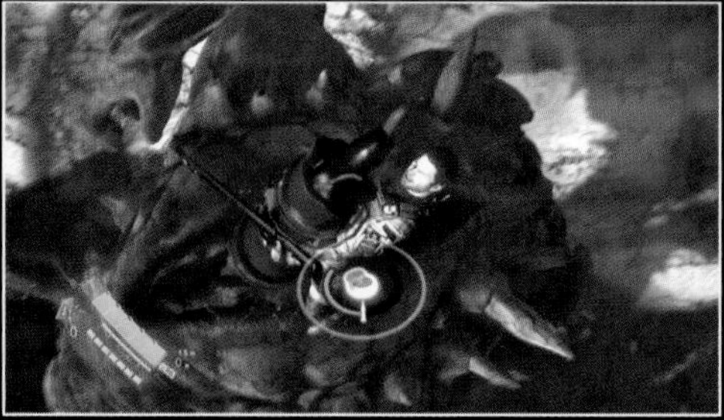

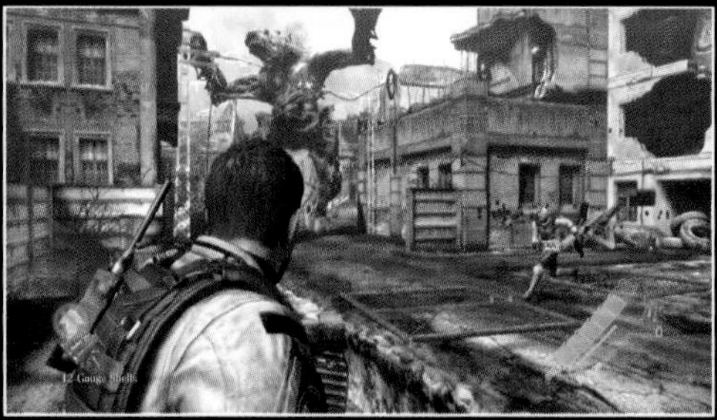

Continue past the turret this time and go to the corner. Kick down the emergency ladder for easier escape from the area below. Then move to the back corner of the balcony and shoot any J'avo in the fenced area below, including the one manning the anti-aircraft cannon. Drop to the ground behind the fence. The Ogroman soon smashes through the gate into this area. Shoot it to deter it from attacking Fin. If the area is clear of enemies and the Ogroman is deterred—by running into a power line, for instance—then you can drop here into a section of the tunnel previously unreachable from where you were exploring before. A couple item crates in this tunnel segment can be smashed for supplies. However, you must return topside to protect Fin and to help him finish destroying the final gun.

When HQ radios that they have a fix on the second Ogroman with its exposed umbilical, climb the ladder on the side of the building to get out of harm's way. The BSAA bombs the Ogroman out of existence, and Chris and Piers send Sherry and her companion on their way.

CITY HALL

CITY HALL INTERIOR MAP

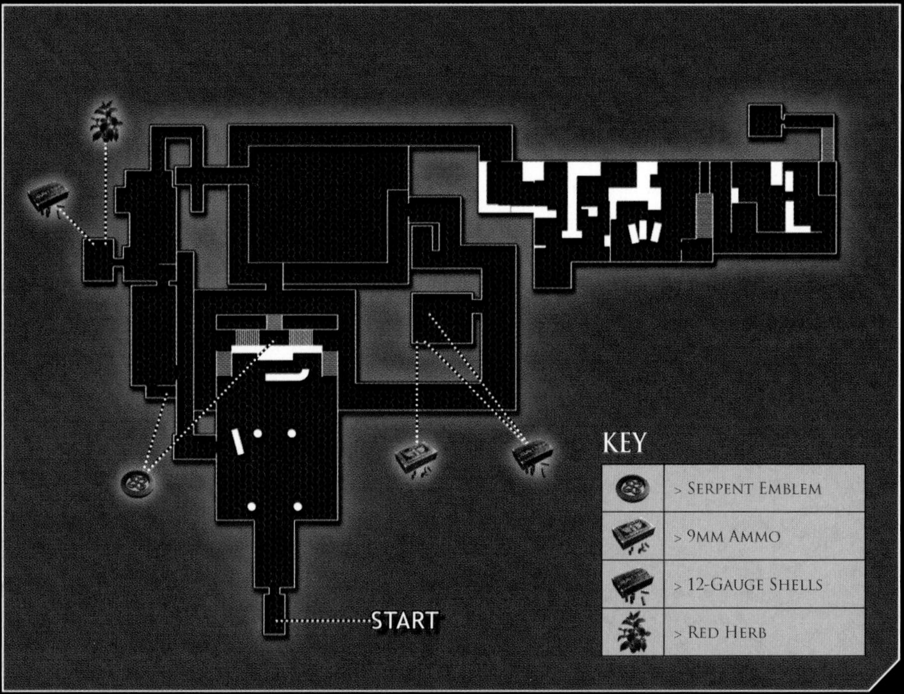

DISTURBING EVIDENCE

Proceed into the foyer. Chris and his men find city hall to be full of people encased in chrysalids that are preparing to hatch new mutations. Move behind the reception desk to smash an item crate.

SERPENT EMBLEM: FOYER STAIRWELL UNDERPASS

Follow the corridors formed by archways to either side of the central stairs. These lead to a corridor running below the stairs where a **Serpent Emblem** hangs on the wall.

CHASE THE WOMAN IN RED

When Fin calls out for Chris, head upstairs and follow the railing to the right. Approach the door where Fin stands and press Partner Action to open it. Proceed down the corridor and around the corner to the left. Chris spots a mysterious and familiar woman at the far end. As you head

Take him down with a Quick Shot and melee. Enter the room he came out of and smash several item crates. Collect the **12-Gauge Shells** on the desk plus another box of shells and **9mm Ammo** on the back shelves in the corner.

Exit the room and continue following the corridor. Smash the small crate in the bathroom at the first corner for another item, then proceed to the door at the end of the hallway and open it.

MEET THE NASTY NAPADS

Move down the railing to the left and drop into the room below. Crossing the center of the room causes a chrysalid to hatch, releasing a Napad. These creatures are covered by extremely hard scales that must be blasted off before the creature sustains damage. Hand Grenades tossed at the Napad's feet are extremely effective. Flash Grenades are also extremely effective at blinding the creature and rendering it vulnerable to a stealth hit from behind, provided its back scales have been blown off. Otherwise, you can still use Flash Grenades to make it vulnerable to melee attacks and knock off those scales. Slide across the tables in the room to put barriers between yourself and the Napads since more hatch and attack. Even with exposed skin, Napads are surprisingly resilient against Shotgun blasts. Instead, stream bullets into them with your Assault Rifle. Each Napad drops **Skill Points (1,500)** when defeated.

CHASE DOWN THAT WOMAN

When the Napads are suppressed, move to the back door and Fin will blow it open with charges. Before moving on, smash one item crate in the room if you haven't already. Proceed down the subsequent corridor and smash three item crates in a niche to the left. Continue following the winding corridor to a door and open it.

J'avo attack from inside the room. Take cover on the left side of the door and return fire, tossing Flash or Hand Grenades if any remain. Once the area opposite the doorway is clear, move in and take cover. Fire on more J'avo that are farther inside. Search a small side room to the right to find a **Red Herb**, **12-Gauge Shells**, and an item crate. When you are done, follow your men into the back passageway and open the exit door with Partner Action.

Chris and his team finally catch up to the mysterious woman, Ada Wong. She accompanies the team through the next several areas, but she is not someone you need to protect or help, since she offers no aid in return.

SERPENT EMBLEM: ADA'S ROOM

After joining up with Ada Wong, move into the small room at the back. A **Serpent Emblem** sits atop the cabinet in the corner of this tiny area.

RETURN TO THE FOYER

Follow Ada and your team through the door she opened at the back. Turn left and smash an item crate, and then catch up with the others gathered around a door at the opposite end. Open the door with a Partner Action.

The chrysalids in the foyer have hatched into Napads. Don't waste your time and ammo fighting them—head directly upstairs. Ada opens a secret door in the center of the second floor. Approach it and kick the gate open with a Partner Action.

STAND OFF AGAINST STRELATS

Move around the balcony to the left. As you progress, more chrysalids in this area hatch into Strelats—fast-moving and dangerous lizard-like monsters. After a Strelats hatches, it is highly susceptible to bright light. Toss a Flash Grenade in front of it to blind it, then dash up to it and perform a melee. To kill a Strelats instantly during the melee, press the Fire button as the timer hand passes through the colored part of the gauge. Otherwise, blast them with your Shotgun until they are dead. You confront three Strelats as you smash item crates and make your way around the balcony. Strelats typically drop **Skill Points (1,000)** when defeated.

THE LABYRINTHINE WAREHOUSE

When the balcony is clear, move to the door at the far end and Fin will blow it with charges. Proceed down the corridor to a wider area and smash an item crate on the far side. Then drop from the nearby ledge into the warehouse. The warehouse is a maze-like structure full of Napads and Strelats, so refer to your Directional Beacon whenever you get lost or confused during combat. Climb any ladders or stairs you encounter and open any doors. These typically lead to high ground from which it is better to fight and to item crates you can smash. As you approach the stairs to the exit, divert into a wide area on the left to smash two last item crates. Then descend the stairs and open the door at the bottom with Partner Action. A terrifying scene plays, marking the end of the chapter.

CHRIS CHAPTER 2: RANKING CRITERIA

RANK	ACCURACY(%)	DEATHS	CLEAR TIME(MIN)	ENEMIES ROUTED
A	70	2	90	70
B	60	5	110	60
C	50	7	120	40
D	*1	*1	*1	*1

*1 Any Below Rank C

POINTS AWARDED PER RANK (ABOVE)				
Rank	A	B	C	D
Points	25	20	15	10

TOTAL RANKING POINTS TABLE

RANK	S	A	B	C	D	E
Total	100	90	75	55	45	*2

*2 Any Below Rank D

WAIYIP, CHINA

June 30, 2013

TENEMENT—POISAWAN ENTRANCE

TENEMENT MAP

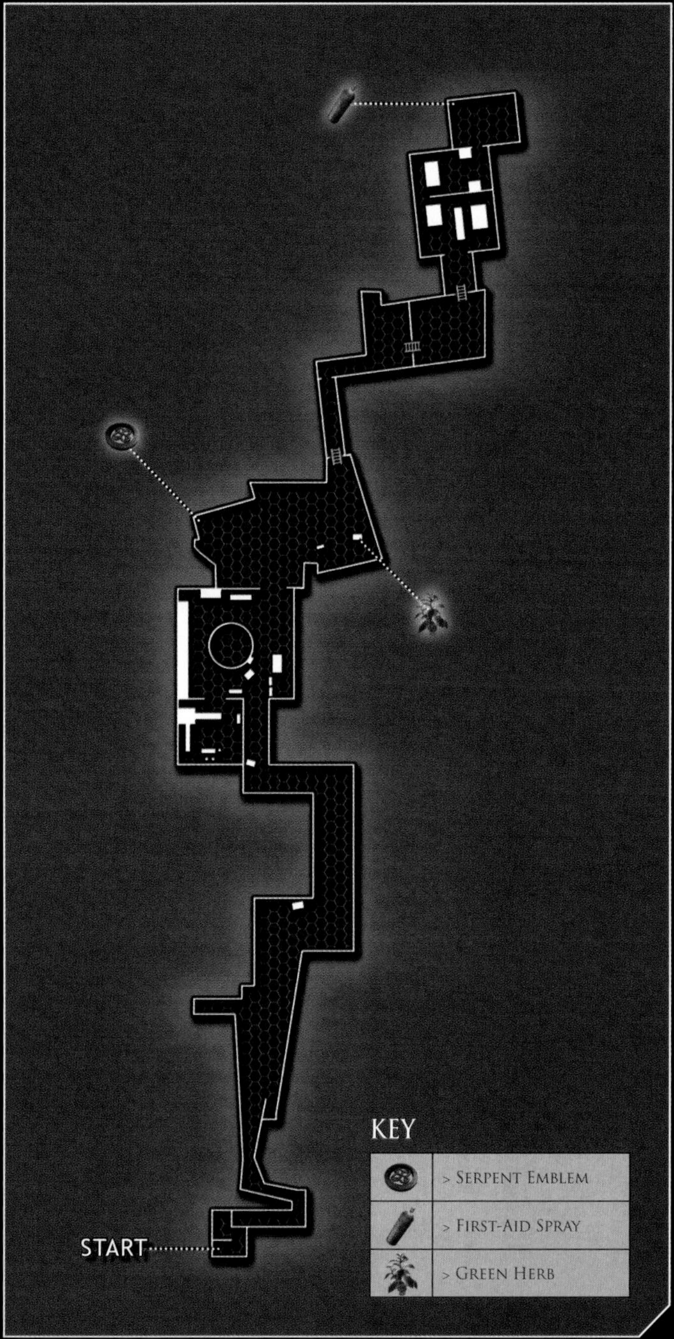

DETERMINATION

Returning to the present with his memories of Edonia restored, Chris Redfield resolves to track down Ada Wong and Neo-Umbrella. Press Action to drop from the ledge and follow the path through the building wreckage.

A NEW TERROR

Arriving at the end, Chris watches in horror as a giant invisible snake seizes a BSAA soldier and drags him off. Go uphill after the huge serpent, following your men through the street, an alley, and then a playground. Approach the red gate and open it with Partner Action. Chris follows a trail of blood and slime into a nearby tenement building.

SERPENT EMBLEM: DESERTED STREET

After emerging from the playground gate, turn left and move to the opposite end of the street. A **Serpent Emblem** rests among some boxes in the corner.

THE SLIME TRAIL ENTERS DANGEROUS TERRITORY

Follow the giant snake's trail to the corner, then turn right and search a table in the corner for a **Green Herb**. Smash a couple item crates in the opposite corner, including one behind the ladder. Then climb up.

Drop from the ledge into a narrow alley. Approach the door at the end and open it with a Partner Action. Head to the right along the next alley and stop just before the end. Toss a Hand or Flash Grenade around the corner to take down a couple J'avo waiting in ambush. Then, climb the ladder in the corner behind the crates.

THE J'AVO GAUNTLET

On the roof, hop over the low wall and head to the right around the small building. Climb the ladder on the next wall. Mutated J'avo drop down and attack, knocking you from the ladder. Take them out with Quick Shots and melee attacks and try climbing the ladder again.

Smash the item crates on both sides and kick open the door. The room is full of J'avo waiting in ambush. Run up behind the nearest crates and shoot the two enemies directly ahead of you. Then take cover, reload, and eliminate the remaining J'avo with a Quick Shot and melee attack combo. Gather any items that dropped and proceed into the next portion of the room. Use a Flash Grenade to stun three more J'avo, and take them down with Stealth Hits, throws, or gunfire.

Open the door in the corner. A **First-Aid Spray** sits on the edge of the large box directly ahead and you have a few item crates to smash. Move to the blue door and initiate a Partner Action to open it.

POISAWAN COURTYARD

COURTYARD MAP

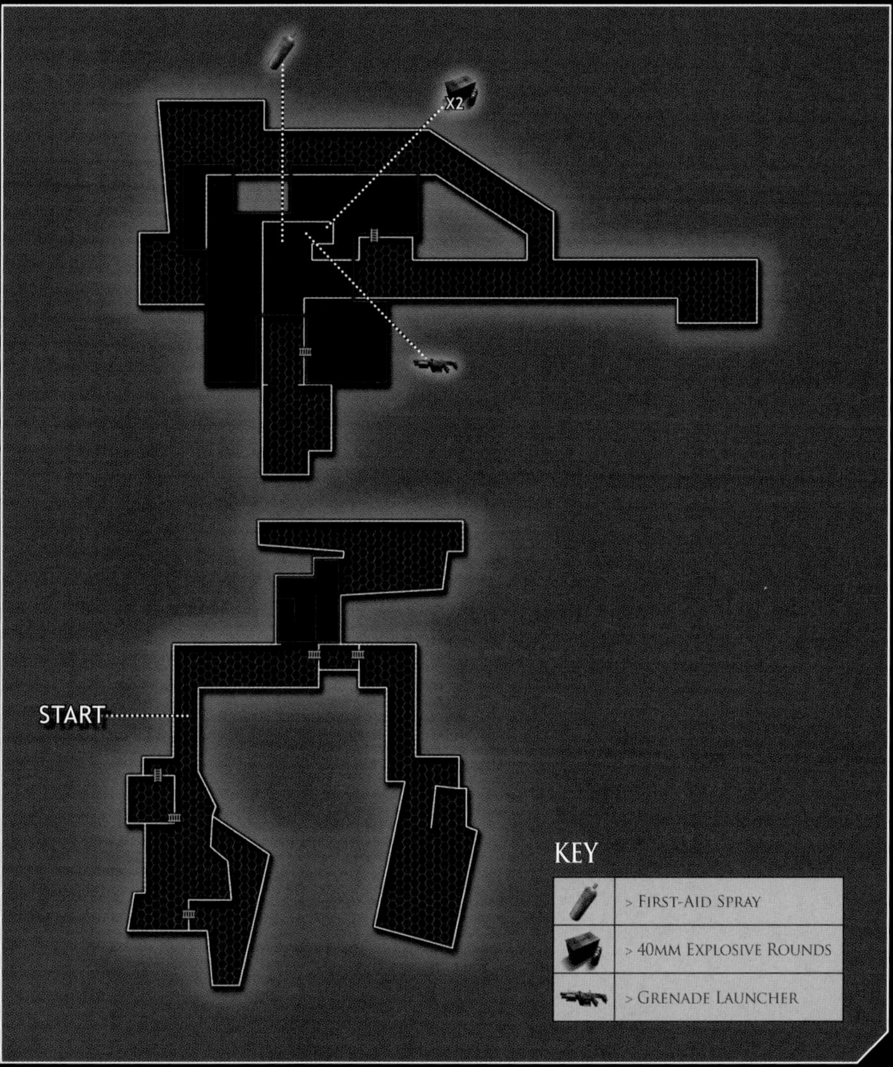

SECOND FATEFUL MEETING

Chris and his team emerge onto a long balcony that half-circles a courtyard. He spots Sherry Birkin and her companion, Jake Muller, surrounded and trapped far below. Chris orders his men to spread out and wipe out the J'avo threatening to kill Sherry and Jake.

SNIPE THEM ALL!

Unable to get down to Sherry's and Jake's level, you must move along the edge of the balcony and target enemies on the ground below. The best vantage point is on the opposite side of the area from which you start. Many of the J'avo you shoot on the ground below mutate into Noga-Skakanje and jump to the upper levels. Other J'avo invade the balconies as well, so keep your head up and be ready to defend yourself with Quick Shots. Watch for the many snipers perched above Sherry and Jake and on the levels above you. Occasionally check the attack helicopter hovering in the sky above. Shoot Noga-Skakanjes standing on the wings and hanging from the belly of the helicopter.

After you've killed a dozen or so enemies, the remaining foes become tagged with little red markers to make them easier to find. The last enemy typically hangs on the wing of the helicopter, so blast it off to end this event.

HEAD TO THE SHOWDOWN

When you've routed the enemies, the helicopter fires one last missile before flying off. Collect any items remaining in the area, and then meet your team by the door in the center of the back balcony. Enter with a Partner Action.

Follow the stairs to the top, and then climb the ladder up to the roof. Smash several item crates around the landing area, move to the opening in the low wall, and jump to the next rooftop. Open the door with a Partner Action. Although there is a ladder on the right, don't climb it yet. Instead, notice the weapon icon hovering directly ahead. Follow it to find the **Grenade Launcher**. You also find a **First-Aid Spray** and two boxes of **40mm Explosive Rounds** nearby. While you gather these items, your team notices that the Attack Chopper has come around again to attack!

ENEMY ATTACK CHOPPER—L

J'avo leap into the area and attack throughout the battle, and they will not stop until you bring down the helicopter. Therefore, it is important to find high ground and prioritize shooting down the chopper as quickly as possible, hitting it repeatedly with grenades. Slide over tabletops and hop over bars to put barriers between yourself and the J'avo, but only switch to another weapon and fire on them if they are directly challenging you. You may kill J'avo to obtain additional dropped items that may help fight the chopper. After a while, the J'avo no longer appear, and you can then deal with the chopper alone.

Stay on the move and return fire on the chopper. Avoid climbing on top of any rises, since this only makes you a better target. Instead, stay close to solid objects around the roof, fire from behind them, and take cover if the chopper's Gatling guns whir up. Be ready to leave cover and dash away if the Attack Chopper swoops around to your side during a bullet barrage. Missiles are also fired, and staying close to cover helps you avoid damage from these as well. The helicopter flies off occasionally, soaring behind the buildings or under the connecting wooden bridge, during which time you should reload all your weapons and take out a J'avo or two.

As the Attack Chopper hovers overhead, track its movements until it stops (unless it's firing on you) and then hit it with grenades as quickly as possible before it starts firing or moving again. Take cover, relocate if necessary, and then fire grenades at it again. Keep hitting it with explosives until it crashes and burns.

PICK UP, CLEAN UP, AND MOVE ON

After the battle, pick up any items or smash any item crates that you may have missed nearby. Then, cross the bridge and open the double doors with a Partner Action.

POISAWAN INNER AREA

INNER AREA MAP

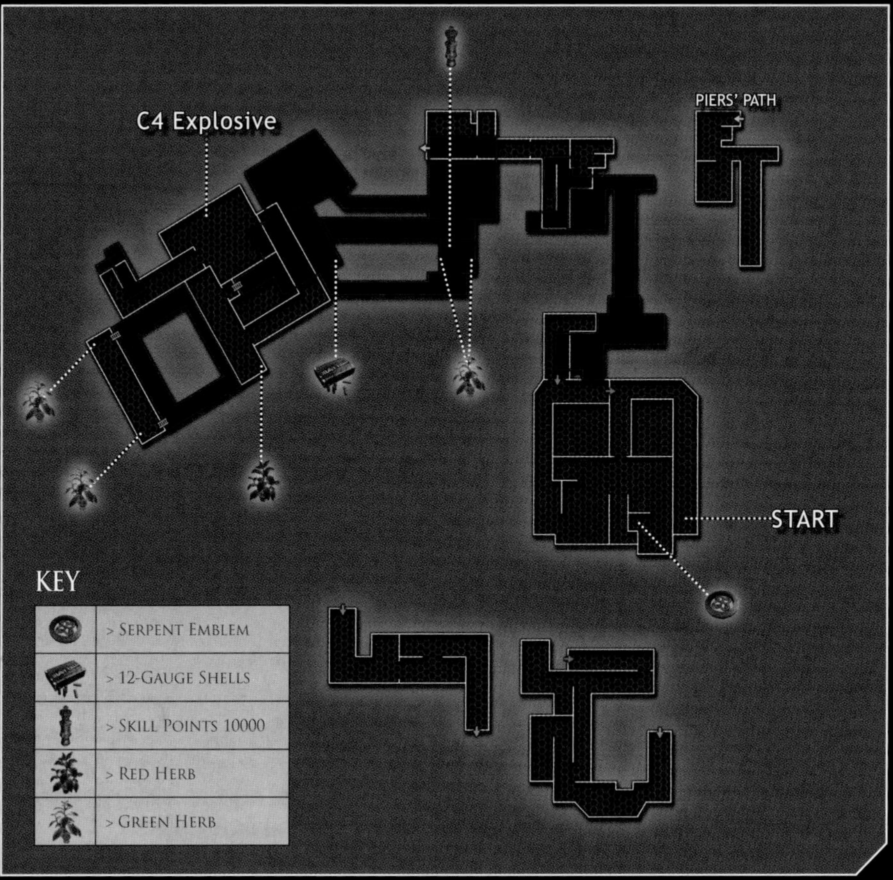

BACK TO THE SNAKE...

Now you can return to tracking the massive invisible snake B.O.W. that dragged off your team member. Head down the corridor and examine the body at the corner. Then follow your other men around two left turns to a door, which they kick down.

SERPENT EMBLEM: FAMILY BEDROOM

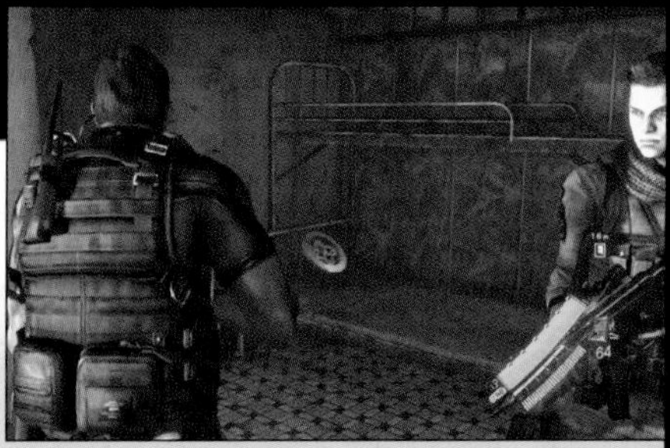

After your men kick down the door and breach the living quarters, go to your left past a Mahjong table into the bedroom. Just inside, turn right and you spot a **Serpent Emblem** on the lower bunk bed.

STAY ON THE TRAIL

Search the washroom to the right, just inside the living quarters, to find an item crate to smash. Proceed through the living quarters and continue out the back door. Turn right and follow the corridor until the huge snake is spotted again. Follow it downstairs and open the damaged door with a Partner Action.

USE THE DIRECTIONAL BEACON TO AVOID GETTING LOST

Move into the next passageway until a scene begins. After the scene, move past your troops and go through the door on the right. Take the next left turn to find an item crate that typically drops some Explosive Rounds, and then follow your Directional Beacon back out of there and down the corridor. Descend the stairs at the end, and open another damaged door with a Partner Action.

Smash item crates around the old barber shop, and then move into the back room. Another of your fellow soldiers is attacked and carried off by the giant snake. He's gone: don't waste your bullets. Proceed through the doorway on your right, kick open the next door, and you see the enormous snake slither by again. Move around the balcony to the opening in the low wall, and press Action to slide down the rope.

REMOVE THE DEBRIS

As you move to the back of the area, an air-conditioning unit falls in your path. Approach it and press the Partner Action button to push it out of the way.

BRIEF SEPARATION

Chris and Piers are separated when the giant snake drags off more of the soldiers while the team is rappelling down. Proceed down the corridor while Chris gets radio updates from his men. When the radio check-ins are complete, enter the niche ahead on the right to smash some item crates. Follow the corridor. You may divert into an open room on your left to find one of your dead troopers and an item crate.

Return to the corridor and approach the stairs at the end. First head left and around the corner to smash another item crate, then backtrack to the stairs and ascend. Piers meets up with you on this floor, where he was dragged by the massive snake. When playing as Piers, you can't do much other than break open some item crates and rejoin Chris as soon as possible. Move down to the broken door in the corner and open it with a Partner Action.

CORNER THIS THING

Proceed down the corridor until the giant snake is spotted again, this time dropping a live man who rejoins your team. Follow the snake into the next room, and drop down through the floor. Another dead soldier can be examined here. Open the gates at the end with a Partner Action.

ILUZIJA

Stand in the room and rotate your camera u
vaguely liquid, invisible snake slithering thr

and knocks you to the ground. You have a ch
this attack by pressing Fire at just the right t
snake will seize you in its maw and shake yo
to knock two full blocks off your Health Gau
may also wrap around you and constrict. Bre
by rotating the Left Stick. To recover, consur
use a First-Aid Spray and reload between att

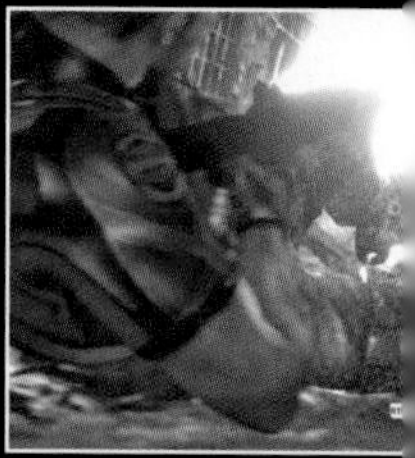

After suffering several attacks to the mouth, the giant snake slides through a vent into the next area. Crawl through the vent until the snake appears. Shoot it quickly before it se
Otherwise, shoot it before it drags you up i
means instant death. Continue crawling thr
next room.

at the creature to bring it out of hiding whi
the room. When it appears, shoot it in the r
it away. Break the available item crates in t
pick up the packs of **12-Gauge Shells** in the
Slide across tables in the quarters to escape
these same tables as cover for firing at it.

Also remember to press Ready/Aim while walking backwards to drop and fire your Shotgun from the ground, which helps to avoid the bite attacks.

When the snake has had enough, it attempts to flee by smashing through the back doors of the room. Search the sweatshop to find any additional 12-Gauge Shells you may have overlooked during the battle. There is another vent in this room that resembles a fireplace, which you can crawl through to reach someone's living quarters. Inside are several item crates to smash, two **Green Herbs**, and a chest in one corner containing **Skill Points (3,000)**. When you are finished here, pursue the snake.

A brush from Iluzija drops Chris and Piers into a sunken and partially flooded area. Marco, one of Chris' men, finds a giant electrical outlet that just might be useful. From your starting position in the pit, run around to the left and dash for the ladder at the far end. The massive reptile may pass by, causing you to stagger. However, this attack does not cause damage and the huge beast has hardened its skin to the point where you can't hurt it, so don't bother trying at this point.

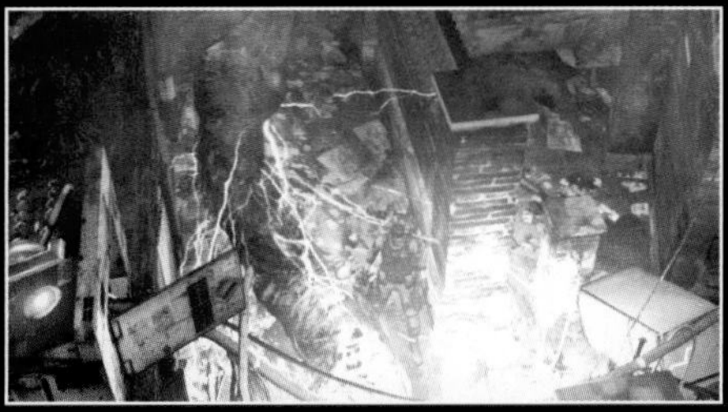

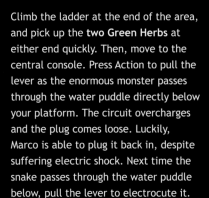

Climb the ladder at the end of the area, and pick up the **two Green Herbs** at either end quickly. Then, move to the central console. Press Action to pull the lever as the enormous monster passes through the water puddle directly below your platform. The circuit overcharges and the plug comes loose. Luckily, Marco is able to plug it back in, despite suffering electric shock. Next time the snake passes through the water puddle below, pull the lever to electrocute it.

NEED A HAND UP?

Hop down from the control platform and dash to the other side of the area. Find where Marco hangs from the upper level, and press Action while standing below him to get a lift up. Grab a **Red Herb** on Marco's platform. Move toward the electric plug but do not touch it or you'll suffer electrocution damage. Instead, head through the open door on the right and down the corridor. Ascend the stairs, head left, and open the door at the end via Partner Action.

DEFEAT THE INSECT SWARM, GNEZDO

Poor Marco is transformed into a Gnezdo, a rather serious enemy that is difficult to kill. Shoot the swirling mass of insects that sometimes takes the form of a walking woman. This should cause a larger insect to appear, which flies separately from the group. This is the queen of the brood, so shoot it and hit it with melee attacks to kill the entire swarm. Watch out for the creature's attacks such as swarming you with insects or forming large swarming projectiles to knock you down.

When the Gnezdo is defeated, its chrysalid shell collapses. Sift through the fragments to find **Marco's C4 Explosive**. Smash the item crates around the room, collect their contents, then approach the red gates. Press the Partner Action button to plant the C4 and blow the gates down. Following a short scene, proceed down the hallway and descend the stairs. Open the door at the bottom with a Partner Action.

STILT HOUSING AREA

STILT HOUSING MAP

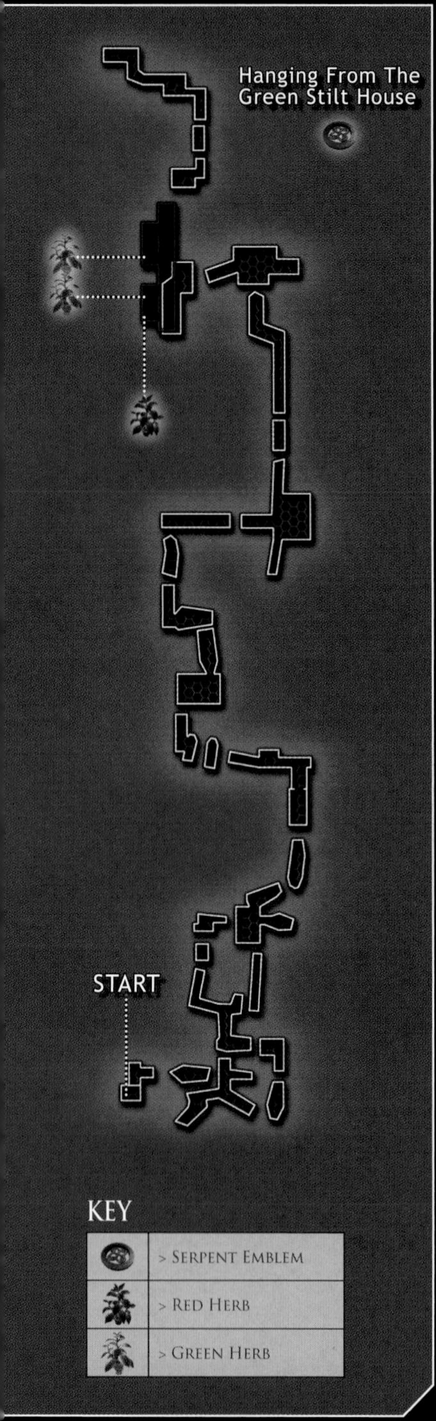

HOP FROM DOCK TO BOAT TO DOCK...

Drop from the platform and smash the item crates below. Now turn right, move to the edge, and leap over to the boat. Move to the bow and jump onto the dock. J'avo snipers to your left draw a bead, so run forward and take cover behind the low wall. Return fire on the snipers and take them out. To get the one on the far left, you must follow the dock up to a tall stack of boxes, take cover on the left corner, and fire between his shots.

Continue following the dock to the right. Climb onto a houseboat and smash the item crates. Jump from the front of the houseboat to a pontoon and then onto the deck. More snipers leap into the area from your right. Move forward, take cover behind the low safety barrier, and return fire on them until the area is clear. Continue left across a series of boats and onto another dock. Keep moving forward until you are behind a threefold safety barrier, and shoot the snipers that are now covering all sides of you. Proceed around the left side of the barrier and head back to the main dock. Some of the enemies you encounter on the water level may take chrysalid form and then hatch as Napads. However, you can easily outrun these foes by jumping from dock to dock.

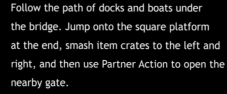

Follow the path of docks and boats under the bridge. Jump onto the square platform at the end, smash item crates to the left and right, and then use Partner Action to open the nearby gate.

OUTRUN THE CHOPPER

Chris and Piers catch sight of Ada getting away on a jet ski. Another attack helicopter swoops in to cover her escape. You must leap from boat to dock to boat, dashing the entire way. If you stay too long in one place, the chopper will sink you into the river. Ignore any enemies on the docks by simply running past them.

Make your way around the docks until you land on the porch of a pagoda-style building. Move left and climb the ladder at the end. Now you must take down another chopper!

SERPENT EMBLEM: ACROSS FROM THE PAGODA

After arriving on the bottom level of the pagoda-style building, move to the left and take cover behind the first segment of the railing that is solid from floor to bannister. Facing the water, look up and to your left at a rustic, greenish hut structure floating over the lake. A **Serpent Emblem** hangs from the front side of the stilt house. Piers can certainly hit it easily with his Anti-Materiel Rifle, but there's no reason why Chris can't hit it with an Assault Rifle shot as well.

SHOOT DOWN THE CHOPPER

As before, take cover while the chopper sprays the railing with gunfire. When there is a break, rise up and fire grenades at the chopper until it moves off. J'avo appear throughout the building and may attack. The helicopter takes down quite a few of them for you by accident. But if the chopper isn't firing at a given moment, then you may need to switch to your Shotgun and deal with enemies directly. Many of them mutate into the disgusting Glava-Begunats, which can glue you to the spot with a sticky spray. You can still fire while immobilized, but rotate the Left Stick and press Action to break free.

Twin banquet rooms on the upper level contain a lot of breakable boxes and vases that contain supplies, so restock from them as necessary. Keep hitting the chopper with grenades until it comes down. Now, run for the end of the balcony and jump off the edge. The pagoda-style building explodes and sinks.

THE END OF THE DOCKS

Follow the dock, jump onto a boat, and then leap from the bow. Blast two J'avo out of your way and go left. Continue to the edge of the dock, and take a bead on the exploding barrel that is high up on the right. Shoot it as J'avo congregate around the top of the ladder ahead to take them all out at once. Otherwise you are forced to peck your way through them, and they all have a high chance of mutation.

Climb the ladder, head right, and smash some item crates near the far wall. Then turn left, move to the door at the end, and use Partner Action to exit.

MEDICAL RESEARCH CENTER

INNER AREA MAP

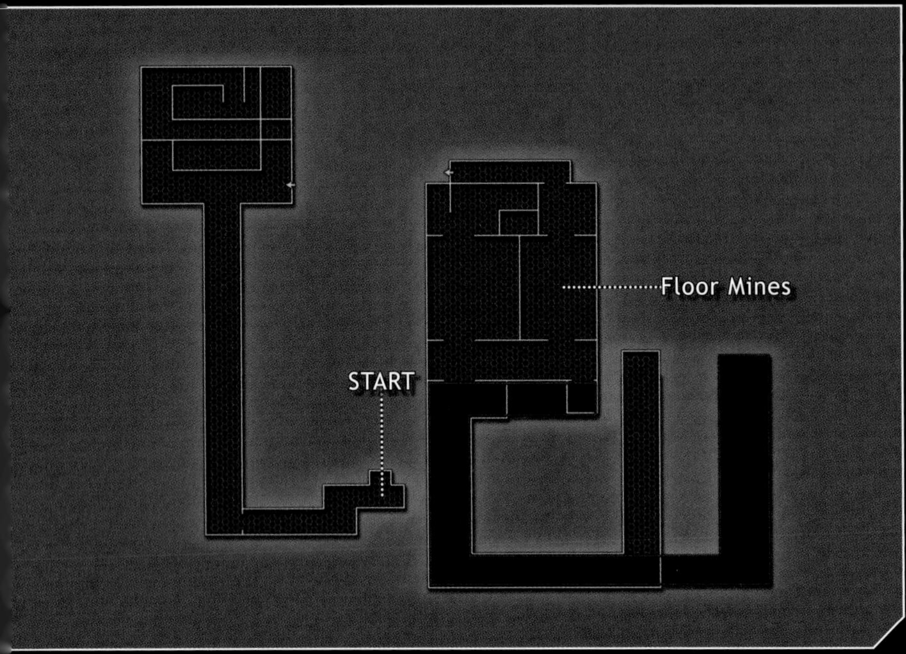

THE LASER TRAP CHAMBER

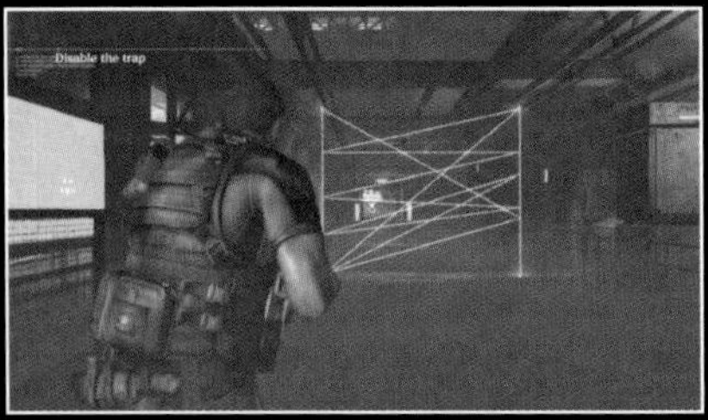

Chris and Piers catch up to Ada as she enters a mysterious research lab. Dash for the red-lit door straight ahead and open it. Turn left and begin dashing along the length of the lab in pursuit of Ada. Seeing your progress, Ada decides to slow you down by triggering moving laser wall traps. Move to the right, aim and press Action to roll forward and lie flat on your back. If done correctly, you'll to pass through a low gap in the array, unharmed. Failure to act in time or missing the gap in the beams inflicts damage.

Continue dashing to the end. Quickly move up to one of the red circuit breakers on either side of the doorway and press Fire to smash it, which deactivates the lasers. In Single player offline mode, your partner will smash the other, but once your circuit is broken you should help with his.

If the Leon and Helena in another room similar to yours break out of confinement first, they get onboard the elevator before you do and get to claim some fabulous prizes. You get stuck taking the stairs, and going to Room 00. However, if you make it onto the elevator before Leon and Helena, then the elevator will take you to Room 01. Outside Room 01 you'll find several extra item crates to smash, as well as two chests, each containing **Skill Points (2,000)**.

ON TO THE NEXT TRAP

Assuming you failed to make it to the elevator first, head around the corner to the right and open the door. Run up the stairs in the next room. Open the door at the top and smash the five item crates on the left. Use a Partner Action to open the doors marked No. 00.

DODGE THE FLOOR MINES

Piers and Chris are trapped inside a room. Smash the item crates in the room, pick up whatever they drop, and then examine the exit door.

Ada activates a prototype testing program that releases homing floor mines into the room. These devices roll up to you or your partner, their lights turn red, and then they explode. You have two ways to deal with these mines: shoot them with your Shotgun or let them roll up to you and then dodge roll to either side or backwards. The second method conserves more bullets, but you must avoid rolling too short, such as into a wall or obstacle.

When Ada becomes bored and leaves, move to the circuit box at the back of the room and press Action. Tap the Reload button rapidly to break into the circuit box, open the exit doors, and shut down the remaining floor mines.

ROOM 01 MUST BE HOTWIRED

A similar scenario involving the floor mines occurs in Room 01, except it is Piers' job to hotwire the control panel at the back of the room while Chris dodges the floor mines. Set off the floor mines before they explode next to Piers, or he takes longer.

CHASE DOWN ADA!

Continue into the next room, head to the far right, and press Action to kick in the vent cover. Crawl through the vent and then begin dashing after Ada, whose position is marked on the level below. You must stay close to her or the game will end if she gets away. When Ada grapples across the room, continue down the path and take the next left turn. Dash to the end of the gantry and drop down to trigger an exciting scene.

MAIN THOROUGHFARE

CAR CHASE FOR THE AGES

Chris and Piers hop into a military jeep and take off after Ada Wong, unfortunately she is driving a much faster vehicle. Chris starts off on the gun while Piers takes the wheel, but they will soon switch. The machine gun fires like any other gun. To drive the jeep, press Fire to hit the gas or Aim to apply the brakes through turns. Pressing Action puts the vehicle in boost for a short period, and you must use it wisely to keep up with Ada. If she gets more than 300 meters ahead, the game ends immediately and you must start over. Your vehicle's remaining integrity is displayed in the lower-right corner of the screen. You must avoid collisions and gunfire to keep from exploding.

1

Enemy cars fall between you and Ada, covering her escape. Shoot the jeeps with prolonged bursts to make them explode. Since this takes a few seconds, shoot any J'avo that stand up in the back of the car and aim machine guns or rocket launchers your way.

2

When you are driving, hit the boost every time you see a straightaway. Ada will do the same, and this is the only way you can keep up with her.

3

Apply the brakes to help steer around wreckage in the streets or to avoid enemy cars that explode.

4

The pursuit leads into a tunnel. Ada and the enemy cars are on your left. Shoot the cars before you get out of the tunnel.

5

More enemy cars fall in as the chase returns to above-ground streets. Shoot them out of your way.

6

Ada exits onto a highway. Shoot a couple more enemy cars out of your path.

7

Ada drops a grenade near a parked tanker truck. Steer hard to the left to avoid crashing. Your jeep jumps onto the train tracks running parallel to the highway Ada is on.

8

Steer left to avoid an oncoming train. Piers jumps the jeep back onto the highway behind Ada. Follow her down the exit ramp to the far right.

9

Ada drives into a parking garage. Drive straight ahead and then to the right. Follow the yellow lines around the garage until you reach the ramp up to the next level.

A large group of enemy cars and J'avo wait in ambush on the second level of the garage. Shoot a **Serpent Emblem** in the background. Then, prioritize shooting the J'avos crouching with rocket launchers in front. Finally, shoot the cars to destroy them.

Follow the last enemy car out of the garage by driving to the right and around the next corner onto another ramp.

Drive straight across the third floor toward a large hole in the wall. Piers stops at the edge, and he trades places with Chris.

If you are playing as Chris, press Reload to smash out the windshield so that you can see clearly.

Hit the boost and follow Ada down the exit ramp to the right and onto trolley-car tracks.

Apply the brakes to make a sharp right turn at the end of the street, and then boost again to pursue Ada down the highway.

Enemy cars carrying rocket-launching J'avo troops join the chase. With little time to react, you must now steer left or right quickly to avoid incoming rockets. Don't follow the enemy cars directly behind, and veer side to side frequently to avoid rockets.

Continue following the highway. After perhaps the longest left curve in history, hit your boost to catch up to Ada.

Follow Ada to the port, where Chris jumps the car onto an aircraft carrier.

SERPENT EMBLEM: PARKING GARAGE

When Piers and Chris run into the J'avo squad in the parking garage, aim at the back wall directly above the central enemy car. A **Serpent Emblem** hangs on a double-decker bus window. Shoot it and then deal with the J'avo.

CHRIS CHAPTER 3: RANKING CRITERIA

RANK	ACCURACY(%)	DEATHS	CLEAR TIME(MIN)	ENEMIES ROUTED
A	70	2	85	55
B	60	4	105	40
C	50	7	130	25
D	*1	*1	*1	*1

*1 Any Below Rank C

POINTS AWARDED PER RANK (ABOVE)				
Rank	A	B	C	D
Points	25	20	15	10

TOTAL RANKING POINTS TABLE

RANK	S	A	B	C	D	E
Total	100	90	75	55	45	*2

*2 Any Below Rank D

AIRCRAFT CARRIER—REAR HANGAR

REAR HANGAR MAP

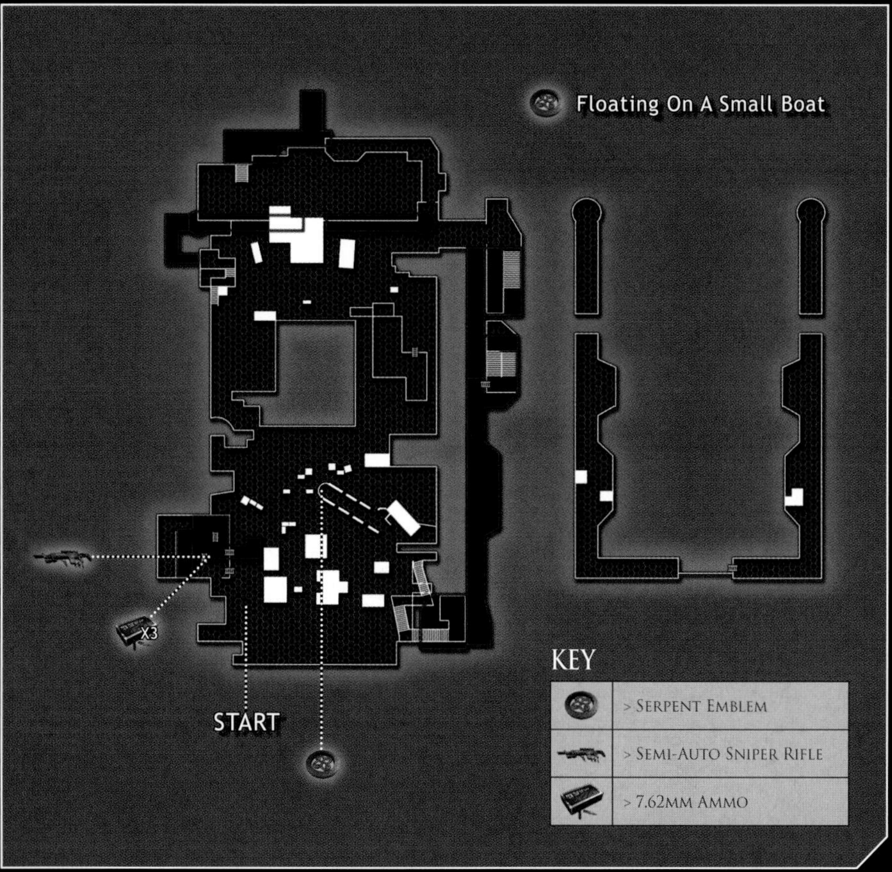

WAKE-UP CALL

If you wake up as Piers, you must rotate the Left Stick rapidly to avoid being murdered by a Neo-Umbrella J'avo attempting to kill you. If you wake as Chris, you find the J'avo attacking Piers and must roll into an aiming position where Chris is lying on his back. Shoot the J'avo to knock it off of Piers.

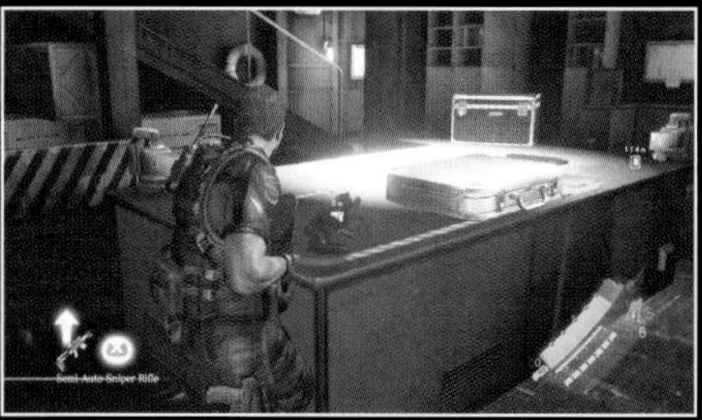

The J'avo runs off and a squad of snipers takes position along the far end of the hangar. Move left to the doorway of the small office. Shoot the J'avo inside this office, which usually makes it mutate, then blast it from behind for an easier take-down. Look for another J'avo to come down the stairs inside. On the central counter of this room, you find a **Semi-Auto Sniper Rifle**. Open the nearby case and collect the three boxes of **7.62mm Ammo**, then you are ready to return fire on the snipers. Ascend the stairs in this room and proceed all the way up to the top level. Smash several item crates along the way and on the gantry suspended over the hangar floor.

From this gantry, take cover behind one of the solid sections of rail and scan the snipers at the far end of the hangar. Find and shoot the exploding barrels between the snipers to take out several of them simultaneously.

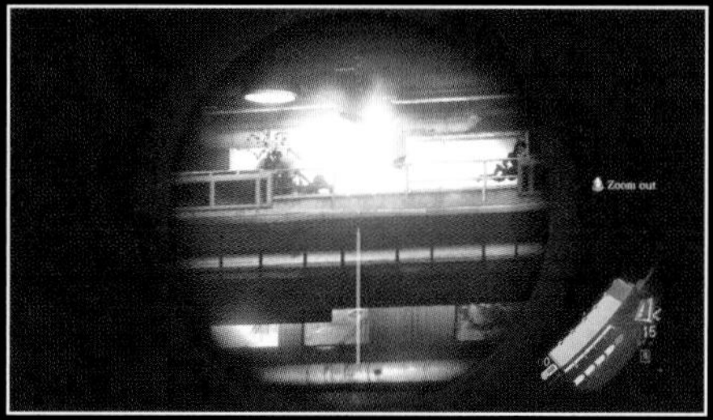

TRACK ADA

Return inside and drop down the ladder on your immediate left. Kick down the nearby emergency ladder and drop to the bottom floor. Keep moving along the left wall of the hangar. You will see Ada Wong walking through the central door on the far wall of the hangar. Another squad of J'avo appears during the scene, so wipe them out as you continue making your way along the hangar on this side.

Approach the stairs that you see directly ahead and against the left wall. A J'avo raises the stairs, blocking access to the exit through which Ada left and releasing another squad of J'avo into the hangar. The J'avo on the ground floor mutate immediately, and there is a sniper perched above. Backtrack a few steps and hide behind some boxes. Draw in the ground mutants and take them out, then equip the Sniper Rifle and take down the J'avo up high. It typically mutates into a Napad, which you can easily deal with by firing Quick Shots with a Sniper Rifle.

Ascend the stairs and you see a bulkhead closing over the door that Ada went through. Piers is right: can this get any worse? At the top of the stairs, proceed through a short corridor and then climb the ladder.

DESTROY THE BULKHEAD

Move across the top bridge to the wide gap in the middle and press Action. You see a missile at the back end of the hangar, which looks like a good way to get through the bulkhead. Press Partner Action to toss Piers across the gap. A few seconds after the toss, the bridge sections rotate inward, connecting you both to the upper balconies that run back to the missile. Fight your way back through hordes of Neo-Umbrella J'avo and meet up at the missile. Chris will be delayed because he must climb hand over hand across a horizontal pole. Once Chris and Piers are on the same side, eliminate any persistent enemies nearby. Now, turn the winch on the missile to aim it down at the bulkhead. In Multiplayer mode, the other player must examine the open circuit panel and hotwire the missile. This is accomplished by pressing Reload several times as the timer needle moves through the colored parts of a revolving command prompt. With that task completed, the missile takes off and destroys the bulkhead.

After the missile launches, drop from the platform. Landing on a lower tower, you can then fire upon the J'avo waiting for you on the ground. Take out several of them before dropping down and finishing off the remainders.

SERPENT EMBLEM: HELICOPTER IN REAR HANGAR

In this same area of the hangar, you spot a large helicopter transport with its doors open and its ramp down. Enter it and move up to the cockpit. There you find a **Serpent Emblem** in the pilot's seat. You may smash a couple item crates on either side.

FIGHT TO THE EXIT

Facing the exit, head for the right side of the hangar and work your way toward the objective marker. On the back side of some cargo containers, locate a ladder that you can climb in order to reach some item crates on the far side. From this vantage point, you can also snipe the J'avo gathering below. Drop down and finish off the last one or two enemies.

Approaching the objective marker, you must take cover behind the cargo container on the right. Two J'avo with machine guns guard the door. Toss a grenade between them or toss a Flash Grenade and move in to mop them up. Approach the white doors at the back of this small area and open them via Partner Action.

MOVE UP THE SIDE OF THE SHIP

After emerging onto an exterior platform, you notice a smaller boat in the water. This boat tracks your movements with a spotlight and also opens fire occasionally, but none of the bullets will hit you.

SERPENT EMBLEM: DINGHY BEHIND THE CRUISER

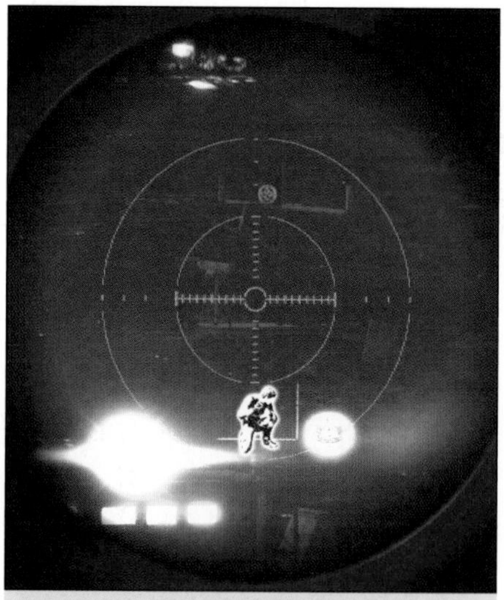

After emerging from the hangar, equip the Sniper Rifle and scope the area above the cruiser out in the water. Spot the **Serpent Emblem** mounted to the dinghy behind the cruiser, zoom in, and shoot it.

LOWER THE STAIRS

Ascend the stairs on the left to find a couple item crates, and then move to the opposite ledge and drop down. Climb onto the raised platform and navigate around to the next set of stairs. Go to the uppermost level, smash some item crates on the right, and then climb the ladder.

Turn left and run the length of the exterior balcony. Go up the stairs at the end, follow the corner to the right, and open the doors with a Partner Action. Move up to the green-lit control panel and press Action to pull the lever, lowering the stairs that were raised earlier. Now you're ready to move on.

FIGHT THROUGH THE HANGAR

Turn around, kick down the emergency ladder behind you, and drop into the room below. Make your way down the stairs back into the hangar. As you reach the second landing, a fighter jet lowers into the hangar and opens fire. J'avo charge you from your right, so turn left and jump through the hole in the railing onto a cargo container.

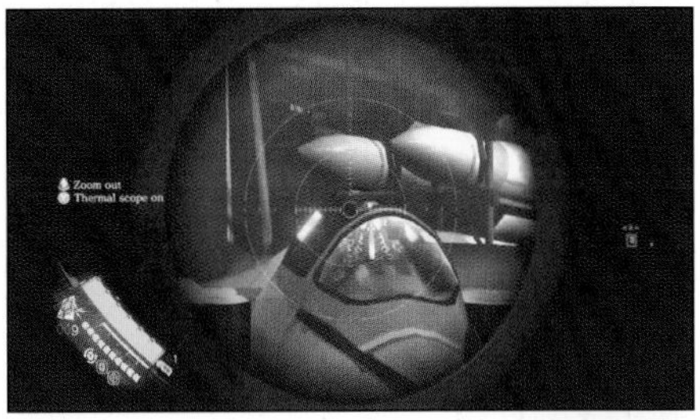

The J'avo will leap after you, but this makes them easier to shoot out of the air. When they're down, equip your Sniper Rifle and take out other J'avo now standing around the hangar. Drop from the cargo container, go right, and go back up the stairs you were just on. From here, snipe the pilot in the fighter jet cockpit to stop him from firing on you.

Facing the exit, work your way back up the right side of the hangar. More J'avo come out to attack, so take them down with Shotgun blasts and melee attacks.

The objective marker now indicates the door to the control room under the platform. Open it with a Partner Action. Move up to the next doorway, take cover on either side, and blast J'avo as they attempt to rush out of the control room. When the area is clear, move into the room and eliminate more enemies entering from the left.

Continue through the exit of the control room, and check your left for more enemies, possibly incoming. Kill them and search the shelves in back for an item crate to smash. Turn around and head for the stairs that were lowered. Go upstairs and to the right, then proceed through the blasted bulkhead and open the door with a Partner Action. After a short scene, open the next door the same way.

AIRCRAFT CARRIER—BRIDGE

BRIDGE MAP

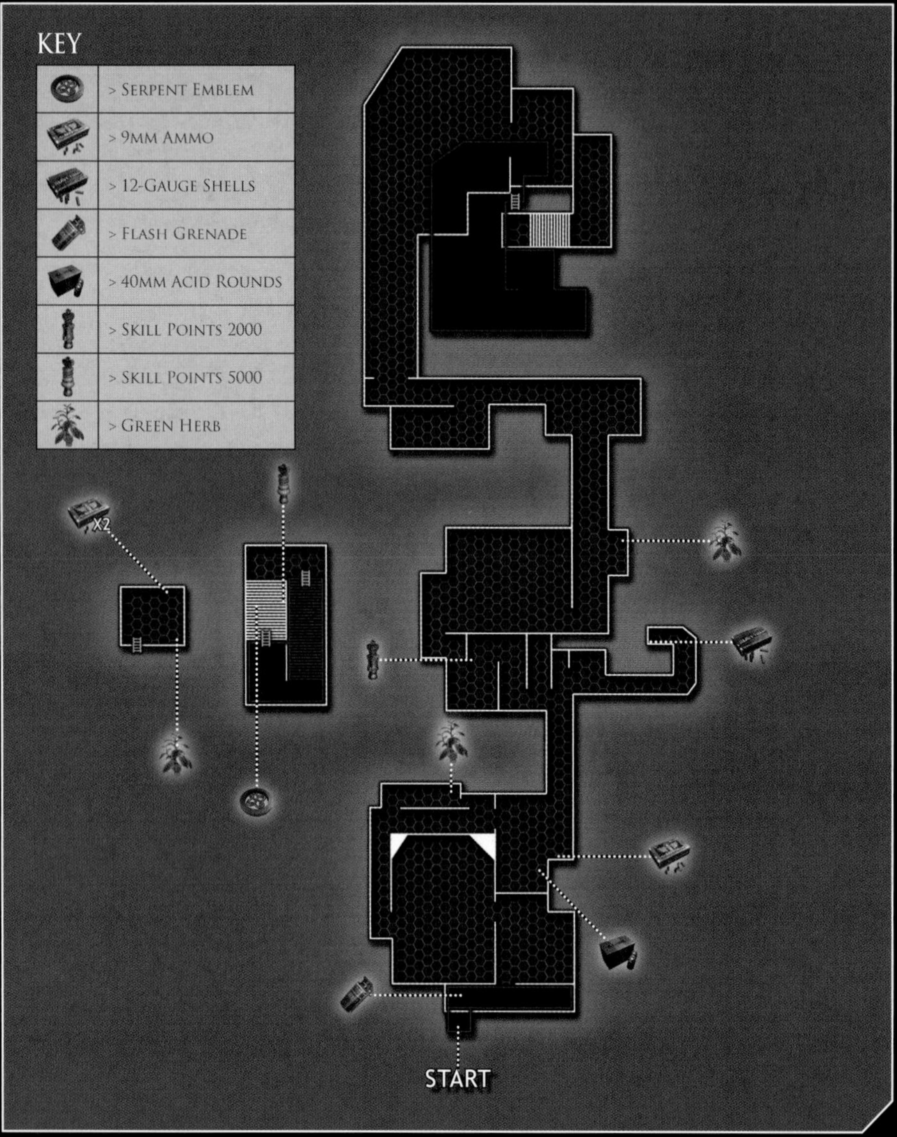

PURSUE THE WOMAN IN RED

Search the shelves straight ahead to find a **Flash Grenade**, then turn right and proceed to the right side of the elevator doors. Press Action to open the doors, go inside, and press Partner Action to ascend to the bridge.

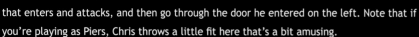

When you spot Ada, follow her through the door ahead on the right. Take down a J'avo that enters and attacks, and then go through the door he entered on the left. Note that if you're playing as Piers, Chris throws a little fit here that's a bit amusing.

NO LECTURES TODAY, PLEASE

Move forward and take cover behind the low shelves. Return fire on Neo-Umbrella J'avo behind the lecture desk.

They mutate automatically into Neo-Umbrella Noga-Trchanje and begin crawling the ceiling. Target them all quickly, if you can, by tossing a Flash Grenade. Then go around stomping on Noga-Trchanje heads while they writhe on the ground. Remember that you can also run up to active Noga-Trchanje and stomp them out of existence.

TAKE A DETOUR

Proceed through the back doorway of the lecture room. Go right down the corridor. The corridor continues to the right, but a bathroom is straight ahead. A J'avo is hidden within. Blast it out of the nook rather than allowing it to sneak up behind you later. A **Green Herb** is located at the far end. Exit the bathroom and proceed down the corridor. Open the door at the end with a Partner Action.

THE OTHER SIDE OF THE SHIP

A J'avo crouched behind the wash bins ahead mutates into a Telo-Eksplozija. Hit it with melee strikes to knock it down and roll away before it bursts. More J'avo come down the stairs behind it. Search the shelves to the right to find **9mm Ammo**, and then check the cart around the corner for **40mm Acid Rounds**. You can switch firing modes while aiming the Grenade Launcher to load different rounds.

Fight your way upstairs and continue onto the exterior balcony. Follow the edge around to the far side, where you'll find **12-Gauge Shells** sitting on the bannister. Return inside and open the door opposite. Hop the counter and open the case in the second half of the room to find **Skill Points (2,000)**.

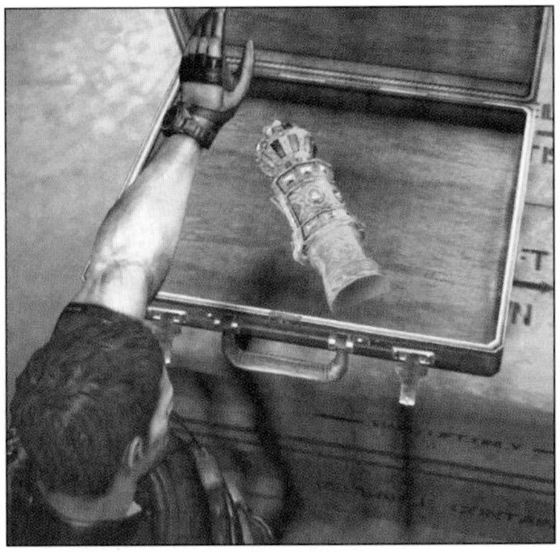

AMBUSH AFTER AMBUSH

Open the door at the back of the room and head around the corner to the right. Hop over the fallen lockers and you spot Ada in the next area. More J'avo burst in through the back door, so take them down. Open the door and follow Ada up the corridor. J'avo crash through the side windows and more pile into the passageway behind you. Take them out with several Quick Shots fired from the Shotgun. Eliminating the enemies raises the bulkhead door that Ada went through. Pick up a **Green Herb** in this area and carry on.

TAKE COMMAND

Head upstairs into the mess hall, then go left. In the center of the left wall in the next corridor, you can slip through the doorway and perform a stealth hit on a J'avo before it turns around. Afterward, smash four item crates in this room to restock. Return to the corridor, continue to the end, and open the door on the right with a Partner Action.

More spider-like Neo-Umbrella Noga-Trchanje cover the ceiling of the command bridge. Throw a Flash Grenade to stun them all and kick in some heads. Proceed into the bridge to spot Ada on the far side. A Gnezdo soon appears and attacks. Blast the swarm to make the queen come out, and then hit the creature repeatedly to kill it. Unlike last time, this enemy drops **Skill Points (2,500)**.

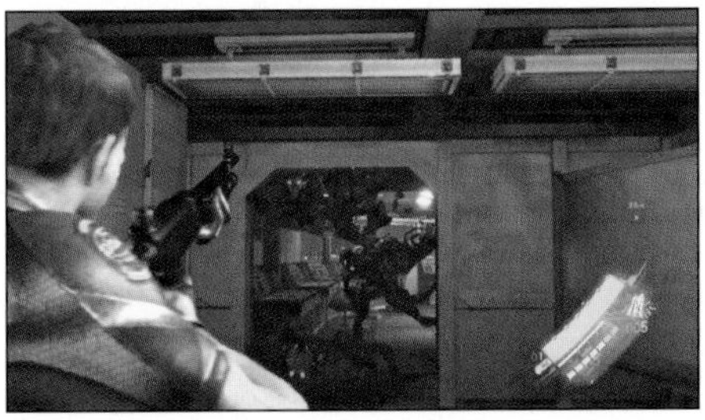

SEE WHAT'S COOKING UPSTAIRS

Follow Ada by jumping out the side window at the back of the bridge. You arrive just in time to see her grapple away. Continue up to the next doorway and go upstairs. Smash the two item crates then open the doors with a Partner Action.

In the radar room, take out the two J'avo directly ahead. Continue right and around the corner into the communications center. J'avo rappel through the windows, so fire a grenade into their midst to take them all out at once.

Move to the far side of the communications center where a ladder leads to the next level up. Climb the ladder and open the briefcase on your immediate right to obtain **Skill Points (5,000)**. Then, move around to the base of the stairs.

SERPENT EMBLEM: BRIDGE STAIRS

A **Serpent Emblem** lies under the stairs behind the case containing Skill Points (5,000), visible between the steps. Shoot it before ascending.

A NICE, QUIET SUPPLY ROOM

Ascend the stairs and climb the ladder. Collect a **Green Herb,** two boxes of **9mm Ammo**, and smash the item crates in the corner. Open the nearby door with a Partner Action.

AIRCRAFT CARRIER—FORWARD HANGAR

BRIDGE MAP

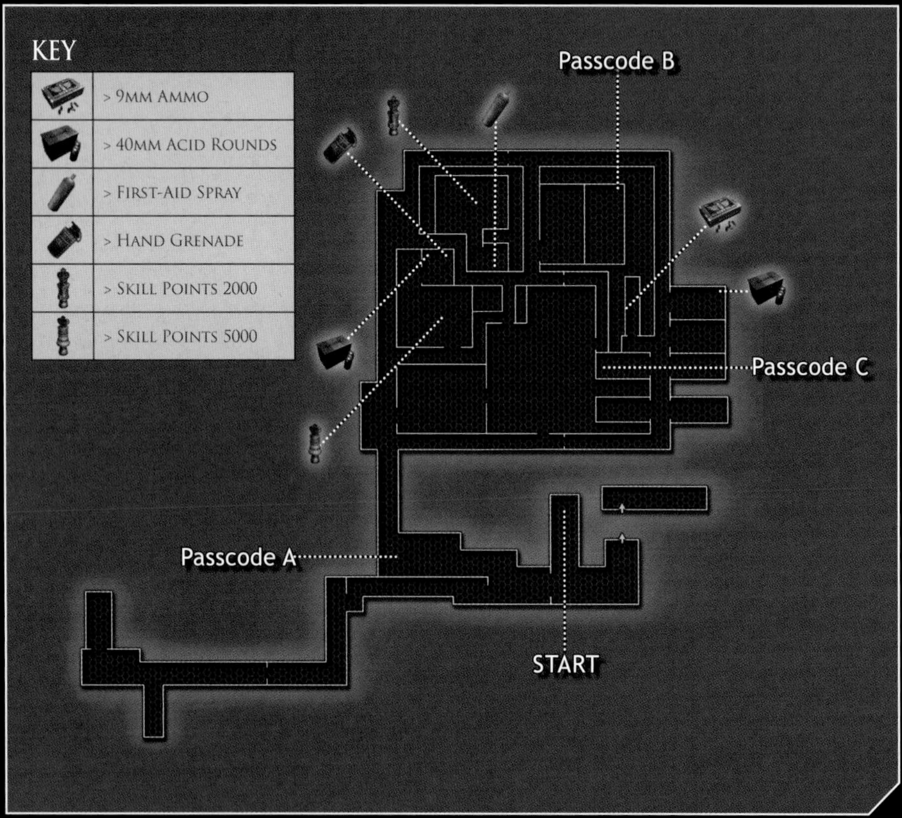

DETERMINE HOW TO ESCAPE

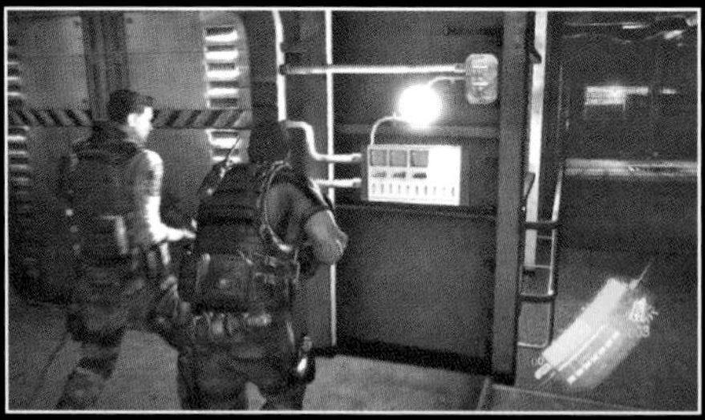

Chris and Piers wind up in the bowels of the ship again, headed for the hangar near the ship's bow. Proceed down the passage and the ship rocks to the side. This happens regularly as you head for the hangar. At the intersection, head left and up the stairs to find an item crate to smash, then return to the main path.

Examine the console with the blinking lights. Chris determines that three separate passcodes are needed to open the door. The passcode locations are marked in the surrounding area with distances to each one. However, you'll have trouble traveling a straight line to most of them, since they are located in the maze of crew quarters.

THE SHAMBLING HORRORS

Head around the corner and up the corridor to locate the first keycard you need, **Passcode A**. Then, open the door on the right. Chris and Piers witness the horror of a Rasklapanje duplicating itself inside a human host. These creatures fall apart when shot, and then the severed torso, legs, and arms crawl after you and attack. The best way to deal with Rasklapanje is *not to*: simply try to stay away from them. However, in some situations you are forced to shoot the Rasklapanje until it separates. After doing so, move on as quickly as possible.

PUT OUT THE KITCHEN FIRE

Head downstairs and past the Rasklapanje and open the door in the wall on the right. Proceed to the back of the kitchen, and you are shut inside with a Rasklapanje when safety protocols activate. Shoot the Rasklapanje until the sprinklers put out the stove fire, then open the rear door with a Partner Action.

PASSCODE C IS EASY TO FIND

In the mess hall, head to the right and open the door in the wall. Follow the passageway to your left into the dark and ominous crew quarters. Although item crates are in several of the compartments, head straight for the location of **Passcode C** (as marked on the map in this section and indicated in your environment).

CIRCLE STRAIGHT TO PASSCODE B

From the crew quarters, simply continue down the same corridor all the way around the perimeter of the area. At the next intersection, turn left and move through the next door on your left. Open the doors at the back of the room with a Partner Action. Chris is sealed inside the back room with a full Rasklapanje. You have about half a second to hit the monster with a Quick Shot before it tackles you to the ground. Rotate the Left Stick rapidly to break free of its grip, and then shoot it and all its pieces until they are still. Pick up **Passcode B** in the corner, smash the item crate on the gurney, and move to the doors to reopen them with a Partner Action.

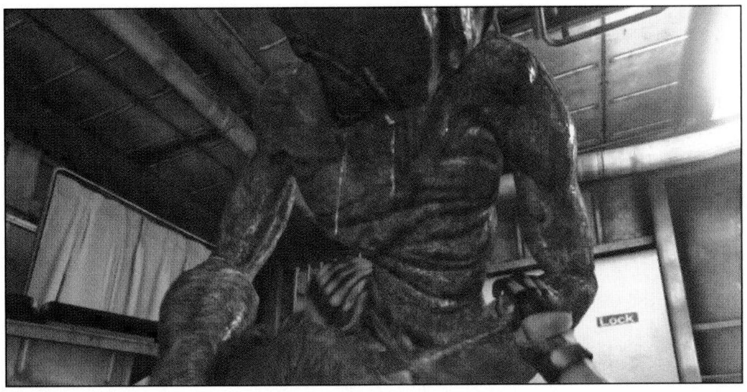

STAY AND PLUNDER OR MOVE ON?

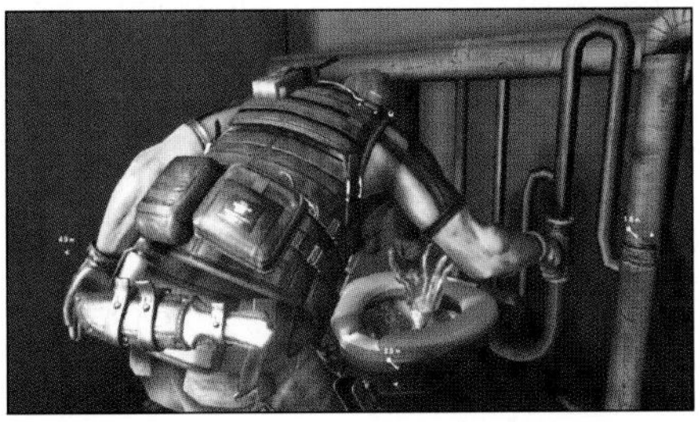

After exiting the examination room, the easiest way out is to turn left and head back through the mess hall and kitchen to the entrance. However, you will miss extra items and loads of Skill Points in the main quarters (as shown on the map). Also, if a Rasklapanje hand is in the bathroom with you, perform a melee action to flush it down the drain.

INPUT THE PASSCODES

Return to the passcode input panel and hit the Action button three times to input all of the passcodes. When the doors open, move down the short passage and smash the two item crates on your left. Open the white doors with a Partner Action and head left.

SURPRISE ATTACK

A Rasklapanje leaps out of the vent, knocking Chris and Piers onto the pipes over a molten vat. The game enters slow motion as the body parts leap out at you. Raise your weapon and shoot each body part one time to knock each of the parts into the vat below.

When you are back on your feet, proceed through the next door. Dash down the corridor and smash an item crate at the end on your left. Open the doors opposite with a Partner Action and run for the fighter jet visible straight ahead.

AIRSPACE OVER AIRCRAFT CARRIER

PILOT LESSONS—DO A BARREL ROLL

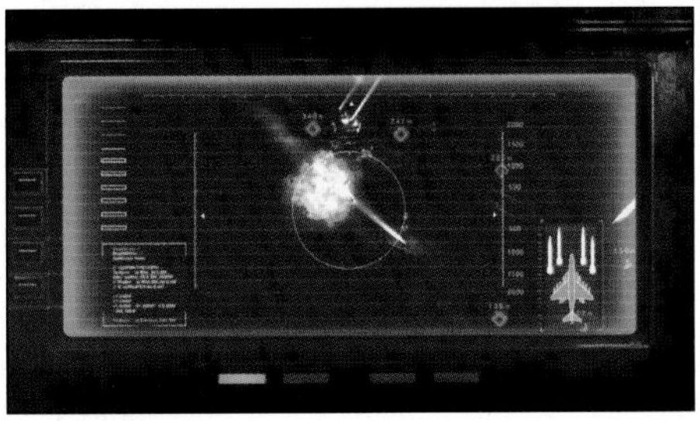

Now flying the fighter jet, you must take out the virus missiles that are aimed at the population. Chris pilots the jet, and is responsible for shooting down missiles or doing barrel rolls to avoid them. Perform a barrel roll whenever a missile alert pops up onscreen. Hold the Aim button to fire from first-person view inside the cockpit if you prefer. Press R1/RB to do a barrel roll in order to escape incoming missiles that are too close to shoot down.

Piers' job is to lock onto targets and fire missiles. Looking through the lock-on screen, move the Right Stick to aim. Align the central circle so that targets marked with green diamonds remain in the circle until lock-on is confirmed. Press the fire button to launch a missile.

FIRST STRIKE

Get used to your individual jobs immediately. While Piers lines up his targeting system on the area marked with a green diamond and fires a missile, Chris must avoid an incoming strike by performing a barrel roll.

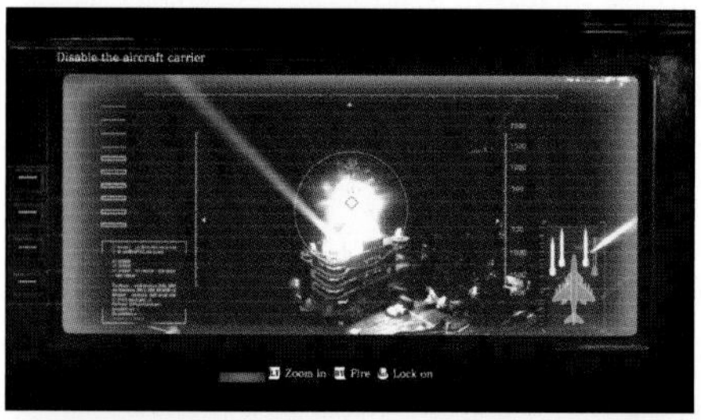

BOMBARD THE CARRIER

Several helicopters take off and hover over the aircraft carrier while firing missiles. Chris' job is to pilot the fighter back and forth over the carrier so that Piers can take out the anti-aircraft guns on the sides and top surface. To this end, Chris must not swerve around so much that Piers cannot establish a lock-on. However, shooting down the helicopters reduces the number of missiles that are fired at the fighter and makes for smoother flying.

Meanwhile, Piers must lock onto each anti-aircraft cannon and send a missile into it. Lock onto targets from right to left as Chris circles around so that you can blow up multiple targets on each pass.

DROP OFF PIERS

When the anti-aircraft guns are destroyed, a J'avo triggers the missile countdown. You have four minutes and counting to drop off Piers and protect him so that he can reach the controls and disarm the missile. After letting Piers out, watch for J'avo approaching his position from below and gun them all down. As he reaches the second cargo container that he must destroy, another squad approaches him from the top. Take out these J'avo easily by shooting the exploding barrel in the narrow passage.

When you are controlling Piers on the ground, quickly advance on the cargo container a few yards away and press Action to examine it. While Piers sets up a bomb below the container, press the Reload button while the timer hand passes through the colored area of the revolving command prompt. Do this repeatedly to set the device and blow up the container.

SERPENT EMBLEM: AIRCRAFT CARRIER DECK

After blowing the first container out of your way, head for the back of the carrier and then go right. Slide over a stack of girders in your path then turn right sharply. A **Serpent Emblem** lies below a tire, through which you can shoot to hit it.

DEACTIVATE THE MISSILE LAUNCH

Continue following the narrow path through the equipment to the second cargo container. Again, press Action to start setting your bomb, then press Reload as the timer hand moves through colored parts of the revolving command prompt. Afterward, head for the train car that houses the missile controls. Approach the console and press Action. Press Reload during the revolving command prompts to shut down the missile launch.

PROTECT PIERS FROM THE OGROMAN

As Piers heads for the control booth, an Ogroman is released on deck. Chris must shoot the monster in the face to make it stagger and to prevent it from chasing Piers. After Piers disarms the missile and avoids the Ogroman's clutches, continue shooting the creature in the face so that Piers can escape. On the deck, Piers must dash for the crane arm at the forward corner of the carrier. Without looking back, climb the ladder and move out on the arm to hop back into the fighter.

After Piers is back in the fighter, both of you must shoot the Ogroman in the face repeatedly to knock it out of the way so that Piers may then lock onto the missile and fire.

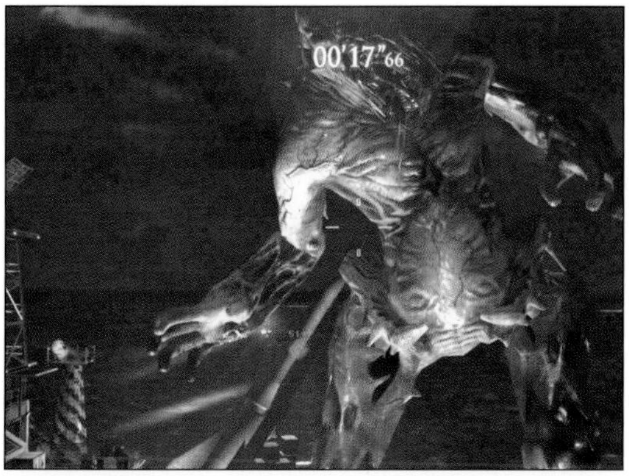

CHRIS CHAPTER 4: RANKING CRITERIA

RANK	ACCURACY(%)	DEATHS	CLEAR TIME(MIN)	ENEMIES ROUTED
A	70	2	75	55
B	60	4	90	45
C	50	7	120	35
D	*1	*1	*1	*1

*1 Any Below Rank C

POINTS AWARDED PER RANK (ABOVE)				
Rank	A	B	C	D
Points	25	20	15	10

TOTAL RANKING POINTS TABLE

RANK	S	A	B	C	D	E
Total	100	90	75	55	45	*2

*2 Any Below Rank D

CHINESE WATERS

July 1, 2013

"MAYBE IT'S FATE"

Chris and Piers land the fighter jet on an offshore oil rig identified as belonging to Neo-Umbrella. Finding an elevator, the two embark on a long ride to an underwater facility hidden on the ocean floor. During the ride, Chris contemplates the series of events that brought him here and the fact that he must now save the son of his former mortal enemy.

UNDERWATER FACILITY

FACILITY MAP

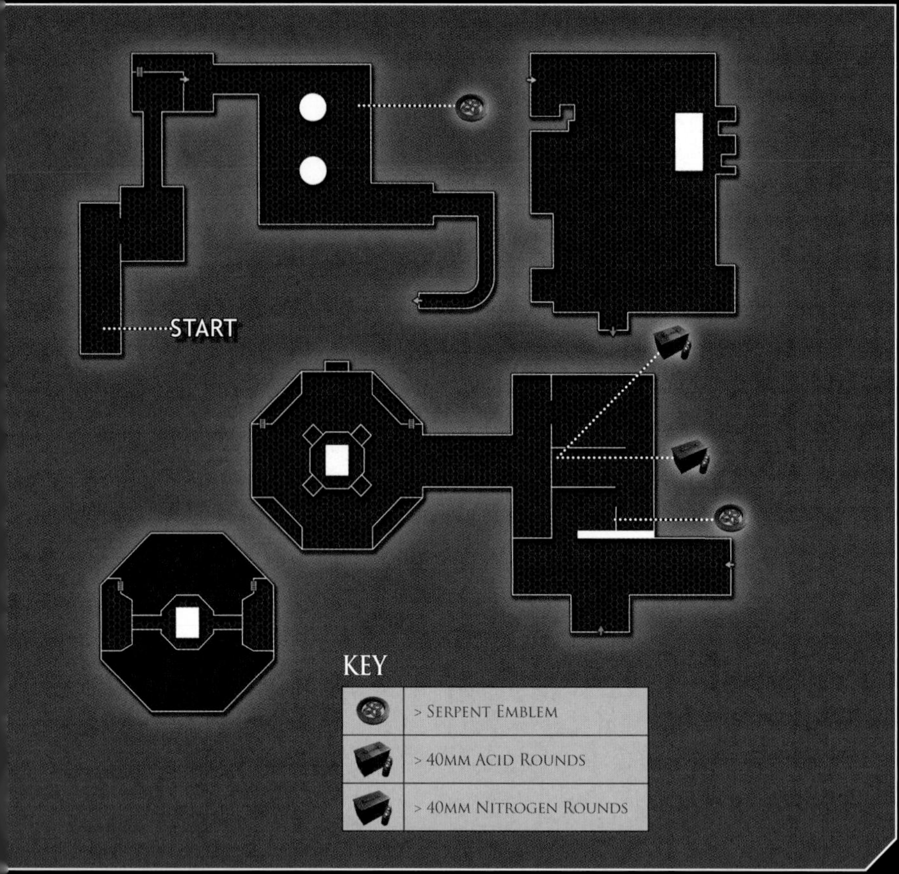

SERPENT EMBLEM: CARGO STORAGE UNDERBELLY

While crawling beneath the fan, angle the camera upward to spot a **Serpent Emblem** straight ahead, resting atop a long tube that runs under the ceiling. Hold the Aim button while crawling to fire on the target.

RELEASE JAKE AND SHERRY

Head down the corridor and open the door on the right with a Partner Action. Piers finds Jake and Sherry on lockdown and releases them. This triggers an alarm. Turn left from the control panel, run to the wall, and crawl through the vent into the next room.

Smash the gray item crates around the area. Approach the ledge above the spinning fan, and initiate a Partner Action to throw Piers across the gap. Piers pulls the lever on the other side, shutting down the fan. Turn around and drop over the ladder into the lower area. Approach the fan and crawl under it, pressing Action repeatedly to use your stamina to go faster.

NAVIGATE THE CARGO BAY UNDERBELLY

Smash item crates in the lower area as you make your way to another spinning fan. Chris radios for Piers and must wait until the sniper makes his way to the lever above. When he shuts the fan off, crawl under the blades. After rising inside the wind tunnel, move down a short distance and enter the low vent duct on the right. Chris slides into a corridor on the level below. Directly ahead are two Neo-Umbrella J'avo walking away.

Run up behind them and take down at least one with a Stealth Hit. Knock out the other J'avo with a Quick Shot and melee attack combo.

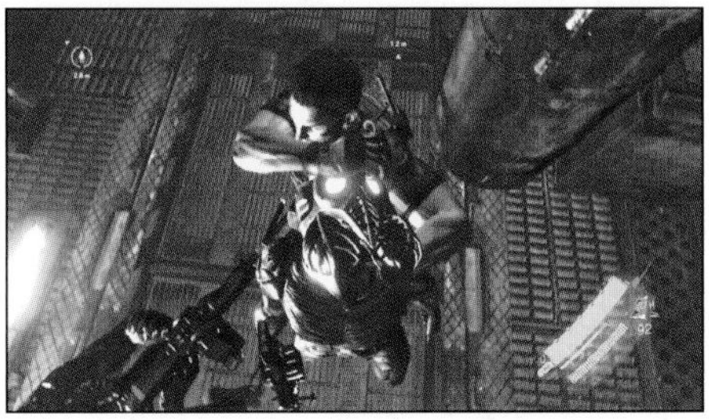

RIDE THE ELEVATOR BACK TO PIERS' LOCATION

Piers needs help! Move to the wall and pull the marked lever to restore elevator power. Approach the red panel on the wall and press Action to open the elevator doors. Press the button inside the elevator on the left to ride back up to the previous level.

Help Piers take out the J'avo he's been fighting while you were below. Watch out for potential snipers with rocket launchers on the upper levels. When it's clear, head from the elevator to the far-right corner of the area to find two separate sets of item crates. Smash them and a last, lone crate on the far wall near the first lever.

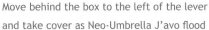

PULL THE LEVERS, STAND TALL

When playing Piers during this section, you must initiate a Partner Action to make Chris toss you across the gap. Turn right, move to the lever, and pull it to deactivate the fan below, allowing Chris to proceed.

Move behind the box to the left of the lever and take cover as Neo-Umbrella J'avo flood the area beyond. From here, snipe the snipers and rocket-launching enemies on the upper levels. Ignore the enemies manning the machine-gun turrets.

With the upper level snipers gone, turn left and dash to the back wall of the cargo bay. Head right to find another lever. Whether Chris requests your help or not, pull the lever to deactivate the second fan that blocks your partner's path.

From the lever, turn right and dash into the center. Work your way behind the first turret. Hit the gunner with a Quick Shot from your Anti-Materiel Rifle to put him down quickly. Dash for the turret closer to the entrance and eliminate that gunner in the same manner. This tactic leaves only a few stragglers that you can deal with at close range until Chris arrives.

A GLUT OF ENEMIES THROUGH ONE DOOR

Return to the elevator and press the button on the left side to open the doors. Board the lift and press the button on the left. When the doors open after the ride, move to the double doors on the other side of the corridor and open them via Partner Action.

Quickly fire a grenade into the far-right corner to take out two J'avo entering the room. Otherwise, run around the central table and take them down fast with Quick Shots and melee. More J'avo try to come through the door, but you can easily gun them down as they try to funnel through the narrow opening. Do not move out of the room until J'avo stop attempting to breach the room—in the corridor beyond, they come from both sides and will surround you. If you step into the corridor and more J'avo appear, retreat into the command center so that enemies must funnel through the doorway choke point.

SERPENT EMBLEM: COMMAND CENTER

From the entrance of this room, look up and to the right to spot a **Serpent Emblem** hidden in a small niche near the ceiling. The emblem is mounted sideways, which makes it difficult to see.

MOVING ON...

When the corridor beyond the command center is perceptibly clear, enter the passageway and head around the corner to the left. In the far-right corner you'll find an item box containing **40mm Acid Rounds** and **40mm Nitrogen Rounds**. The Nitrogen Rounds serve a special purpose in an upcoming boss fight, so reserve all of this ammo that you find for the upcoming event.

Move to the sliding door at the corner of the corridor. It opens automatically, allowing you into a medical bay. Do not proceed, however, as two J'avo with rocket launchers wait in ambush around the corner to the left. Take cover behind the boxes stacked near the door and hit them with grenades or Sniper Rifle shots to eliminate them. Smash the item crate to the left of the sliding-door exit.

Go left and pull the lever to power up the nearby elevator. Move to the left side of the doors and press the button to open them. Once aboard the elevator, press the button on the left.

A FUN-FILLED LITTLE ROOM

Disembark from the elevator and head left to the exit. Pull the levers in unison via Partner Action. The pressure-lock corridor will take two minutes to connect, and then an additional minute and thirty seconds to pressurize. J'avo breach the room and pull levers next to the conveyor belts, which dispense chrysalids into the room. You must fight off J'avo, Napads, and Gnezdo until the connection and pressurization process is complete. The best strategy for dealing with this is to merely run around the outskirts of the lower level, stopping only to blast J'avo away from the conveyor belt levers with your Shotgun. Do not linger on the spot waiting to kill an individual pulling a lever. Instead, make a quick circle nearby until your foe gets back up, then hit him with another Shotgun Quick Shot. Enemies continue appearing in the room so, as soon as the pressurization process is complete, move to the exit door and open it with a Partner Action.

UNDERWATER FACILITY— LOWER LEVELS

LOWER LEVELS MAP

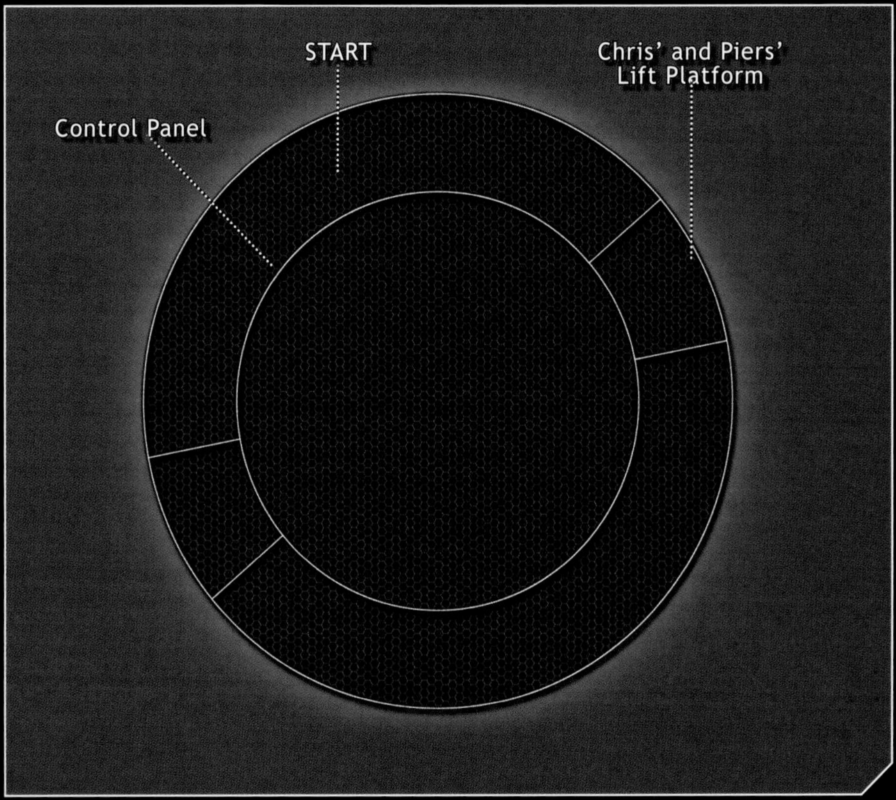

CROSSOVER LIFT ACTION

Chris and Piers meet up with Jake and Sherry inside a wide silo surrounding a massive chrysalid. The four must work together to reach the exit, which is at the very top of the silo, while fending off hordes of heavily armed Neo-Umbrella J'avo.

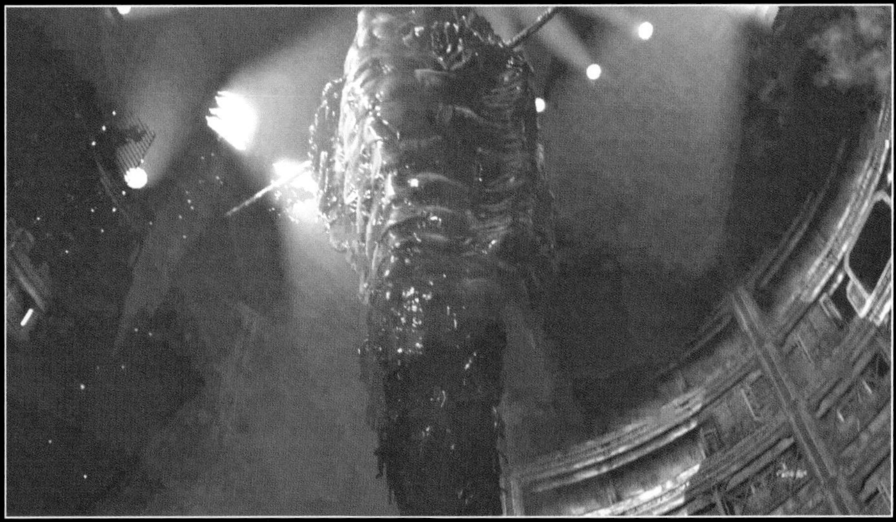

Run toward the central control panel. Approach the button on the left side and press it to activate two platforms in the area. Jake and Sherry head for one platform while Chris and Piers should head for the other. Move to one of the levers and press Partner Action to activate the platform.

As the platforms rise and circle the chamber, hardcore Neo-Umbrella J'avo soldiers drop on Chris' and Piers' platform. Hit them with Quick Shots and melee combos to take them out. Your platform also passes open doorways from which J'avo soldiers fire rocket launchers. Switch to your Assault Rifle or handgun and take out these foes before they adjust their aim on you. Furthermore, snipers may take up positions in doorways on the opposite side of the chamber. Watch for sniper laser sights and equip your Sniper Rifle to deal with these enemies before they knock you down.

SWITCH PARTNERS, TALK IT UP!

Jake won't grab the lever on his side until you grab yours. Therefore, you can run over to Jake's and Sherry's platform and become Sherry's partner! This changes the dialog completely, although listening to this dialog while fighting may be difficult.

UPPER LEVELS MAP

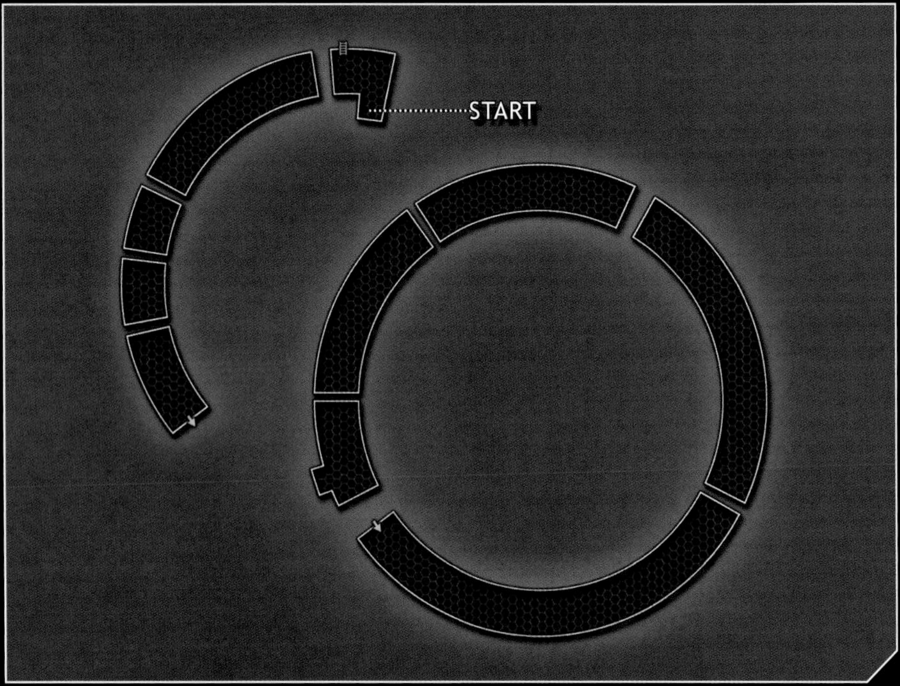

Perform another Partner Action to surmount a high ledge. Haos blocks your way again, so shoot it in the face to make it move. Yet another high ledge blocks your path. Press Partner Action again to boost up your partner. You, however, are put in danger when Haos rips the platform you're standing on out of the wall. Press the Action button rapidly to beat the timer hand three times to hang on. Continue dashing when Haos drops the loose platform segment. Board the elevator with Piers.

A SEVERE OBSTACLE COURSE

Jake and Sherry depart, leaving Chris and Piers to deal with the giant B.O.W. called Haos that hatched from the massive cocoon. You must dash along the circular route and ascend farther up the silo. Turn around and climb the ladder behind you. At the top, leap the gap, turn left, and start dashing along the circular path.

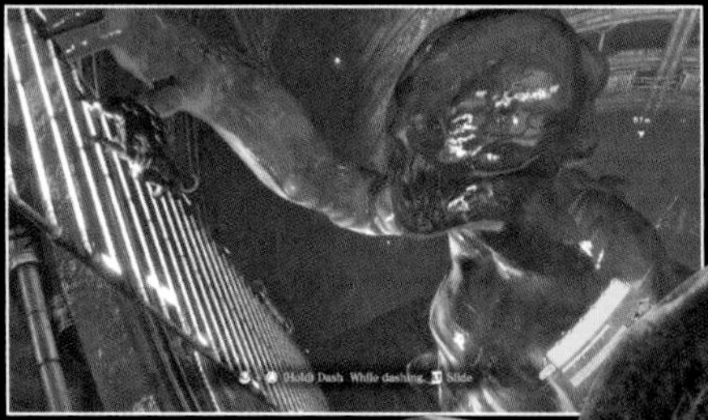

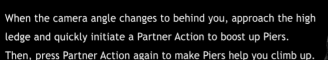

When the camera angle changes to behind you, approach the high ledge and quickly initiate a Partner Action to boost up Piers. Then, press Partner Action again to make Piers help you climb up.

As you leap onto the next circular segment, Haos slams an arm on the platform and blocks your way. Shoot the creature in the face with your Assault Rifle or handgun until it screams in pain and lifts its arm. Continue dashing along the circular path around the silo.

HAOS (UPPER LEVELS)

The monster pulls itself up through a flood drainage hatch to attack Chris and Piers. Move around the outskirts of the area, where you'll find plenty of item crates to break for supplies. Shoot Haos with the Grenade Launcher. Nitrogen Rounds will slow the creature down considerably, so switch weapon modes twice to load these and then switch back to Explosive Rounds. This battle is really just the warm-up, and Haos falls unconscious after you hit it with roughly ten Explosive Rounds.

EMERGENCY ESCAPE ROUTE

EMERGENCY ESCAPE ROUTE MAP 1

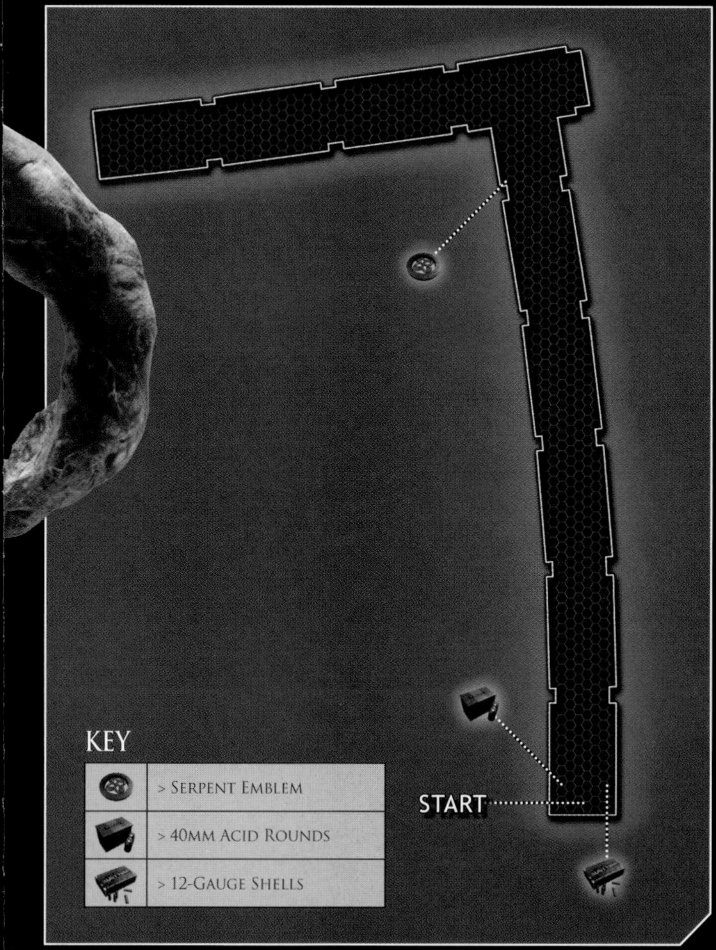

STRUGGLE TO THE FINISH LINE

Time to go! Chris and Piers enter the tunnels that connect to a room full of emergency escape pods. On the floor directly in front of you are **40mm Acid Rounds** and **12-Gauge Shells**. Proceed up the passage until Haos attacks. Dash forward to keep from falling into the ocean. If you fall into a crawling position, crawl for the top of the sloping floor and press Action repeatedly to go faster.

In the next segment, Haos slams its hand through the sidewall. Shoot the hand with your Assault Rifle, handgun, or Shotgun until it pulls back. Then, dash up the sloping floor and press Ready/Aim to slide under the sealing hatch. Keep dashing and sliding under the compartment doors before they close and blast Haos' hand out of your way.

When you reach the last compartment of the first corridor, a strong tremor throws you into the previous area, which is sinking. Press the Action button to climb up the sloping floor and under the closing compartment door, which your partner holds open for you. In co-op mode, the player using the partner must press the Action button repeatedly to keep the door open long enough for the other to climb through.

HAOS' LAST RUSH

Press Partner Action to open the double doors together. Haos attacks again, so turn left and dash, sliding under the closing compartment door. Continue dashing away from Haos as it smashes into the tunnel and gives chase.

SERPENT EMBLEM: EMERGENCY ESCAPE ROUTE

At the final segment of the first leg of the emergency escape route, look down at the floor behind you to your left to spot a **Serpent Emblem** that appears to have fallen among the pipes.

EMERGENCY ESCAPE ROUTE (CONT.)

EMERGENCY ESCAPE ROUTE MAP 2

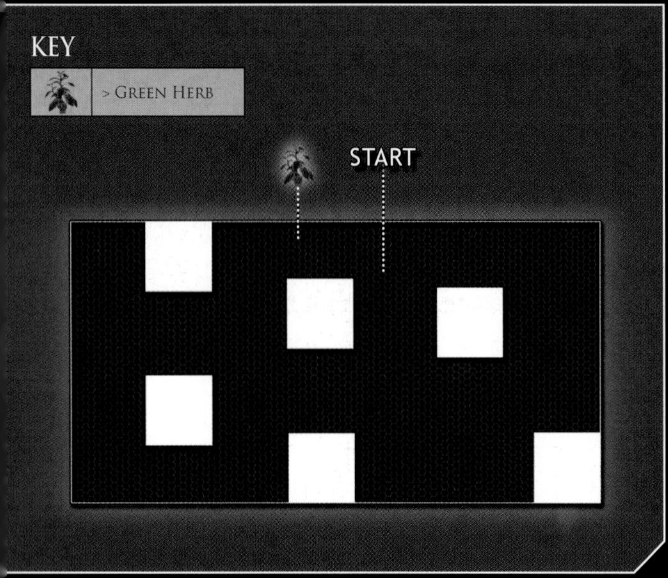

FACE TO FACE WITH FATE

Chris and Piers fail to outrun Haos, and Piers pays a high price. Haos seizes Chris in hand, and Piers must use a newfound ability to free him.

After the scene, approach the control panel next to the door. Press the button to activate the depressurization process. Haos breaks free of its chrysalid and attacks, so at least you'll have something to do while you wait.

HAOS (ESCAPE ROUTE)

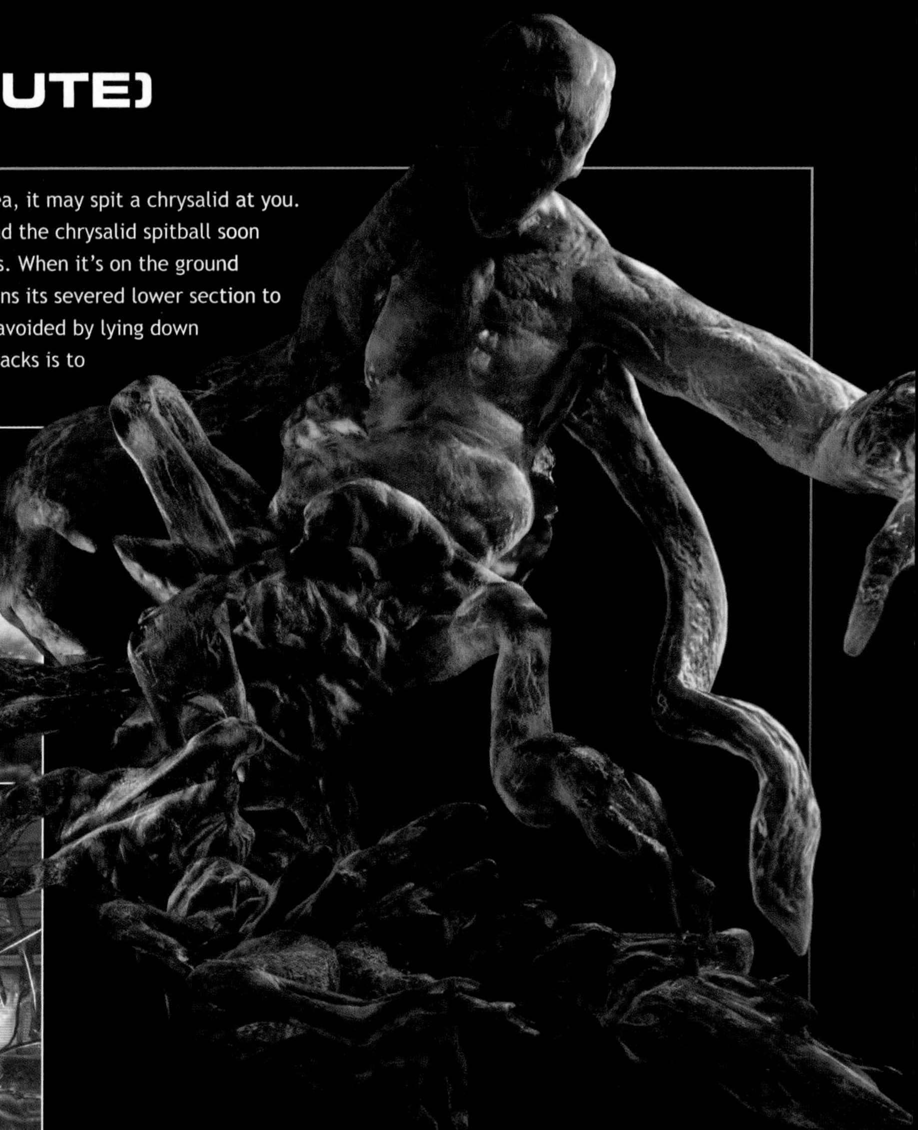

When Haos climbs atop one of the large containers in the area, it may spit a chrysalid at you. The collision knocks you down and inflicts severe damage, and the chrysalid spitball soon bursts and causes further damage if you're in the blast radius. When it's on the ground floor, Haos attacks by claw swipes and tackles. It also summons its severed lower section to transform into a cloud of whipping tentacles that cannot be avoided by lying down or ducking. The only strategy necessary to avoid all these attacks is to stay back at all times.

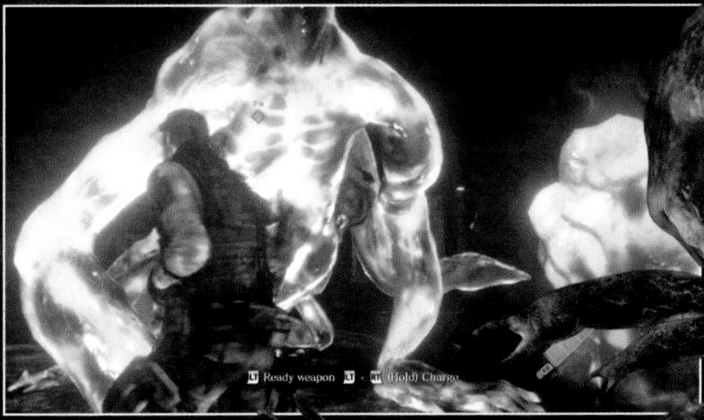

Eliminate Haos as quickly as possible to conserve life and ammo. Load your Grenade Launcher with Nitrogen Rounds and shoot Haos with these to slow it down considerably when it is crawling in the water. Otherwise, load Explosive or Acid Rounds. Spot the twin organ sacks on either side of its lower abdomen and shoot them until they explode. The creature rolls in pain after the first organ explodes, during which time you should navigate around to its other side. Shoot the other organ sack until it explodes.

The same strategy applies to Piers, who can now use only an electric cannon to attack. Hold Ready/Aim and Fire to charge up an attack and then release them to fire. The longer you hold these two buttons, the stronger the charge that is released. Therefore, hold the two buttons only a couple of seconds to release a stinging shot or hold them a while to fire a massive electrical storm. Be aware that the longer you charge the attack, the more your aim wavers. Also, Haos is likely to change positions, and you might not hit the organ sack that you are aiming for.

When both organ sacks are blasted off, the creature encases itself in a chrysalid. Blast the chrysalid with a grenade or full electric current to destroy it. At this point, Haos writhes in pain. Dash up to its lower torso and press the Fire button to stab its main, central organ. Repeat this process two more times.

If you need ammunition or supplies, move to the outer edges of the room and smash item crates in the hopes of getting what you need.

After you stab the creature's main organ three times, it bashes Chris away and seizes Piers. The actions you need to take depend on the character you're playing. As Chris, you'll be in a Dying state. Crawl back over to Piers as quickly as possible and press Partner Action to stab Haos in the heart. Rotate the Left Stick rapidly to twist your knife and gut the organ. As Piers, tap the Action button repeatedly to hold the creature at bay until Chris can stab it.

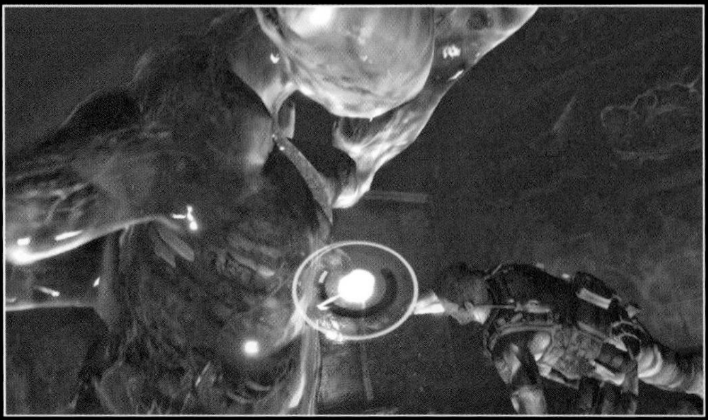

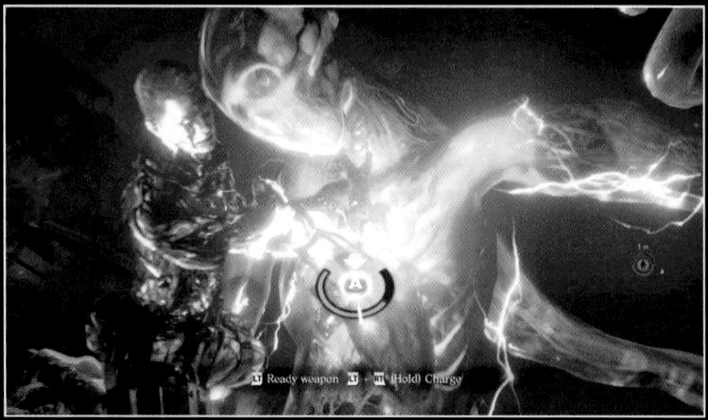

TIME TO GET OUT

When Haos lies still again, approach the exit door. Pick up the **Green Herb** that appears in the water to the left to heal any wounds that have been inflicted. Approach the door, press Action, and rotate the Left Stick to unlock it. Press Partner Action to proceed.

Dash across the collapsing platforms quickly or you fall into the abyss. At doorways covered by mucous membranes, Piers must charge up a full blast and fire it to burn away the barriers. Continue dashing through the area without regard for hatching chrysalids. Dash to the exit to complete Chris' Campaign.

SERPENT EMBLEM: ROUTE TO ESCAPE PODS

Reaching the last mucous membrane blockage that Piers must clear, equip your handgun and move to the right side of the platform. Look down and to the right to spot a **Serpent Emblem** resting on top of a bright light. Piers is unable to shoot this emblem.

ENDING

Having completed Chris' Campaign, you may unlock several features if this is your first campaign, including Agent Hunt mode and eight Skill Sets. The Steel Beast map is unlocked in The Mercenaries game. If this is the last campaign you complete, this will also unlock Ada's campaign.

CHRIS CHAPTER 5: RANKING CRITERIA

RANK	ACCURACY(%)	DEATHS	CLEAR TIME(MIN)	ENEMIES ROUTED
A	70	3	80	40
B	60	5	110	30
C	50	9	120	25
D	*1	*1	*1	*1

*1 Any Below Rank C

POINTS AWARDED PER RANK (ABOVE)				
Rank	A	B	C	D
Points	25	20	15	10

TOTAL RANKING POINTS TABLE

RANK	S	A	B	C	D	E
Total	100	90	75	55	45	*2

*2 Any Below Rank D

JAKE

NORMAL DIFFICULTY

The walkthrough provided for Jake's Campaign has been simplified to pertain only to Normal difficulty mode, in single player, offline. Most of the strategies described herein pertain to using Jake's unique abilities. However, certain areas that are only accessible when playing as Sherry are described with special notes. The walkthrough does not account for changes due to gaming online with other players. Therefore it is recommended that you play as Jake during your first attempt at this campaign in order to follow this walkthrough more closely.

JAKE CHAPTER 1

DECEMBER 24, 2012

Edonia, Eastern Europe

Jake Muller is a mercenary hired by Neo Umbrella to take part in a battlefield experiment. He survives by injecting himself with the C-Virus, proving to Sherry Birkin that he possesses antibodies that fight the virus. Sherry accompanies Jake and provides assistance as they attempt to escape from Edonia.

THE SEWER

SEWER MAP

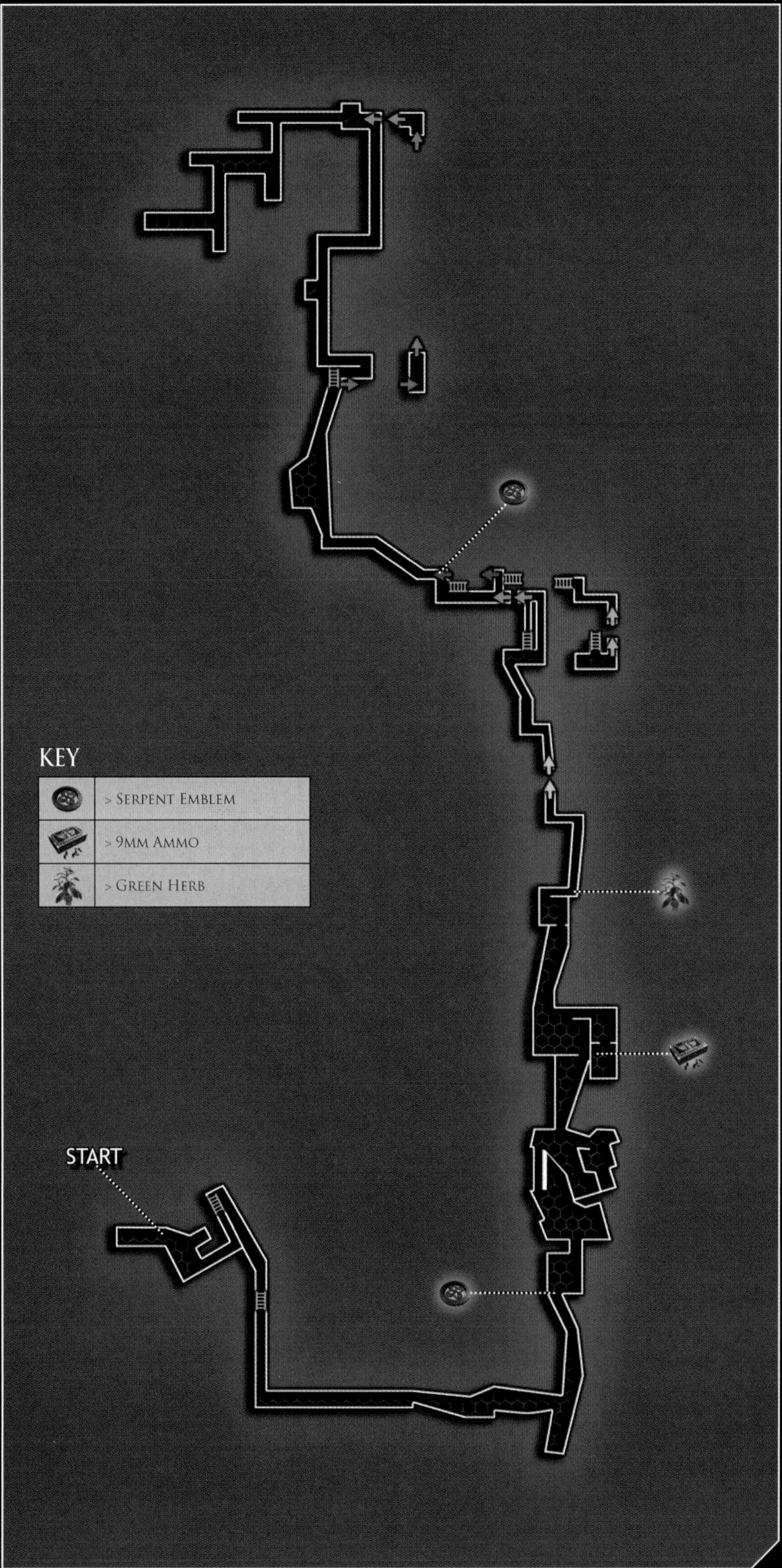

CLIMB OUT OF THE MUCK

Exit the tunnel into the main room, move right, and ascend the stairs. Turn left and run to the ladder. Press Action (⊗ on PlayStation 3, Ⓐ on Xbox 360) to climb the ladder. Follow the upper passage and climb another ladder out.

PARTNER UP

Through the windows directly ahead, infected J'avo engage the BSAA. Proceed directly through the corridor to avoid damage. The door at the end is locked and requires Jake and Sherry to work together to open it. Approach the door until the Partner Action button icon (◉ on PlayStation 3, Ⓑ on Xbox 360) appears onscreen. Press the button to initiate partner co-op action and open the door.

INTO THE FRAY

A BSAA helicopter hovers over the path ahead and sprays all targets with gunfire. Hold the Action button while moving to dash. Jake should take cover in the small niche to the left while Sherry takes cover to the right. Because Jake is dressed the same as the other J'avo, the helicopter occasionally targets and fires at both characters throughout this area. Wait behind cover for the helicopter to move off, then continue down the path and around the corner to the left.

FIND YOUR WAY WITH THE DIRECTIONAL BEACON

If you're ever unsure of where to go next, hold the left shoulder button (L1 on PlayStation3, LB on Xbox 360). A holographic arrow appears and shows the way.

SERPENT EMBLEM: OLD BUILDING

As you proceed down the path, look above the doorway of the building ahead to spot a **Serpent Emblem.** Shoot these to unlock additional content regarding Jake's campaign in the Collections screen of the Special Features menu. Four Serpent Emblems can be found in every chapter.

AMBUSH THE J'AVO

Proceed down the path and into the small building. Unaware of your presence, J'avo exit the other side. Move to the doorway, take cover on the left side by holding the Aim Weapon button (L2 on PlayStation 3, LT on Xbox 360), and fire on the J'avo in the courtyard outside. Take out the J'avo holding the rocket launcher first by aiming for his head. Then, take down the others. Since ammo is still extremely limited, run into the courtyard and stun one of the remaining enemies with a Quick Shot (L2 + R2 or LT + RT, simultaneously), then approach the stunned enemy and kick him to the ground by pressing Fire (R2 on PlayStation 3, RT on Xbox 360). While standing over the prone enemy, press Fire again to stomp his head in. Pick up any items dropped by defeated enemies and enter the small building off to the left side.

JAKE RULES BY FIST

Unlike the characters of other campaigns, you'll note that Jake Muller does not carry a combat knife for survival. As demonstrated in the opening movie, Jake is a better-than-average martial artist. Therefore you can conserve a lot of ammo and health throughout Jake's campaign by switching to his "Hand-to-Hand" when facing just one or two remaining foes. As with other weapons, hold the Aim button (L2 on PlayStation 3, LT on Xbox 360) to assume a fighting stance and tap Fire (R2 on PlayStation 3, RT on Xbox 360) to execute quick jabs, or hold the Fire button to perform a powerful uppercut that knocks down a J'avo immediately. Then, follow up by approaching the downed J'avo and throw him to take him out. If possible, try to throw one J'avo into others to knock them all down. However, like physical attacks, Jake's Hand-to-Hand uppercut and the follow-up throw consume stamina, which requires time to recharge. Therefore, you should stand still and rest for a few seconds in order to ready Jake for his next melee attack. However, this is not a good idea while under BSAA bombardment, so keep moving!

SHOCK 'EM, SHERRY!

Sherry Birkin also does not carry a survival knife like most characters. Instead, she carries the Stun Rod, which she can use to shock enemies by delivering an electric charge to the body. Hold the Ready/Aim button to raise the Stun Rod and press the Fire button to swing it. Continue to hold the Fire button to charge the rod for your next attack. Deliver an incapacitating charge that knocks an enemy to the ground. Then deal with other enemies or finish off the downed foe with a head stomp.

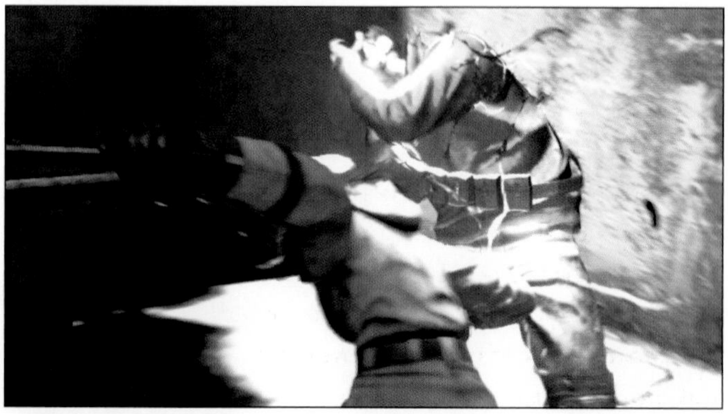

NAVIGATE THE WAR ZONE

Approach the window at the back of the small building. A J'avo toting a rocket launcher runs past the window. With extremely quick reflexes, you might be able to press the Fire button in time to take him down with a Stealth Hit. Otherwise, press the Action button to hop outside. Follow the J'avo to the right, but don't worry about taking him down. The BSAA will handle that for you.

The helicopter fires missiles into the area. Quickly drop over the low ledge and follow the dividing barrier back up the hill to the small building where the J'avo are emerging. If you ignore the enemies in the area, they will ignore Jake and attack the chopper. In turn, the chopper takes them all out for you. If you are caught in a missile blast, press Action as you land to get back up quickly. Run up the short hill and continue up the stairs into the building.

A CLOSE CALL

Proceeding into the building triggers a missile volley from the BSAA helicopter, destroying the structure and dropping Jake into a subterranean passage. Pick up the **9mm Ammo** on the chair to the left, and hop out the window to rejoin Sherry. Ascend the steps to the left and follow the path around the corner to the right. Drop from the ledge, move to the next door, and press the Partner Action button to open the door in unison with Sherry.

SMASH CRATES FOR ITEMS

After a short scene where Jake attempts to extort money from Sherry, approach the tall crates across from Jake's location and press the Fire button to smash them. Crates contain random items such as Green Herbs, Red Herbs, various ammo or Skill Points (in the form of Chess Pieces). Skill Points can be used to purchase Skills at the end of each Chapter, or between games.

WATCH YOUR STEP

Proceed through the doorway and head right to find a **Green Herb** at the corner. Approach the ledge cautiously, however, or Jake may topple over the side. If this happens, you'll have a brief opportunity to climb back up, which is accomplished by rotating the Left Stick rapidly. In Single mode, your partner will probably help you up. If your partner falls over the side, approach the ledge where they are hanging and press the Partner Action button to help them up. Thank your partner afterward—hold the Partner Action button to display a list of partner commands, and press one of the other buttons shown to interact with your follower.

STEALTH HITS

Continue along the ledge until Jake spots J'avo patrolling the area ahead. Move down the path and directly up behind the first enemy while his back is turned. Press the Fire button to instantly eliminate the unwary enemy with a Stealth Hit. Stick around only long enough to pick up whatever item he may drop, then move to the ledge and press Action to leap across. Use a Quick Shot to knock the next J'avo off balance, then knock him over the side with a physical attack. Run along the curving ledge and take out another J'avo in the same fashion.

TAKEDOWNS THROUGH WINDOWS

Peek around the next corner to spot a J'avo standing inside the building. Tilt the Left Stick slightly to creep up behind the unwary foe until the Fire button icon appears onscreen, then press the button to execute a stealthy takedown. Continue around the corner to the left.

CREATE A PATH FOR SHERRY

Press Action at the edge to perform an acrobatic pole swing across the chasm. Sherry cannot follow Jake and shouts that she'll use the lower route. However, she cannot make it without Jake's help. Smash the crates near Jake's landing point to obtain items, then jump across the next gap and dash across the crumbling ledge. Climb up the ladder at the corner, then turn around and go back to a raised emergency ladder. Kick the emergency ladder down, drop down, then move into the niche on the left and face the opening to pull Sherry up to your level via Partner Action. Climb the emergency ladder, move to the next ledge and drop back down, and then cross the bridge to the exit. Use a Partner Action to open the door together.

TAKE THE LOWER ROUTE

Sherry cannot swing across long gaps or chasms using horizontal poles the way Jake can. So as he leaps across, hop through either window into the small guarded structure. Drop through the hole in the floor to the lower level, and go through the doorway to the exterior ledge. Follow the ledge to the left, jump the gap, and dash around the corner. Take out the J'avo positioned here and approach the ladder. When the Partner Action button icon appears, press the Partner Action button to make Jake pull you up to his level. Smash the tall crates to the left and jump the crumbling gap and cross the bridge.

SERPENT EMBLEM: DAMAGED BEAM

After climbing to the uppermost level, before the wooden bridge, turn to the right and notice the **Serpent Emblem** resting on the front side of the damaged vertical beam that is connected to the bridge.

TAKE COVER AND RETURN FIRE

Follow the passage around the corner. You'll spot a squad of J'avo waiting in ambush down the slope to the right. Use the sandbags to take cover and return fire. To take cover, stand against a sandbag, hold the Ready Weapon button, and then press Action to crouch behind cover. From this position, you can move the Left Stick to pop out and aim. Release the Left Stick to resume cover. Eliminate the J'avo firing from the higher ledge first, then dash down the slope and leap over the barricade. Take down the remaining foes with Quick Shots followed by physical combos. Do not attempt to shoot every enemy from a distance or you'll run out of ammo.

SHERRY CREATES THE PATH

When the area is clear, move to the corner and initiate a Partner Action to hoist Sherry to the level above. In turn, she knocks down a horizontal pole that Jake can use to leap the chasm to the right. Press Action to jump the gap, then dash across the crumbling path to the next corner.

FIGHT THROUGH THE CORRIDOR

After taking down the J'avo guarding the barricade, move to the bottom of the ledge. When the button icon appears, press the Partner Action button to make Jake hoist Sherry up to the ledge. Move down the ledge a bit and press the Action button to kick down a horizontal pole so Jake can cross the area below.

Proceed around the corner, drop down, and dash up the corridor to fight several J'avo guarding a few item crates. More J'avo drop from the ceiling when the first few are defeated. If you are having trouble taking out the J'avo with Sherry alone, race past them to the end of the corridor and rejoin Jake for easier corridor clearing, crate smashing, and item collection.

UNDER THE GUN

The BSAA helicopter flies up to Jake's area and begins chasing him with gunfire. Hold Action while running along the ledge to leap gaps and climb ledges automatically.

When you cross the second segment, the camera swings to the left to show you the helicopter, then it returns to normal view after you jump the next gap.

EXPLORE YOUR PARTNER'S PATH FOR ITEMS

Ascend the stairs, turn left, and jump the gap by swinging from the horizontal pole. Here you'll rejoin Sherry. Move past her and go upstairs to explore the area she passed through. A few item crates are found along this path, as well as a few J'avo that Sherry obviously left alive. Follow the path back to the stairs and the point where you reunited with Sherry and continue.

DASH THROUGH THE TURRET TRAP

Open the door with a Partner Action. A J'avo takes control of the machine-gun turret at the next corner. Dash quickly through the area and turn left at the first junction. Another manned machine-gun turret is directly ahead, so dash through and take the first corner on the right. A great number of J'avo begin flooding the area to fight, so avoid combat and run through. Take the next left, dash toward the last gun turret, and move through the doorway to the right to exit the area. Press the right shoulder button (R1 on PlayStation 3, RB on Xbox 360) to heal up if necessary, then open the large metal doors with a Partner Action.

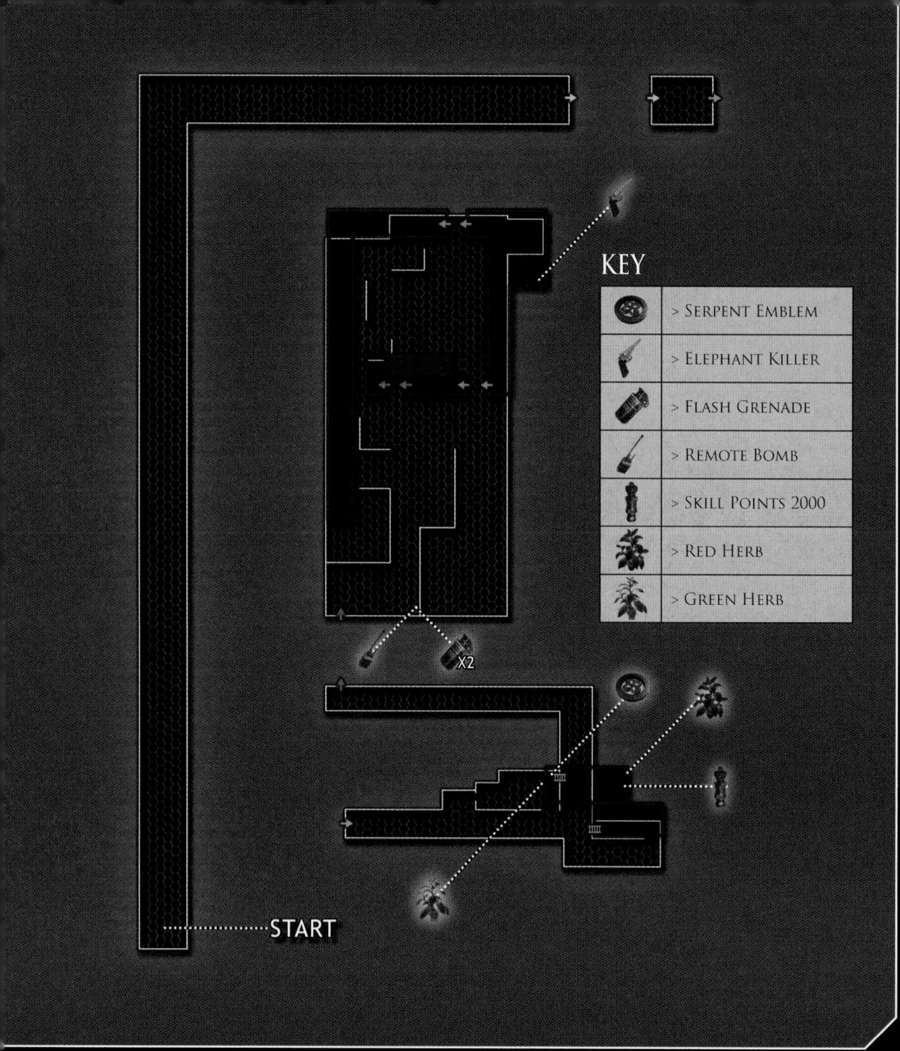

TIME FOR A PIT STOP

Move up the corridor and move to the left into a small bathroom. Take out a J'avo patrolling this area with a Quick Shot followed by a physical attack and head stomp. Grab the **Green Herb** in the corner.

SERPENT EMBLEM: EXPOSED CEILING COMPARTMENT

This Serpent Emblem can only be found when playing as Sherry. At the same corner where the Green Herb is located, press the Partner Action button—as indicated by the onscreen icon—to make Jake hoist Sherry to the upper level. Turn around to find a **Serpent Emblem** hidden on the upper level. This area also features a couple of crates to smash and a **Red Herb**, which is only available for Sherry.

FLEE FROM USTANAK

A large monster called Ustanak begins chasing Sherry and Jake. Hold Action to dash away from the monster while guiding your character using the Left Stick. When the camera angle changes to behind Jake and Sherry, run toward the ledge and jump off. Jake lands on a wooden scaffold, and Ustanak lands behind him. Run to the ledge and press the Partner Action button to tackle Sherry and dive through a window into the next building. When playing as Sherry, there is nothing to do. Once inside you're safe from the tenacious Ustanak, but only for the time being.

THE LURKER IN THE BASEMENT

Exit the bathroom, head left, and then go right to locate a crate on a shelf, next to a door. Smash the crate to obtain an item and press Action to open the door normally or press Action twice quickly to kick it open. Smash another crate on the shelves in the back corner, then turn around and drop down the ladder to the level below. Take out a single J'avo waiting in ambush, then smash three more crates in the basement to obtain other items. Climb out and follow the corridor to the exit. Open the door via Partner Action.

SEARCH THE CRUMBLING WAREHOUSE

Jake and Sherry enter a large warehouse that appears to be crumbling in on itself. Follow the railing down to the left and drop off the edge. Smash the crate opposite your landing point to reveal an item, then turn to the right and move to the other corner to find a briefcase on shelves. Open the briefcase to find **Flash Grenades x2** and a **Remote Bomb**. When ready, move to the exit and use a Partner Action to open it.

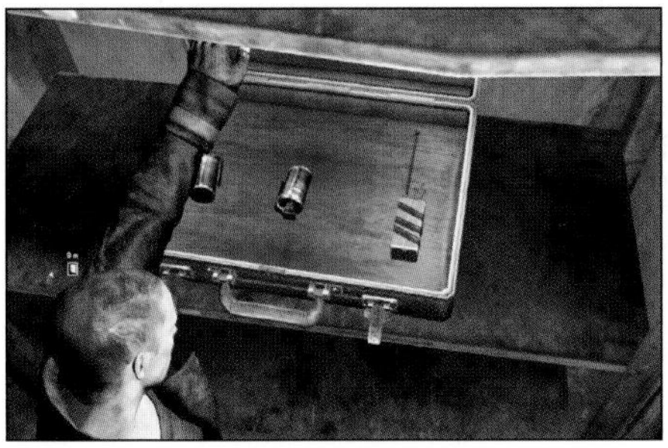

J'avo blow through the warehouse roof and rope down from above. Wait until all three enemies land on the ground. Now, shoot the red exploding barrel off to the right to take them all out instantly. Finish off any stragglers and collect any dropped items.

Search the warehouse for crates and items, including the **Elephant Killer** pistol on the upper level. Knock down any emergency ladders pulled to the upper level. When you are finished searching the area, drop to the lower level and approach the exit. Perform a Partner Action at the marked exit.

SAVE THOSE EXPLODING BARRELS... AND THE ELEPHANT KILLER

Avoid using the Elephant Killer against any of the J'avo present. You should also avoid shooting any of the other exploding barrels in the warehouse. You'll soon see why this is recommended...

USTANAK (WAREHOUSE)

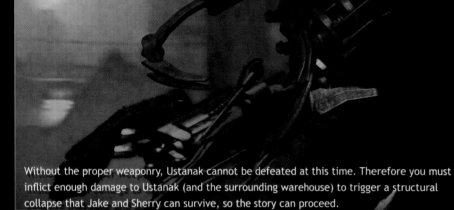

Without the proper weaponry, Ustanak cannot be defeated at this time. Therefore you must inflict enough damage to Ustanak (and the surrounding warehouse) to trigger a structural collapse that Jake and Sherry can survive, so the story can proceed.

At the outset of the battle, Ustanak charges toward the exit doors. Dash out of its path, then stop, turn around, and shoot the exploding barrel next to the doors. Ustanak staggers in pain. Equip the Elephant Killer and fire all five rounds into its head, slowly, one shot at a time, waiting for the monster to recover and straighten up slightly following each shot. Spend the remaining time baiting Ustanak toward the remaining barrels around the warehouse. When the monster and J'avo surround a red barrel, shoot the object to inflict damage to Ustanak and wipe out the J'avo. Quickly pick up dropped items on the run.

J'avo sidekicks appear in the warehouse throughout the encounter. Killing them only triggers the appearance of reinforcements. Try to ignore the J'avo as best you can. Detonating the exploding barrels and other traps will take out most of the minor enemies as collateral damage, leaving a bevy of items and Skill Point pieces to pick up afterward.

If the lower level becomes too difficult, or if too many J'avo interfere with your work, ascend the central stairs to the upper level. More exploding barrels dot the higher paths, so use them to damage Ustanak.

Remote Bombs provide another way to damage the creature. Equip one of these by pressing up or down on the D-pad, then face Ustanak. Press Aim to set the bomb, then wait for the monster to spot Jake and hunker down for a dash attack. Run to the left or right to avoid Ustanak, then press Aim + Fire to detonate the Remote Bomb while the beast is standing on it.

Ustanak may occasionally cover his face with his hand and shake his head as if dazed. During this state, you may approach and kick Ustanak with a physical attack. However, the monster recovers quickly, so don't put yourself at risk by going for the free shot. Flash Grenades detonated directly in front of Ustanak will bring it to this state immediately, allowing for a follow-up attack.

As far as Ustanak's attacks go, he mainly dashes toward Jake and knocks him over. At close range, he attempts to snatch Jake or Sherry in his metal claw and impale his captive several times. You must then rotate the Left Stick to break free. Likewise, if you see your partner in this predicament, approach Ustanak's front side and perform physical kicks to his knee until he drops your partner. The creature may also throw small grenades that soon detonate, canceling your attack pose and inflicting medium damage. However, this battle can be won by detonating three to five barrels very close to Ustanak and also through wise use of the Elephant Killer and any Remote Bombs that you may have on hand.

UNDERGROUND PASSAGE

UNDERGROUND PASSAGE MAP

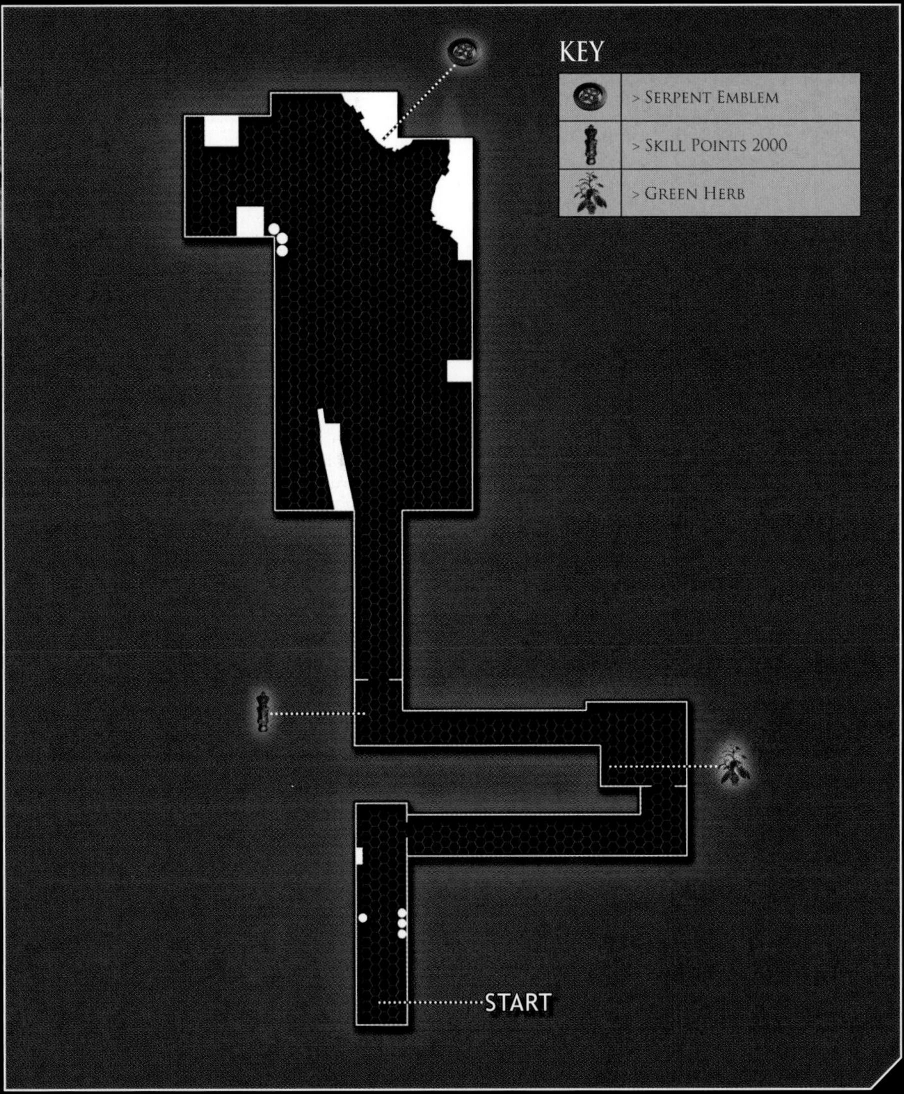

SERPENT EMBLEM: CONNECTED COURTYARD RUINS

Upon emerging from the dark underground passage, look high on the wall directly ahead to spot a **Serpent Emblem**, just above ground level. Shoot it from a safe distance, since J'avo guards are standing to the far left.

WELCOME RESPITE

Follow the hallway. Smash a low crate at the first corner to obtain an item and continue through the doorway to the right. Jake and Sherry automatically turn on flashlights to illuminate dark areas. Proceed to the next corner and smash a tall crate, then go left into the next corridor. Turn to your left in the mannequin area to spot a **Green Herb** on the shelves. Smash another low crate at the next corner. When you approach the exit ladder, open the metal trunk on the left to obtain **Skill Points (2,000)**. Climb the ladder to travel to the outdoors.

TWO TO TAKE DOWN

Proceed further into the courtyard, move to the left wall, and follow it to the end. Take cover behind the crates at the corner and move to the edge in order to spot the two J'avo standing guard in front of the exit gate. Throw a Flash Grenade if one is available, then switch to Hand-to-Hand and rush in to perform two quick takedowns while the guards are blind. Hold the Aim + Fire buttons to perform an uppercut. Then approach knocked-down enemies and press Fire to grab their legs and hurl them. Move to the exit gate and initiate a Partner Action to open it.

IN FRONT OF CITY HALL

IN FRONT OF CITY HALL MAP

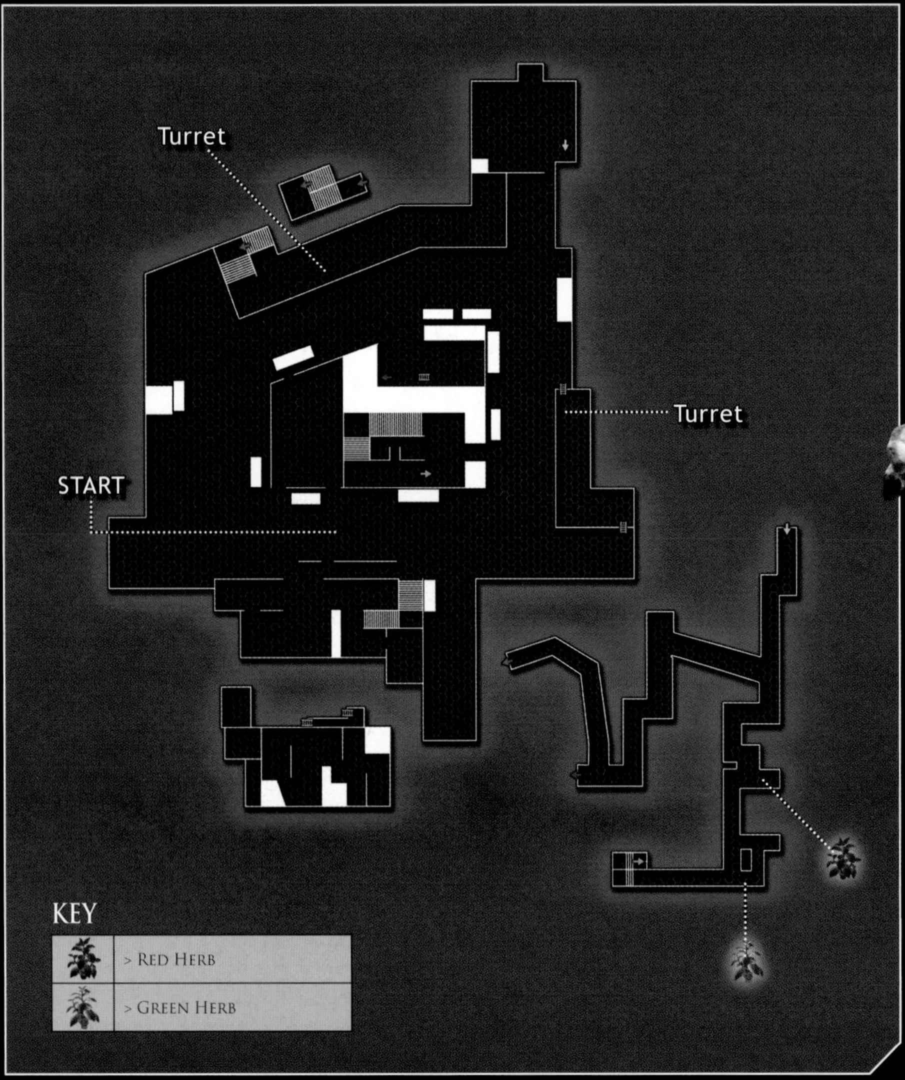

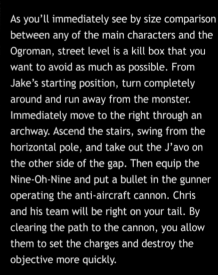

CHRISTMAS EVE CROSSOVER!

Jake and Sherry join forces with Chris Redfield and Piers Nivans to fight giant B.O.W.s in a ruined downtown area. Those who've played Chris's Campaign previously will no doubt be familiar with the objectives and methods for killing each Ogroman, but we'll repeat a large portion of the information here for convenience.

As you'll immediately see by size comparison between any of the main characters and the Ogroman, street level is a kill box that you want to avoid as much as possible. From Jake's starting position, turn completely around and run away from the monster. Immediately move to the right through an archway. Ascend the stairs, swing from the horizontal pole, and take out the J'avo on the other side of the gap. Then equip the Nine-Oh-Nine and put a bullet in the gunner operating the anti-aircraft cannon. Chris and his team will be right on your tail. By clearing the path to the cannon, you allow them to set the charges and destroy the objective more quickly.

OGROMAN (x2)

Meanwhile, you must now deal with an Ogroman and an endless stream of J'avo emanating from a hole in the ceiling in the backroom. Kill J'avo to restock with dropped items. The backroom also has several crates you can break for additional supplies. Ignore the J'avo unless they attack you or the soldier placing charges.

Aim for the Ogroman's soft tissue umbilical, which the helicopter accidentally pulled out of his back. This is its weakest spot; the face is also a weak point, but not to the same degree. By shooting the umbilical or face, you may cause the monster to stagger and lean against the building. When this happens, quickly approach the creature's elbow resting on the edge and press the Fire button to initiate a Quick Time Event where Jake leaps onto the Ogroman's shoulder and begins twisting a large bone protrusion out of its back. To succeed, tap the Action button rapidly to fill the onscreen gauge before the timer reaches the left side. Good controller technique for this requires lifting your left hand off the controller and tapping the Action button rapidly with your left forefinger, taking care to lift your pointer only the minimum amount off the button between every tap. Doing so causes Jake to impale the monster with its own bone, inflicting massive damage. Jake then drops to the street, where you should seek shelter or higher ground. Failure to rip the bone out in time allows the giant monster to seize and crush Jake. You can escape this attack by rotating the Left Stick rapidly.

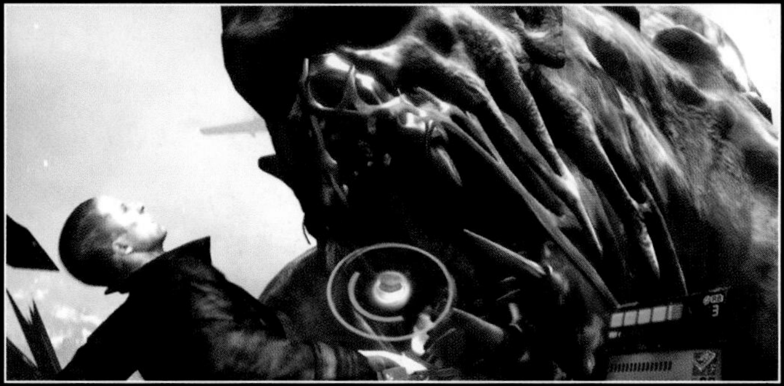

The second anti-aircraft cannon is located atop an old church tower in the center of the area. While Chris and his team break into the building, provide them with some cover. Dash past the church tower to the very top end of the street. You'll find a ladder connected to a balcony where J'avo fire upon the heroes. Climb the ladder, kill the J'avo, and take control of one of the gun turrets by holding the Aim button. Rotate the turret using the Left Stick and hold the Fire button to shoot.

Try to target and hit the Ogroman's exposed umbilical enough times to make it lean against the building, allowing for another QTE attack. However, should the Ogroman reach the turret, he will rear back and smash it with his fist, and you don't want to be standing there when he does.

Once Chris's team has blown the door on the tower across the street, go inside and help them fight the J'avo descending the stairs. Smash crates on the ground floor, then ascend the stairs, and climb the ladder to reach the roof.

Shoot the two J'avo manning the anti-aircraft cannon, then protect the team while they set up charges on the cannon. To do this effectively, you must fight enemies from two sides—endless J'avo drop from a high ledge at the back of the rooftop before the cannon is destroyed; occasionally the Ogroman climbs up the side of the building and begins swatting at the soldiers. The teammate planting the charges will stop working in order to drive away the Ogroman. Therefore, prioritize shooting the Ogroman in its weak spot to make it climb down from the building. As a result, the bombardier can resume setting charges as quickly as possible. Take down J'avo quickly with a Hand-to-Hand uppercut followed by a full-body toss, hopefully into other J'avo.

at some point you should kill the first Ogroman, it will melt into a large pile of toxic goo that you should avoid for a while. Once the material dissipates, search the area where it died to find **Skill Points (4,000)**.

Whether or not the first Ogroman is dead, a second one appears after the tower anti-aircraft cannon has been taken out. The second Ogroman's back umbilical is not pulled out and exposed like the first one. Do not shoot at the second Ogroman until the first is dead.

When the tower cannon is destroyed, climb back down through the ceiling hole and descend the stairs. Collect any Skill Point prizes that may be in the street from killing the first Ogroman. Follow the soldiers underground by dropping through the ground floor hatch into a subterranean tunnel. Chris and his team tend to pave the way while you can explore and smash crates for items. Don't miss the **Green Herb** sitting inside the exposed drain pipe at the first corner. Continuing to follow the soldiers, you'll find more items and crates, such as a **Red Herb** and items dropped by defeated enemies.

Although you eventually reach a ladder mounted in concrete, don't climb it. Instead, turn right and follow a short dirt tunnel to another ladder. This is where the soldiers went. Climb the ladder, ascend the stairs, and cross the exposed upper level. J'avo snipers fire from the church tower rooftop, but luckily there is a gun turret nearby that you can use to kill them and fire on the Ogroman. Just remember that if the Ogroman reaches the gun turret, he will smash it. Jake and Sherry shouldn't be anywhere near the turret when that happens.

Since the second Ogroman's umbilical is not exposed, shoot its head until it covers its face in pain and leans against the building. Then run out onto its shoulders and rapidly rotate the Left Stick to pull out its umbilical. The timer hand moves quickly, and you'll find it hard to beat, so try this little trick with the controller: release the controller with your left hand, pinch the Left Stick with all the fingers of your left hand, and then rotate it as rapidly as possible. You'll get more rotations per second this way and yank the umbilical out easily. Upon dropping to the street, dash away from the Ogroman quickly so the air strike can commence!

INSIDE THE HELICOPTER

QUITE A RIDE!

Although they are safe on board a helicopter and already well on their way out of danger, things suddenly take an unexpected turn for Sherry and Jake when a familiar face reappears.

USTANAK (HELICOPTERS)

Run to the front of the compartment to find **9mm Ammo x2** and a **First Aid Spray**. Reload your Nine-Oh-Nine and stay near the cockpit, facing the back. Soon Ustanak smashes through one of the bulkhead doors. Look for the red targeting marker to determine where Ustanak is about to break through and avoid that area. In emergencies, remember to leap away from the creature by pressing the Aim button while walking backwards. Then lay on the ground and fire until it withdraws. Once Ustanak has a door off, it leans inside and attempts to grab Jake. Avoid its metal claw swipes and pop a few shots into its head to drive it away. Otherwise, if it's allowed to hang from the hull without resistance, Ustanak will cause the helicopter to crash. Reload your weapon each time it vanishes. Also watch out for any grenades it tosses into the cockpit or cabin and avoid any explosions.

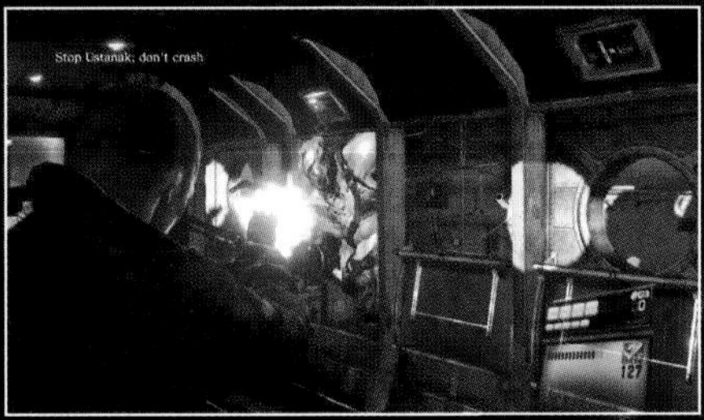

As the damage to the helicopter intensifies, you must avoid standing near the smoking cockpit area. Otherwise, Jake and Sherry will be too choked up to fire on Ustanak.

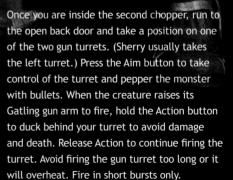

Eventually, the commander orders you to jump to the next chopper. Dash to the front side door and press the Partner Action button to fling Sherry across. Then face the doorway and press Action to leap over. Jake winds up missing slightly and hangs out the helicopter doorway. Quickly rotate the Left Stick to climb up into the cabin before Ustanak kills Jake with Gatling gun fire. When you are playing as Sherry, approach the open cabin door while Jake hangs and press the Partner Action button to lift him up.

Once you are inside the second chopper, run to the open back door and take a position on one of the two gun turrets. (Sherry usually takes the left turret.) Press the Aim button to take control of the turret and pepper the monster with bullets. When the creature raises its Gatling gun arm to fire, hold the Action button to duck behind your turret to avoid damage and death. Release Action to continue firing the turret. Avoid firing the gun turret too long or it will overheat. Fire in short bursts only.

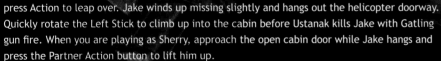

Shooting Ustanak alone is not enough to win this second leg of the battle. However, firing on Ustanak is useful because it makes the creature cover itself in defense rather than return fire. Meanwhile, focus the majority of your bullets on the three choppers flying behind yours and take out any homing missiles they fire. Each chopper displays two stages of damage before it falls from the sky—burning and *really* burning. Shoot each of the choppers until they are burning, then shoot each of them again until they are *really* burning. You must shoot strategically to bring down all three choppers quickly: shoot down the two side choppers first, and then shoot down the chopper where Ustanak is hanging. Any deviation from this strategy allows Ustanak to leap from chopper to chopper while replacement choppers fly into formation, potentially stretching the time of the battle to lengths that you cannot survive.

When you shoot down Ustanak's chopper, it collides with yours, causing Jake and Sherry to fall to the ground and slide toward the hatch. Aim for the gas tank near Ustanak and shoot it to blow the creature off the back end. As Jake and Sherry slide out of the chopper, press the Action button swiftly before the timer expires to grab a parachute and bail out. The strategy is the same when you are playing through the campaign as Sherry.

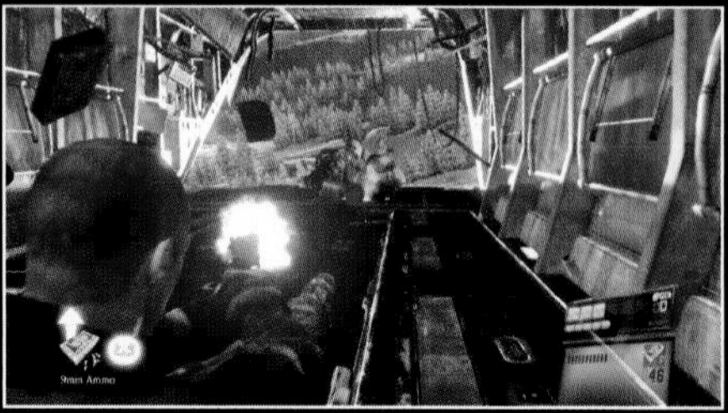

CHAPTER RANKING

As in the other campaigns, the player is awarded a rank for prowess in four criteria regardless of difficulty selected: hit accuracy percentage, player deaths suffered, total clear time, and number of enemies defeated. For each letter grade rank obtained, a specific number of points are awarded as determined by the "Points Awarded Per Rank" table. These points are then added together to determine an overall rank for the chapter as determined by the "Total Ranking Points Table," with S being a perfect score, requiring A ranking for all four criteria.

JAKE CHAPTER 1: RANKING CRITERIA

RANK	ACCURACY(%)	DEATHS	CLEAR TIME(MIN)	ENEMIES ROUTED
A	70	2	60	40
B	60	5	85	30
C	50	7	105	20
D	*1	*1	*1	*1

*1 Any Below Rank C

POINTS AWARDED PER RANK (ABOVE)				
Rank	A	B	C	D
Points	25	20	15	10

TOTAL RANKING POINTS TABLE

RANK	S	A	B	C	D	E
Total	100	90	75	55	45	*2

MOUNTAIN PATH

MOUNTAIN PATH MAP

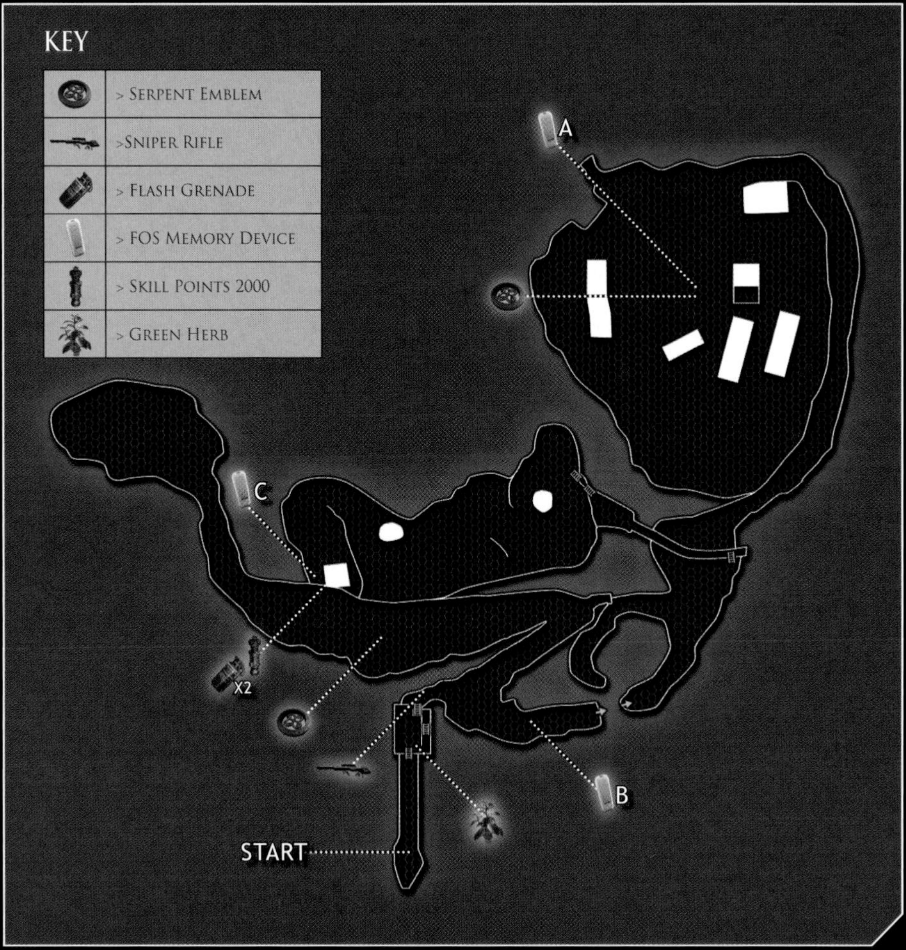

SNOW BLIND

Jake and Sherry must explore the mountainous area where their plane crashed, find three scattered memory units that Sherry lost in the recent chaos, and seek shelter from wintery weather conditions. Proceed uphill along the path and climb the tall ladder. Jake and Sherry spot a cabin some distance away where they might be able to seek shelter.

WHITEOUTS WILL HAPPEN

The unstable weather sometimes reduces visibility to just a few yards. Luckily, a mini-map appears in the upper-right corner of the screen until you reach the cabin. Refer to this mini-map to determine the lay of the land and where the lost memory units are located.

SOMEONE LEFT YOU PRESENTS...

Pick up the **Green Herb** at the top of the stairs hanging over the side of the rise and combine it with any herbs left in your inventory. Descend the stairs and drop to the level below. Head to the left past the next ladder and stomp a wooden barrel to reveal an item. Then, drop from the platform.

Directly across from the drop point, you'll find supplies on some stacked wood covered with a tarp, including three item crates to smash and the **Sniper Rifle**.

Refer to the mini-map to get your bearings. For navigational purposes, the top of the mini-map will be north. Head east from the Sniper Rifle location and follow the northeast path. The southeast path leads to a dead end, so avoid it.

BIRTH OF MESETS

Eventually you'll arrive at what remains of an old wooden bridge with J'avo chrysalid cocoons nearby. Giant winged creatures called Mesets break free of the chrysalids and attack. Quickly arm yourself with a Flash Grenade (press up or down on the D-pad) and toss it at the cocoon's location before the flying monsters disperse around the area. The flash kills them both easily. These monsters typically drop **Skill Point (500)** treasures.

THE CLOSEST MEMORY DEVICE ISN'T THAT CLOSE

Move to the edge of the wooden platform and jump off. Upon landing on the path below, you won't be able to climb back up. Turn right, follow the curved path southeast, and continue south. Look for a little broken bridge that Jake can still leap across. Quickly dash west up the slope and search near the tree at the top to find **FOS Memory Device B**. Dashing up the slope allows you to stay ahead of some J'avo sentries that will pick up your trail at this point. You'll have to fight them in order to return to the main path to the north. Use Jake's Hand-to-Hand skills as much as possible to conserve ammo.

Jump back across the little broken bridge and start to follow the northeast path. Just a short way up the hill, you may spot a sniper's laser sight piercing the darkness, depending on whiteout conditions. Equip your Sniper Rifle and shoot the opposing snipers in the head before they spot you or Sherry. Use the Sniper Rifle to take down other enemies that charge down the slopes from the northeast. J'avo keep appearing until you reach a raised mine cart railway that is accessible by a ladder. Kill the J'avo snipers around the base of the ladder but do not climb up. Nothing worthwhile is up there, but remember this ladder for later. Smash the barrels around the ladder for supplies. Do not linger at the ladder; fight your way up the northeast slope. Dash at J'avo and slide into them to knock them down, creating an advantage.

ONE TALL ICY SLOPE

Nearing the top of the long east slope, you may hear an engine revving up ahead. By looking through the sniper scope you may spot a J'avo piloting a snowmobile. He rides around quite a bit, making him a difficult target. One of the surest ways to knock him off the snowmobile is by shooting him with your Nine-Oh-Nine as he approaches, either by aiming or with a Quick Shot. However, with bad timing or positioning, the shot is extremely tricky to gauge, and this strategy may allow the pilotless snowmobile to run you over. If successful, you can hop on the snowmobile and pilot it to the top of the slope. Another sniper may be waiting at the top on your left. Suffering a sniper shot here may cause you to slide all the way down the slope.

ONE SLIPPERY SLOPE

You may have noticed that the northeast slope is extremely icy. Falling on this slope at any point may cause Jake and Sherry to slide all the way to the bottom. If you fall into an unstoppable slide, angle your camera downward and use the Left Stick to steer Jake away from damaging rocks and trees.

ANOTHER MEMORY DEVICE FOUND

After reaching the top of the long, icy slope, head southwest across a wide snow-covered timber yard. Another J'avo on snowmobile patrols this area, so prepare to knock him from his ride. Follow the closest memory unit marker to the center of the area. Inside a fenced area you'll find **FOS Memory Device A** near a parked construction crane. Smash the item barrels around the area to resupply.

SERPENT EMBLEM: TIMBER YARD CRANE

Find the crane near the center of the snow-covered timber yard area. Move to the driver's side of the crane and look at the operator's seat to easily spot a **Serpent Emblem**.

THE SHACK ACROSS THE BRIDGE

Head southwest across the timber yard to find a rickety wooden bridge across the gorge. Cross the bridge and stick to the north wall as you proceed west; item crates lie along this wall. Continue to follow the north wall until you reach the west end. Ascend the slope and follow the ledge south to locate a small shack (not the cabin seen previously) housing several item barrels and item crates. Open the silver case in the corner to obtain **Skill Points (4,000)** and **Flash Grenades x2**. The last **FOS Memory Device C** lies outside the hut. Taking the device causes the chrysalid cocoon below the ledge to hatch, releasing a Mesets. Toss a Flash Grenade at the edge of the raised level to blind and kill the Mesets instantly.

SERPENT EMBLEM: RADIO TOWER

After locating the last FOS Memory Device on the western rise, turn south and look at the radio tower rising from the level below. At the top of the tower you'll spot a **Serpent Emblem**. Shoot it with either your Nine-Oh-Nine or the Sniper Rifle.

RETURN TO THE MINE CART RAIL

Go back across the wooden bridge to the timber yard and follow the road to the northeast. Either dash down the long, icy slope or walk backward and press Ready/Aim Weapon to leap onto your back and slide down to the bottom without hitting any rocks or trees. Return to the ladder attached to the raised mine cart rails and climb it.

SLIDE THROUGH THE CAVE

Follow the mine cart rail until you reach a small mountain. Smash the item barrel to the right. Here you will find a small opening that Jake can crawl into at the base of the rock wall. Climbing in, Jake enters a slide. Sliding through the tunnel takes you back to the starting point. During the slide, you might be able to pick up a **Green Herb** and a **Red Herb**. Simply tap the Pickup button rapidly while sliding.

TO THE TOWER, AND THE CABIN BEYOND

After Jake and Sherry recover from the hard fall, head up the northeast path once again. Upon reaching the area where the chrysalid cocoons broke open (near the drop off point), turn around and follow the northwest slope up to the base of the radio tower. Continue dashing past the radio tower and up the northwest slope to a gate. When approaching the cocoon near the gate, equip Flash Grenades and blind-kill the hatchling Mesets. Move to the gate and initiate Partner Action to enter the cabin.

SNOW-COVERED MOUNTAIN MAP

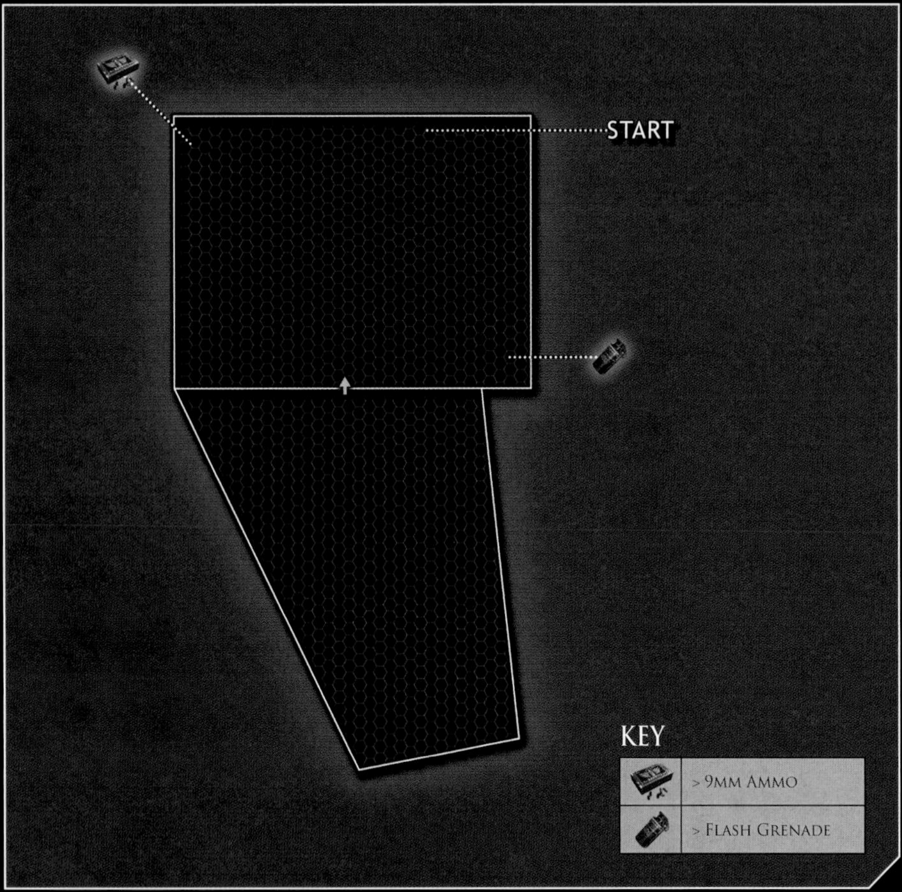

CABIN STANDOFF!

The cabin is surrounded by dozens of J'avo. Fortunately, most of them try to make their way into the cabin by the same window, so you can pick them off as they come through. Shoot them outside the window as well.

Adapting quickly, some of the J'avo climb up on the cabin rooftop and drop inside. Move behind the central table. Stay near Sherry and assist her in taking down J'avo with Partner Attacks. Reload with **9mm Ammo** that is located on a workbench to the side.

After a short duration, or after you've killed a large number of the J'avo, they become smarter and decide to breach the back wall of the cabin. Move to the side of the central table opposite the new breach point and press Action to kick over the table, creating makeshift cover against the shooters outside. Toss a Flash Grenade between you and the breached wall, turn your camera away to avoid the glare, and kick down all the stunned J'avo before they recover their sight. Head stomp the last one down, then shoot the others as they try to rise.

AVALANCHE!

As soon as possible, exit the cabin via the breached wall. An avalanche begins, either when you step out or after a short duration following the wall breach. You have approximately 30 seconds to run out of the cabin and board one of the two snowmobiles waiting outside before a wall of snow and ice kills you instantly. Pick up any dropped items on the run and don't risk going back for anything missed. Press the Partner Action button to board the snowmobile.

The Fire button is the accelerator and the Ready/Aim Weapon button is the brakes. Avoid the avalanche behind you by holding the accelerator button down until you come to any sharp curve. When there is a curve ahead, you should be ready to tap and release the brakes to help navigate it before accelerating again.

OUTRUN THE AVALANCHE

1

Pick up items along the path while driving, such as Skill Points (100) and Skill Points (300). Rapidly tap the Pickup button while driving to collect these.

2

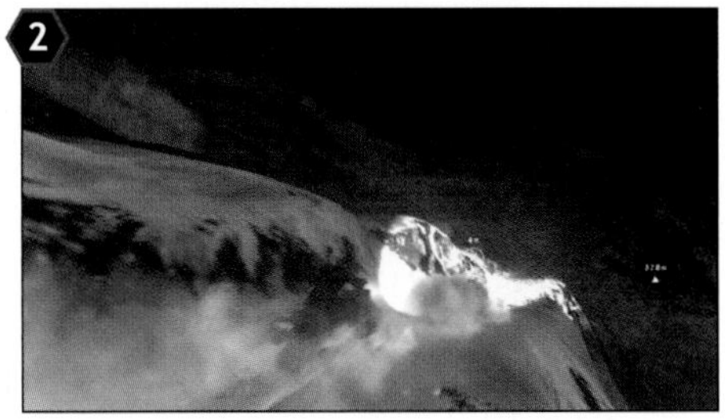

When the camera moves out to the side to show the avalanche is now on Jake and Sherry's left, you must avoid steering off the side of the slope—this causes instant death.

3

Sherry warns you to veer right as the avalanche slides down from the left. Follow her partner marker if you're too far behind.

4

After a low jump, you'll drive into a field full of trees. Veer to the left to avoid an avalanche coming from the right.

5

Navigate through the trees by veering slightly left or right, but avoid making sharp turns.

6

As the trees get thicker and harder to avoid, another avalanche slides in from the left. Steer to the right to outrun it. Tap the Pickup button to collect more Skill Points (300) near certain trees in the area.

7

Past the tree fields you'll hit a frozen river, which can bounce you around and slow you down a bit. Hold the accelerator to get over the frozen rapids while steering to the right to avoid the avalanche.

8

*Beyond the frozen ledges, as soon as the ground is smooth again, steer to the far right to hit a **Serpent Emblem** on the way down.*

9

Entering a tunnel, repeatedly tap the Pickup button to collect three Skill Points (300) just inside the entrance.

10

Emerging from the tunnel and making a short drop, you must now navigate an ice field that is breaking up. Steer left and then sharply to the right while accelerating.

11

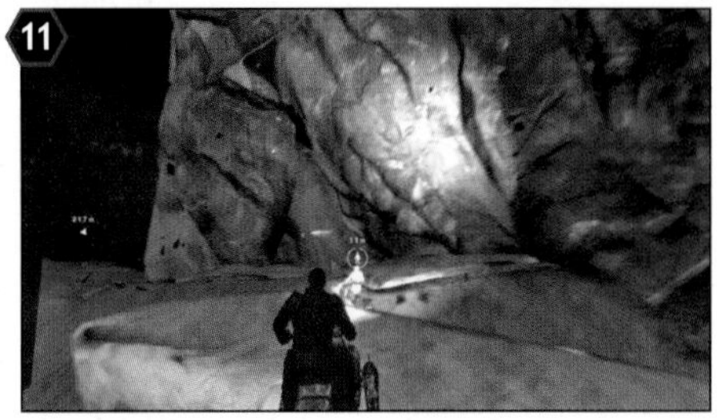

Brake when a massive wall of ice rises directly ahead, steer left, and accelerate into the end of the turn.

12

Continue accelerating off the ledge directly ahead. Press the Action button before the timer elapses to finally reach safety.

SERPENT EMBLEM: AVALANCHE ESCAPE ROUTE

The **Serpent Emblem** mentioned above can only be hit by sticking to the right side of the route and then veering to the right at the correct moment.

CAVE

CAVE MAP

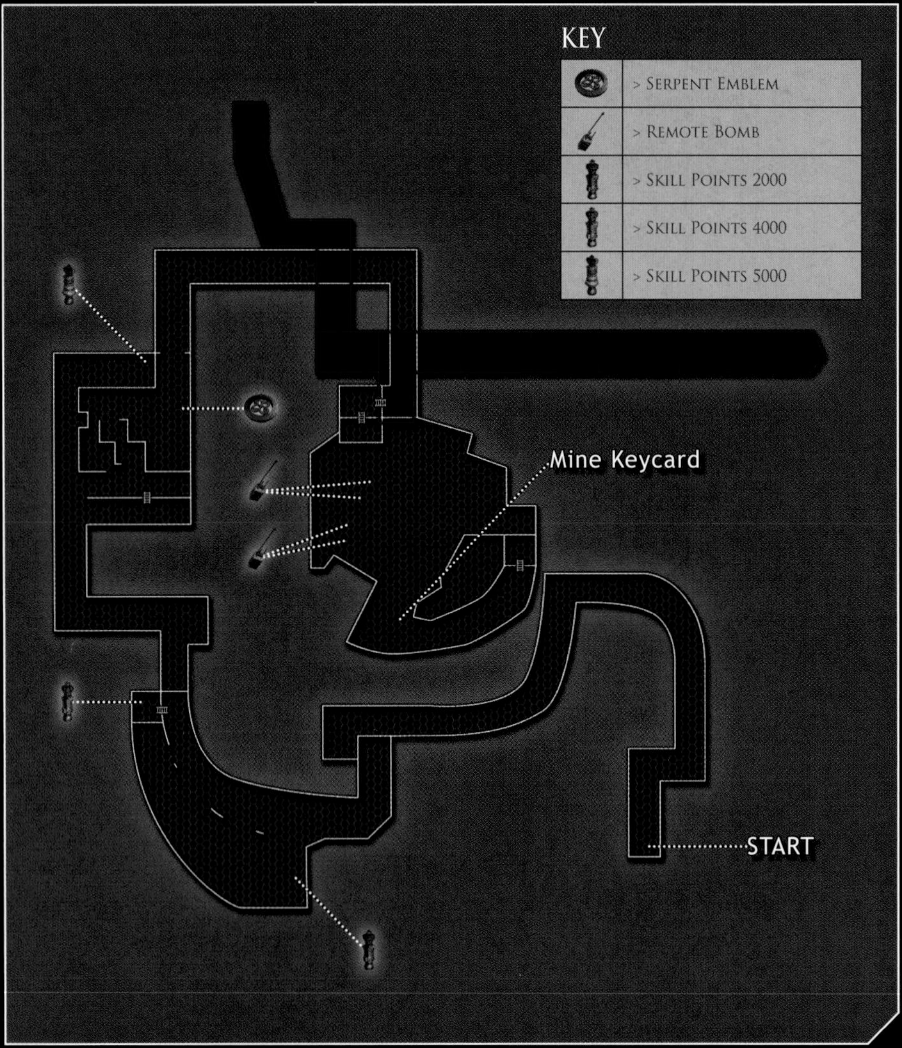

CRUNCHY FLOORS

Following the avalanche, Jake and Sherry appear to be trapped in an old mine and must follow the tunnels to escape. Proceed into the mine until you reach a floor covered in frozen ice. Stepping on the ice makes a good deal of noise, awakening a swarm of bats that fly by. This is unavoidable, but there is a lesson to be learned about floors with crunchy ice.

THE USTANAK'S SILENT DOMAIN

Press the Action button and then rotate the Left Stick to unlock the bulkhead door at the end of the tunnel. Initiate a Partner Action to open it. Jake and Sherry enter into a large chamber guarded by an Ustanak, who is using flying bug J'avo called Oko to look for intruders. Turn left from the entrance and move down the path while the Oko is moving away. Climb inside the dumpster here and wait for the Oko to pass back and forth. When you see the Oko heading off to the left, jump out and move up behind it. Quickly eliminate the Oko with a stealth attack.

Failure to hit the Oko before it turns around and spots you will alert the Ustanak, who will confront you in a second. If spotted, dash back to the dumpster and hide inside until the huge creature goes away. The bugs can "detect" your presence with the line of bugs flying near the ground in front of them.

To sneak up on the second Oko, wait just behind the top of a small rise in the tunnel for it to approach and turn. Then, run up behind it and smash it. Proceed to the end of the path, turn left, and drop over the ledge.

THE DIVIDED CAVE

Note the dumpster on the left. This is where you need to hide if anything goes wrong in the next chamber. Wait at the corner for an Oko to approach and turn back. Then head around the corner, run up behind it, and smash it to the ground. Turn to your left for a moment to notice a metal box on the other side of the chamber and behind a dividing wall of icicles. The Ustanak and another bug patrol the other side. Once you have your bearings, proceed down your side of the tunnel until you reach a small light bulb mounted to the cave floor. Wait for another bug to approach and turn away before sneaking up behind it for a stealth hit. Continue to the end and climb up the ladder on the left. Open the chest on the concrete ledge above to obtain **Skill Points (2,000)**.

ONE TRICKY CHESS PIECE TO CLAIM!

The Duralumin case on the other side of the icicles is extremely tricky to reach. The following strategy can only be attempted in co-op mode with a sentient and competent partner. While one player drops down into the back side of the divided chamber, the other needs to return to the dumpster area. The partner near the dumpster must have a Remote Bomb. Place the bomb near the very first icicles to obliterate them, then retreat to the dumpster. Allow the partner standing on the concrete block at the other end to drop to the ground, sneak up on the bug patrolling the back area, and smash it. Then the partner near the dumpster must detonate the Remote Bomb and immediately jump into the container to avoid detection. While the Ustanak goes searching for someone near the dumpster, the partner not hiding must dash over to the Duralumin case, open it, snatch the **Skill Points (4,000)** inside, and then dash back to where the concrete ledge is and drop down the ledge in the corridor below. When the Ustanak stops looking for the partner who is safe inside the dumpster, he or she can jump out and catch up with the other.

HEAVILY PATROLLED MAINTENANCE ROOM

Note two things about this room as you enter. First, the only dumpster in which you can hide is the first one on the left. The others are full of junk and not usable. So if a bug spots you in the next area and the Ustanak comes a-running, you must dash to this dumpster and get inside before the monster sees you doing so.

Second, Oko patrol the low area through which you must cross to reach the exit. From the entrance, head directly to your right and follow the rail to an opening. Watch the bug patrolling the area directly below. This bug makes a circle around the entire area. When it turns the corner directly below your spot and is headed left, drop to the ground behind it and perform a stealth hit.

Continue to the left and hide at the corner in order to peek into the next section. Two bugs patrol a very short strip of area. Watch both bugs approach and, when both turn away, you can run up and use a stealth attack on each of them, one at a time. By the time you're scraping the second off your boot heel, another one should be turning at the next corner. Pursue it and smash it. That leaves only one more bug that moves up the stairs toward the exit and then back into a little niche. You can catch the stair bug at the top of the stairs or in the niche, but cornering it in the niche is easier.

At the top of the area is a railing over which you can hop to fall into a low passage. Open the Duralumin case at the end of this depression to collect **Skill Points (5,000)**.

SERPENT EMBLEM: MAINTENANCE ROOM

Ascend the stairs to the exit and turn around. A **Serpent Emblem** rests on the side of a water tower directly ahead. However, shooting it draws the attention of the Ustanak in the next room, and the beast will catch you in a heartbeat. You cannot shoot it from the stairs and make it back to the dumpster near the entrance in time to hide. Therefore, return to the dumpster and command your partner to wait there (Partner Action button + D-pad Left). Equip the Sniper Rifle and hop the rail to drop into the low area at the top of the room. Ascend the stairs and stop at the corner. From here, you can use the Sniper Rifle to aim through the gap between the two railings and shoot the Serpent Emblem from the side. When the Ustanak is alerted, dash back to the dumpster and jump inside to safety.

THE HUNT IS OVER

Open the bulkhead door and proceed through with a Partner Action. Proceed along the ledge until you start stepping on more crunchy ice. If the Ustanak hears any noise, the creature smashes through the wall. Hold the Action button while guiding your character to dash through the area. When the view switches to below a small opening, run a few more steps and press the Ready/Aim button while still dashing. You will slide under the opening and into a small crevice that the Ustanak cannot penetrate.

EXPLOSIVE DIVERSION

Climb two ladders to finally reach the back side of the main chamber, which you have seen before. Turn left and drop over the ladder. Move around the edge of the room toward the door to trigger a short scene, the keycard for the door is seen in a dead man's hand across the room. After the scene, continue around the outskirts of the chamber to the far side. Initiate Partner Action to fling Sherry onto a concrete rise, and then return to the far side of the area. There you can collect **four Remote Bombs** that are scattered around. Return to the exit, plant a Remote Bomb near the door, then turn left. Run over to the closest column and hide behind it with your back pressed to it. Detonate the bomb to draw the Ustanak over to the door, allowing Sherry to collect the **Keycard**. Remain hidden behind the column until the Ustanak moves away from the door, then approach the exit and initiate a Partner Action to open it. When playing as Sherry, you must carefully and quickly collect the keycard yourself when Jake sets off a Remote Bomb on the other side of the room.

BULKHEAD BY BULKHEAD

The Ustanak detects Jake and Sherry escaping from the main chamber. Run down the short corridor and press Action to open the next bulkhead door. You must then rotate the Left Stick and press Partner Action to proceed to the next chamber. The enormous creature is hot on your heels and smashing his way through the bulkhead door. Proceed to the next door and work furiously to open it and pass through. Continue opening bulkhead doors and fleeing until you reach an area where a tunneling drill is parked.

DRILL THE USTANAK!

Operate the tunneling drill by rotating the Left Stick rapidly to beat the timer hand on the gauge. Press the Fire button when the timer bar is within the blue section of the gauge to drive the Ustanak back. Repeat this until you knock the beast back to the end, where you must rotate the Left Stick and then press Action when the timer bar is within the blue part of the gauge. Doing so successfully pins the creature to the back wall of the cave, ending the chase. Failure to press the buttons correctly allows the monster to push the tunneling drill back, meaning you must regain lost ground. After pinning the monster, dash up the tunnel to the exit to complete the chapter.

JAKE CHAPTER 2: RANKING CRITERIA

RANK	ACCURACY(%)	DEATHS	CLEAR TIME(MIN)	ENEMIES ROUTED
A	70	5	60	50
B	60	7	80	40
C	50	9	110	20
D	*1	*1	*1	*1

*1 Any Below Rank C

POINTS AWARDED PER RANK (ABOVE)				
Rank	A	B	C	D
Points	25	20	15	10

TOTAL RANKING POINTS TABLE

RANK	S	A	B	C	D	E
Total	100	90	75	55	45	*2

*2 Any Below Rank D

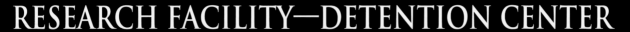

RESEARCH FACILITY—DETENTION CENTER

DETENTION CENTER MAP

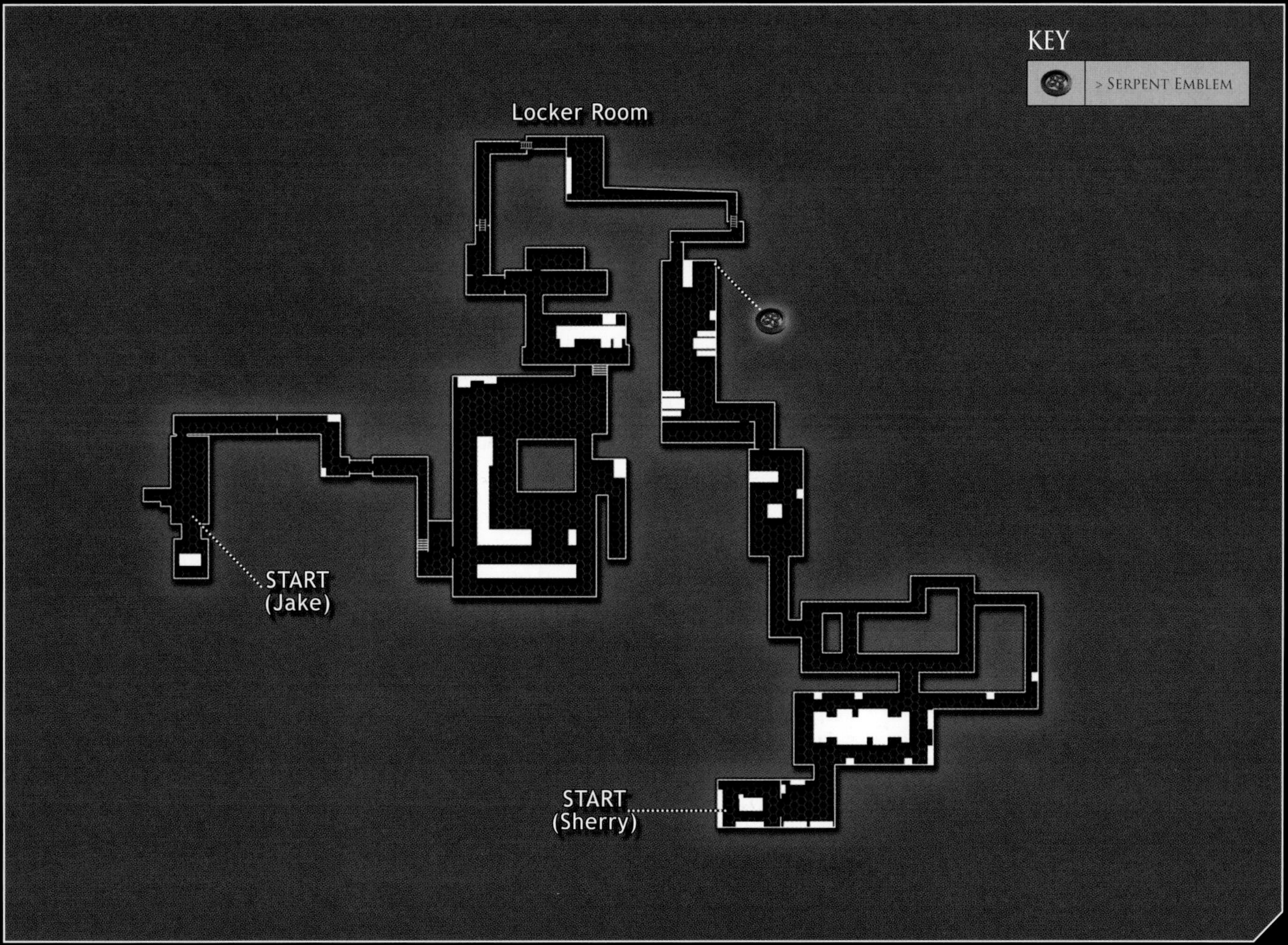

ALL LOCKED UP

Captured by the mysterious Neo-Umbrella organization, Jake and Sherry have now spent the last six months confined in a secret research facility. Having cooperated with his captors for the last several weeks, Jake has successfully lulled the guards into thinking that he won't try anything. But they are mistaken. Seeing an opportunity, Jake determines that it is time to leave.

JAKE AND SHERRY'S SEPARATE PATHS

Since Jake and Sherry are separated in the Detention Center, your choice of character affects many elements when you begin Chapter 3—start point, navigation, environmental interaction, and enemy encounters. The following paragraphs describe how to break out and reunite with Sherry. It is ***strongly recommended*** that you play Chapter 3 for the first time as Jake, since many solutions for navigating Sherry's side are revealed during his playthrough. For those playing as Sherry, skip past the following section and look for the special column "Sherry's Escape from the Detention Center."

GUARD BY GUARD

Stripped of weapons, you must fight your way out of the Detention Center with Hand-to-Hand. Combat gauge management is crucial. Dash across the long room and slide into one or both of the guards. If you are shot and knocked down, tap the Action button rapidly while falling to perform a roll and get right back up. Knock down one guard with a Palm Strike by holding the Attack button to charge. While he's down, move to the other guard and knock him off his feet as well. Then, move back to the other guard and try to finish him off while the other guard gets back on his feet.

When the two armed guards are down, a third J'avo wielding a Stun Rod enters. The best way to avoid being electrocuted is to Quick Counter when the Fire button icon appears during his wind-up. If you're not reflexive or just not close enough, then hold Ready/Aim + Fire to charge a Palm Strike during his pull-back move, and release before he strikes. Grab the guard's legs and toss him. He is resilient, so you may need to stomp or punch him again as he gets back up. The guard with the Stun Rod drops the **Switchboard Key**. Pick up the key, move to the white box with red Chinese characters mounted to the wall, and press Action to escape your cell.

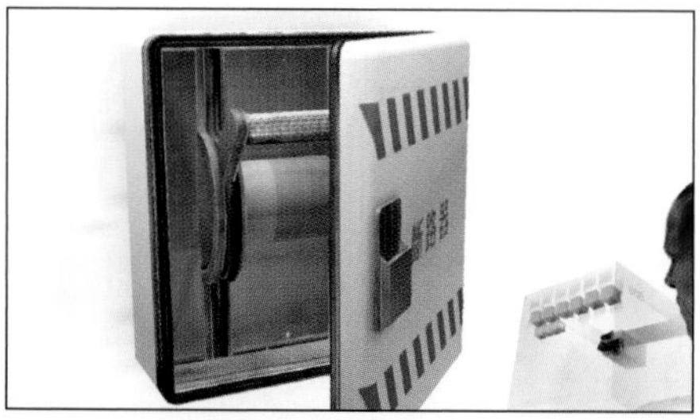

OUT AND ABOUT

After a short scene where Jake shuts down the power, which releases Sherry from her cell elsewhere, Jake finds himself in the hall outside the vault. Dash down the corridor and slide into a lone oncoming guard. Finish him with Hand-to-Hand and a full body toss, then pause a few moments to catch your breath and let the Combat Gauge refill.

SOLID STEALTH TACTICS

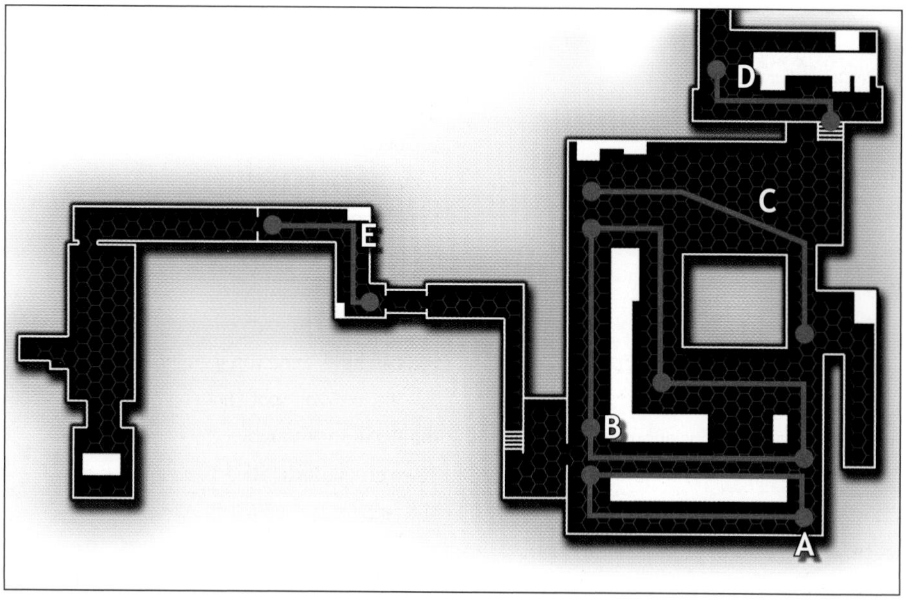

At the end of the corridor, you'll enter a lab. Move to the railing across from the door, hold Ready/Aim, and press Action to crouch below the railing. Tilt the Left Stick to the right to slide down the wall until you reach the top of some stairs. Wait there and watch the room below until you're certain no guards are present. Release Ready/Aim to stand and press Action to hop over the rail. Move up to the railing between the machine on the left and the metal detector on the right. Press Ready/Aim and then Action to hide below the wall.

While hiding below this rail, angle your camera to watch a guard patrolling the aisle on the right (marked A on the map) as well as a J'avo who comes strolling in from the far left (B). If the timing is still good, J'avo A on the right will move up the far aisle while the J'avo B on the left will move up the inside aisle. When you can see both of their backs, stand, hop the rail, and move over to the far aisle. Run up behind J'avo A before he reaches the end of the aisle and perform a Stealth Hit takedown.

Continue up to the end of the aisle and press Ready/Aim at the corner to watch guard B moving up the inside aisle. As he turns away and moves around a low worktable, make sure that guard C is not approaching from far away, beyond a short drop. When the inside aisle guard moves around the corner, and when the area beyond is clear, run up behind him for a Stealth Hit.

Backtrack to the previous corner near the short drop ledge. Wait for guard C to come close and stop just below the drop. Guard D in the far back area is not a concern at this point, but make sure that he is not about to turn your way as you attempt this next kill. When guard C turns, leave the corner, drop over the short ledge, run up behind the guard, and perform a Stealth Hit from behind.

Quickly turn around and run to the corner nearest the stairs up to the final area. Hide at the corner and watch guard D as he emerges from the next room and checks the stairs. When he turns back, run around the corner, press Action to climb up the low ledge, and run up behind guard D to perform a Stealth Hit.

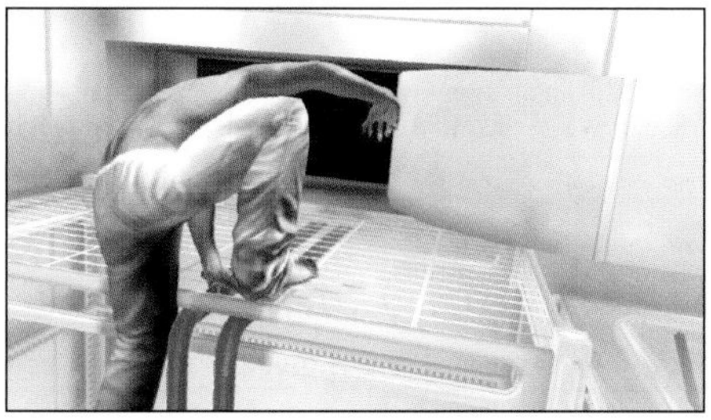

From the top of the stairs, go through the door on your right. A large cart blocks the aisle on your left. Press the Action button to push the cart all the way down the aisle. Back up out of the aisle, go back through the door, and continue to the other side of the cart. Climb onto the cart, then crawl into a vent opening.

THE EYE IN THE SKY

Jake drops into a corridor outside a surveillance room. The door at the end of the passage is locked and requires a passcode input. The panel buttons are marked with strange symbols. To determine the passcode, enter the surveillance room and approach the console with the joystick. Press Action to take control of a surveillance camera elsewhere in the facility.

Camera 1 has a mounted machine gun, so you can have some fun gunning down a few J'avo if you spot them on patrol. Use the Right Stick to move the camera, press down on the Right Stick to zoom in and out, and press the Fire button to shoot.

Press the Action button to switch to Camera 2, which is inside a locker room. Here you'll spot Sherry hiding in a locker just as a J'avo guard enters. Angle the camera downward to see a guard input the passcode to get through the door directly below. Then you'll see Sherry learn the same passcode and use it to get through the door.

Switch to Camera 3, which surveys a waiting room. This camera also has a mounted machine gun. Sherry soon enters and engages the guards. Provide assistance by gunning them all down with the machine gun on the camera. When the area is clear, move the camera to follow Sherry over to the exit. Press down on the Right Stick to zoom in as she inputs the passcode into the panel. Make a note of the passcode symbols she inputs to open the door. The passcode is different every time you play, so this guide cannot provide a single answer. Once you have the passcode, press the Partner Action button to exit camera control.

SERPENT EMBLEM: DETENTION CENTER WAITING ROOM

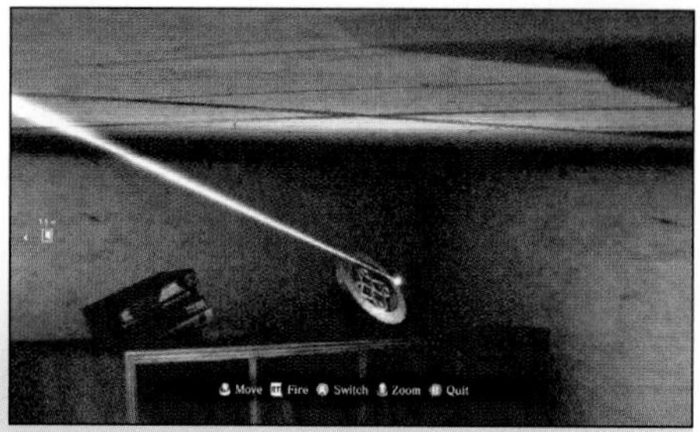

After helping Sherry make her way through the Waiting Room, but before exiting camera control, press down on the Right Stick and zoom in on the shelves in the corner to the right of the exit. A **Serpent Emblem** rests atop the shelves. Shoot it with the machine gun mounted on the camera.

INPUT THE PASSCODE

With the passcode symbols memorized (or written on a piece of paper), exit the surveillance room and return to the passcode panel. Press the Action button to interact with the panel. Use the Left Stick to move Jake's finger over the button bearing the first symbol. Hit the Pickup/Reload button to press the button on the panel. Repeat for the other two symbols to open the door.

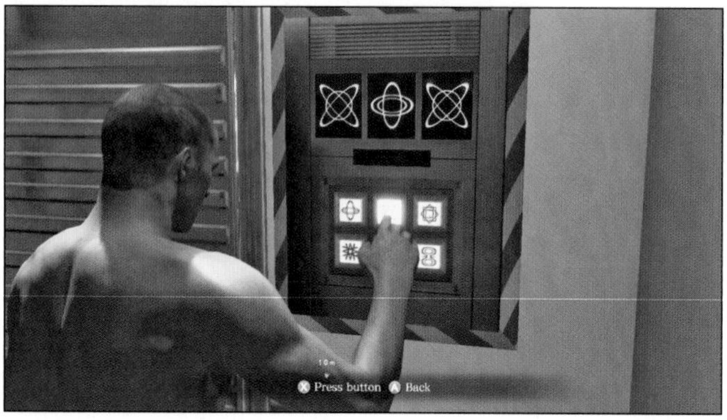

Enter the dark hallway, face the floor vent duct on the right, and press Action to crawl inside. Climb the ladder in the small room, move forward a few feet, and crawl into another vent duct. Press the Action button repeatedly to crawl through faster. When Jake stands, run down the remaining passage and climb another ladder. At the top, crawl into the small opening and press Action to drop down on the other side.

SHERRY'S ESCAPE FROM THE DETENTION CENTER

When starting Chapter 3 of Jake's Campaign and playing as Sherry, you must escape from a completely different area and follow a very different route in order to rendezvous with Jake. Playing this Chapter as Jake first provides a clear idea of what to expect and what to do, and it is highly recommended. However, the following Stealth Hit strategies do not require this.

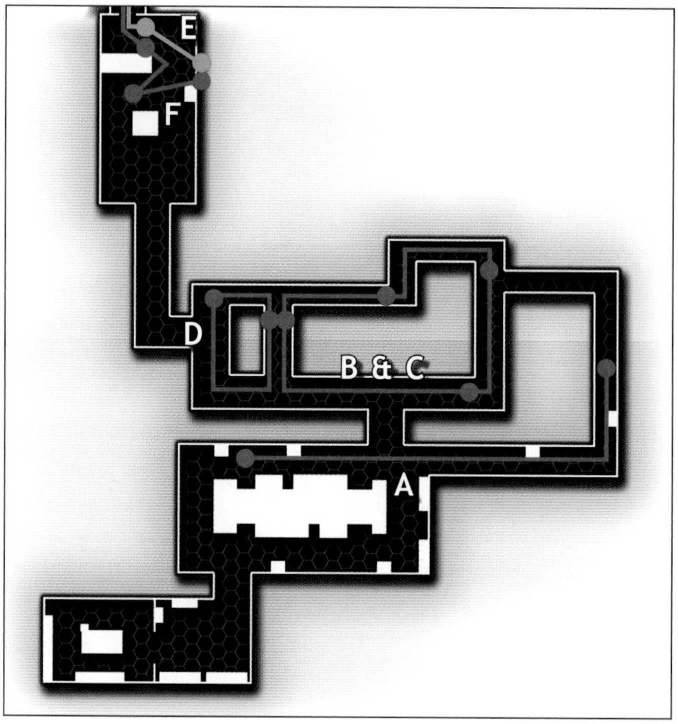

At first, Sherry is suffering a normal day of confinement, although it seems "quieter than normal." Move to the table against the wall and activate the stereo if you wish to listen to some music. You won't be staying long, however.

After a few seconds, Jake breaks free of the vault that he's been kept in all these months and shuts down the power. The power goes out in Sherry's room as well, allowing her to overpower a J'avo guard and obtain a Stun Rod. Exit the dark room and follow the corridor to your left. Continue to the far corner, then press Ready/Aim to hide at the corner and peek down the long passage. With good timing, a J'avo guard (marked "A" on the map) should be walking away. Move up the corridor and note the small niches between computer server cabinets on your right. Move up to the second one, which is across from a small pushcart, and hide behind it. The guard will take a long while to return but the wait is worth it.

When the guard moves past your position, look for the Fire button icon to appear onscreen, and press it to take him down with a Stealth Hit.

Leave your hiding spot and move up to the closest door. Hide on the left side of the door and watch the two J'avo guards patrolling the open central area. The closest guard strolls past, but the guard on the far side stops and peers straight across, in your direction. It is a clear disadvantage to attack from this position, so wait until the farthest guard moves on. Move past the doorway to the end of the corridor. Continue around the next two left turns and move down the left side of the hall, toward the stairs, and into the central area.

Press up against the corner on the left side of the stairs. Angle your camera to look through the various windows into the central area, but mainly keep an eye on the corner behind you. Wait for both J'avo guards to walk past your position. Walk up slowly behind the second one and perform a Stealth Hit before he moves on. Return to your hiding place, wait for the front guard to come around again, and eliminate him the same way.

Looking straight ahead from the bottom of the stairs, you should be able to see J'avo guard D appear at the bottom of the opposite stairs on the far side of the area. As he makes his way up the stairs, run around the corner to the right and hide at the corner down the hall from the stairs as shown in the screenshot.

When guard D heads up the stairs, run up behind him for a Stealth Hit. Because Sherry is lower than the guard, you may merely knock him down. Quickly follow with a finishing Stun Rod stab.

Ascend the stairs and go around the corner to the right. As you enter a locker room, J'avo guard E emerges from the doorway on the right wall. Wait for him to move to the far door, input the passcode, and exit.

When you hear the exit door close, run around the corner toward the door. Turn to your left and hide in the central lockers in the row opposite the door. The view from inside this locker is fixed on the passcode panel. Wait for another J'avo guard to enter the area, approach the door, and input the passcode symbols. Pause the game for a moment and make a mental note of the code or draw the symbols on a piece of paper. Also note whether the J'avo guard is wearing a vest (guard E) or a suit (guard F). If a suit, then stay where you are until a guard wearing a hunting vest appears and inputs the code. Then step out of the locker, and move to the panel. Press Action at the panel, use the Left Stick to move Sherry's hand to the button for the first symbol, and press the Reload/Pickup button to press it. Repeat for the second two symbols and ignore any scary noises you hear in the room.

The sounds should be coming from J'avo guard F in a suit, who pauses in the center of the room for a moment, or J'avo guard E in a vest, who moves straight to the passcode panel.

Quickly move around the corner to your left, enter the doorway, press up against the wall, press Action to duck, and crawl along the low wall to see the room beyond. In a few seconds, Jake will use the machine gun mounted to the security camera on the far side of the room to gun down two of the J'avo guards, leaving only J'avo guard G free to approach your position. As guard G turns away, stand, hop over the low wall, and run up behind him for a stealth takedown. If the Stealth Hit does not go well and another J'avo appears in the room, run under the security camera and wait for Jake to take him out. Then, move to the exit door and input the same passcode as before.

Enter the concrete corridor, run down the short passage to the right, and hop over the railing to drop. Run upstairs and press the Action button to emerge from a fake locker into a dressing room. Wait a few moments, and Jake will join you.

RESEARCH FACILITY—LIVING QUARTERS

LIVING QUARTERS MAP

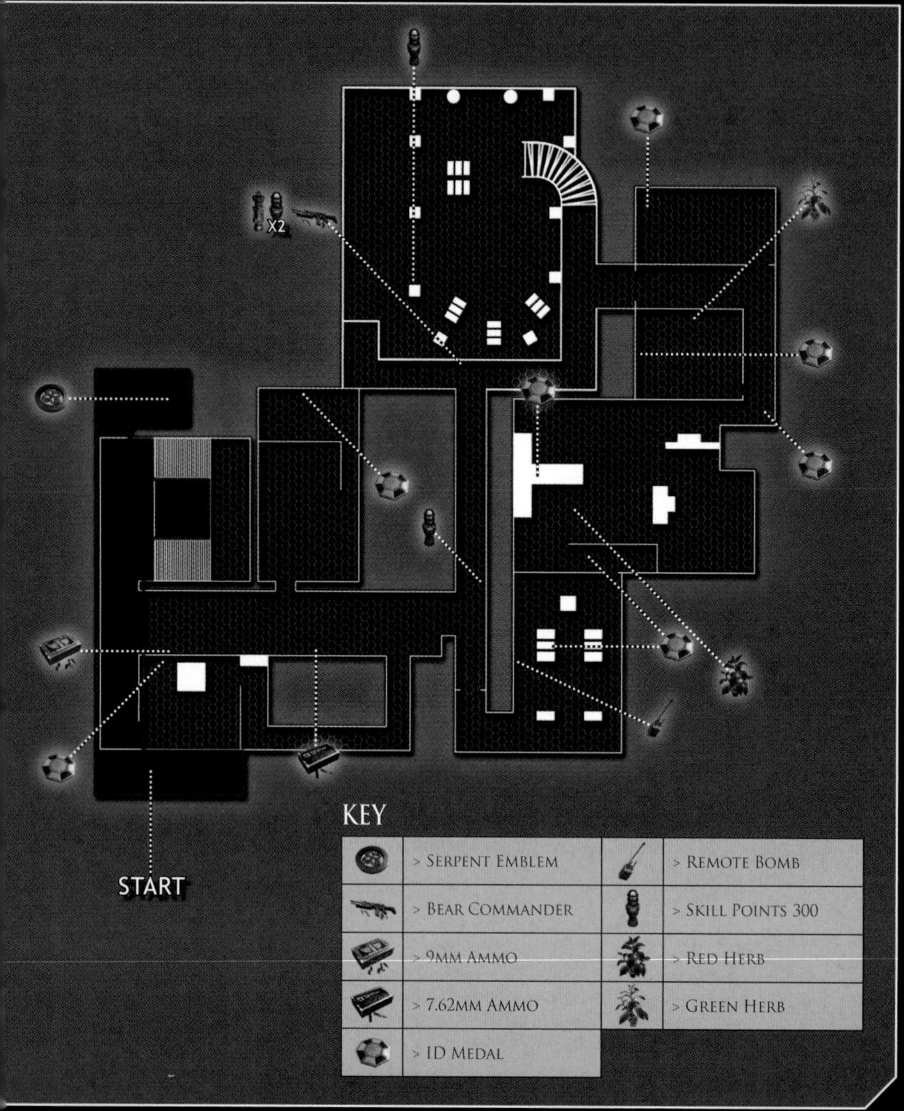

RETURN TO THE OLD "RUN-N-GUN" STYLE

Jake and Sherry reunite, awkwardly put their clothes on, and reacquire their gear. It's time to quit Stealth Hit tactics, since armed enemies throughout the rest of the area are well-positioned to spot Jake and Sherry and to open fire immediately.

Exit the locker room and head down the long corridor to the right. Take cover at the corner and open fire on the J'avo guard wearing a white suit at the top of the stairs. A more preferable tactic is to toss a Flash Grenade, dash upstairs, and take down the guard plus two others with Hand-to-Hand. There's a high probability that shooting the guard in the white suit may cause it to shift into chrysalid form and then hatch a Strelats. However, the chances of transformation drop significantly when the guard is defeated via melee, although it is still possible. The same guard drops an **ID Medal**, a key item carried by several guards throughout the Living Quarters area, which you must collect to escape this facility.

IN CASE THIS IS YOUR FIRST STRELATS...

Strelats are large lizard-like monsters that hatch from mutating J'avo chrysalids. At close range they exhale gas, and at long range they rear up on their hind legs and fire a cone-shaped blast of darts. The best way to deal with them is to use high-powered weaponry, such as the Elephant Killer or a Quick Shot from the Sniper Rifle to knock them on their backs. Then, quickly approach the Strelats while down and finish it off with a melee attack. If a Strelats is focused on your partner, approach it unnoticed from behind for an instant Stealth Hit. Flash Grenades also render Strelats prone to Stealth Hit attacks from behind but are best utilized in wider spaces. Using any other weaponry or tactics against these extremely strong creatures is highly inefficient and wastes ammo. Strelats drop **Skill Points (1,000)** when defeated.

CHECK OUT THE SECOND FLOOR

Continue to the top of the stairs, head to the left, take cover behind the column against the railing, and gun down another J'avo guard at the next corner. Move to his position, take cover at the corner, and aim down the golden hallway. Guards soon emerge from the far connecting corridor. Shoot through the glass panels to drop them from a distance. Equip your Sniper Rifle for more efficient work.

HEAD BACK DOWNSTAIRS?

The following advice may seem illogical, but it's actually to your benefit. After clearing the golden corridor on the second floor, do not investigate the second level any further at this time. Instead, return to the stairwell and hop over the rail. Turn to your left to spot a blue door in the corner. Quickly dash to the door and press Action twice to kick it open. Inside you'll find J'avo guards dropping from the ceiling behind the row of shelves dividing the room. These enemies do not appear unless you return to this room ***after*** visiting the second level. Use Quick Shots plus melee attacks to take down the guard or guards in the room at this time. Wait approximately ten seconds in the room and another J'avo guard will drop from the ceiling. Keep taking down the guards until they stop dropping from the ceiling vent. Use melee to defeat them all since one is programmed to transform into Strelats if shot. This same guard drops another **ID Medal** when defeated. Between guard appearances, smash a Chinese box in this room to acquire an item.

SERPENT EMBLEM: LIVING QUARTERS STORAGE ROOM

A **Serpent Emblem** is located between the boxes on the dividing shelves in the room. The best angle to see it is from the spot where the J'avo guards drop from the ceiling. To conserve bullets, Jake can punch the emblem.

CONTINUING THE SEARCH UPSTAIRS

When guards stop dropping into the downstairs storage room, go back upstairs. Move past the wide golden corridor to the end of the small hallway and open the door. Approach the desk next to the bed and open the central drawer to obtain another **ID Medal**.

Go through the back door of the bedroom and follow the corridor. Kick open a Chinese box at the second corner for an item. Proceed through the next door back to the wide golden corridor. Smash the golden urns on the marble pedestals to your left—if they weren't already destroyed during the previous gun battle here—to reveal **9mm Ammo** and **7.62mm Ammo** for your Sniper Rifle. Proceed through the double doors across the hallway.

LIBRARY STANDOFF

Several J'avo wait in ambush on both levels of the two-story library. Move quickly into the center of the room and take a position behind one of the tables. Press the Ready/Aim button to knock the table over and take cover. Shoot the J'avo with the heavy machine gun on the upper level to the left and the man at the top of the stairs. Another guard pops out from behind the central bookcase on the lower level. Listen for the sounds of a J'avo pulling a grenade pin and tossing it your way. Roll out of harm's way by quickly pushing Action twice while running left or right.

Smash the Chinese box in the corner on the ground floor to obtain an item, and then move to the stairs and dash to the top. Take out any J'avo on the upper level, then move behind the dividing bookcase. More J'avo guards emerge from the sliding door at the end, which you cannot enter. Take down these J'avo with melee attacks to reduce the chances of one of them transforming into a Strelats. One of the guards appearing in this area drops an **ID Medal** and another can be found on the back shelf, upstairs.

EVERYONE TAKES COVER

Exit the library, turn left, and head through the open doorway at the end of the corridor. J'avo guards wait in ambush on your left, so quickly press Ready/Aim to throw over a table and take cover. Equip the Sniper Rifle and take out the guards at the end of the narrow corridor. One of them will probably transform into a Strelats, so switch to the Elephant Killer to deal with it efficiently. If the guards toss grenades, move to the marble pedestal on your right and take cover there or retreat to the golden corridor. One of these guards drops an **ID Medal** when defeated. After the battle, move to the golden urn on the marble pedestal and smash it—if it wasn't shot previously—to reveal **Skill Points (300)**.

BOMB THE LOUNGE

After the gun battle in the narrow corridor, turn around and go the opposite direction up the hallway, and follow the corners to the left. Search this empty sitting room and you'll notice that the glass back door is blocked by something large. An **ID Medal** lies on the floor beneath one of the coffee tables. To obtain it, smash the golden urn against the wall to obtain a **Remote Bomb**. Move to the coffee table and press Ready/Aim to set the Remote Bomb. Then, move behind one of the tables at the back of the room and press Ready/Aim to push it over. Call your partner to your side if needed, take cover behind the table you turned over, and then press Ready/Aim and Fire to detonate the Remote Bomb and blow up the furniture. You can then pick up the ID Medal.

LOBBY TAKEOVER

Return to the long narrow corridor and approach the far end. Be wary of new or additional guards that may be hiding just outside the corridor's end. Proceed onto the balcony overlooking the main lobby. Move a few feet to the left or right, equip your Sniper Rifle, and take out the two guards posted by the double doors at the far end of the room. If the Sniper Rifle cannot zoom twice and you find aiming difficult from this distance, move to the right and follow the balcony down to the end, jumping across the gap using a horizontal pole. Stop at the top of the curved staircase and snipe the front door guards from there. One of the guards will probably mutate into a Strelats while the other drops an **ID Medal**.

INSERT COINS

Explore the lobby. One of the golden urns, located on a marble pedestal to the right side of the central statue, can be smashed to obtain **Skill Points (300)**. A golden gate beneath the rear balcony is sealed, even though several item boxes and the Bear Commander can be seen inside from this position.

Move to the front side of the statue and press Action to examine it. Jake and Sherry determine that this is where the ID Medals you've collected will come in handy. Insert three ID Medals to turn the statue's head to the left. The other statue on the side of the lobby slides forward, providing access to the door hidden behind it. Go upstairs, move behind the statue, and enter the corridor behind it.

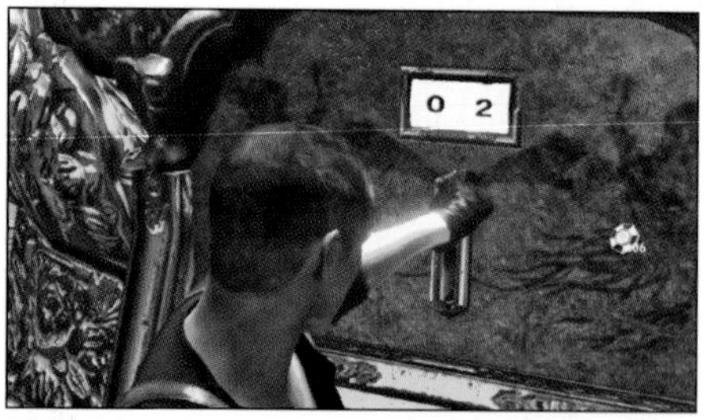

BLAST THE BILLIARD HALL

When you're halfway up the corridor, the doors on the left burst open and a J'avo guard runs out to attack. Take him down with a Quick Shot and melee follow-up to save your ammo for the firefight to come. Standing outside the double doors, shoot any J'avo you see inside the billiard hall and on the balcony above. When your view is clear, dash all the way across the room and slide over the bar. Take cover here and return fire on the J'avo in the opposite corner, both on the ground floor and the balcony above. Hop back over the bar and use the billiard tables as cover while taking out any remaining guards on the upper level. One of the J'avo who drops from the upper level, typically near the end, drops an **ID Medal**. Use the piano in the chamber to play a melody and another **ID Medal** will pop out.

SECOND WAVE

Exit the billiard hall, move to the single door across the hallway, and kick it open. Smash the golden urn directly to your right to obtain a **Green Herb**. Another **ID Medal** is lodged in a crest above the fireplace on the far side of the room. Taking it triggers another wave of enemies that emerges from the billiard hall. Take cover on the left side of the doorway and shoot each J'avo in the face as they charge across the corridor and attempt to breach the room. Trigger another wave by banging the gong in the room. One of the last enemies that you trigger by ringing the gong drops another **ID Medal**.

TIME FOR A SWIM

Return to the corridor and follow it to the glass doors at the end. Open the doors and move to the water fountain at the corner to find an **ID Medal**.

Go through the second set of glass double doors to enter a swimming pool area. Climb down into the pink (but harmless) waters, move to the back of the pool, and crawl under the second archway. Under here you'll find another **ID Medal**.

Exit the water and move down the opposite side of the room toward the stairs. Smash the first golden urn near the stairs to obtain a **Red Herb**. Ascend the stairs and press Action to push the large cart farther down the balcony, which unblocks the glass door on your right and reveals yet another **ID Medal** on the floor.

BACK TO THE LOBBY

The unblocked glass door in the pool room takes you back to the sitting room where you probably detonated a bomb earlier. Follow the connecting corridor back out toward the large lobby. Another squad of J'avo appear from the wide golden hall on your left. Take cover at the doorway and gun them all down. A couple of these guys will transform into Strelats, and one of the last to appear drops an **ID Medal** when defeated.

THE OTHER LOBBY DOOR AND THE BEAR COMMANDER

At this point, having searched all the areas and eliminated all the enemies described in this section of the walkthrough, you should now possess 13 ID Medals (having already used three in the lobby). Return to the giant central statue in the lobby and insert ID Medals until the counter reaches 10. This opens the door on the other side of the lobby, behind the reception desk. However, inserting more ID Medals until the counter reaches 16 lowers the golden bars at the back of the lobby. This allows access to the **Bear Commander**, an item chest containing **Skill Points (2,000)**, **Skill Points (300) x2**, and two Chinese Boxes you can smash to obtain items. One of the Chinese boxes typically yields **40mm Explosive Rounds** that you may load into the Bear Commander.

BEAR COMMANDER MODES OF FIRE

The Bear Commander's standard mode of fire is fully automatic and reloads using 5.56mm Ammo. Press the Toggle Fire Mode button (△ on PlayStation 3, Ⓨ on Xbox 360) while aiming the Bear Commander to switch to firing the grenade launcher, which shoots 40mm Explosive Rounds. The grenade launcher must be reloaded after each round fired. This is accomplished by pressing either Fire or Reload/Pickup.

ENTER THE SECURITY ROOM

Enter the newly revealed corridor behind the reception desk and move to the door at the end. Initiate Partner Action to open the security room door. Sherry downloads all of the medical data Neo-Umbrella has collected about Jake and her. She also determines that her superiors are in China and sets up a rendezvous.

RESEARCH FACILITY—ENTRANCE

DETENTION CENTER MAP

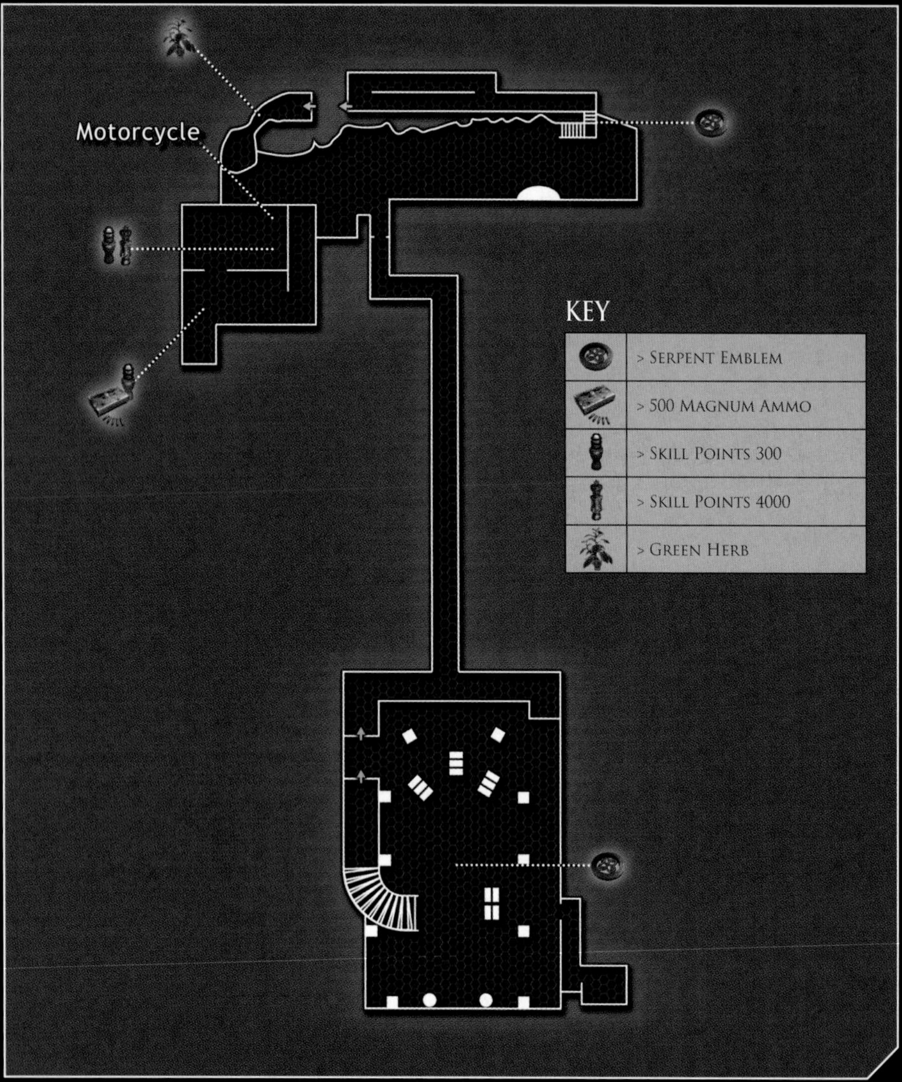

TANK INVASION

Exit the security room, return to the lobby, and take cover behind the reception desk. New J'avo guards run downstairs and take up positions in the lobby. Use your handgun to shoot the guards on the ground floor, then switch to your Sniper Rifle to take out the J'avo firing from the upper level.

When the area is clear, go across the lobby to the stairs. A giant tank smashes through the front doors! As the time frame shifts to slow motion, move out of the center of the lobby. The tank rolls into the center of the lobby, smashes the central statue, and parks there. The tank tracks Jake with its cannon and fires shells at intervals, so you must keep moving to avoid injury! Swing back across the horizontal pole, take out any J'avo positioned near the central double doors, and continue to the other side. At the far ledge, initiate a Partner Action to pull Sherry to the upper level. Then initiate a Partner Action to open the double doors and proceed down the corridor.

SERPENT EMBLEM: ENTRANCE LOBBY

After the tank runs over the central statue, a **Serpent Emblem** appears among the debris beneath the tank. To shoot it, you must move to either the front or rear of the tank, depending on where the turret is aiming. Then, walk backward and press Ready/Aim + Action to fall back and lie on the ground. Aim beneath the tank and shoot the Serpent Emblem. If the turret rotates your direction, roll to the left or right while in this position to avoid incoming blasts.

ESCAPE FROM THE TANK

Proceed down the corridor until the floor gives way, which drops Jake and Sherry into a hidden passageway. The tank smashes through the wall behind you. Dash away from the tank by tilting the Left Stick downward while holding Action. Watch the tank turret and move to the other side of the corridor as needed to avoid any shells as they are fired.

When you reach the end of the corridor, the view swings to the left to reveal an exit. Quickly change directions to escape the corridor and jump through the window opening into the alley below.

Smash the nearby crates for items, then move to the end of the alley and initiate a Partner Action to open the door. Take cover on either side of the doorway, equip your Sniper Rifle, and take out the J'avo guards on the deck of the pagoda-style building opposite. When J'avo approach at close range, move into the water and take them out.

Outside the door, turn to your right and continue toward the stone stairs at the far end. The tank smashes through the wall on the right, so adjust your position while the game is stuck in slow motion to avoid being crushed. Continue dashing for the stone stairs at the far end and ignore any J'avo in the water.

SERPENT EMBLEM: ENTRANCE COURTYARD

Move to the far side of the stone stairs leading up to the pagoda-style building. You will find a **Serpent Emblem** leaning against the back side.

TAKE THE PAGODA

Ascend the stone stairs to the pagoda building's deck level. Take cover against either concrete column to the left or right and shoot any J'avo blocking the deck. Dash down the aisle and enter the doorway on the right. Quickly smash two Chinese boxes in the corner to acquire items. Dash to the next corner and do the same with two more boxes. Pull the lever on the wall to rotate the statue outside, which moves a horizontal pole within Jake's reach.

MAKE THE TANK ROTATE THE STATUE

Blasting away chunks of the wall, the tank begins targeting this little side room now. Sherry will be more secure here than outdoors but not for long. While Sherry pushes over tables and returns fire on additional J'avo invading the room, Jake must run outside and swing across the horizontal pole to the stone platform opposite. From there, he spots a motorcycle inside the executive suite of the main building across the water. Follow the curved wooden bridge to the back side of another statue and pick up the **Green Herb** along the way. Continue to another stone platform where two more Chinese boxes can be smashed for items. Stand on this platform until the tank rolls forward, striking the statue and rotating it. The horizontal pole on this statue is still not in the right position, so run back across the wooden bridge to the previous stone platform. This causes the tank to back up. Run back across the bridge to the second stone platform and stand there until the tank moves forward and rotates the statue again. Do this once more until the horizontal pole hangs parallel to the first stone platform. Return to that platform and swing across to the main building.

COMMANDEER THE EXECUTIVE MOTORCYCLE

Naturally, you must take out a squad of J'avo in the corridor. They don't usually mutate, which provides easy takedowns. However, for the sake of your partner, consider using the grenade launcher on the Bear Commander to clear the passage quickly.

Proceed into the suite and open the briefcase on the nearest table to obtain **Skill Points (300)** and **.500 Magnum Ammo**. The suite is again invaded by another J'avo squad coming from the entrance corridor. Use another grenade to quickly take them out before they get too far into the room and spread out.

Enter the other half of the suite, move to the table on the far right, and open another case to acquire **Skill Points (4,000)** and **Skill Points (300).** Now, move to the motorcycle and press Action to escape from the building and to end this chapter.

JAKE CHAPTER 3: RANKING CRITERIA

RANK	ACCURACY(%)	DEATHS	CLEAR TIME(MIN)	ENEMIES ROUTED
A	70	2	60	55
B	60	3	80	40
C	50	5	110	30
D	*1	*1	*1	*1

*1 Any Below Rank C

POINTS AWARDED PER RANK (ABOVE)				
Rank	A	B	C	D
Points	25	20	15	10

TOTAL RANKING POINTS TABLE

RANK	S	A	B	C	D	E
Total	100	90	75	55	45	*2

*2 Any Below Rank D

CITY AND HIGHWAY

HOT PURSUIT

Jake and Sherry may have escaped captivity at the secret Neo-Umbrella facility, but they're not in the clear. J'avo quickly launch on motorcycles and an attack helicopter. They attempt to run down the heroes on the open highway and the city streets of China. If Jake and Sherry won't surrender willingly, then Neo-Umbrella is committed to taking them out!

1

Like the snowmobiles earlier, the motorcycle accelerates by holding the Fire button and the Ready/Aim button applies the brakes. Accelerate your speed only on straightaways and clear roads and allow the bike to coast on turns and around obstacles.

2

Steer away from any missile explosions to the left and right. When the helicopter settles ahead, steer to one side of the road. As the helicopter draws a line of fire across the road, steer to the other side.

3

Stop accelerating as Jake and Sherry enter the city. Avoid the railings and debris in the street to maintain the bike's structural health (displayed on the lower right).

4

During a jump, a J'avo with a rocket launcher takes aim. Sherry automatically handles the situation for you.

5

As Jake steers through a narrow alley, brake if necessary to avoid damage from slamming into either wall.

6

Sliding onto a main street, the duo encounter J'avo on motorcycles. Sherry automatically takes care of the ones behind you. Meanwhile, watch the J'avo ahead and be ready to swerve when they drop Molotovs on the street. Slow down to make this easier.

7

Watch for cars and more J'avo dropping Molotovs as Jake swings onto a wider street. Hitting a car at this speed means instant death.

8

Wreckage blocks the end of the street. Steer to the far right in order to hit a ramp and jump onto scaffolding.

9

Accelerate while driving on the scaffolding to avoid being shot by the attack helicopter, which flies in from your left.

10

Sherry flies off the motorbike during a jump but manages to catch onto a helicopter.

11

Sherry can't hold onto the helicopter forever, so be ready to accelerate by pressing the Fire button when the timer hand moves through the green portion of the gauge. Press Fire just before the timer hits for greater chance of success.

12

Accelerate through the wall of falling pipes.

13

Steer slightly right of center to hit a ramp.

14

Jake catches Sherry as she falls from the chopper.

15

Back on the city streets, avoid accelerating to make steering easier around vehicles, debris, and exploding Molotovs.

16

The helicopter fires a missile, causing an oil tanker truck to block the street. Prepare to press the Reload and Action buttons simultaneously before the timer gauge shown onscreen expires or you will die instantly. (On a second try, you need to press only the Action button.)

17

Jake stops after a 180-degree turn, facing the oil tanker. Sherry shoots it automatically.

18

Accelerate down the street until you're ahead of another J'avo biker gang so that Sherry can shoot them behind you. Avoid the accelerator as you start encountering more burning vehicles.

19

At the end of the street, steer to the left in order to hit a ramp and jump into a building corridor.

20

When the helicopter settles ahead, be ready to press the Action button to escape instant death before the timer gauge expires.

21

Even though you land back on a highway section, the amount of debris makes acceleration unwise. Carefully steer between the burning vehicles at normal speed.

22

Accelerate again when you see less debris. Another J'avo biker gang overtakes you, and enemies ahead resume dropping Molotovs. Steer clear of flames to avoid damage.

23

Ahead, the helicopter opens fire on a car carrier, releasing the gate. Rolling, flaming cars head your way. Steer to the far right to avoid the first two and then the far left.

24

The car carrier crashes ahead. Steer onto the car carrier to use it as a ramp.

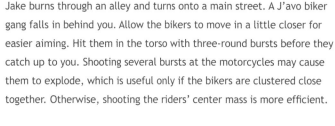

HANDLE THE SHOOTING

When you are playing as Sherry, Jake handles all the driving while her job is to fend off attackers and shoot exploding objects. Firing is accomplished with the usual controls, and ammo is infinite during this segment with no reloading required. Press down on the Right Stick to switch hands and view the other side of the motorcycle, or hold the Action button to hug Jake's torso.

During the first leg of the run, you can do little to prevent the chopper from firing. However, shooting at the helicopter's cockpit may throw off the pilot's aim a bit and prevent damage from machine-gun fire.

After jumping and landing in the city, Jake drives through a street and then makes another jump. Time slows as a J'avo with a rocket launcher rises up. Aim at the exploding barrel on the scaffolding and shoot it before the J'avo fires his missile... or it's an instant death.

Jake burns through an alley and turns onto a main street. A J'avo biker gang falls in behind you. Allow the bikers to move in a little closer for easier aiming. Hit them in the torso with three-round bursts before they catch up to you. Shooting several bursts at the motorcycles may cause them to explode, which is useful only if the bikers are clustered close together. Otherwise, shooting the riders' center mass is more efficient.

Following a ride along scaffolding and a jump through an explosion, Sherry flies off the bike and grabs hold of the helicopter's landing skid. Tap the Reload button repeatedly to maintain your grip until Jake gets his bike turned around and rides below.

After Jake slides the motorcycle under a skidding oil tanker, he executes a 180-degree turn to face the rig. First, shoot the **Serpent Emblem** above the sign to the left. Then aim at the leaking, red oil tank on the side of the rig and shoot it to blow up the vehicle.

When Jake gets rolling again, another J'avo biker gang falls in behind you. Before Jake jumps into a building corridor, quickly shoot at their gas tanks to blow them up as a group.

Jake lands the bike on a highway and navigates through some treacherous wreckage. Sherry will turn back to aim at more J'avo bikers swarming behind. Shoot the closest enemies first before they kick you and switch sides to shoot at enemies as needed.

This emblem can only be claimed while playing as Sherry. When the game enters slow motion so that you can shoot the oil tanker, look to the left and upward to spot a **Serpent Emblem** resting on top of a building sign. Shoot it, and then shoot the oil tanker as quickly as possible.

POISAWAN COURTYARD

POISAWAN COURTYARD MAP

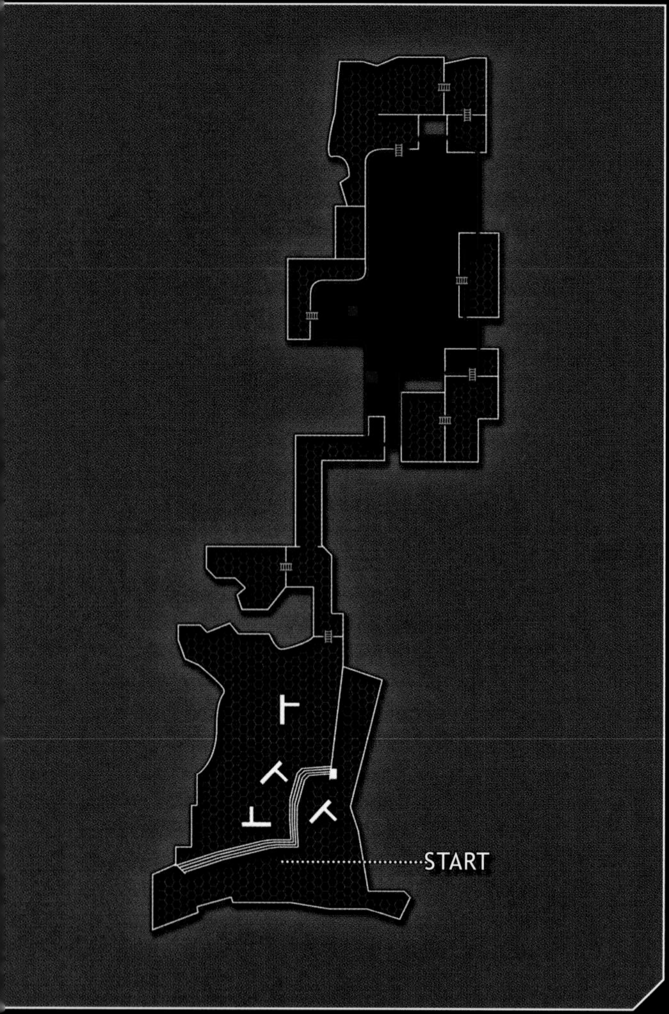

The attack chopper circles overhead supporting J'avo ground soldiers by firing on Jake and Sherry. The chopper's machine gun will track you every movement, so don't linger too long in one place. Stay on the move by running around the area, but you should also remain close to the concrete ruins. Doing so reduces the number of bullets the chopper can hit you with. You can eliminate some J'avo simply by running behind them while the chopper is firing. Shooting at the chopper is useless at this point, so don't bother.

If you approach a J'avo at a point when the chopper isn't firing, perform a Quick Shot with anything more powerful than your handgun. Follow up with a roundhouse kick to take out the enemy. Do not stay near the spot where you perform melee attacks or head stomps for long, or you'll take bullets when the chopper resumes firing again.

CORNERED, SURROUNDED!

Jake and Sherry crash their motorcycle in a courtyard surrounded by tall buildings. The attack helicopter settles overhead, determined to take

THE MARKED WAVE

Continue circling the area. Perform Quick Shots on several waves of J'avo, or let the helicopter shoot them for you, until all are eliminated. Noga-Skakanje and more J'avo drop from the chopper and flood the upper levels. Chris and the BSAA will handle the enemy on the platforms. You must take out those that drop into the courtyard and fly on the attack chopper's wings. All enemies are marked, making them easier to locate. Stop and snipe enemies whenever the chopper

HEAD OUT FOR ROUND TWO

When the attack chopper finally flies off, move toward the exit marker. Smash a crate near the raised emergency ladder to obtain an item. Then, turn left and head to the far side. Swing across the gap on a horizontal pole, turn right, and climb the ladder. Move to the other side of the platform and kick down the emergency ladder so that Sherry may climb up. Approach the door and initiate a Partner Action to open it. Follow the short corridor to the next courtyard, turn left, and drop from the ledge. Defeat a group of Noga-Skakanje that strolls casually into the courtyard. Now, climb the ladders to take on the attack chopper directly.

ENEMY ATTACK CHOPPER—L

Jake has access to more areas of the upper levels than Sherry, but both still have access to item crates and the highest rooftops. Pay attention to the distance indicated next to the chopper's red marker and climb the ladders closest to its position. Smash any crates you find on the way up and pick up anything useful. When you reach the highest level, equip the Bear Commander and switch to grenade launcher firing mode. Carefully watch the chopper while it fights Chris on the upper levels. Whenever it flies within clear range, hit it with a grenade and quickly reload.

As Jake, you should stay on the rooftop where the chopper hovers most frequently while fighting with Chris. Sherry cannot reach this rooftop. Sometimes the chopper flies off in a wide circle around the area. When it swoops back in from the other side, J'avo will be clinging to a rope hanging from below the chopper. Hit the cockpit with a grenade as it flies low across your level. Fire a grenade to blast these enemies off the rope. If the rope is clear, the Action button icon may appear onscreen. Press Action to grab the rope and fly off with the chopper.

While hanging from the chopper's rope, tap the Reload button repeatedly to climb up to the cockpit. Aim at the pilot's head through the cockpit glass and Fire when the button icon appears onscreen. This feat earns an Achievement or Trophy.

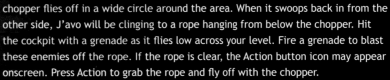

POISAWAN—SHOPPING DISTRICT

POISAWAN—SHOPPING DISTRICT MAP

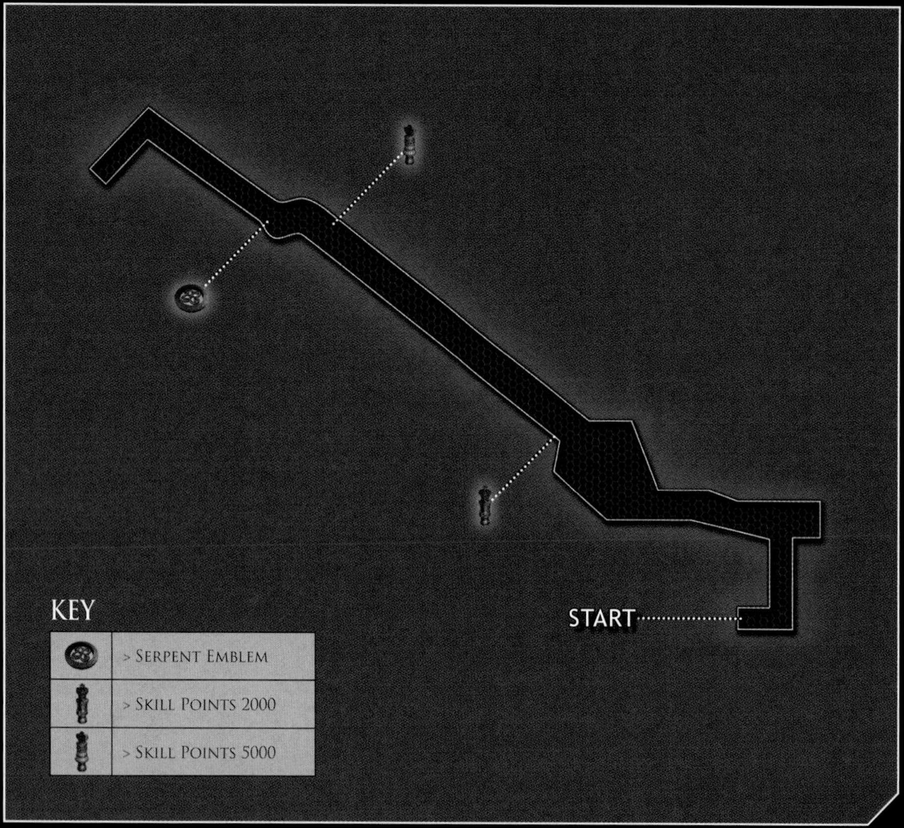

SERPENT EMBLEM: LONG ALLEY

On the side of the alley that is on the opposite side of the two crates that are behind the truck mentioned previously, a **Serpent Emblem** rests on the windshield of a parked car with its lights on.

ONWARD

Enter the next alley, hop a traffic barricade, smash two crates on the right, and continue around the next corner. Open the next door with a Partner Action.

REWARD ALLEY

Follow the corridor out to an alley, turn right, and smash a crate to obtain an item. Turn around, proceed down the alley, hop over a traffic barricade, and continue forward. Just beyond the cluster of barrels on your left, move into the niche behind the barrels to find more crates to smash. Another duo of crates lies on the other side of the alley. Search behind the truck opposite these to find three more crates. Hop another traffic barricade, turn left, and open the box in the corner niche to obtain **Skill Points (2,000)**. Continue down the alley, smash two crates on the left, and then look for an item box tucked behind the dumpster opposite the crates, which contains **Skill Points (5,000)**. Past the next truck are two more crates to smash.

SHOPPING DISTRICT

SHOPPING DISTRICT MAP

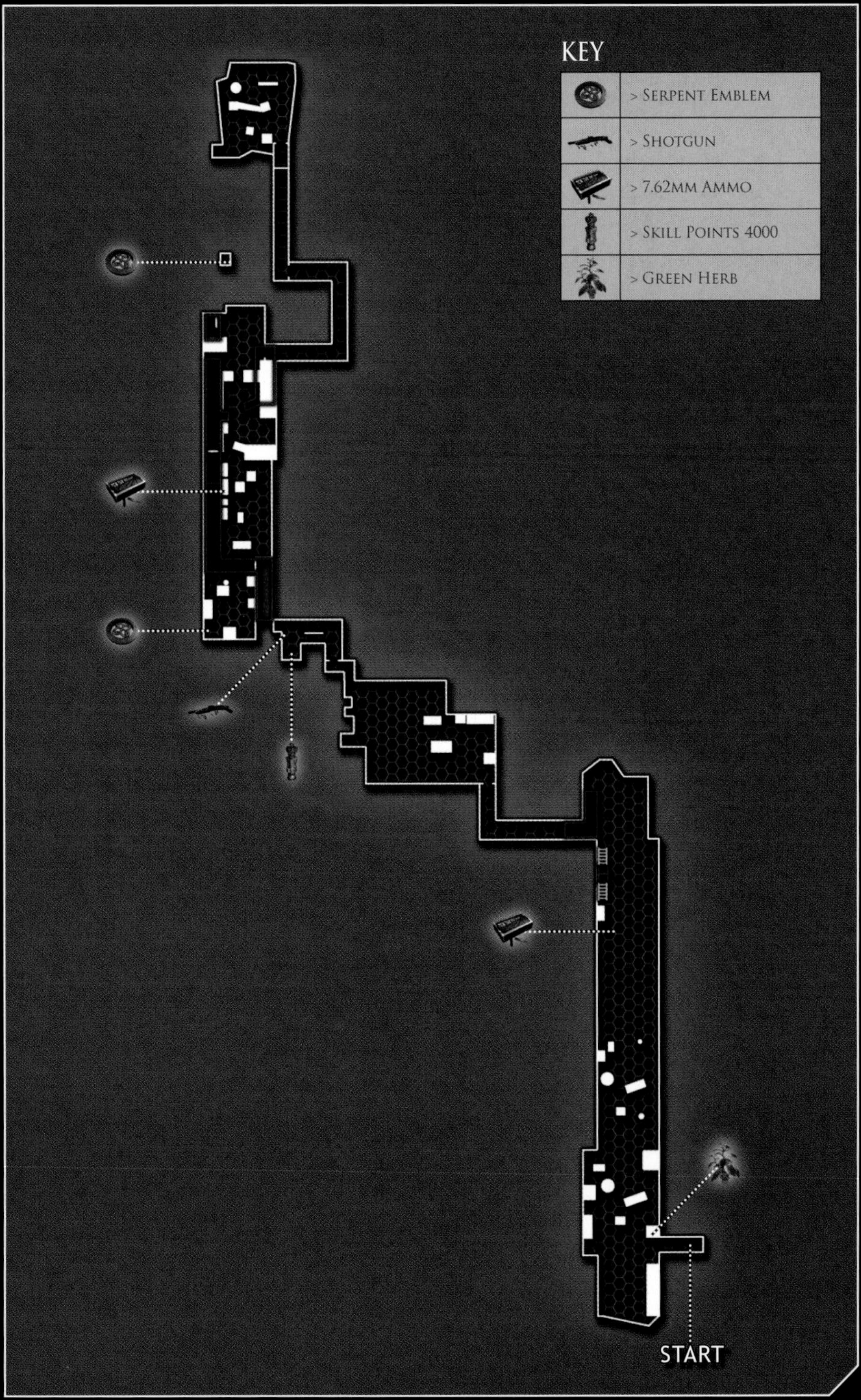

THE SHOOTING GALLERY

The J'avo marching down the street ahead quickly notice Jake and Sherry and attack. Confine the battle in the narrow entryway to avoid being surrounded. One of the enemies usually mutates into a chrysalid and then hatches as a Strelats. Prepare a Flash Grenade to blind it, approach it and apply melee attacks, and fire off a finishing move when prompted. Pick up the **Green Herb** from the boxes on the right. Smash the crates to the left and behind the boxes to the right for items.

Equip your Sniper Rifle and fire on the J'avo standing guard at the far end of the street. This usually causes them to mutate, but at least they won't be able to hold their heavy machine guns anymore. Gun them down with the Bear Commander and your Nine-Oh-Nine as they run down the street to attack at close range.

On the right side of the street, you'll find a ladder to climb on the side of a newsstand. Climb the sign above the newsstand to reach a platform where a couple of crates can be smashed for items. Drop from the platform back to the street, then move down the street and cross to the center to find more crates and a box of **7.62mm Ammo**. Near the ammo box, you'll find another series of ladders. The nearby exit door is locked, and Jake must swing across a gap using a horizontal pole to reach the platform above it. Drop down behind the exit door and press Action to unbolt it and open it for Sherry. Any chrysalid cocoons left in the street at this point hatch into Strelats, but there's no need to stick around and fight. Quickly move to the exit door, smash two crates to the left for items, and then open the door with Partner Action.

COMBAT OVER CORPSES

The small square is full of dead bodies, which you should avoid only because your character may trip over them. Continue avoiding them as a large squad of J'avo enters from the other side of the area. Throw a Flash Grenade to stun them before they fan out. Quickly dash into their midst, plant a Remote Bomb, run away, and detonate it to kill most of them instantly. If you don't have such supplies on hand, climb the ladder mounted to the newsstand on one side of the area and shoot the enemies from above. A second wave of enemies enters the area when the first are mostly defeated, or they may wait for you in the alley beyond.

STAIRWAY TO SHOTGUN

Kick open the exit, smash two crates around the corner to the left for items, and open the next door with a Partner Action. Head up several flights of stairs. At the top of the fourth flight on your left, open the box in the niche to obtain **Skill Points (4,000)**. Continue upstairs to the top of the building and smash the crate on the left for an item. The **Shotgun** sits in the open locker behind this crate.

SEPARATED ON THE STREET

Climb onto the little platform hanging off the side of the building and jump across. The structure collapses, dropping you to the street level. Whether you are playing as Jake or Sherry, your partner will navigate the upper level and provide cover fire from above.

SERPENT EMBLEM: STREET AREA 2—NEAR ENTRANCE

After falling to the street, turn around and head toward the parked taxi. Turn right to spot a **Serpent Emblem** mounted on a newsstand in the corner. Shoot it quickly since enemies are headed your way.

CLEAR THE LOW ROAD

A J'avo squad converges immediately on the location where you fell. Several of them mutate into Strelats, so don't hesitate to use the Shotgun against them for faster kills. However, you shouldn't waste all of your grenades on these creatures, since you will need some shortly.

Quickly make your way down the street, moving from cover to cover and sliding over low platforms. A box of **7.62mm Ammo** sits on a newsstand on the left side of the street. Smash a couple crates within a niche formed by tall boxes on the right side of the street farther up. Continue to a long line of newsstands and tall boxes. Shoot between them to hit J'avo armed with heavy machine guns near the end of the street.

Throw Flash Grenades to stun the gunners and give yourself a fighting chance. A couple more item crates rest against the wall to the right. Some of the gunners will mutate into Strelats. Luckily, your partner can drop to the street here and help you kill these monsters off.

Go through the exit door opened by your partner on the left side of the street. Follow the short alley as it turns twice and leads back to the street. Smash some item crates at the second corner. Then, climb the ladder at the end.

SERPENT EMBLEM: STREET AREA 2—NEAR EXIT

After climbing the ladder up to the scaffolding, look down in the street and to your right to spot yet another **Serpent Emblem** mounted on a newsstand below. Shoot it from here before moving on.

ENTER THE SMALLEST STREET SECTION

Proceed down the scaffolding by hopping the low support bars. Drop over the end, turn around, and smash the three item crates in the corner. Open the exit door with Partner Action. Step into the street area, turn to the left, and smash some item crates in the far corner. Then head toward the other end of the street.

UBISTVO (SHOPPING AREA)

A bizarre enemy with a chainsaw-like, mutated hand leaps into the area and attacks. Avoid the back corners of the area during this battle since those areas are now engulfed in flames. The monster advances slowly on Jake or Sherry and attempts to slice them in half with its chainsaw hand. If attacked, press the button displayed onscreen quickly to break free. Otherwise you face instant death.

Back away from the Ubistvo and shoot it in the head. Even the Nine-Oh-Nine is good for dealing with this situation, depending on your ammo reserves at this point. Meanwhile, watch out for instances when it staggers or lunges wildly. These are tactics designed to throw you off and to allow it to get really close, really fast. The creature may also leap across the area to attack, so don't shoot too many times from one place. Climb either ladder and cross the central structure to give yourself some breathing room to shoot from above. When the creature leaps onto the upper level, hop down immediately.

Continue shooting the Ubistvo in the torso and face until it staggers. Approach it and perform melee attacks to hurry this encounter, then move away immediately. When the monster staggers badly and Sherry shouts, "Now's our chance!" run up to the Ubistvo and perform a special melee attack where Jake rips the metal rod out of the creature's back and impales it through the chest. Then Sherry must approach the creature and finish it off using her Stun Rod. Ubistvo drops **Skill Points (4,000)**.

UBISTVO IS DOWN

When the creature falls, proceed into the corridor opening that lies between the burning wreckage in the corner. An airplane crashes as you continue down the corridor. Follow the corner to the right and smash five item crates to restock. Open the double doors opposite the crates with a Partner Action.

AIRPLANE CRASH SITE

CRASH SITE MAP

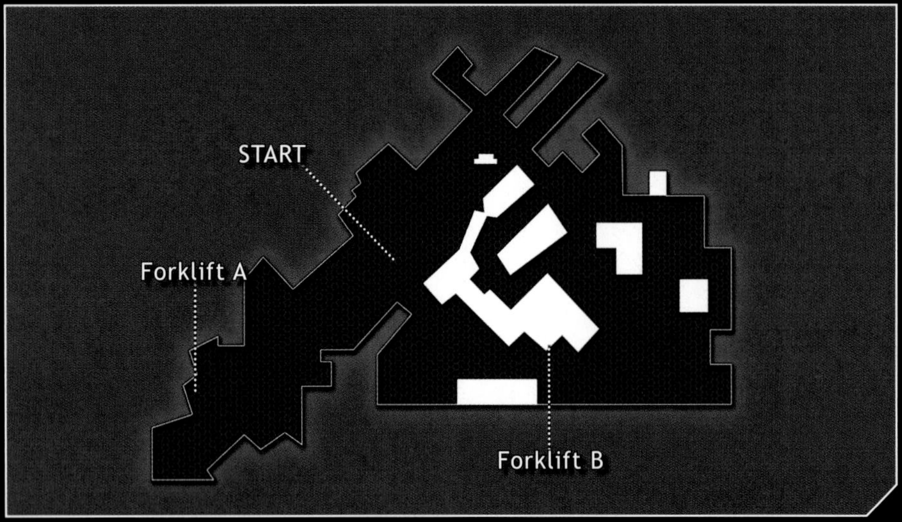

FAMILIAR FACES ALL AROUND

Jake and Sherry meet Leon and Helena near the airplane crash site just as the Ustanak arrives on the scene! If ever a titanic showdown was in the making, this has to be it.

USTANAK (SHIPYARD)

Although this battle is also fought during Leon's Campaign, we'll repeat the monster's attacks and strategies for dealing with them for convenience's sake. The Ustanak has equipped itself for this battle with a giant cage on its back. If it catches hold of Jake, it will put him in the cage. In order to get out, you'll have to rotate the Left Stick, then press the button displayed onscreen three times as a timer gauge moves through three green zones around the circle. Failure to do so leaves you trapped in the cage, but you'll get another opportunity to try.

Any other character whom the Ustanak grabs merely suffers damage for several seconds and can break free by rotating the Left Stick. Free a partner caught in the Ustanak's hold by moving beside the creature and pressing the Partner Action button when the icon is displayed onscreen. This action unlocks the "Lifesaver" Achievement/Trophy. The only other attack that the Ustanak employs is a charging shoulder butt, which knocks you down and inflicts significant damage. You'll roll around in pain for several seconds afterward, allowing the Ustanak to scoop you up. If you're Jake, he'll put you into the cage, which makes this an attack to avoid.

One of the keys to avoiding capture is to stay off the ground as much as possible. At the start of the battle, turn to your left and climb the ladder mounted on the cargo container. From here, you can shoot the monster repeatedly in the head, preferably with the Elephant Killer or 40mm Explosive Rounds. If the creature climbs up, merely hop down and shoot him from below. Climb back up when the Ustanak drops down, and continue playing this game of levels as much as possible.

On top of the cargo container is a large bin full of propane tanks. Move behind the bin and press Action to push the container over the side, spilling them on the ground. When the Ustanak is near these, shoot one of them with the Nine-Oh-Nine to create a huge explosion, engulfing the Ustanak in pain.

You can climb the larger cargo container a few yards away from the first one by pressing the red button on the forklift next to it. This will lower the arms and the pallet resting on them. Hop onto the pallet and climb on top of the container. Up here you'll find several item crates to smash as well as two more bins of propane tanks to push over the side. Hop down and stand near the tanks to bait the Ustanak over. Dash a few yards away and shoot the tanks before the creature runs off.

After the Ustanak suffers considerable damage, the dramatic music ends and it runs off. Let him go and avoid wasting any bullets on it at this time. Move to the back wall of the area and press the Partner Action button to hoist Sherry up and over.

The Ustanak returns and separates Leon and Sherry from Jake and Helena. The creature now sports a shotgun arm and fires from a distance. Take cover behind cargo containers and return fire, shooting any remaining propane tanks that are near the monster.

Meanwhile, Leon and Sherry must find a way to get back into the game. Quickly smash the item crates around the enclosed area and restock. Move to the back of the wrecked bus. Press the Partner Action button, then tap Reload repeatedly to open the engine hatch. Leon says he can fix it, so run up the side of the bus to the door and press Partner Action to climb inside. Then press Reload before the timer expires to start the engine. Sherry crashes the bus through the barrier.

Sherry's and Leon's actions open up the back area, providing access to another forklift. It can be lowered in order to reach four more bins of propane tanks. Knock these over and use them against the Ustanak. After suffering further damage, the Ustanak will retrieve his claw arm and switch it out. Thereafter, he returns to attempts at capturing Jake. If you're playing as Jake, then stay off ground level as much as possible. Continue blowing up propane tanks around the Ustanak and shooting him in the head until the battle is over.

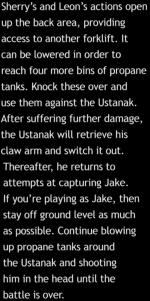

ESCAPE TO THE RIVER

Following the battle, turn away from the blaze and enter the small courtyard on your right. Smash the three item crates in this area to restock, then drop into the open hole in the ground.

Head down the corridor. Open the first door on your right to smash some more item crates and continue to the end. Break another crate at the end, then open another door and smash more item boxes. Grab the **Green Herb** off the workbench and use Partner Action to open the double doors.

STILT HOUSING AREA

STILT HOUSING MAP

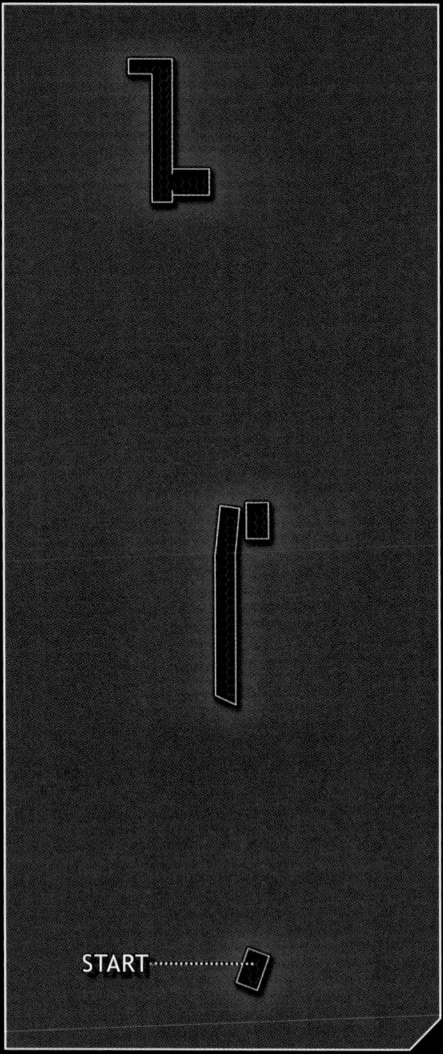

If playing as Jake, you'll take control of the flats boat automatically. As Sherry, you must turn around, move to the steering wheel, and press Action to take control. As debris floats into your path, rotate the Left Stick to steer the boat away. Failing to steer the boat in time causes a collision and stops the engine. Move to the engine, press Action, then press the reload button twice as the timer needle moves through green areas while circling the gauge. When the flats boat arrives at a sunken pagoda-style building, move to the bow and hop off. Proceed along the roof until the Ubistvo reappears.

REVENGE OF THE UBISTVO

Jake and Sherry reach the river but encounter the irrepressible Ubistvo. Hopping onto a flats boat, they have to navigate the treacherous and debris-strewn river to get away from the creature and reach the rendezvous point.

UBISTVO (STILT HOUSING AREA)

The creature merely staggers back and forth, following you around and attempting to saw you in half. The best tactic to employ here is to plant Remote Bombs in the path, move away, and detonate them as the Ubistvo walks by. Hopefully the blast will take out some of the J'avo dropping onto the roof as well. The blast causes the Ubistvo to stagger, allowing you to dash in and perform a follow-up roundhouse kick. Roughly three Remote Bombs detonated close to the Ubistvo should be enough to stagger and defeat the monster in this fight.

If you run out of Remote Bombs or don't have any, then equip your most powerful weapon with ammo, such as the Elephant Killer, the Bear Commander with Explosive Rounds, or the Shotgun. Blast the creature until it staggers, then hit it with a roundhouse. Repeat until it is knocked into the water by a falling signboard.

START UP YOUR NEW BOAT

After the Ubistvo is knocked off the roof, move to the far end and run down the signboard, which now serves as a ramp. When the camera swings out to view another flats boat in the water below, move to the ledge and press Action to jump across. Approach the engine at the rear of the boat and press Action to start it up. You must then press the reload button as the timer needle moves through the green portions of the gauge. Take your time and press the button just as the needle enters these areas.

ATTACKED FROM UNDERWATER

Grab the steering wheel and rotate the Left Stick to turn the boat as the Ubistvo saws down smokestacks and drops other obstacles in your path. A pile of beams hanging from a nearby crane then begins to swing back and forth over the boat. Allow the pile to swing past the boat twice, then dash up to the bow in order to miss the third swing. Otherwise you'll be knocked over and take significant damage.

The boat collides with an overturned barge, and the Ubistvo leaps onto your deck. The tactics for dealing with it are the same as before: plant Remote Bombs if you have any left or shoot it until a scene occurs and the creature is knocked off the boat.

SEPARATED BY A CHAINSAW MANIAC

Your boat continues floating over to the dock. Jake disembarks, but Sherry is trapped onboard the boat by the Ubistvo, which makes a final appearance. If you are playing as Jake, fire on the creature until a mysterious stranger swoops in and saves Sherry. If you are playing as Sherry, continue shooting the Ubistvo with your Triple Shot handgun until help arrives.

HEAD TO THE RENDEZVOUS

First breathe a deep sigh of relief that you'll never see the Ubistvo again! Then climb the ladder on the dock and follow the ledge to the right. Take a left at the far corner and open the doors with Partner Action.

END OF CHAPTER 4

BETRAYAL

Jake and Sherry are captured again—this time by none other than Simmons. The evil genius has sinister new plans for the biologically superior heroes.

JAKE CHAPTER 4: RANKING CRITERIA

RANK	ACCURACY(%)	DEATHS	CLEAR TIME(MIN)	ENEMIES ROUTED
A	70	5	80	40
B	60	7	110	30
C	50	9	140	20
D	*1	*1	*1	*1

*1 Any Below Rank C

POINTS AWARDED PER RANK (ABOVE)				
Rank	A	B	C	D
Points	25	20	15	10

TOTAL RANKING POINTS TABLE

RANK	S	A	B	C	D	E
Total	100	90	75	55	45	*2

*2 Any Below Rank D

UNDERWATER FACILITY 1

UNDERWATER FACILITY 1 MAP

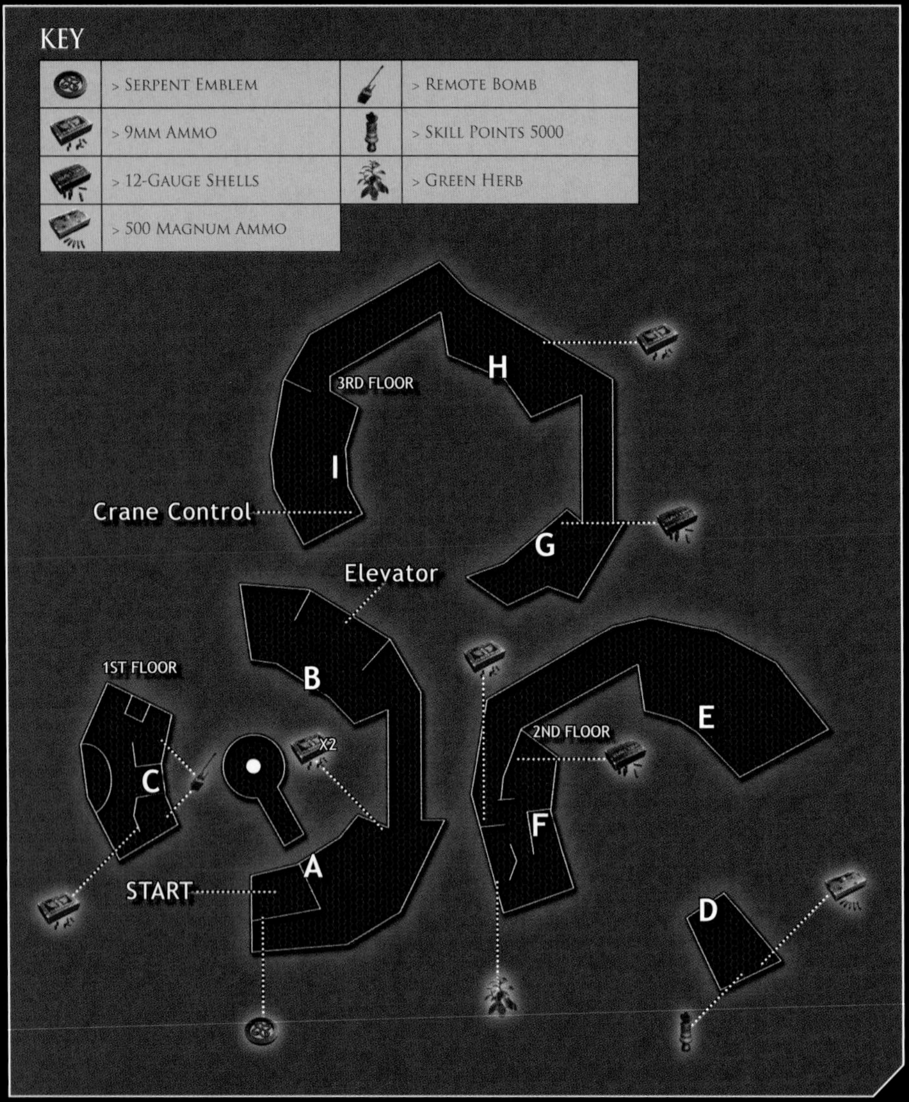

THE FAMILIAR BONDS OF CAPTIVITY

Jake and Sherry awaken from unconsciousness to find themselves once again in captivity, this time in Neo-Umbrella's secret undersea lab. After a few minutes, they are released from their shackles. Now it's time to escape from the facility and hook up with the BSAA to make the most of a potential virus cure circulating within Jake's veins.

After regaining control of Jake, move to the window on the left side of the exit door and press Action. You will spot your equipment on a table across from the door. Turn right and move below the high ledge on the nearby wall. Press Partner Action to boost Sherry up to the vents. Move to the windows and press Action if you wish to track her progress through the ducts to the outer room. She grabs your gear and shoots the lock on the door, which releases you. Unfortunately, she's brought something rather foul and nasty down from the vents with her.

DEALING WITH RASKLAPANJE

The tottering, gelatinous humanoid creature that falls from the vent with Sherry is called a Rasklapanje. These annoying creatures follow you everywhere and repeatedly perform grab attacks. You must rotate the Left Stick to break free of them. However, shooting them only makes things worse because the creature's torso separates from the legs, creating two enemies that pursue you. If you blast the creature's hands off, they transform into hand creatures that leap onto your face.

The best way to deal with a Rasklapanje is to steer clear of it. One good strategy is to lead it to the far side of the room, away from where you need to go or interact with controls, and then dash away from it. Perform all required actions quickly when it catches up. If a Rasklapanje gets too close, switch to Hand-to-Hand or use Sherry's Stun Rod to knock them back. Even these methods can cause Rasklapanje to fall apart, so use them sparingly.

In Single mode, your AI partner won't be as tolerant of these creatures. Monitor the situation and don't hesitate to suppress Rasklapanje body parts created by your partner. Flash Grenades are useless against them, but Remote Bombs detonated with proper timing can suppress all Rasklapanje body parts at once. Notice the use of the term "suppress" instead of "defeat" or "kill." Rasklapanje body parts revive after a few minutes and either rejoin themselves or grow into two, new full-size Rasklapanje. Leave the area as quickly as possible after successful suppression.

CRAWL THROUGH THE VENT

When playing as Sherry, move to the window left of the door and press Action to spot your gear. Move under the ledge indicated and press Partner Action to get a boost from Jake. Crawl through the vent and press Action twice quickly to move a little faster. At the end of the vent, you encounter a Rasklapanje, but don't stop crawling! Continue forward until Sherry falls through a weak panel.

After getting on your feet, quickly move to the bench against the wall and press Action to reclaim your gear. Avoiding the Rasklapanje, move over to the cell, and shoot the circle pressure pad, below the red light, on the right side of the door. When Jake is free of confinement, you can both proceed to shoot the Rasklapanje until it separates, at which point the exit door can be opened.

SHOOT THE MONSTER TO EXIT

Unfortunately, the game requires you to attack the Rasklapanje that falls from the vent with Sherry, at least until the torso separates. The light on the exit door turns green, meaning you can leave. Grab two boxes of **9mm Ammo** on the bench where your gear was located. Move to the left side of the door and initiate a Partner Action to open it.

SERPENT EMBLEM: SPECIMEN CONFINEMENT LAB

After reclaiming your gear and dealing with the Rasklapanje, step back inside and aim at the ledge above, where Jake hoisted up Sherry. To the right you'll easily spot a **Serpent Emblem** resting in the corner.

DETERMINE THE ELEVATOR'S PROBLEM

Although the doors of the previous room seal shut behind you, the Rasklapanje rejoins itself soon and squeezes through the vent system, following you from room to room. Quickly dash down the long corridor and examine the marked control console inside the elevator. The power has been rerouted to an incubation chamber elsewhere and must be switched back on again.

HOP ON THE LIFT PLATFORM

Exit the elevator and move to the red lever on the left side—Sherry must go to the right lever. Press Partner Action to pull the levers simultaneously. The Rasklapanje typically squeezes into the room at this time, but ignore it. Turn around and move to the door behind you on the left side. Again, Sherry must move to the right side. Press Partner Action to open the door to the interior shaft. Jake and Sherry move into the shaft automatically, so just run to the edge and press Action to jump onto the moving platform. While doing so, note that you just left room B.

JUMP INTO ROOM E

The elevator carries you to Room E. Jump into the room, lead the Rasklapanje to the far side of the central consoles, then dash back to the controls on either side of the door you jumped through. Press Partner Action to pull the levers simultaneously. The elevator in the shaft now rotates as it descends, and the door to Room C opens. The door in your current area seals shut, so you must find another way back to the elevator.

From the door, turn to your right and run to the back corner of the room. Enter the corridor and dash to the next area, Room F. Follow the corners to a T-intersection and move left into a small area with several control panels. A box of **12-Gauge Shells** rests on the nearest console.

RASKLAPANJE RECIPE #1: FLASH-FRIED HAND!

If a severed Rasklapanje hand follows you into this area, approach it and press the Fire button when it displays onscreen to perform a special kill action. Peel the sticky creature off the ground, slam it into the nearby incinerator, and burn it up!

SEARCH THE REFRIGERATED SPECIMEN AREA

Return to the T-intersection, follow the other passage, and move into the small room to the immediate right. Pick up the box of **9mm Ammo** on the bench, then move down the connecting wall and smash the glass on the second refrigerator to collect a **Green Herb**.

SERPENT EMBLEM: REFRIGERATION/INCINERATION LAB

A **Serpent Emblem** is plainly visible inside the central refrigerator. Shoot through the glass to destroy it for credit.

ROOM C

Jump off the platform at Room C. Quickly run around the dividing wall to the right—Sherry must go left. Move to the lever on the console and press Partner Action to pull the levers together. Doing so activates another lift platform higher up, which will now be your ride to the upper levels. A **Remote Bomb** rests on the console to Jake's left and another one plus **9mm Ammo** sits on the control panels around Sherry's lever. Get away from the Rasklapanje in the room, run back to the doorway, and jump onto the lift platform again.

RASKLAPANJE RECIPE #2: GROUND HANDBURGER!

If you stand next to either of the grinders in the room and a Rasklapanje hand moves to your location, press the Fire button when prompted to perform a melee attack. Your character tosses the severed hand into the grinder.

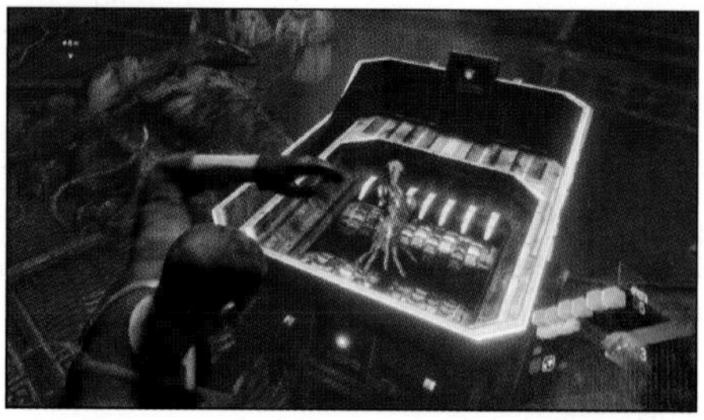

JAKE RIDES TO ROOM D

Ride the lift platform to Room D. Thanks to a horizontal bar, Jake (and only Jake) can jump across the gap and collect several items in this room. Smash two item crates on the left, then slide across the table to the refrigerator at the back. Kick in the glass doors to reveal **.500 Magnum Ammo**. Move to the table on your right and open the briefcase to obtain **Skill Points (5,000)**.

RIDE AROUND TO ROOM G

Return to the doorway and wait for the upper lift platform (the one with blue lights) to descend. Hop onto it, ride it up to Room G, and jump off. Turn left and search the nearest console to find **12-Gauge Shells**. Enter the hallway in the back corner of the room and proceed to the next room. Pick up the **9mm Ammo** on the console directly ahead, then turn left and run to the lever near the window. Sherry will find her way to the other side of the room on her own. Pull both levers simultaneously with a Partner Action to activate the elevator all the way back in Room B.

SHERRY'S ROUTE TO THE UPPER ROOMS

When you ride the top lift platform up from Room C to Room D, Jake jumps off by himself. Meanwhile, Sherry must continue up to Room I and jump off the lift platform. Smash the two item crates on your left, then turn the other direction and run through the corridor to the next room.

Smash the two item crates at the first corner, then head over to the red lever near the windows and press Partner Action. After Jake joins you and pulls the lever on his side of the electric beams dividing the room, aid him in shooting the Rasklapanje until it falls into the electric beams.

STOP THE MALFUNCTIONING LIFT PLATFORM

Knock the Rasklapanje into the electric beams that bisect the room by shooting it repeatedly until it weakens. Move away from the beams to the far side of the Rasklapanje and shoot it with your Nine-Oh-Nine until it falls into the electricity. The creature's arm breaks one of the levers, creating a dangerous power surge.

When the electric beams go out, move to Sherry's side of the room. Smash two item crates around the corner to the right. Continue into the corridor beyond and dash to the next room, which is Room I. Move to the far side of Room I and smash two more item crates. Then go left to the red lever near the window and press Action to pull it. This lowers the crane arm outside and stops the malfunctioning lift platform long enough for you to hop on.

THE SNAILS' RACE

The Rasklapanje hops onto the lift platform with Jake and Sherry. Shoot it repeatedly until all parts of the creature are suppressed and pick up any items it drops.

The lift platform breaks free from the crane arm and plummets. Jake and Sherry are dropped to the lower platform. Rotate the Left Stick rapidly to climb onto the lower platform. Jake and Sherry must now crawl through a shrinking space. Press Action repeatedly and rapidly by tapping your index finger on it, which makes Jake crawl across the platform to Room B.

ON TO THE NEXT MECHANICAL NIGHTMARE

Turn around, enter Room B, and move to the elevator control console. Press the Partner Action button to move on to the next area.

UNDERWATER FACILITY—LOWER LEVELS

LOWER LEVELS MAP

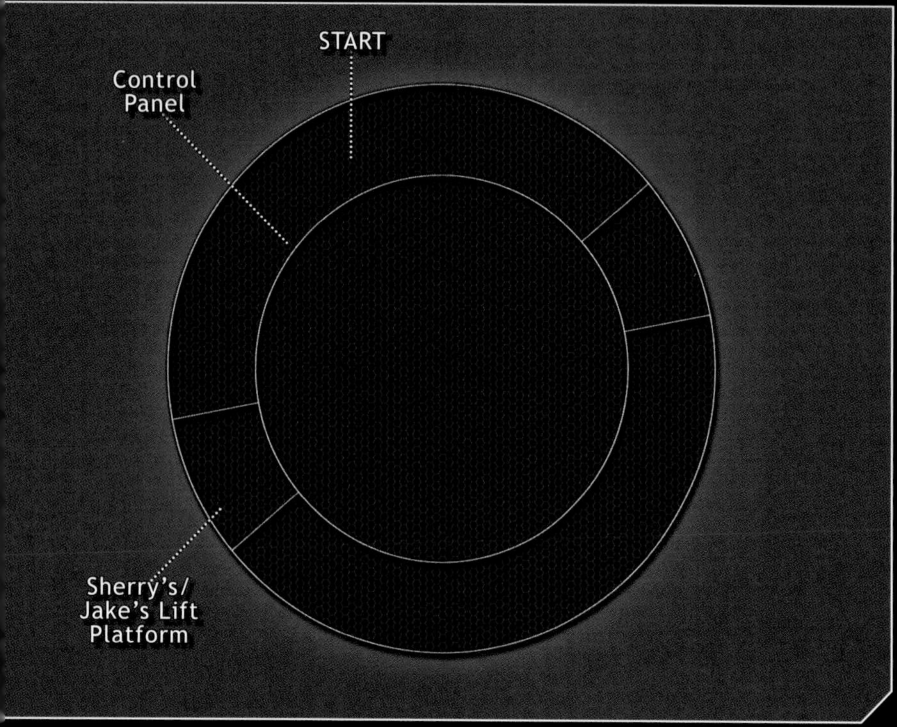

As the platform rises and circles the chamber, Neo-Umbrella J'avo soldiers drop on the platform occupied by Chris and Piers. Save your bullets, however, since they are about to drop on yours as well. Switch to the Shotgun to assist in close encounters, and use plenty of melee attacks between blasts to keep your platform clear. Your platform also passes open doorways from which J'avo soldiers fire rocket launchers. Switch to your Nine-Oh-Nine or Triple Shot and take these foes out with Quick Shots, which improve your aim, and follow-up bursts. Snipers may take up positions in doorways on the opposite side of the chamber. Watch for sniper laser sights and equip your Sniper Rifle to shoot these enemies before they take you out.

SWITCH PARTNERS!

Chris won't grab the lever on his side until you grab yours. Therefore, you can run over to Chris's and Piers' platform and become Piers' partner! This changes the dialog completely, but you may have a hard time hearing it during all the shooting.

A BRIEF CROSSOVER

Jake and Sherry meet up with Chris and Piers in a large silo surrounding a massive chrysalid cocoon. The team must figure out a way to get to the exit, which is at the very top of the silo, while fending off hordes of heavily armed Neo-Umbrella monsters.

Turn around and run back toward the central control panel. Approach the button on the left side and press it to activate two platforms in the area. Chris and Piers head for one platform while Jake and Sherry must go to the other. Move to one of the levers and press Partner Action to activate the platform.

UNDERWATER FACILITY 2

LOWER LEVELS MAP

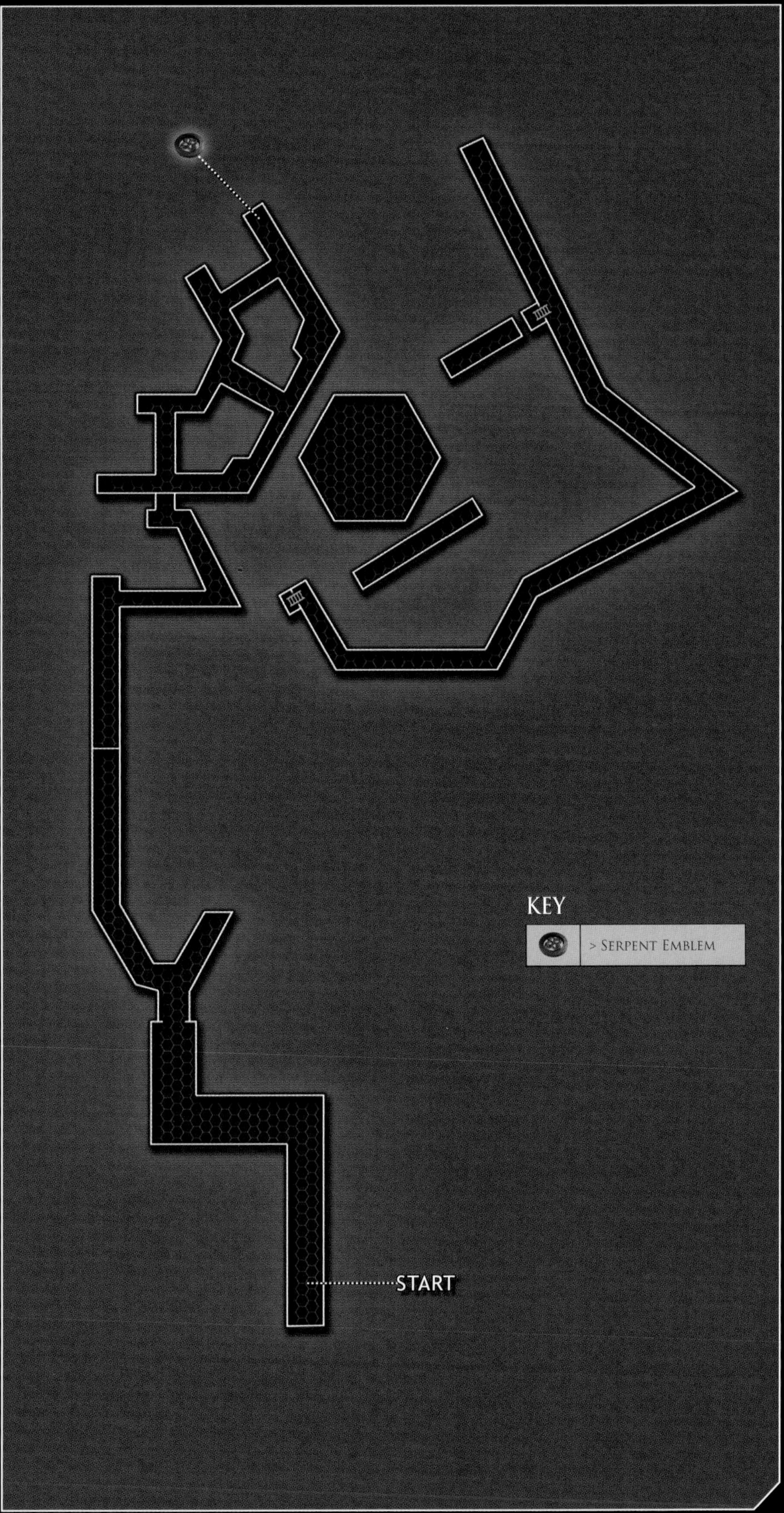

STOCK UP AND GET READY

Jake and Sherry find themselves in a long corridor with lots of item crates. Dash through the corridor, slide into the crates, and stock up on items. Follow this corridor to the end and press the Partner Action button to proceed. Enter the magma-filled chamber and drop to the level below.

(MAINTENANCE LEVEL)

As Sherry points out at the beginning, fighting the Ustanak on the suspended gantries is too dangerous (not to mention, a waste of time). Back away from the monster, turn to your right, and dash all the way out to the end of the longer gantry. Press Action to jump from the end to the level below. Navigate the next zig-zagging gantry quickly and move to the cargo container blocking the drop point. Press Partner Action to push the container off the platform. Jake and Sherry drop to the level below and so does the Ustanak. Now the battle can actually begin...

The Ustanak swings its new flail arm, flinging the ball in your direction. The best way to avoid this attack is to hold Ready/Aim and press Action to duck below the spiked ball. Time your duck for when the Ustanak swings the ball forward and you'll dodge the attack. Another way to dodge the swinging ball is to jump backward by pressing Ready/Aim and Action. Then you can fire from the ground until the Ustanak's next swing. Meanwhile, shoot the creature repeatedly, even with your handgun. Break the item crates scattered around the area to restock, primarily with **9mm Ammo**.

After you inflict significant damage to the Ustanak, it smashes the gantry apart with its flail arm, dropping everyone onto an extremely hot platform on the magma's surface. The creature continues swinging its arm and also charges across the area to deliver shoulder-butt attacks. Whenever the Ustanak's flail arm slams the ground, it creates a small magma pool that remains for a short duration and you have to avoid it. Items appear within these magma pools, which you can claim as the pool begins to cool and diminish. To cool off the magma pools more quickly, stay near them and bait the Ustanak into throwing its flail in a nearby spot—the previous magma pool vanishes more quickly.

Continue ducking and running to avoid the Ustanak's flail swings and throw everything you have at it. You do not need to conserve any ammo beyond this point in the game, so fire off all your Elephant Killer, Sniper Rifle, and Shotgun rounds. Pound it with any 40mm Explosive Rounds left. When it begins aiming for your partner instead of you, plant Remote Bombs next to it, then run away and detonate them.

Continue hitting the creature with your most powerful weapons until the Ustanak staggers badly. When you are playing as Sherry, this is your cue to approach it quickly and press Partner Action. Sherry leaps onto the creature's back while Jake attacks from the front. When you are playing as Sherry, press the Action button rapidly to maintain your chokehold. As Jake, you'll see Sherry leap onto the creature first. Approach it and press Partner Action to seize it by the arm, and then press Action rapidly to tear off its flail.

The Ustanak and Jake fall onto a short gantry section. Completely disarmed, you must now perform Hand-to-Hand attacks to finish off the creature. Move in close to the Ustanak and wait until it starts to raise an arm to attack. Deliver a punch combo or palm strike to throw it off balance. If you aren't close enough to the creature or fail to cancel its attacks in time, press Reload and Action when prompted to sidestep its attacks. Only perform a palm strike occasionally when the creature is staggering badly. Otherwise, although your Combat gauge is not currently displayed, you will not have the stamina needed to perform the palm strike attack. Patience is the most important tactic to employ here. Don't throw punches or palm strikes randomly in a panic. Wait, dodge attacks, and look for opportunities to attack while it recovers from its own misses. After enough damage has been inflicted on the Ustanak, you'll see the Action button icon displayed onscreen. Press the button repeatedly before the timer expires to finish off the creature.

While Jake is fighting the monster one-on-one, Sherry has her own route to travel. Climb up the ladder, dash around to the far side of the level, and examine the control lever on the machinery positioned just above the fight. The console controls a shipping container launching device that can be used once or twice to assist Jake in the battle. Tilt the Left Stick to either side to rotate the inner track. When it is aligned with the path that is closest to the Ustanak's location below, press the Reload button to launch the container. If you properly aim, the container drops right into the Ustanak's side, weakening the monster and making it easier for Jake to defeat. After a few seconds, the cargo container will winch back up and give you another opportunity to hit the creature.

SERPENT EMBLEM: MAINTENANCE LEVEL

While fighting the Ustanak on the lowest gantry level, dash to the two crates positioned on the far extension. Look at the column rising from the magma a few feet away to spot a **Serpent Emblem.** Shoot it quickly with the Nine-Oh-Nine or Triple Shot and return to the battle immediately.

EXIT THE MAGMA AREA

After the Ustanak is dropped into the magma, run across the gantry and leap to the ladder. Climb the ladder to join Sherry on her level and together head for the exit. Perform a Partner Action to open the door.

SHIPPING CENTER

LOWER LEVELS MAP

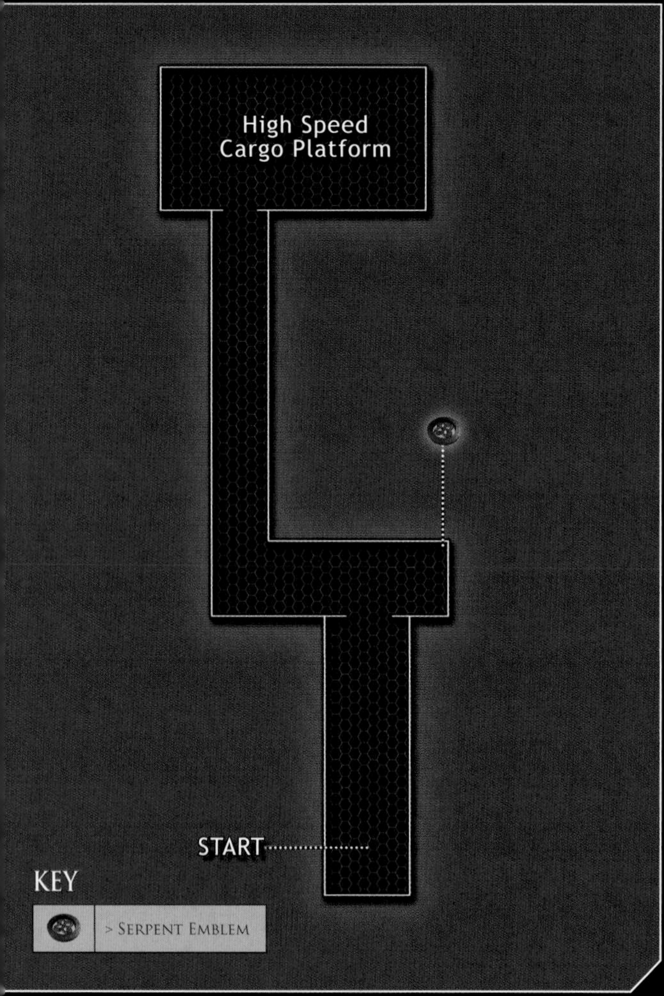

SERPENT EMBLEM: MAINTENANCE CORRIDOR

Leave the Ustanak battle area, proceed down the corridor, and head to the right. The last **Serpent Emblem** in Jake's Campaign rests against the gas tank in the right corner. Unarmed, you must move up to it and perform a melee kick to take it out.

BOARD THE HIGH-SPEED CARGO PLATFORM

Go down the corridor and to the left. Open the double sliding doors with Partner Action. Proceed onto the high-speed cargo delivery platform and find the activation levers at the front. Pull the levers with Partner Action.

CRAWL AWAY FROM USTANAK!

The cargo platform takes off at high speed, driving Jake and Sherry to the floor. The Ustanak hops onboard for one last chase. Press and release the Fire button, and then the Ready/Aim button, to move each of your arms and crawl forward on the platform. Once you find the rhythm of moving Jake's or Sherry's arms, continue pressing and releasing the buttons one at a time. Stay away from the Ustanak or it throws you off the platform for an instant death. You have one last chance to dodge its grab attack by pressing Reload and Action to roll away at the last second.

SEND THE USTANAK PACKING

When you reach the first cargo containers, press the Partner Action button to release the locks and hit the Ustanak with the cargo. Although this knocks the creature back and gives you some breathing room, it still keeps coming! Resume crawling up the platform by moving each of your character's arms. Continue until the duo reach a stack of pipes. Press Partner Action to release them. The gate doesn't go down completely, so press the Action button rapidly to fill the onscreen gauge before the timer hand reaches the end.

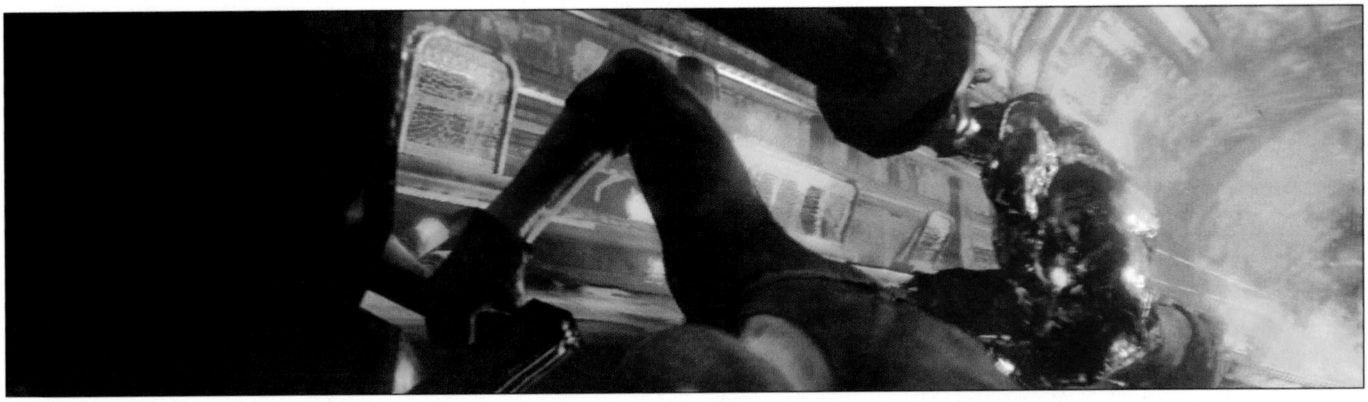

The Ustanak lands back on the platform for one last attack. Continue crawling up the platform, hand over hand, until you reach the Elephant Killer. When you reach it, press Partner Action one last time to quickly end Jake's scenario.

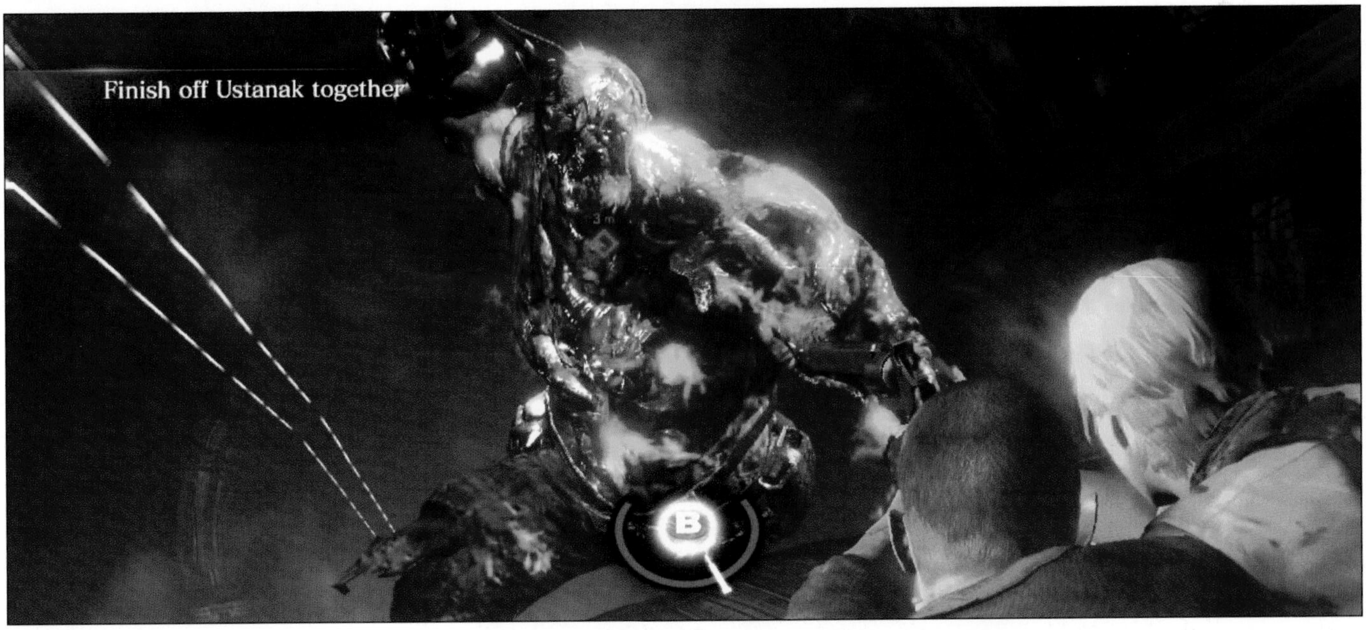

ENDING

After viewing the end of Jake's campaign, you unlock a new Dog Tag just as you've done in previous chapters. If this is your first completed campaign, you also unlock all eight skill sets. You are now able to choose sets and switch skills on the fly while replaying this or other campaigns. Agent Hunt is also unlocked in the Extra Content menu. If all three campaigns are complete at this time, Ada's Campaign is added to the Campaign Select menu.

JAKE CHAPTER 5: RANKING CRITERIA

RANK	ACCURACY(%)	DEATHS	CLEAR TIME(MIN)	ENEMIES ROUTED
A	70	2	55	5
B	60	3	85	3
C	50	5	110	2
D	*1	*1	*1	*1

*1 Any Below Rank C

POINTS AWARDED PER RANK (ABOVE)				
Rank	A	B	C	D
Points	25	20	15	10

TOTAL RANKING POINTS TABLE

RANK	S	A	B	C	D	E
Total	100	90	75	55	45	*2

ADA

NORMAL DIFFICULTY

The walkthrough provided for Ada's campaign has been simplified to pertain only to Normal difficulty mode, in single player, offline. Most of the strategies described herein pertain to using Ada's unique abilities.

ADA CHAPTER 1

JUNE 27, 2013

Deep Sea, Northern Atlantic

While escaping pursuers, Ada Wong stumbles into a room that looks like a study with a curious blue cube located on top of it. The voice and face of National Security Advisor Derek Simmons appears on the cube and invites Ada to investigate a research submarine. Sometime later, Ada enters the submarine via an advanced deep-sea diving suit and begins her search for Derek's secret, which somehow involves her.

SUBMARINE INTERIOR

SUBMARINE INTERIOR MAP

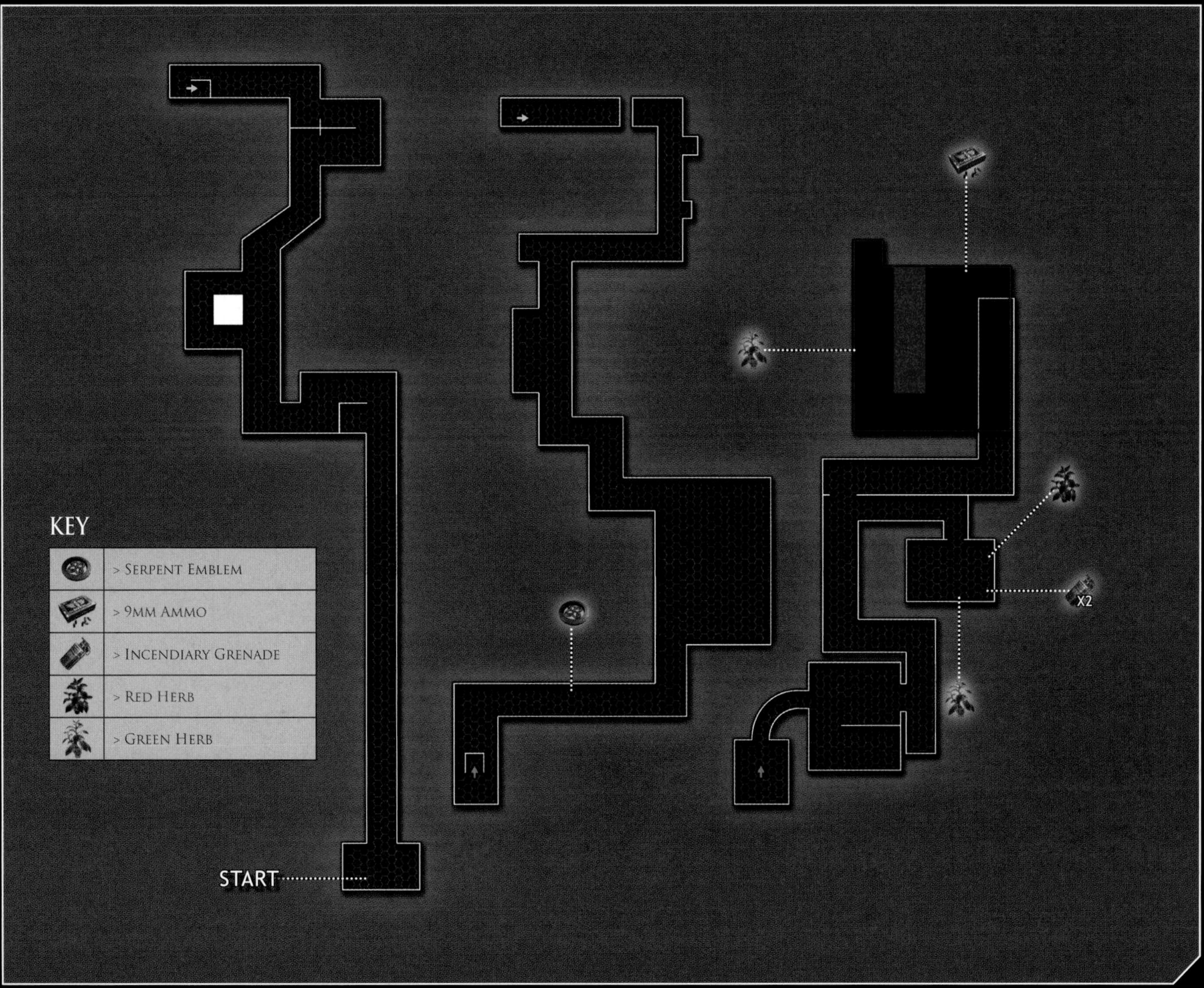

ENTERING THE SUBMARINE

Walk forward and unlock the door by pressing Action and open it by pressing Action again. To maintain stealth, don't throw any doors open in this stage (by pressing the Action button while the door is opening).

TAKE THEM BY SURPRISE

Walk forward down the corridor until you see an enemy Neo-Umbrella J'avo in your way. The key to this mission is stealth, so take out every enemy without alerting any of the others. Walk behind the J'avo and perform a Stealth Hit by using a melee attack while its back is turned.

STAY CALM AND KEEP QUIET

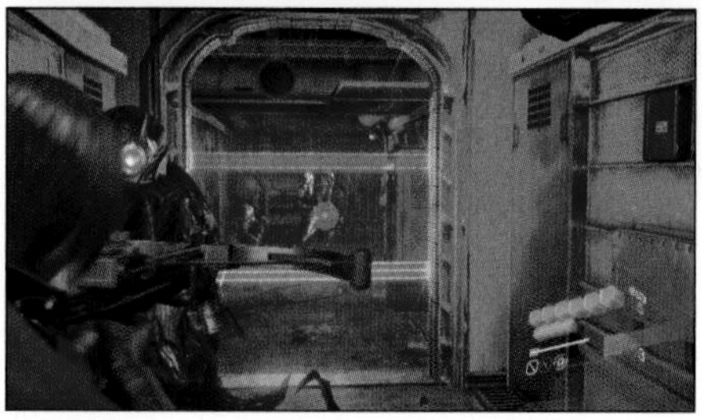

Ada's Campaign focuses on stealth as much as it does action. When you play as Ada, it is important to take out enemies quickly and silently. If you kill an enemy with a melee finisher from behind or use the Crossbow to shoot them in the head, they die without alerting any other enemies. This is very important because any enemies that are alerted will chase after you *and* will set off an alarm, sending waves of enemies to your position. If this happens, an endless stream of foes will attack you until you can move to a different level of the ship.

Avoid the doorways protected by yellow lasers. If you touch them, they set off an alarm that sends waves of enemies toward you. Look for a way around them before walking through them.

Ignore the path to the left since it's protected by yellow lasers. Continue walking forward into a room with a small opening in the wall on the left. Move to the opening and press Action to crawl through it, or run and slide by dashing with Action then pressing Aim to slide through it.

DEATH FROM BEHIND

Continue beyond the laser door and walk down the hallway to the corner. Enter into cover until you can see down the hall, where a Neo-Umbrella J'avo is on patrol. Wait for the guard to come near then use a melee attack to attack from behind cover and instantly kill it. If you move too far in the passage, you'll peek past the corner and the J'avo will be able to see you.

Continue walking forward and you encounter an area with another yellow laser door. Take a left and enter into the sleeping chambers. This is another area that you can choose to crawl or slide under. However, don't slide under this one because a J'avo is waiting for you on the other side. Crawl under the opening, walk behind the J'avo, and take it down with a Stealth Hit.

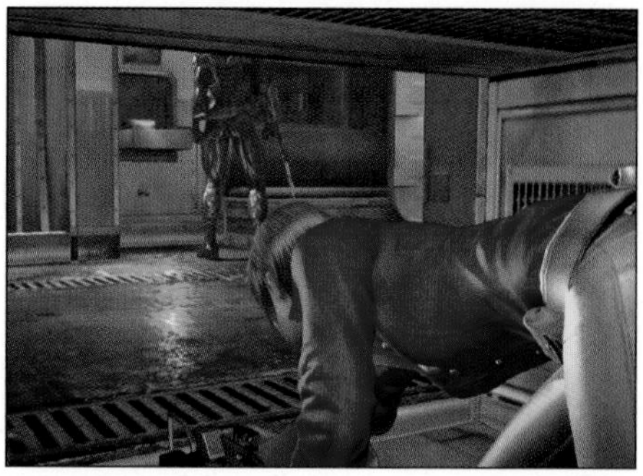

SURPRISING ANOTHER

After you kill the J'avo, go near the door and enter into cover. Look down the hallway to the left. A J'avo walks back and forth down the hall and will spot you if you run out of the room. This enemy won't come close enough for you to finish it from behind cover. Wait for it to get close and turn around. At that moment, run after it and use a melee attack from behind.

ARROW THROUGH THE HEAD

Continue along the path but take caution. You encounter another laser door with a J'avo hiding behind it. If you move too close, the enemy will spot you. Use this as an opportunity to practice your Crossbow aim. Steady your Crossbow and wait for the J'avo to stop moving. Fire at its head to instantly kill it without alerting other enemies.

MUTANT IN WAITING

Before the laser-covered door is a room to the right with a J'avo waiting inside. This J'avo won't set off an alarm, but that doesn't mean it's safe to just run in and kill it. If it sees you, it transforms into a Glava-Sluz, a J'avo mutation that attacks by spitting webs out of its mutated head. To take this enemy out and prevent its mutation, first seek cover. Aim and shoot at the monster's head with the Crossbow. If you miss, it automatically mutates. Wait for it to finish its mutation, then shoot the Glava-Sluz with the Crossbow to pin it to the wall. Run up and complete a kill with a melee finisher.

ANYONE CALL FOR A WEB-SLINGER?

The first chapter of Ada's Campaign features many J'avo that will mutate into the Glava-Sluz, a J'avo with the ability to spit webs out of its head. On their own, these monsters aren't very threatening because they're easy to avoid, and you can easily take them out with melee attacks. When they're in groups, however, they can be extremely dangerous. Getting hit by their web freezes you in place, and you still take damage from other enemies while you're confined. To escape from the webs, you must complete a rotation action on the controller as quickly as possible. When fighting a group of enemies, choose Glava-Sluz as your first targets.

After defeating that J'avo, walk beyond the fence and enter the crawlspace by pressing Action. Crawl around the winding duct until you emerge from the other end. Use a melee attack to destroy the crate. Then, move to the end of the hall, turn around, and jump down the open hatch by pressing Action.

ANOTHER ONE UNAWARE

Walk down the hall and destroy the item crate. Continue to the end of the area and press Action to use Ada's grappling hook. Climb to the upper level of the submarine. Continue to the doorway, enter cover, and you see a J'avo walking up and down the hall. Wait for it to turn around, then run up behind it and use Stealth Hit for an instant kill.

Walk to the end of the hall and enter some cover by the corner to see a J'avo walking up and down the stairs. Wait for a melee finisher prompt to appear when it gets close. Use a melee attack to pull it towards you. Slam it into the wall for an instant kill.

THE FIRST REAL FIGHT

Walk to the end of the hall before the descending staircase and enter into cover. Three Neo-Umbrella J'avo stand there but they cannot be eliminated with a Stealth Hit. Don't worry about an alarm, but you will have to dispatch them the old-fashioned way. Before starting this battle, prepare your Crossbow and take out an enemy with a headshot to even your odds. You can also use a grenade to kill one or more of them. Use the strategies you've employed up to this point and make an effort to conserve as much ammo as possible.

A TRIO OF J'AVO

After taking out the enemies, break the item crate at the top of the stairs. Descend the staircase and continue down the hallway. Move around the crates and climb down another set of stairs. Continue walking down the hallway, then turn left and walk down another hallway. Through a window, you see J'avo in a room and additional foes walking through the hallway.

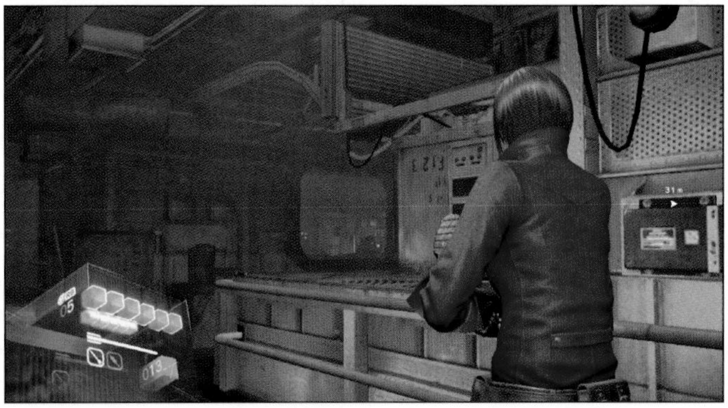

FIRST, THE ONE IN THE ROOM

Walk near the boxes to remain concealed and press Action to crouch and go into cover. Hold the button and walk to the end of the boxes, but don't exit just yet. When both enemies in the hallway start walking away, quickly run past the hall toward the breakable crates. Enter cover again to stay hidden and observe the lone J'avo in the room. Silently take it out with the Crossbow. Or, you may wait for it to turn around and then you can run to the wall between the two windows.

THEN, THE ONE IN THE HALL

Wait for the J'avo on patrol to turn around again. Jump over one of the partitions, run up, and perform a Stealth Hit. Once it's defeated, jump back over the partition and destroy the item box you ignored before. Jump over the partition again and move to the far side of the room and away from the window that is open to the hallway with the J'avo. Wait for it to walk past and stop, then fire you Crossbow for the kill.

FINALLY, THE LONE SURVIVOR

Smash the item crate in the room. Enter cover by the door and wait for the other J'avo in the hall to stop moving. Then, run out and finish with a Stealth Hit. Continue down the hall, take a right, and climb up the stairs.

SERPENT EMBLEM: IN PLAIN SIGHT

After you take out the J'avo in the hallway, you find a tiny sleeping area with little more than a bed and a cabinet. A **Serpent Emblem** sits on top of the cabinet. You may destroy it with any weapon, but the Crossbow is best—it helps to avoid calling attention to yourself.

THROUGH THE GRATE

Continue down the hallway and enter the room to the left. Smash the crate at the end of the hall, then immediately turn around and jump down the open hatch. Continue forward and crawl through the vents at the end of the room. Turn right and continue to the grate, then press Action to open it.

AN OLD-FASHIONED PUZZLE

Press Action again to jump down from the ducts. Unlike the rest of the cold interior of the submarine, this is a warm, fully furnished room fit for a fancy home. Ada will notice a picture and mention that this room was probably decorated by National Security Advisor Derek Simmons. Walk to the door and examine it by pressing Action. Ada notes that it's locked and that you must solve the puzzle of the room to open it.

To start this puzzle, move behind the partition and try to look through the goggle-like object in the wall. Ada will notice that the picture is blocked by something. Move back to the other side of the wall and over to the goat head hanging off the wall. Examine it with Action. The horns will move away from the goat's eyes.

Walk behind the wall in the room and examine the object in the middle of the wall. You see the picture as it truly is—a hellish scene with an animal in the center. This animal changes every time you visit this puzzle. It can be a snake, a fish, or an eagle.

Change the picture on the console near the door to match the painting in the center. Each console controls a different section of the puzzle—the first section of the puzzle is controlled by the console to the right of the painting, the second, by the console to the left of the painting, the third by the console across from the second, and the final section is controlled by the other console behind the partition.

First, move to the console to the left of the door and examine it with Action. Press Reload (Ⓧ on Xbox 360 and ▢ on PlayStation 3) to cycle through the available pictures on the console. You need to press it only once to get the image you need. Press Action to exit the console.

Once the console on the wall matches the image in the painting, move to the console by the door and press Action to activate it and unlock the door.

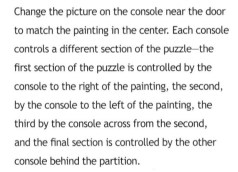

TURNING THE TURRETS

After solving the puzzle, press Action to open the door and walk through. Ada will step on a glowing spot that activates a ceiling-mounted turret that takes out a Neo-Umbrella J'avo. These turrets will become a useful tool for advancing through the upcoming rooms.

Walk to the end of the hallway, turn left, then walk to the end of the hall near the glowing panel. You see an enemy at the end of the hall near another turret. Walk into the hall and step on the panel, then move back and wait until the turret finishes off the J'avo.

WATCHING A SHOW

Continue to the end of the hallway and take a right. Move to the end of the next hallway and take another right, then press Action on the console near the door to open it. Enter the room and grab the **Green Herb** on the desk, the two **Incendiary Grenades** to the right of the projector, and the **Red Herb** on the projector's left. Press Action to activate the projector and Ada will learn about the son of Albert Wesker: Jake Muller.

AMBUSH IN THE ROOM

Once the show's over, an alarm sounds and three Neo-Umbrella J'avo attack. If you want to take them out quickly, throw one of your Incendiary Grenades into the doorway and finish off any survivors with melee attacks.

LURE THEM TO THEIR DOOM

Walk out of the room and turn left, then enter the newly opened room on the right. Three J'avo will be waiting for you. Quickly run out of the room and down the hallway past the camera turret. Wait behind the wall in cover and watch as the three J'avo mindlessly run into the turret's path where they are soon dispatched.

Return to the room, break the two item boxes, then run beyond the crates. At the end of the hall, two J'avo drop into the room from the ceiling. Take them out with melee attacks before they recover from their landing.

USE YOUR ENEMY'S WEAPONS AGAINST HIM

Press Action to jump to the top of the crates and press Action again to crawl through the ducts above them. After you exit the ducts, Aim and press Action to enter into cover and to avoid a J'avo ambush.

Once there's a break in the gunfire, run to the end of the hallway and press Action to jump down. Run to the glowing panel to activate the ceiling turrets.

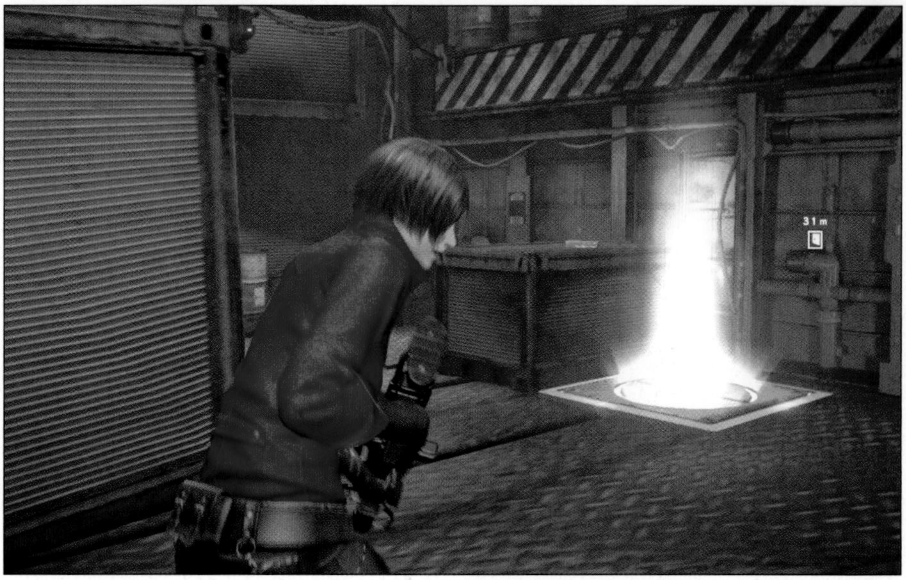

Run toward the breakable boxes to goad enemies into the path of the turret. Then run past them, take a left, and activate the other turret panel. Now that the turrets are active, run around the area, avoid attacks, and wait for the turrets to finish off all of your foes. If any enemies get near you, use melee attacks and continue dodging.

When most of the J'avo are finished, wait in cover behind the large crate near the breakable boxes until you don't see any more enemies. Smash these item boxes and collect the **9mm Ammo** located on the crate near them. Walk around the crates and enter into cover before moving into the next area on the right. A J'avo controls a mounted turret and fires on you. Use the Action button to crouch and wait until the enemy stops firing, then advance forward to a set of crates on the opposite side of the hall.

Pick up the **Green Herb** and wait for the turret to stop shooting again. Jump over the crates by pressing Action, run toward the next set of crates, and step on the ceiling turret activation panel. The turret will take out the J'avo manning the turret, allowing you to advance.

TO THE REACTOR

Go back to any item boxes that you might have missed and destroy them, then return to the door near the mounted turret and press Action to open the gate. Walk through the doorway and press Action to move on to the next area.

SUBMARINE REACTOR

SUBMARINE REACTOR MAP

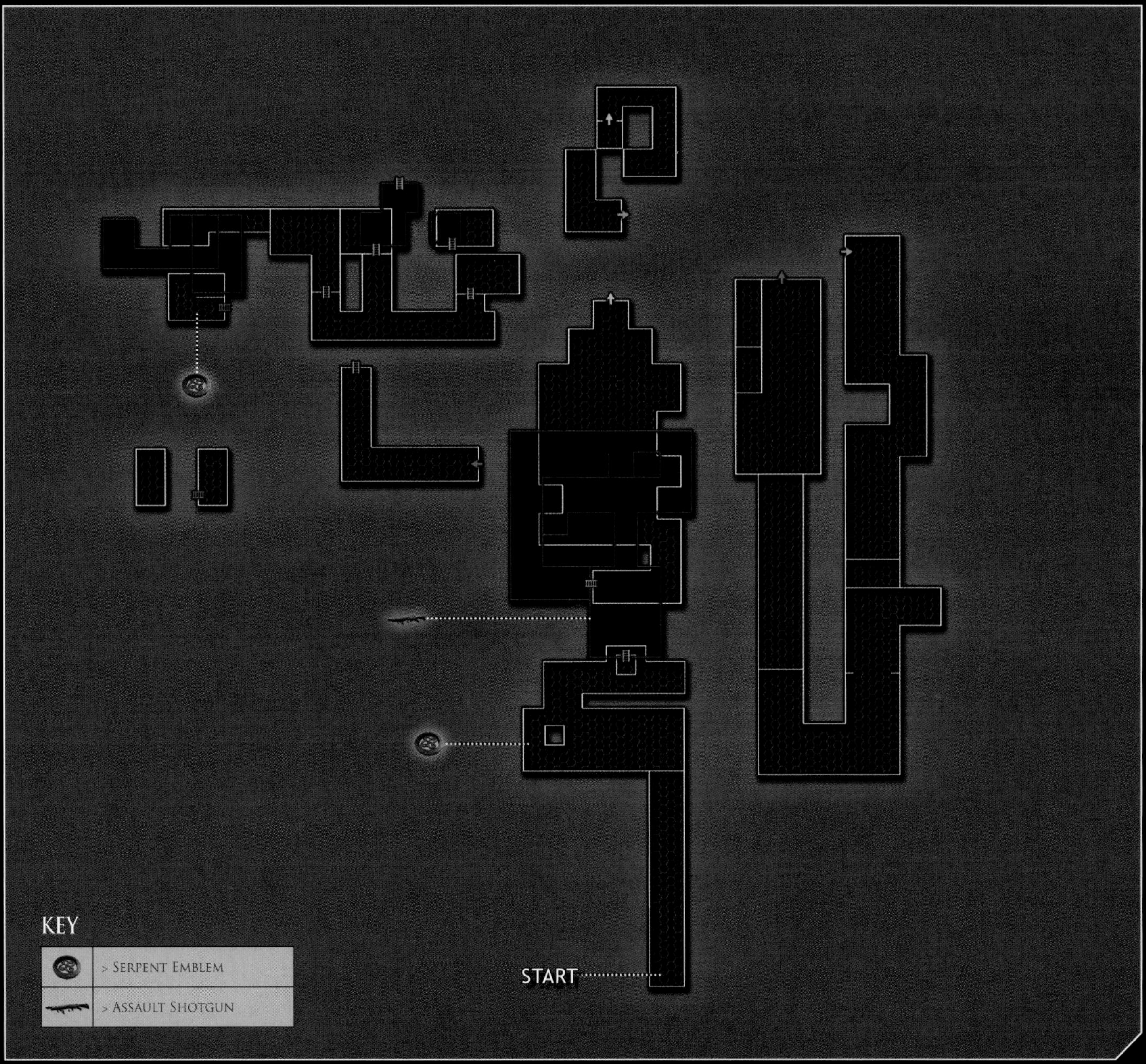

ENTERING THE REACTOR

Walk past the bunk beds, go up the stairs, and press Action once to unlock the door and a second time to open it.

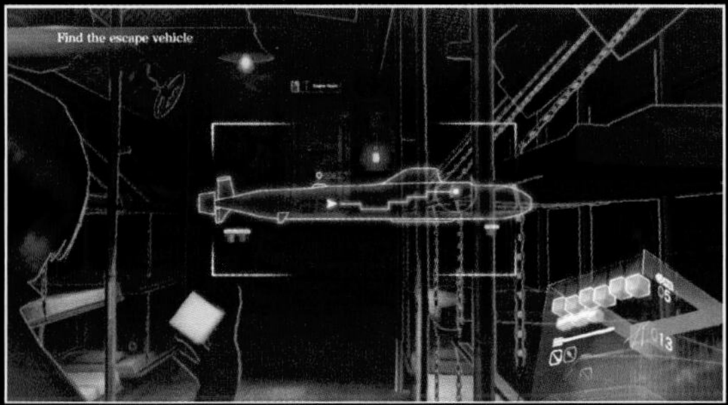

SERPENT EMBLEM: BARELY HIDDEN

After you open the door, turn left and walk to the end of the room. Turn around and you will be staring at a **Serpent Emblem**. Strike it with a melee attack to collect it.

FINDING THE ASSAULT SHOTGUN

Smash the box behind the pillar, walk to the wall, and turn right. Destroy the crate at the end of the hall, walk to the hatch, and press Action to jump down. Walk forward and you find the **Assault Shotgun**, a powerful new weapon for Ada.

Go down the hall and take a right at the T-intersection. A Glava-Smech and a destructible box are on the left. However, fighting the Glava-Smech may be more trouble than the item box is worth.

KILL TO AVOID A FIGHT

Take a left and enter cover. You see a lone J'avo in the hall. Take it out with a Crossbow headshot to keep it from alerting the Glava-Smech. If you miss and the Glava-Smech is alerted, you will have to take out both creatures. Don't forget to smash the box in the room with the Glava-Smech.

Walk down the hall and enter cover at the corner. You see another J'avo but this one is walking up and down the corridor. Wait for it to turn around then run up to it and use a Stealth Hit to eliminate it.

FIGHTING BY THE REACTOR

Go to the end of the hall, take a left, and press Action to climb the ladder. Walk to the end of the hall, turn to the left, and prepare to fight. Three enemies—two J'avo and a Ruka-Khvatanje—come straight at you. Equip your Assault Shotgun, wait for them, and then take them out. Run to the box on the left side of the room and destroy it. Another J'avo attacks you there. Wait for it to stop shooting then kill it. Afterward, run to the crate on the other side of the room.

A MAJOR BLUNDER

Two additional J'avo appear and attack you from across the gap in the room. If you shoot one of them a couple times it will fall while shooting and start a cinematic. The J'avo hits an explosive canister, damages the submarine, and allows water to flood the vessel.

FIGHTING IN THE CONTROL ROOM

Run to the platform at the center of the walkway and press Action to fire Ada's grappling hook. Move to the door, unlock it, then open it with Action. Move through the doorway and then to the right. A J'avo appears. Save your ammo by using melee attacks against it.

RUNNING THROUGH THE CATWALKS

Destroy the box to the left, turn around, and move to the locked door. Unlock and open it, then move through the doorway. Turn to the left and press Action to jump across the gap. Now, turn right and continue down the catwalk until you run into another spot where you can use Ada's grappling hook. Ada will jump but her landing area becomes unstable, so quickly move forward.

Dash through the area so you can easily bypass the various obstacles that you must jump over.

Move around the catwalk and over another set of pipes. Jump onto the upper area with Action. Move toward the locked door, unlock it, then open it. Follow the curving hallway until you reach the end, then press Action to jump away with Ada's grappling hook.

Walk down the hallway and you encounter a pair of J'avo, one with a wrist blade and one with a machine pistol. Use a Quick Shot and a melee finisher on the J'avo with the wrist blade. Move into cover and wait for the gun-wielding J'avo to stop firing. Once it stops, run toward it and perform melee attacks until it is eliminated.

THE SUB IS SINKING

Walk through the doorway and destroy the item crate on your left. Move to the end of the hallway and press Action to use the grappling hook. At this point, the submarine will begin to flood and turn on its axis. Move forward as quickly as you can and avoid the falling debris.

Before you can reach the end of the hallway, Ada will slip and fall on top of a crate. Wait for an Action prompt and press the button when it appears to roll to safety.

ESCAPING THE FLOOD

Walk to the end of the hall and take a right. When you reach the end of the hall, rushing water floods the area. At this point, you must constantly move or Ada will be overtaken by the rushing water. Press Action to ascend using the grappling hook, run to the ladder on the left, and press Action to climb.

At the top of the ladder, run forward and press Action to jump across the gap on the left. Move to the end of the hall and press Action to climb up the ladder on the right. Run to the gap on the left and press Action to jump across it. Press Action again to climb up the ladder. Now, run to the end of the hall and look to your left. You see a small opening near the ground. Press Action to crawl under it.

You are immediately ambushed by a Noga-Trchanje, a J'avo whose legs have mutated into spider-like appendages. Shoot it with the Ammo Box 50 or Assault Shotgun. After it's dead, run forward and turn to the left.

SERPENT EMBLEM: NO TIME FOR EXPLORATION

Before climbing the ladder in front of you, you see a **Serpent Emblem** to the right of the ladder. Quickly shoot it and keep moving.

Climb the ladder, run down the walkway, and jump down by pressing Action. Turn right and move to the valve located on the wall. Press Action and a Quick Timing Event will start. Quickly rotate or shake the left stick to turn the valve.

Retrace your steps to the crawl space, walk to the end of the hall, then climb the ladder to your right. Run to the end of the walkway, turn right, and press Action to crawl under the pipe. To crawl under the pipe faster, repeatedly press Action. Crawl to the end of the area and run forward until you can use the grappling hook.

Turn around and walk down the grates toward the ladder. Press Action to climb it. At the top of the ladder, turn right, then right again to another ladder, and press Action to climb. Move around the crates on the ground. Dash forward while holding Action to jump across the gap. Move toward the ladder and climb it.

Run forward and press Action to climb on top of the crates. Then, turn right and press Action again to jump over additional crates. Run up the stairs and turn right to run over the grates. Press Action to use the grappling hook and ascend to safety.

SUBMARINE TORPEDO ROOM

SUBMARINE TORPEDO ROOM MAP

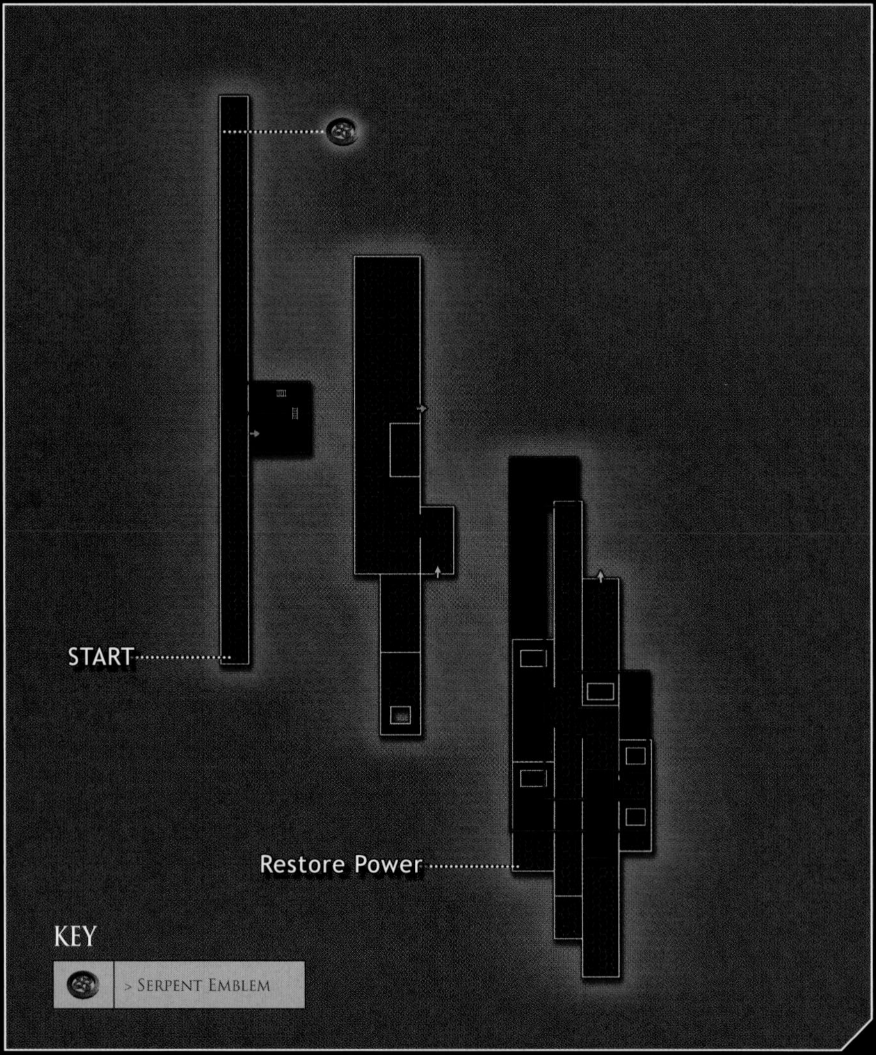

A MAJOR PEST

Walk to the end of the room and press Action to jump over the partition. You drop down to a room containing a Gnezdo. Fire the Ammo Box 50 or Assault Shotgun whenever you see its core—the flying "queen" insect—appear.

SERPENT EMBLEM: BEHIND THE WALL

After killing the Gnezdo, move forward and jump over the partition. Then turn around to see a **Serpent Emblem** that you can break with a melee attack.

CLIMBING DOWN THE SUB

Destroy the boxes behind the partition. Jump over it and move to the end of the hall. Take a right, climb up the ladder, then climb the next ladder to your right. Turn right and walk to the hole in the wall. Press Action to crawl through it then press Action to jump down.

OUT OF POWER

Ada will land on a platform with a console on it. Press Action to examine it. She notices that no power is flowing to it. You must restore the power before this console can be activated.

Press Action to jump off the platform. Move to the partition at the end of the hall. Jump over it then walk forward and jump over another partition. Press Action again to jump down into the area below.

INSECT INFESTATION

Once you land, you immediately see a pair of Gnezdo in front of you. You need to conserve your ammo for the battles to come, so prepare to run past them.

MARCO POLO

This section of the submarine is swarming with Gnezdo, which are difficult to kill and can quickly overwhelm you. An upcoming battle will require most of your ammunition, so you should avoid these Gnezdo wherever possible. This section is also home to a maze of underwater entrances and exits that you can use to avoid the Gnezdo, since they won't chase you underwater. As a result, you may have to deviate from this walkthrough at various points. Use the map to find the best place to emerge, advance to the next section, and avoid the Gnezdo.

RUNNING TO THE WATER

Move into the opening on the left, jump over the partition, and destroy the box. Move to the end of the room and destroy another box for its contents. Turn around and jump through the partition on the right. Now, turn right and jump down the opening in the floor and into the water.

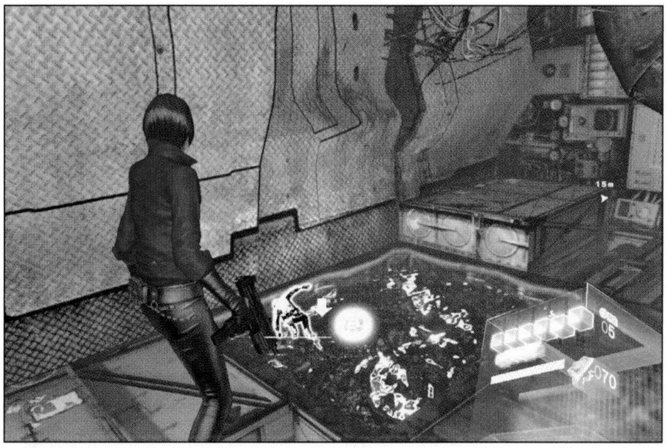

SWIMMING TO THE SWITCH

Dive down and take a slight right, then swim forward past the ladders on the ground until you reach a wall. When you look up you can see an opening that can be used to escape the water.

RESTORE POWER

Emerge from the water, move forward, climb the wall, and then press Action to pull the lever, which restores power to the submarine. Turn around and return to the water. Go back the way you came to the opening by swimming over the ladders.

After you emerge, move to the opening across the room and jump into the water. Swim forward, take a left, then exit the water through the opening above you. Move forward and press Action to kick the console, which opens the doors in front of you.

BACK TO THE CONSOLE

Climb into the doors, move forward, and then press Action to use the grappling hook. Continue forward and press Action to climb the crates. Turn left and press Action to climb under the opening on the wall. When you reach the grating, press Action to kick it out of your way.

POP QUIZ

Press action to drop from the ducts then move to the raised platform with the console on it. Approach the console and press Action to activate it. You will be surprised to hear the voice of Ada Wong. This other Ada will ask you questions that you must answer by pressing Partner Action whenever you're prompted.

Be prepared to fight—as soon as the Ada voice starts talking, J'avo begin to flood the room. Your best chance of survival is to avoid their attacks. As you kill the J'avo in the room, more will appear to take their place. When the Partner Command prompt appears, move near the console (you don't need to be on the platform) and press the button to answer the questions asked of you.

KEEP THEM ALIVE

Immediately target the J'avo with the machine gun and keep the J'avo with wrist blades alive. Attacking them might cause them to mutate into other J'avo forms like the Glava-Dim, which spews poison that will quickly incapacitate you. They might even turn into a Gnezdo, which will be incredibly difficult to beat while you answer the computer's questions.

The easiest way to avoid the J'avo is to jump onto the platform, wait for them to follow you up there, then jump off. Repeat this process until you've answered all of the voice's questions.

ESCAPE THE SUB

You must answer five questions before you can move on. When you've answered all of the questions, move back to the platform with the console. A grappling hook prompt will appear. Press the Action button to escape the sub and complete the chapter.

ADA CHAPTER 1: RANKING CRITERIA

RANK	ACCURACY(%)	DEATHS	CLEAR TIME(MIN)	ENEMIES ROUTED
A	70	2	50	45
B	60	3	90	40
C	50	5	110	30
D	*1	*1	*1	*1

*1 Any Below Rank C

POINTS AWARDED PER RANK (ABOVE)				
Rank	A	B	C	D
Points	25	20	15	10

TOTAL RANKING POINTS TABLE

RANK	S	A	B	C	D	E
Total	100	90	75	55	45	*2

*2 Any Below Rank D

TALL OAKS, U.S.A.

June 29, 2013

After escaping the submarine, Ada Wong travels to the Simmons family estate to investigate their mysterious cathedral for more information on the strange voice in the submarine. Arriving at the Tall Oaks Cathedral, she spots Leon and Helena but moves in a separate direction to perform her own investigation.

FOREST CEMETERY

FOREST CEMETERY MAP

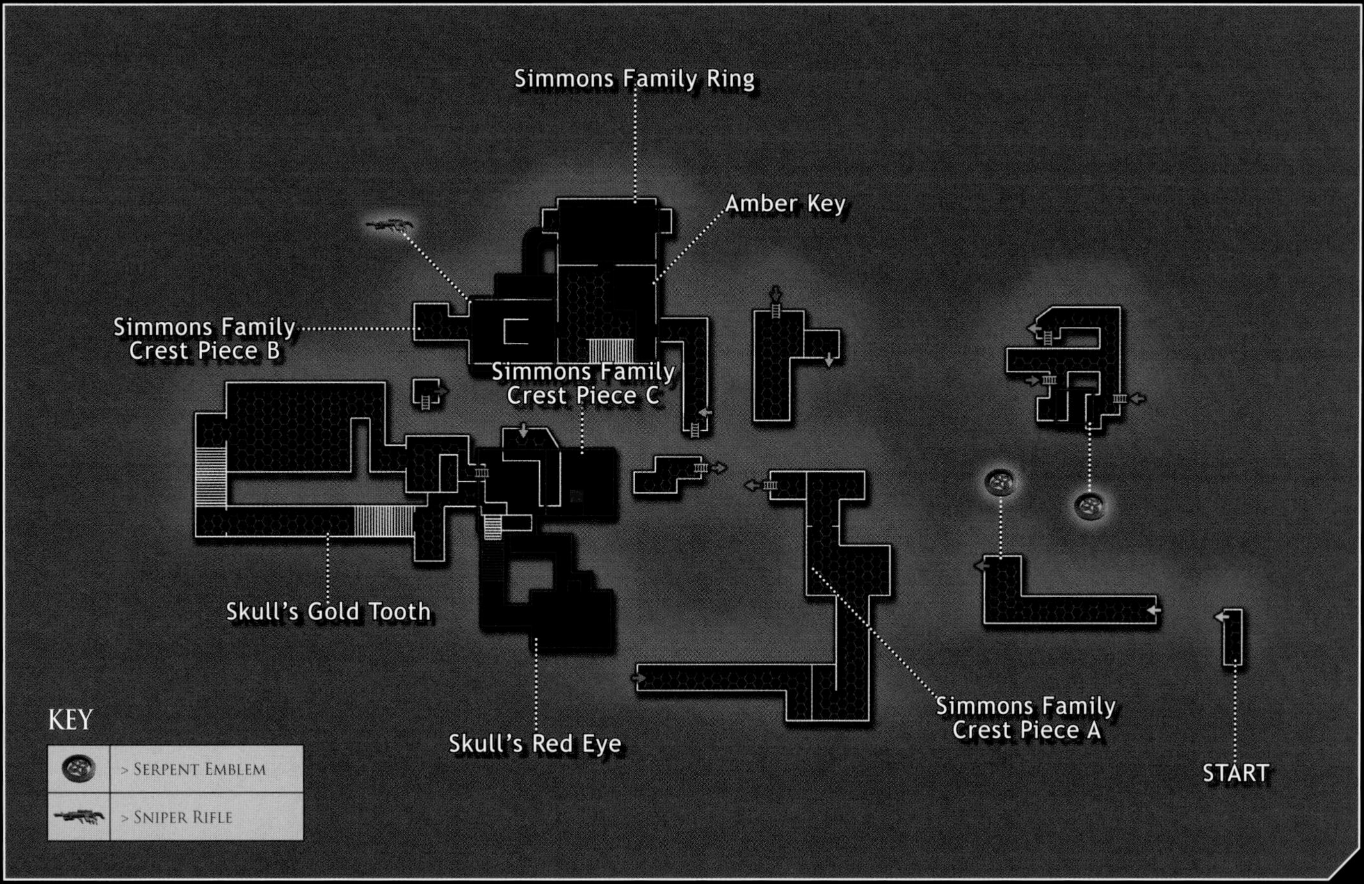

ENTERING THE CATHEDRAL

Take a few steps forward and Ada spots Leon and Helena entering the cemetery. Once you are back in control, move forward and press Action to move to the cathedral grounds. When you land, move forward until you see a trio of graves on your right.

SERPENT EMBLEM: BEHIND THE GRAVE

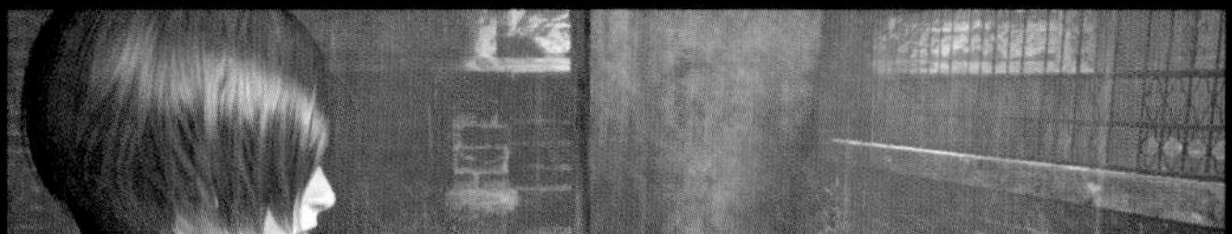

Before jumping into the open hole, move behind the large grave and look down to see a **Serpent Emblem**. Use a melee attack to break it.

WELCOME TO YOUR GRAVE

Smash the box behind the large grave then return to the front of the headstones. Jump into the opening in the ground by pressing Action. Walk forward then move down the stairs. Make a slight right turn and jump down the opening where the ladder is.

Destroy the three barrels on the left and continue out the doorway. Take a left and walk down the hallway, move through the doorway, then take a left. Examine the chest in the room by pressing Action. You notice it's locked with a large, yellow padlock. Destroy the padlock by shooting it.

COAT OF ARMS, PART A

Move to the chest and open it by pressing Action. It contains the **Simmons Family Crest Piece A**, which you need to complete the puzzle of the cathedral. Pick it up from the chest by pressing Reload.

After you pick up the crest, you find that the entrance to the room is sealed by iron bars. Two zombies appear to your right. The zombies are crawling on the ground, so move back and wait for them to try to grab you. When they miss, run up and crush their heads with a melee finisher.

STRANGELY SHAPED KEY

After the zombies are defeated, a door opens. Move through the door and destroy the barrels inside. Then, move to the end of the walkway. Press Action to use the grappling hook, then move forward and climb up the ladder to return to ground level. Continue forward and examine the door with Action. You notice an indentation on the door. Press Action again to place the first part of the Simmons Family Crest into the indentation, which opens up a door to a crypt across the graveyard.

TO THE CRYPT

Turn around and walk down the stone path. When the path diverges, take a left, walk forward, then take another left and destroy the barrels in front of you. Turn around, take a right, and return to the original path. Take a left and walk down the path to the end. Turn left at the wall and you find the open crypt on your left. Press Action to jump into the crypt then continue forward and down the stairs. Turn left at the corner and continue toward the door.

Open the door by pressing Action and continue through the door. You arrive in a large room with several areas blocked off by steel gates. Ignore these for now and go up the stairs to your left.

COLLECTING AND USING THE AMBER KEY

At the top of the stairs, destroy the box then turn left and shoot the padlock to your left. Walk over the bridge that is lowered. After crossing the bridge, press Action to open the chest to reveal the **Amber Key**. Now, return to the ground floor of the room. Move to the door with a green jewel on it and press Action to unlock it using the Amber Key.

A HANGING PUZZLE

Pass through the door and Ada sees a zombie pull a handle, which drops the chest in the center of the room down a hole that immediately closes. This is a hint for the puzzle you soon must complete. Run up and kill the zombie with melee attacks, then break the barrels at the end of the room. Be sure to pick up the **Sniper Rifle** lying on the ground against the switch.

You notice that many zombie corpses are hanging from the ceiling in this room. Padlocks are near the heads of each one. When you shoot the padlocks, the zombies drop and give you an item. Shoot them down to collect some ammo. Once you shoot a zombie down, it will give you an item only once, so don't waste your time repeatedly shooting the same zombie.

To solve the puzzle in this room, move to the left side of the switch—the side the Sniper Rifle was resting against—and push it using the Action button. Push it once more by pressing Action, then shoot the corpse hanging above the switch. The corpse will fall on the switch and remain there, keeping the hole open.

COAT OF ARMS, PART B

Move to the top of the platform and press Action to jump down the hole. You land in a room with two zombies in chairs and three panels on the floor sparking with electricity. Open the chest and retrieve the **Simmons Family Crest Piece B**.

SHOCKING

To solve this second puzzle, stand in front of the zombie that is behind the chest. Press Action twice to move it to the electrified panel. The zombie begins shaking as if the panel is an electric chair and you receive a slight shock. Next, go to the other zombie in a chair and push it forward six times. Move to its left side and push it forward once to place it on the panel.

After both zombies are on electrified panels, another zombie will drop from the ceiling. Don't kill it immediately because you need it to finish the puzzle. Lure it to the final electrified space and use a melee attack on it. This causes the zombie to fall on the electrified panel, which completes the circuit and solves the puzzle.

PUT A PIN IN IT

The door in the room will open, allowing you to escape. Go through the doorway, turn right, and climb up the ladder to return to the room in which you found the Amber Key. Now that the power has been restored, pull the lever near the unmarked steel gate. Move to the gate and press Action to open it. Three zombies will walk onto the panel and start milling about. Jump to this platform by pressing Action.

You fall to the floor below, which kills the three zombies. The floor collapses when too much weight is placed on it. For now, collect any items dropped from the zombies and destroy the three item boxes in the room. Move to the small opening on the wall and press Action to crawl through it. Follow the passage to the end and climb up the ladder to your left to return to the chamber.

To solve the third puzzle, equip the Crossbow and shoot each zombie in the chest to pin it to the wall. If a zombie is too far from the wall, wait for it to stand up then shoot it again. If you require more arrows, jump onto the platform to kill the remaining zombies, collect the arrows they drop, then climb back up.

Once all three zombies are attached to the wall, jump onto the platform and approach the chest. Open it and pick up the **Simmons Family Ring** inside.

KEY RING

Return to the room with the hanging zombies and move toward the door with the purple jewels at the end of the room. Press Action to unlock the door using the Simmons Family Ring.

Walk through the doorway and press Action to use the grappling hook. Climb up the ladder to return to the graveyard.

Move on top of the grave near the broken ladder and press Action to grapple to the top of a crypt. Move forward here and press Action again to use the grappling hook to swing through an open roof of a crypt.

INCOMPLETE FACE

Walk forward and press Action to jump down to the level below. You notice a statue of a skull with one jeweled eye and a missing gold tooth. Move toward it and press Action to examine it.

Two cloaked zombies appear, one with a gold tooth and another with a jeweled eye. The items probably belong in the skull statue. Move toward the ladder, break the two boxes to its right, then climb the ladder. At the top of the ladder, move forward and take a right at the wall. Move toward the barrels and destroy them.

A TOOTH FOR A TOOTH

Continue to the door on the left. You encounter a cloaked zombie again. It escapes through a door and shuts it, leaving you in a room full of zombies. To conserve ammo, take out these monsters with melee attacks as much as possible. You won't have much trouble from them since they're slow-moving. Watch out for the zombie holding the dynamite, which explodes when he dies, potentially hurting you and any zombies nearby. To quickly complete this area, kill him from a distance when he is close to other zombies.

Continue through the door that opens and chase after the cloaked zombie. After you pass through the doorway, the prison cells open and release a horde of undead. You must kill all of them before you can move on. Use the Assault Shotgun to keep from being overrun—you won't have much space to escape if they surround you. Locate and kill the Shrieker first among the zombie mob. If it shrieks, the zombies become enraged, making them faster and stronger.

Once you've defeated the zombies, move through the door at the end of the hall, take a left, and go down the stairs. Destroy the barrels then turn left and enter the doorway. More zombies will appear in the hallway. Ignore them and run down the hall toward the cloaked zombie. Perform a melee attack as you run at it, then use a melee attack to finish it off after it's hit the ground. Upon its death, it drops the **Skull's Gold Tooth**. Pick it up with Reload and run out the door before the other zombies can catch you.

ADA WONG, D.D.S.

Climb up the stairs and press the Action button to crawl through the hole on the left. Follow the crawl space to the end, then jump off the platform to return to the room with the skull statue. Return to it and press Action to insert the Skull's Gold Tooth. After it's inserted, turn around and move to the red spot on the ground. Press Action to use the grappling hook to travel to the upper level of the area.

AN EYE FOR AN EYE

Take a few steps into this area and the ground collapses underneath you. Ada drops into a crawl space with giant spinning blades behind her. Press Action repeatedly to crawl away from them as fast as possible.

The path diverges to the right and you encounter two spitting zombies. Equip the Ammo Box 50 and take them out before they hit you with spit—it incapacitates you and makes you more vulnerable to the spinning blades.

Continue crawling to the exit where a Whopper blocks your path. When you see an opening on the left, quickly turn and follow it until you can escape the crawl space.

As soon as you exit, rush toward the cloaked zombie and take him out before the Whopper stands up. Pick up the **Skull's Red Eye** with Reload and destroy the barrels at the back of the room.

ADA WONG, OPTOMETRIST

Leave the room and continue down the hallway until you reach some barrels. Destroy them then turn right and travel up the stairs. Crawl through the opening at the end of the stairs then jump down to return to the room with the skull statue. Press Action in front of the statue to insert the Skull's Crystal Eye, which will open the gate to the left.

COAT OF ARMS, PART C

Continue through the gate and open the chest to find the **Simmons Family Crest Piece C**. Move around the chest and go to the back of the room. Press Action to grapple to the upper levels. Take a left, then make a right, and climb back to the graveyard.

OPENING THE CRYPT

Go down the walkway to the left. Turn right at the T-intersection and return to the front of the cathedral. Press Action in front of the door to insert Piece B of the Simmons Family Crest. Press Action again to insert Piece C, which will open the door to the crypt. Enter the crypt by pressing Action. Then walk to the door and open it by pressing Action to complete the stage.

SERPENT EMBLEM: LOOK BEHIND YOU

Before moving on, turn around and look up after you jump down into the opening in the crypt. You see a **Serpent Emblem** that you should shoot down and collect.

ALTAR CORRIDOR

ALTAR CORRIDOR MAP

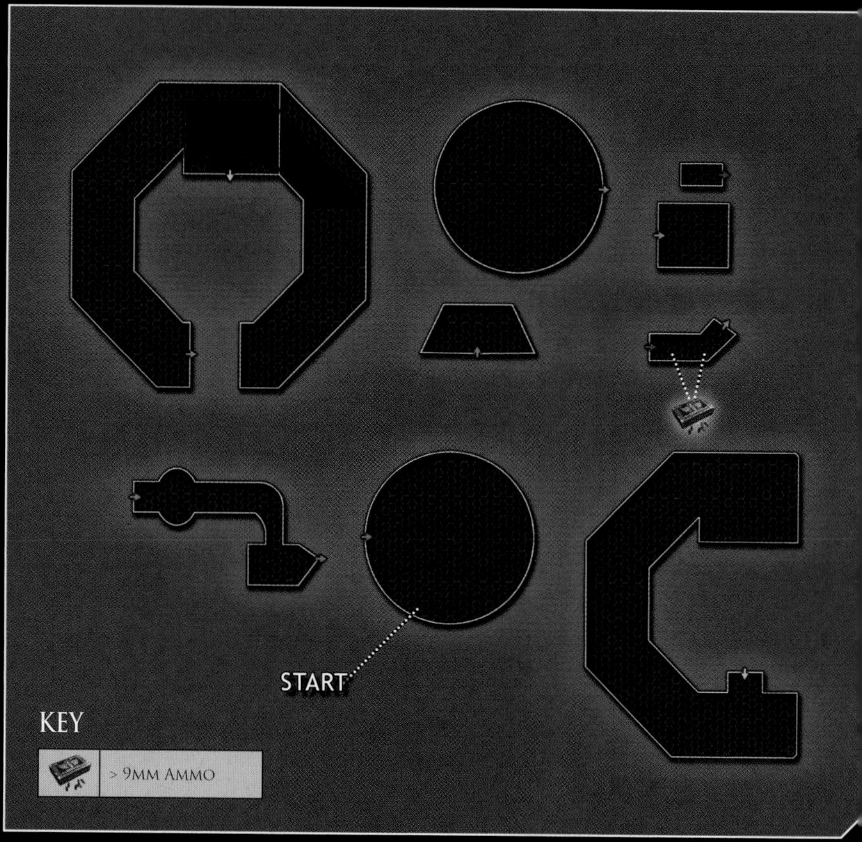

REUNION WITH LEON

Ada encounters Leon and Helena standing near the mutated Deborah Harper. Ada shoots Debora in the head to save Helena from Deborah's grasp, and then jumps down to help further.

SISTER SQUABBLE

Helena is sobbing over the mutated Deborah, who comes alive and attacks with a spinning attack that knocks you off your feet. Deborah will then jump on Helena, attacking her again. Although it seems cruel, allow Deborah to attack Helena without interfering. After a short time, Deborah will jump off, wounded, destroying the floo beneath you.

DOWN TO THE DEPTHS

You find yourself in a lower level of the catacombs with Leon. Follow the wooden path downward. A pair of zombies falls onto the walkway, dropping ammo or items for you. Keep following the path and destroy the pots at the end of the walkway. Turn left then press Partner Action to jump across the gap.

Ada gives Leon the Simmons Family Ring. Continue downward through the catacombs. Break the pot in front of you then continue down the walkway. Jump across the gap by pressing Action and continue by pressing Action to jump down several walls. You eventually reach an elevator blocked by a large object. Press Action to investigate it. Helena will pull a switch that moves the elevator out of your way and allows you to continue forward.

Press Partner Action to jump over the gap. Deborah attacks you in mid-air, knocking you farther down the catacombs.

TAKE A SHOT AT HER

You land on a raised platform away from Deborah. Pull out the Sniper Rifle and wait for Deborah to unleash her tentacles. Shoot at the glowing spot on her tentacle with the Sniper Rifle. When Deborah falls down to the lower levels, chase after her.

DEBORAH

You fight Deborah again, this time as Ada. While you can't kill her just yet, you can at least force her to retreat. To wound her, aim for the glowing spots on her tentacles that appear after she performs an attack. After you destroy one, she retreats and you must avoid another one of her attacks before you can damage her again.

Before an attack, Deborah jumps to a higher elevation and poses with her tentacles out. This is your opportunity to shoot her tentacles and damage her. She will occasionally walk around the arena and stare at you from above. You can injure her while she is up there and knock her onto the ground. This exposes a tentacle and allows you to deal significant damage.

After roughly 10 seconds of posing, Deborah hides her tentacles and either jumps to the other side of the room or jumps down onto your level with a flying kick. You can tell when she is going to kick because she screams at you before attacking. Avoid her kick by attacking her from the other side of the room. If she jumps to the other side, she shortly comes down with a kick from the other side. Run to the opposite side of the area to avoid her. If she hits you with the kick, she jumps on top of you, and you must perform a Quick Timing Event to escape. If you don't escape, you are instantly killed.

After Deborah lands, she jumps at you with a swipe of her tentacles. Keep moving around the edge of the arena to avoid her attack, which exposes her tentacles and gives you the chance to damage her. She either repeats this attack or swings a horizontal slash that you can avoid by keeping your distance.

Zombies will walk around the area and attack you, and you can kill them if you need additional ammo. For the most part, ignore them and focus your assault solely on Deborah's tentacles. This ensures a quick victory before she has an opportunity to use most of her attacks.

HE CAN TAKE CARE OF HIMSELF

After defeating Deborah, she destroys the floor. When this happens, you fall onto an area with Helena. Destroy the pots on the platform then jump onto the mine cart by pressing Action. You ride this cart with Helena while Leon must walk down by himself. You can help Leon by shooting the zombies in his way, but letting him fend for himself doesn't cause any issues for you.

A RELAXING RIDE?

Once Leon reaches the end of the walkway, he rotates a crank and joins you on the mine cart. The mine cart accelerates and you must duck under three obstacles by pressing Action and Reload simultaneously. To easily avoid all obstacles, use Aim and then press Action and back on the left stick to jump backward and to land on your back. The obstacles will harmlessly pass over your head.

Deborah will catch up and jump on top of the mine cart to attack you. She performs three attacks in a sequence while on the mine cart: a horizontal swipe, a vertical slash, then a horizontal swipe in the other direction. She then jumps to the other side of the mine cart and repeats this sequence.

Avoid the horizontal attacks by ducking: use Action and Reload or the backward-jump trick described above. This won't help you avoid her vertical slash, however, so prepare to roll by moving left or right after her first slash.

After she goes through both attack sequences, Deborah jumps off the mine cart and you suddenly notice an explosive barrel in your path. Shoot it with the Ammo Box 50 or the Assault Shotgun just in case you miss with your first shot. You must dodge two more obstacles and destroy another explosive barrel in your way. At this point, the pattern repeats and you have to dodge two more obstacles and obliterate another barrel.

HOPE YOU HAVE INSURANCE

After the second barrel and obstacle sequence, Deborah returns to the mine cart. You must dodge a single horizontal attack and then the cart crashes, sending you and Deborah flying out of the cart.

You hang from a ledge until Leon helps you up. Quickly grab the **9mm Ammo** lying on the ground, then destroy the two barrels and pick up the second **9mm Ammo**. Pull out a weapon and aim at Deborah, who moves toward Helena with the intent to kill. You have only a few seconds to take her out, so make your shots count. The number of hits matters more than the power behind them, so use the Ammo Box 50.

ANOTHER GOODBYE

Deborah's head explodes and she wanders around aimlessly before plummeting to her death off the edge of the walkway. Helena will say her final goodbyes. Then, you see a scene showing what Derek Simmons did to Helena and Deborah to force her into helping him assassinate the President. Ada bids Leon goodbye. From her communicator, the voice of Derek Simmons informs her of a nearby research laboratory's location.

TO THE LAB

Once you regain control of Ada, follow the path until you reach three destructible pots. Walk into the elevator, turn around, and press Action to activate the elevator. It takes you to the next stage.

UNDERGROUND LAB

UNDERGROUND LAB MAP

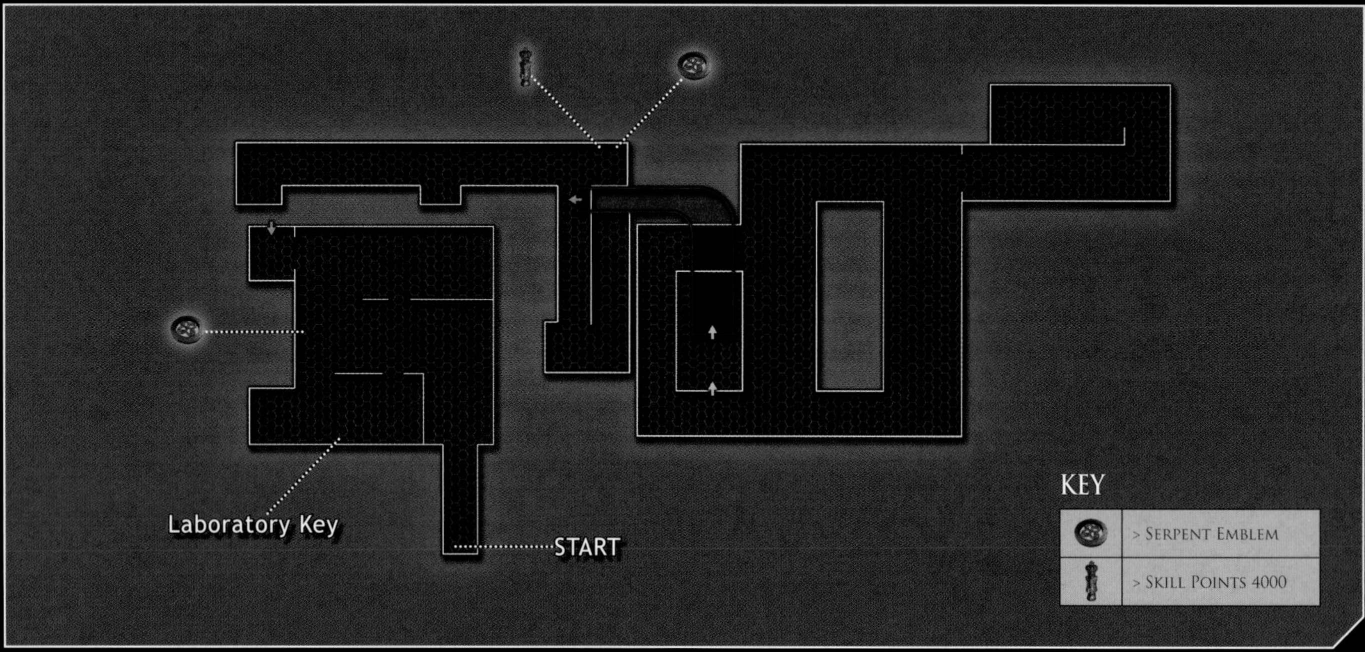

DON'T DAWDLE

Your elevator ride ends and you enter a small room with a breakable item box and a door. Destroy the box and exit the room quickly. If you linger in this room too long, a Whopper bursts in and proves to be an incredibly difficult challenge in such a confined area.

When you enter the next room, a Whopper charges toward you and destroys the gates in your way. Wait for it to begin its charge then move to the side to avoid being hit. Take it out by using the Crossbow. A single shot anywhere on its body and a second shot to the head immediately ends the fight.

A Whopper Supreme stands behind the gates ahead of you but ignore it for now. Take a left at the fence and destroy the box to your left. Take another left, then a right, and walk to the three boxes next to a staircase leading to the water. Destroy them and shortly a Whopper emerges from the water. Shoot it with the Crossbow, but wait for it to reach land before killing it. Then you can collect the Skill Points that drop.

SERPENT EMBLEM: NEAR THE WATER

Return to the staircase leading to the water and look down. You find a **Serpent Emblem** leaning against the fence and facing the water. Shoot it to collect it.

SUPER-SIZE BEAST

Now is the time to deal with the Whopper Supreme. Move toward the entrance and take a left when your path is blocked. Look down at the fence in the center of the room. You see a small opening in the fence under which you can crawl. Crawl under the fence but immediately turn around and crawl back under it again. This prompts the Whopper Supreme to chase you, and it destroys the gate on the left.

To defeat the Whopper Supreme, run laps around the area near the staircase and crawl space. Wait for the Whopper Supreme to charge and then stop. Aim for its head with the Crossbow and fire. It should go down in about four shots to the head. If it stops next to the generator near the fence with the crawl space, shoot it with the Ammo Box 50 to electrocute the Whopper Supreme.

IT WON'T NEED THIS ANYMORE

Walk to the door near the fences and destroy the two item boxes nearby. Use Action to examine the door. You notice that it's locked. Return to the area where the Whopper Supreme was contained and examine its corpse to find the **Laboratory Key**. Destroy the two crates to the right, return to the door, and open it with the key.

SUPREME SURPRISE

Walk through the doorway then turn right. Move to the end of the walkway and press the Action button to travel across the gap. A Whopper Supreme will fall from the ceiling and attack. Avoid the beast's attacks and shoot it repeatedly with the Crossbow each time it stops.

THE MATADOR

Equip the Assault Shotgun then continue forward and destroy the two boxes on your right. As soon as you move down the path, a Napad will burst through the door in front of you and charge. Quickly move to the left or right, which causes it to miss you. Then turn around and blast it in the back with the Shotgun to destroy its armor. Blast it in the back again and it quickly falls.

Walk into the area in which the Napad was contained and open the chest inside to find a **Silver Queen,** which awards 4,000 Skill Points.

THE MATADOR RETURNS

Turn around and go to the left. Walk to the end of the passage and break the box there. Walk through the doorway, turn left, and continue through the hallway. Another Napad charges at you from behind a set of doors. Dodge to the side then turn around and destroy it with the Assault Shotgun. Walk to the end of the hallway and jump down the gap in the floor.

SERPENT EMBLEM: NOT EVEN TRYING

After you jump, immediately turn around. A **Serpent Emblem** is available there. Crush it with a melee attack.

NOT A GOOD SIGN

Move down the path to the right, destroy the boxes, then turn around and continue down the path. Once you've reached the end, press Action to crawl under the grating. Move forward and press Action again to use the grappling hook. You land in an area surrounded by chrysalids. Move to the right and destroy the box in front of you, then turn around and continue down the catwalk. Destroy the two item boxes you encounter, turn to the right, and continue toward another set of boxes. Jump to the lower left and smash another crate.

After destroying the boxes, turn left and walk up the stairs to a room full of chambers containing C-Virus experiments. Turn to the right, smash another box, then turn around and continue down the walkway toward a set of boxes at the end of the hall. Smash them, then continue down the walkway toward another item box.

HARD ROCK GAUNTLET

Before you can reach the box, an alarm sounds and the doors on your right shut. Napads suddenly emerge from the chrysalids in the room, and you must destroy them before you can move on. Keep your distance from the Napads by standing on the opposite side of the raised platforms in the room. When one jumps on top of the platform, quickly run around the platform to get behind its back and shoot it. You will quickly destroy the Napads in this room by using this tactic.

Destroy the five boxes in the room and wait for two other Napads to enter. Use the same tactics to kill these two as you did the others. If you run out of Shotgun shells, use the Crossbow or the Sniper Rifle and continue leading the Napads to the raised platforms.

Another Napad emerges from the room with the experimental chambers. Run behind it while it's still spawning and, after it fully emerges, shoot it in the back for a quick kill.

HAPPY BIRTHDAY ADA WONG

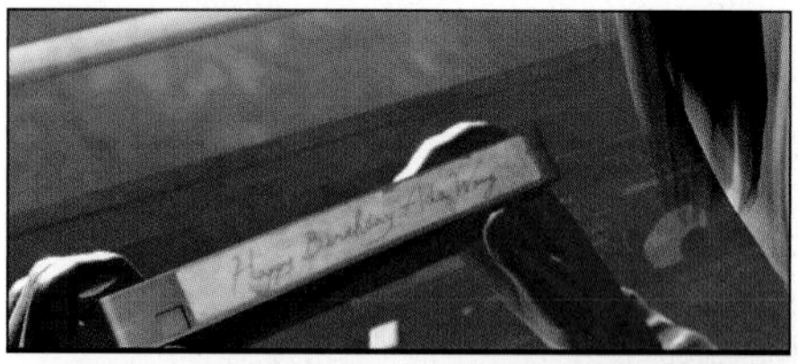

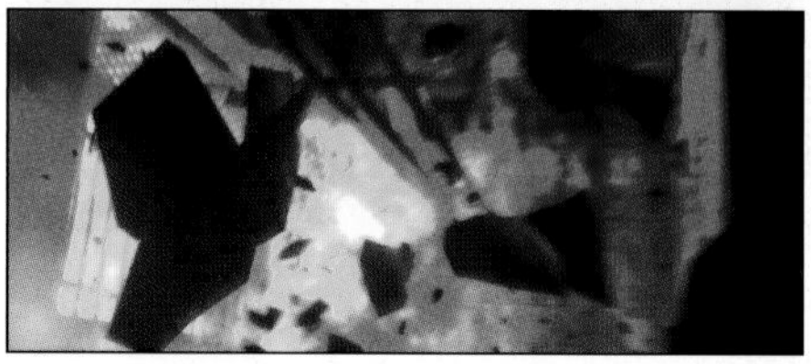

After you destroy the fifth Napad, the alarm ends and the doors in the room with the platforms open. Go through the doorway and take a left at the corner. Take another left then move into a room containing more spawning chambers and a computer. You discover a tape labeled "Happy Birthday Ada Wong."

Ada places the tape into the VCR and footage of a creature emerging from a chrysalid is displayed. Surprisingly, the creature looks eerily similar to Ada Wong. Ada then notices a familiar ring on the hand of a man in the room.

Derek Simmons contacts Ada over the communicator and they start to chat about what Ada's currently seeing. Ada quickly realizes that she hasn't been talking to Derek Simmons at all. Ada then calls the actual Derek Simmons and confronts him with the information she learned from the Ada Wong impostor. Ada then exits the facility, leaving a bomb behind to destroy the research laboratory.

ADA CHAPTER 2: RANKING CRITERIA

RANK	ACCURACY(%)	DEATHS	CLEAR TIME(MIN)	ENEMIES ROUTED
A	70	2	45	30
B	60	3	70	20
C	50	5	90	10
D	*1	*1	*1	*1

*1 Any Below Rank C

POINTS AWARDED PER RANK (ABOVE)				
Rank	A	B	C	D
Points	25	20	15	10

TOTAL RANKING POINTS TABLE

RANK	S	A	B	C	D	E
Total	100	90	75	55	45	*2

*2 Any Below Rank D

WAIYIP, CHINA

June 30, 2013

Ada arrives in China just as Chris and Piers take off to her last known location. Knowing that they are also chasing the Ada Wong doppelganger, she follows after them to find out more about this fake Ada's plans.

TENEMENT—BIN STREET

TENEMENT—BIN STREET MAP

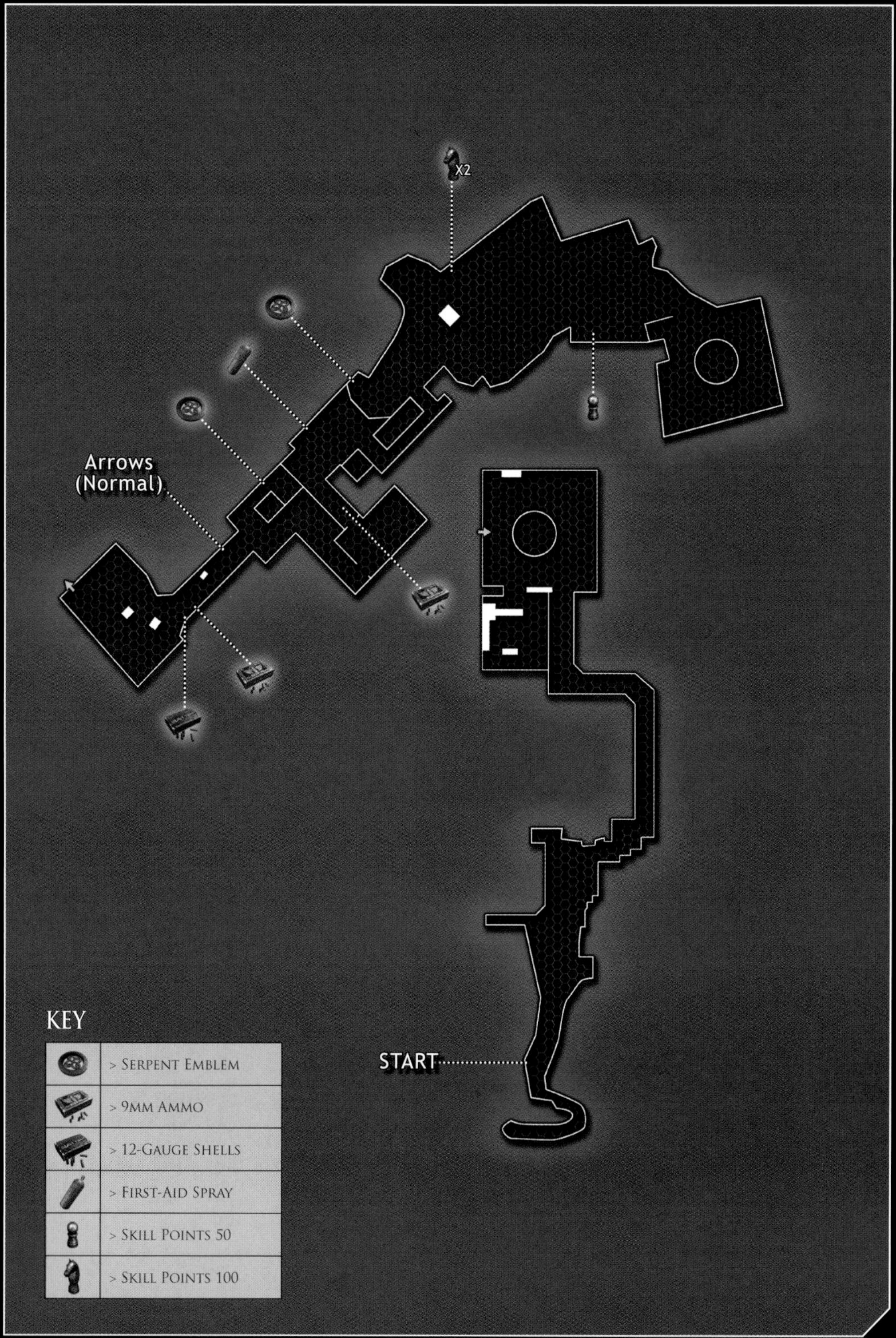

WHEE!

Walk up the destroyed path, go right, and continue through the alleys. Go left, then right, and continue past the park on the left. Take a left then enter the park. Climb on top of the playground equipment then press Action to take a fun ride down the slide to collect a medal at the end of the chapter.

Exit the park and move to the crate near the red fence. Press Action to climb up the crate, then press Action again to climb onto the fence. Walk to the end of the fence and press Action to grapple to the gate in the distance.

MARKET MAYHEM

You land in a park near two J'avo. Eliminate them with melee attacks and the Ammo Box 50. Exit the park and walk toward the stalls. Two Ruka-Srp emerge and attack you. Keep your distance and fight them with guns unless you stun them. When you do, run at them and attack with a melee finisher.

SHEEP TO THE SLAUGHTER

Continue forward and destroy the item crate on your left. Then turn around and move toward the covered stall to find another item box tucked away in the corner near a produce stand. Move back to the main pathway. Two J'avo run at you from across the top of the stalls. Wait for them to come to you, then remove them from existence. Finish this area by destroying the box on your right.

SERPENT EMBLEM: AMONG THE TRINKETS

Head past the covered stall and down the main street until your path is blocked by partitions. Look to your left to see a stall full of fans, necklaces, and other trinkets. At the top of the stall's right wall, a **Serpent Emblem** is hidden among the other objects. Shoot it to collect it.

BATTLE IN THE MARKET

Go back down the main street until you see a gap between the stalls on the right. Walk through the gap and continue down the path on the right behind the stalls. Smash the box on the left, then keep moving until your path is blocked. You confront a pair of J'avo. Take them out with a combination of headshots and melee attacks.

Return to the main street, take a left, and break the box in the stall to the left. Continue down the path until you're blocked by more partitions. Take a left toward the building. Before you enter, grab the **9mm Ammo** sitting on a table near the door.

HIDE OUTSIDE

Open the door and prepare for a fight. A J'avo armed with a machine pistol is directly across from the door and another one stands to the right. Immediately back out of the room and enter some cover outside the building, facing the doorway. One of the J'avo you shoot will probably mutate into a Strelats. If so, take it out and exit the room.

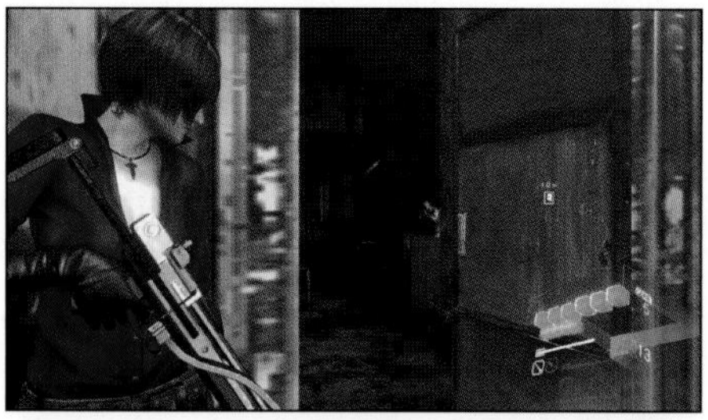

STOPPING THE STRELATS

In this chapter, you will encounter the lizard-like Strelats mutation on occasion when you attack J'avo. When you fight a Strelats, hide behind an object to avoid its needle attacks. After it fires, run toward the beast and strike with a melee attack to stun it. Then, perform a multi-prompt melee finisher—use a melee attack, then quickly press melee attack again, then Action, then either Action, Reload, or melee attack again to finish the combo. Two of these will finish this monster off for good, even if the prompt is missed. If you run at this creature haphazardly, it will either emit a cloud of smoke, stunning you, or spit an acidic fluid which can damage you. The best way to take it down is to rush it after it attacks from a distance.

UNNECESSARY FORCE

Exit the building and take a right. Smash the three boxes in the hallway then walk out to the main street. You witness a J'avo gun down a trio of civilians in cold blood. Take the J'avo out with melee attacks or any weapon that you have a lot of ammo for.

SERPENT EMBLEM: IN THE HOLE

Continue down the main street and take a right to reach the area behind the stalls. When you reach the wall, take another right and head toward partitions blocking off a section of the main street. A **Serpent Emblem** is lodged in one of the partitions. Approach it and hit it with a melee attack to collect it.

SNIPING A STRELATS

Destroy the box on your way back to the main street. Continue walking down the street until a J'avo and a Strelats attack. Run back to the hallway near the building and equip the Sniper Rifle.

The Strelats runs to the top of the stalls, which makes him difficult to hit. If you move to the hallway, the stalls block its needles while you are able to shoot it safely.

Return to the main street and take out the J'avo, which will be hiding in cover behind a stall. Take aim at its legs with the Crossbow and shoot them out from under it.

COMPLETELY UNAWARE

Walk to the end of the street where you see a chrysalid and a J'avo to the right. Catch the J'avo off guard with the Sniper Rifle or Crossbow.

Afterward run to the bus at the end of the street before Strelats emerge from the chrysalids. Don't waste your resources fighting them at this point. Instead, run to the bus and press Action to grapple toward the next area.

SHOPPING DISTRICT

SHOPPING DISTRICT MAP

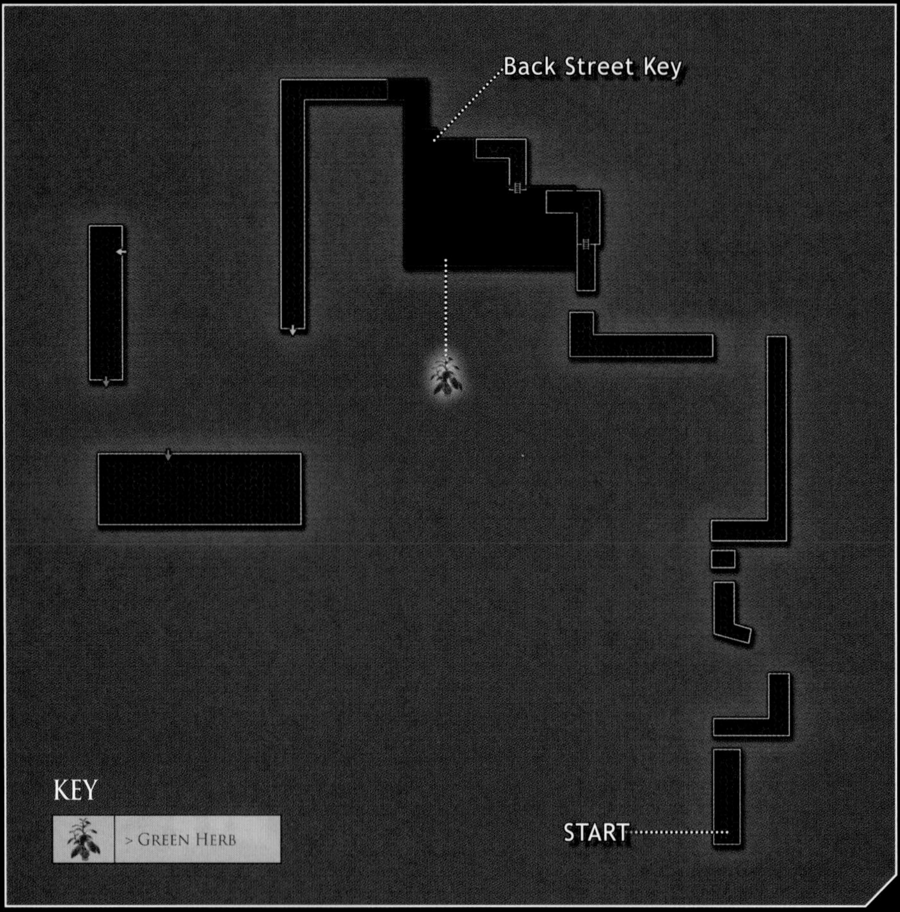

ESCAPE FROM DANGER

You land in the street and witness the birth of the chainsaw-wielding Ubistvo from a chrysalid cocoon. When you see this danger, grapple away to a flimsy scaffolding and prepare to run for your life.

ESCAPE ACROSS THE SCAFFOLDS

You must move quickly or the Ubistvo will destroy the platforms you stand on. Constantly hold down Action to dash through this section, to automatically cross gaps, and to jump over obstacles. Begin by dashing down the scaffolding until you reach a gap.

Turn right, dash until the path ends, then take a left. Dash to the end of the path until you reach a point where you must press Action to grapple across the street.

Continue holding down Action to dash and automatically jump over the low obstruction in your way. Dash forward and jump to the next walkway.

The area you jump to collapses. You must complete a Quick Timing Event to regain your footing. As soon as you make the jump, begin rotating the stick to easily pass it.

Resume holding Action and move forward to jump to the next area. Turn right and run until the path continues to the left. Move while holding Action to automatically jump over the low obstruction. Tap Aim to slide through the gap between the sign and the scaffolding.

Jump off the end of the walkway and grapple across the street into an alleyway. Continue through the doorway and pull a steel bar down to lock the door in place. For now, you don't have to worry about the Ubistvo.

DOESN'T SEEM FAIR

Walk down the alleyway and turn to the right. Press Action to grapple to the next area. You must collect a key from the other side of the plaza, which is full of zombies. While it may seem like overkill, you should take out all of these threats with the Sniper Rifle to make the upcoming confrontation easier. A total of nine zombies are in the area, so count each kill. Move down to the plaza once you've finished all of them off.

After the zombies are removed from the scene, walk around the area and collect any items they dropped. Pick up other items located around the area, including a **Green Herb** on a table across the plaza from the locked door. You should also bash the five crates in the area.

PICK UP THE KEY

When you've gathered the items, move to the zombie corpse and pick up the **Back Street Key**. A zombie nearby will come to life after you pick up the key. Wait near it and use a melee attack. Then move to the door and press Action to open it.

ATTACK FROM BEHIND

The Ubistvo attacks you from behind, but you dodge at the last second. It also grabs the key with its chainsaw, so you need to take him down and reclaim the key before you can move on. The Ubistvo is incredibly deadly and can kill you in a single hit. Keep your distance and attack it with the Assault Shotgun. It's easy to avoid the Ubistvo if you climb a ladder to get to the top of a stall and fire at it from above until it jumps after you. When it does, jump off the stall and wait for it to follow you down. Then, climb back up the ladder and repeat this process until you defeat it.

More zombies enter the area during the Ubistvo fight. While your primary foe may take some of the zombies out, it will probably knock them to the ground and force you to deal with an army of crawling zombies. Fire at them while backing away to safely exterminate them.

GET ON THE BUS

After the Ubistvo and the zombies have been defeated, go to the Ubistvo's corpse and retrieve the **Back Street Key**. Move to the door, unlock it using the key, go through the doorway, and then turn left. Move to the end of the hall and press Action to grapple to the scaffolding above. Destroy the box in the corner. Then, turn left and run to the end of the walkway. You will automatically grapple onto an oncoming bus.

Shortly after you land on the bus, the Ubistvo returns and gives chase. Don't worry about fighting it now since you won't be able to stop it. Instead, run away to the edge of the bus and press Action to use the grappling hook to swing to the other side. Repeat this process several times on the bus to keep it from reaching you.

Eventually, the bus passes under a low-hanging billboard that the Ubistvo crashes into, knocking him off the vehicle. Quickly press Action to prevent the same thing from happening to you.

SERPENT EMBLEM: BRIEF OPPORTUNITY

When the bus stops, pull out the Ammo Box 50 or another weapon that can fire quickly and look to the left. A **Serpent Emblem** is attached to the building in front of you. You have only a short amount of time to destroy this, so make sure your aim is true before shooting.

After a brief stop, the bus reverses direction and the Ubistvo climbs back on top. Wait at the front of the bus for it to approach then press Action to grapple to the back of it.

The Ubistvo turns around then comes after you again. Wait by the back of the bus and press Action to grapple to the front of the bus to avoid it. Repeat this process two more times before you escape from the bus to the railroad tracks above.

FINISH THE FIGHT

The Ubistvo chases you onto the railroad tracks for one final, decisive battle. During this fight, it's much easier to avoid the attacks because it moves much slower and doesn't attack as often. Before it attacks, it slowly walks toward you then suddenly speeds up. Fire at it while it's moving slowly, then prepare to evade when it speeds up. It only charges in a straight line, so move out of its path to avoid getting hit. Even if it gets close to you, it has a long wind-up before it strikes. Simply roll out of the way before it attacks.

Use Pipe Bomb Arrows and Incendiary Grenades to stun the Ubistvo. The explosions will keep it stunned long enough for you to reload and to fire again.

After you inflict a large amount of damage to the monster, a train roars down the tracks. Quickly press Action or you are instantly killed. Another prompt will appear, this time for Reload, then another prompt for Action. When you miss your chance to escape via the train, the battle goes on.

Continue damaging the Ubistvo and avoiding its attacks—its tactics do not change. Eventually, you intercept a BSAA radio transmission that alerts you to the current movements of the fake Ada Wong. While you listen to this transmission, you are unable to attack the Ubistvo, so focus solely on dodging its attacks.

Another train passes by and this time you need to complete a Quick Timing Event. If you're successful, you will kick the Ubistvo, stunning it. Next, grapple onto the train. It crashes into the monster at full speed, finishing the fight.

TRAIN

TRAIN MAP

KEY

(Serpent Emblem icon)	> SERPENT EMBLEM
(Skill Points icon)	> SKILL POINTS 4000

MORE DESTRUCTION

At this point, Ada is still riding on the train. Walk through the train car until you can press Action to grapple to the top of it. Begin walking down the train. You then witness the plane containing Leon and Helena crash.

INTO THE APARTMENT

After a while, you fire your grappling hook and land on an apartment building. Walk into the building and head down the staircase on the right. Destroy the four boxes on your way down.

SERPENT EMBLEM: CAREFULLY HIDDEN

As you walk down the stairs, you might catch a glimpse of a **Serpent Emblem** at the bottom of the stairs. Take out your Sniper Rifle and shoot it from the top of the stairs.

OUT OF THE APARTMENT

Walk up the other staircase in the hall and open the door at the top. Directly left of the door you find a box that you can destroy. Continue behind the partition and turn right. Destroy the box in the left corner of the room and enter the door.

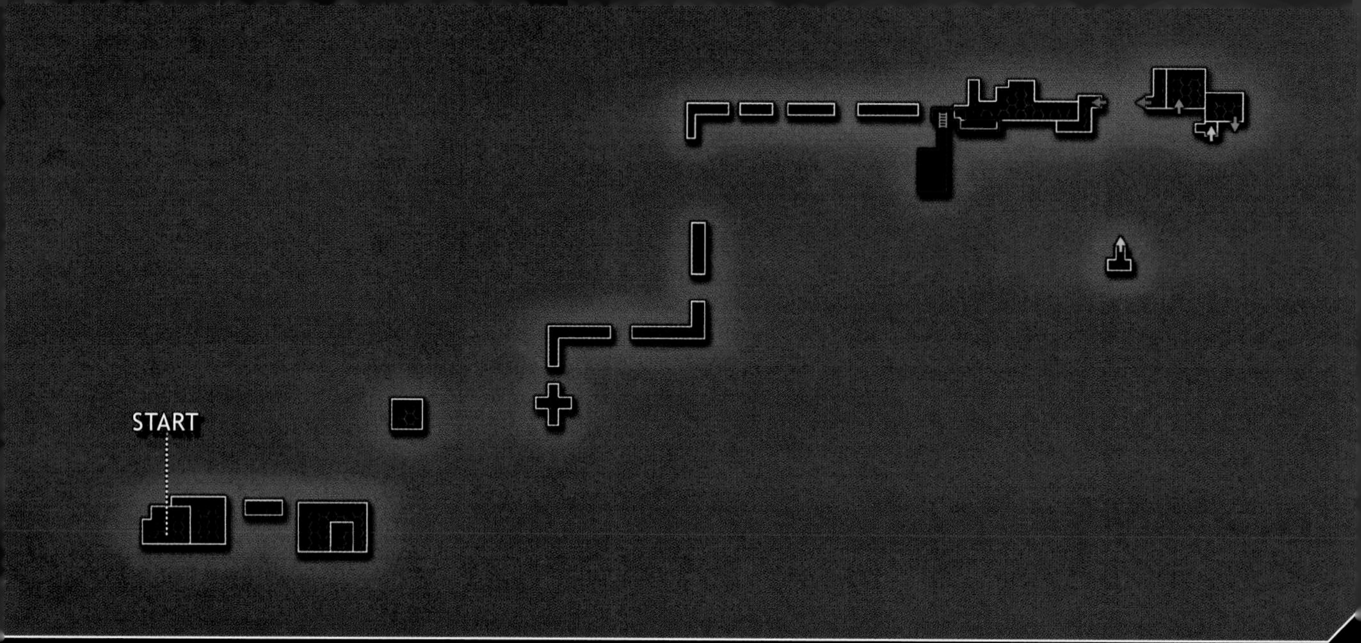

WESKER'S SON

You emerge into the Stilt Housing Area and spot Jake and Sherry through the scope of your Sniper Rifle. The Ubistvo also appears and attacks Jake and Sherry.

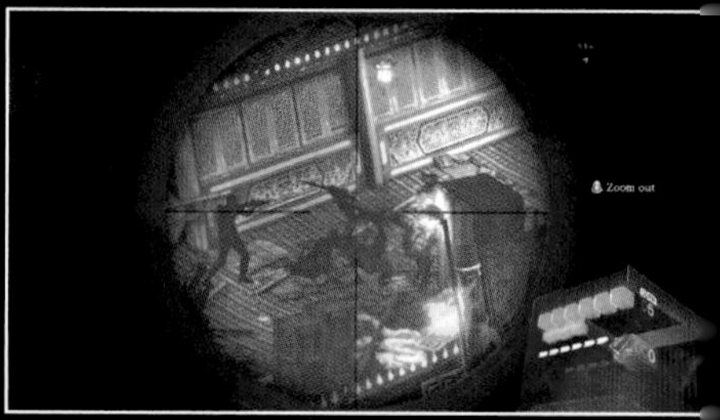

Shoot the chainsaw-wielding beast in the head with the Sniper Rifle to give Jake and Sherry time to escape on a motorized raft.

SNIPER SUPPORT

You must protect Jake and Sherry from afar by taking enemies out with the Sniper Rifle. Begin by moving forward then press Action to jump to a lower level. Walk to the right until you reach a pot on the right then destroy it.

Resume walking down the path that you were traveling on and jump over the gap to the next area. Move to the end, turn right, and smash a crate.

Run to the red-colored plate and press Action to grapple to the next area. Destroy three boxes on the platform and use the Sniper Rifle to take out some of the J'avo fighting Jake and Sherry.

Some of the J'avo might mutate into the flying Noga-Let, which will move straight to your position. Stop trying to help Jake and Sherry at this point and take out the Noga-Let when they approach.

YOUR OWN PROBLEMS

You can move on whenever you like. When you're ready, walk to the end of the platform and press Action to grapple to the next area. Once you're there, take a left at the intersection then jump over the gap by pressing Action. Continue along this path until it diverges to the right.

AIM FOR THE UBISTVO

Run down the passageway until you reach a four-way intersection and then head to the right. Jump over the gap and you land on a set of girders suspended in mid-air. Destroy the six crates on the girders but watch for any Noga-Let that might fly toward you.

Once you've destroyed the crates, equip the Sniper Rifle. Shoot the Ubistvo to send it flying into an electrified sign and to enable Jake and Sherry to continue on their way.

CONTINUE OVER THE AREA

Continue to the end of the girders and grapple to the next area. Run to the end of the walkway and take a right at the corner. Jump across the various gaps until you can grapple to an area with plants and a shack. Hop over the pipe and destroy the three pots in the corner on the left.

HE WON'T GO AWAY

The Ubistvo returns and attacks Jake and Sherry while they are on their raft. Hop over another pipe and destroy the crate along the wall. Head to the end of the area and press Action to grapple onto the crane located in the river. Keep an eye on Jake and Sherry until they manage to turn the tide against the Ubistvo. An Action prompt appears and, when pressed at the right time, drops the hanging girders onto the monster.

BYE BYE UBISTVO

The crane rotates and enables you to jump onto another platform. Jake and Sherry get separated, and Sherry is stuck on her own to fend off the Ubistvo. Move to the end of the platform and wait for an Action prompt to appear. Quickly press Action when it appears to grapple from the crane and to save Sherry from the raft. The stunned Ubistvo is destroyed once and for all by the blades of a helicopter spinning in the water.

OFF TO THE CARRIER

After saving Sherry, move to the red plate on the ground and press Action to jump down to the lower level. Walk down the path and grapple to the next area. Continue along the scaffolding until you reach the docks. Climb down the ladder and move toward the jet ski located at the end of the docks. Press Action near the jet ski and zoom off toward the aircraft carrier you heard about while eavesdropping on the BSAA.

ADA CHAPTER 3: RANKING CRITERIA

RANK	ACCURACY(%)	DEATHS	CLEAR TIME(MIN)	ENEMIES ROUTED
A	70	2	45	40
B	60	5	70	30
C	50	9	100	20
D	*1	*1	*1	*1

*1 Any Below Rank C

POINTS AWARDED PER RANK (ABOVE)				
Rank	A	B	C	D
Points	25	20	15	10

TOTAL RANKING POINTS TABLE

RANK	S	A	B	C	D	E
Total	100	90	75	55	45	*2

*2 Any Below Rank D

WAIYIP, CHINA

June 30, 2013

After saving Jake and Sherry from the Ubistvo, you head toward an aircraft carrier located off the coast of China. By intercepting a BSAA radio transmission, you learn that the fake Ada Wong was last seen heading toward this ship, which is operated by J'avo.

AIRCRAFT CARRIER—FORWARD HANGAR

AIRCRAFT CARRIER—FORWARD HANGAR MAP

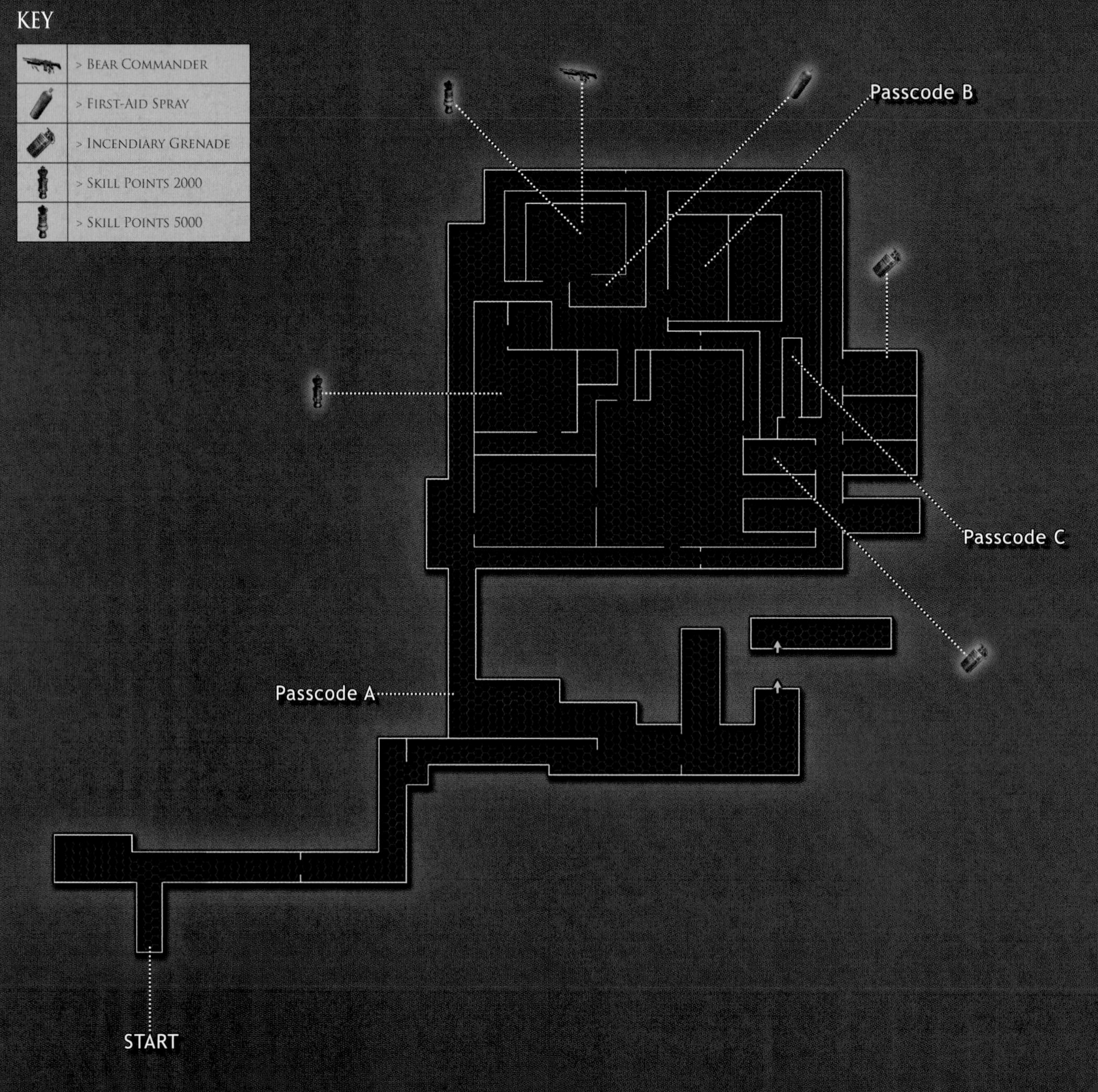

TAKING THEM OUT SILENTLY

When you first enter the carrier, you see a J'avo standing guard unawares. Run behind this foe and use a Stealth Hit.

Turn around, smash the item box in the corner, then return to where you killed the J'avo. Continue toward the door, unlock it, then open it. Slowly advance through this area and watch for the J'avo creeping ahead. Wait for it to turn around then you can finish with a Stealth Hit.

Go through the doorway and observe the J'avo walking through the opposite end of the hall. When it turns around, run down the hall and take cover outside the doorway. Wait for it to approach you and turn around again. Use a Stealth Hit to eliminate this potential threat.

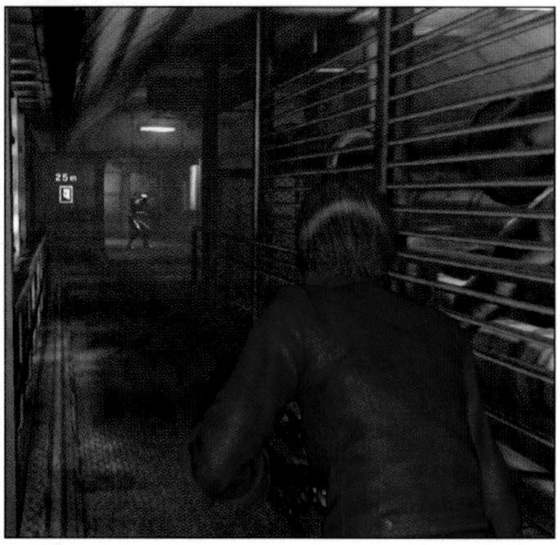

THREE PASSCODES

Press Action to activate the console on the wall. You learn that Ada must find three different Passcodes to open the door.

PASSCODE A

Turn around and enter cover against the wall that separates the doorway and the right hallway. A J'avo enters the room. Wait for it to walk toward you and turn around. Then, move behind it for a Stealth Hit. It drops **Passcode A**, the first of the three passcodes required for the door.

A SUDDEN RASKLAPANJE ATTACK

After you pick up Passcode A, a Rasklapanje slides into the room from the grates above. Shoot it with the Assault Shotgun to break it in half and keep firing at it to take out its legs and torso.

RASCALLY RASKLAPANJE

Within this area you encounter several of the grotesque Rasklapanje. Often these enemies aren't much trouble. You can destroy them quickly in a single Shotgun blast. However, this stage is a complex maze and, when left alone, the Rasklapanje revives and pursues you. To prevent an attack from behind, listen for the stumbling Rasklapanje's movement and its screams.

RETURN TO ASSASSINATING

Walk to the door and press Action to open it. Move down the stairs, turn to the right, and ready your Crossbow. You see a J'avo walking around. Finish it off with an Arrow to the head. Enter cover and look down the hallway facing the door through which you entered. Wait for the J'avo in the hallway to turn around, then run behind it to perform a Stealth Hit.

Look for the hallway that extends from the side of the hallway you're in. Enter cover, look down this second hallway, and wait for a J'avo to walk past. When it faces away from you, run behind it and use a Stealth Hit for an instant kill.

RASKLAPANJE RETURN

Around this time, the Rasklapanje will revive if you were unable to finish it off for good. Listen for the legs to slosh behind you and shoot them out if the beast comes close.

DON'T LET THEM KNOW

Unlock the white door at the end of the hall using Action to open it. Don't move through the doorway too quickly or a J'avo in the hall to the left spots you. Wait for it to turn around then perform a Stealth Hit.

WAITING IS THE HARDEST PART

You see a room with a porthole in the hallway that the J'avo once walked in. Look through the porthole and wait for the J'avo to walk by and to turn around. Then you can open the porthole. Quickly run behind it and finish it off with a deadly Stealth Hit.

PASSCODE B?

The J'avo drops Passcode B. But as you move to pick it up, a Rasklapanje torso appears from a grate, swallows it, then moves back into the grates. You must chase it down but, if you wait in the room, it eventually comes to you. Use this opportunity to finish off the Rasklapanje and reclaim **Passcode B**.

BEAR COMMANDER

Exit the room and walk down the hallway to the left. Take a right and continue until the path diverges to the right. Follow its twists then open the door on your right. Enter the room and move near the case on the table to pick up the Bear Commander, an assault rifle with a grenade launcher for its alternate fire.

Open the suitcase next to the Bear Commander and grab the **Silver King** inside the case. This item is worth significant Skill Points (5,000). Turn around and break the crate on the sofa.

DON'T NEED TO GO?

A box is in the bathroom but you might summon a Rasklapanje by moving the near grate, which makes approaching the box more trouble than it's probably worth. Go after the box or simply ignore it. Exit the room and turn right then move to the right again. Move to the end of the hall and walk through it.

TRIAL BY FIRE

Walk down the hallway until it splits to the right, then continue down the hall. As you walk through the hallway, a pipe ruptures and begins spewing fire. A Rasklapanje attacks you from a grate. When prompted, quickly press Action to take it out.

Another Rasklapanje attacks from behind and you must fight it in a very cramped area. Battle the Rasklapanje with melee attacks to knock it into the spewing fire.

BLOW 'EM AWAY

Continue down the hall and walk up the stairs. Several J'avo and a Rasklapanje torso appear in the hall. Use this as an opportunity to test the Bear Commander's grenade launcher attachment. Change modes on the gun and fire an explosive round into the hallway to take out several of the enemies. Then, fire another shot at any stragglers.

PASSCODE C

Walk into the doorway on the right and open the door. Kill the single J'avo inside and grab **Passcode C** from its corpse.

Exit the room, head back to the hallway, and turn right. Enter the door on the left and destroy the box on the lower bed. Then return to the hall and enter the other door. Grab an **Incendiary Grenade** from the top-left bunk.

Go back down the hall and enter the room on the left. Break the crate at the far end of the room, go across the hall into the other room, and break the box on the left. Return to the hall, take a right, then unlock and open the door. Enter the cafeteria on the right and destroy the two boxes inside. Now, return to the hallway.

INPUT THE PASSCODES

Continue down the hall, go up the stairs on the left, then walk down the hall on your left to go back to the console. Press Action to activate the console—the three passcodes will activate the device.

GOODBYE TO THE RASKLAPANJE

Open the door and enter the room. Two Rasklapanje attack you. Use the Bear Commander's grenades to break them apart. You can then choose to kill the separated pieces with another grenade (if they're close by) or simply run past them.

TO THE BRIDGE

Walk up the stairs and smash the item box. Take a left and walk to the crates. Press Action to use the grappling hook to ascend to the upper level. You will hear the voice of the fake Ada over the intercom as you move to the door at the end of the hall. Activate the door to move to a different level of the aircraft carrier.

AIRCRAFT CARRIER—BRIDGE

AIRCRAFT CARRIER—BRIDGE MAP

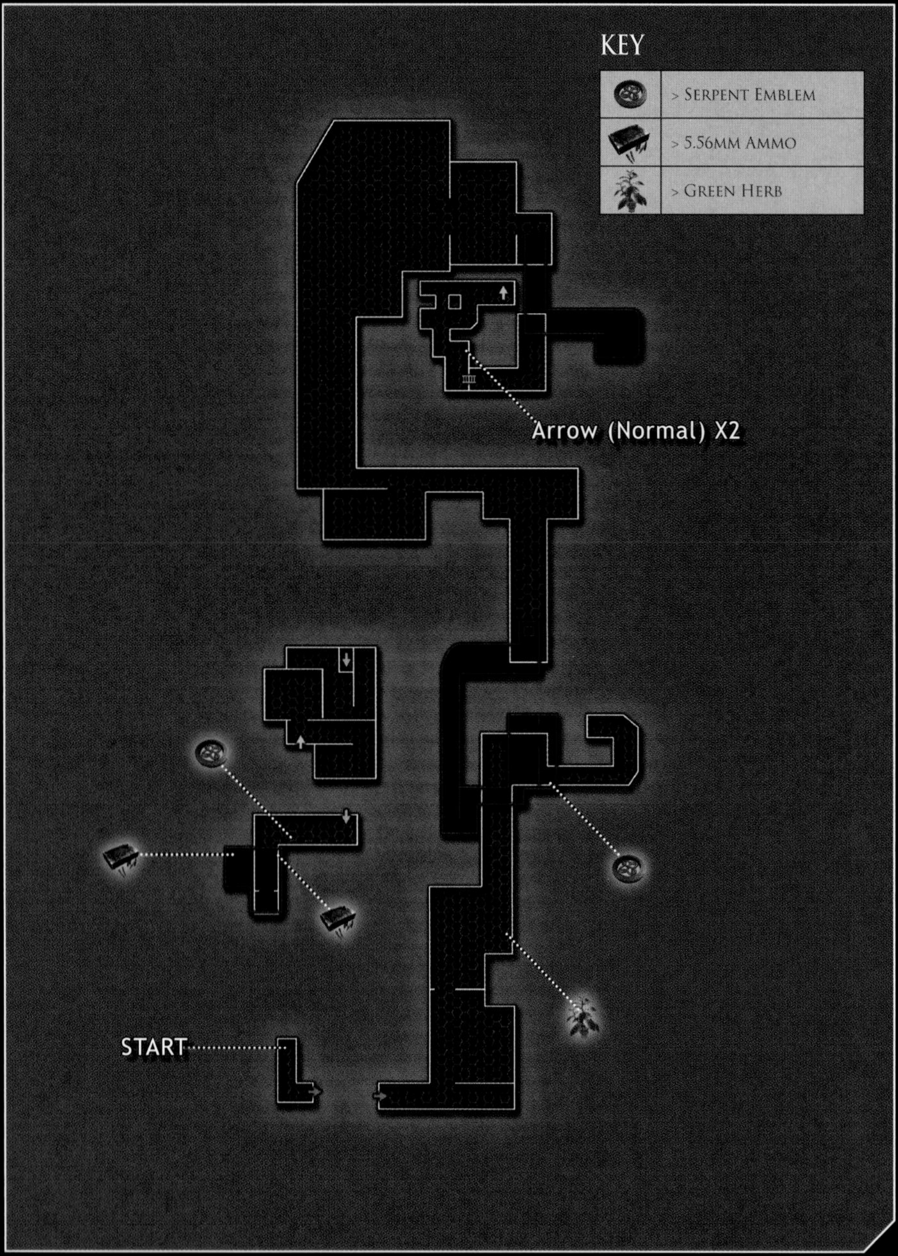

GRAPPLING AWAY

You emerge from an elevator on a platform outside of the carrier. Move to the ledge and press Action to grapple to a higher area outside the bridge.

Move to the door on the left and press Action to unlock it. Chris and Piers emerge from the elevator on the right and begin to chase you. Quickly enter the room and shut the door behind you. Dash forward and press Aim to slide under the automatically closing door. If you miss it, Chris bursts into the room and captures you, causing a mission failure.

DISCRETION RECOMMENDED

After you escape, you see a **Green Herb** on your right. Pick it up and move through the open doorway. Head up the stairs and press Action when prompted. A large group of J'avo mills about inside a room. From this point, you need to be stealthy to avoid detection.

SNEAKING AROUND

You can earn the Sneaking Around Achievement/Trophy in this stage by avoiding your enemies' notice. If they spot you, you cannot obtain this Achievement unless you start the chapter over again.

AVOIDING THE SPOTLIGHTS

Head through the open doorway and you see a smaller boat shining a spotlight around the exterior of the carrier. If one of these lights falls on you, enemies quickly surround you. Dash down the corridor, take a left until you can't move forward, then take another left. Run to the end of the walkway where you can grapple to safety.

SERPENT EMBLEM: THE FAMILY STOPPED TRYING

After grappling away from the patrol boat, look to your left to find a **Serpent Emblem** on the ground. Break it with a melee attack.

A BATTLE BELOW

Head to the open doorway then take a left and then a right at the corner. Take a left at the end of the path and go around the yellow bars. Press Action to jump into the ducts and press Action again to crawl through the ducts. As you crawl, you see Chris and Piers fighting a horde of J'avo. Ignore their battle and keep moving.

Exit the ducts and move to the end of the room. Press Action to jump down the hole there. Move forward to avoid being spotted, and then climb up the stairs. Walk into the room, take a left, and move through the open doorway. A J'avo waits in the room, but you must avoid it without being seen. If he sees you, you must take him out quickly. There are also several item boxes that you can break in this room for supplies.

AVOID THE GNEZDO

Walk through the open doorway, take a right, then head to the control room. In here you find a Gnezdo that you must avoid. Run to the right side of the room and then run toward the big red button. Move to the button, press Action to unlock the door, then head through the doorway. Move around the consoles in the middle of the room then head toward the window and jump out.

AVOID THE SPOTLIGHTS AGAIN

Take a right and jump down the open hatch. Prepare to run when you encounter another area covered by a patrol boat.

Hold down Action and move to the left to jump over any obstacles. You cannot completely outrun the light, but there is a crawl space available ahead. Press Action to crawl through it when the prompt appears. Crouch and wait until the light passes by.

Once it passes by, crawl forward to the next steel wall and wait for the search light to come back around. When it leaves again, continue forward into the crawl space on the left.

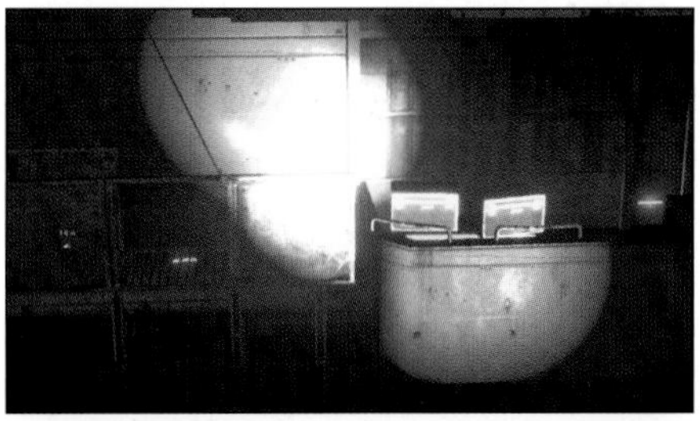

Dash quickly and efficiently to escape the spotlight. When the camera angle changes, run to the left then loop around to reach the grapple point. Press Action to escape the spotlight for good.

DON'T LET THEM KNOW

Break the item crates on the right then continue to the left. You see three enemies in a room to the right, but you don't need to worry about them. Enter into cover and sneak to the end of the wall. Peek out and shoot the lone J'avo near the ladder with a Crossbow headshot.

Stay in cover to sneak past the J'avo in the room. Press Action when you are in cover to crouch under the windows.

SPIDERS IN THE DUCTS

Go into the doorway and pick up the **Arrows** on the shelf to the right. Head back through the doorway on the left and jump into the ducts at the end of the room. Crawl through the ducts but don't move too far forward. Two Noga-Trchanje are crawling through the ducts, as well. Wait for them to stop moving then shoot each of them with the Crossbow.

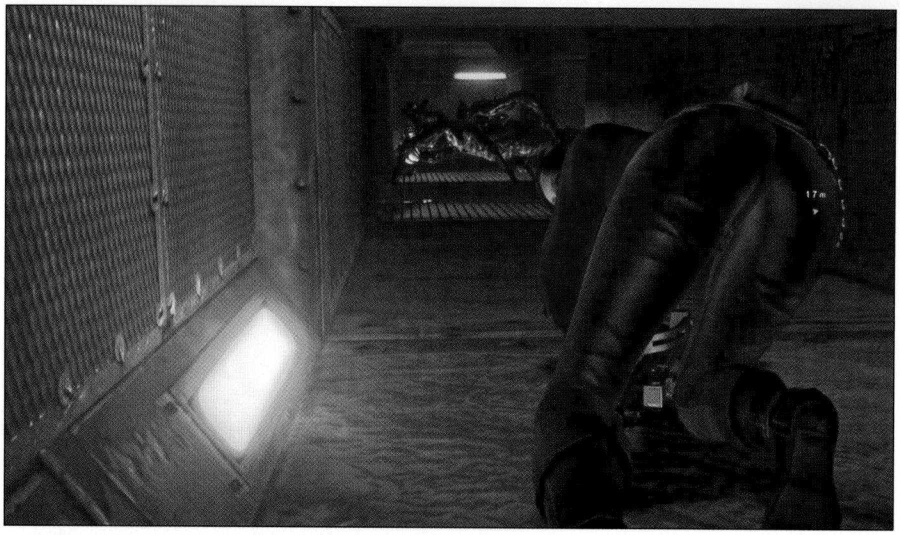

THE TRUTH ABOUT CARLA

Take a right at the T-intersection and jump down the hole at the end of the duct. Head left through the door then left again up the stairs. Open the door to the right and walk into the room. You find a suitcase on the desk and learn about the project to build another Ada Wong using the C-Virus.

Ada will also learn the name "Carla Radames," which appears to be the name of the Ada doppelganger, and she finds a model of the Quad Tower, which she takes. The fake Ada Wong suddenly falls from the roof of the carrier onto the ground. It looks like Carla died before Ada even had a chance to meet her.

Once you regain control of Ada, look over the side of the carrier. Press Action to view Carla's corpse then turn around and head toward the doorway on the right.

TAKE OUT ANOTHER

Go down the stairs, take a left, then a second left, and go around the stairs toward a hatch in the ground. Jump down the hatch. Head forward but stop before reaching the corner. A J'avo walks by. Wait for it to turn around then run behind it and perform a stealth kill. Go back and destroy the box.

SERPENT EMBLEM: EMBLEM IN THE LOCKER

Look in the broken lockers on the left side of the wall. In the locker farthest to the right, a **Serpent Emblem** sits on the top shelf. Destroy it to collect it.

INVESTIGATE THE BODY

Run to the end of the hall and press Action to activate the elevator. Move into the elevator shaft and press Action again.

When the elevator stops, exit and head forward. Grab the **5.56mm Ammo**, head left, and grab another box of **5.56mm Ammo**. Move toward the open space and toward Carla's corpse.

NOT WHAT IT SEEMS

As she moves toward Carla, Ada expresses pity for her—until Carla suddenly revives and mutates into a monster. The mutated form of Carla chases Ada back into the aircraft carrier, where you lock the door on the creature.

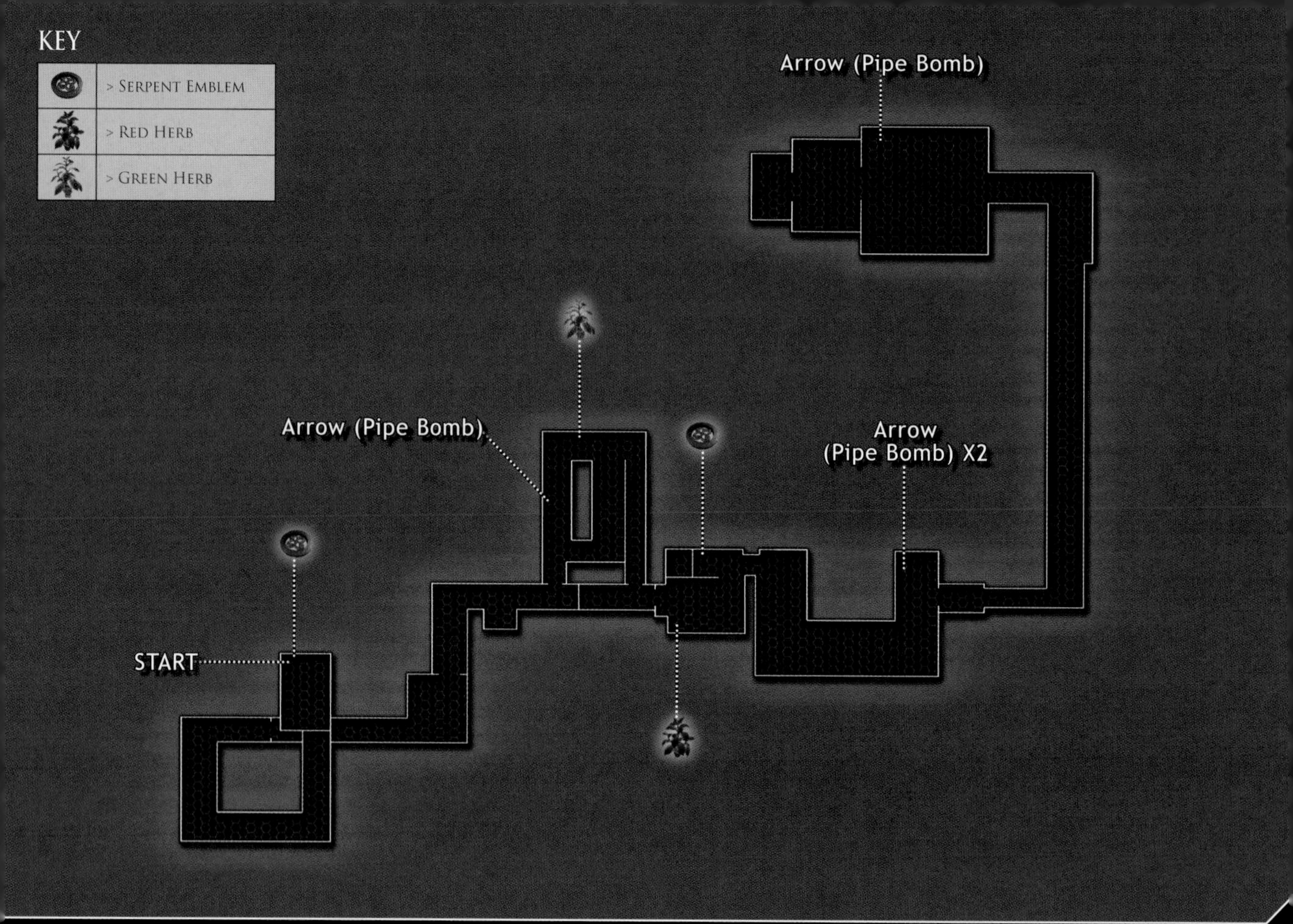

ESCAPE THROUGH THE CARRIER

Turn around and destroy the box behind you. Head toward the hatch.

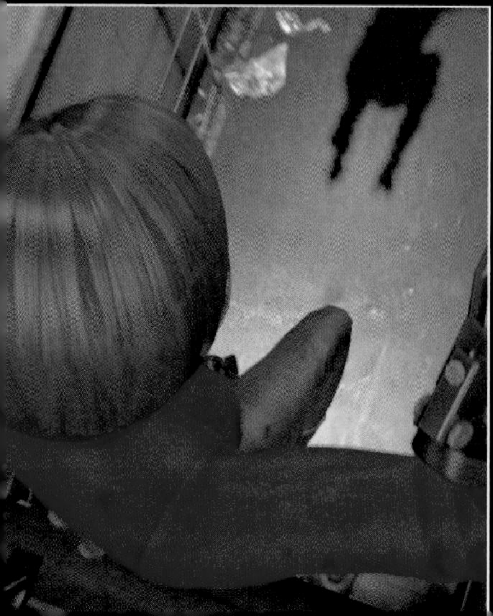

SERPENT EMBLEM: DON'T JUMP YET

Before jumping down the hatch, you see a **Serpent Emblem** to the left of the hatch. Destroy it to collect it.

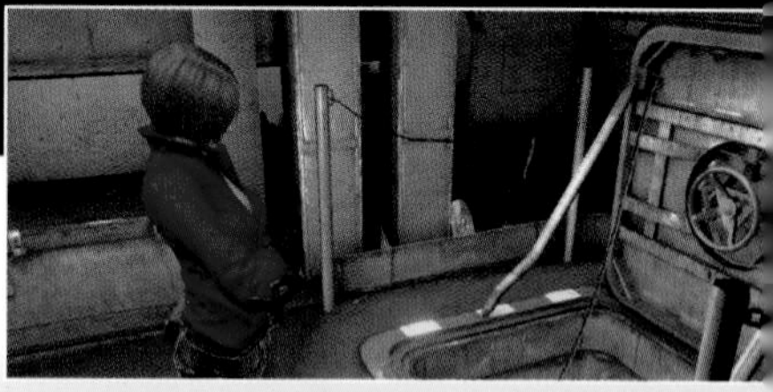

WHOSE SIDE ARE YOU ON?

Jump down the hatch then move forward down the hallway. Two J'avo attack you. Before you can counterattack them, the mutated Carla mercilessly crushes them. At this point, you should run.

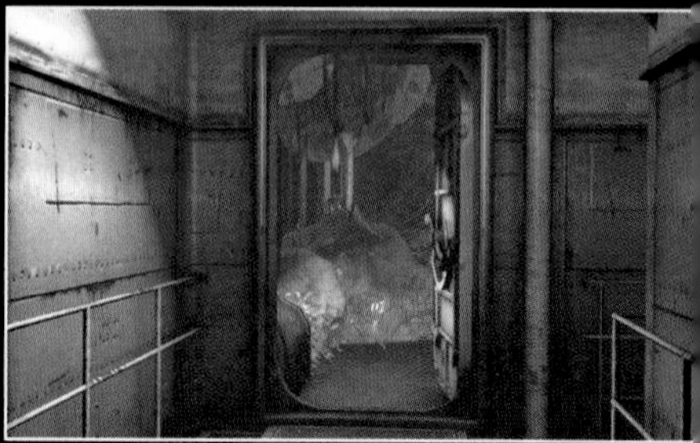

FARTHER DOWN THE CARRIER

Turn right then head down the stairs. Turn right again and head down another staircase. Go down yet another staircase and move toward the door. Press Action to unlock it and then again to open it. Continue down the hallway.

Once you enter a room, turn to the left and destroy a box. Then, destroy the two red blobs on the door. They drop items, which you should pick up before exiting the room. Unlock the door and open it.

CARLA SPORES

Continue down the hallway and you encounter a mutant in the shape of the woman. These Carla Spores are slow but deadly and incredibly hard to kill. Avoid them whenever you can.

Run past the Carla Spore and go right. At your next opportunity, take a left when you can. Unlock and open the door you find. Head into the conference room. Take a right at your first opportunity then a left. Grab the **Green Herb** on the table then take a right.

THE WALLS HAVE HANDS

As you move down this hall, the wall grabs you and you must complete a Quick Timing Event. Rotate the left stick quickly to break free. Continue to the left and then another wall grabs you. Shake free, head to the door, and throw it open.

TURN QUICKLY

Head to the left and you encounter a valve. Press Action to activate it. Furiously rotate the stick to open the valve before a Carla Spore is able to interrupt you.

DEADLY OBSTACLES

After you open the door, run through and throw it shut behind you. This prevents the Carla Spores from reaching you. Break the boxes to your left. Look above the box near the door and where you see a blob in the shape of a face. This Carla Spore face attacks you if you go too close to it and it inflicts huge damage. Use the Bear Commander or Ammo Box 50 to stun it and then run underneath it.

SERPENT EMBLEM: AVOID THE SPORE

Stun the Carla Spore face but take a left instead of continuing through the doorway. Move into the hall to find a **Red Herb** and a **Serpent Emblem**. Move to the Serpent Emblem and break it. Then turn around, shoot the Carla Spore face, and run to the doorway.

ANOTHER IN YOUR WAY

In the next room, another Carla Spore face waits to attack you. Shoot it and run past it to avoid injury. Go through the hall and you find a corner containing another Carla Spore face and a blue canister of liquid nitrogen. Shoot the canister to destroy the face, which reveals a weakness of the Carla mutation.

RUN FROM YOURSELF

On your right is another door with a valve. Activate it with Action, then quickly rotate the left stick to open it. Head down the stairs and break the box on your left. Head around the corner and an enormous Carla Spore face appears. You must run for your life!

Dash down the hall. A wall on the right grabs you, and you must rotate the left stick to escape. Keep running down the hall while holding Action to avoid any hurdles you need to jump over.

Reach the end of the hall and use the grappling hook to quickly move through the carrier.

Ada will eventually stumble. When this happens, she turns around to see the giant face coming straight toward her. At this point, Ada will automatically equip the Ammo Box 50, no matter how much ammo you have. If you're out of ammo, switch to the Assault Shotgun and shoot at the blue canisters on the ground. When you destroy one, the Carla Spore face will crumble.

Three red blobs that you can destroy for additional ammo are nearby. Don't take them out with melee attacks because they spray an acidic fluid that can injure you.

FACE YOUR DESTINY

Take a left through the hallway. You reach another door with a valve. Open it and enter a room with the largest Carla Spore you've seen so far.

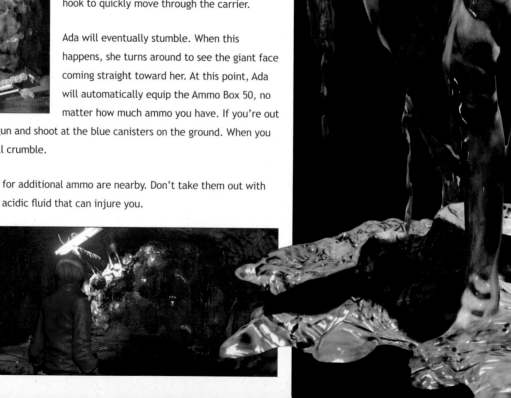

CARLA SPORE

This giant Carla Spore looks intimidating and can be incredibly easy or incredibly difficult to defeat, depending on how much ammo you have conserved. Equip the Crossbow and pull out your Pipe Bomb Arrows. Prepare your assault on Carla. Focus on a single point and shoot at her—as the arrows explode, a hole will begin to open in her face.

As the hole opens, you see blue liquid-nitrogen canisters behind her. Whenever you can, shoot an arrow through the hole that you've opened before it closes. You might have to fire a couple Pipe Bomb Arrows before the canisters detonate.

Carla attacks by building up an acidic fluid in her eye and shoots it at you by winking. To prevent this attack from happening, fire at her eye until it's destroyed. The eye won't regenerate for a while, so use the opportunity to focus your firepower on her face.

Small Carla Spores walk around and try to interrupt your attacks. Watch for them and avoid them when they get close.

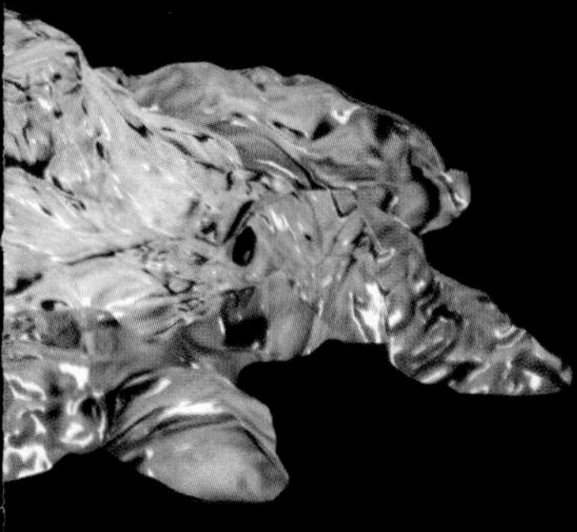

Focus on using only Pipe Bomb Arrows. If you run out, use the Assault Shotgun. If you run out of Assault Shotgun ammo, take out another weapon and break the red blobs on the wall to acquire more ammo. Your other weapons are unable to open a hole in the giant Carla Spore face, so don't bother using them.

When you've done significant damage to the nitrogen canisters, they explode and freeze the Carla Spore. It then shatters and is destroyed. Head for the elevator and investigate the console to escape the aircraft carrier.

ADA CHAPTER 4: RANKING CRITERIA

RANK	ACCURACY(%)	DEATHS	CLEAR TIME(MIN)	ENEMIES ROUTED
A	70	2	50	15
B	60	3	65	10
C	50	5	85	5
D	*1	*1	*1	*1

*1 Any Below Rank C

POINTS AWARDED PER RANK (ABOVE)				
Rank	A	B	C	D
Points	25	20	15	10

TOTAL RANKING POINTS TABLE

RANK	S	A	B	C	D	E
Total	100	90	75	55	45	*2

*2 Any Below Rank D

TATCHI, CHINA

July 1, 2013

Having defeated Carla once and for all, Ada travels to Tatchi via a stolen helicopter from the aircraft carrier. Ada sees the destruction caused by Carla's missile firsthand and witnesses the horrific scene of a city overrun by zombies. Surprisingly, Ada encounters Leon and Helena as they attempt to fight off a horde of zombies.

HIGH-RISE AREA

FLIGHT OF THE VALKYRIE

Through most of this chapter, Ada pilots an attack helicopter armed with machine guns and five powerful missiles. Start by helping Leon and Helena survive a zombie onslaught by attacking the zombies around them.

SERPENT EMBLEM: IN THE TRUCK

Move the chopper to the right and shine its spotlight on the yellow truck to the left. You see a **Serpent Emblem** in the truck bed near the cabin, and you can shoot it with the helicopter's machine guns.

Take out all the zombies to allow Leon and Helena to move on. Then pilot the helicopter farther through the city.

ONE-ON-ONE DUEL

While flying through the streets of Tatchi, you encounter another attack helicopter piloted by J'avo. Take it out with your machine guns.

Another helicopter will attack you but this one is occupied by J'avo using rocket launchers. Keep moving from side to side to avoid the rockets and keep your crosshair fixed on the sides of the helicopter. Damage it with machine-gun fire while you shoot down its missiles.

TWO-ON-ONE

Next, a pair of choppers attacks, one with rockets and the other with machine guns. The chopper with machine guns will attempt to block you from shooting the other chopper when it fires rockets at you. Take out the one in front while moving side to side to avoid the rockets from the distant chopper. Use a missile on the closest helicopter to take it out more quickly. After it's down, take out the second chopper and keep moving.

When the choppers are defeated, Ada will fly to a high-rise building where she encounters a different, more powerful helicopter equipped with formidable missiles. Duck under the building to avoid the enemy copter's missiles. Then pop out and blast it after it fires. After a few seconds of gunfire, drop back down to avoid the helicopter's missiles. Repeat this process until the enemy helicopter is destroyed.

SERPENT EMBLEM: SEE THE SIGN

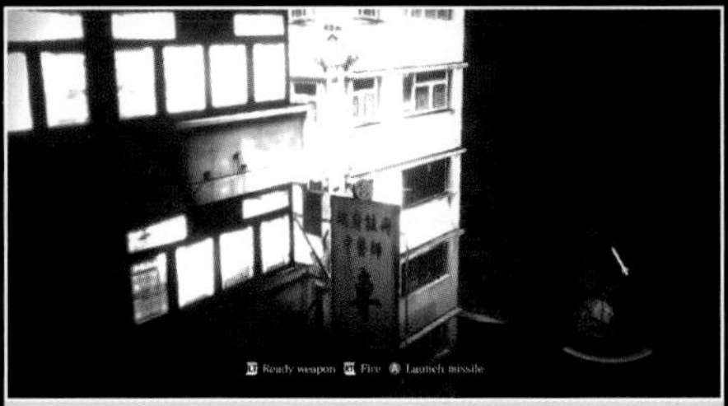

While fighting the attack helicopter, move down and to the right to find a **Serpent Emblem** teetering on top of a sign. Shoot it with the machine gun to collect.

QUAD TOWER ENTRANCE

REUNION WITH SIMMONS

Leon and Helena encounter the mutated form of Derek Simmons again at the entrance of the Quad Tower. You must fly in to provide support. Derek transforms into a grotesque Tyrannosaurus Rex and begins chasing Leon and Helena.

DEREK SIMMONS (TYRANNOSAURUS)

Keep your distance and fire at the weak points on his back and mouth to damage the beast. The mutated Simmons occasionally tries to attack you by jumping directly at you. Keep moving to avoid his strikes.

After suffering a large amount of damage, Simmons will transform back into a human. Use this opportunity to pummel him with machine-gun fire.

Continue fighting Simmons until a BSAA Agent arrives to help Leon and Helena. At this point, Ada automatically pilots the helicopter and all you must do is keep your crosshair aimed on Simmons' weak points. Simmons eventually destroys the jeep and at that point you regain control of the chopper. Continue shooting at his weak points with the machine gun.

Simmons also attacks you by picking up a car in his mouth and throwing it at you. If you see him pick up a vehicle, move the helicopter so the pillar in the center of the arena is between you and him. The car will fly straight into it and explode and you can resume firing at him. Eventually Derek Simmons collapses, which ends the fight. Ada flies the helicopter away from the entrance and to the roof.

QUAD TOWER ROOF

QUAD TOWER ROOF MAP

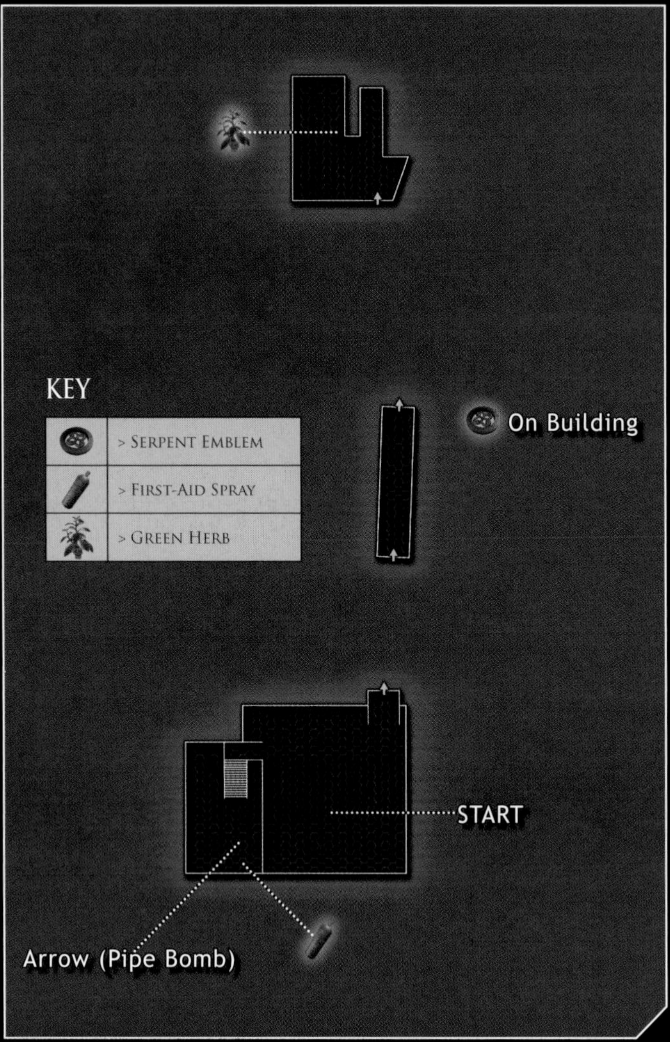

FIRST ROOF

Ada moves to the roof of the Quad Tower and spots humans under siege by zombies. Take out the zombies with the helicopter's machine gun to save the humans.

SECOND ROOF

After you slay the zombies, fly to the roof of another part of the Quad Tower. A BSAA Agent and two civilians stand on a roof while under attack by zombies. Take out the zombies to again save the humans.

SERPENT EMBLEM: BLINK AND YOU'LL MISS IT

Before you finish off the zombies on the second roof, move the helicopter to the left and look at the area next to the roof. A **Serpent Emblem** lies on the roof where it can be shot.

One of the zombies carries dynamite. Shoot it and it blows up a needle on the roof, which impales a zombie below. You might remember this needle from Leon's final boss fight.

THIRD ROOF

Maneuver the chopper to a third building with a helipad that is covered in BSAA zombies and a few Whopper Supremes. Take them out so you can safely land the helicopter. Avoid shooting the boxes below so you can collect the items inside after you land.

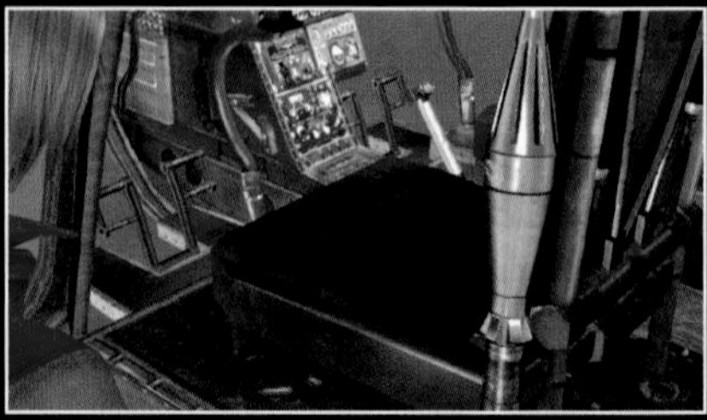

After you've taken out the enemies, Ada will land the helicopter and remove a Rocket Launcher and sign it with a kiss.

STOCK UP

Collect the objects dropped by the zombies you've killed then go down the stairs and destroy the boxes to procure more items. Open the chest near the boxes to find **First-Aid Spray** and a set of **Pipe Bomb Arrows**.

SWINGING IN AIR

Climb back up the stairs and move to the platform on the opposite side of the helipad. Press Action to grapple to the girders that are suspended in the air.

SERPENT EMBLEM: THE FINAL EMBLEM

After landing on the girders, take out your Sniper Rifle and look to the left. The 80th and final **Serpent Emblem** is on the top of the roof near a pipe. Shoot it to complete your collection.

INTO THE TOWER

Continue down the girder then use the grappling hook to move to the next roof. Jump down and pick up the **Green Herb** lying on the ground. Move to the door and open it to enter the Quad Tower.

QUAD TOWER

QUAD TOWER MAP

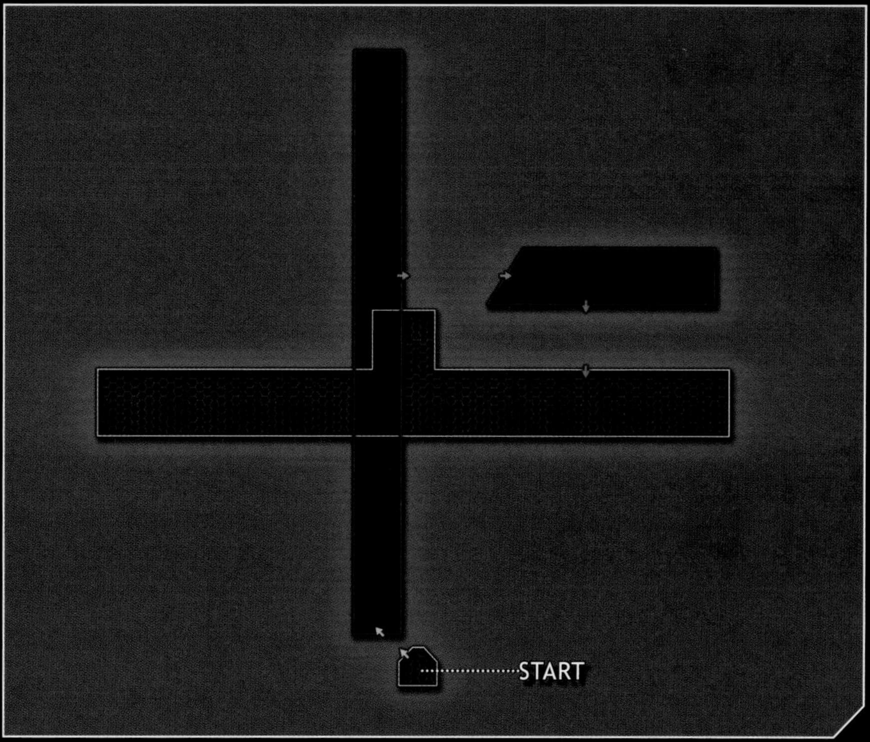

CLOSE CALL FOR LEON

You enter the Quad Tower as Leon and Helena jump out of an exploding elevator.

SIMMONS RETURNS

An explosion occurs in the room next to you. Jump onto a descending elevator. The beast form of Derek Simmons reappears. Simmons shoots needles at you from his tail. Move to the side to avoid the projectiles.

THE FINAL BATTLE

The elevator falls to the ground. Use your grappling hook to swing to the section that Simmons is standing on. Here is where your final fight begins.

DEREK SIMMONS (BEAST)

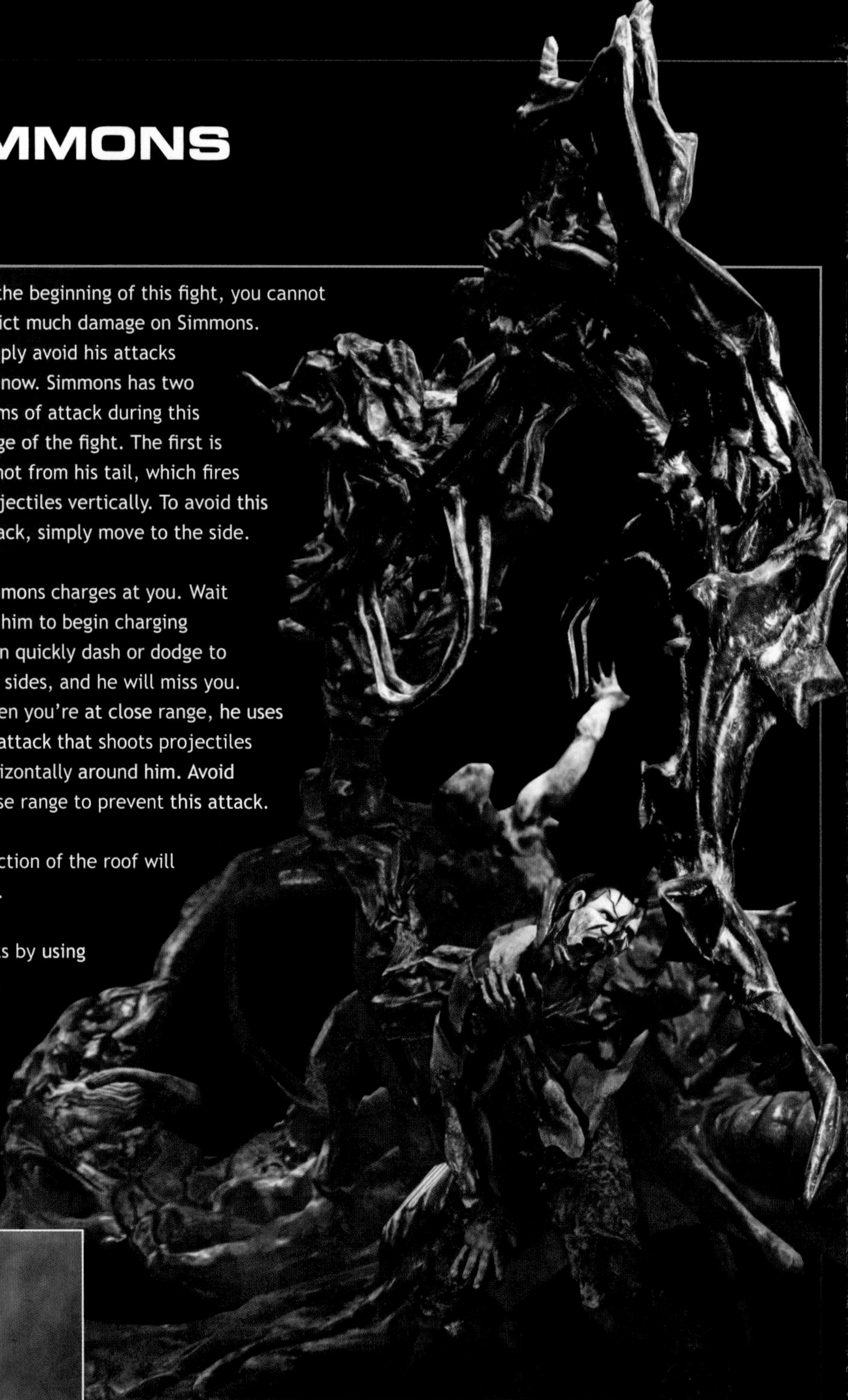

At the beginning of this fight, you cannot inflict much damage on Simmons. Simply avoid his attacks for now. Simmons has two forms of attack during this stage of the fight. The first is a shot from his tail, which fires projectiles vertically. To avoid this attack, simply move to the side.

Simmons charges at you. Wait for him to begin charging then quickly dash or dodge to the sides, and he will miss you. When you're at close range, he uses an attack that shoots projectiles horizontally around him. Avoid close range to prevent this attack.

When you survive Simmons' attacks long enough, a section of the roof will collapse, and you can take the fight to a larger venue.

After you land on the roof, Simmons primarily attacks by using his tail. One of Simmons' next attacks is a horizontal tail swipe. Avoid this by staying out of his range or by ducking and sliding under it. Simmons can also attack vertically with his tail. Avoid this by moving to the side before it reaches you. The vertical attack has more range than the horizontal attack, so move to the side if you're outside of the horizontal attack's range.

Leon and Helena regain their footing and assist you from a distance. Let them assault Simmons while you focus on avoiding his attacks and wait for him to transform back into a human. When he does, run to him and hit him with melee attacks until you can perform a finisher. When the time is right, press the melee attack button and mash the Action button furiously to perform a devastating combo.

If Simmons hits you with a charge, from then on he performs a more powerful grab attack. He picks you up by the neck then throws you to the ground, which results in massive damage.

Zombies meander out on the platform waiting for you to kill them. If you need ammo, shoot them. Otherwise, avoid them.

After Simmons has suffered a considerable amount of damage, grapple onto another walkway while Leon and Helena start climbing up elevator cables. At this point, it's your turn to help Leon and Helena. Shoot Simmons with the Sniper Rifle when he gets close to your climbing friends. After you hit him, he slides down the elevator.

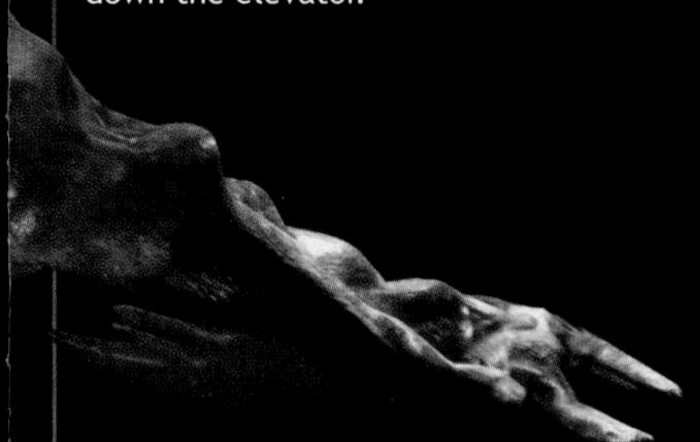

When Leon and Helena finish climbing the cables, Simmons will change targets and attack you directly, knocking you out. Leon heroically comes to your aid and keeps Simmons away until you recover. Simmons then fires a barrage of projectiles from his tail and Leon responds by moving in front of them to protect you.

After you recover, you rejoin Leon to fight Simmons together.

Simmons is equipped mostly the same as before except for a new, quick, short-range tail stab. If his stab hits, you suffer significant damage. Maintain distance to prevent injury.

At this point, you reach the final battle. Unload all your available firepower into Simmons. When you inflict enough damage to him, Simmons reverts to a human. Run up to him then and perform a melee finisher.

After suffering considerable damage, Simmons thrashes around and knocks Leon off the walkway. Move to Simmons and taunt him as Leon hangs on for dear life. At this point, run behind Simmons, stab him with an arrow, and send him into the fire below to finally defeat him!

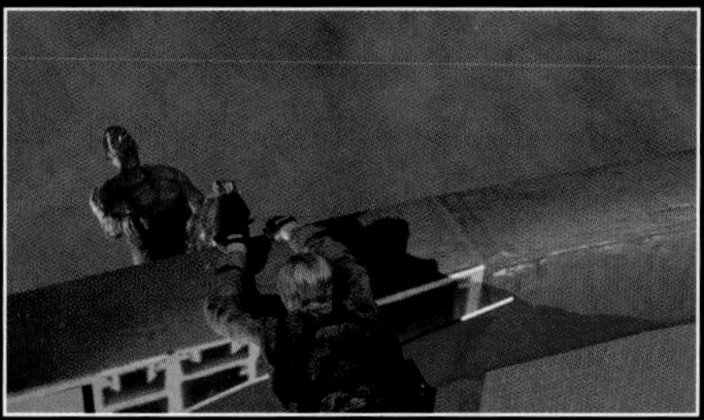

Saying Goodbye

After the battle, Ada is separated from Leon once again. Ada sends Leon a message through her communicator and walks away as Leon cries Ada's name.

GENETICS LAB

WRAPPING UP LOOSE ENDS

Ada's mission isn't over yet. She enters a strange laboratory in an unknown location. Walk through the strange hallway.

You emerge from the hallway to find a room surrounded by monitors. Move down the stairs and examine the console in the middle of the room by pressing Action.

Insert the model of the Quad Tower you picked up at the aircraft carrier into the console. Screens begin showing bizarre images of Carla and several researchers. Various images of Carla's research on the C-Virus and victims in chrysalid state appear. The clip ends with Carla describing what she calls her "greatest work yet."

Walk around the console to the door in the center of the room. Walk through the hallway to find a lone chrysalid isolated in some kind of chamber.

The chrysalid begins to hatch. Before it can finish, empty a clip from your Ammo Box 50 into it, destroying it. Proceed to reload. Use your weapon to destroy the equipment and notes located in the room. Empty clip after clip into them.

Out of the corner of her eye, Ada spots an image of Carla and Simmons in happier times. Ada throws the communicator toward it and walks away. With the lab in flames, she receives a call asking if she's ready for a new job. Congratulations! You've completed *Resident Evil 6*!

ADA CHAPTER 5: RANKING CRITERIA

RANK	ACCURACY(%)	DEATHS	CLEAR TIME(MIN)	ENEMIES ROUTED
A	70	2	55	40
B	60	3	70	30
C	50	5	90	20
D	*1	*1	*1	*1

*1 Any Below Rank C

POINTS AWARDED PER RANK (ABOVE)				
Rank	A	B	C	D
Points	25	20	15	10

TOTAL RANKING POINTS TABLE

RANK	S	A	B	C	D	E
Total	100	90	75	55	45	*2

*2 Any Below Rank D

PART III: DOG TAGS

Dog Tags are customizable icons that represent you online to other players. You can fill your Dog Tag with three different elements: Templates, Emblems, and Titles.

TEMPLATES

Templates are the background of your customizable Dog Tag and can be unlocked by completing chapters in the campaign.

Customize your Dog Tag with a Template that fits your style and best represents you to other online players!

ICON	TEMPLATE NAME	UNLOCK REQUIREMENTS
	Default	–
	Silencer	Clear Leon's Campaign Chapter 1
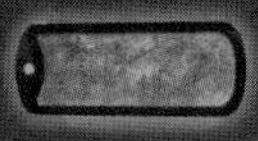	Silencer—Gold	Clear Leon's Campaign Chapter 2
	Silencer—Copper	Clear Leon's Campaign Chapter 3
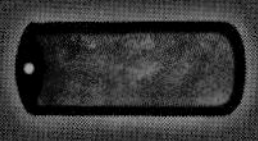	Silencer—Red	Clear Leon's Campaign Chapter 4
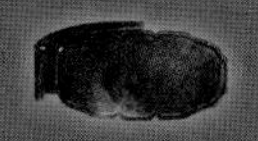	Hand Grenade	Clear Leon's Campaign Chapter 5
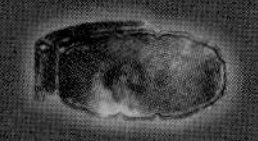	Hand Grenade—Gold	Clear Chris' Campaign Chapter 1
	Hand Grenade—Copper	Clear Chris' Campaign Chapter 2
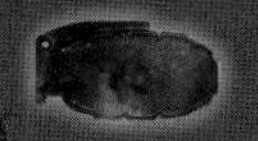	Hand Grenade—Green	Clear Chris' Campaign Chapter 3
	Virus Shot	Clear Chris' Campaign Chapter 4
	Virus Shot—Gold	Clear Chris' Campaign Chapter 5
	Virus Shot—Copper	Clear Jake's Campaign Chapter 1
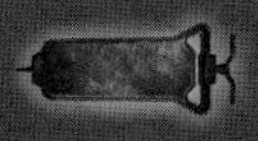	Virus Shot—Light Green	Clear Jake's Campaign Chapter 2
	Wings	Clear Jake's Campaign Chapter 3
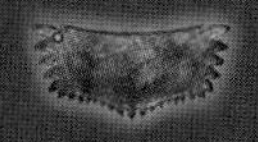	Wings—Gold	Clear Jake's Campaign Chapter 4
	Wings—Copper	Clear Jake's Campaign Chapter 5
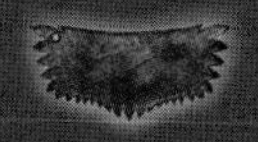	Wings—Pink	Clear Ada's Campaign Chapter 1
	Tank	Clear Ada's Campaign Chapter 2
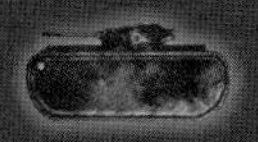	Tank—Gold	Clear Ada's Campaign Chapter 3
	Tank—Copper	Clear Ada's Campaign Chapter 4
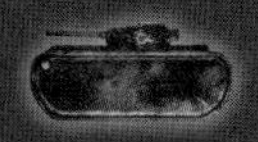	Tank—Yellow	Clear Ada's Campaign Chapter 5

EMBLEMS

Emblems are placed on your Dog Tag and are gained by unlocking Achievements or Trophies. Show off your best Achievement/Trophy to everyone online!

ICON	ACHIEVEMENT/TROPHY NAME	UNLOCK REQUIREMENTS
	The Longest Night	Complete Prelude
	Gone to Hell	Complete Chapter 1 in Leon's Campaign
	Buried Secrets	Complete Chapter 2 in Leon's Campaign
	Get on the Plane	Complete Chapter 3 in Leon's Campaign
	Big Trouble in China	Complete Chapter 4 in Leon's Campaign
	The Trouble with Women	Complete Chapter 5 in Leon's Campaign
	Rescue the Hostages	Complete Chapter 1 in Chris' Campaign
	Tragedy in Europe	Complete Chapter 2 in Chris' Campaign
	After Her!	Complete Chapter 3 in Chris' Campaign
	There's Always Hope	Complete Chapter 4 in Chris' Campaign
	Duty Calls	Complete Chapter 5 in Chris' Campaign
	Money Talks	Complete Chapter 1 in Jake's Campaign
	A Revolting Development	Complete Chapter 2 in Jake's Campaign
	Let's Blow this Joint	Complete Chapter 3 in Jake's Campaign
	Still on the Run	Complete Chapter 4 in Jake's Campaign
	See You Around	Complete Chapter 5 in Jake's Campaign
	I Spy	Complete Chapter 1 in Ada's Campaign
	Counterintelligence	Complete Chapter 2 in Ada's Campaign
	This Takes Me Back	Complete Chapter 3 in Ada's Campaign
	Ada's Demise	Complete Chapter 4 in Ada's Campaign
	What's Next	Complete Chapter 5 in Ada's Campaign

ICON	ACHIEVEMENT/TROPHY NAME	UNLOCK REQUIREMENTS
	Green Around the Ears	Complete the game in Amateur mode
	Normal Is Good	Complete the game in Normal mode
	Back in My Day	Complete the game in Veteran mode
	Leave It to the Pro	Complete the game in Professional mode
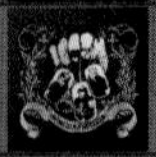	Check Out My Dogs	Customize your dog tags
	Titular Achievement	Earn 10 different titles
	One Is Better Than None	Purchase one skill
	Mad Skillz	Max out all the skills that allow you to level up
	Silent Killer	Use a stealth attack to take down five enemies
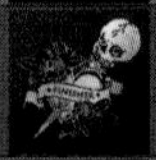	Finish What You Start	Perform a coup de grâce on ten enemies
	Bob and Weave	Counter an enemy's attack three times in a row
	Down, Not Out	Defeat an enemy while dying then recover without any help
	Lifesaver	Help or rescue your partner ten times
	Weapons Master	Use all the weapons in the game and kill ten enemies with each of them
	Give a Little Push	Knock ten enemies off a high place
	Rising Up	Earn a level-four title
	They're ACTION Figures!	Collect 3 figures
	Stuntman	Defeat 20 enemies with the Hydra using a Quick Shot
	Bring the Heat	Take down an enemy from 50 meters away with a headshot using a thermal scope
	High Voltage	Defeat ten enemies with a Stun Rod charge attack
	Zombie Massacre	Defeat 500 Zombies

ICON	ACHIEVEMENT/TROPHY NAME	UNLOCK REQUIREMENTS
	J'avo Genocide	Defeat 500 J'avo
	B.O.W.s Are Ugly	Defeat 100 enemies that have come out of a chrysalid cocoon
	I Prefer Them Alive	Rescue two female survivors at the cathedral in Leon Chapter 2
	Flying Ace	Pilot the VTOL without getting a scratch on it in Chris Chapter 4
	Hard Choice	Shoot the helicopter pilot with a Magnum at point-blank range in Jake Chapter 4
	Sneaking Around	Get through the aircraft carrier's bridge area without being noticed in Ada Chapter 4.
	Covered in Brass	Earn 150 different medals
	Heirlooms	Collect all the Serpent Emblems

TITLES

Titles are essentially in-game achievements that are unlocked after you've performed a unique action. These Titles can be added to your Dog Tag so you can show off some of the difficult objectives you've accomplished online!

For most of the titles, as you make progress towards a title you'll gain additional stars until you reach four stars. Some titles have only one level, so you'll need to complete that objective just once. Some of these Titles can take a long time to unlock. But for many you can progress in Extra Content modes, so keep on playing!

TITLE NO.	NAME	DESCRIPTION	★	★★	★★★	★★★★
1	Resident Evil	Unlocked by default	–	–	–	–
2	Curious Fan	Have a completed Resident Evil 5 save on your system	1 time	–	–	–
3	Newbie	Play Resident Evil 6 for a long time	5 hours	15 hours	50 hours	100 hours
4	Global Player	Meet different people online	10 people	50 people	100 people	300 people
5	Rollin' with the Homies	Play online with people on your Friends list	5 times	30 times	100 times	300 times
6	My Skills	Earn a large number of Skill Points over the course of the game	10,000 points	50,000 points	100,000 points	200,000 points
7	Skill Collector	Unlock many skills across each game mode	10 skills	20 skills	40 skills	80 skills
8	File Collector	Read the files found by destroying Serpent Emblems	10 Files	30 Files	50 Files	All Files
9	Figure Collector	Collect a large number of figures	20 figures	40 figures	60 figures	All figures
10	Earning Them Medals	Earn a large number of medals across all modes	100 medals	300 medals	1,000 medals	2,000 medals
11	Title Collector	Unlock a large number of titles	20 titles	50 titles	100 titles	200 titles
12	People Eater	Play as a zombie in extra content modes	10 times	30 times	100 times	300 times
13	J'avo Juice	Play as a J'avo in extra content modes	10 times	30 times	100 times	300 times
14	Left My Mark	Tag an enemy as a target	10 times	30 times	100 times	300 times
15	Tag Master	Allow co-op partners to destroy enemies you've tagged	10 times	30 times	100 times	300 times
16	Enjoying the Scenery	Walk a long distance	300 meters	1,000 meters	3,000 meters	5,000 meters

TITLE NO.	NAME	DESCRIPTION	★	★★	★★★	★★★★
17	Running My Shoes Off	Run a long distance	10,000 meters	30,000 meters	50,000 meters	100,000 meters
18	Mad Dasher	Dash a long distance in event scenes	300 meters	1,000 meters	3,000 meters	5,000 meters
19	Rock-Hard Buns	Move a long distance on your back	50 meters	100 meters	300 meters	500 meters
20	Big Baby	Crawl a long distance through small spaces	20 meters	50 meters	100 meters	300 meters
21	Like a Duck to Water	Swim a long distance	100 meters	300 meters	500 meters	1,000 meters
22	Joyrider	Travel a long distance in any vehicle	50kilometers	100 kilometers	200 kilometers	500 kilometers
23	Easy Target	Need help from a co-op partner	10 times	30 times	100 times	300 times
24	Rescue Me	Receive help from a co-op partner	10 times	30 times	100 times	300 times
25	Hero	Help a co-op partner	10 times	30 times	100 times	300 times
26	Death Wish	Enter dying state by losing health	10 times	30 times	50 times	100 times
27	Resuscitated Agent	Receive help from a co-op partner while in dying state	10 times	30 times	50 times	100 times
28	Phoenix	Return from dying state without any help	10 times	30 times	50 times	100 times
29	Last Hurrah	Take out enemies while in dying state	1 enemy	3 enemies	10 enemies	100 enemies
30	Lifesaver	Help a co-op partner while they're in dying state	10 times	30 times	50 times	100 times
31	Dead Ringer	Die in any game mode	10 times	50 times	100 times	200 times
32	Going Out in Style	Die in a unique cutscene or from an instant kill attack	5 times	10 times	30 times	50 times
33	Headshot Master	Shoot enemies in the head	30 times	100 times	300 times	1,000 times
34	Gunslinger	Hit enemies with Quick Shot attacks	30 times	100 times	300 times	1,000 times
35	Potent Pugilist	Attack enemies with Martial Arts attacks	30 times	100 times	300 times	1,000 times
36	Relentless Attacker	Use a special Martial Arts finisher attack against a stunned enemy	10 times	30 times	100 times	300 times
37	Combat Master	Perform a coup de grâce attack	10 times	30 times	100 times	300 times
38	By Any Means	Attack an enemy with their own weapon by countering or using a finisher	5 times	10 times	30 times	100 times
39	Badass	Use Martial Arts while your Combat Gauge is empty	5 times	10 times	30 times	100 times
40	Executioner	Finish off a grounded enemy	10 times	30 times	100 times	300 times
41	Counter Attacker	Counter an enemy's attack	10 times	30 times	100 times	300 times
42	Stealth Killer	Kill an enemy from behind without being noticed	10 times	30 times	100 times	300 times
43	Slip Slider	Slide while running	50 times	100 times	300 times	500 times
44	Slide 'n' Smash	Break a box or other stage fixture by sliding	10 times	50 times	100 times	300 times
45	Bone Breaker	Kill an enemy by sliding	5 times	10 times	50 times	100 times
46	Nine-Oh-Nine Expert	Kill an enemy with the Nine-Oh-Nine	30 times	100 times	300 times	1,000 times
47	Picador Expert	Kill an enemy with the Picador	30 times	100 times	300 times	1,000 times
48	Wing Shooter Expert	Kill an enemy with the Wing Shooter	30 times	100 times	300 times	1,000 times
49	Shotgun Expert	Kill an enemy with the Shotgun	30 times	100 times	300 times	1,000 times
50	Assault Shotgun Expert	Kill an enemy with the Assault Shotgun	30 times	100 times	300 times	1,000 times
51	Hydra Expert	Kill an enemy with the Hydra	30 times	100 times	300 times	1,000 times
52	Lightning Hawk Expert	Kill an enemy with the Lightning Hawk	30 times	100 times	300 times	1,000 times
53	Elephant Killer Expert	Kill an enemy with the Elephant Killer	30 times	100 times	300 times	1,000 times
54	Sniper Rifle Expert	Kill an enemy with the Sniper Rifle	30 times	100 times	300 times	1,000 times

TITLE NO.	NAME	DESCRIPTION	★	★★	★★★	★★★★
55	Semi-Auto Sniper Rifle Expert	Kill an enemy with the Semi-Auto Sniper Rifle	30 times	100 times	300 times	1,000 times
56	Anti-Materiel Rifle Expert	Kill an enemy with the Anti-Materiel Rifle	30 times	100 times	300 times	1,000 times
57	Ammo Box 50 Expert	Kill an enemy with the Ammo Box 50	30 times	100 times	300 times	1,000 times
58	Triple Shot Expert	Kill an enemy with the Triple Shot	30 times	100 times	300 times	1,000 times
59	MP-AF	Kill an enemy with the MP-AF	30 times	100 times	300 times	1,000 times
60	A.R. for Special Tactics Expert	Kill an enemy with the Assault Rifle for Special Tactics	30 times	100 times	300 times	1,000 times
61	Bear Commander Expert	Kill an enemy with the Bear Commander	30 times	100 times	300 times	1,000 times
62	Assault Rifle RN	Kill an enemy with the Assault Rifle RN	30 times	100 times	300 times	1,000 times
63	Explosive Round Expert	Kill an enemy with Explosive Rounds	30 times	100 times	300 times	1,000 times
64	Acid Round Expert	Kill an enemy with Acid Rounds	30 times	100 times	300 times	1,000 times
65	Nitrogen Round Expert	Kill an enemy with Nitrogen Rounds	30 times	100 times	300 times	1,000 times
66	Rocket Launcher Expert	Kill an enemy with the Rocket Launcher	3 times	10 times	30 times	100 times
67	Crossbow Expert	Kill an enemy with the Crossbow	30 times	100 times	300 times	1,000 times
68	Crossbow Master	Stick an enemy to the wall with the Crossbow	30 times	100 times	300 times	1,000 times
69	Survival Knife Expert	Kill an enemy with the Survival Knife	30 times	100 times	300 times	1,000 times
70	Combat Knife Expert	Kill an enemy with the Combat Knife	30 times	100 times	300 times	1,000 times
71	Stun Rod Expert	Kill an enemy with the Stun Rod	30 times	100 times	300 times	1,000 times
72	Hand-to-Hand Expert	Kill an enemy with Jake's Hand-to-Hand attacks	30 times	100 times	300 times	1,000 times
73	Gatling Gun Expert	Kill an enemy with a turret emplacement	10 times	30 times	100 times	300 times
74	I Spy	Kill an enemy with the camera-operated turret found in Jake's Chapter 3	10 times	30 times	100 times	300 times
75	ATV Gun Expert	Kill an enemy with the ATV's mounted gun in Chris' Chapter 3	10 times	30 times	100 times	300 times
76	I Got Hand	Kill an enemy with Piers' mutated arm in Chris Chapter 5	3 times	10 times	30 times	100 times
77	Hand Grenade Expert	Kill an enemy with a Hand Grenade	30 times	100 times	300 times	1,000 times
78	Incendiary Grenade Expert	Kill an enemy with an Incendiary Grenade	30 times	100 times	300 times	1,000 times
79	Flash Grenade Expert	Kill an enemy with a Flash Grenade	3 times	10 times	50 times	100 times
80	Flash Grenade Master	Blind an enemy with a Flash Grenade	30 times	100 times	300 times	1,000 times
81	Demolitions Expert	Kill an enemy by detonating an explosive drum or other exploding items located in stages	30 times	100 times	300 times	1,000 times
82	Pipe Bomb Expert	Kill an enemy with Arrow (Pipe Bomb)	30 times	100 times	300 times	1,000 times
83	Remote Bomb Expert	Kill an enemy with a Remote Bomb	30 times	100 times	300 times	1,000 times
84	Manipulator	Allow an enemy to kill another enemy	10 times	30 times	100 times	300 times
85	Need a Pick-Me-Up	Consume a Healing Tablet	100 times	300 times	1,000 times	2,000 times
86	The Chemist	Combine Herbs with other Herbs	30 times	100 times	300 times	1,000 times
87	Need My Meds	Use First Aid Spray	3 times	10 times	30 times	100 times
88	Not an Acrobat	Use Ada's grappling hook	10 times	30 times	100 times	300 times
89	Undercover	Spend a long time in cover cumulatively	5 minutes	10 minutes	30 minutes	100 minutes
90	Reloader	Reload a weapon	500 times	1,000 times	3,000 times	5,000 times
91	Zombie Hunter	Kill a Zombie	100 times	300 times	1,000 times	3,000 times
92	Shrieker Hunter	Kill a Shrieker	20 times	50 times	200 times	500 times

TITLE NO.	NAME	DESCRIPTION	★	★★	★★★	★★★★
93	Whopper Hunter	Kill a Whopper	20 times	50 times	200 times	500 times
94	Zombie Dog Hunter	Kill a Zombie Dog C	20 times	50 times	200 times	500 times
95	Bloodshot Hunter	Kill a Bloodshot	20 times	50 times	200 times	500 times
96	J'avo Hunter	Kill a J'avo	100 times	300 times	1,000 times	3,000 times
97	Cocoon Hunter	Destroy a chrysalid	10 times	30 times	100 times	300 times
98	Glava-Sluz Hunter	Kill a Glava-Sluz	30 times	100 times	300 times	1,000 times
99	Glava-Smech Hunter	Kill a Glava-Smech	30 times	100 times	300 times	1,000 times
100	Glava-Begunats Hunter	Kill a Glava-Begunats	30 times	100 times	300 times	1,000 times
101	Glava-Dim Hunter	Kill a Glava-Dim	30 times	100 times	300 times	1,000 times
102	Ruka-Srp Hunter	Kill a Ruka-Srp	30 times	100 times	300 times	1,000 times
103	Ruka-Khvatanje Hunter	Kill a Ruka-Khvatanje	30 times	100 times	300 times	1,000 times
104	Ruka-Bedem Hunter	Kill a Ruka-Bedem	30 times	100 times	300 times	1,000 times
105	Noga-Trchanje Hunter	Kill a Noga-Trchanje	30 times	100 times	300 times	1,000 times
106	Noga-Let Hunter	Kill a Noga-Let	30 times	100 times	300 times	1,000 times
107	Noga-Skakanje Hunter	Kill a Noga-Skakanje	30 times	100 times	300 times	1,000 times
108	Noga-Oklop Hunter	Kill a Noga-Oklop	30 times	100 times	300 times	1,000 times
109	Telo-Eksplozija Hunter	Kill a Telo-Eksplozija	30 times	100 times	300 times	1,000 times
110	Telo-Krljusht Hunter	Kill a Telo-Krljusht	30 times	100 times	300 times	1,000 times
111	Telo-Magla Hunter	Kill a Telo-Magla	30 times	100 times	300 times	1,000 times
112	Strelats Hunter	Kill a Strelats	20 times	50 times	200 times	500 times
113	Mesets Hunter	Kill a Mesets	10 times	30 times	100 times	300 times
114	Napad Hunter	Kill a Napad	20 times	50 times	200 times	500 times
115	Gnezdo Hunter	Kill a Gnezdo	10 times	30 times	100 times	300 times
116	Lepotitsa Hunter	Kill a Lepotitsa	5 times	20 times	50 times	200 times
117	Brzak Hunter	Kill a Brzak	2 times	5 times	20 times	50 times
118	Ubistvo Hunter	Kill an Ubistvo	5 times	20 times	50 times	200 times
119	Iluzija Hunter	Kill an Iluzija	2 times	5 times	20 times	50 times
120	Deborah Hunter	Kill Deborah	3 times	10 times	30 times	100 times
121	Rasklapanje Hunter	Kill a Rasklapanje	5 times	20 times	50 times	200 times
122	Ogroman Hunter	Kill an Ogroman	5 times	20 times	50 times	200 times
123	Ustanak Hunter	Kill an Ustanak	5 times	20 times	50 times	200 times
124	Oko Hunter	Kill an Oko	10 times	30 times	100 times	300 times
125	Derek Hunter	Kill Derek Simmons	5 times	20 times	50 times	200 times
126	Carla Hunter	Kill Carla Spore	10 times	30 times	100 times	300 times
127	Haos Hunter	Kill a Haos	3 times	10 times	30 times	100 times
128	Road Rage	Kill an enemy with a vehicle	10 times	30 times	100 times	300 times
129	Open Season	Kill an animal	10 times	30 times	100 times	300 times
130	Metal Muncher	Destroy a helicopter or tank	10 times	30 times	100 times	300 times

TITLE NO.	NAME	DESCRIPTION	★	★★	★★★	★★★★
131	Kickin' Ass & Takin' Names	Kill a large number of enemies cumulatively	1,000 enemies	3,000 enemies	5,000 enemies	10,000 enemies
132	Fire Hazard	Kill a zombie with fire	30 times	100 times	300 times	1,000 times
133	Face Smasher	Destroy a J'avos mask	30 times	100 times	300 times	1,000 times
134	Any Port in a Storm	Use a chrysalid cocoon for cover for several minutes	1 minute	3 minutes	10 minutes	20 minutes
135	Chuter Shooter	Kill a parachuting enemy	3 times	10 times	30 times	100 times
136	Getting Good Grades	Achieve an S-Rank in the campaign	5 chapters	10 chapters	15 chapters	20 chapters
137	Decorated Agent	Receive unique medals in the campaign	50 medals	100 medals	150 medals	193 medals
138	Medal Agent	Receive a large number of medals cumulatively in the campaign	200	500	1,000	1,500
139	Amateur	Clear chapters in the campaign in Amateur mode	5 chapters	10 chapters	15 chapters	20 chapters
140	Got Some Experience	Clear chapters in the campaign in Normal mode	5 chapters	10 chapters	15 chapters	20 chapters
141	I Know What I'm Doing	Clear chapters in the campaign in Veteran mode	5 chapters	10 chapters	15 chapters	20 chapters
142	Professional	Clear chapters in the campaign in Professional mode	5 chapters	10 chapters	15 chapters	20 chapters
143	???	Keep an eye out for additional content!	??	??	??	??
144	Action Junkie	Complete any chapter in the campaign in any difficulty mode	35 times	70 times	100 times	200 times
145	Respect the Skills	Complete different campaign chapters without dying	5 chapters	10 chapters	15 chapters	20 chapters
146	Lone Wolf	Complete the campaign without playing co-op	5 chapters	10 chapters	15 chapters	20 chapters
147	Amazon	Complete all chapters in the campaign using female characters	15 chapters	–	–	–
148	Party Time!	Play with three other players in the campaign	1 time	3 times	10 times	30 times
149	Props to You	Praise a co-op player	10 times	20 times	50 times	100 times
150	Herb Sharer	Feed a co-op partner health tablets	10 times	30 times	100 times	200 times
151	Emblem Finder	Destroy the Serpent Emblems found in the campaign	20 emblems	40 emblems	60 emblems	80 emblems
152	Treasure Hunter	Open a treasure chest in the campaign	10 times	30 times	50 times	100 times
153	Exterminator	Kill an enemy that's being controlled by another player	10 times	30 times	100 times	200 times
154	Still in Training	Die in the campaign and continue	10 times	30 times	50 times	100 times
155	Survivalist	Complete a chapter in the campaign using only Leon's Survival Knife	1 time	–	–	–
156	Hydra Tamer	Complete a chapter in the campaign using only Helena's Hydra	1 time	–	–	–
157	Combat Specialist	Complete a chapter in the campaign using only Chris' Combat Knife	1 time	–	–	–
158	Snipe This!	Complete a chapter in the campaign using only Piers' Anti-Materiel	1 time	–	–	–
159	Martial Artist	Complete a chapter in the campaign using only Jake's Hand-to-Hand	1 time	–	–	–
160	Beat-Down King	Complete a chapter in the campaign using only Sherry's Stun Rod	1 time	–	–	–
161	Eagle Eyed	Complete a chapter in the campaign using only Ada's Crossbow	1 time	–	–	–
162	Trigger Happy	Use all the ammo in your weapon during the campaign	50 times	100 times	300 times	1,000 times
163	Button Masher	Complete an action button event	1,000 times	3,000 times	5,000 times	10,000 times
164	Spin Doctor	Complete a rotation action event	10 times	30 times	100 times	200 times
165	The Right Touch	Press an action button at the exact time	10 times	30 times	100 times	200 times
166	Hired Killer	Play The Mercenaries	10 times	30 times	100 times	200 times
167	Decorated Mercenary	Earn unique medals in The Mercenaries	10 medals	20 medals	30 medals	50 medals
168	Medal Mercenary	Earn many medals in The Mercenaries	30 medals	100 medals	200 medals	300 medals

TITLE NO.	NAME	DESCRIPTION	★	★★	★★★	★★★★
169	S.T.A.R.S. Trainee	Receive an S-Rank in different stages of The Mercenaries	3 stages	5 stages	7 stages	9 stages
170	Professional Mercenary	Receive an A-Rank in different stages of The Mercenaries	3 stages	5 stages	7 stages	9 stages
171	Soldier of Fortune	Complete different stages of The Mercenaries	3 stages	5 stages	7 stages	9 stages
172	A Cut above the Rest	Receive an S-rank with different characters in The Mercenaries	3 characters	7 characters	14 characters	All characters
173	Killing's What I Do	Kill many enemies in The Mercenaries	300	1,000	3,000	5,000
174	Gettin' My Hands Dirty	Kill enemies with physical attacks in The Mercenaries	100	500	1,000	3,000
175	Combo Master	Pull off high combos in The Mercenaries	40 Combo	80 Combo	120 Combo	150 Combo
176	Man of the Hour	Get time bonuses from Hourglasses in The Mercenaries	100 times	200 times	300 times	500 times
177	Under the Wire	Finish a round of The Mercenaries with extra time	1 minute	2 minutes	3 minutes	5 minutes or more
178	Killin' Like a Boss	Find and kill a hidden boss in The Mercenaries	10 times	30 times	100 times	200 times
179	Let's Work Together!	Chain physical attacks with a co-op partner in The Mercenaries (Duo)	10 times	50 times	100 times	200 times
180	Team Player	Rescue a partner from dying state in The Mercenaries (Duo)	5 times	10 times	20 times	30 times
181	Agent Hunter	Play Agent Hunt	10 times	30 times	100 times	200 times
182	Brutal Hunter	Kill an Agent while playing Agent Hunt	10 times	30 times	100 times	200 times
183	Decorated Hunter	Collect unique medals in Agent Hunt	10 medals	20 medals	30 medals	50 medals
184	Medal Hunter	Cumulatively collect medals in Agent Hunt	50 medals	100 medals	200 medals	300 medals
185	Assassin	Perform a coup de grâce on an Agent in Agent Hunt	1 time	3 times	10 times	30 times
186	Stay Outta My Turf!	Stay on the same stage with the same agent for a long time in Agent Hunt	1 hour	–	–	–
187	Mutant	Mutate a body part as a J'avo in Agent Hunt	30 times	100 times	200 times	300 times
188	Metamorph	Transform from a J'avo into a different creature in Agent Hunt	10 times	30 times	100 times	200 times
189	Vagabond	Play different stages in Agent Hunt	3 stages	6 stages	9 stages	12 stages
190	Mad Dog	Play as a Zombie Dog C in Agent Hunt	5 times	20 times	100 times	200 times
191	Blood on My Hands	Play as a Bloodshot in Agent Hunt	5 times	20 times	100 times	200 times
192	Shrieking Awesome	Play as a Shrieker in Agent Hunt	5 times	20 times	100 times	200 times
193	Disjointed	Play as a Rasklapanje in Agent Hunt	5 times	20 times	100 times	200 times
194	Ultimate Hunter	Play as all enemy types in Agent Hunt	1 time	–	–	–
195	Cannon Fodder	Die in Agent Hunt without harming an Agent	10 times	30 times	100 times	300 times

Part IV: Extra Content

Agent Hunt

RULES OF ENGAGEMENT

Agent Hunt allows you to assume the role of *Resident Evil 6* monsters and gives you an opportunity to take out other players while they are playing through the campaign!

In the start of most Agent Hunt stages, you enter as a basic enemy like a J'avo or zombie and then gain the ability to upgrade into a mutated J'avo or a stronger creature.

Each creature has its own attacks and abilities, and each has its own strengths and weaknesses. To successfully take out an Agent, study your creature's abilities and learn how to best take advantage of them.

CREATURES

Each creature has different stats, including health, stamina regeneration, and attacks. In each creature's section, you'll find its stats as well as how to control it.

Each creature has 500 stamina unless you equip it with skills to increase stamina, although some creatures can regenerate stamina faster than others.

Some creatures may not be available when you start an Agent Hunt but will become available as you continue the mission. Save up for a strong creature so you can surprise the campaign player's Agent before they finish their mission!

J'AVO/NEO-UMBRELLA J'AVO

J'avo have very little health and have only melee weapons. But they are deadly in a group. When playing as a J'avo, attack Agents when other groups of J'avo are attacking them, so you can sneak in and get a hit while they are unaware!

Neo-Umbrella J'avo are slightly different and are equipped with a wrist blade instead of a knife and other attacks.

The J'avo's defining element is their ability to transform into a different J'avo mutation. You cannot mutate in the beginning of a match—you earn the ability to purchase new mutations as you progress through the match. You can even earn the ability to equip two mutations at a time!

Normal J'avo can only mutate into three different forms: Glava-Sluz, Ruka-Srp, and Ruka-Khvatanje. The Neo-Umbrella J'avo can mutate into many more forms, however, from the exploding Telo-Eksplozija to the deadly Glava-Smech!

When you mutate your first form, the J'avo's health is restored and increased, although mutating into a second form doesn't restore your health. J'avo have the unique ability to hide in lockers in chapters where you're fighting against Jake. This gives you the chance to hide until after he passes by and then pop out to attack from behind!

STATS

Stamina Recovery	100 per second
Default Health	800
J'avo Found in	Chris Chapter 3—Stilt Housing Area Jake Chapter 3—Research Facility—Living Quarters Jake Chapter 4—Shopping District
Neo-Umbrella J'avo Found in	Chris Chapter 4—Aircraft Carrier—Rear Hangar Chris Chapter 5—Underwater Facility

COMMANDS

L3	Move	0 Stamina
L3 + A/X	Dash	0 Stamina
START	Taunt	Recovers 100 Stamina per second
RT/R2	Slash	100 Stamina
RT/R2 + A/X	Dashing Attack	100 Stamina
LT/L2	Guard	0 Stamina
LT/L2 + RT/R2	Guarding Attack	100 Stamina
LB/L1	Side-Step Left	0 Stamina
RB/R1	Side-Step Right	0 Stamina
LB/L1 + RB/R1	Dodge Roll	100 Stamina
(Agent knocked down) RT/R2	Normal: Stab Rush Neo-Umbrella: Kick	0 Stamina
LT + A/X	Crouch	0 Stamina

GLAVA-SMECH

The Glava-Smech has only one attack, but it is very deadly. If you hit an Agent with your Bite attack, you lift them into the air with your giant pincers and hold them in place until they break free!

The Glava-Smech is very slow, however, so attack in a group where you are able to grab an Agent while they're distracted.

STATS

Mutates From	Neo-Umbrella J'avo
Stamina Recovery	100 per second
Default Health	1,200
Found in	Chris Chapter 4—Aircraft Carrier—Rear Hangar Chris Chapter 5—Underwater Facility

COMMANDS

L3	Walk	0 Stamina
L3 + A/⊗	Run	50 Stamina per second
START	Taunt	Recovers 100 Stamina per second
RT/R2	Bite	100 Stamina

GLAVA-SLUZ

STATS

Mutates From	J'avo & Neo-Umbrella J'avo
Stamina Recovery	100 per second
Default Health	1,200
Found in	Chris Chapter 3—Stilt Housing Area Chris Chapter 4—Aircraft Carrier—Rear Hangar Chris Chapter 5—Underwater Facility Jake Chapter 3—Research Facility—Living Quarters Jake Chapter 4—Shopping District

COMMANDS

L3	Walk	0 Stamina
L3 + A/⊗	Run	50 Stamina per second
START	Taunt	Recovers 100 Stamina per second
RT/R2	Spit	100 Stamina
LT/L2	Sticky Thread	200 Stamina

When playing as the Glava-Sluz, you can spit sticky webs over Agents, limiting their maneuverability and giving other creatures the chance to attack while the player is immobile! While playing as the Glava-Sluz, take your time and look for a chance to attack in groups since your own damage-dealing ability is limited.

RUKA-KHVATANJE

At close range, the Ruka-Khvatanje is weak—weaker than even the standard J'avo. The Ruka-Khvatanje shines at a distance, where you can grab Agents using an insect-shaped arm!

When playing as the Ruka-Khvatanje, get behind groups of enemies and sneak in attacks from a distance. If Agents start approaching you, run away and wait around another group of enemies to best take advantage of your powers.

STATS

Mutates From	J'avo & Neo-Umbrella J'avo
Stamina Recovery	100 per second
Default Health	1,200
Found in	Chris Chapter 3—Stilt Housing Area Chris Chapter 4—Aircraft Carrier—Rear Hangar Chris Chapter 5—Underwater Facility Jake Chapter 3—Research Facility—Living Quarters Jake Chapter 4—Shopping District

COMMANDS

L3	Walk/Run	0 Stamina
L3 + A/X	Dash	50 Stamina per second
START	Backstep	0 Stamina
RT/R2	Punch	100 Stamina
LT/L2	Stretch Attack	100 Stamina
LB/L1	Side-step Left	0 Stamina
RB/R1	Side-step Right	0 Stamina

RUKA-SRP

The Ruka-Srp gains an enormous claw for attacks, giving you extreme damage-dealing ability. Unlike many other mutations, the Ruka-Srp has the ability to fight an Agent head-on, since you can dodge and maneuver towards your opponent. Guard their attacks until they run out of ammo, then run toward them and strike!

The Ruka-Srp moves slowly when not running, however, so monitor your stamina. Getting close to your opponent is pointless if you don't have the stamina to attack them!

STATS

Mutates From	J'avo & Neo-Umbrella J'avo
Stamina Recovery	100 per second
Default Health	1,200
Found in	Chris Chapter 3—Stilt Housing Area Chris Chapter 4—Aircraft Carrier—Rear Hangar Chris Chapter 5—Underwater Facility Jake Chapter 3—Research Facility—Living Quarters Jake Chapter 4—Shopping District

COMMANDS

L3	Walk	0 Stamina
L3 + A/X	Run	50 Stamina per second
START	Guard	0 Stamina
RT/R2	Horizontal Slash	100 Stamina
LT/L2	Crouching Attack	100 Stamina
LB/L2	Backward Dodge	50 Stamina
RB/R2	Forward Dodge	50 Stamina

TELO-EKSPLOZIJA

If you mutate into a Telo-Eksplozija, you should prepare to die. You have only one attack. Once you've used it, you die. However, when you die, you explode, potentially taking an Agent with you!

When you trigger the Telo-Eksplozija's explosion, you lose most of your movement ability and then explode 5 to 10 seconds later. Be careful when using this explosion—while you can take out an Agent, you can also take out any other creatures, lessening your total offensive ability!

STATS

Mutates From	Neo-Umbrella J'avo
Stamina Recovery	100 per second
Default Health	1,200
Found in	Chris Chapter 4—Aircraft Carrier—Rear Hangar Chris Chapter 5—Underwater Facility

COMMANDS

L3	Walk	0 Stamina
L3 + A/⊗	Run	100 Stamina per second
START	Feint	0 Stamina
RT/R2	Explode	0 Stamina

RUKA-BEDEM

On its own, the Ruka-Bedem is mostly useless. While you are difficult to damage, it is also difficult to attack Agents because you have to break your own defense when trying to attack.

When you purchase two upgrades, the Ruka-Bedem becomes a devastating powerhouse, giving the other mutations enhanced attacking and defensive ability! Combine Ruka-Bedem with the Ruka-Srp to gain offensive power or use the Ruka-Khvatanje to become a long-range sniper-type attacker with an unbreakable defense!

STATS

Mutates From	Neo-Umbrella J'avo
Stamina Recovery	100 per second
Default Health	1,200
Found in	Chris Chapter 4—Aircraft Carrier—Rear Hangar Chris Chapter 5—Underwater Facility

COMMANDS

L3	Walk	0 Stamina
L3 + A/⊗	Run	50 Stamina per second
START	Guard	0 Stamina
RT/R2	Slam	100 Stamina
LT/L2	Rush Attack	100 Stamina

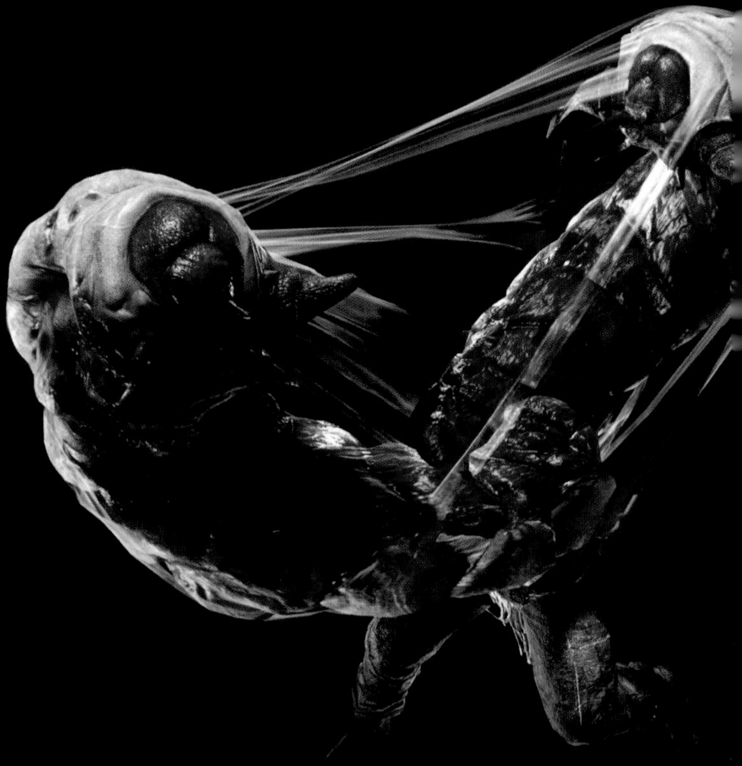

MESETS

The elusive Mesets is rarely seen in the campaign, but you control it at your leisure in Agent Hunt! The Mesets has the unique ability to fly, offering the chance to attack Agents from the air.

While playing as the Mesets, keep your distance by flying around the Agent and attack them while they're unaware. The Mesets is incredibly weak on the ground, so stay airborne as much as possible.

STATS

Stamina Recovery	100 per second
Default Health	2,000
Found in	Jake Chapter 2—Mountain Path

COMMANDS

L3	Walk	0 Stamina
L3 + A/⊗	Fly	0 Stamina
START	Taunt	0 Stamina
RT/R2	Beak Attack	100 Stamina
LT/L2	Rush Attack	100 Stamina
(In-flight) RT/R2	Homing Grab	100 Stamina

STRELATS

The Strelats is an advanced mutation with strong, long-range attacks but weak close-range attacks. When playing as Strelats, run away while attacking a group of enemies from behind and at a distance.

If enemies get close, spray spit around the ground and look for a chance to escape. Avoid close proximity to Agents, since their Martial Arts attacks can completely devastate you.

If you are hit, play dead and hope the Agent diverts their attention, then try to escape! If you utilize this strategy too often, you are punished for it, so don't overuse it.

STATS

Stamina Recovery	50 per second
Default Health	3,000
Found in	Jake Chapter 3—Research Facility—Living Quarters Jake Chapter 4—Shopping District

COMMANDS

L3	Walk	0 Stamina
L3 + A/⊗	Dash	100 Stamina per second
START	Steam Injection	50 Stamina
RT/R2	Spit Poison	100 Stamina
LT/L2	Enter Stance	0 Stamina
LT/L2 + RT/R2	Needle Attack	100 Stamina
RB/R1	Play Dead (Face Down)	Recovers 100 Stamina per second
LB/L1	Play Dead (Face Up)	Recovers 100 Stamina per second

NAPAD

The burly Napad is heavily armored and hard to take down, making it a difficult target for enemy Agents. When playing as a Napad, attack your enemy relentlessly.

Equip a skill that gives you additional stamina so you can keep attacking Agents. Each of the Napad's attacks requires stamina, and its slow movement speed makes it difficult to escape. Keeping your stamina up is very important!

STATS

Stamina Recovery	50 per second
Default Health	5,000
Found in	Chris Chapter 3—Stilt Housing Area Chris Chapter 4—Aircraft Carrier—Rear Hangar

COMMANDS

L3	Walk	0 Stamina
START	Taunt	Recovers 100 Stamina
RT/R2	Punch	100 Stamina
LT/L2	Multi-Punch	0 Stamina
LT/L2 + RT/R2	Rush	100 Stamina
Hold LT/L2, Press X/■	Charge	0 Stamina
(After charging) RT/R2	Super Rush	100 Stamina
(During Super Rush) RT/R2	Tackle	0 Stamina
LB/L1	Punch to the Left	50 Stamina
RB/R1	Punch to the Right	50 Stamina
LB/L1 + RB/R1	2-Hit Punch	100 Stamina

GNEZDO

While the Gnezdo is a difficult enemy to take down in the campaign, it's also a very difficult creature to control. The Gnezdo's offensive capabilities are not very strong and, when its humanoid form is broken, it has no offensive or defensive capabilities at all!

When playing as the Gnezdo, rush down your enemy while summoning decoys and occasionally firing at an Agent. If you surround yourself with additional enemies, you are much harder to defeat than you are when attacking alone.

STATS

Stamina Recovery	100 per second
Default Health	2,000
Found in	Chris Chapter 5—Underwater Facility

COMMANDS

L3	Walk	0 Stamina
L3 + A/X	Run	50 Stamina per second
START	Fake Attack	0 Stamina
RT/R2	Big Attack	100 Stamina
LB/L1 or RB/R1	Decoy Shot	100 Stamina
LT/L2	Stance	0 Stamina
LT/L2 + RT/R2	Insect Bullet	100 Stamina

ZOMBIE

The staple *Resident Evil* creature is not terribly powerful but, in numbers, can easily overwhelm an Agent. When playing as the zombie, take your enemy by surprise because you have little to no chance in a head-to-head fight.

Your zombie might be equipped with a weapon. But while your offensive capability is slightly stronger, you are easier to counter and instantly destroy. When equipped with a weapon, act as if you're going to attack with it and instead throw it at your enemy at the last second.

Be careful if you carry an item that can explode (like dynamite), a fire extinguisher, or a ladder. If you drop it or die, you kill any other creatures around you, reducing your overall offensive force!

STATS

Stamina Recovery	Standing—100 per second Crawling—150 per second
Default Health	600-1500
Found in	Leon Chapter 1—Gun Shop Leon Chapter 2—Forest Cemetery Leon Chapter 3—Cavern

COMMANDS

UNARMED

L3	Walk	0 Stamina
L3 + A/⊗	Dash	0 Stamina
START	Point at Agent	Recovers 100 Stamina per second
RT/R2	Punch	0 Stamina
L3 + A/⊗ + LT/L2	Diving Grab	100 Stamina
LT/L2	Grab	0 Stamina
LB/L1	Side-step Left	100 Stamina
RB/R1	Side-step Right	100 Stamina
LB + RB/L1 + L2	Enter Crawling	0 Stamina
(Near face-down Agent) R2	Grab Agent	0 Stamina

ARMED

L3	Walk	0 Stamina
L3 + A/⊗	Dash	0 Stamina
START	Taunt	Recovers 100 Stamina per second
RT/R2 > RT/R2	Horizontal Swing > Vertical Swing	0 Stamina
L3 + RT/R2 > RT/R2	Vertical Swing > Side Swing	0 Stamina
LT/L2	Aim	0 Stamina
LT/L2 + RT/R2	Throw Weapon	0 Stamina
LB/L1	Side-step Left	100 Stamina
RB/R1	Side-step Right	100 Stamina

SPITTING ZOMBIE

L3	Walk	0 Stamina
L3 + A/⊗	Dash	0 Stamina
START	Taunt	Recovers 100 Stamina per second
RT/R2	Punch	0 Stamina
L3 + A/⊗ + LT/L2	Diving Grab	100 Stamina
LT/L2	Aim	0 Stamina
LT/L2 + RT/R2	Spit	0 Stamina
LB/L1	Side-step Left	100 Stamina
RB/R1	Side-step Right	100 Stamina
LB/L1 + RB/R1	Crawl	0 Stamina
(Near face-down Agent) RT/R2	Grab Leg	0 Stamina

CRAWLING

L3	Crawl	0 Stamina
L3 + A/⊗	Crawl Fast	0 Stamina
RT/R2	Crawling Punch	100 Stamina
LT/L2	Unarmed—Crawl Acid Aim	0 Stamina
LT/L2 + RT/R2	Unarmed—Acid: Spit	0 Stamina
LB/L1	Rotate Left	0 Stamina
RB/R1	Rotate Right	0 Stamina
LB/L1 + RB/R1	Rise	0 Stamina

BLOODSHOT

Muscular Bloodshot zombies are much stronger than normal zombies and have the capability to attack an enemy directly. When playing as a Bloodshot, rush the Agent and attack them directly, diverting their attention away from other creatures.

Be careful when using the diving attack against Agents. Although you move quickly, an Agent's counter deals massive damage, potentially killing you in a single hit! Attack enemies primarily with punches and dive when an Agent turns their back to you.

STATS

Stamina Recovery	100 per second
Default Health	3,000-6,000
Found in	Leon Chapter 1—Gun Shop Leon Chapter 2—Forest Cemetery Leon Chapter 3—Cavern

COMMANDS

L3	Walk	0 Stamina
L3 + A/⊗	Dash	0 Stamina
START	Backstep	Recovers 100 Stamina per second
RT/R2	Uppercut	0 Stamina
LT/L2	Flying Grab	100 Stamina
LB/L1	Side-step Left	100 Stamina
RB/R1	Side-step Right	100 Stamina
LB/L1 + RB/R1	Crawl	0 Stamina
(Near facedown Agent) RT/R2	Grab leg	0 Stamina

ZOMBIE DOG

The Zombie Dog is very weak and can be taken out in a single shot from many weapons. However, it is still a threatening and powerful creature. As a Zombie Dog, hide from your enemy until they come in contact with other enemies, then quickly run at them and attack them from behind.

When running at an enemy, use the rotate abilities to make yourself a more elusive target because your plans are useless if you take a hit. If you manage to hit an Agent, retreat and circle behind them again to attack them as they rise!

STATS

Stamina Recovery	100 per second
Default Health	500-1,000
Found in	Leon Chapter 1—Gun Shop Leon Chapter 2—Forest Cemetery

COMMANDS

L3	Walk	0 Stamina
L3 + A/⊗	Run	10 Stamina per second
START	Sniff Sniff	200 Stamina per second
RT/R2	Flying Grab	100 Stamina
LB/L1	Side-step Left	100 Stamina
RB/R1	Side-step Right	100 Stamina
LB/L1 + RB/R1	Backstep	100 Stamina
(While running) LB/L1	Rotate Left	0 Stamina
(While running) RB/R1	Rotate Right	0 Stamina
(While running) LB/L1 + RB/R1	180-degree turn	0 Stamina
X/□	Bark	Recovers 200 Stamina per second

SHRIEKER

The Shrieker has limited offensive ability but summons zombies to its position, giving you the chance to overwhelm Agents!

When playing as the Shrieker, keep away from Agents and hide while charging up a shriek. It's very important to remain hidden from Agents while charging since this creature's throat swells up, making it vulnerable to attack! If you die while charging, you destroy any creatures around you, reducing your offense even further. Stealth is key when playing as the Shrieker.

STATS

Stamina Recovery	100 per second
Default Health	5,000
Found in	Leon Chapter 1—Gun Shop Leon Chapter 2—Forest Cemetery

COMMANDS

L3	Walk	0 Stamina
L3 + A/X	Dash	0 Stamina
START	Look for Agent	0 Stamina
LT/L2	Punch	0 Stamina
RT/R2	Shriek	0 Stamina
X/□	Charge Shriek	0 Stamina

RASKLAPANJE

The Rasklapanje is a unique creature that generally must fight off Agents individually without assistance. It is a powerful creature, however, and is even a good match-up for two Agents!

Your tactics should change depending on what kind of encounter you're in. If the Agents are separated, focus on grabbing Agents, which leads to an instant kill no matter how much health they have! If two Agents are near each other, however, your attack is easily broken up.

If you are defeated, you break, depending on how much damage your body parts take. When separated, focus on surviving until your other body parts regenerate and combine into a full creature again. If you manage to hold out, all of your health is restored, giving you another chance to take down the Agents!

STATS

Stamina Recovery	100 per second
Default Health	3,000
Found in	Leon Chapter 4—Market Chris Chapter 4—Aircraft Carrier—Forward Hangar Jake Chapter 5—Underwater Facility

COMMANDS

WHOLE BODY

L3	Walk	0 Stamina
L3 + A/X	Run	0 Stamina
START	Taunt	Recovers 100 Stamina per second
RT/R2	Grab	100 Stamina
LT/L2	Throw Arm (unless arm is already thrown)	100 Stamina
LB/L1	Left-moving Attack	100 Stamina
RB/R1	Right-moving Attack	100 Stamina

LOWER BODY ONLY

L3	Walk	0 Stamina
L3 + A/X	Run	0 Stamina
RT/R2	Kick	100 Stamina
LT/L2	Running Blow	100 Stamina per second
LB/L1 + RB/R1	Stance	0 Stamina

UPPER BODY ONLY

L3	Walk	0 Stamina
L3 + A/X	Run	50 Stamina per second
START	Taunt	Recovers 100 Stamina per second
RT/R2	Grab Leg	100 Stamina
LB/L1 + RB/R1	Stance	0 Stamina

STAGES & GOALS

Your goal and method of attack should change depending on the stage and the creature you are playing. Generally, when you're a weak monster like a zombie or a J'avo, bide your time and attack when Agents run into other groups of monsters. In turn, you build up points so you can become a stronger monster. Check each stage's description for the best way to win!

LEON CHAPTER 1 | GUN SHOP

CREATURES AVAILABLE—*Zombie, Zombie Dog, Bloodshot*

In this stage, the Agents are trapped in a small room and you are part of an attacking horde. Focus on attacking Agents who look away from you and try to upgrade to a stronger enemy as quickly as possible.

This stage can be difficult to win. You don't have many ways to take Agents by surprise, and the creatures you control are rather weak. Instead of isolating an Agent and killing them, whittle their health and ammo down, drain their resources, and use the attacking horde to your advantage.

LEON CHAPTER 2 | FOREST CEMETERY

CREATURES AVAILABLE—*Zombie, Shrieker, Zombie Dog, Bloodshot*

This stage is dark and provides multiple places where you can wait for an Agent and ambush them. This should be your general strategy. Unless you are a Bloodshot, you have very little chance of success in a one-on-one fight against an Agent, let alone two!

Conserve upgrades for most of the level and ambush Agents with normal zombies and Zombie Dogs. Stay away from the Shrieker for most of the level since you are an easy target if an Agent spots you.

Once the Agents reach the Cathedral, the Shrieker becomes a powerful enemy because you can increase the mass of enemies attacking the Agents. The Bloodshot is also a great enemy here. Many other powerful creatures are in this area, giving you the chance to overwhelm Agents with sheer power!

LEON CHAPTER 3 | CAVERN

CREATURES AVAILABLE—*Zombie, Shrieker, Bloodshot*

This winding section places the Agents in small areas, making direct combat difficult. Instead of fighting the Agents head-on, sneak around them and ambush them from areas they can't reach.

Identify the Agent who tends to lag behind the other and take that Agent out. If the lead Agent jumps to another area while you're attacking the slower Agent, it is more difficult for them to assist and allows you to deal more damage!

LEON CHAPTER 4 | MARKET

CREATURES AVAILABLE—*Rasklapanje*

This level is essentially a maze and offers many chances to ambush Agents. Wait for the Agents to separate and then attack them when they're isolated.

If you attack the Agent directly, you have very little room to evade, so be careful when attacking two Agents at once. In situations where you must fight and you take damage, escape when you're separated and hide to regenerate your health.

CHRIS CHAPTER 3 | STILT HOUSING AREA

CREATURES AVAILABLE—*J'avo, Napad*

You have several chances to attack Agents in this stage and each should be handled differently. In the first area, the Agents are mobile and under attack from multiple snipers located around the area. Stay away from the Napad and stick to the normal J'avo, Glava-Sluz, and Ruka-Khvatanje mutations. The Glava-Sluz can trap the Agents in place, making them easy targets for snipers, while the Ruka-Khvatanje can grapple enemies from afar while they're running, preventing them from making progress.

Once the Agents make it past the snipers, they are in an area where they're mostly trying to run from an attack helicopter. It is very difficult to attack Agents in this section since they can generally run straight past you. If you must use a mutation, use the Glava-Sluz and trap the agents in the line of helicopter fire, try to stand in their way, and prevent them from running through the area.

In the final area, the Agents do battle with the helicopter directly. In this area, the Napad becomes useful because the Agents are preoccupied with fighting the helicopter. A strong target like the Napad is a powerful distraction. The Glava-Sluz and Ruka-Srp are also useful here. You can attack the Agent directly but also keep them exposed to attacks from the helicopter!

CHRIS CHAPTER 4 | AIRCRAFT CARRIER—REAR HANGAR

CREATURES AVAILABLE—*Neo-Umbrella J'avo, Napad*

In this stage, Agents are bombarded with a multitude of other J'avo, some with sniper rifles. In this stage, you don't need to attack the enemy directly since they are often occupied. Sneak behind the Agents and take them out!

Since you have access to Neo-Umbrella J'avo, you can use a variety of mutations, including Telo-Eksplozija. The Telo-Eksplozija's explosion requires time to trigger, so you need ample time to prepare. Since you have many chances to ambush the enemy, you have more chances to use this transformation to attack enemies from behind!

CHRIS CHAPTER 4 | AIRCRAFT CARRIER—FORWARD HANGAR

CREATURES AVAILABLE—*Rasklapanje*

This area is a giant maze for the Agents, which offers a great stage for the Rasklapanje. This stage is mostly similar to other Rasklapanje stages. As a result, you should primarily hide and attack the Agents when they get separated.

Look at this chapter's walhthrough map and use it to your advantage—find where Agents need to go to find Passcodes and wait for them in ambush. If you get damaged, it is very difficult to regenerate. The spaces are very small, making it difficult to find time to regenerate.

CHRIS CHAPTER 5 | UNDERWATER FACILITY

CREATURES AVAILABLE—*Neo-Umbrella J'avo, Gnezdo*

The Agents are mostly separated in this stage, giving you plenty of time to attack them on one-on-one. When fighting Piers, you are one of many J'avo, so you won't need to focus directly on an Agent to do damage. You can use many levers and buttons to cause stage elements to attack the Agent, so take advantage of them.

If you get to a turret before an Agent, it is difficult for them to progress, so get there as soon as possible. Fighting Chris is far more difficult because he encounters very few enemies and will force you to fight him one-on-one. If you must fight him, save up for a Gnezdo, which will put you in a much better position to fight him.

JAKE CHAPTER 2 | MOUNTAIN PATH

CREATURES AVAILABLE—*Mesets*

The only creature you can control in this stage is the Mesets, which has the unique ability of flight. This is the only chance you can control the Mesets, so you probably won't have much practice with it. Devote some time to learning its unique controls before trying to confront the Agents.

Visibility in this stage is very low, so use that to your advantage. Keep your distance from the Agents and attack sparingly. Look for Agents to begin fighting other enemies, then use that opportunity to attack them from behind. If one of the Agents jumps onto a snowmobile, use this as an opportunity to attack the other one while they're separated.

JAKE CHAPTER 3 | RESEARCH FACILITY—LIVING QUARTERS

CREATURES AVAILABLE—*J'avo, Strelats*

This stage is mostly straightforward, and you fight Agents head-on. You can hide in several areas that are nearly impossible to for Agents to predict unless they know about them beforehand. The most notable of these are the lockers located around the area. Hide in them until you see an Agent enter and leave, then sneak up behind them!

Otherwise, save up for a Strelats and attack your enemy from afar, especially in the larger areas. The more distance you can gain while playing as a Strelats the better.

JAKE CHAPTER 4 | SHOPPING DISTRICT

CREATURES AVAILABLE—*J'avo, Strelats*

In this area, and until you can afford stronger mutations, use the other J'avo to cover you as you run in and attack. Focus on the Ruka-Srp. Simply distracting the enemy while other J'avo open fire could be enough to take down the Agents.

When you can turn into a Strelats, follow the same strategy, but be sure to keep your distance to maintain your health. Focus strictly on hit-and-run tactics and completely avoid fighting the Agents head-on.

JAKE CHAPTER 5 | UNDERWATER FACILITY

CREATURES AVAILABLE—*Rasklapanje*

In this stage, the Agents are separated, giving you ample opportunities to instantly kill them. Learn the order in which this stage must be completed and focus on the busiest Agent—one Agent is idle for most of the stage, making them more likely to anticipate your attacks.

Find places where you can wait in ambush or for Agents to run by. The Agent will be busy working on an action-prompt in many places, giving you the perfect opportunity to attack them from behind!

THE MERCENARIES

RULES OF ENGAGEMENT

This famous mini-game mode returns to *Resident Evil 6* and features eight characters, each with their own unique load-outs and abilities.

n The Mercenaries, you have two minutes to rack up as many points as possible by defeating enemies quickly and continuously. Each stage in The Aercenaries has a unique distribution of enemies, which come out in the same order each level. Learning this order will help you rack up huge scores.

Although your time is initially very limited, you can increase your available time by five seconds if you finish off enemies with any variety of melee ıttacks, including counters and coups de grâce. Melee weapons like the Stun Rod, knives, and Jake's Hand-to-Hand also increase the timer by five ;econds for each kill and don't use any of your Combat Gauge, making these powerful attacks even more useful!

HOURGLASSES

Each stage in The Mercenaries contains several large hourglass-shaped items that provide unique bonuses. The most common fixtures are the yellow ıourglasses that, when destroyed, give you extra time to complete the stage. The amount of time each object provides is fixed. But each of them looks the ;ame, so you can't tell the time they contain unless you break them (or use the maps found in this guide)! You can't break a yellow hourglass by shooting t—they can only be broken by melee attacks or by sliding. Therefore, plan a path around the level that allows you to run into each of them!

Jse gunfire to break green hourglasses, which allow you to enter "Combo Time." When you're in Combo Time, you get an extra 1000 points for each ıdditional combo you perform as long as it is active. Combo Time only lasts for 30 seconds, so use it only when many enemies are grouped together.

TIME BONUSES

You will often find that earning additional time is as important as killing enemies in The Mercenaries. There are several ways to earn time, most notably by destroying yellow hourglasses and finishing enemies with melee attacks.

TIME BONUS ITEMS	BONUS GRANTED
Yellow Hourglasses	30, 60 or 90 seconds
Melee Weapon Kills and Melee Attacks	5 seconds
Coup de Grâce	7 seconds
Finish with Counter	10 seconds

The bonus granted by a yellow hourglass differs, depending on which one you break. The amount is pre-determined, but you can't tell how many seconds you'll be given until you break the hourglass. Use the maps in this guide for each stage to learn where the most valuable hourglasses are located.

You can earn five seconds of additional time by killing enemies with melee attack finishers, or melee weapons—the Combat Knife, Survival Knife, Stun Rod, and Hand-to-Hand. If you finish an enemy with a coup de grâce, you receive a bonus of seven seconds, allowing you to continue building your remaining time! If you kill an enemy with a counter-attack, you gain a bonus of 10 seconds, although you shouldn't rely on this—you'll probably spend as much time as you'd gain just waiting for the enemy to attack!

Mixing up all three options—melee attacks, finishers, and melee weapons—is key to racking up high scores in The Mercenaries. When you have stamina remaining, you should finish off enemies with melee attacks to keep building up time.

SCORING

COMBO	BONUS	BOSS BONUS
2 Combo	40	750
3 Combo	100	1,500
4 Combo	200	2,250
5 Combo	400	3,000
6 Combo	500	3,750
7 Combo	600	4,500
8 Combo	700	5,250
9 Combo	800	6,000
20-29 Combo	1,200	7,500
30-39 Combo	1,400	8,250
40-49 Combo	1,700	9,000
50-59 Combo	2,000	10,500
60-69 Combo	2,400	12,000
70-79 Combo	2,800	15,000
80-89 Combo	3,400	18,000
90-99 Combo	4,000	22,500
100-109 Combo	6,000	30,000
110-119 Combo	8,000	45,000
120-129 Combo	12,000	60,000
130-139 Combo	20,000	75,000
140-149	30,000	90,000
150	60,000	150,000

If you kill a secret boss in a combo, your combo bonus will increase depending on the portion of the combo that you killed that enemy with. If you don't have much of a combo bonus when one of these large monsters spawns, kill some smaller enemies before finishing off the large enemies to maximize your score—if you can manage to keep that boss alive.

Each enemy is worth a specific number of points, no matter how you kill them. Note that the enemies worth high point values also tend to increase your combo bonus. Even though Zombie Dogs are worth only 100 points, they give you the same Combo Bonus as a normal zombie or J'avo.

POINT VALUES	SCORE AWARDED
Zombies	300
J'avo	300
Zombie Dog	100
J'avo with 1 Mutation	500
Bloodshot	600
Shrieker	800
Whopper	1,000
Napad	1,500
Strelats	1,500
Gnezdo	3,000

If you finish all 150 enemies in a stage before time is over, you earn a 200-point bonus for every second left on the clock!

At the end of a Mercenaries stage, you're graded based on how many points you earn. To get the highest scores, you must complete a combo bonus for almost the entire stage! If you're playing in Splitscreen (or Duo), you need to score more points to reach higher ranks. Remember this if you're trying to help each other unlock characters! In multiplayer modes, enemies are stronger and faster—normally you'll face monsters with Normal difficulty strength. But in multiplayer modes, you face Veteran-difficulty enemies!

RANK	SCORE REQUIRED—SOLO	SCORE REQUIRED—DUO
E Rank	0–39,999	0–59,999
D Rank	40,000–59,999	60,000–89,999
C Rank	60,000–79,999	90,000–119,999
B Rank	80,000–99,999	120,000–179,999
A Rank	100,000–139,999	180,000–219,999
S Rank	140,000+	220,000+

In the beginning, the only available stage in The Mercenaries is Urban Chaos and you will be limited to using Leon, Chris, and Jake. Additional stages and Ada become available by completing the full story campaign.

Depending on the character you use, the stage you completed, and the rank you receive, you can unlock additional characters and costumes. These unique costumes not only give most characters new clothing but also a unique load-out—they are essentially new characters!

REWARD	UNLOCK REQUIREMENT
Steel Beast stage	Complete Chris' Campaign.
Mining the Depths stage	Complete Jake's Campaign.
Ada	Complete Ada's Campaign.
Helena	Complete Urban Chaos with a B rank or better.
Piers	Complete Steel Beast with a B rank or better.
Sherry	Complete Mining the Depths with a B rank or better.
Carla	Unlock every character and every character's Costume 1.
Costume 1	Complete any stage with an A rank or better as that character.

MERCENARIES SKILLS

The Mercenaries mode has its own unique Skills that are usable only in The Mercenaries mode. Many of these Skills are straightforward, but you can equip only one Skill at a time. As a result, you should equip them based on the character you're going to use. Several only benefit you when playing with another player, so don't equip those when going solo.

NAME	POINTS	DESCRIPTION
Eagle Eye	3,000	Adds an extra level of magnification to sniper rifle scope.
Item Drop Increase	3,500	Causes more defeated enemies to drop items.
Go for Broke!	60,000	Makes it easier to complete combos as time runs out.
Time Bonus +	90,000	Increases time awarded by a Time Bonus.
Combo Bonus +	50,000	Increases time for a Combo Bonus.
Limit Breaker	60,000	Increases the points earned for surpassing 50 combos.
Blitz Play	5,000	Increases your attack power if you attack immediately after another player.
Quick Shot Damage Increase	15,000	Increases power of quick shots.
Power Counter	8,000	Greatly increases the power of counters.
Second Wind	6,000	Increases power to firearms and melee attacks when life gauge is low.
Martial Arts Master	25,000	Increases strength of physical attacks, but the power of firearm-related attacks is greatly reduced.
Target Master	25,000	Increases strength of firearm-related attacks, but the power of physical attacks is greatly reduced.
Last Stand	30,000	Greatly increases attack power, but attacks on you cause three times normal damage.
Preemptive Strike	7,000	Increases attack power when you attack from behind.
Dying Breath	15,000	Greatly increases attack power when dying, but recovery time is comparably shortened.
Pharmacist	17,000	Increases the potency of Healing Tablets.
Medic	12,000	Heals a teammate that's far away when you use a Healing Tablet.
First Responder	15,000	Makes it easier to rescue dying teammates.
Take It Easy	20,000	Increases speed of natural recovery when using cover.
Natural Healing	15,000	Increases speed of natural recovery.

CHARACTERS AND DEFAULT LOAD-OUTS

LEON S. KENNEDY

UNLOCK CONDITIONS: Default

LOAD-OUT

- Wing Shooter x18
- Shotgun x8
- Remote Bomb x4
- 9mm Ammo x50
- 12-Gauge Shells x8
- Healing Tablets x8

RECOMMENDED SKILLS: Quick Shot Damage Increase, Item Drop Increase, Power Counter

GENERAL STRATEGIES

Leon's default load-out is surprisingly underpowered because his only weapons are his Wing Shooter, which isn't terribly powerful, and the Shotgun, which has a long delay between shots and is difficult to use as crowd control. Focus on using the Wing Shooter and melee attacks to build up time while using the Shotgun and your Remote Bombs against stronger enemies.

Even though you can dual-wield with the Wing Shooter, it's often better not to. Dual-wielding adds a considerable aiming penalty, causing you to miss important distance shots or miss hitting weak points at close range. Be sure your Shotgun is always fully loaded so you won't have to reload at a critical time.

The Wing Shooter has a unique Quick Attack when dual-wielding that can be performed as long as you have stamina. If you're surrounded, consider using all five hits of Leon's special Quick Attack to stun the surrounding enemies and finish them off with melee attacks.

LEON S. KENNEDY—COSTUME 1

UNLOCK CONDITIONS: Complete any stage as Leon with A Rank or better

LOAD-OUT

- Assault Rifle RN x30
- Sniper Rifle x6
- Grenade Launcher x5
- 5.56mm Ammo x60
- 7.62mm Ammo x30
- Healing Tablets x4

RECOMMENDED SKILLS: Target Master, Item Drop Increase

GENERAL STRATEGIES

Unlike Leon's default load-out, this swashbuckling Leon is loaded with powerful weapons and is capable of taking out any stage without much difficulty.

The Assault Rifle RN in The Mercenaries is incredibly powerful and can take down many normal enemies in only a couple shots. Use it to stun enemies and finish them off with melee attacks to build up time and ammo. When you are fighting enemies from a distance, pick them off with the Sniper Rifle to keep your Combo Timer up and to save ammo for your Assault Rifle. If your inventory ever becomes full, consider dropping your 7.62mm Ammo in favor of 5.56mm Ammo since the Assault Rifle RN is really the only weapon you need.

The Assault Rifle RN is very powerful, even for an assault rifle! It can be used effectively against every enemy, even at long range!

Save your grenade launcher rounds for stronger enemies only. The Assault Rifle RN is powerful enough on its own to quickly take out the stronger normal enemies like Bloodshots. This load-out doesn't have many Healing Tablets, so watch for Green Herbs to add to your case.

HELENA HARPER

UNLOCK CONDITIONS: Complete Urban Chaos as any character with B Rank or better

LOAD-OUT

- Picador x16
- Hydra x3
- Grenade Launcher x6
- 9mm Ammo x50
- 10-Gauge Shells x30
- Healing Tablets x6

RECOMMENDED SKILLS: Quick Shot Power Increase, Counter Master, Pharmacist

GENERAL STRATEGIES

Helena's default load-out is packed with weapons, giving you the chance to take out almost any enemy quickly. The Hydra is a unique weapon that fires rapidly and does huge damage, but it is only effective on enemies directly next to you. Use it to stun enemies and finish them off with melee attacks to build up your timer.

When you run low on Hydra ammo, switch to the Picador and follow the same strategy. Against larger enemies, use your Grenade Launcher to take them down. You don't have much ammo, so make sure each shot counts.

The Hydra has three unique Quick Attacks that deal big damage and function as a crouch, which allows her to avoid many attacks!

HELENA HARPER—COSTUME 1

UNLOCK CONDITIONS: Complete any stage as Helena with A Rank or better

LOAD-OUT

- Ammo Box 50 x50
- Sniper Rifle x6
- Herb(Red) x1
- First-Aid Spray x1
- Incendiary Grenade x3
- 9mm Ammo x50
- 7.62mm Ammo x20

RECOMMENDED SKILLS: Eagle Eye, Target Master, Take It Easy

GENERAL STRATEGIES

Helena's alternate costume is a challenge because she has little in terms of offensive power and no Healing Tablets. As a result, you must immediately search out herbs in order to restore your health. Although she begins with considerable ammo for the Ammo Box 50, it's a weak weapon, which means you need to rely on the Sniper Rifle to do damage to larger enemies.

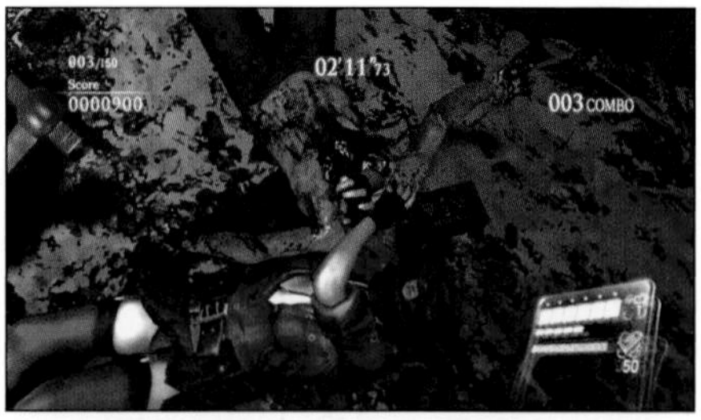

You must build up extra time with Helena as often as possible since you need to spend extra time looking for healing items—she starts with only one First-Aid Spray and no Healing Tablets!

Your first priority is to use the Ammo Box 50 to stun enemies and then finish them with melee attacks. Build up your timer and get some herbs. When you start suffering damage, you should immediately retreat, find the Green Herbs in the stage, and build up your tablet case. While running, use your Sniper Rifle to take out enemies from a distance to keep your Combo Timer up.

CHRIS REDFIELD

UNLOCK CONDITIONS: None

LOAD-OUT

- Assault Rifle for Special Tactics x30
- Lightning Hawk x7
- Combat Knife
- Hand Grenade x3
- 5.56mm Ammo x60
- .50 Action-Express Magnum Ammo x7

RECOMMENDED SKILLS: Item Drop Increase, Target Master, Natural Healing

GENERAL STRATEGIES

The default version of Chris is fairly powerful and includes an assault rifle, a magnum, and a melee weapon that doesn't cost stamina to use. Use the Combat Knife to take down weaker enemies and build up time. Use the Assault Rifle when you're overwhelmed, and use the Lightning Hawk against stronger enemies.

Chris doesn't have anything to heal himself except for Healing Tablets, so retreat whenever your health is getting too low while using the Combat Knife. If enemies surround you, throw a Hand Grenade at them to instantly take them out.

The Lightning Hawk is capable of killing many enemies in a single shot no matter where it hits them! You can also shoot through multiple enemies, making it a tremendously powerful weapon.

CHRIS REDFIELD—COSTUME 1

UNLOCK CONDITIONS: Complete any stage as Chris with A Rank or better

LOAD-OUT

- Nine-Oh-Nine x15
- Shotgun x8
- Rocket Launcher x1
- 9mm Ammo x50
- 12-Gauge Shells x20
- Healing Tablets x6

RECOMMENDED SKILLS: Power Counter, Item Drop Increase, Quick Shot Damage Increase

GENERAL STRATEGIES

This load-out is underpowered and contains only a weak handgun and the slow, normal Shotgun... but it also has the incredibly powerful Rocket Launcher! You get only one shot with the Rocket Launcher, so you have to make it count. Don't just save it for a powerful enemy. Instead, save it for a group of enemies to take them all out at once.

Follow the general strategy of using the Nine-Oh-Nine and melee attacks to build up time. Use the Shotgun against stronger enemies or when you have tons of Shotgun ammo to expend.

Although you only get one shot, Chris' Alternate load-out is the only place where you can use the Rocket Launcher outside of the end of Leon's Campaign. So you can use this costume to build up progress toward Titles and Achievements!

PIERS NIVANS

UNLOCK CONDITIONS: Complete Steel Beast as any character with B Rank or better

LOAD-OUT

MP-AF x30
Anti-Materiel Rifle x10
First-Aid Spray x1
Remote Bomb x3
9mm Ammo x50
AM Rifle Ammo x20
Healing Tablet x1

RECOMMENDED SKILLS: Target Master, Item Drop Increase

GENERAL STRATEGIES

Piers' default load-out contains both the powerful MP-AF and the Anti-Materiel Rifle. The MP-AF functions as either a handgun or an automatic rifle, depending on which firing method you use. Stick with single-shot mode and kill enemies with finishers instead of using automatic fire.

The Anti-Materiel Rifle is a powerful single-shot weapon that functions as a sniper rifle with the capability to take out multiple targets. It doesn't have much ammo, but you can quickly take out even the strongest enemies in a single shot. Save your Anti-Materiel Rifle Ammo for big enemies, like Bloodshots and Whoppers, that can only be dropped with lots of 9mm Ammo.

Use the Quick Shot to fire the Anti-Materiel Rifle without a scope, allowing you to deal big damage to large enemies without obstructing your view.

PIERS NIVANS—COSTUME 1

UNLOCK CONDITIONS: Complete any stage as Piers with A Rank or better

LOAD-OUT

Ammo Box 50 x50
Semi-Auto Sniper Rifle x5
Assault Shotgun x7
9mm Ammo x30
7.62mm Ammo x15
12-Gauge Shells x10
Healing Tablets x4

RECOMMENDED SKILLS: Eagle Eye, Item Drop Increase, Target Master

GENERAL STRATEGIES

Much like his default load-out, this version of Piers has many weapons but load-outlacks the extreme firepower of the Anti-Materiel Rifle. Primarily use the Ammo Box 50 and finishers to build up time. Save the Semi-Auto Sniper Rifle and Assault Shotgun for bigger enemies.

Make free use of any of your weapons depending on how much ammo you have for each. Use the weapon that you have the most ammo for while you build up stocks of other ammo.

The Assault Shotgun fires rapidly, allowing you to quickly mow down enemies. If you don't take out an enemy in a single shot, you'll probably knock them down, giving you the chance to finish them off for some additional time.

Jake Muller

UNLOCK CONDITIONS: Default

Load-Out

Nine-Oh-Nine x15
Elephant Killer x5
Hand-to-Hand
Flash Grenade x2
9mm Ammo x50
.500 Magnum Ammo x10
Healing Tablets x10

RECOMMENDED SKILLS: Martial Arts Master, Power Counter, Natural Healing

General Strategies

Jake's default load-out is the only one that feature's Jake's unique Hand-to-Hand ability. Rely on this to take out enemies since Hand-to-Hand builds up time after every kill and doesn't drain your Combat Gauge. Unlike other melee-heavy load-outs, Jake doesn't have First-Aid Spray. So use a Flash Grenade when you're running low on health, which gives you time to use standard Healing Tablets.

Save the Elephant Killer for bigger enemies and use the Nine-Oh-Nine for faster-moving or flying enemies. Magnum ammo tends to be rare, so make sure you have enough available when stronger enemies spawn in the stage.

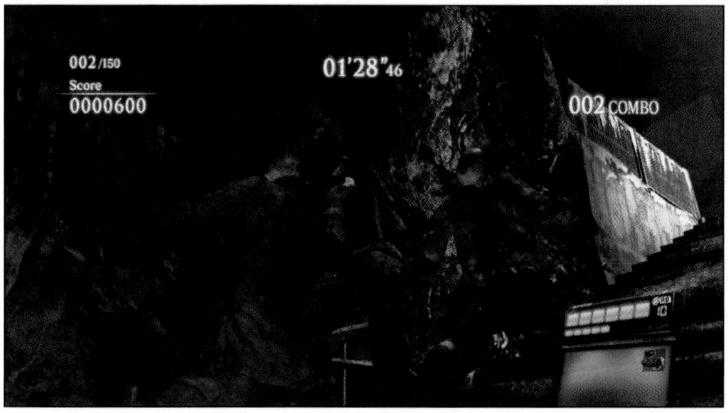

Jake's Hand-To-Hand attacks don't cost any stamina, earn you time for every kill, can be charged to use from a distance, and do tons of damage—especially his charged uppercut. Use them as much as possible to build up time.

Jake Muller—Costume

UNLOCK CONDITIONS: Complete any stage as Jake with A Rank or better

Load-Out

Survival Knife
Semi-Auto Sniper Rifle x5
Grenade Launcher x6
First-Aid Spray x1
7.62mm Ammo x20
40mm Explosive Rounds x12
Healing Tablets x8

RECOMMENDED SKILLS: Martial Arts Master, Power Counter, Natural Healing

General Strategies

Jake's alternate costume trades handguns and Hand-to-Hand for a Survival Knife and a grenade launcher. Even though this load-out has a Sniper Rifle, focus on using the Survival Knife to quickly take out enemies at close range. The Survival Knife inflicts huge damage and doesn't cost stamina, which helps you quickly build up time while taking out enemies.

You suffer some damage when using the knife, so save your First-Aid Spray for when you're low on health. Take out bigger enemies with the Semi-Auto SR or your Grenade Launcher. You have plenty of Grenade Rounds, so don't worry about conserving ammo.

The Survival Knife is surprisingly powerful for a last-resort weapon and adds to your time after every kill! When you're surrounded by weak enemies, take them out with the Survival Knife.

SHERRY BIRKIN

UNLOCK CONDITIONS: Complete Mining the Depths with any character with B Rank or better

LOAD-OUT

Triple Shot x20
Lightning Hawk x7
Stun Rod
Herb (Red) x2
First-Aid Spray x1
9mm Ammo x30
.50 Action-Express Magnum Ammo x10
Healing Tablet x1

RECOMMENDED SKILLS: Pharmacist, Quick Shot Power Increase, Item Drop Increase

GENERAL STRATEGIES

Sherry's default load-out requires keeping yourself safe. She has First-Aid Spray for quick healing and Red Herbs to quickly fill up your tablet case with healing items. Since each of those Red Herbs takes up a slot in your inventory, find Green Herbs to combine them with. Then you can carry more ammo and grenades.

Attack with Sherry's Triple Shot in single-shot mode and with her Stun Rod. Use the single-shot mode to conserve ammo and melee attacks to finish off enemies. The Stun Rod doesn't cost any stamina but isn't as strong as the knife weapons. Use it as long as you have the stamina available to finish off enemies. If you hit an enemy with the charged attack on the Stun Rod but they die by being set on fire, you won't be awarded extra time. Hit an enemy with the Stun Rod's normal attack before using the charged attack.

The Stun Rod counts as a melee weapon and allows you to build up time with every kill. But it's weaker than the others. You can charge the Stun Rod to deal enormous damage. But if enemies die from incineration, you won't get the bonus!

Save the Lightning Hawk for larger enemies like the Bloodshot and Napad since magnum ammo isn't very common. If you find yourself with plenty of magnum ammo, switch to using the Lightning Hawk exclusively. It can often kill basic zombie and J'avo enemies in a single shot.

SHERRY BIRKIN—COSTUME

UNLOCK CONDITIONS: Complete any stage as Sherry with A Rank or better

LOAD-OUT

Bear Commander x30
Assault Shotgun x7
Herb (Red) x2
First-Aid Spray x1
Flash Grenade x2
5.56mm Ammo x60
12-Gauge Shells x20
40mm Explosive Rounds x3
Healing Tablet x1

RECOMMENDED SKILLS: Target Master, Pharmacist, Item Drop Increase

GENERAL STRATEGIES

Sherry's alternate costume trades in her Stun Rod and Triple Shot for a heavier arsenal suited to quickly killing enemies. Use the Bear Commander to take out enemies and look for opportunities to finish off enemies with melee attacks to build up your time.

Save your Bear Commander grenades and Assault Shotgun for bigger enemies to conserve Bear Commander ammo. Also find out where Green Herbs are located in a stage and make them part of your circuit through the stage. This ensures that you make space in your inventory as soon as possible.

The Bear Commander's alternate fire mode switches the weapon from an assault rifle to a grenade launcher. When you see a large group of enemies or a larger, stronger enemy, enter into alternate fire and unleash explosive fury!

ADA WONG

UNLOCK CONDITIONS: Complete Ada's Campaign

LOAD-OUT

- Ammo Box 50 x50
- Crossbow x1
- Incendiary Grenade x3
- 9mm Ammo x30
- Arrows (Normal) x60
- Arrows (Pipe Bomb) x30
- Healing Tablets x8

RECOMMENDED SKILLS: Target Master, Power Counter, Item Drop Increase

GENERAL STRATEGIES

Ada's default load-out is built around her Crossbow, which is difficult to aim but very powerful. The Crossbow kills most enemies in a single hit if it hits their weak point, allowing you to quickly dispatch even the strongest enemies!

Use the Ammo Box 50 to stun enemies, use coups de grâce to build up time, then focus on the Crossbow to quickly kill enemies. When you've reduced the enemies surrounding you, switch to the Ammo Box 50 and use melee attacks to build up your time.

Ada's Arrow (Pipe Bomb) takes out multiple enemies, but it has a short delay before it explodes. Don't use it unless you think a group of enemies will stay together before it explodes!

Some enemies like the Napad and Whopper won't die in a single Crossbow hit, so save your Arrow (Pipe Bomb) and Grenades for them. The explosion caused by a Pipe Bomb Arrow can also take out several enemies at a time. However, it explodes after a delay, making it hard to time a shot that kills multiple enemies.

ADA WONG – COSTUME 1

UNLOCK CONDITIONS: Complete any stage as Ada with A Rank or better

LOAD-OUT

- MP-AF x30
- Sniper Rifle x6
- Herb (Red) x2
- Hand Grenade x3
- Flash Grenade x2
- 9mm Ammo x30
- 7.62mm Ammo x6
- Healing Tablet x1

RECOMMENDED SKILLS: Target Master, Eagle Eye, Item Drop Increase

GENERAL STRATEGIES

Ada's alternate costume drops the Crossbow in favor of multiple guns. This load-out is similar to Piers' default load-out but with a normal Sniper Rifle, instead of the Anti-Materiel Rifle, and more grenades.

Attack most enemies with the MP-AF in single-shot or automatic-fire mode. Use the Sniper Rifle against enemies when you've gained some distance or against stronger enemies. You won't have much 7.62mm Ammo in the beginning, and most of your inventory slots will be occupied by grenades and herbs. So look for Green Herbs to combine with your Red Herbs to fill up your tablet case.

The Flash Grenade doesn't do much damage, but it can stun any enemies it hits. Throw it at a group, then run in and finish them off with melee attacks to gain some additional time!

Save your Hand Grenades for bigger enemies or groups since you might not always have a chance to use your Sniper Rifle. If enemies overwhelm you, drop a Flash Grenade and run off to a distance.

CARLA RADAMES

UNLOCK CONDITIONS: Unlock every character and their Costume 1

LOAD-OUT

Picador x16
Grenade Launcher x6
9mm Ammo x50
40mm Acid Rounds x12
40mm Nitrogen Rounds x6
Healing Tablets x6

RECOMMENDED SKILLS: Item Drop Increase, Quick Shot Power Increase

GENERAL STRATEGIES

Unlike the other characters, Carla does not have an alternate costume. Although she is a menace throughout the campaign, Carla's load-out is limited. She has a Grenade Launcher with a smorgasbord of ammo, and her only other weapon is the weak Picador, leaving her without much stopping power beyond her limited Grenade Launcher ammo.

Enemies don't drop Grenade Launcher rounds, so conserve that ammo as much as possible. Save your Explosive Rounds for bosses and larger enemies since you only have the six you started with. The Nitrogen and Acid Rounds are more flexible and can be used against any enemy. But save them for large groups of enemies.

Nitrogen rounds encase enemies in ice, allowing you to finish them off quickly and effectively.

Use Quick Shot on enemies and coup de grâce finishers instead of trying to take down enemies with the Picador alone. Since you only have one weapon, and 9mm Ammo is abundant, you don't need to worry about running out.

MAPS

URBAN CHAOS

ENEMY WAVES

- Zombies
- Zombie Cops
- Zombie Dogs x9
- Firefighter Zombies
- BSAA Zombies
- Bloodshot BSAA Zombies x2
- Zombies
- Whopper x1
- Spitting Zombies
- Bloodshots x9
- Firefighter Zombies
- Zombies
- Whoppers x2
- Zombie Cops
- Zombie Dog x7
- Bloodshot BSAA Zombies x2
- BSAA Zombies
- Zombies

SECRET BOSS: Napad—Kill 15 enemies with counters before you've killed 80 enemies

GENERAL STRATEGY

Urban Chaos is a straightforward level comprised of an overhead bridge area and a few rooms hiding items and Time/Combo Bonus hourglass items. You begin fighting zombies. After several are killed, they are replaced with Zombie Cops, which often carry weapons. If you hear gunfire, move to avoid being shot from behind.

Zombie Cops are followed by Zombie Dogs, which can quickly overwhelm you. You can easily dispatch them, so make them a priority until the next wave of zombies attacks.

Firefighter Zombies are also easy to defeat quickly—shoot them in the arm, then shoot the canister on their back, which causes them to explode. They're followed by BSAA Zombies that carry weapons and can turn into Bloodshots. Be sure they're really dead before moving on.

Your first big challenge is a Whopper, which isn't much of a threat, but it can take a while to kill. Take it out with your strongest weapons as soon as possible.During your fight with the Whopper, you encounter zombies that vomit poison on you. This poison seals you in place while causing damage, so it is important to remove these threats as soon as possible to keep your momentum. You can see a spitting zombie wind up before it attacks. Start running if you see it charging up.

A pack of Bloodshots will then appear, which can be difficult to take out if spitting zombies are around. Take a few out quickly but wait until the Firefighter Zombies appear. You can kill them with the Firefighter Zombie's explosions.Shortly after the Firefighter Zombies are dispatched, you run into a pair of Whoppers. They are difficult to take down, especially if you've already used up your strong ammo. Unload your strongest weapons into them since they are the last challenges in this fight.

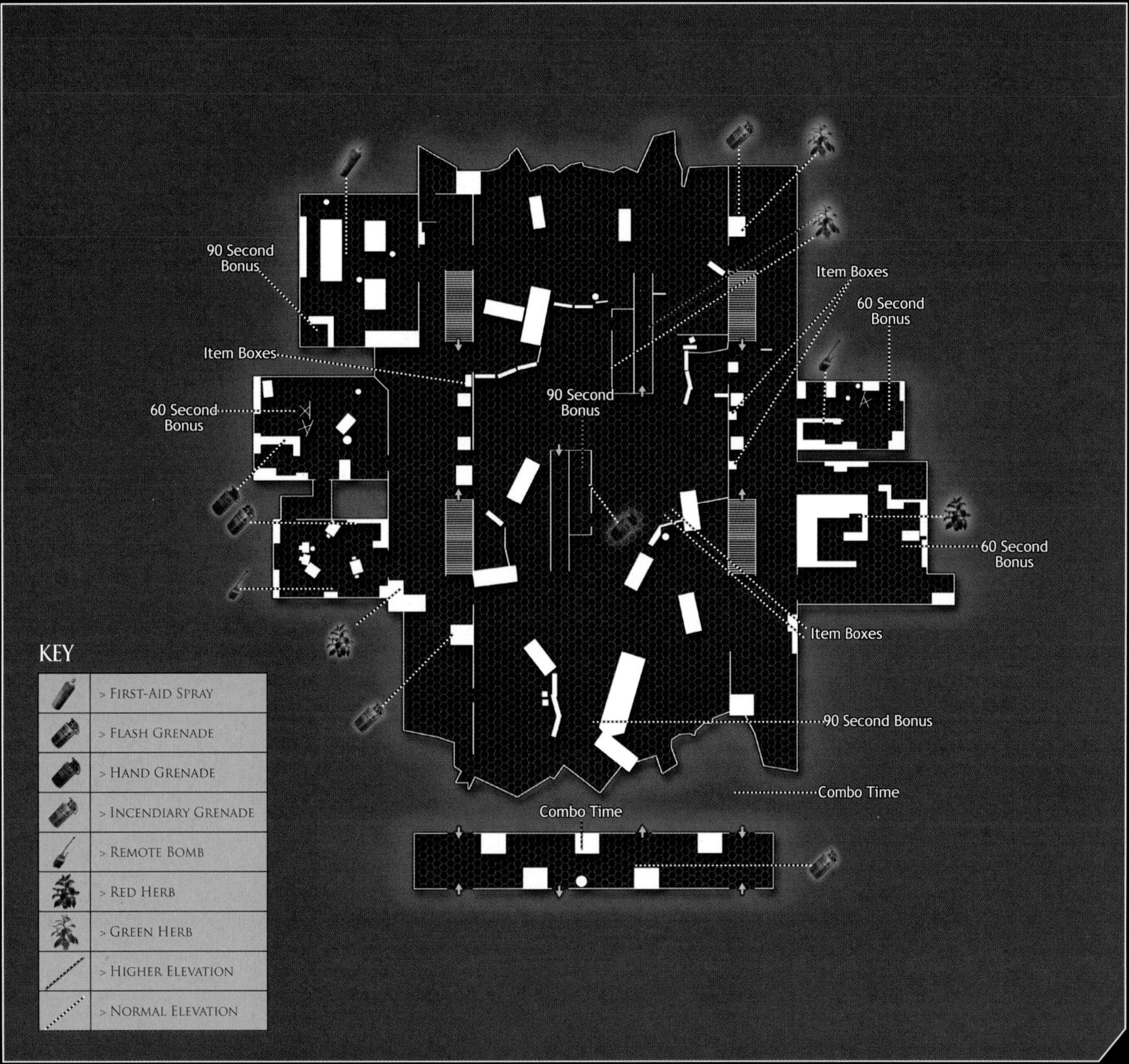

Near the end of the stage, a pair of Whoppers will appear. These monsters require some time to kill, so build up time by defeating other enemies while you're fighting them.

The secret boss of Urban Chaos is a Napad who is easy to beat and poses little threat. Keep the Napad alive as long as possible to get more points!

These zombies carry guns and can only be defeated by a headshot or a finisher. Take them out quickly by shooting them in the head and using a finishing move on them.

A few zombies will turn into Bloodshots after you kill them, so save your heavy ammo for their transformed form.

STEEL BEAST

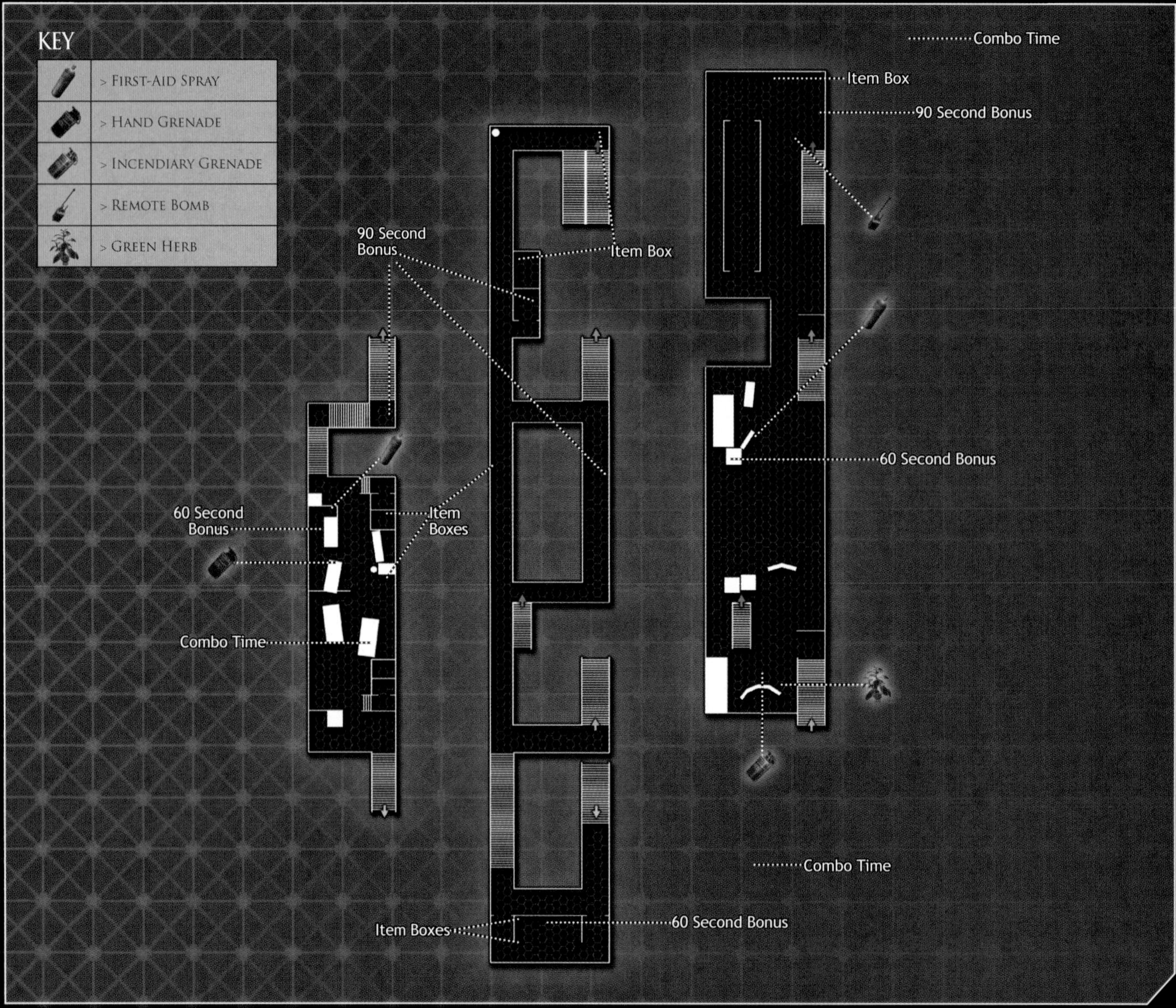

WAVES

Melee J'avo
Ruka-Srp x4

STRATEGY

This area pits you against a horde of J'avo, most of which will charge at you with knives and other melee weapons. You should use them to build up your timer at relatively little risk. After a few waves of J'avo, you encounter a series of Ruka-Srp and Noga-Let, both of which are not terribly threatening.

A J'avo with a Rocket Launcher will appear in the top floor of the bridge and a sniper J'avo on the middle floor of the structure. Be careful of both when trying to run through the stage. Eventually, several waves of Napad will spawn. These are tough to take down quickly, so use your heavy weapons on them. While they're attacking, Telo-Eksplozija will also appear—shoot their feet out and use their explosions against the Napad.

After you defeat the Napad, several waves of Noga-Skakanje will spawn. They are fairly easy to defeat because they use only melee attacks. Your biggest challenge will be to take them down quickly due to their erratic movements.

Another sniper J'avo will appear with J'avo that mutate into Ruka-Srp. Don't waste your ammo shooting a J'avo that's transforming. They are invulnerable to damage until their transformation is finished. Several waves of Ruka-Bedem will appear with Glava-Smech and Telo-Eksplozija. Use the same strategy of killing Telo-Eksplozija near other enemies to take down multiple targets at once. Ruka-Bedem are unscathed if you fight them with conventional weapons. So focus on melee attacks and getting behind them while they're defending.

Glava-Smech are harmless since they can only attack at close range and are slow. Simply shoot their glowing areas to take them down before they surround you.

Two J'avo spawn in this location every time you play Steel Beast and will sit here until they're defeated. Fewer enemies will spawn while they're alive, so take them out quickly to cause more random enemies to appear.

At some point, a parade of Napad will appear, one after the other. They are easy to defeat but require a lot of ammo to kill. Use your strongest weapons on them to get rid of them quickly.

Occasionally you will see and hear explosions—a rocket launcher J'avo has appeared. They won't move from this location, so take them out before they shoot you in the back with a rocket.

The secret boss of Steel Beast is the Gnezdo and can be difficult to summon since he requires 25 coup de grâce finishes to appear. After he appears, he spends most of his time shooting slow-moving projectiles at you. They can catch you off-guard if you aren't paying attention to the Gnezdo.

MINING THE DEPTHS

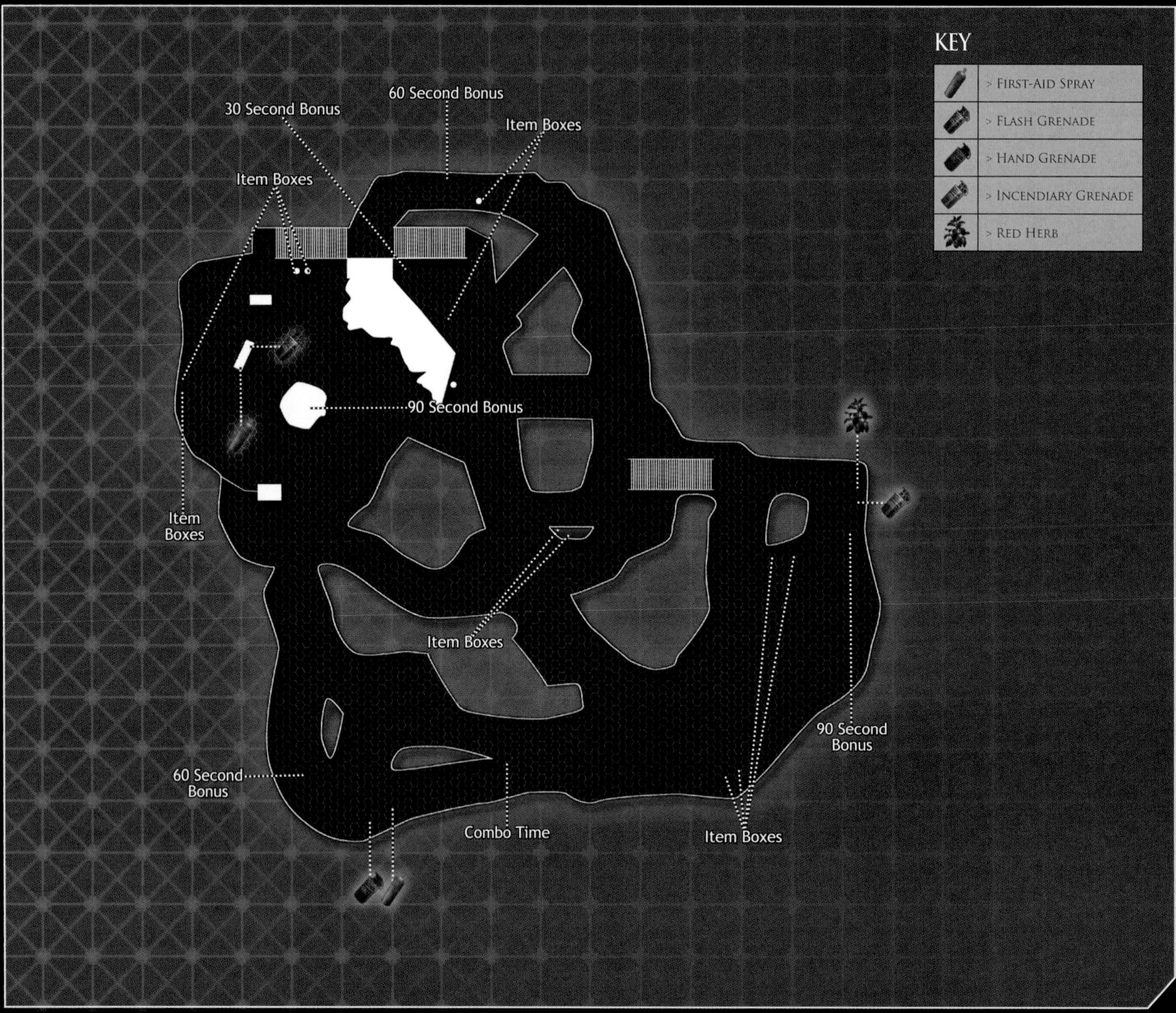

WAVES

Firefighter Zombies
Zombies
Zombie Dog x7
Shriekers x2
BSAA Zombies
Zombie Dog x5
Firefighter Zombies
Bloodshots x11
Dynamite Zombies
Shrieker x1
Bloodshots x7
Firefighter Zombies
BSAA Zombies
Zombie Dog x12
Shrieker x1
Zombies

STRATEGY

This area is large and you can easily lose enemies in the system of tunnels. You'll also find it hard to build a combo if enemies are located throughout them. Go through the tunnels to break the Time Hourglasses, then move to the central area and fight everyone from there.

You are generally fighting a parade of zombies along with Shriekers and Zombie Dogs. Shriekers in The Mercenaries aren't much of a threat since you want as many enemies as close together as possible. Save them for when you've already built a substantial combo.

Bloodshots are difficult to defeat since you're in such confined quarters. While you can instantly take them out by countering their diving attack, it's difficult to time. Focus on shooting them. After the first wave of Bloodshots, zombies holding dynamite will spawn. Don't use melee attacks on these zombies because they drop the dynamite they're carrying and explode, damaging you. Shoot them from a distance.

Due to the successive waves of Bloodshots and dynamite zombies, you might run out of time when fighting them. Watch for opportunities when you can finish an enemy with a coup de grâce to keep your timer high.

Due to the Shriekers, Bloodshots, and general weakness of most of the enemies in this stage it's very easy to obtain a high rank. As long as you maintain a combo, you should be able to easily reach A Rank. This is the preferred stage for unlocking costumes.

A Shrieker spawns here and can occasionally be hard to see. Once his chest puffs up, quickly shoot him with any weapon a few times and kill him.

Numerous Bloodshots spawn and can be difficult to kill. Take them out with counters whenever possible to obtain additional time!

Occasionally, zombies carrying dynamite will appear. Watch out for them since the dynamite they drop severely damages other enemies but also deals

If you quickly and efficiently kill enemies, it's easy to cause the Strelats to appear. Unlike other secret bosses, the Strelats effectively attacks you from

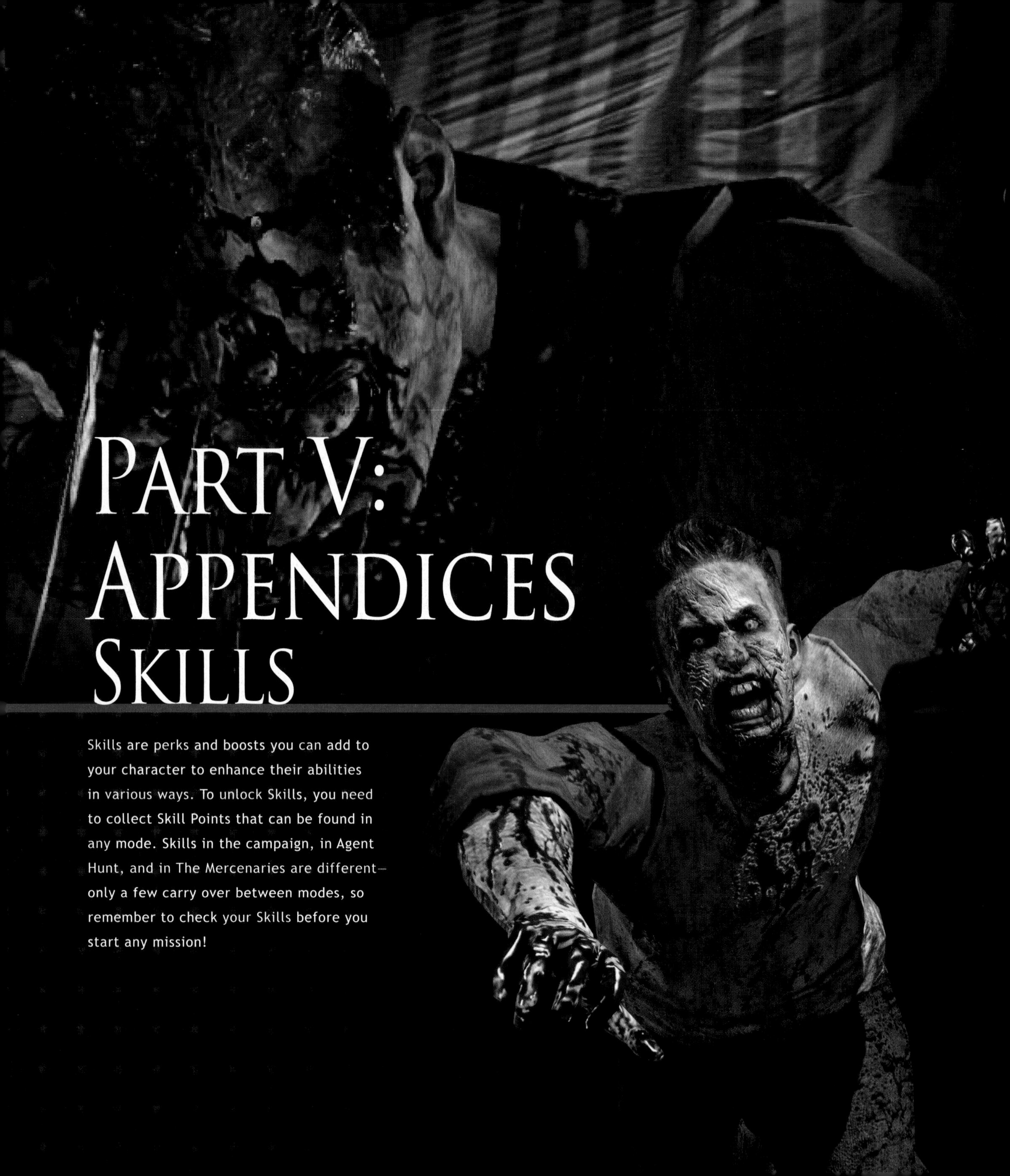

Part V: Appendices

Skills

Skills are perks and boosts you can add to your character to enhance their abilities in various ways. To unlock Skills, you need to collect Skill Points that can be found in any mode. Skills in the campaign, in Agent Hunt, and in The Mercenaries are different—only a few carry over between modes, so remember to check your Skills before you start any mission!

CAMPAIGN SKILLS

A variety of Skills are available in the campaign mode and provide various boosts to your attack and defense. Some Skills unlock only after you complete a large portion of the game, so check for new Skills often!

NAME	FUNCTION	COST	UNLOCK REQUIREMENTS
Firearm Lv. 1	Increase damage of guns by 10%	12,000	–
Firearm Lv. 2	Increase damage of guns by 20%	29,000	Purchase Firearm Lv. 1
Firearm Lv. 3	Increase damage of guns by 50%	75,000	Purchase Firearm Lv. 2
Melee Lv. 1	Increase damage of physical attacks, Stun Rod, Combat Knife, Surival Knife, and Hand-to-Hand by 10%	10,000	–
Melee Lv. 2	Increase damage of physical attacks, Stun Rod, Combat Knife, Surival Knife, and Hand-to-Hand by 20%	25,000	Purchase Melee Lv. 1
Melee Lv. 3	Increase damage of physical attacks, Stun Rod, Combat Knife, Surival Knife, and Hand-to-Hand by 50%	75,000	Purchase Melee Lv. 2
Defense Lv. 1	Enemy attacks deal 80% damage	3,200	–
Defense Lv. 2	Enemy attacks deal 70% damage	28,000	Purchase Defense Lv. 1
Defense Lv. 3	Enemy attacks deal 50% damage	80,000	Purchase Defense Lv. 2
Lock-On Lv. 1	Small decrease in the movement of the red dot sight after firing a gun	2,800	–
Lock-On Lv. 2	Large decrease in the movement of the red dot sight after firing a gun	31,000	Purchase Lock-On Lv. 1
Rock Steady Lv. 1	Small decrease in the movement of the aiming reticle after firing a shot	3,500	–
Rock Steady Lv. 2	Large decrease in the movement of the aiming reticle after firing a shot	33,000	Purchase Rock Steady Lv. 1
Critical Hit Lv. 1	Increase chance of critical hit by 50%	3,500	–
Critical Hit Lv. 2	Increase chance of critical hit by 75%	13,000	Purchase Critical Hit Lv. 1
Critical Hit Lv. 3	Increase chance of critical hit by 100%	32,000	Purchase Critical Hit Lv. 2
Piercing Lv. 1	Increase piercing capacity by 1. Does not affect Crossbow or Grenade Launchers.	12,000	–
Piercing Lv. 2	Increase piercing capacity by 2. Does not affect Crossbow or Grenade Launchers.	28,000	Purchase Piercing Lv. 1
Piercing Lv. 3	Increase piercing capacity by 3. Does not affect Crossbow or Grenade Launchers.	55,000	Purchase Piercing Lv. 2
J'avo Killer Lv. 1	Deal 20% more damage to J'avo	3,000	Kill 30 J'avo
J'avo Killer Lv. 2	Deal 50% more damage to J'avo	25,000	Purchase J'avo Killer Lv. 1
Zombie Hunter Lv. 1	Deal 20% more damage to zombies	3,000	Kill 30 zombies
Zombie Hunter Lv. 2	Deal 50% more damage to zombies	25,000	Purchase Zombie Hunter Lv. 1
Eagle Eye	Gain an additional level of zoom on the Sniper Rifle, Semi-Auto Sniper Rifle and Anti-Materiel Rifle	3,000	–
Quick Reload	Increase reload speed by 20%	10,000	–
Last Shot	Increase damage dealt by the last shot in a clip by 300%	55,000	–
Shooting Wild	Removes aiming reticle and sniper scope but increases damage dealt by 50%	65,000	–
Combat Gauge Boost Lv. 1	Increase size of the combat gauge to 8 blocks	70,000	–
Combat Gauge Boost Lv. 2	Increase size of the combat gauge to 10 blocks	90,000	Purchase Combat Gauge Boost Lv. 1
Breakout	Decrease the amount of rotations needed to escape rotation-action prompts	2,800	–
Item Drop Increase	Increase the rate of item drops by defeated enemies	3,500	–
Recovery Lv. 1	The revival gauge in dying state will fill in 10 seconds instead of 15	10,000	–
Recovery Lv. 2	The revival gauge in dying state will fill in 7 seconds instead of 15	70,000	Purchase Recovery Lv. 1
Team-Up	When within 5 meters of your partner in single player, your AI partner will deal as much damage as the player.	14,000	–
Field Medic Lv. 1	Receive 1-2 health tablets whenever you're rescued: single-player only	12,000	–
Field Medic Lv. 2	Receive 2-3 health tablets whenever you're rescued: single-player only	95,000	Purchase Field Medic Lv.1
Lone Wolf	Your partner won't help you in single-player	100	–

NAME	FUNCTION	COST	UNLOCK REQUIREMENTS
AR Ammo Pickup Increase	Increase drop rate of 5.56mm Ammo	8,000	–
Shotgun Shell Pickup Increase	Increase drop rate of 12-Gauge and 10-Gauge Shells	8,000	–
Magnum Ammo Pickup Increase	Increase drop rate of .50 Action-Express Magnum Ammo	25,000	–
Rifle Ammo Pickup Increase	Increase drop rate 0f 7.62mm Ammo and AM Rifle Ammo	8,000	–
Grenade Pickup Increase	Increase drop rate of 40mm Explosive, Acid, and Nitrogren rounds	22,000	–
Arrow Pickup Increase	Increase drop rate of Arrow (Normal) and Arrow (Pipe Bomb)	20,000	–
Grenade Power-Up	Increase damage dealt by thrown grenades by 100%	40,000	Get 800 kills with grenades
Handgun Master	Increase damage dealt by the Nine-Oh-Nine, Wing Shooter, Triple Shot, and Picador by 100%	37,000	Get 1,500 kills with handguns
Shotgun Master	Increase damage dealt by the Shotgun and Assault Shotgun by 100%	38,000	Get 1,000 kills with shotguns
Magnum Master	Increase damage dealt by the Lightning Hawk and Elephant Killer by 100%	40,000	Get 800 kills with Magnums
Sniper Master	Increase damage dealt by the Sniper Rifle and Semi-Auto Sniper Rifle by 100%	39,000	Get 1,000 kills with sniper rifles
Machine Pistol Master	Increase damage dealt by the MP-AF and Ammo Box 50 by 100%	38,000	Get 1,500 kills with machine pistols
Assault Rifle Master	Increase damage dealt by the Assault Rifle RN, Assault Rifle for Special Tactics, and Bear Commander by 100%	37,000	Get 1,500 kills with assault rifles
Grenade Launcher Master	Increase damage dealt by the Grenade Launcher and the Bear Commander's Alternate Fire by 100%	40,000	Get 800 kills with grenade launchers
Crossbow Master	Increase damage dealt by the Crossbow by 100%	40,000	Get 800 kills with crossbows
Infinite Handgun	Infinite ammo for the Nine-Oh-Nine, Triple Shot, Picador, and Wing Shooter	79,000	Complete all campaigns
Infinite Shotgun	Infinite ammo for the Shotgun and Assault Shotgun	89,000	Complete all campaigns
Infinite Magnum	Infinite ammo for the Lightning Hawk and Elephant Killer	99,000	Complete all campaigns
Infinite Sniper Rifle	Infinite ammo for the Sniper Rifle and Semi-Auto Sniper Rifle	79,000	Complete all campaigns
Infinite Machine Pistol	Infinite ammo for the MP-AF and Ammo Box 50	89,000	Complete all campaigns
Infinite Assault Rifle	Infinite ammo for the Assault Rifle RN, Assault Rifle for Special Tactics, and Bear Commander	89,000	Complete all campaigns
Infinite Grenade Launcher	Infinite ammo for the Grenade Launcher and Bear Commander Alternate Fire	99,000	Complete all campaigns
Infinite Crossbow	Infinite ammo for the Crossbow	79,000	Complete all campaigns

AGENT HUNT SKILLS

Skills in Agent Hunt generally boost various parameters like offense or defense. Pick Skills that complement your abilities or use them to make up for deficiencies in your character. You can only equip one Skill, so make it count!

NAME	FUNCTION	COST	UNLOCK REQUIREMENTS
CREATURE OFFENSE Lv. 1	Damage dealt increases by 10%	5,000	–
CREATURE OFFENSE Lv. 2	Damage dealt increases by 20%	15,000	Purchase CREATURE OFFENSE Lv. 1
CREATURE OFFENSE Lv. 3	Damage dealt increases by 30%	60,000	Purchase CREATURE OFFENSE Lv. 2
CREATURE DEFENSE Lv. 1	Damage sustained decreases by 10%	5,000	–
CREATURE DEFENSE Lv. 2	Damage sustained decreases by 20%	15,000	Purchase CREATURE DEFENSE Lv. 1
CREATURE DEFENSE Lv. 3	Damage sustained decreases by 30%	60,000	Purchase CREATURE DEFENSE Lv. 2
CREATURE HEALTH Lv. 1	Health increases by 20%	5,000	–
CREATURE HEALTH Lv. 2	Health increases by 50%	15,000	Purchase CREATURE HEALTH Lv. 1
CREATURE HEALTH Lv. 3	Health increases by 100%	60,000	Purchase CREATURE HEALTH Lv. 2
CREATURE STAMINA Lv. 1	Stamina gauge increases to 6 units	5,000	–
CREATURE STAMINA Lv. 2	Stamina gauge increases to 7 units	15,000	Purchase CREATURE STAMINA Lv. 1
CREATURE STAMINA Lv. 3	Stamina gauge increases to 10 units	60,000	Purchase CREATURE STAMINA Lv. 2

THE MERCENARIES SKILLS

Skills in The Mercenaries offer a variety of bonuses, some focused on reaching higher scores and some making it easier to survive. Find skills that match your character or pick a Skill that helps you get the highest scores!

NAME	FUNCTION	COST	UNLOCK REQUIREMENTS
Eagle Eye	Gain an additional level of zoom on the Sniper Rifle, Semi-Auto Sniper Rifle, and Anti-Materiel Rifle	3,000	–
Item Drop Increase	Increase the rate of item drops by defeated enemies	3,500	–
Go for Broke!	When time is under 30 seconds, you receive an extra 2 seconds to perform a combo (17 seconds total)	60,000	–
Time Bonus+	Gain an additional 10 seconds when you break a Yellow Hourglass	90,000	–
Combo Bonus+	Gain an additional 10 seconds when you break a Green Hourglass	50,000	–
Limit Breaker	Gain an additional 50 points for every combo performed over 50	60,000	–
Blitz Play	If you attack an enemy right after another player, damage dealt is increased by 50%	5,000	–
Quick Shot Damage Increase	Quick Shot Damage increased by 50%	15,000	–
Power Counter	Counter damage increased by 25%	8,000	–
Second Wind	Increase damage by 10% when your health is at 2 blocks or lower	6,000	–
Martial Arts Master	Increase damage of Martial Arts, Hand-to-Hand, Survival Knife, Combat Knife, and Stun Rod by 25% but decrease gun damage by 50%	25,000	–
Target Master	Increase gun damage by 25% but decrease melee attack damage by 50%	25,000	–
Last Stand	Increase damage dealt by 30% but damage you suffer is increased 300%	30,000	–
Preemptive Strike	Increase damage dealt to enemies from behind by 75%	7,000	–
Dying Breath	Increase damage dealt to enemies while you're in dying state by 300% and shortens recovery time from dying state to 5 seconds	15,000	–
Pharmacist	One tablet restores two blocks of health	17,000	–
Medic	Co-op partner's health will restore no matter where they are on screen if you eat a Healing Tablet	12,000	–
First Responder	You can rescue your teammates from dying state without using any items	15,000	–
Take It Easy	In cover, health and Combat Gauge recovery is doubled	20,000	–
Natural Healing	Healing and Combat Gauge recovery is increased by 25%	15,000	–

ITEMS

Items have been a part of the *Resident Evil* series since the beginning, and *Resident Evil 6* features both the classic assortment of herbs as well as First-Aid Spray. While playing Extra Content and the campaign, watch for these valuable items. They can save your life!

GREEN HERB

This classic *Resident Evil* item is used to fill your tablet case with additional healing items. Each Green Herb, on its own, adds a single healing item when added to your case. You can combine Green Herbs with other Green Herbs to gain extra healing tablets. Combining with a Green Herb gives you an extra Green Herb for a total of three tablets, while combining with a Red Herb gives you a total of six tablets!

Green Herbs can be found in specific places around many stages or dropped from enemies and boxes. For maximum efficiency, save your Green Herbs until you have a Red Herb to combine with them. Or if you need the space, combine two Green Herbs for an extra tablet in your case.

RED HERB

These unique herbs do nothing on their own and cannot be stored in your case. However, when combined with a Green Herb, the Red Herb turns a Green Herb into six tablets, which is twice as many as when you combine two Green Herbs!

Red Herbs are found in many stages but are rarely dropped by enemies. Save your Green Herbs to combine with Red Herbs except in extreme emergencies.

FIRST-AID SPRAY

Unlike herbs, First-Aid Spray doesn't go into your case—it's equipped and used like a Grenade or weapon. The First-Aid Spray restores all of your character's health as well as your partner's! If both of you are running low on health, consider using a First-Aid Spray to restore full health.

First-Aid Sprays are rarely found in stages and enemies never drop them. Conserve your First-Aid Sprays for when you and your partner need them the most.

First-Aid Spray activates quickly and can also be used while running, giving you the chance to restore your health while avoiding enemy attacks! If you're in a bind, don't just sit there; run away and use your First-Aid Spray!

Depending on their size, these unique items increase your available skill points. The value of the item dropped depends on the strength of the enemy—more powerful enemies drop higher-value chess pieces.

While this is primarily true in The Mercenaries mode, you more often find high-value chess pieces after gaining a large combo or defeating more enemies in the area. The closer you get to the 150-enemy cap, the more often enemies drop 1,000-point items or higher!

In some stages you find enormous, high-value chess pieces in different chests or simply sitting alone. In many instances, these items won't respawn in future play-throughs, so grab them as soon as you see them!

WEAPONS

Resident Evil 6 features a variety of weapons, each capable of taking down zombies, J'avo, and other B.O.W.s with varying degrees of efficiency. Unlike the past two entries in the series, *Resident Evil 6* does not feature a shopkeeper, and you will simply find new weapons as you progress through the campaign. Learn every weapon's abilities, strengths, and weaknesses to best defeat your enemies!

NINE-OH-NINE (909)

AMMO	9MM AMMO
Characters	Chris, Jake
Alternate Fire	None
Shots Per Clip	15
Power	150
Crit. Chance	12.5
Reload Speed	A
Firing Speed	A

The starting weapon for Chris and Jake, the Nine-Oh-Nine is a standard handgun with a decent-sized clip and a fast rate of fire. As a weapon, it's rather unremarkable but useful in a pinch.

If you have no other options available, handgun ammo can be stacked much higher than other ammunition—you can unload into enemies even if you can't quickly dispatch them. When planning your inventory, consider keeping some handgun ammo as a precaution.

WING SHOOTER

AMMO	9MM AMMO
Characters	Leon
Alternate Fire	Dual-Wield
Shots Per Clip	18 / 36
Power	120
Crit. Chance	8
Reload Speed	A
Firing Speed	A
Firing Speed (Alt. Fire)	A+

Leon's unique handgun has a larger clip than most other handguns and can be dual-wielded, allowing you to unload numerous bullets into enemies without reloading. As a result, the Wing Shooter proves to be a useful weapon during the entirety of Leon's Campaign.

The Wing Shooter also features a unique combo performed by using Quick Attack up to five times in a row while dual-wielding. While this isn't the best way to use your Action Gauge, it sure does look cool!

PICADOR

Helena's unique starting weapon is similar to the Nine-Oh-Nine but can fire an additional round before reloading. Like the Nine-Oh-Nine, the Picador should be used until you find stronger weapons or are otherwise out of ammo.

AMMO	9MM AMMO
Characters	Helena
Alternate Fire	None
Shots Per Clip	16
Power	160
Crit. Chance	6
Reload Speed	A
Firing Speed	A-

SHOTGUN

AMMO	12-GAUGE SHELLS
Characters	Leon, Helena, Jake, Sherry
Alternate Fire	None
Shots Per Clip	8
Power	Far—140x7, Close—180x7
Reload Speed	C
Firing Speed	C

This classic weapon fires in a large spread, allowing you to attack multiple enemies with a single shot and dealing big damage to enemies at close range. You can also use the Shotgun's wide spray of buckshot to hit fast-moving enemies that avoid single-shot weapons like handguns.

The Shotgun is also stronger at long ranges than it would seem, making it a decent weapon against distant enemies as long as you have the extra ammo.

ASSAULT SHOTGUN

AMMO	12-GAUGE SHELLS
Characters	Chris, Piers, Ada
Alternate Fire	None
Shots Per Clip	7
Power	Far—150x7, Close—170x7
Reload Speed	C
Firing Speed	B

This version of the Shotgun doesn't hold as many shots per clip as the normal Shotgun, but it allows you to fire rounds much faster.

HYDRA

AMMO	10-GAUGE SHELLS
Characters	Helena
Alternate Fire	None
Shots Per Clip	3
Power	Far—120x7, Close—170x7
Reload Speed	C
Firing Speed	S

Unlike the other Shotgun weapons, Helena's Hydra is a sawed-off shotgun that fires a large spread in front of her as quickly as you can pull the trigger. The Hydra isn't as strong as the Shotgun at long- and medium-range, but it's devastating at short-range.

Helena has a unique Quick Attack combo when the Hydra is equipped, allowing her to perform three unique attacks. The Hydra can only fire three rounds before reloading and uses a different ammo type than the other Shotguns. Therefore, consider how much space you devote to its ammo.

ELEPHANT KILLER

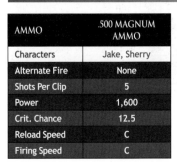

AMMO	.500 MAGNUM AMMO
Characters	Jake, Sherry
Alternate Fire	None
Shots Per Clip	5
Power	1,600
Crit. Chance	12.5
Reload Speed	C
Firing Speed	C

This revolver-style handgun functions like the Lightning Hawk but with additional damage, additional delay between shots, and a smaller clip size.

Like the Lightning Hawk, the Elephant Killer is incredibly useful and should be a frequent go-to when you need a powerful weapon.

LIGHTNING HAWK

Although this looks like a standard handgun, it's incredibly powerful and features stopping power at any range. It fires slowly, but it knocks down any enemies it hits, allowing you to quickly clear a path. The Lightning Hawk is especially effective in constricted areas like hallways.

Magnum ammo is scarce, but you can hold up to 50 using a single slot, making it a useful and powerful weapon.

AMMO	.50 ACTION-EXPRESS MAGNUM AMMO
Characters	Leon, Helena
Alternate Fire	None
Shots Per Clip	7
Power	1,200
Crit. Chance	8
Reload Speed	A
Firing Speed	B

SNIPER RIFLE

The Sniper Rifle has an attached scope that allows you to precisely target enemies at long ranges. The Sniper Rifle has two levels of zoom that can be triggered by pressing (R3 XBOX/R3 PS3).

Use this weapon to attack enemies at long ranges from the back of the battlefield to support a partner at the front lines. While the Sniper Rifle has a six-shot clip, a long delay occurs between firing each round, so make each shot count!

AMMO	7.62MM AMMO
Characters	Jake, Sherry, Ada
Alternate Fire	None
Shots Per Clip	6
Power	700
Crit. Chance	100
Reload Speed	C
Firing Speed	C-

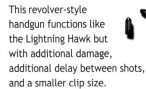

SEMI-AUTOMATIC SNIPER RIFLE

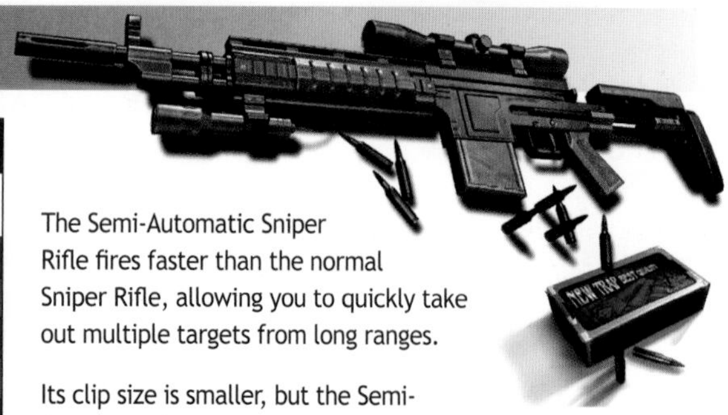

AMMO	7.62MM AMMO
Characters	Leon, Helena, Chris, Piers
Alternate Fire	None
Shots Per Clip	5
Power	600
Crit. Chance	75
Reload Speed	B
Firing Speed	B+

The Semi-Automatic Sniper Rifle fires faster than the normal Sniper Rifle, allowing you to quickly take out multiple targets from long ranges.

Its clip size is smaller, but the Semi-Automatic Sniper Rifle remains scoped after every shot, allowing you to stay locked on distant targets.

ANTI-MATERIEL RIFLE

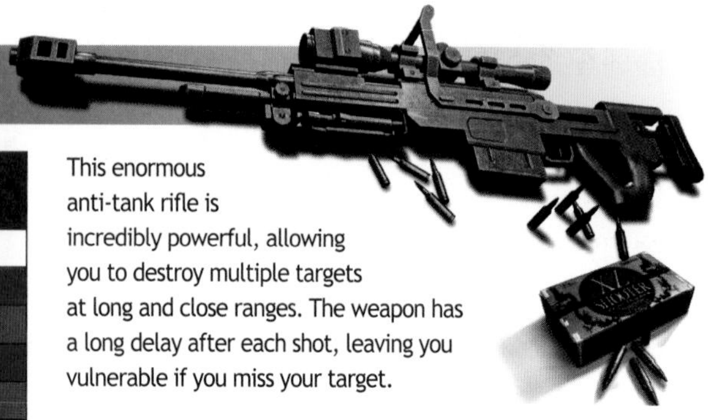

AMMO	ANTI-MATERIEL RIFLE AMMO
Characters	Piers
Alternate Fire	Thermal Scope
Shots Per Clip	10
Power	1,000
Crit. Chance	100
Reload Speed	B
Firing Speed	D-

This enormous anti-tank rifle is incredibly powerful, allowing you to destroy multiple targets at long and close ranges. The weapon has a long delay after each shot, leaving you vulnerable if you miss your target.

The Anti-Materiel Rifle features two levels of zoom as well as a thermal scope that can be activated through alternate fire. This highlights living creatures, allowing you to pick out distant or partially hidden targets.

ASSAULT RIFLE FOR SPECIAL TACTICS

AMMO	5.56MM AMMO
Characters	Chris
Alternate Fire	None
Shots Per Clip	30
Power	200
Crit. Chance	6
Reload Speed	B
Firing Speed	S

This automatic-rifle is a powerful weapon with a high rate of fire. Use it to attack groups of enemies at medium and short ranges.

This is Chris' most useful weapon and will be your go-to attack option throughout his campaign. Given its flexibility, prioritize this weapon's ammo over Chris' other weapons.

MP-AF (MACHINE PISTOL—ACCURATE FIRE)

AMMO	9MM AMMO
Characters	Piers
Alternate Fire	Automatic Fire
Shots Per Clip	30
Power	100
Crit. Chance	6
Reload Speed	B
Firing Speed	A
Firing Speed (Alt. Fire)	S

Piers' unique weapon functions as both a pistol and an automatic rifle. In single-shot mode, it's a useful handgun that holds a large clip and requires minimal reloading.

As an automatic rifle, it isn't very strong, but its high rate of fire can easily dispatch enemies. The MP-AF uses 9mm ammo, which is readily available and can be stored in 150-shot units in a single inventory slot. As a result, you can carry a lot of ammo without sacrificing herbs or grenades.

TRIPLE SHOT

This unique handgun features a large clip size as well as the ability to switch between single- and triple-shot burst fire.

In single-shot mode, the weapon is an average handgun. Use the triple-shot function of this weapon against stronger enemies that you can't drop with a single handgun shot.

AMMO	9MM AMMO
Characters	Sherry
Alternate Fire	3-shot burst
Shots Per Clip	20
Power	130
Crit. Chance	8
Reload Speed	A
Firing Speed	S

AMMO BOX 50

This machine pistol features a large clip and a fast rate of fire, allowing you to quickly attack a number of enemies or simply unload on a single target.

Unfortunately, the weapon deals very little damage per hit, so it should be used only as a last resort during Ada's sneaking segments or if you lack ammo for more powerful weapons.

AMMO	9MM AMMO
Characters	Ada
Alternate Fire	None
Shots Per Clip	50
Power	90
Crit. Chance	5
Reload Speed	B
Firing Speed	S

Bear Commander

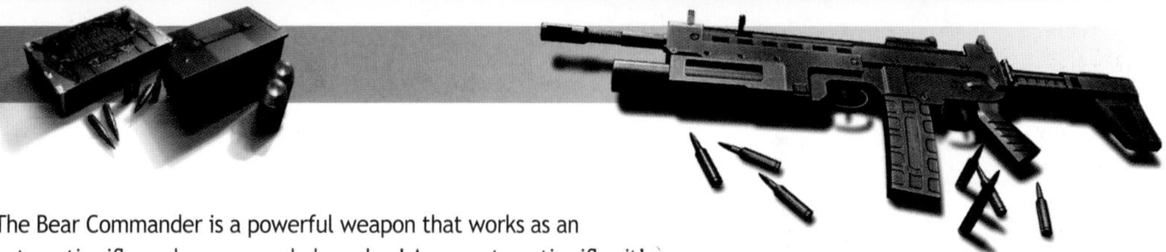

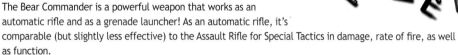

AMMO	5.56MM AMMO, 40MM EXPLOSIVE ROUNDS
Characters	Jake, Sherry, Ada
Alternate Fire	Explosive Rounds
Shots Per Clip	30
Power	190
Crit. Chance	4
Reload Speed	B

The Bear Commander is a powerful weapon that works as an automatic rifle and as a grenade launcher! As an automatic rifle, it's comparable (but slightly less effective) to the Assault Rifle for Special Tactics in damage, rate of fire, as well as function.

The Bear Commander uses only Explosive grenade rounds, but you can quickly switch between grenade and rifle functions. It is versatile and suited to taking out groups of enemies and strong, single targets.

Assault Rifle RN

AMMO	5.56MM AMMO
Characters	Leon, Helena
Alternate Fire	None
Shots Per Clip	30
Power	210
Crit. Chance	2.5
Reload Speed	B
Firing Speed	S

This variation of Assault Rifle is similar to the others but offers an attached bayonet for close-combat attacks. The bayonet increases damage during martial arts attacks that use the Assault Rifle RN, making it ideal at both medium and close ranges.

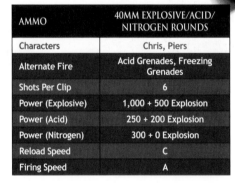

Grenade Launcher

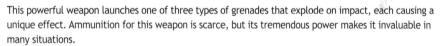

AMMO	40MM EXPLOSIVE/ACID/ NITROGEN ROUNDS
Characters	Chris, Piers
Alternate Fire	Acid Grenades, Freezing Grenades
Shots Per Clip	6
Power (Explosive)	1,000 + 500 Explosion
Power (Acid)	250 + 200 Explosion
Power (Nitrogen)	300 + 0 Explosion
Reload Speed	C
Firing Speed	A

This powerful weapon launches one of three types of grenades that explode on impact, each causing a unique effect. Ammunition for this weapon is scarce, but its tremendous power makes it invaluable in many situations.

Explosive Rounds cause a small explosion resulting in massive damage to enemies with blast range. Use them to take out groups or severely damage, if not destroy, larger enemies. Acid Rounds spray a corrosive fluid over a small area that damages enemies on contact. They are highly effective against the Iluzija. Nitrogen Rounds freeze enemies around its point of impact, allowing you to quickly destroy them with martial arts or other weapons.

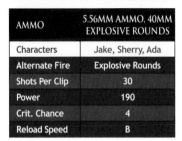

HAND GRENADE

AMMO	HAND GRENADE
Characters	Chris, Piers, Ada
Power	1,200 + 600 Explosion

These thrown weapons create a large explosive blast that is powerful enough to destroy many enemies in a single attack.

Each grenade can only be thrown once before it is used up. But you can stack up to five in a single inventory slot. Grenades are uncommon, so use them only when they'll take out a large group.

INCENDIARY GRENADE

AMMO	INCENDIARY GRENADE
Characters	Leon, Helena, Ada
Power	800+400 Explosion

After you throw an Incendiary Grenade, it spreads napalm in a short area and covers enemies caught in its blast radius in flames.

Incendiary Grenades easily dispatch normal enemies and are especially effective against enemies like Rasklapanje and Lepotitsa.

FLASH GRENADE

AMMO	FLASH GRENADE
Characters	Chris, Piers, Jake, Sherry
Power	1

This grenade variation creates a large flash, stunning any enemies caught near it and destroying some outright.

Use Flash Grenades when you're surrounded by enemies and need to move to a safer position or simply avoid them altogether.

REMOTE BOMB

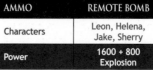

AMMO	REMOTE BOMB
Characters	Leon, Helena, Jake, Sherry
Power	1600 + 800 Explosion

Unlike grenades, when you use a remote bomb, you place it to be remotely detonated. The explosion caused by the Remote Bomb is large, so gain some distance from it before activating it.

Remote Bombs require some planning, since you can't simply throw them like grenades. Lure groups of enemies into them or set one and bait a charging enemy like the Ustanak to its position then let it go!

CROSSBOW

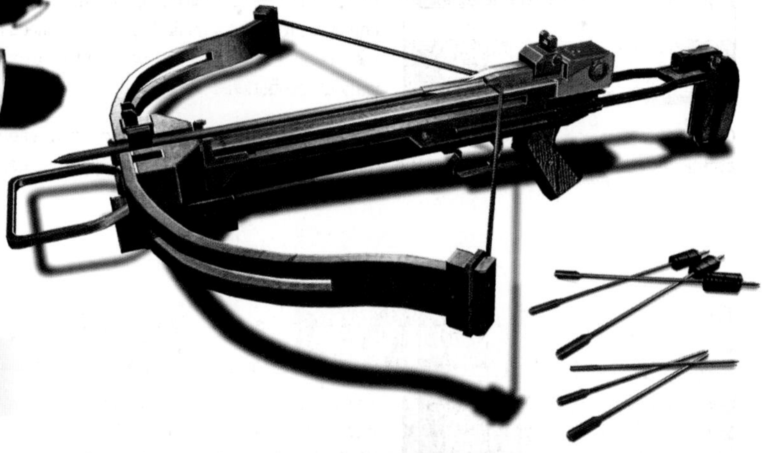

AMMO	ARROWS (NORMAL), ARROWS (PIPE BOMB)
Characters	Ada
Alternate Fire	Pipe Bomb Arrows
Shots Per Clip	1
Power (Normal)	550
Power (Pipe Bomb Impact)	150
Power (Pipe Bomb Explosion)	1000 + 500 Explosion
Crit. Chance	100
Reload Speed	B

Ada's Crossbow is a silent but deadly weapon that can shoot two types of arrows, each with a specialized function. Shortly after a Pipe Bomb arrow strikes an enemy, it detonates and creates a small explosion. It's not as powerful as a Grenade Launcher's Explosive Round, but it can severely damage enemies caught in its blast radius.

Normal Crossbow arrows are highly effective, depending on where they hit the opponent and where your opponent is standing. A single Crossbow arrow is enough to instantly kill many opponents during a headshot! If your arrow hits another part of the body, it inflicts minimal damage. However, you can impale enemies against a wall, leaving them vulnerable to additional attacks!

SURVIVAL KNIFE

AMMO	NONE
Characters	Leon
Power	180

Unlike martial arts, the Survival Knife doesn't require Stamina to use, giving you the ability to melee attack enemies without waiting to recharge. The Survival Knife inflicts low damage and isn't very fast. Avoid using it whenever possible and only in situations when it's the only option.

COMBAT KNIFE

AMMO	NONE
Characters	Chris
Power	180

Chris uses this weapon to relentlessly attack enemies at close range without worrying about spending or recharging Stamina. The Combat Knife is strong, but save it for when you've fully depleted your ammunition.

STUN ROD

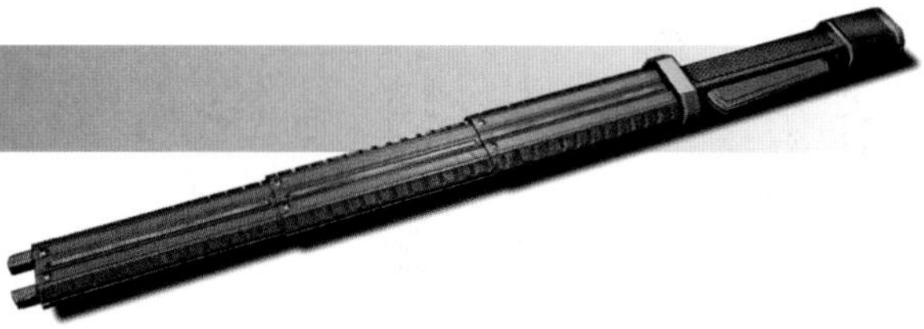

AMMO	NONE
Characters	Sherry
Power	140
Power (Charge)	280+40+80

This is a close-range melee weapon that you can use continuously without spending Stamina. When an enemy is hit by the Stun Rod, they are stunned for a short period, allowing you or your partner to hit them without retribution.

Charge the Stun Rod by holding down the Attack button. This charged attack stuns enemies for longer and can potentially take out weaker enemies in a single attack. You can move while charging the Stun Rod but only slowly, which makes you defenseless. Use this only against enemies with melee weapons.

ROCKET LAUNCHER

AMMO	1 SHOT PER ROCKET LAUNCHER
Characters	Leon
Power	30,000 + 2,000 Explosion

This powerful *Resident Evil* mainstay is rare but also very powerful. In the Campaign, you'll encounter this weapon only once but you can use it freely in The Mercenaries.

Any enemy you fire this weapon at will be instantly destroyed, along with anything around it. Since you have limited opportunities to fire the Rocket Launcher, however, you won't be able to fully enjoy its destructive capabilities.

ENEMIES

Resident Evil 6 features a variety of weapons, each capable of taking down zombies, J'avo, and other B.O.W.s with varying degrees of efficiency. Unlike the past two entries in the series, *Resident Evil 6* does not feature a shopkeeper, and you will simply find new weapons as you progress through the campaign. Learn every weapon's abilities, strengths, and weaknesses to best defeat your enemies!

J'AVO

J'avo are mutated soldiers that carry a variety of weapons and are found throughout China and Edonia, often in groups. J'avo have been mutated by the C-Virus, which makes them difficult to kill and capable of surviving multiple shots to the head.

How you choose to deal with J'avo depends upon the weapons they carry. Those with melee weapons are the easiest to attack because they do not have any tactics other than running straight at you. Shoot them as they run, then move out of the way or counter their attacks to take them out.

For J'avo with machine pistols or assault rifles, stand behind cover and wait for them to fire. J'avo aren't very bright, and will fire for a specified amount of time before stopping, giving you the opportunity to return fire.

Occasionally you encounter J'avo with sniper rifles and rocket launchers. Unless you have a sniper rifle, simply avoid sniper J'avo by constantly moving and placing obstacles between you and their laser sight. Don't waste your ammo trying to shoot them with something other than a sniper rifle unless they're fairly close. When you see J'avo with rocket launchers, dispatch them as quickly as possible. These J'avo generally sit in place and fire on you. Spot them and drop them with a handgun or an assault rifle.

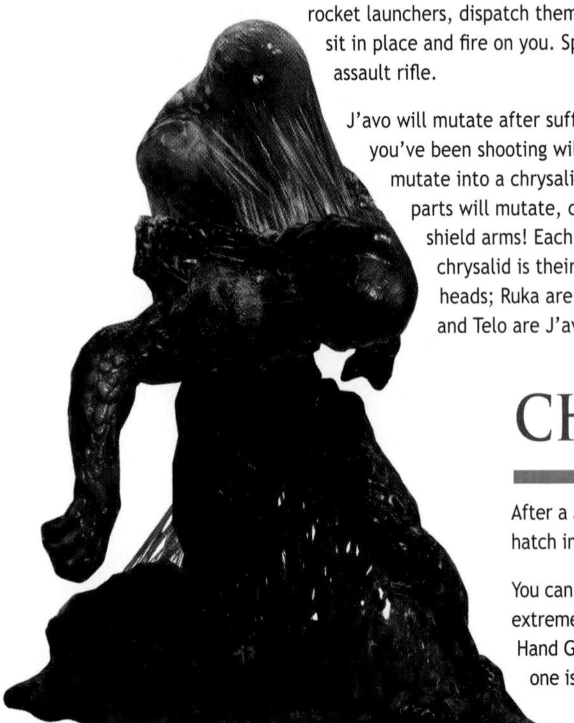

J'avo will mutate after suffering considerable damage. The body part you've been shooting will mutate, but occasionally their entire body will mutate into a chrysalid after death. Occasionally, a J'avo's multiple body parts will mutate, creating spider-legged J'avo or mutants with shield arms! Each mutated J'avo is discussed in its own section—a chrysalid is their after-death form; Glava are J'avo with mutated heads; Ruka are J'avo with mutated arms; Noga are J'avo with leg mutations; and Telo are J'avo whose bodies have turned into a particularly grotesque form.

CHRYSALID

After a J'avo is defeated, it will occasionally transform into a hard cocoon. If left alone, the cocoon will hatch into an advanced J'avo—a Strelats, Napad, Mesets or Gnezdo!

You can destroy a chrysalid before it hatches, although it is difficult and ammo-intensive because they're extremely durable. Don't use something as weak as a handgun. Instead, use a Shotgun, Grenade Launcher, Hand Grenade, or Incendiary Grenade to destroy one. Chrysalids are vulnerable to electricity, however. If one is near a generator—or you have access to Sherry's Stun Rod—use electricity to take them out!

GLAVA

A Glava mutation occurs when a J'avo has been significantly damaged in the head, usually enough to kill an average J'avo. Head mutations are common and can happen in many stages. It's best to avoid Glava mutations as you would other mutations. However, they're all manageable.

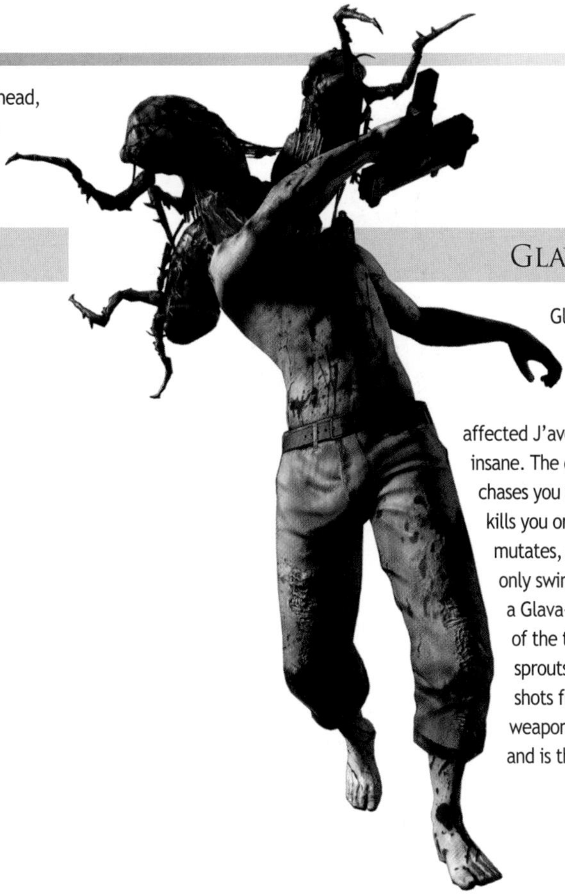

GLAVA-SLUZ

The Glava-Sluz mutation isn't very deadly but can be extremely lethal when it's grouped with normal J'avo or other B.O.W.s. The Glava-Sluz's only attack is a stream of spider webs that imprison you on contact. If you cause a Glava-Sluz mutation, get rid of it immediately to prevent other enemies from killing you while you're imprisoned.

GLAVA-BEGUNATS

Glava-Begunats is a mutation that causes three insect heads to emerge from the affected J'avo's head, driving it insane. The crazed J'avo endlessly chases you at a fast pace until it kills you or vice versa. When it mutates, a Glava-Begunats will only swing at you. To take out a Glava-Begunats, shoot each of the three insect parts that sprouts from its neck. A few shots from even the weakest weapon will destroy each head and is the easiest way to kill it.

GLAVA-SMECH

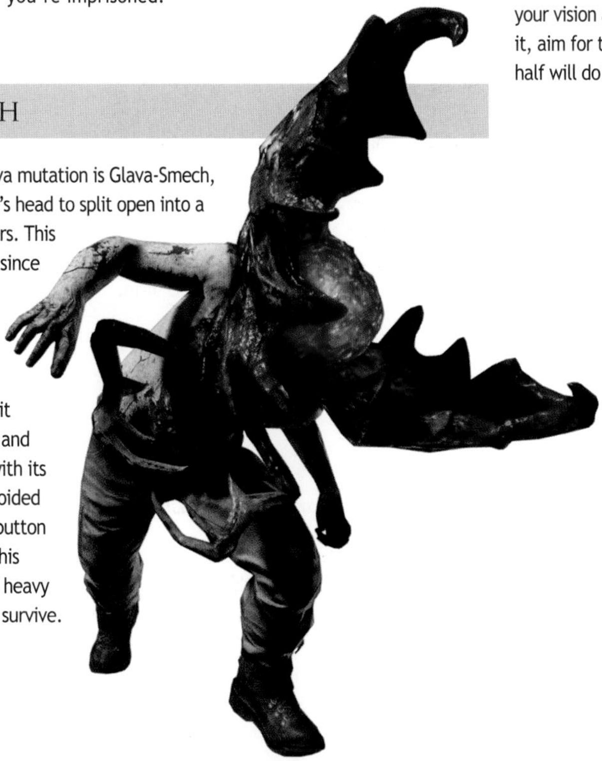

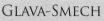

The most common Glava mutation is Glava-Smech, which causes the J'avo's head to split open into a grotesque pair of pincers. This enemy is easy to avoid since it has only one attack that is very slow—even if the attack is close, you can safely roll away. If one does hit you, it will pick you up and attempt to crush you with its pincers. This can be avoided with a properly timed button press. Even if you fail this event, you suffer some heavy damage but ultimately survive.

GLAVA-DIM

The rarest Glava mutation is the Glava-Dim, which only appears in two stages of the campaign. When the Glava-Dim is activated, the J'avo's head splits into two halves, each half-insect, half-horrible-flesh-orb. The Glava-Dim attacks by spitting red poison at you, which blurs your vision and slowly drains your health. To destroy it, aim for the mutated sections of its head—either half will do!

RUKA

Sometimes when a J'avo takes damage in the arm, its appendage will mutate into a weapon, making it slightly more dangerous than before. The Ruka mutations are common and hard to avoid. Even a single shot hitting a J'avo arm will cause it to mutate!

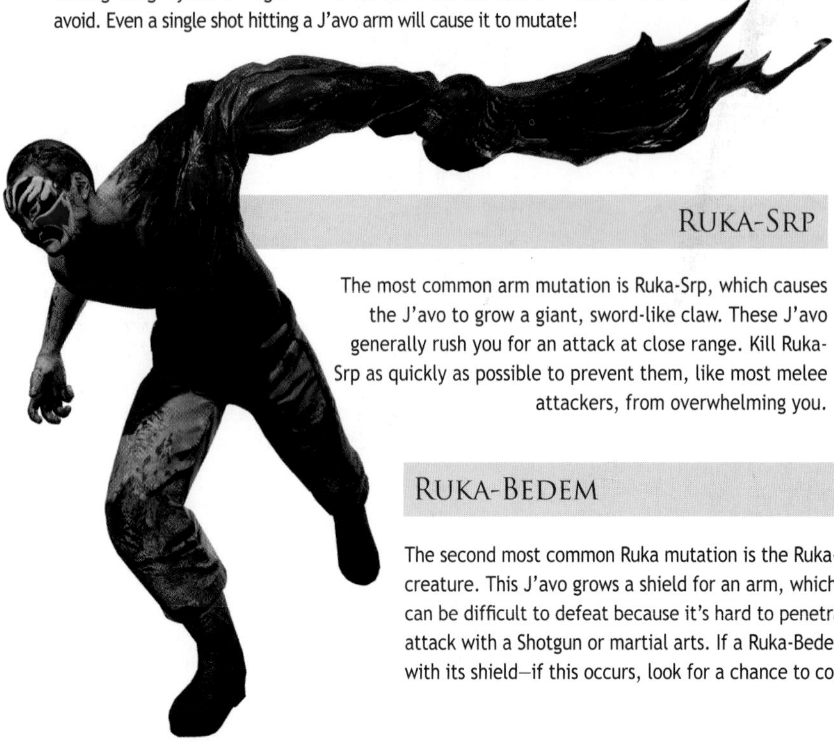

RUKA-SRP

The most common arm mutation is Ruka-Srp, which causes the J'avo to grow a giant, sword-like claw. These J'avo generally rush you for an attack at close range. Kill Ruka-Srp as quickly as possible to prevent them, like most melee attackers, from overwhelming you.

RUKA-BEDEM

The second most common Ruka mutation is the Ruka-Bedem, which results in a defensive creature. This J'avo grows a shield for an arm, which protects it from any frontal assault. They can be difficult to defeat because it's hard to penetrate their defense. Move behind them and attack with a Shotgun or martial arts. If a Ruka-Bedem gets close, it will try and bash you with its shield—if this occurs, look for a chance to counter and inflict big damage.

RUKA-KHVATANJE

The Ruka-Khvatanje is slightly less common and causes the J'avo to grow an insect-shaped appendage from its arm. Unlike the Ruka-Srp, these J'avo tend to attack from long-range. The insect-arm stretches and can grab you from a long distance. If the arm grabs you, it picks you up and slams you to the ground without any chance to break free. Kill them before they can attack to prevent them from tossing you around.

NOGA

Noga mutations occur when a J'avo is damaged in the legs and generally give the J'avo different movement capabilities. Many of these mutations should be treated as completely different threats because their maneuverability and tactics radically change with the mutation.

NOGA-TRCHANJE

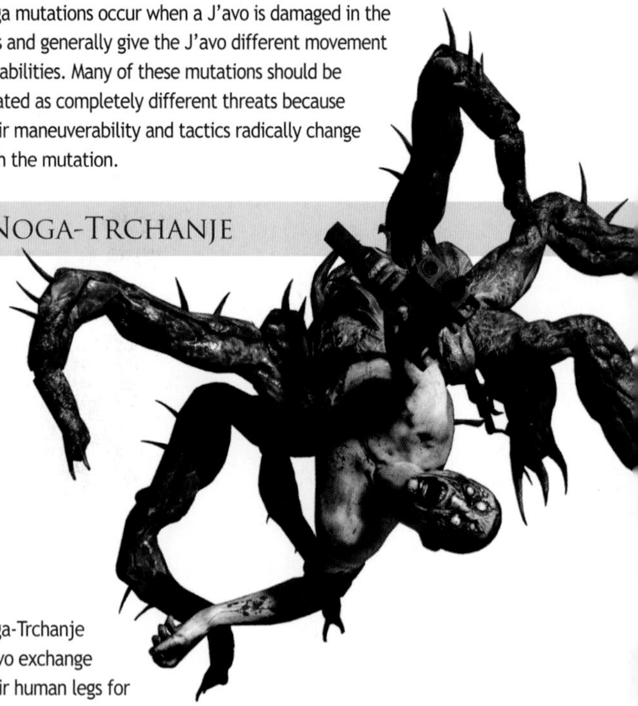

Noga-Trchanje J'avo exchange their human legs for those of a spider. These J'avo move differently and gain the ability to climb on walls. Noga-Trchanje are also low to the ground, so some martial arts attacks might miss. Otherwise, they're similar to normal J'avo and will attack you from a distance with guns. As a result, you may not want to change your tactics too much.

Noga-Let

The Noga-Let J'avo's legs are removed and replaced with insect wings. These J'avo are much harder to hit, but they're not very threatening because they rarely attack. Even if these J'avo are equipped with a weapon, the weapon simply hangs there limp since they are unable to fire it. When a transformation occurs, Noga-Let fly straight toward you. Shoot it before it has a chance to do anything.

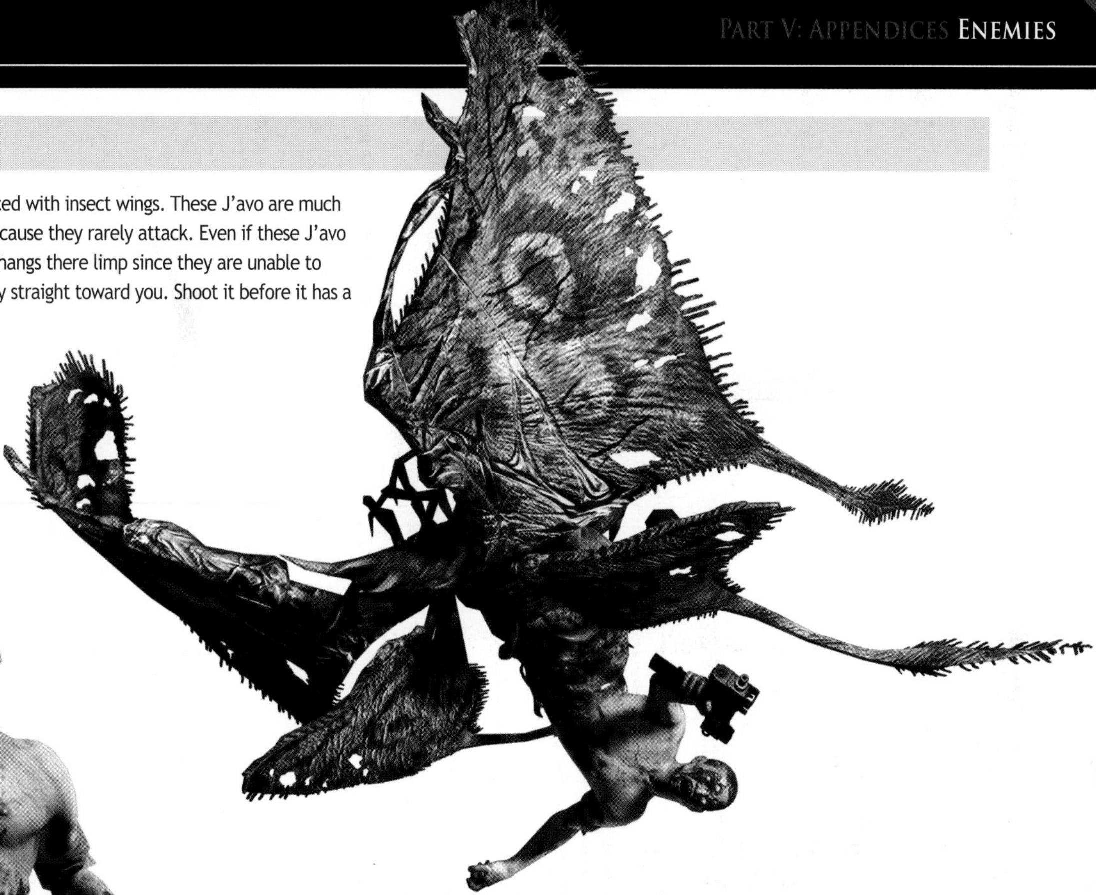

Noga-Oklop

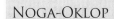

Unlike the other Noga mutations, Noga-Oklop gain no additional movement capabilities—in fact, they lose them! These J'avo have completely invincible legs. If a J'avo becomes a Noga-Oklop, fire away at its head or torso to take it down. At close range, it can kick you, but you shouldn't worry too much about this attack.

Noga-Skakanje

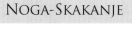

Noga-Skakanje are J'avo with insect legs that they use to jump long distances, generally away from you. These J'avo can be annoying as they can jump very far and snipe away at you! Treat Noga-Skakanje as a normal sniper J'avo—take them out from a distance while your partner covers you.

TELO

These J'avo mutations occur when a J'avo's torso absorbs a significant amount of damage. These forms are rare—usually when you hit the torso, it triggers a Ruka or Glava mutation instead. This is actually beneficial—the Telo mutations are incredibly deadly and can cause damage without contact!

Telo-Eksplozija

The most common mutation is Telo-Eksplozija, which causes the J'avo's torso to mutate into a grotesque cocoon. Telo-Eksplozija has no attacks and simply tries to get as close to you as possible. Upon death, it explodes and damages anything in the vicinity, including you! If you cause a Telo-Eksplozija mutation, take it out from a distance so you aren't caught in the explosion. If you shoot a Telo-Eksplozija in the legs, it falls over, keeping it in position and away from you when it explodes!

Telo-Magla

A J'avo affected by the Telo-Magla mutation begins writhing on the ground before growing strange appendages then finally spews a poison gas around its vicinity. The gas slowly drains health from you if you're near it but can be avoided by simply moving away from it. Kill the J'avo while he's writhing on the ground by stomping on its head, but make sure you finish him off before he releases the gas.

Telo-Krljusht

The Telo-Krljusht is the rarest but also easiest mutation to confront. When this mutation is triggered, the J'avo grows a set of armor around its torso that is impervious to gunfire. Easily dispatch these mutations by shooting their legs or their head.

STRELATS

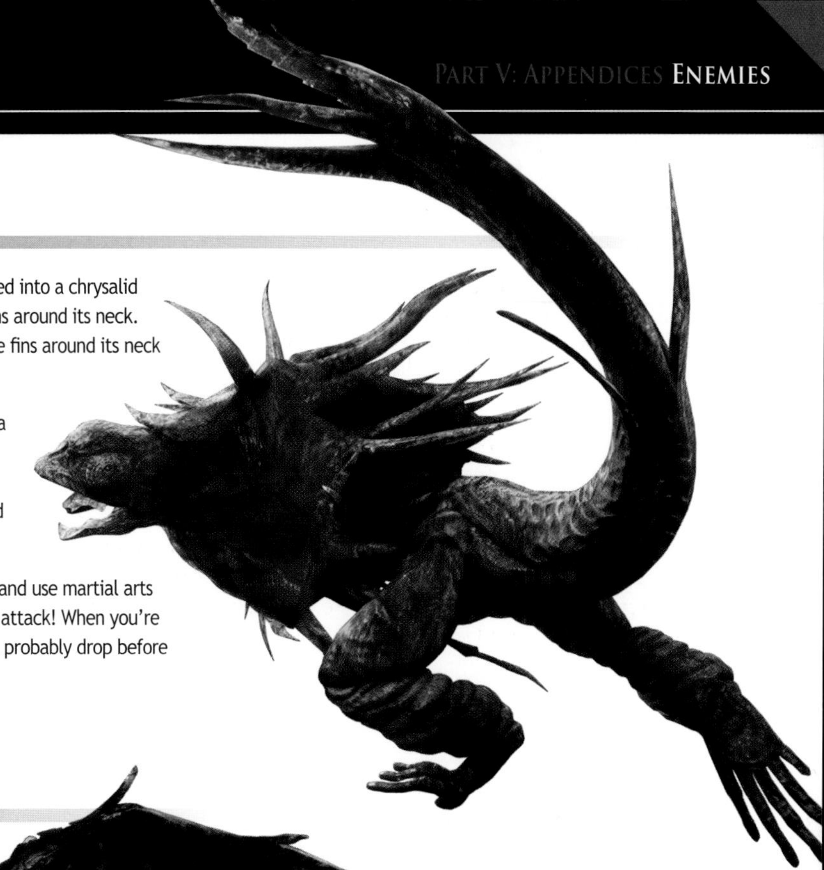

This B.O.W. looks and moves like a lizard and generally appears after a J'avo has turned into a chrysalid cocoon. Strelats tend to attack from long range with needles that it emits from the fins around its neck. These projectiles move fast, but it's easy to see them coming—it emits steam from the fins around its neck before firing. To keep Strelats from firing at all, chase it down whenever it runs off.

At close range, the Strelats has a few defense mechanisms for escape. If it's charging a needle attack from close range, it can instead release a poisonous fog. This is meant as a smoke screen and does little damage, though it gives the Strelats time to escape. When it is not charging, the Strelats spews a poisonous liquid that is more lethal. Avoid this liquid even if doing so allows the Strelats to get away.

When you get close, wait for it to start smoking while charging a needle or fog attack and use martial arts on it. This will dizzy the Strelats, allowing you to perform another special martial arts attack! When you're at long range, aim for his head and move closer. If you avoid his needle attack, he will probably drop before you have a chance to get close.

MESETS

This rare B.O.W. has a bird-like appearance and behavior. The Mesets typically avoids confrontation by flying around your position and eventually diving in to attack. This attack cannot be countered, so roll out of the way or shoot it down before he gets a chance to attack.

After he dive-bombs, the Mesets will land and perform one of two attacks—a repeated short-range peck attack or a mid-range charge that it telegraphs by quickly moving in place. The short-range attack is difficult to avoid, so keep some distance from it while it's on the ground. The mid-range attack can be countered easily and allows you to inflict big damage without using any ammo.

The Mesets is very rare—you might play through the campaign and never see one! Even though you won't see it much, it's an easy opponent to defeat. Use any machine gun or handgun and shoot it down while it's in the air. It doesn't move fast enough to avoid your attacks and doesn't have much health. If you let one fly around while you're fighting other enemies, it can be a huge distraction that divides your attention. If you're playing co-op, one partner should focus on the Mesets while the other keeps grounded enemies at bay.

NAPAD

The Napad is a heavily armored B.O.W. that is seemingly indestructible. Its attacks are straightforward—it charges at you or punches you, both of which can be countered or easily avoided by staying out of its way. If the Napad connects with a punch, it grabs you and slams you to the ground if you don't mash out of its attack. Stay out of its range as much as possible.

The easiest way to take one out is by striking its weak point, which is located under its heavily armored back. The Napad's armor is brittle—a single round from a shotgun should knock it right off! After you remove its armor, target the glowing area on its back and you will drop it quickly.

GNEZDO

This unique B.O.W. appears as a swarm of insects shaped like a human, but its true form is that of a large, bee-like insect. In battle, it hides within the swarm and only emerges when the swarm is dispersed after suffering a certain amount of damage.

Although the Gnezdo seems threatening, it's easy to kill. The Gnezdo has only one attack—a slow-moving projectile that targets you or your partner. Avoid this attack by moving out of its way and guiding the projectile into a wall to keep it from surprising you from behind.

Don't use martial arts or melee weapons on the Gnezdo. If you get too close, you'll be engulfed in a swarm of insects that will slowly damage you. Instead, shoot at the Gnezdo until its true form emerges, then unload on it.

Certain weapons like Ada's Crossbow, a Shotgun, or a Magnum can take out the true form almost instantly, although the small target is difficult to hit with single-shot weapons.

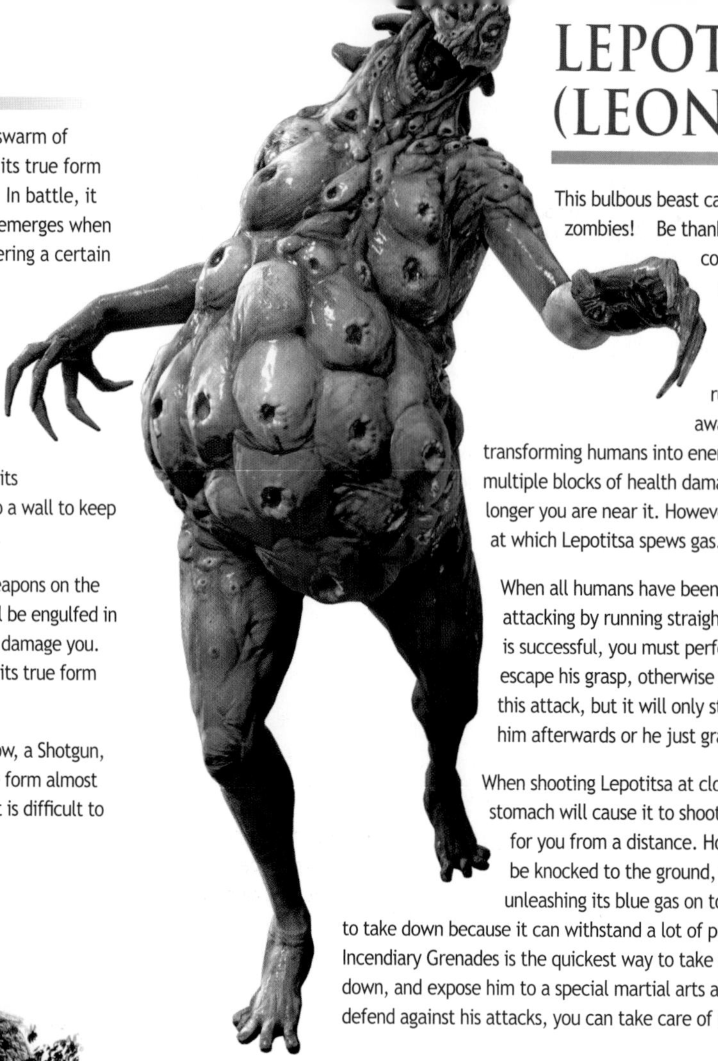

LEPOTITSA (LEON BOSS 1)

This bulbous beast carries gas inside that can turn humans into zombies! Be thankful you encounter this mid-boss only a couple times because the Lepotitsa is difficult to conquer.

Depending on how many humans are in the area, the Lepotitsa will run away from you or run toward you. If humans are present, he runs away from you and constantly spews blue gas, transforming humans into enemy zombies. This dangerous blue gas inflicts multiple blocks of health damage in one hit and continues to hurt you the longer you are near it. However, you will be hurt only if you're near the point at which Lepotitsa spews gas.

When all humans have been turned to zombies, the Lepotitsa begins attacking by running straight toward you in an attempt to grab you. If he is successful, you must perform a short "timing mini-game" in order to escape his grasp, otherwise you suffer significant damage. You can counter this attack, but it will only stop the Lepotitsa for a moment—don't shoot him afterwards or he just grabs you again!

When shooting Lepotitsa at close range, hit it only in the head. Any shot to its stomach will cause it to shoot a stream of gray gas. This isn't much problem for you from a distance. However, if this gas hits you at close range, you'll be knocked to the ground, which makes you vulnerable to the Lepotitsa unleashing its blue gas on top of your head! The Lepotitsa is difficult to take down because it can withstand a lot of punishment from any weapon. Liberal use of Incendiary Grenades is the quickest way to take one out. They inflict big damage, knock him down, and expose him to a special martial arts attack! As long as you keep your distance and defend against his attacks, you can take care of Lepotitsa without trouble.

ILUZIJA (CHRIS BOSS 2)

This giant snake B.O.W. has optic camouflage that makes it very difficult to see. However, dispatching this monster is fairly easy since it has only one attack that is very easy to avoid. The Iluzija rears its head back, opening its mouth, and giving away its position before it charges at you. If you are hit, Iluzija can do massive damage, especially if you miss the escape event. To avoid injury, simply roll to the side when it starts to attack and it will harmlessly move past you.

To defeat the Iluzija, simply fire on it with any of your weapons when it appears and prioritize shooting its mouth. You inflict more damage in this area, especially with grenade rounds. Be careful when shooting its mouth because it only opens up shortly before the Iluzija attacks. If it stares directly at you, move to avoid and let your partner attack. Likewise, attack only when it targets your partner. If you take your time and prioritize safety, this mini-boss is an easy challenge.

To finish off the Iluzija, electrocute it using a switch and a puddle of water. When you reach this point, don't waste your time shooting it—either you or your partner should lead the Iluzija away from the platform with the switch while the other prepares to electrocute it. Once the generator is fully charged, wait until Iluzija moves over the puddle of water. Then flip the switch to end the fight!

RASKLAPANJE

This grotesque B.O.W. has a humanoid shape but can barely walk. Its only attack is to clumsily grab at you or your partner. If a Rasklapanje contacts you, your partner should immediately knock him off you. If you have no partner available or they're indisposed, be prepared to mash out of its attack—if you don't, it instantly kills you! This grab can be countered, but it's incredibly risky to be anywhere near a Rasklapanje, so keep your distance.

Destroying a Rasklapanje is fairly easy—keep your distance and shoot it with mid-range weapons. You can take one down quickly with Incendiary Grenades—a giant pouch of flesh emerges from its mouth and you can attack it for massive damage.

When you kill the Rasklapanje for the first time, its torso separates from his legs and crawls around looking for something to punch. This form is simply annoying—it has only one attack, a simple punch, and can't do significant damage as long as you stay away from it and take it down at your leisure. Occasionally, the Rasklapanje's hand will separate after one of its two forms are killed. If this happens, kill it—it will always drop an item or Skill Points!

OKO

These tiny, insect-like B.O.W.s are completely harmless on their own. However, when they contact you or if they're destroyed, they alert the Ustanak to your location!

Whether or not you should kill an Oko depends upon where you are in the stage—some Oko's must be destroyed to advance, but others will deliver you straight to the Ustanak! See the campaign walkthrough for more details.

UBISTVO

This humanoid B.O.W. has a chainsaw as an arm and is exceptionally deadly. In many stages, the Ubistvo cannot be killed and, as a result, must be avoided. Its chainsaw attack instantly kills you no matter how it hits you! Thankfully, Ubistvo's tactics are straightforward and easy to avoid.

To take down the Ubistvo, shoot at its head with powerful weapons while keeping a safe distance. As long as you attack it at an angle, you should be safe. If it faces you directly, don't bother fighting it—you should only prepare to escape! The Ubistvo doesn't have much health, so keep pressure on it and you will win quickly.

USTANAK

This burly B.O.W. appears throughout Jake's campaign—like the classic *Resident Evil* enemy Nemesis—each time with a new tool of destruction attached to its arm. Many encounters with the Ustanak require that you simply run away or hide. But there are a few instances when you're forced to fight.

When you do fight the Ustanak, pay attention to his arm—if it looks like it could kill you up close, it probably can! Many of his arms are meant for long-range attack. But you should still keep your distance because it hits hard and fast.

Remain at a mid-range distance and watch for attacks from its arm, which can grab you from a distance. When you are at mid-range his charge attacks have a surprising amount of maneuverability. For more details on the various Ustanak Boss Fights, check the specific Ustanak encounter in the campaign walkthrough.

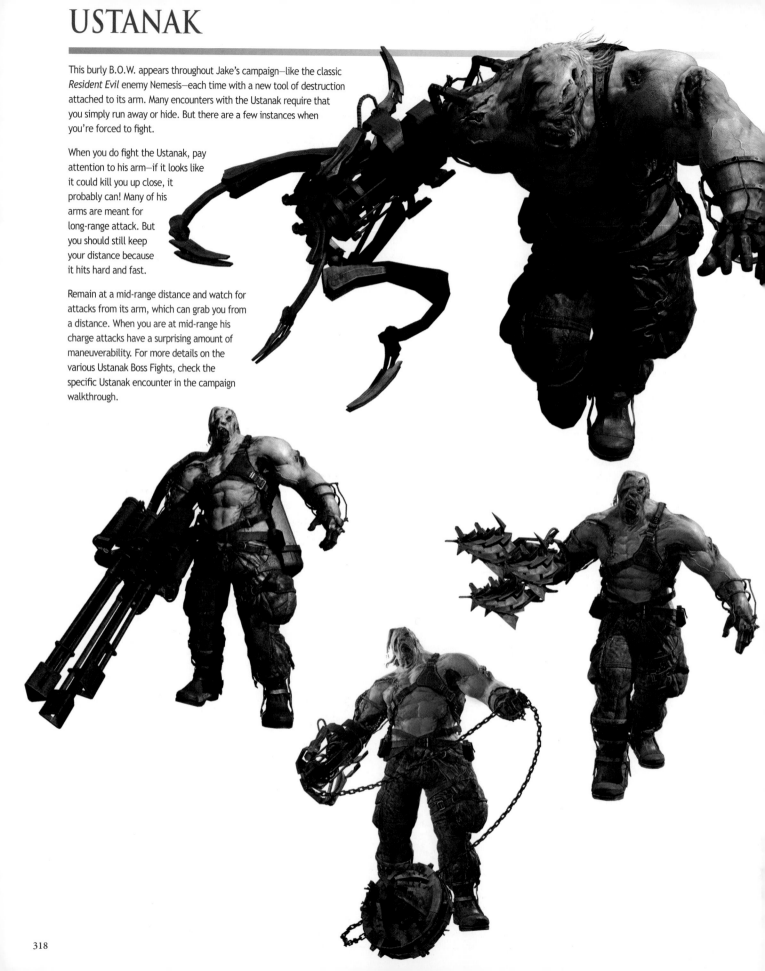

HAOS (CHRIS FINAL BOSS)

This enormous B.O.W. appears at the end of Chris' Campaign and looks like an enormous Rasklapanje but is much more lethal. This vicious monster is at times invincible and can only be damaged during specific stages. If he chases you, don't waste your ammo—just run! More details on how to take down this B.O.W. can be found in the campaign walkthrough.

CARLA SPORE—S (BOSS)

Carla mutates into a grotesque J'avo version that is practically invincible! When you first meet Carla, you have only one choice—run! Carla Spore makes no attempt to kill you but likewise can't be killed. So don't waste ammo trying to take her down.

CARLA SPORE—L (BOSS)

After an intense chase, Carla mutates into this horrible monstrosity in an attempt to finish off Ada. This gigantic boss continuously regenerates and cannot be killed directly—for more information on how to take down this monster, consult the specific boss fight in the campaign walkthrough!

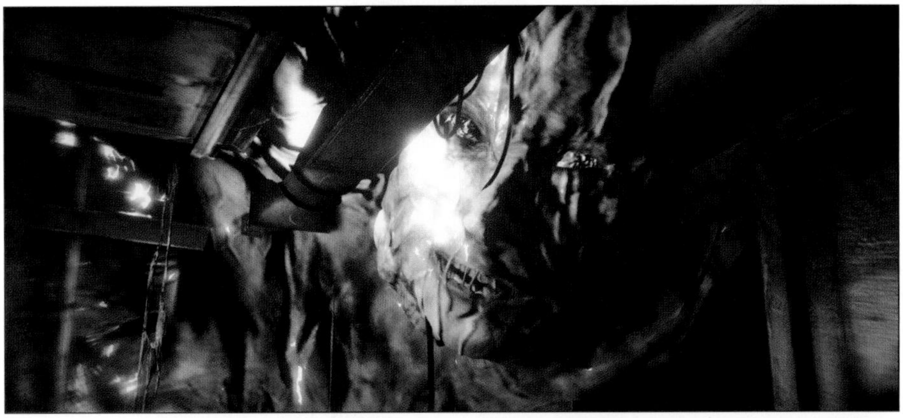

ZOMBIE

The original *Resident Evil* villain returns in its full, undead glory! The shambling undead generally try to get close and grab you. They come in many different forms, each with different abilities and attacks.

Many forms of zombie carry melee and long-range weapons, but they are inaccurate and should be treated as any other zombie. Watch for zombies dressed as firefighters—you can shoot the extinguisher on their backs, which explode, destroying nearby enemy zombies!

Be careful with zombies holding dynamite. They drop it when they die, damaging anything within the blast radius!

Some zombies appear heavily armored, making them invincible to most attacks. While certain armored zombies have exposed heads, others have almost complete body armor and are best dispatched with martial arts.

Bloodshot

Upon death, red-eyed zombies occasionally mutate into these grotesque B.O.W.s. The Bloodshot is a skinless, humanoid creature that is faster than normal zombies but difficult to take down.

Bloodshots attack and act mostly like zombies but are less vulnerable—if you knock down a Bloodshot, they stand up instantly! Bloodshots are killed only by destroying their hearts, which erupt after they've sustained a significant amount of damage. If you see a Bloodshot drop to its knees, attack its chest area immediately!

Shrieker

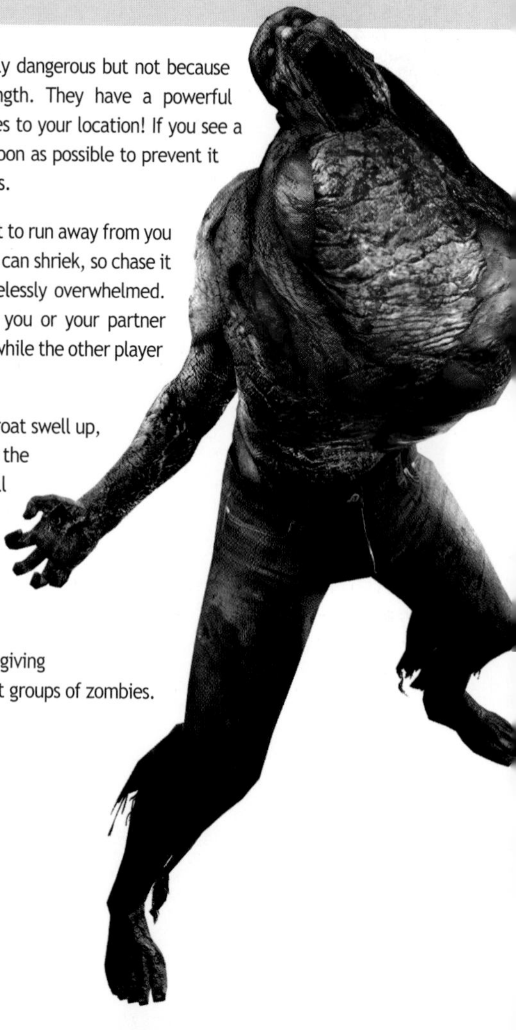

These B.O.W.'s are highly dangerous but not because of their offensive strength. They have a powerful scream that calls zombies to your location! If you see a Shrieker, take it out as soon as possible to prevent it from summoning zombies.

The Shrieker will attempt to run away from you and find a place where it can shriek, so chase it down unless you're hopelessly overwhelmed. If you're playing co-op, you or your partner should target a Shrieker while the other player keeps enemies at bay.

If you see a Shrieker's throat swell up, be careful. Quickly shoot the pulsating bulge. It will fall to its knees and unleash one last powerful scream before death! Instead of summoning zombies, however, the shriek will destroy them, giving you a useful tactic against groups of zombies.

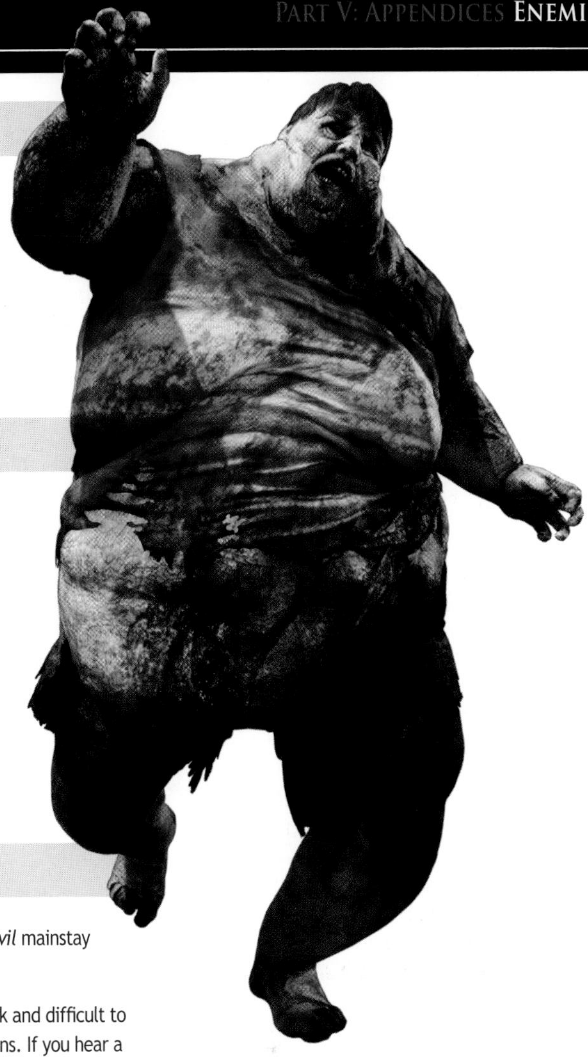

WHOPPER

This super-sized zombie isn't tricky or threatening but is durable and difficult to defeat. They require significant ammo to take down and aren't easily thwarted by counters or martial arts.

If you have high-powered weapons, use them on a Whopper—handguns are ineffective and simply provide time for other enemies to gather. Ignore the Whopper's head and chest and aim for its stubby legs. After a few rounds to the feet, it falls to its knees, allowing you to finish without fear of retribution.

WHOPPER SUPREME

The Whopper Supreme is nearly identical to the Whopper, except it's twice the size! This enormous beast functions like the Whopper, although it mostly charges at you.

Fight the Whopper Supreme much as you would a normal Whopper—take out its legs, then run up and perform a special martial arts attack. You might have to do this several times due to the Whopper Supreme's health. It is sometimes better to avoid it altogether, since it requires a considerable amount of ammo to take down and with little reward for doing so.

ZOMBIE DOG C

After a long absence, this legendary *Resident Evil* mainstay returns, this time mutated from the C-Virus.

Zombie Dogs are easy to kill but are very quick and difficult to hit with semi-automatic weapons like Handguns. If you hear a Zombie Dog coming near, use Quick Shot to quickly turn and take it down or wait for a chance to counter it.

BRZAK

This shark-like creature chases Leon and Helena through the underground of the Cathedral and is nearly impossible to kill. You can't fight the Brzak. You can only run from it, so save your ammo if you encounter it.

OGROMAN

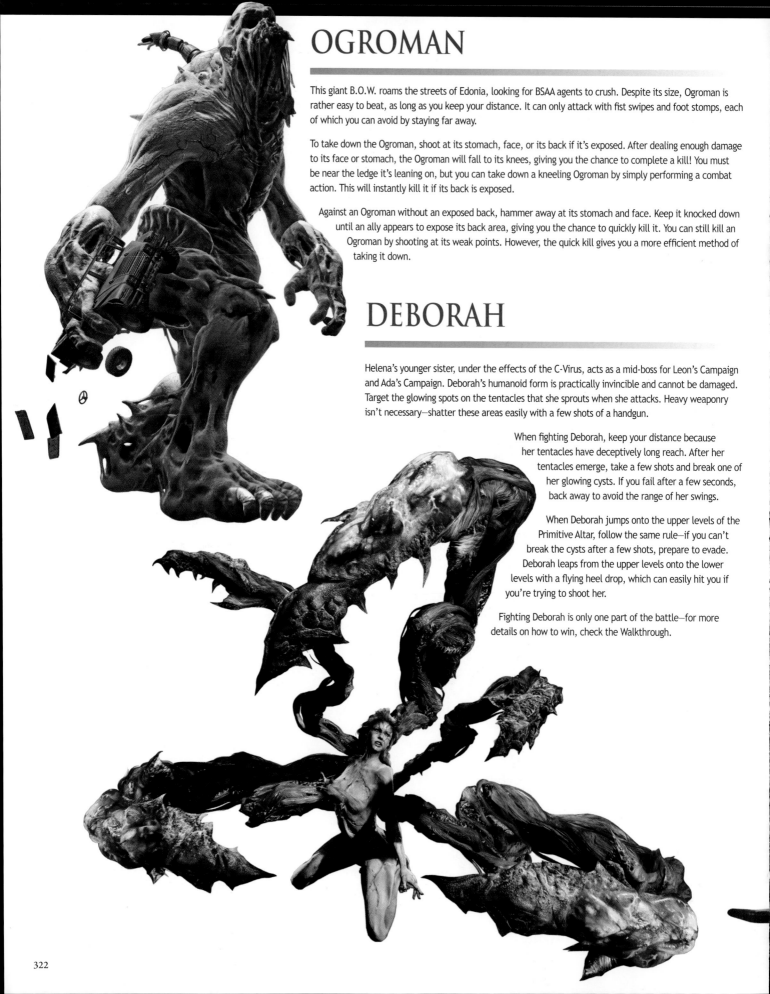

This giant B.O.W. roams the streets of Edonia, looking for BSAA agents to crush. Despite its size, Ogroman is rather easy to beat, as long as you keep your distance. It can only attack with fist swipes and foot stomps, each of which you can avoid by staying far away.

To take down the Ogroman, shoot at its stomach, face, or its back if it's exposed. After dealing enough damage to its face or stomach, the Ogroman will fall to its knees, giving you the chance to complete a kill! You must be near the ledge it's leaning on, but you can take down a kneeling Ogroman by simply performing a combat action. This will instantly kill it if its back is exposed.

Against an Ogroman without an exposed back, hammer away at its stomach and face. Keep it knocked down until an ally appears to expose its back area, giving you the chance to quickly kill it. You can still kill an Ogroman by shooting at its weak points. However, the quick kill gives you a more efficient method of taking it down.

DEBORAH

Helena's younger sister, under the effects of the C-Virus, acts as a mid-boss for Leon's Campaign and Ada's Campaign. Deborah's humanoid form is practically invincible and cannot be damaged. Target the glowing spots on the tentacles that she sprouts when she attacks. Heavy weaponry isn't necessary—shatter these areas easily with a few shots of a handgun.

When fighting Deborah, keep your distance because her tentacles have deceptively long reach. After her tentacles emerge, take a few shots and break one of her glowing cysts. If you fail after a few seconds, back away to avoid the range of her swings.

When Deborah jumps onto the upper levels of the Primitive Altar, follow the same rule—if you can't break the cysts after a few shots, prepare to evade. Deborah leaps from the upper levels onto the lower levels with a flying heel drop, which can easily hit you if you're trying to shoot her.

Fighting Deborah is only one part of the battle—for more details on how to win, check the Walkthrough.

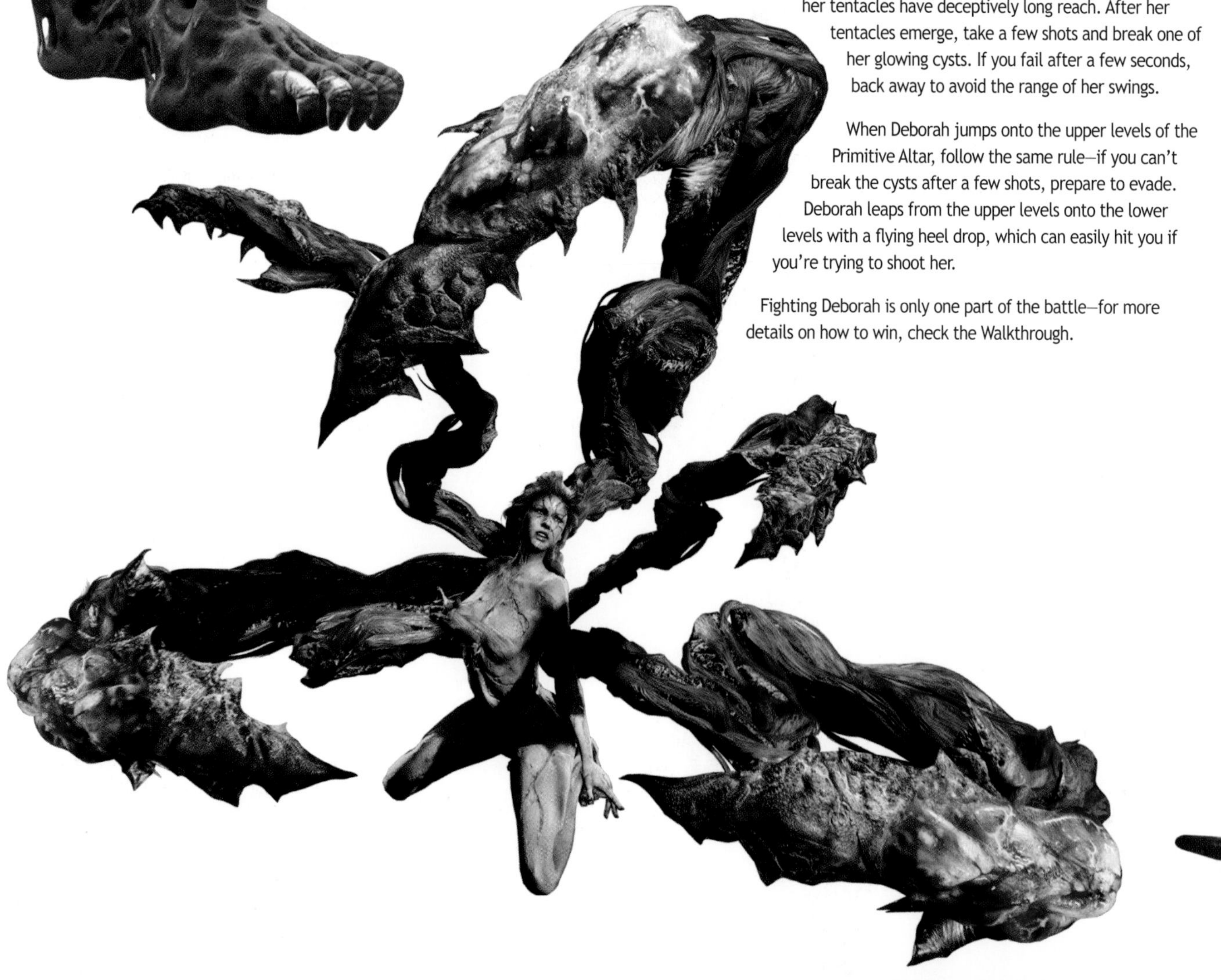

SIMMONS

Mutated by the C-Virus, the National Security Advisor serves as the final boss of Leon's Campaign and Ada's Campaign. Like many J'avo, Simmons has the ability to transform, although he can transform into several giant beasts, including a centaur and a Tyrannosaurus Rex, each with its own unique abilities. For more details on how to take down the various forms of Simmons, check out the Walkthrough.

ANIMALS

Rat

These little critters are found in many levels and can be used for target practice. Unfortunately, they don't drop anything—and if they do, it's incredibly rare. Shooting at these animals is a waste of ammo.

Rooster

Roosters are only found in the Market level during Leon Chapter 4. So if you want to fill your enemies list, take out at least one! Much like shooting rats, shooting a rooster offers no benefit. You're better off not wasting ammo.

Crow

Shooting these flying critters, like the others, offers no benefit to you. You may shoot some to fill out the Enemies section of Records, but otherwise it's best to leave them alone.

Bat

These animals also fly but drop no items. They're found mostly in cave and underground areas, so keep your eyes open.

Spider

These creatures are smaller than the other animals but provide no reward to you when killed.

Snake

These reptiles are incredibly rare but offer no bonus when you kill them.

MEDALS

When you complete a chapter in the campaign or a stage in Agent Hunt or The Mercenaries, you earn a medal based on your achievements. Medals are awarded for tasks that range from difficult to easy, and some are even awarded for performing badly!

When you unlock a medal for the first time, it appears in your Records, which indicates how many times you've collected each medal and it also shows medals that you still need to earn. Your goal is to earn every medal to fill out the section!

CAMPAIGN MEDALS

Medals earned in the campaign are awarded only at the successful completion of a chapter. If you managed to achieve something difficult, don't exit to the menu! Complete the chapter to earn credit. Medals can be earned by any character in any chapter unless otherwise noted. Play through the Campaign as each character and sub-character in order to unlock them all!

MEDAL	VALUE	REQUIREMENTS
Accuracy—A Rank	Gold	Accuracy—A Rank
Accuracy—B Rank	Silver	Accuracy—B Rank
Accuracy—C Rank	Bronze	Accuracy—C Rank
Accuracy—D Rank	Green	Accuracy—D Rank
Deaths—A Rank	Gold	Deaths—A Rank
Deaths—B Rank	Silver	Deaths—B Rank
Deaths—C Rank	Bronze	Deaths—C Rank
Deaths—D Rank	Green	Deaths—D Rank
Clear Time—A Rank	Gold	Clear Time—A Rank
Clear Time—B Rank	Silver	Clear Time—B Rank
Clear Time—C Rank	Bronze	Clear Time—C Rank
Clear Time—D Rank	Green	Clear Time—D Rank
Enemies Routed—A Rank	Gold	Enemies Routed—A Rank
Enemies Routed—B Rank	Silver	Enemies Routed—B Rank
Enemies Routed—C Rank	Bronze	Enemies Routed—C Rank
Enemies Routed—D Rank	Green	Enemies Routed—D Rank
Rescued partner.	Green	Help a downed or struggling partner.
Saved a partner from dying.	Bronze	Rescue a partner while they're in dying state.
Aided a partner in need during a story intersection.	Silver	Help a partner while playing with another group—for example, save Chris as Jake.
Rescued by partner 10 times.	Bronze	Help your partner 10 times in one Chapter.

MEDAL	VALUE	REQUIREMENTS
Killed an enemy while dying.	Silver	Kill an enemy while in dying state.
Recovered from dying.	Green	Survive in dying state long enough to recover.
Beat the Chapter without entering the dying state.	Bronze	Beat a Chapter without running out of health.
Beat the game after having entered the dying state at least 5 times.	Green	Beat a chapter while having entered dying state 5 times or more.
Killed an enemy with a counterattack.	Silver	Kill an enemy with a counterattack.
Successfully countered one of Ustanak's attacks.	Silver	Counter an attack from Ustanak—you don't have to kill it.
Killed an enemy with a physical attack.	Green	Kill an enemy with physical attacks.
Killed 10 or more enemies with physical attacks.	Bronze	Kill at least 10 enemies with physical attacks.
Killed an enemy with a coup de grâce.	Bronze	Kill an enemy with a coup de grâce finishing attack.
Killed an enemy with a Quick Shot.	Green	Kill an enemy with a Quick Shot.
Killed an enemy with a stealth attack.	Green	Kill an enemy with a physical attack from behind while they don't know you're there.
Killed an enemy while sliding.	Green	Kill an enemy by sliding (run and use a physical attack).
Destroyed an item box while sliding.	Green	Slide into an item box.
Used a weapon lodged in a zombie to kill it.	Bronze	Counter or use a finisher attack against a stunned zombie holding a weapon.

MEDAL	VALUE	REQUIREMENTS
Killed an enemy by chaining a physical attack with your partner.	Silver	Use a physical attack on an enemy after your partner or vice versa.
Successfully inputted commands at the exact moment.	Green	Complete an action prompt when you have to hit a button at a precise time.
Successfully executed a counterattack.	Bronze	Perform a counter on an enemy.
Correctly executed all revolving-action command prompts.	Green	In chapters with revolving-action prompts, successfully complete each one.
Saved partner from falling off a high ledge.	Green	Help your partner when they might fall off a ledge.
Praised a partner's actions 3 times.	Green	Use partner commands to praise your partner three times in one chapter.
Killed an Agent Hunt player.	Bronze	Kill an enemy controlled by another player.
Killed by an Agent Hunt player.	Green	Killed by an enemy controlled by another player.
Matched online in a story intersection.	Green	Encounter other players playing through the campaign in certain chapters.
Killed 5 enemies with explosive drums.	Bronze	Kill 5 enemies by shooting explosive drums.
Executed a headshot.	Green	Shoot an enemy in the head.
Executed 10 headshots.	Bronze	Shoot 10 enemies in the head.
Executed 5 consecutive headshots.	Bronze	Shoot five enemies in the head in a row without missing or hitting a different body part.
Killed an enemy with grenade.	Green	Kill an enemy with a grenade.
Killed 10 enemies with grenades.	Bronze	Kill 10 enemies with grenades.
Burned 10 enemies with Incendiary Grenades.	Bronze	Hit 10 enemies with the explosion caused by Incendiary Grenades.
Killed an enemy using the environment.	Bronze	Kill an enemy using items located in stages, like generators.
Used an enemy's attack to kill another enemy.	Bronze	Kill an enemy by redirecting another enemy's attack.
Beat the chapter without taking any damage.	Gold	Clear a chapter without suffering any damage.
Beat the chapter without getting knocked down.	Silver	Clear a chapter without getting knocked down.
Killed an animal.	Green	Kill an animal like a rat or spider.
Tripped a running enemy.	Green	Shoot an enemy that's running at you in the legs.
Knocked an enemy off a high ledge.	Bronze	Use a finisher attack to push an enemy off a ledge.
Killed an enemy with a Flash Grenade.	Bronze	Kill an enemy with a Flash Grenade.
Blinded 10 enemies with Flash Grenades.	Bronze	Hit 10 enemies with the explosion from a Flash Grenade.

MEDAL	VALUE	REQUIREMENTS
Shot an enemy-thrown object in mid-air.	Bronze	Shoot an object out of the air when thrown at you by an enemy.
Knocked down an enemy-thrown object with your knife.	Silver	Use the Combat or Survival Knife to knock an enemy-thrown object out of the air.
Killed an enemy in mid-jump.	Bronze	Kill an enemy when they jump at you.
Killed an enemy in mid-jump with a headshot.	Silver	Use a headshot to kill an enemy when they jump at you.
Beat the Chapter using only a handgun.	Silver	Clear a chapter using only the Picador, Nine-Oh-Nine, or Wing Shooter.
Beat the Chapter using only a shotgun.	Silver	Clear a chapter using only the Shotgun or Assault Shotgun.
Beat the Chapter using only a Magnum.	Silver	Clear a chapter using only the Lightning Hawk or Elephant Killer.
Beat the Chapter using only a sniper rifle.	Silver	Clear a chapter using only the Sniper Rifle or Semi-Automatic Sniper Rifle.
Beat the Chapter using only an MP-AF.	Silver	Clear a chapter using only the MP-AF.
Beat the Chapter using only an assault rifle.	Silver	Clear a chapter using only the Bear Commander, Assault Rifle RN, or Assault Rifle for Special Tactics.
Beat the Chapter using only a grenade launcher.	Silver	Clear a chapter using only the Grenade Launcher.
Beat the Chapter using only physical attacks.	Silver	Clear a chapter without firing a weapon.
Beat the Chapter without the use of physical attacks.	Bronze	Clear a chapter without using Martial Arts.
Beat the Chapter without reloading.	Silver	Clear a chapter without reloading a gun.
Beat the Chapter without the use of grenades.	Bronze	Clear a chapter without using grenades.
Beat the Chapter using only grenades.	Silver	Clear a chapter only using grenades.
Beat the Chapter without using health items.	Bronze	Clear a chapter without restoring your health with items.
Kill 50 enemies with a knife.	Gold	Kill 50 enemies in one chapter with the Survival or Combat Knife.
Beat the chapter without picking up any ammo or health items.	Silver	Complete a chapter without picking up items (Skill Points are okay).
Beat the chapter without equipping any Skills.	Bronze	Complete a chapter without any equipped Skills.
Destroyed 3 helicopters with the VTOL's barrel gun.	Silver	Destroy 3 helicopters as Chris in Chris Chapter 4.
Shot 10 J'avo off their motorcycles.	Silver	Shoot 10 J'avo off their motorcycles as Sherry in Jake Chapter 4.
Escaped the zombie-infested campus.	Green	Complete Leon Chapter 1—Campus.

MEDAL	VALUE	REQUIREMENTS
Made it back to the surface.	Green	Complete Leon Chapter 1—Underground.
Cooperated with survivors to fend off zombies.	Green	Complete Leon Chapter 1—Gun Shop.
Made it to the cathedral.	Green	Complete Leon Chapter 2—Forest Cemetery.
Solved the mysteries of the cathedral.	Green	Complete Leon Chapter 2—Cathedral.
Relieved Deborah of her suffering.	Green	Complete Leon Chapter 2—Altar Corridor.
Acquired the Simmons Family ring.	Green	Complete Leon Chapter 3—Catacombs.
Discovered the exit from the underground cavern.	Green	Complete Leon Chapter 3—Cavern.
Defeated the B.O.W. lurking in the water.	Green	Complete Leon Chapter 3—Underground Water Channel.
Piloted the aircraft.	Green	Complete Leon Chapter 4—Inside the Airplane.
Provided Jake and Sherry with backup.	Green	Complete Leon Chapter 4—Airplane Crash Site.
Agreed to fight toward a common goal.	Green	Complete Leon Chapter 4—Medical Research Center.
Made it to Quad Tower.	Green	Complete Leon Chapter 5—High-Rise Area.
Parted ways with Ada once again.	Green	Complete Leon Chapter 5—Quad Tower.
Sent Derek to his grave.	Bronze	Complete Leon's Campaign.
Returned to the fight after 6 months.	Green	Complete Chris Chapter 1—Main Street.
Saved a valuable hostage.	Green	Complete Chris Chapter 1—Tenement.
Escaped from a building being bombed.	Green	Complete Chris Chapter 1—Tenement.
Provided cover while Finn set the bombs.	Green	Complete Chris Chapter 2—City in Eastern Europe.
Gained control of the bridge.	Green	Complete Chris Chapter 2—The Bridge.
Neutralized 3 anti-aircraft guns.	Green	Complete Chris Chapter 2—In Front of City Hall.
Shot down the helicopter.	Green	Complete Chris Chapter 3—Poisawan Courtyard.
Avenged your fallen comrades.	Green	Complete Chris Chapter 3—Poisawan Inner Area.
Infiltrated the aircraft carrier.	Green	Complete Chris Chapter 4—Aircraft Carrier—Rear Hanger.
Witnessed Ada's end.	Green	Complete Chris Chapter 4—Aircraft Carrier—Bridge.
Saw an unavoidable nightmare.	Green	Complete Chris Chapter 4—Airspace over Aircraft Carrier.
Saved Jake and Sherry.	Green	Complete Chris Chapter 5—Underwater Facility.
Escaped from the giant B.O.W.	Green	Complete Chris chapter 5—Underwater Facility—Upper Levels.

MEDAL	VALUE	REQUIREMENTS
Said farewell to your partner.	Bronze	Complete Chris' Campaign.
Made a promise to your partner.	Green	Complete Jake Chapter 1—The Sewer.
Escaped from a collapsing building.	Green	Complete Jake Chapter 1—Water Channel.
Teamed up with the BSAA in the square.	Green	Complete Jake Chapter 1—In Front of City Hall.
Recovered all the lost data.	Green	Complete Jake Chapter 2—Mountain Path.
Escaped the avalanche on snowmobile.	Green	Complete Jake Chapter 2—Snow-Covered Mountain.
Defeated Ustanak with the drill.	Green	Complete Jake Chapter 2—Cave.
Successfully escaped captivity.	Green	Complete Jake Chapter 3—Research Facility—Detention Center.
Reunited with your partner.	Green	Complete Jake Chapter 3—Research Facility—Living Quarters.
Evaded the tank attacks.	Green	Complete Jake Chapter 3—Research Facility—Entrance.
Avoided the helicopter attacks.	Green	Complete Jake Chapter 4—City and Highway.
Lit the approaching B.O.W. on fire.	Green	Complete Jake Chapter 4—Shopping District.
Defeated Ustanak with Leon and Helena.	Green	Complete Jake Chapter 4—Airplane Crash Site.
Escaped from the underwater facility.	Green	Complete Jake Chapter 5—Underwater Facility—Lower Levels.
Landed the finishing blow to Ustanak.	Green	Complete Jake Chapter 5—Shipping Center.
Fulfilled your promise to your partner.	Bronze	Complete Jake's Campaign.
Acquired information about Jake.	Green	Complete Ada Chapter 1—Submarine Interior.
Outran the incoming flood of water.	Green	Complete Ada Chapter 1—Submarine—Reactor.
Escaped from the sinking submarine.	Green	Complete Ada Chapter 1—Submarine—Torpedo Room.
Acquired Simmons' ring.	Green	Complete Ada Chapter 2—Forest Cemetery.
Gave Simmons' ring to Leon.	Green	Complete Ada Chapter 2—Altar Corridor.
Obtained information about your doppelganger.	Green	Complete Ada Chapter 2—Underground Lab.
Experienced a little taste of China.	Green	Complete Ada Chapter 3—Tenement—Bin Street.
Witnessed an airplane crash.	Green	Complete Ada Chapter 3—Shopping District.
Saved Sherry from the attacking B.O.W.	Green	Complete Ada Chapter 3—Stilt Housing Area.
Shook off the BSAA tail.	Green	Complete Ada Chapter 4—Aircraft Carrier—Bridge.
Witnessed your own death.	Green	Complete Ada Chapter 4—Aircraft Carrier—Bridge.

MEDAL	VALUE	REQUIREMENTS
Faced your own destiny.	Green	Complete Ada Chapter 4—Aircraft Carrier Interior.
Approached Quad Tower from the outside.	Green	Complete Ada Chapter 5—High-Rise Area.
Jumped off the 80th floor.	Green	Complete Ada Chapter 5—Quad Tower.
Settled things once and for all.	Bronze	Complete Ada's Campaign.
Killed 3 zombies hiding on the rooftop.	Bronze	Kill 3 or more zombies hiding on roofs in Leon Chapter 1—The Town and Gun Shop.
Killed all enemies in front of the cathedral.	Bronze	Kill all the enemies at the end of Leon Chapter 2—Forest Cemetery.
Saved one or more survivors in the cathedral.	Bronze	Prevent at least one civilian from turning into a zombie from the Lepotitsa's gas in Leon Chapter 2—Cathedral.
Stopped the flames without your partner's help.	Bronze	Kill the zombies turning the cranks in Leon Chapter 2—Catacombs without Helena's help.
Blew up all the fuel tanks at the crash site.	Bronze	Blow up all the fuel tanks in Leon Chapter 4—Airplane Crash Site.
Put a B.O.W.'s hand into the microwave.	Bronze	Place the Rasklapanje's hand in the microwave in Leon Chapter 4—Market.
Beat the Chapter without using a Rocket Launcher.	Bronze	Kill Simmons without using the Rocket Launcher in Leon Chapter 5—Quad Tower Roof.
Rescued a hostage from certain death.	Bronze	Save the hostage from the J'avo in Chris Chapter 1—Tenement.
Defeated a flying B.O.W. with the snowmobile.	Bronze	Kill a Mesets by running into it with a snowmobile in Jake Chapter 2—Mountain Path.
Defeated the giant B.O.W. through its weak spot.	Bronze	Pull the tube out of the Ogroman's back in Jake Chapter 1 or Chris Chapter 2—In Front of City Hall.
Killed a paratrooper enemy in mid-air.	Bronze	Kill a paratrooper as they fly into the stage in Chris Chapter 2—The Bridge.
Slid down the slide.	Bronze	Slide down the slide in the park in Chris Chapter 3—Tenement—Poisawan Entrance or Ada Chapter 3—Tenement—Bin Street.
Beat Leon and Helena in the race.	Bronze	Beat Leon's team to the elevator in Chris Chapter 3—Medical Research Center.
Cleared the stage without opening the one-way doors.	Bronze	Clear the chapter without opening the one-way doors in Chris Chapter 4—Aircraft Carrier—Forward Hanger.
Reached the missile in 3 minutes or less.	Bronze	Reach the missile as Piers in Chris Chapter 4—Airspace over Aircraft Carrier.
Killed 3 enemies armed with gatling guns.	Bronze	As Piers, kill three enemies carrying Gatling Guns in Chris Chapter 5—Underwater Facility.

MEDAL	VALUE	REQUIREMENTS
Killed more enemies than Jake and Sherry (1).	Bronze	Kill more enemies than Jake and Sherry in Chris Chapter 5—Underwater Facility—Lower Levels.
Discovered the hidden storage room.	Bronze	Find the hidden room in the bathroom area in Jake Chapter 1—Water Channel.
Wiped out all enemies around the cabin.	Bronze	Kill all enemies surrounding the cabin in Jake Chapter 2—Snow-Covered Mountain.
Beat the cave area without killing any enemies (excluding Ustanak).	Bronze	Complete the cave area without killing any Oko in Jake Chapter 2—Cave.
Destroyed 5 or more enemies using the turret-mounted cameras.	Bronze	Use Camera Turrets to kill 5 enemies in Jake Chapter 3—Research Facility—Detention Center.
Found all ID medals.	Bronze	Find every ID Medal in Jake Chapter 3—Research Facility—Living Quarters.
Personally killed the helicopter pilot.	Bronze	Kill the pilot of the attack helicopter in Jake Chapter 4—Poisawan Courtyard.
Beat Chris and Piers in the race.	Bronze	Beat Chris' team to the elevator in Leon Chapter 4—Shopping District.
Ground up a B.O.W.'s hand.	Bronze	Place a Rasklapanje hand in the shredder in Jake Chapter 5—Underwater Facility 1.
Killed more enemies than Chris and Piers.	Bronze	Kill more enemies than Chris and Piers in Jake Chapter 5—Underwater Facility—Lower Levels.
Discovered a shortcut.	Bronze	Find the shortcut in Ada Chapter 1—Submarine Reactor.
Killed 5 zombies while in the minecart.	Bronze	Kill five zombies from the minecart in Ada Chapter 2—Altar Corridor.
Had 10 walls broken down by enemies.	Bronze	Allow the Whoppers to break 10 walls in Ada Chapter 2—Underground Lab.
Used a B.O.W.'s attacks to kill all zombies in the area.	Bronze	Allow the Ubistvo to kill all the zombies in Ada Chapter 3—Tenement—Bin Street.
Killed more enemies than Jake and Sherry (2).	Bronze	Kill more enemies with your Sniper Rifle than Jake and Sherry in Ada Chapter 3—Stilt Housing Area.
Killed off your imperfect doppelganger.	Bronze	Destroy all the Carla Spores in Ada Chapter 4—Aircraft Carrier Interior.
Cleared the chapter without being spotted by the enemy.	Bronze	Clear Ada Chapter 4—Aircraft Carrier—Bridge without being spotted by any enemies.
Protected Leon and Helena.	Bronze	Prevent Simmons from harming Leon and Helena while they're climbing the elevator cables in Leon Chapter 5—High Rise Area.
Rescued Leon from becoming B.O.W. chow.	Bronze	Prevent Simmons (in T-Rex form) from biting Leon in Ada Chapter 5—Quad Tower Entrance.

AGENT HUNT MEDALS

Medals earned in Agent Hunt are awarded only at the end of a hunt, whether or not it's successful. Just like in the campaign, you must see a hunt through in order to earn credit for the medals earned.

MEDAL	VALUE	REQUIREMENTS
Hunt Successful.	Gold	Succeed in Agent Hunt.
Hunt Failed.	Green	Fail in Agent Hunt.
Finished off an agent.	Gold	Defeat an Agent in Agent Hunt.
Put an agent into dying state.	Bronze	Put an agent into dying state.
Attacked and inflicted damage upon an agent.	Bronze	Damage an Agent.
Played as a Zombie.	Green	Play as a Zombie.
Played as a J'avo.	Green	Play as a J'avo.
Played as a Rasklapanje.	Bronze	Play as a Rasklapanje.
Played as a Shrieker.	Bronze	Play as a Shrieker.
Played as a Zombie Dog C.	Bronze	Play as a Zombie Dog C.
Played as a Bloodshot.	Bronze	Play as a Bloodshot.
Mutated into a Strelats.	Bronze	Mutate from a J'avo into a Strelats.
Played as Mesets.	Bronze	Play as a Mesets.
Mutated into a Napad.	Bronze	Mutate from a J'avo into a Napad.
Mutated into a Gnezdo.	Bronze	Mutate from a J'avo into a Gnezdo.
Played as a Glava-Sluz.	Bronze	Play as a Glava-Sluz.
Played as a Glava-Smech.	Bronze	Play as a Glava-Smech.
Played as a Ruka-Srp.	Bronze	Play as a Ruka-Srp.
Played as a Ruka-Khvatanje.	Bronze	Play as a Ruka-Khvatanje.
Played as Ruka-Bedem.	Bronze	Play as a Ruka-Bedem.
Played as Telo-Eksplozija.	Bronze	Play as a Telo-Eksplozija.
Hit an agent with a thrown object.	Silver	As a Zombie, hit an agent with a thrown weapon.
Performed a successful dynamite punch.	Silver	As a Zombie, hit an agent with a stick of dynamite.

MEDAL	VALUE	REQUIREMENTS
Sprayed acid on an agent.	Silver	As a Zombie, hit an agent by spitting acid on them.
Assembled 5 zombies by shrieking.	Silver	Summon 5 zombies by screaming as a Shrieker.
Mutated two different body regions as a J'avo.	Silver	Mutate multiple body parts as a J'avo.
Hid behind cover as a J'avo.	Silver	Hide behind cover as a J'avo.
Bit and lifted up an agent.	Silver	Successfully bite an agent as a Glava-Smech.
Immobilized an agent with a sticky substance.	Silver	Hit an enemy with your spray as a Glava-Sluz.
Attacked an agent with a mutated scythe arm.	Silver	Hit an enemy with your claw arm as a Ruka-Srp.
Grabbed an agent with an extended arm.	Silver	As a Ruka-Khvatanje, grab an enemy with your long-range arm.
Blocked an agent's attack with a shield.	Silver	As a Ruka-Bedem, block an agent's attack with your shield.
Stomped on an agent.	Silver	As a Rasklapanje, hit an Agent with a stomping attack.
Killed by an agent's coup de grâce.	Silver	As an enemy other than a Rasklapanje, die from an agent's coup de grâce.
Travelled over 1,000 meters in one session.	Green	Travel over 1,000 meters in a single session of Agent Hunt.
Killed by an agent in a single attack.	Green	Die in one attack from an agent.
Attacked an agent being held by another creature.	Green	Attack an agent while another creature is holding the agent.
Killed by physical attacks.	Green	Die from an agent's physical attacks.
Killed a creature as a creature.	Green	Kill another creature as a monster in Agent Hunt.
Killed in an explosion.	Green	Die in an explosion.
Played for less than 1 minute.	Green	Have a session finish in one minute; you will not earn this medal by leaving intentionally.
Played for 10 minutes.	Green	Play 10 minutes in a single session.
Did not inflict any damage to agents.	Green	Finish a session without damaging an agent.
Finished a game without dying once.	Green	Finish a session without dying.
Killed by an agent 10 times.	Green	Die 10 times due to an agent.

THE MERCENARIES MEDALS

The Mercenaries contains medals that you can earn alone, but many must be earned while playing The Mercenaries (Duo). To earn all the medals, you must complete a stage by killing every enemy you can—you must defeat 150 enemies!

MEDAL	VALUE	REQUIREMENTS
Cleared Urban Chaos.	Green	Complete the stage Urban Chaos.
Cleared the Steel Beast.	Green	Complete the stage Steel Beast.
Cleared Mining the Depths.	Green	Complete the stage Mining the Depths.
???	Green	Keep an eye out for additional content!
???	Green	Keep an eye out for additional content!
???	Green	Keep an eye out for additional content!
???	Green	Keep an eye out for additional content!
???	Green	Keep an eye out for additional content!
???	Green	Keep an eye out for additional content!
???	Green	Keep an eye out for additional content!
Killed 120 enemies.	Gold	Kill 120 enemies in one session.
Killed 100 enemies.	Silver	Kill 100 enemies in one session.
Killed 70 enemies.	Bronze	Kill 70 enemies in one session.
Killed 40 enemies.	Bronze	Kill 40 enemies in one session.
Executed a 120—hit combo.	Gold	Acquire a combo of 120 or more.
Executed a 100-hit combo.	Silver	Acquire a combo of 100 or more.
Executed a 50-hit combo.	Bronze	Acquire a combo of 50 or more.
Executed a 20-hit combo.	Green	Acquire a combo of 20 or more.
Survived for 120 seconds.	Gold	Survive for two minutes.
Survived for 90 seconds.	Silver	Survive for 90 seconds.
Survived for 60 seconds.	Bronze	Survive for 60 seconds.
Survived for 30 seconds.	Green	Survive for 30 seconds.
Killed an enemy with a physical attack.	Green	Kill an enemy with martial arts.

MEDAL	VALUE	REQUIREMENTS
Killed an enemy with a coup de grâce.	Gold	Kill a large enemy with a coup de grâce.
Killed an enemy with a Quick Shot.	Silver	Kill an enemy with a Quick Shot.
Killed an enemy with a counterattack.	Bronze	Kill an enemy with a counter.
Destroyed a time bonus item while sliding.	Green	Destroy a Yellow Hourglass by sliding into it.
Found a Time Bonus.	Green	Destroy a Yellow Hourglass.
Found all Time Bonuses.	Bronze	Destroy all Yellow Hourglasses in a stage.
Found a Combo Bonus.	Green	Destroy a Green Hourglass.
Found all Combo Bonuses.	Bronze	Find all Green Hourglasses.
Caused the hidden boss to appear.	Bronze	Complete the conditions to summon a hidden boss.
Defeated the hidden boss.	Silver	Defeat a hidden boss.
Defeated the hidden boss during a combo chain.	Gold	Defeat the hidden boss during a combo.
Defeated the hidden boss with a physical attack.	Silver	Defeat the hidden boss with martial arts.
Executed a 150-hit chain combo with a partner.	Gold	Acquire a 150 combo in The Mercenaries (Duo).
Cleared the stage with a partner with over 150 seconds left.	Silver	Clear a stage in The Mercenaries (Duo) with over 150 seconds remaining.
Killed 150 enemies with a partner.	Bronze	Kill all enemies in a stage in The Mercenaries (Duo).
Cleared the stage with a partner.	Green	Complete a stage in The Mercenaries (Duo).
Cleared the stage without taking any damage.	Gold	Complete a stage without taking any damage.
Cleared the stage without the use of any Skills.	Silver	Complete a stage without equipping any Skills.
Killed an enemy using the stage surroundings.	Green	Kill an enemy using an explosive drum or another deadly stage emplacement.
Cleared the stage with 100% accuracy.	Gold	Complete a stage without missing a shot.
Cleared the stage without the use of any health items.	Bronze	Complete a stage without healing yourself.

ACHIEVEMENTS/ TROPHIES

Resident Evil 6 features a variety of Achievements or Trophies that can be gained by playing through the game. All of the Achievements or Trophies are earned by playing through the campaign, although some are easier to obtain by playing through Extra Content. If you are alert while playing through the game, you will unlock these rather easily!

ICON	TITLE	REQUIREMENT	GAMERSCORE AWARDED	TROPHY EARNED
	The Longest Night	Complete the tutorial.	10	Bronze
	Gone to Hell	Complete Chapter 1 in Leon's Campaign.	15	Bronze
	Buried Secrets	Complete Chapter 2 in Leon's Campaign.	15	Bronze
	Get on the Plane	Complete Chapter 3 in Leon's Campaign.	15	Bronze
	Big Trouble in China	Complete Chapter 4 in Leon's Campaign.	15	Bronze
	The Trouble with Women	Complete Chapter 5 in Leon's Campaign.	15	Bronze
	Rescue the Hostages	Complete Chapter 1 in Chris' Campaign.	15	Bronze
	Tragedy in Europe	Complete Chapter 2 in Chris' campaign.	15	Bronze
	After Her!	Complete Chapter 3 in Chris' Campaign.	15	Bronze
	There's Always Hope	Complete Chapter 4 in Chris' Campaign.	15	Bronze
	Duty Calls	Complete Chapter 5 in Chris' Campaign.	15	Bronze
	Money Talks	Complete Chapter 1 in Jake's Campaign.	15	Bronze
	A Revolting Development	Complete Chapter 2 in Jake's Campaign.	15	Bronze
	Let's Blow This Joint	Complete Chapter 3 in Jake's Campaign.	15	Bronze
	Still on the Run	Complete Chapter 4 in Jake's Campaign.	15	Bronze

ICON	TITLE	REQUIREMENT	GAMERSCORE AWARDED	TROPHY EARNED
	See You Around	Complete Chapter 5 in Jake's Campaign.	15	Bronze
	I Spy	Complete Chapter 1 in Ada's Campaign.	15	Bronze
	Counter-intelligence	Complete Chapter 2 in Ada's Campaign.	15	Bronze
	This Takes Me Back	Complete Chapter 3 in Ada's Campaign.	15	Bronze
	Ada's Demise	Complete Chapter 4 in Ada's Campaign.	15	Bronze
	What's Next	Complete Chapter 5 in Ada's Campaign.	15	Bronze
	Green Around the Ears	Complete the game in Amateur mode.	15	Bronze
	Normal Is Good	Complete the game in Normal mode.	30	Silver
	Back in My Day	Complete the game in Veteran mode.	30	Silver
	Leave It to the Pro	Complete the game in Professional mode.	90	Gold
	Check Out My Dogs	Customize your Dog Tags.	15	Bronze
	Titular Achievement	Earn 10 different titles.	15	Bronze
	One Is Better Than None	Purchase one Skill.	15	Bronze
	Mad Skillz	Max out all the Skills that allow you to level up.	90	Gold
	Silent Killer	Use a stealth attack to take down five enemies.	15	Bronze
	Finish What You Start	Perform a coup de grâce on 10 enemies.	15	Bronze
	Bob and Weave	Counter an enemy's attack three times in a row.	15	Bronze
	Down, Not Out	Defeat an enemy while dying, then recover without	15	Bronze

ICON	TITLE	REQUIREMENT	GAMERSCORE AWARDED	TROPHY EARNED
	Lifesaver	Help or rescue your partner 10 times.	15	Bronze
	Weapons Master	Use all the weapons in the game and kill 10 enemies with each of them.	30	Silver
	Give a Little Push	Knock 10 enemies off a high place.	15	Bronze
	Rising Up	Earn a level-4 title.	30	Silver
	They're ACTION Figures!	Collect 3 figures.	15	Bronze
	Stuntman	Defeat 20 enemies with the Hydra using a Quick Shot.	15	Bronze
	Bring the Heat	Take down an enemy from 50 meters away with a headshot using the Thermal Scope.	15	Bronze
	High Voltage	Defeat 10 enemies with a Stun Rod charge attack.	15	Bronze
	Zombie Massacre	Defeat 500 zombies.	15	Bronze
	J'avo Genocide	Defeat 500 J'avo.	15	Bronze
	B.O.W.s Are Ugly	Defeat 100 enemies that have come out of a chrysalid.	30	Silver
	I Prefer Them Alive	Rescue two female survivors at the cathedral.	15	Bronze
	Flying Ace	Pilot the VTOL without getting a scratch on it.	15	Bronze
	Hard Choice	Shoot the helicopter pilot with a Magnum at point-blank range.	15	Bronze
	Sneaking Around	Get through the aircraft carrier's bridge area without being noticed.	15	Bronze
	Covered in Brass	Earn 150 different medals.	30	Silver
	Heirlooms	Collect all the Serpent Emblems.	30	Silver

ACHIEVEMENT/TROPHY STRATEGY

General Tips—You can gather many of these Achievements/Trophies simply by playing through the campaign in various difficulty modes. After playing through all four campaigns, you should have about half the Achievements/Trophies!

You can unlock Check Out My Dogs, Titular Achievement, and One Is Better Than None after completing a few missions in any campaign and by entering the menus attached with those Achievements/Trophies.

Several Achievements/Trophies will probably unlock just from trying to play through the game, like Down, Not Out and Weapons Master. Heirlooms, Covered in Brass, Rising Up, and They're ACTION Figures! will take some grinding before they unlock, however. To unlock Covered in Brass more easily, play The Mercenaries and Agent Hunt to unlock those modes' specific medals. They're ACTION Figures! and Rising Up will unlock as you complete the Heirlooms Achievement or Trophy.

COLLECTION TROPHIES

Monster Killing Achievements/Trophies—While 500 seems like a massive number, you can unlock these Achievements or Trophies by playing through the game and playing through The Mercenaries a few times. Unfortunately, you can't unlock B.O.W.s Are Ugly in The Mercenaries because J'avo do not mutate into chrysalids in multiplayer modes. Go through levels like Chris Chapter 4 and Ada Chapter 2 to ultimately make your way to these Achievements/Trophies. Both feature many enemies that will mutate into J'avo.

Mad Skillz—Unlocking this Achievement/Trophy requires you to purchase all levels of the following Skills: Firearm, Melee, Defense, Lock-On, Rock Steady, Critical Hit, Piercing, J'avo Killer, Zombie Hunter, Combat Gauge Boost, Recovery, and Field Medic. This requires at least 954,000 skill points, which will take quite a while to accumulate. This is best accomplished by playing The Mercenaries, although you must gain some incredibly high scores to begin earning Skill points.

Finish What You Start—This Achievement/Trophy requires you to perform 10 coup de grâce attacks on stunned large enemies. Find an enemy greater than a J'avo or Zombie to perform this, like a Lepotitsa. This is most easily done with Bloodshots. After taking enough damage, they drop to their knees. Simply perform a Martial Arts attack on 10 Bloodshots and you quickly unlock this Achievement/Trophy!

Bob and Weave—To unlock this Achievement/Trophy, counter three times on the same enemy in a single battle. Against most enemies, you'll probably kill them before this triggers, unfortunately. This is most easily done on the Lepotitsa found in Leon Chapters 2 or 4, since it typically attacks only once. Leon Chapter 4 begins with a boss battle against the B.O.W., making it the best place to retry this tactic if you're having trouble.

Lifesaver—While you may be able to trigger this by yourself, this Achievement/Trophy can be earned in co-op in a single enemy encounter! Find a friend to take damage against any creature, then revive them when they're put into a Dying state.

Weapons Master—This Achievement/Trophy can be easily achieved because all you must do is use each weapon you have. However, you must also kill 10 enemies with the Rocket Launcher, which you get to use only once in Leon's Campaign. To rack up kills with the Rocket Launcher, unlock Chris' Costume 1 and use him in The Mercenaries to kill enemies.

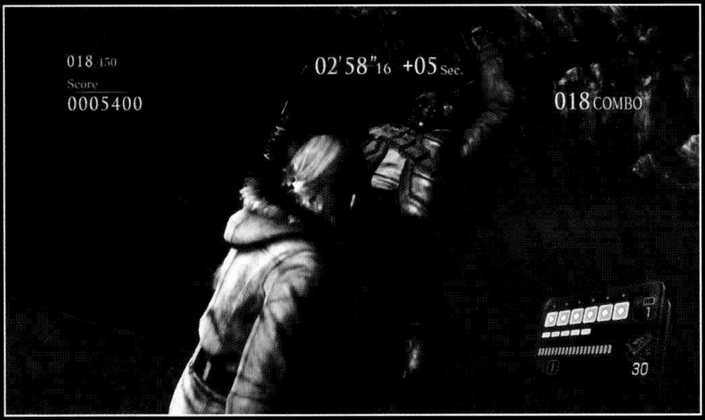

Give a Little Push—While you can make some progress in this Achievement/Trophy by playing through the campaign, you can more quickly finish this by playing the Steel Beast stage in The Mercenaries. Stay on the top area of the stage, the area without a railing, and attack J'avo until they're stunned (or use a Quick Shot). Then use a finisher to push them off the bridge.

Stuntman—This Achievement/Trophy is easily unlocked by playing through Leon's Campaign as Helena but also can be completed once you've unlocked Helena in The Mercenaries. Simply enter into any area and focus only on killing enemies with Quick Shots. You should unlock the Achievement/Trophy before the time has expired!

Bring the Heat—To unlock this Achievement/Trophy, play Chris Chapter 4 as Piers and take out a sniper using the Anti-Materiel Rifle in Thermal Scope mode.

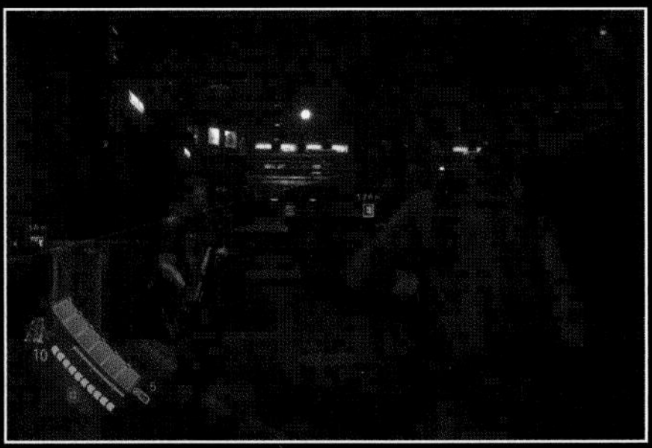

High Voltage—This Achievement/Trophy requires you to take down 10 enemies using the charged attack with Sherry's Stun Rod. Hold the trigger until electricity starts to build up on the rod then release to attack an enemy. This will take down many weaker enemies in a single hit! You can unlock this Achievement/Trophy in the campaign or The Mercenaries, but be sure you kill the enemy with the Stun Rod attack directly. If they die by being set on fire, it doesn't count toward the Achievement/Trophy.

I Prefer Them Alive—You can only unlock this Achievement/Trophy in Leon's Campaign Chapter 2 during the boss fight against the Lepotitsa in the cathedral. This can be difficult to unlock since you can't directly save the civilians in the cathedral—you can only hope the Lepotitsa doesn't convert them before you kill him. Two female civilians have to survive to unlock this Achievement/Trophy, which adds to the difficulty. You might need to wait until you've already completed the campaign and have access to more powerful weapons before you can unlock this.

Flying Ace—At the end of Chris' Campaign Chapter 4, you pilot a VTOL against an aircraft carrier. To unlock this Achievement/Trophy, you must complete the stage without incurring any damage. To achieve this, focus on taking out enemy helicopters while destroying the anti-aircraft emplacements on the carrier. This Achievement/Trophy is easier to obtain in co-op when another player is available to battle enemies or in Amateur mode, which allows you to defeat enemies more quickly and easily finish the rest of the chapter to reach this section.

Hard Choice—After the motorcycle chase in Jake's Campaign Chapter 4, you battle an attack helicopter. After the first encounter, you are in a courtyard area around two tall buildings. To get this Achievement/Trophy, climb to the top of one of the buildings. Wait for the helicopter to stop firing at Chris' team, fly toward the courtyard, and drop off J'avo soldiers. Move toward the rope that the J'avo climbed down and perform the Action button prompt. You'll climb up and shoot the helicopter pilot with the Elephant Killer!

Silent Killer & Sneaking Around—You might be able to unlock Silent Killer by yourself, but you'll definitely unlock it by completing Sneaking Around. To unlock Sneaking Around, make your way through the first area in Ada's Campaign Chapter 4 without being spotted. This requires you to take out each enemy with stealth attacks. As long as you're careful, you won't have much difficulty with this Achievement/Trophy.

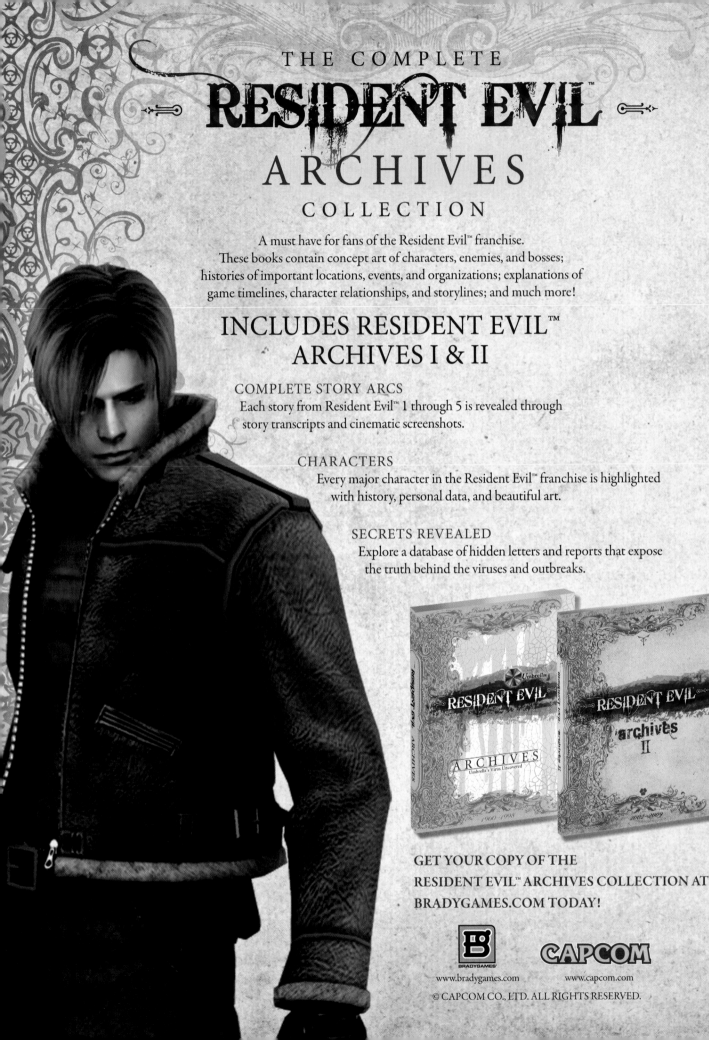

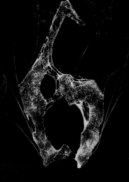

RESIDENT EVIL 6

SIGNATURE SERIES GUIDE

Written by Dan Birlew and Logan Sharp

DK/BradyGames, a division of Penguin Group (USA) Inc.
800 East 96th Street, 3rd Floor
Indianapolis, IN 46240

ISBN 13 EAN: 978-0-7440-1422-8

Printing Code: The rightmost double-digit number is the year of the book's printing; the rightmost single-digit number is the number of the book's printing. For example, 12-1 shows that the first printing of the book occurred in 2012.

15 14 13 12 4 3 2 1

Printed in the USA.

BRADYGAMES STAFF

PUBLISHER
Mike Degler

EDITOR-IN-CHIEF
H. Leigh Davis

LICENSING MANAGER
Christian Sumner

MARKETING MANAGER
Katie Hemlock

OPERATIONS MANAGER
Stacey Beheler

CREDITS

SENIOR DEVELOPMENT EDITOR
Chris Hausermann

MANUSCRIPT EDITOR
Matt Buchanan

EDITORIAL ASSISTANT
John Gehner

BOOK DESIGNER
Carol Stamile

PRODUCTION DESIGNER
Tracy Wehmeyer

AUTHOR ACKNOWLEDGEMENTS

Dan Birlew would like to thank:
Everyone at BradyGames for entrusting me with this amazing project, and for all their patience and hard work; Christopher Hausermann most of all. I would also like to thank everyone at Capcom USA, especially Brian Oliveira for his attention to our concerns and for answering our questions. Great thanks also to co-author Logan Sharp for picking up several passes I dropped, and running with them. I would especially like to thank my wife, Laura, for understanding that Resident Evil is simply more important than trivial everyday things, but certainly not more important than her.

Logan Sharp would like to thank:
Chris Hausermann, Leigh Davis, Dan Birlew, and especially Brian Oliveira for all the help and support and thanks again to Vanessa for being my number one dame.